DRAMA
for Students

Advisors

Jayne M. Burton is a teacher of English, a member of the Delta Kappa Gamma International Society for Key Women Educators, and currently a master's degree candidate in the Interdisciplinary Study of Curriculum and Instruction and English at Angelo State University.

Tom Shilts is the youth librarian at the Okemos branch of Capital Area District Library in Okemos, Michigan. He holds an MSLS degree from Clarion University of Pennsylvania and an MA in U.S. History from the University of North Dakota.

Amy Spade Silverman has taught at independent schools in California, Texas, Michigan, and New York. She holds a bachelor of arts degree from the University of Michigan and a master of fine arts degree from the University of Houston. She is a member of the National Council of Teachers of English and Teachers and Writers. She is an exam reader for Advanced Placement Literature and Composition. She is also a poet, published in *North American Review*, *Nimrod*, and *Michigan Quarterly Review*, among others.

DRAMA

for Students

**Presenting Analysis, Context, and Criticism
on Commonly Studied Dramas**

VOLUME 31

Sara Constantakis, Project Editor

Foreword by Carole L. Hamilton

GALE
CENGAGE Learning·

Farmington Hills, Mich • San Francisco • New York • Waterville, Maine
Meriden, Conn • Mason, Ohio • Chicago

Drama for Students, Volume 31

Project Editor: Sara Constantakis

Rights Acquisition and Management:
    Sheila Spencer

Composition: Evi Abou-El-Seoud

Manufacturing: Rhonda Dover

Imaging: John Watkins

Product Design: Pamela A. E. Galbreath,
    Jennifer Wahi

Digital Content Production: Kevin Duffy

For product information and technology assistance, contact us at
Gale Customer Support, 1-800-877-4253.
For permission to use material from this text or product,
submit all requests online at **www.cengage.com/permissions.**
Further permissions questions can be emailed to
permissionrequest@cengage.com

Gale
27500 Drake Rd.
Farmington Hills, MI, 48331-3535

ISBN-13: 978-0-7876-9641-2

ISSN 1094-9232

This title is also available as an e-book.
ISBN-13: 978-1-4144-4943-2
Contact your Gale, a part of Cengage Learning sales representative for ordering information.

Table of Contents

The Study of Drama

We study drama in order to learn what meaning others have made of life, to comprehend what it takes to produce a work of art, and to glean some understanding of ourselves. Drama produces in a separate, aesthetic world, a moment of being for the audience to experience, while maintaining the detachment of a reflective observer.

Drama is a representational art, a visible and audible narrative presenting virtual, fictional characters within a virtual, fictional universe. Dramatic realizations may pretend to approximate reality or else stubbornly defy, distort, and deform reality into an artistic statement. From this separate universe that is obviously not "real life" we expect a valid reflection upon reality, yet drama never is mistaken for reality—the methods of theater are integral to its form and meaning. Theater is art, and art's appeal lies in its ability both to approximate life and to depart from it. For in intruding its distorted version of life into our consciousness, art gives us a new perspective and appreciation of life and reality. Although all aesthetic experiences perform this service, theater does it most effectively by creating a separate, cohesive universe that freely acknowledges its status as an art form.

And what is the purpose of the aesthetic universe of drama? The potential answers to such a question are nearly as many and varied as there are plays written, performed, and enjoyed. Dramatic texts can be problems posed, answers asserted, or moments portrayed. Dramas (tragedies as well as comedies) may serve strictly "to ease the anguish of a torturing hour" (as stated in William Shakespeare's *A Midsummer Night's Dream*)—to divert and entertain—or aspire to move the viewer to action with social issues. Whether to entertain or to instruct, affirm or influence, pacify or shock, dramatic art wraps us in the spell of its imaginary world for the length of the work and then dispenses us back to the real world, entertained, purged, as Aristotle said, of pity and fear, and edified—or at least weary enough to sleep peacefully.

It is commonly thought that theater, being an art of performance, must be experienced—seen—in order to be appreciated fully. However, to view a production of a dramatic text is to be limited to a single interpretation of that text—all other interpretations are for the moment closed off, inaccessible. In the process of producing a play, the director, stage designer, and performers interpret and transform the script into a work of art that always departs in some measure from the author's original conception. Novelist and critic Umberto Eco, in his *The Role of the Reader: Explorations in the Semiotics of Texts* (Indiana University Press, 1979), explained, "In short, we can say that every performance offers us a complete and satisfying version of the work, but at the same time makes it incomplete for us, because it cannot simultaneously give all the other artistic solutions which the work may admit."

Thus Laurence Olivier's coldly formal and neurotic film presentation of Shakespeare's *Hamlet* (in which he played the title character as well as directed) shows marked differences from subsequent adaptations. While Olivier's Hamlet is clearly entangled in a Freudian relationship with his mother Gertrude, he would be incapable of shushing her with the impassioned kiss that Mel Gibson's mercurial Hamlet (in director Franco Zeffirelli's 1990 film) does. Although each of performances rings true to Shakespeare's text, each is also a mutually exclusive work of art. Also important to consider are the time periods in which each of these films was produced: Olivier made his film in 1948, a time in which overt references to sexuality (especially incest) were frowned upon. Gibson and Zeffirelli made their film in a culture more relaxed and comfortable with these issues. Just as actors and directors can influence the presentation of drama, so too can the time period of the production affect what the audience will see.

A play script is an open text from which an infinity of specific realizations may be derived. Dramatic scripts that are more open to interpretive creativity (such as those of Ntozake Shange and Tomson Highway) actually require the creative improvisation of the production troupe in order to complete the text. Even the most prescriptive scripts (those of Neil Simon, Lillian Hellman, and Robert Bolt, for example), can never fully control the actualization of live performance, and circumstantial events, including the attitude and receptivity of the audience, make every performance a unique event. Thus, while it is important to view a production of a dramatic piece, if one wants to understand a drama fully it is equally important to read the original dramatic text.

The reader of a dramatic text or script is not limited by either the specific interpretation of a given production or by the unstoppable action of a moving spectacle. The reader of a dramatic text may discover the nuances of the play's language, structure, and events at their own pace. Yet studied alone, the author's blueprint for artistic production does not tell the whole story of a play's life and significance. One also needs to assess the play's critical reviews to discover how it resonated to cultural themes at the time of its debut and how the shifting tides of cultural interest have revised its interpretation and impact on audiences. And to do this, one needs to know a little about the culture of the times which produced the play as well as the author who penned it.

Drama for Students supplies this material in a useful compendium for the student of dramatic theater. Covering a range of dramatic works that span from 442 BCE to the 1990s, this book focuses on significant theatrical works whose themes and form transcend the uncertainty of dramatic fads. These are plays that have proven to be both memorable and teachable. *Drama for Students* seeks to enhance appreciation of these dramatic texts by providing scholarly materials written with the secondary and college/university student in mind. It provides for each play a concise summary of the plot and characters as well as a detailed explanation of its themes. In addition, background material on the historical context of the play, its critical reception, and the author's life help the student to understand the work's position in the chronicle of dramatic history. For each play entry a new work of scholarly criticism is also included, as well as segments of other significant critical works for handy reference. A thorough bibliography provides a starting point for further research.

This series offers comprehensive educational resources for students of drama. *Drama for Students* is a vital book for dramatic interpretation and a valuable addition to any reference library.

Sources

Eco, Umberto, *The Role of the Reader: Explorations in the Semiotics of Texts*, Indiana University Press, 1979.

Carole L. Hamilton
Author and Instructor of English at Cary Academy, Cary, North Carolina

Introduction

Purpose of the Book

The purpose of *Drama for Students* (*DfS*) is to provide readers with a guide to understanding, enjoying, and studying dramas by giving them easy access to information about the work. Part of Gale's "For Students" literature line, *DfS* is specifically designed to meet the curricular needs of high school and undergraduate college students and their teachers, as well as the interests of general readers and researchers considering specific plays. While each volume contains entries on "classic" dramas frequently studied in classrooms, there are also entries containing hard-to-find information on contemporary plays, including works by multicultural, international, and women playwrights. Entries profiling film versions of plays not only diversify the study of drama but support alternate learning styles, media literacy, and film studies curricula as well.

The information covered in each entry includes an introduction to the play and the work's author; a plot summary, to help readers unravel and understand the events in a drama; descriptions of important characters, including explanation of a given character's role in the drama as well as discussion about that character's relationship to other characters in the play; analysis of important themes in the drama; and an explanation of important literary techniques and movements as they are demonstrated in the play.

In addition to this material, which helps the readers analyze the play itself, students are also provided with important information on the literary and historical background informing each work. This includes a historical context essay, a box comparing the time or place the drama was written to modern Western culture, a critical essay, and excerpts from critical essays on the play. A unique feature of *DfS* is a specially commissioned critical essay on each drama, targeted toward the student reader.

The "literature to film" entries on plays vary slightly in form, providing background on film technique and comparison to the original, literary version of the work. These entries open with an introduction to the film, which leads directly into the plot summary. The summary highlights plot changes from the play, key cinematic moments, and/or examples of key film techniques. As in standard entries, there are character profiles (noting omissions or additions, and identifying the actors), analysis of themes and how they are illustrated in the film, and an explanation of the cinematic style and structure of the film. A cultural context section notes any time period or setting differences from that of the original work, as well as cultural differences between the time in which the original work was written and the time in which the film adaptation was made. A film entry concludes with a critical overview and critical essays on the film.

To further help today's student in studying and enjoying each play or film, information on audiobooks and other media adaptations is provided (if available), as well as suggestions for works of fiction, nonfiction, or film on similar themes and topics. Classroom aids include ideas for research papers and lists of critical and reference sources that provide additional material on each drama. Film entries also highlight signature film techniques demonstrated, as well as suggesting media literacy activities and prompts to use during or after viewing a film.

Selection Criteria

The titles for each volume of *DfS* are selected by surveying numerous sources on notable literary works and analyzing course curricula for various schools, school districts, and states. Some of the sources surveyed include: high school and undergraduate literature anthologies and textbooks; lists of award-winners, and recommended titles, including the Young Adult Library Services Association (YALSA) list of best books for young adults. Films are selected both for the literary importance of the original work and the merits of the adaptation (including official awards and widespread public recognition).

Input solicited from our expert advisory board—consisting of educators and librarians—guides us to maintain a mix of "classic" and contemporary literary works, a mix of challenging and engaging works (including genre titles that are commonly studied) appropriate for different age levels, and a mix of international, multicultural and women authors. These advisors also consult on each volume's entry list, advising on which titles are most studied, most appropriate, and meet the broadest interests across secondary (grades 7–12) curricula and undergraduate literature studies.

How Each Entry Is Organized

Each entry, or chapter, in *DfS* focuses on one play. Each entry heading lists the full name of the play, the author's name, and the date of the play's publication. The following elements are contained in each entry:

Introduction: a brief overview of the drama which provides information about its first appearance, its literary standing, any controversies surrounding the work, and major conflicts or themes within the work. Film entries identify the original play and provide

understanding of the film's reception and reputation, along with that of the director.

Author Biography: in play entries, this section includes basic facts about the author's life, and focuses on events and times in the author's life that inspired the drama in question.

Plot Summary: a description of the major events in the play. Subheads demarcate the play's various acts or scenes. Plot summaries of films are used to uncover plot differences from the original play, and to note the use of certain film angles or techniques.

Characters: an alphabetical listing of major characters in the play. Each character name is followed by a brief to an extensive description of the character's role in the play, as well as discussion of the character's actions, relationships, and possible motivation. In film entries, omissions or changes to the cast of characters of the film adaptation are mentioned here, and the actors' names—and any awards they may have received—are also included.

Characters are listed alphabetically by last name. If a character is unnamed—for instance, the Stage Manager in *Our Town*—the character is listed as "The Stage Manager" and alphabetized as "Stage Manager." If a character's first name is the only one given, the name will appear alphabetically by the first name. Variant names are also included for each character. Thus, the nickname "Babe" would head the listing for a character in *Crimes of the Heart,* but below that listing would be her less-mentioned married name "Rebecca Botrelle."

Themes: a thorough overview of how the major topics, themes, and issues are addressed within the play. Each theme discussed appears in a separate subhead. While the key themes often remain the same or similar when a play is adapted into a film, film entries demonstrate how the themes are conveyed cinematically, along with any changes in the portrayal of the themes.

Style: this section addresses important style elements of the drama, such as setting, point of view, and narration; important literary devices used, such as imagery, foreshadowing, symbolism; and, if applicable, genres to which the work might have belonged, such as Gothicism or Romanticism. Literary terms are explained within the entry, but can also be found in the Glossary. Film entries cover how the director conveyed the meaning, message, and mood of the work using film in comparison to the author's use of language, literary device, etc., in the original work.

Historical Context: in play entries, this section outlines the social, political, and cultural climate in which the author lived and the play was created. This section may include descriptions of related historical events, pertinent aspects of daily life in the culture, and the artistic and literary sensibilities of the time in which the work was written. If the play is a historical work, information regarding the time in which the play is set is also included. Each section is broken down with helpful subheads. Film entries contain a similar Cultural Context section, because the film adaptation might explore an entirely different time period or culture than the original work, and may also be influenced by the traditions and views of a time period much different than that of the original author.

Critical Overview: this section provides background on the critical reputation of the play or film, including bannings or any other public controversies surrounding the work. For older plays, this section includes a history of how the drama or film was first received and how perceptions of it may have changed over the years; for more recent plays, direct quotes from early reviews may also be included.

Criticism: an essay commissioned by *DfS* which specifically deals with the play or film and is written specifically for the student audience, as well as excerpts from previously published criticism on the work (if available).

Sources: an alphabetical list of critical material used in compiling the entry, with full bibliographical information.

Further Reading: an alphabetical list of other critical sources which may prove useful for the student. It includes full bibliographical information and a brief annotation.

Suggested Search Terms: a list of search terms and phrases to jumpstart students' further information seeking. Terms include not just titles and author names but also terms and topics related to the historical and literary context of the works.

In addition, each entry contains the following highlighted sections, set apart from the main text as sidebars:

Media Adaptations: if available, a list of audiobooks and important film and television adaptations of the play, including source information. The list may also include such variations on the work as musical adaptations and other stage interpretations.

Topics for Further Study: a list of potential study questions or research topics dealing with the play. This section includes questions related to other disciplines the student may be studying, such as American history, world history, science, math, government, business, geography, economics, psychology, etc.

Compare and Contrast: an "at-a-glance" comparison of the cultural and historical differences between the author's time and culture and late twentieth century or early twenty-first century Western culture. This box includes pertinent parallels between the major scientific, political, and cultural movements of the time or place the drama was written, the time or place the play was set (if a historical work), and modern Western culture. Works written after 1990 may not have this box.

What Do I Read Next?: a list of works that might give a reader points of entry into a classic work (e.g., YA or multicultural titles) and/or complement the featured play or serve as a contrast to it. This includes works by the same author and others, works from various genres, YA works, and works from various cultures and eras.

The film entries provide sidebars more targeted to the study of film, including:

Film Technique: a listing and explanation of four to six key techniques used in the film, including shot styles, use of transitions, lighting, sound or music, etc.

Read, Watch, Write: media literacy prompts and/or suggestions for viewing log prompts.

What Do I See Next?: a list of films based on the same or similar works or of films similar in directing style, technique, etc.

Other Features

DfS includes "The Study of Drama," a foreword by Carole Hamilton, an educator and author who specializes in dramatic works. This essay examines the basis for drama in societies and what drives people to study such work. The essay also discusses how *DfS* can help teachers show students how to enrich their own reading/viewing experiences.

A Cumulative Author/Title Index lists the authors and titles covered in each volume of the *DfS* series.

A Cumulative Nationality/Ethnicity Index breaks down the authors and titles covered in each volume of the *DfS* series by nationality and ethnicity.

A Subject/Theme Index, specific to each volume, provides easy reference for users who may be studying a particular subject or theme rather than a single work. Significant subjects from events to broad themes are included.

Each entry may include illustrations, including photo of the author, stills from stage productions, and stills from film adaptations, if available.

Citing Drama for Students

When writing papers, students who quote directly from any volume of *DfS* may use the following general forms. These examples are based on MLA style; teachers may request that students adhere to a different style, so the following examples may be adapted as needed.

When citing text from *DfS* that is not attributed to a particular author (i.e., the Themes, Style, Historical Context sections, etc.), the following format should be used in the bibliography section:

> "*Candida.*" *Drama for Students.* Ed. Sara Constantakis. Vol. 30. Detroit: Gale, Cengage Learning, 2013. 1–27. Print.

When quoting the specially commissioned essay from *DfS* (usually the first piece under the "Criticism" subhead), the following format should be used:

> O'Neal, Michael J. Critical Essay on *Candida*. *Drama for Students*. Ed. Sara Constantakis. Vol. 30. Detroit: Gale, Cengage Learning, 2013. 12–15. Print.

When quoting a journal or newspaper essay that is reprinted in a volume of *DfS*, the following form may be used:

> Lazenby, Walter. "Love and 'Vitality' in *Candida.*" *Modern Drama* 20.1 (1977): 1–19. Rpt. in *Drama for Students*. Ed. Sara Constantakis. Vol. 30. Detroit: Gale, Cengage Learning, 2013. 18–22. Print.

When quoting material reprinted from a book that appears in a volume of *DfS*, the following form may be used:

> Phelps, William Lyon. "George Bernard Shaw." *Essays on Modern Dramatists*. New York: Macmillan, 1921. 67–98. Rpt. in *Drama for Students*. Ed. Sara Constantakis. Vol. 30. Detroit: Gale, Cengage Learning, 2013. 26. Print.

We Welcome Your Suggestions

The editorial staff of *Drama for Students* welcomes your comments and ideas. Readers who wish to suggest dramas to appear in future volumes, or who have other suggestions, are cordially invited to contact the editor. You may contact the editor via e-mail at: **ForStudentsEditors@cengage.com.** Or write to the editor at:

Editor, *Drama for Students*
Gale
27500 Drake Road
Farmington Hills, MI 48331-3535

Literary Chronology

1564: William Shakespeare is born in April in Stratford-Upon-Avon, England.

1597: William Shakespeare's *Romeo and Juliet* is published in the first quarto edition.

1616: William Shakespeare dies on April 23 in Stratford-Upon-Avon, England.

1854: Oscar Wilde is born on October 16 in Dublin, Ireland.

1871: Jesse Lynch Williams is born on August 18 in Sterling, Illinois.

1874: Owen Davis is born on January 29 in Portand, Maine.

1881: Hatcher Hughes is born on February 12 in Polkville, North Carolina.

1895: Oscar Wilde's *The Importance of Being Earnest* is produced.

1900: Oscar Wilde dies of cerebral meningitis on November 30 in Paris, France.

1910: Frank Loesser is born on June 20 in New York, New York.

1910: Abe Burrows is born Abram Solman Borowitz on December 18 in New York, New York.

1916: Willie Gilbert is born William Gomberg on February 24 in Cleveland, Ohio.

1917: Jesse Lynch Williams's *Why Marry?* is produced.

1918: Jesse Lynch Williams's *Why Marry?* wins the Pulitzer Prize for Drama.

1923: Owen Davis's *Icebound* is produced.

1923: Owen Davis is awarded the Pulitzer Prize for Drama for *Icebound*.

1924: Hatcher Hughes's *Hell-Bent fer Heaven* is produced.

1924: Hatcher Hughes is awarded the Pulitzer Prize for Drama for *Hell-Bent fer Heaven*.

1929: Jesse Lynch Williams dies on September 14 in Herkimer, New York.

1938: Joyce Carol Oates is born on June 16 in Lockport, New York.

1939: Terrence McNally is born on November 3 in St. Petersburg, Florida.

1945: Hatcher Hughes dies of coronary thrombosis on October 18 in New York, New York.

1956: Owen Davis dies on October 14 in New York, New York.

1957: Warren Leight is born on January 17 in Queens, New York.

1959: Jane Martin is born in Kentucky.

1959: Frank Loesser dies of lung cancer on July 26, in New York, New York.

1961: Frank Loesser's *How to Succeed in Business without Really Trying* is produced.

1962: Frank Loesser is awarded the Pulitzer Prize for Drama for *How to Succeed in Business without Really Trying*.

1968: The film *Romeo and Juliet* is released.

1969: Pasqualino De Santis is awarded the Academy Award for Cinematography for *Romeo and Juliet*.

1969: Jack Weinstock dies on May 23 in New York, New York.

1969: Danilo Donati is awarded the Academy Award for Costume Design for *Romeo and Juliet*.

1969: Frank Loesser dies of lung cancer on July 28 in New York, New York.

1969: David Lindsay-Abaire is born on November 11 in Boston, Massachusetts.

1974: Sarah Ruhl is born on January 24 in Wilmette, Illinois.

1980: Willie Gilbert dies on December 2 in New York, New York.

1985: Abe Burrows dies of Alzheimer's disease on May 17 in New York, New York.

1988: Terrence McNally's *Andre's Mother* is produced.

1993: Terrence McNally wins a Tony Award for Best Book of a Musical for *Kiss of the Spider Woman*.

1995: Terrence McNally wins a Tony Award for Best Play for *Love! Valour! Compassion!*.

1995: Terrence McNally wins a Tony Award for Best Play for *Master Class*.

1998: Terrence McNally wins a Tony Award for Best Book Musical for *Ragtime*.

1998: Joyce Carol Oates's *When I was a Little Girl and My Mother Didn't Love Me* is produced.

2001: Jane Martin's *Beauty* is produced.

2001: Warren Leight's *Nine-Ten* is produced.

2002: The film *The Importance of Being Earnest* is released.

2006: David Lindsay-Abaire's *Rabbit Hole* is produced.

2006: Cynthia Nixon is awarded the Tony Award for Best Performance by a Leading Actress in a Play for *Rabbit Hole*.

2007: David Lindsay-Abaire is awarded the Pulitzer Prize for Drama for *Rabbit Hole*.

2010: Sarah Ruhl's *Passion Play* is produced.

Acknowledgements

The editors wish to thank the copyright holders of the excerpted criticism included in this volume and the permissions managers of many book and magazine publishing companies for assisting us in securing reproduction rights. We are also grateful to the staffs of the Detroit Public Library, the Library of Congress, the University of Detroit Mercy Library, Wayne State University Purdy/Kresge Library Complex, and the University of Michigan Libraries for making their resources available to us. Following is a list of the copyright holders who have granted us permission to reproduce material in this volume of *DfS*. Every effort has been made to trace copyright, but if omissions have been made, please let us know.

COPYRIGHTED EXCERPTS IN *DfS*, VOLUME 31, WERE REPRODUCED FROM THE FOLLOWING PERIODICALS:

Back Stage, Vol. 51, No. 50, December 16, 2010. Copyright © 2010 by Nielsen Company. All rights reserved. Reproduced by permission.—*Booklist*, Vol. 98, No. 16, April 15, 2002. Copyright © 2002 by American Library Association. All rights reserved. Reproduced by permission.—*Commonweal*, Vol. 133, No. 5, March 10, 2006. Copyright © 2006 by *Commonweal Magazine*. All rights reserved. Reproduced by permission.—*Daily Mail*, February 13, 2010. Copyright © 2010 by *The Daily Mail*. All rights reserved. Reproduced by permission.—*Dramatics*, November 1999. Copyright © 1999 by Educational Theatre Association. All rights reserved. Reproduced by permission.—*Educational Theatre Journal*, Vol. 11, No. 3, October 1959. Copyright © 1959 by Johns Hopkins University Press. All rights reserved. Reproduced by permission.—*Journal of Popular Film and Television*, Vol. 21, No. 1, Spring 1993. Copyright © Taylor and Francis Group. All rights reserved. Reproduced by permission.—*Library Journal*, Vol. 127, No. 8, May 1, 2002. Copyright © Library Journals LLC. All rights reserved. Reproduced by permission.—*Literature/Film Quarterly*, Vol. 1, No. 4, 1973; Vol. 36, No. 2, 2008. Copyright © 1973, 2008 by *Literature/Film Quarterly*. All rights reserved. Reproduced by permission.—*The New York Post*, October 10, 2005. Copyright © 2005 by *The New York Post*. All rights reserved. Reproduced by permission.—*Sight and Sound*, Vol. 12, No. 9, 2002. Copyright © 2002 by *Sight and Sound*. All rights reserved. Reproduced by permission.—*The Spectator*, 2007. Copyright © 2007 by *The Spectator*. All rights reserved. Reproduced by permission.—*Spokesman-Review*, August 21, 2008. Copyright © 2008 by the *Spokesman-Review*. All rights reserved. Reproduced by permission.—*Syracuse New Times*, April 25, 2012. Copyright © 2012 by *Syracuse New Times*. All rights reserved. Reproduced by permission.—*United Press International*, May 28,

2002. Copyright © 2002 by *United Press International*. All rights reserved. Reproduced by permission.—*Variety*, September 14, 2006. Copyright © 2006 by *Variety*. All rights reserved. Reproduced by permission.

COPYRIGHTED EXCERPTS IN *DfS*, **VOLUME 31, WERE REPRODUCED FROM THE FOLLOWING BOOKS:**

From *Sarah Ruhl: A Critical Study of the Plays*. © 2011 James Al-Shamma by permission of McFarland & Company, Inc., Box 611, Jefferson, NC 28640. www.mcfarlandpub.com.— Creighton, Joanne V. From *Joyce Carol Oates*. Twayne Publishers, 1992. Copyright © 1992 by The Gale Group. All rights reserved. Reproduced by permission.—Davis, Owen. From *Discussions of Modern American Drama*. Edited by Walter J. Meserve. D.C. Heath, 1966.—Davis, Owen. From *Icebound: A Play*. Little, Brown, 1923.— Dickinson, Thomas H. From *Playwrights of the New American Theater*. Books for Libraries Press, 1925.—Friedman, Ellen G. From *Joyce Carol Oates*. Frederick Ungar Publishing, 1980. Copyright © 1980 by Ellen G. Friedman. All

rights reserved. Reproduced by permission.— Lehmann, Courtney. From *Screen Adaptations: Shakespeare's "Romeo and Juliet": The Relationship between Text and Film*. Methuen Drama, 2010. © 2010 Courtney Lehmann. All rights reserved. Reproduced by permission.— Newlin, Keith. From *American Plays of the New Woman: Six Plays from the Early Twentieth Century about the "Proper" Role of Women*. Ivan R. Dee, 2000. Copyright © 2000 by Rowan & Littlefield. All rights reserved. Reproduced by permission.—Paige, Linda Rohrer. From *A Companion to Twentieth-Century American Drama*. Edited by David Krasner. Blackwell Publishing, 2005. Copyright © 2005. Reproduced with permission of Blackwell Publishing Ltd.— Riis, Thomas L. From *Frank Loesser*. Edited by Geoffrey Block. New Haven, CT: Yale University Press, 2008. Copyright © 2008 by Yale University Press. All rights reserved. Reproduced by permission.—Shumacher, Michael. From *Joyce Carol Oates: Conversations 1970-2006*. Edited by Greg Johnson. Ontario Review Press, 2006. Copyright © 2006 by Ontario Review Press. All rights reserved. Reproduced by permission.

Contributors

Susan K. Andersen: Anderson holds a PhD in literature. Entry on *Passion Play*. Original essay on *Passion Play*.

Bryan Aubrey: Aubrey holds a PhD in English. Entries on *How to Succeed in Business without Really Trying* and *Icebound*. Original essays on *How to Succeed in Business without Really Trying* and *Icebound*.

Rita M. Brown: Brown is an English professor. Entry on *Nine-Ten*. Original essay on *Nine-Ten*.

Catherine Dominic: Dominic is a novelist and a freelance writer and editor. Entry on *Why Marry?* Original essay on *Why Marry?*

Kristen Sarlin Greenberg: Greenberg is a freelance writer and editor with a background in literature and philosophy. Entry on *Beauty*. Original essay on *Beauty*.

Sheri Karmiol: Karmiol is a lecturer in interdisciplinary studies at the University of New Mexico. Entry on *Romeo and Juliet*. Original essay on *Romeo and Juliet*.

David Kelly: Kelly is a professor of creative writing and literature. Entry on *The Importance of Being Earnest*. Original essay on *The Importance of Being Earnest*.

Amy Lynn Miller: Miller is a graduate of the University of Cincinnati and currently resides in New Orleans, Louisiana. Entry on *Rabbit Hole*. Original essay on *Rabbit Hole*.

April Paris: Paris is a freelance writer with an extensive background writing literary and educational materials. Entry on *Andre's Mother*. Original essay on *Andre's Mother*.

Bradley A. Skeen: Skeen is a classicist. Entry on *When I Was a Little Girl and My Mother Didn't Want Me*. Original essay on *When I Was a Little Girl and My Mother Didn't Want Me*.

Leah Tieger: Tieger is a freelance writer and editor. Entry on *Hell-Bent fer Heaven*. Original essay on *Hell-Bent fer Heaven*.

Andre's Mother

TERRENCE MCNALLY

1988

Andre's Mother is a brief one-act play by Terrence McNally that explores the themes of love, loss, family, and acceptance within the context of the homosexual community. The Manhattan Theater Club first performed the play on May 18, 1988, as part of an off-Broadway event called Urban Blight.

Written during the height of the AIDS epidemic, the story begins after Andre's death. Cal, Andre's boyfriend, holds an informal memorial where he attempts to connect with Andre's mother. However, she had no idea that her son was gay, dating Cal, or dying of AIDS. Her reaction symbolizes the rejection that many in the gay community have faced from their own families. The play was adapted for television in 1990, earning McNally an Emmy Award. The original play can be found in the collections *Terrence McNally: 15 Short Plays* (1994) and *Andre's Mother and Other Short Plays* (1995).

AUTHOR BIOGRAPHY

McNally was born on November 3, 1939, in St. Petersburg, Florida, but he grew up in Corpus Christi, Texas. In an interview with Toby Silverman Zinman, McNally commented that he developed a love for the theater as a child when his parents took him to New York to see *Annie*

Terrence McNally (© Ron Galella / Ron Galella Collection / Getty Images)

Get Your Gun and *The King and I* and by listening to opera on the radio.

McNally attended Columbia University and graduated with a degree in English and as a member of the honors society Phi Beta Kappa in 1960. After receiving an Evan's Traveling Scholarship, McNally traveled to Mexico, where he wrote a play. After sending the Actor's Studio a copy of the play, he was invited to become the stage manager. He also traveled with noted American author John Steinbeck as a tutor to his children, and the two developed a close friendship.

McNally's first commercially produced play was *And Things That Go Bump in the Night*. After finding success in smaller venues, it premiered on Broadway in 1965, but there it garnered harsh criticism. Discouraged, McNally briefly left his work as a playwright and worked instead as an editor and critic. In 1966, he earned a Guggenheim Fellowship, which allowed him to focus on his writing. He salvaged his career as a

playwright with the one-act play *Next* in 1969. According to his Kennedy Center biography, this play secured his reputation as a satirist addressing important themes in modern culture, such as the Vietnam War, and allowed him to write full-time.

Over the years, McNally has become known for his unconventional stories, commentary on modern life, and honest views of homosexuality in America. He has written plays, musicals, and film and television scripts, and he has collaborated on operas. Zinman comments in the introduction to *Terrence McNally: A Casebook* that McNally's work matured in the 1980s after the deaths of his friends Robert Drivas and James Coco. Two of his most highly regarded works, *Frankie and Johnny in the Clair de Lune* and *TheLisbon Traviata*, were written during this period. *Frankie and Johnny in the Clair de Lune* was staged in 1987 and adapted for a film released in 1991, and *The Lisbon Traviata* was performed in 1985 and revised in 1989.

McNally has never been afraid of controversy, and the play *Corpus Christi* is one of his most controversial. First performed in 1998, the play is a retelling of the biblical Gospels, but the Christ figure is gay. The play was protested, and its author received death threats. The Islamic Shari'ah Court of the United Kingdom found it blasphemous and ordered a death sentence for McNally after the London stage production in 1999.

McNally's later career has earned him numerous awards, including an Emmy for the 1990 television adaptation of *Andre's Mother*. He was nominated for a Pulitzer Prize in 1995 for *A Perfect Ganesh*. He was the recipient of the Tony Award for Best Book Musical in 1993 for *Kiss of the Spider Woman* and in 1998 for *Ragtime*, and of the Tony Award for Best Play in 1995 with *Love! Valour! Compassion!* and again in 1996 for *Master Class*. As of 2013, McNally continued to write plays, including *Mothers and Sons*.

PLOT SUMMARY

Andre's Mother is a one-act play with four characters: Cal, Penny, Arthur, and Andre's mother, who is nameless. It is set in New York City's Central Park in the late 1980s. Each character

MEDIA ADAPTATIONS

- The 1990 Emmy Award–winning "Terrence McNally's *Andre's Mother*" was released on DVD in 2006. This episode of the PBS series *American Playhouse* runs approximately fifty minutes.

enters the stage holding a white balloon, and the group is described as "well dressed."

Cal begins the dialogue by saying that he does not know how to say goodbye, even though he is known for being good with words. The first lines of the play thus reveal to the audience something of the purpose of the gathering. Cal's sister, Penny, asks about a structure nearby, and Cal explains that it is an outdoor theater, which hosts performances of Shakespearean plays. Cal tells Andre's mother that Andre had always wanted to play Hamlet. In fact, Cal continues, Andre did play Hamlet in Boston once, and he recalls how happy Andre was to play his favorite role and live his dream. Andre's mother does not respond to the anecdote, and Penny warns Cal, "It's not the time. Later."

Cal and Penny's father, Arthur, speaks to Andre's mother, telling her how fond he and his wife were of Andre. He acknowledges that his relationship with his own son has been strained. Andre, however, he says, "helped me to know my own boy." Again, Andre's mother does not reply.

Penny asks why they are holding balloons, and Cal explains that they represent Andre's soul. A stage direction (a note within the written play that is not spoken by the actors) specifies that the balloons are white—a traditional symbol of innocence or purity. The gathered people are going to say goodbye and release the balloons, symbolizing, as Cal explains, that they are "willing to let go. Breaking the last earthly ties." Penny jokingly asks whether the pope knows about the ritual. Her father finds the

joke in poor taste, but Penny says that Andre enjoyed her sense of humor. She says that she can hear him laughing. This sense of his laughter allows Penny to symbolically release Andre.

Penny is the first in the group to say goodbye to Andre and release her balloon. As she does so, she admits to having a crush on Andre and wishing that he had been straight. "But if any man was going to have you," she says, "I'm glad it was my brother!" This statement removes any doubts about Andre and Cal's relationship; the audience now knows that they were a couple. As the balloon rises, Penny hopes that the speed of its ascent is a good omen.

Arthur is the next to say goodbye to Andre. He simply releases the balloon, with the words "Goodbye. God speed." Penny questions Cal, but he tells her that he is not ready to let go yet. To give him some privacy, Penny leads Arthur away, telling him that he can buy her ice cream.

Left alone, Cal addresses Andre's mother, who remains silent. He begins by saying, "I wish I knew what you were thinking." He understands that they do not know anything about each other, but he had hoped that they would be friends one day. Now, though, Cal has doubts that a friendship would have been possible because Andre never told her about their relationship. Cal is not sure that Andre would have ever told his family the truth about his sexuality. The audience learns that Andre refused to call his mother and tell her the truth even after he learned that he was dying.

Cal does not understand the relationship between Andre and his mother. He says that he told Andre, "She's your mother. She won't mind." This statement highlights the different relationships that Cal and Andre have had with their families. The audience has seen Cal enjoying an honest and open relationship with his father and sister, but Andre shared little with his mother. Cal explains that fear prevented Andre from contacting her: he was more afraid of disappointing and hurting her than he was of dying. Andre's mother remains silent, refusing to discuss anything Cal.

Cal continues speaking. He compares others within the gay community in New York City to Andre. He says that many gay men in New York choose to leave their homes to keep from hurting their mothers. They are open in the city but hide their full lives from people like her. He describes

New York as "a city of fugitives from our parents' scorn or heartbreak." Cal says that Andre never returned home even when he suffered from bouts of homesickness. In fact, Cal says he accused Andre of being a country boy pretending to be a New Yorker. Again, Andre's mother refuses to say anything.

As it becomes clear that Andre's mother does not intend to acknowledge Cal or his relationship with her son, Cal becomes more frustrated. He tells her that she reminds him of Lulu's mother, the silent character in the comic strip *Little Lulu*. She is like this anonymous character in being "so remote, so formidable." Cal tells her that he will answer the questions that she refuses to ask and then she will never have to see him again. He explains that Andre died of AIDS. They are not sure how Andre contracted the disease; Cal is not infected. He tells her that Andre bravely endured the illness that killed him. He was not afraid to die. The only fear that Andre had was of his mother's disappointment.

Cal continues the one-sided conversation by promising to send Andre's belongings to her. He says that she should have seen Andre when he played Hamlet in Boston—"you would have been proud of him," he says. Cal confesses to Andre's mother that he is bitter about losing Andre, and he is bitter that he cannot reach her. He says he can feel her condemnation, and her judgment makes him feel sick.

Cal then addresses Andre. As he looks at the balloon, he says, "I blew it." Cal quotes a line from *Hamlet* as he releases the balloon, echoing the last words that are said to Hamlet himself in the play. He says goodbye to Andre's mother and exits the stage.

Andre's mother is alone on the stage, where she still remains silent. The audience watches as she fights back a flood of emotions. She finally kisses the balloon and releases it. Her eyes remain on the balloon until the lights go out.

CHARACTERS

Andre

Andre does not appear in the play, but he is symbolically present in the balloons that the characters hold. This young man was Cal's boyfriend and had a good relationship with Cal's

father and sister. He was an actor who loved *Hamlet* and once played the title character in Boston. Andre kept his life a secret from his mother. He refused to tell her that he was gay or had been diagnosed with AIDS. Andre faced death bravely, but he continued to fear disappointing his mother and causing her pain. He died before finding the courage to tell his mother the truth.

Andre's Mother

Andre's mother remains nameless throughout the play, and little is known about her. She refuses to speak when Arthur and Cal try to talk to her. Andre never told his mother that he was gay, in a relationship with Cal, or dying of AIDS. She learns the truth only after his death. She is the last to say goodbye to Andre, and she kisses the balloon before silently releasing it.

Arthur

Arthur is Cal and Penny's father. He was close to Andre and believes that Andre helped him better understand Cal. He says goodbye to Andre after Penny does.

Cal

Cal was Andre's boyfriend and is Arthur's son and Penny's brother. He brings his family together with Andre's mother to say goodbye to Andre after his death. Cal attempts to include Andre's mother in their gathering, but she refuses to speak to him or his family. Cal admits that he hoped to be friends with her, but he finally grows frustrated with her silence. He tells her that her disapproval was all Andre feared when he was dying.

Cal stayed with Andre while he was dying of AIDS, but Cal does not have the disease himself. He offers to pay to send Andre's things to his mother, and he is bitter about his loss as well as her rejection. Cal quotes *Hamlet* to Andre as he says goodbye.

Penny

Penny is Cal's sister and Arthur's daughter. She admits to having had a crush on Andre, but she is happy that Andre and Cal were together. Penny is the first to say goodbye to Andre, and she fondly remembers that he loved her sense of humor.

TOPICS FOR FURTHER STUDY

- Read *Chandra's Secret*. This Michael L. Printz Honor Book by Allan Stratton is a young-adult story about a South African teenager, Chandra, who loses her mother and family stability because of the AIDS epidemic. Soon she questions whether she has AIDS herself. Create social network pages (Twitter, Facebook, or Tumblr, for example) or blog pages for Andre and Chandra, as if they were both living in the present day. What experiences would the two characters share with each other? What can they learn from each other?

- Research the history of AIDS. How has the way society views AIDS and people with AIDS changed over time? What advances in treatment and prevention have been made? Create a multimedia presentation that focuses on the history of the illness and society's reactions. Be sure to include representations in the arts such as theatrical performances.

- Research the history of gay rights in America from the early twentieth century to the present day. Examine the political actions and reactions that have occurred because of the movement. Create a website that offers a time line of the movement. Provide links to important events and individuals within your time line.

- Read the play *Angels in America* or watch the miniseries. Write a one-act play in which the angel and Andre's mother meet. What would the characters say to each other? Ask a classmate to perform the play with you. Record the performance and post it on a website or blog.

- Choose a play from *Collected Plays of Edward Albee: 1978–2003* to compare and contrast with *Andre's Mother*. McNally has been compared to Albee. Based on what you have read, what similarities and differences do you find? Write a paper that compares the characters, style, and themes of the two works. Explain why you believe people draw a connection between Albee and McNally.

THEMES

Loss

Andre's Mother explores the concept of loss on multiple levels. Andre's death is a loss that all of the characters share, although it affects each one differently. For Penny, losing Andre is like losing a dear friend. He appreciated her sense of humor, and she remembers him with laughter. Arthur, on the other hand, has lost a confidant. As Arthur explains, "Andre and I could talk about anything under the sun." Arthur credits Andre's influence for improving his relationship with Cal.

Cal experiences Andre's death on a deeper level. He shared his life with Andre, and he suffers the death of the man he loved. His anecdotes show the close relationship that the couple shared, and

the loss leaves him "bitter." Cal's bitterness is compounded by the loss of hope that he will ever be able to reach Andre's mother. Her rejection only increases his feelings of loss and anger.

Andre's mother experiences a different type of loss. While she mourns the death of her son, Cal makes it very clear that she lost him years before. Andre hid his life from his mother because of fear—fear of hurting her, and fear of facing her disapproval. Her supposed prejudice cost her an honest relationship with her son, and, equally, Andre lost the chance to have a meaningful relationship with his mother.

Acceptance

Despite the sad tone of the play, *Andre's Mother* explores the theme of acceptance. It is clear that Andre found acceptance before his death, but it

Andre's Mother is set in Central Park in New York City. *(© Songquan Deng / Shutterstock.com)*

never came from his own family. Instead, he had been accepted into Cal's family, as Penny and Arthur's anecdotes make clear. Andre also found acceptance as part of the gay community in New York. He and Cal became part of a group united by their experience of rejection by society. This sense of community is evident from the pronouns that Cal uses—"we" and "our," for example, when he says, "We don't want to hurt our mothers."

Although Cal identifies with the rejected members of the homosexual community, he has experienced greater acceptance from his family than did Andre. He did not experience the disapproval that he feels from Andre's mother. His parents and sister were supportive of his relationship with Andre. The support of Cal's family makes it difficult for him to understand the relationship between Andre and his mother. Cal encouraged Andre to contact his mother because he was certain that she would be accepting. As he said, "She's your mother." After attempting to accept Andre's mother into his life, he learns that nothing will overcome her disapproval of his relationship with Andre.

Love

Cal's anecdotes provide insight into a loving and supportive relationship. He says that he loved Andre, and his conversation with Andre's mother shows it. For example, he talks about Andre's love of Shakespeare and how happy he was to play Hamlet. Cal proved his love by taking care of Andre when he was dying. He reaches out to Andre's mother out of love for Andre. He attempts to share pieces of Andre's life with her, but he meets with the rejection that Andre had feared. This interaction causes Cal to come to a deeper understanding of Andre's feelings.

Paradoxically, Andre had refused to tell his mother the truth about his life out of both fear and love. He knew that telling her he was gay would hurt her, and her reaction during the play suggests that he was right. Although her reaction to Cal seems cold and heartless, there is evidence that she loves her son at the end of the play: she kisses the balloon that represents Andre's soul before she releases it.

Homosexuality

In this short play, McNally explores deeply some of the ways families may be affected by homosexuality. Cal's family is supportive of him, but McNally hints that there has been some strain on the family dynamic. For example, Arthur says, "Even my own son isn't always like a son to me." Cal's family is able to navigate the strain, but Andre's family was not so accommodating.

Andre felt the need to keep his relationship with Cal a secret to protect his mother and himself. The disapproval that Cal feels from Andre's mother seems to confirm Andre's belief that she could not handle having a gay son, although there is no way to know her reaction had Andre told her the truth. The fear of rejection by his family that Andre felt echoes a genuine concern for many in the homosexual community. As Cal explains, many homosexual people who transplant to New York are "fugitives from [their] parents' scorn or heartbreak."

STYLE

One-Act Play
Andre's Mother is a brief one-act play. According to William Harmon's *A Handbook to Literature*, one-act plays were part of the "little theater" movement and became prominent in the 1890s. They were originally confined to vaudeville (light variety shows of brief sketches, comedy, musical numbers, and so forth) and opening acts, but they evolved into a medium used to address a variety of themes and topics.

Most plays are divided into a few (often three or five) major divisions, or acts, which are further divided into scenes. A one-act play may be broken into more than one scene, but *Andre's Mother* takes place in a single scene. Rather than shifting locations, McNally has characters exit to create the desired dramatic divisions. Penny and Arthur exit, allowing Cal to face Andre's Mother, and Cal's exit provides the audience with a glimpse of the emotions Andre's mother is feeling by the end of the play.

Symbolism
According to M. H. Abrams in *A Glossary of Literary Terms*, a symbol is "anything which signifies something." The obvious symbols in *Andre's Mother* are the white balloons that the characters hold; Cal explains that "they represent the soul"—specifically, Andre's soul. The color white symbolizes purity and innocence.

By having the characters address the balloons, McNally creates a sense of Andre's presence on stage.

Additionally, Andre's mother acts as a symbol within the play. Because she is nameless and silent, she is seen less as an individual. The audience knows nothing about her, and she comes to represent every parent who refuses to accept a homosexual child. Cal makes this connection when he explains how many gay people in New York City are hiding from unsupportive parents like her.

Emotional Drama
McNally's play is one that makes distinctive appeals to the emotions of the audience. It allows the audience to sympathize with the characters' feelings of loss. McNally further manipulates the audience's feelings as the play progresses.

The silence of Andre's mother elicits a one-sided conversation in which Cal is able to explain how Andre's fear of rejection kept him from his mother, creating empathy for Andre's situation. Additionally, when Andre's mother refuses to ask about her son's death, the audience understands the consequences of her fear and judgment. When she kisses the balloon at the end of the play, it is possible to sympathize with her love and loss.

HISTORICAL CONTEXT

1980s
The 1980s was a time of cultural and political change. Ronald Reagan was elected president in 1980 and served two terms in office. A former actor, Reagan was known for his speaking ability, earning him the title of "the Great Communicator," according to *Encyclopædia Britannica*. He was a great supporter of capitalism and opposed Communism. His political stance highlighted the tension of the Cold War between the Eastern Bloc, led by the Soviet Union, and the United States. The Cold War ended in 1991 with the fall of the Soviet Union.

In the closing decades of the Cold War, Americans also faced a turbulent economy. Although a cut in taxes brought some improvement in the early 1980s, the stock market crashed on Black Monday in 1987, making life difficult for many Americans. As Joyce E. Salisbury and

COMPARE
&
CONTRAST

- **1980s:** The virus that causes AIDS—human immunodeficiency virus, or HIV—is identified in 1981. The first people to contract the disease are gay men, leading to a social stigma surrounding the disease. HIV/AIDS patients face discrimination and are rejected from society—for example, three young brothers, the Rays, are removed from a public elementary school in Florida after being diagnosed with HIV in 1986. A federal court later rules that they must be allowed to attend, but they face opposition and controversy.

  Today: Legal protections exist for people with HIV and AIDS, such as their inclusion in the Americans with Disabilities Act. America's ban on international travelers with HIV/AIDS is lifted in 2010, and drug therapies increase the life expectancy of individuals with HIV and AIDS.

- **1980s:** The rights of homosexuals are limited, but steps are being taken for equality. Wisconsin passes a law prohibiting discrimination based on sexuality. The Democratic

Party includes the rights of homosexuals in its platform.

  Today: Homosexual rights are still debated. The "Don't Ask, Don't Tell" policy of the US military has ended, allowing openly gay people to serve. Several states allow same-sex couples to marry, and the Defense of Marriage Act, the federal law limiting marriage to heterosexual couples, is declared unconstitutional in 2013.

- **1980s:** Gay people face social discrimination, causing many to hide their sexual identity. Homosexual people are not included in mainstream American society, and their presence in the media is rare and stereotyped. Activists encourage them to "come out of the closet" and live openly. National Coming Out Day is established.

  Today: Discrimination still exists, although American society is becoming more tolerant. Many average citizens and celebrities are open about their sexuality, and gay characters are found in movies and television shows.

Andrew E. Kersten explain in *Daily Life through History*, "Workers across the country suffered a number of setbacks during the 1980s, particularly as companies 'downsized' by laying off workers and by cutting benefits."

Amidst this political and financial insecurity, the United States also saw many changes in technology that altered the country's culture. Cable television, invented in the 1970s, was widely embraced in the 1980s. Additionally, the 1980s saw a rise in portable entertainment devices. The Sony Walkman allowed people to travel with cassette tapes as well as radio. The VCR gave people the opportunity to record shows from television and to watch movies in their own homes. The popularity of the personal

computer increased as the devices became more affordable.

With all of the change and uncertainty, however, many Americans shifted their focus to traditional values. This focus brought a public backlash against unconventional behaviors and lifestyles. Laws and campaigns were implemented in attempts to protect traditional values. This moral backlash extended to the gay community, which was seen as a threat. For example, the Supreme Court upheld state laws that made homosexuality illegal.

AIDS Epidemic
The Centers for Disease Control first recognized the existence of a new disease in 1981. The first

people to contract this illness were gay men, and 270 were diagnosed by the end of the year, according to "A Timeline of AIDS" on AIDS. gov. This led to the name "gay related immune deficiency" (GRID), but the name *acquired immunodeficiency syndrome* (AIDS) came into use after people outside the homosexual community were diagnosed with the illness. In 1982, it was discovered that the virus could be transmitted through blood transfusions, and the first cases among women were diagnosed in 1983. In 1984, HIV, the virus that causes AIDS, was identified. Despite the spread of the disease beyond the gay community, there was a stigma attached to the illness because of its prevalence among gay men and intravenous drug users.

Fear of the disease led to discrimination against people with the illness. For example, the job of a doctor in New York who treated patients with AIDS was threatened in 1983. The Ray brothers, three young boys who acquired HIV through blood transfusions, were kept from attending public school in 1987. A week after they won the right to return to class, their home was burned down. The stigma of the disease made it difficult to obtain research funding and treatment. Despite the spread of the disease, little was done to educate the country about AIDS.

In 1988, when *Andre's Mother* was first performed, AIDS still held a stigma; however, the HOPE Act allowed for federal funding to support AIDS prevention and education. Awareness about the disease and the lives of those affected by it spread in the 1990s after the launch of the Red Ribbon Foundation in 1991. By 1997, the death rate due to AIDS dropped 47 percent because of the effectiveness of drug therapies.

Homosexual Rights in the Twentieth Century

The history of homosexual rights in the United States is long and complex. The first national gay rights organization, the Mattachine Society, was established in 1950. This coincided with the "lavender scare," according to the PBS website. This was the purging of more than four thousand military employees based on their sexuality, under the official belief that they were a security threat. The lavender scare was just one example of discrimination that homosexuals faced in the twentieth century. In 1952, the handbook of

Cal recalls how important Hamlet *was to Andre.*
(© Robbie Taylor / Shutterstock.com)

psychiatry, the *Diagnostic and Statistical Manual of Mental Disorders*, listed homosexuality as a psychotic disorder, validating legal prejudice against the homosexual community.

There was not a strong political push for equal rights in the early twentieth century. As Michael Levy explains in the *Encyclopædia Britannica*, "Political activity by homosexuals was generally not very visible. Indeed, gays were often harassed by the police wherever they congregated." This began to change in the 1960s and 1970s. Illinois became to first state to reverse a law making homosexuality illegal in 1962.

In 1969, police raided the Stonewall Inn, a gay bar in Greenwich Village, in New York City. Police clashed with the patrons, and the rioting that followed lasted almost a week. The violence of the Stonewall riots spurred a gay rights demonstration in 1970, the first gay pride parade. Soon, political progress was made. In 1973, homosexuality was removed from the *Diagnostic and Statistical Manual*, and Kathy Kozachenko became the first openly homosexual candidate elected to public office. In 1980, the Democratic Party included homosexual rights in the party platform, and the AIDS epidemic became a focus of gay rights in the 1980s.

The 1990s saw a mix of progress and setbacks for the movement. In 1993, the "Don't Ask, Don't Tell" policy prevented military recruiters from asking applicants about their sexual orientation, but neither were members of the military allowed to be open about their sexuality. The Defense of Marriage Act, defining marriage as being between a man and woman, was signed into law in 1996. In 1998, the brutal murder of a gay college student, Matthew Shepard, placed hate crimes against homosexuals in the spotlight.

CRITICAL OVERVIEW

Although McNally was the winner of four Tony Awards, the critics have not always been kind to him. Critics were merciless in their reviews of his first commercially produced Broadway play, *And Things That Go Bump in the Night*. The play, however, was criticized more for its dark subject matter and perceived homosexual subtext than for its merits and failures, according to Raymond-Jean Frontain's article "McNally and Steinbeck." He quotes a letter in which Steinbeck wrote, "It's a dreadful play—not in the writing but in what it says. And I am afraid it is going to get clobbered by the critics." In fact, many of McNally's early plays were written with the same dark, satirical tone which critics disliked.

Although his talent was recognized with the successful performance of *Next* in 1969, reviews remained a mixture of praise and revulsion until the 1980s. Zinman writes, "*The Lisbon Traviata* (1985, revised 1989) is pivotal in McNally's transformation into a mature and contemplative theatrical voice." One of his most beloved plays, however, was *Frankie and Johnny in the Clair de Lune*. As Alvin Klein states in a review for the *New York Times*, "Out of a one-night stand between two ordinary people in a drab apartment, Mr. McNally fashioned a contemporary romantic fairy tale." McNally later adapted *Frankie and Johnny in the Clair de Lune* for

film, a creative action he also took with *Andre's Mother*.

Andre's Mother was adapted as part of PBS's *American Playhouse* series. The fifty-minute film retains much of the dialogue from the original play and won McNally an Emmy Award. John J. O'Connor's review of the presentation for the *New York Times* explains that McNally created realistic characters representing a particular subculture: "The tasteful surfaces of *Andre's Mother* capture perfectly a certain segment, almost militantly cultivated, of gay life in Manhattan."

McNally's work has been criticized for more than its dramatic content. The 1997 play *Corpus Christi*, in which the Christ figure is gay, brought criticism from different religious leaders. A revival of the play in 2008 was not met with the same political firestorm, allowing critics to focus on the merits of the play itself. *New York Times* reviewer Jason Zinoman concludes that the play is not McNally's best, but "there are moments of hard-won sentiment that will win over the biggest skeptic."

Over the decades, McNally has experienced the highs and lows of his profession. He has been vilified and has received numerous awards. McNally's versatility and fearlessness have helped make him "one of the most beloved and prolific modern-day playwrights," according to the performing arts venue the Kennedy Center.

CRITICISM

April Paris

Paris is a freelance writer with an extensive background writing literary and educational materials. In the following essay, she argues that Andre's fear of rejection is a universal theme that allows the audience to sympathize with the characters in Andre's Mother.

In the handful of minutes necessary to perform *Andre's Mother*, Terrence McNally does more than provide the audience with a glimpse into the struggles the homosexual community faced in the midst of the AIDS epidemic. He tells a universal tale of love, loss, and family. Although the play addresses the complex issues of AIDS, prejudice, and death, it also shows the audience that everyone has the same needs and desires. Andre's story is, basically, a human

WHAT DO I READ NEXT?

- *The 1980s* (American Popculture through History series), by Bob Batchelor and Scott F. Stoddart, is a nonfiction book published in 2007 that explains the changing culture of the 1980s. The text helps explain the setting and culture of *Andre's Mother*.

- *Gay Rights and Moral Panic: The Origins of America's Debate on Homosexuality*, by Fred Fejes, was published in 2008. The nonfiction text examines two political movements, the movement to advance gay rights and the movement to restrict them.

- *Broadway Song and Story: Playwrights/ Lyricists/Composers Discuss Their Hits* is a collection of discussions, criticism, and articles edited by Otis L. Guernsey. Published in 1986, the volume includes contributions from McNally and other notable playwrights.

- *Forbidden Acts: Pioneering Gay and Lesbian Plays of the Twentieth Century*, written by Ben Hodges and published in 2003, is an anthology of plays that explore homosexuality. With works dating from 1918 to 1994, the text exposes the reader to a variety of pioneering plays.

- Andrew Holleran's *Chronicle of a Plague, Revisited: AIDS and Its Aftermath* (2008) is a collection of essays that examine the AIDS epidemic on a global scale. The book provides an in-depth look at the effect of AIDS on the homosexual community.

- *Making Gay History: The Half-Century Fight for Lesbian and Gay Equal Rights*, written by Eric Marcus in 2002, is a collection of firsthand accounts of changes in society with respect to gay rights over fifty years. The accounts come from celebrities, politicians, journalists, and the general public.

- *Frankie and Johnny in the Clair de Lune* (1998) is one of McNally's most popular plays, and he later wrote the screenplay for its film adaptation. The romantic tale showcases the author's versatility and his skill in writing long plays.

- Written by Lutz van Dijk and translated by Dr. Karin Chubb, *Themba: A Boy Called Hope* is the story of a young boy in South Africa who must face the difficulty of having AIDS while pursuing his dream of playing soccer for the national team. Published in 2012, the novel shows the effects of AIDS on South African society.

- Published in 1991, *Ryan White: My Own Story* is an autobiography written for young adults. White and his coauthor, Ann Marie Cunningham, tell the story of his struggle to find normality after he contracted AIDS through a blood transfusion. He fought to end discrimination and expand education about the illness.

story. It is the story of a man who searched for love and acceptance in life.

Andre's Mother obviously explores the dynamics within families. Andre's sexuality has a profound impact on his relationship with his family. His story is a familiar one within the gay community. As John M. Clum explains in "Where Are We Now: *Love! Valour! Compassion!* and Contemporary Gay Drama," homosexuals as a minority group are unique because they "do not share their minority status with their parents—[they] are, in fact, usually educated by their parents to believe that what they are is wrong." It is evident in what is learned of the relationship between Andre and his mother that he had been taught that being gay is wrong. This upbringing caused him to separate his family from his life in New York City. First, he refused to tell his mother about his relationship with Cal. Later, when he was dying of AIDS,

BY POINTING OUT THE NORMALITY OF
ANDRE'S EMOTIONS, MCNALLY CREATES SYMPATHY
IN THE AUDIENCE MEMBERS, WHO, LIKE ANDRE'S
MOTHER, ARE CHALLENGED TO SEE BEYOND THEIR
OWN VIEWS AND BIASES."

Andre was unable to tell his mother the truth. He feared both hurting her and facing her disappointment. His fear was motivated by the shame that had been instilled by his family.

The self-loathing and fear that lived in Andre caused him to distance himself from his family even as he longed to be part of it. He hid the truth and refused to go home, even though it was obvious to Cal that he wanted to go back. As Cal explains to Andre's mother, "This funny sweet, sad smile would cross his face, and he'd say, 'Just a little homesick, Cal, just a little bit.'" Andre knew that he no longer fit in with his biological family. He was not able to live up to their expectations and no longer attempted to try. This caused him to remain in New York City, where he was accepted into new familial structures.

Both the homosexual community and Cal's family met Andre's need for love and acceptance in a way that his own family could not. The idea of rejected individuals creating their own communities and families is common. Clum explains how this concept relates to the gay community: they "came together because they were gay and, therefore, misfits. . . . McNally's characters have forged a gay family." Although no close friends of Andre's appear in the play, Cal indicates that he and Andre were part of a larger community that was united by rejection. He says that they were part of "a city of fugitives from our parents' scorn or heartbreak." Andre found himself part of a large communal family whose members shared his struggles, but he also became part of a couple and gained an extended family through his partner.

Cal and Andre created their own family. They were a devoted couple, and their love was proven when Cal remained with Andre throughout his illness and is further proven when Cal attempts to connect with Andre's mother at the memorial ceremony. As often happens with life partners, Andre became a part of Cal's family. The role that Andre played in the family is clear in the anecdotes that Penny and Arthur share. Penny remembers his sense of humor and how happy he made her brother. Arthur valued his relationship with Andre, who, he says, "helped me know my own boy." Andre was loved and supported in New York, but this support system did not replace his own family or remove his desire to be accepted by his mother.

Andre lived with the feeling that his very existence would be a disappointment to his mother if she knew the truth about him. This is why he hid the truth about his relationship with Cal from her. By refusing to risk rejection, however, Andre continually denied his mother the chance to understand or accept him. The belief that his mother would see him as a disappointment was compounded when he was diagnosed with AIDS. Rather than trying to connect with his mother in the last months of his life, Andre chose to remain hidden. He refused to take a chance, and he died without telling his mother the truth or attempting to reconcile.

The stigma attached to AIDS when *Andre's Mother* was first performed would make Andre's decision to live in secret understandable. As Steven Drukman points out in "You Got to Have Friends: Gay Reception of *Love! Valour! Compassion!*," AIDS was the "gay plague" of the 1980s. The general sentiment at that time was that homosexuality was in a way the cause of the disease. *Andre's Mother* explores how the social disgrace of contracting AIDS affected individuals and their relationships. The disgrace a having a child die of AIDS weighs so heavily on Andre's mother that she does not even ask how her son died. Cal addresses this fear when he says, "Let me answer the questions you can't ask." She learns the truth, but it is too late for her and Andre to face the harsh reality of AIDS together.

Andre's Mother addresses the conflict between family expectations and reality in the midst of tragedy. As in many parent-child relationships, the characters place expectations on each other that are not met. Andre's family expected him to live a traditional life as a heterosexual male. Andre failed to meet this expectation, and this perceived failure kept him from his family. Their unmet expectations increased his fear that he was a disappointment, which caused Andre to place his own expectations on his mother. He anticipated her rejection of him, as Cal explains: "He was so afraid of hurting you and of your disapproval." The expectations that Andre and his mother placed on each other created a superficial relationship and kept them from seeing each other realistically.

Not knowing Andre's mother, Cal places his own expectations on her. Cal's expectations are based on his experience with his own family. He expects her maternal instinct to outweigh her disapproval. When Andre was dying, Cal told him to call his mother. He said, "She's your mother. She won't mind." He also expects that he will be able to connect with her after Andre's death. His expectations are left unmet, however, when she refuses to speak to him. He is able to look at the situation realistically when he leaves her, promising that she will never have to see him again. Both of them are left to grieve their loss alone.

The death of Andre means both the loss of love and the loss of potential. The love that Andre had yet to offer both Cal and his mother ended with his death. His mother loses the potential of having an open and honest relationship with her son, and Cal loses the future that he planned to share with Andre. His death is also a loss to society, as his life and his talent are gone. His death is symbolic of the numerous lives lost to AIDS. As Benilde Montgomery explains in "*A Perfect Ganesh*: McNally's Carnival in India," McNally "hopes that death, particularly untimely death, can recover a significance and meaning."

Ultimately, *Andre's Mother* is a play that addresses human emotions. The audience does not need to be gay to relate to the emotional needs of the characters. McNally's "characters reveal human needs, longings, and failings. They want to be heard, accepted, and loved," according to Kathleen Motoike in the *Continuum Encyclopedia of American Literature*. Through Cal's monologue, McNally illustrates how members of the homosexual community have the same emotional needs as everyone else.

The characters' emotional experiences are universal. Many parents, for example, place expectations on their children, and the failure to meet these expectations is not a fear localized in the gay community. Additionally, children hiding information that their parents would not approve of is not restricted to the gay community. Like any other child, Andre longs for the love and acceptance of his mother and fears her rejection. He searches for love, and becomes part of a community that accepts him as he is.

Andre's mother desired a normal life for her son, a sentiment that many parents share. Her expectations were based on her understanding of the world. Like many parents, she had her own idea of who Andre should have chosen as a romantic partner. She rejects Cal because he represents a part of her son's life that she cannot understand; he represents the life that she feared for her son. Andre's mother is a cold, anonymous figure until the end of the play. The loss of her son and Cal's allegation that Andre feared her, however, challenge her to see her son realistically, and she kisses the representation of his soul goodbye.

Fear had dominated the relationship between Andre and his mother. She had feared that he would not have a normal life, which caused her to live in denial. Andre feared her disappointment, causing him to break away from his family and find his own way in New York. It was this fear, however, that made Andre normal. By pointing out the normality of Andre's emotions, McNally creates sympathy in the audience members, who, like Andre's mother, are challenged to see beyond their own views and biases.

Source: April Paris, Critical Essay on *Andre's Mother*, in *Drama for Students*, Gale, Cengage Learning, 2014.

Frank Pilipp and Charles Shull
In the following excerpt, Pilipp and Shull explain how Andre's Mother *reflects society's attitudes about AIDS and stereotypes of gay men.*

Among the media of popular culture, television, over the past decade, has hesitantly become a mouthpiece for reporting and responding to the AIDS epidemic. In addition to documentary and news-related coverage, a small array of fictional accounts, that is full-length feature films spawned by the disease, have constituted a general, albeit basic, chronicle of the multi-faceted dimensions of the epidemic. As a set, these movies both challenge and reinforce a number of basic values and stereotypes linked to nurturing, caretaking, parenting, and sexuality. Consequently, these movies generate an imagery

The white balloon is an important symbol in Andre's Mother. *(© Zlatko Guzmic | Shutterstock.com)*

of the first AIDS decade as multifarious and, perhaps, as confusing as the epidemic itself. Contrasting the presentations of the gay male AIDS protagonists and their families in the films *An Early Frost* (1985), *As Is* (1986), *Andre's Mother* (1990), and *Our Sons* (1991) should not only show the degree to which the AIDS epidemic has been a cultural catalyst and influenced American society but also how cultural values predetermine public and personal perceptions of such an issue as AIDS.

These films present the views of the AIDS issue through images of those who are either "inside" or "outside" the social worlds of gay men and/or of AIDS. This division reflects the parallel worlds of the "gay"/"straight" and AIDS involved/non-involved experiential worlds of contemporary American society. The films illustrate the tensions generated when a terminal illness forces strangers to acknowledge the experiences of the other; to confront, accept, and interact with a social (or medical) world alien to them. The walls that divide these worlds have been built by the dynamics of fear: families fearing and rejecting those who are gay and/or AIDS infected and gay men fearing rejection by their families. That insider/outsider dichotomy

has also been identified as the worlds of the immune and the implicated. In a compelling manner, Goldstein illustrates how popular culture and the arts have reacted differently to the AIDS epidemic. He indicates that although the treatment or representation of AIDS in the arts reflects the insider perspective of the implicated, often the traumatized view of the artist himself, popular culture represents the unassailable refuge of the immune, the unaffected, and presumably non-infected, outside platform of the broad masses. Unquestionably this premise is well argued, though we must disagree with Goldstein's view that "TV movies about AIDS shy away from gay male protagonists" and that "the typical protagonist is a young, virtuous, and vulnerable woman." Although this holds true for most of those films of the '80s that deal with terminal diseases in general (which are generically indebted to the AIDS epidemic), the films to be discussed here all introduce single, white, professionally successful, gay, male protagonists experiencing AIDS.

. . . *Andre's Mother*, a film adapted from a play by Terrence McNally, displays an unmistakable staginess with its monologues and its often-times too brisk dialogues. The two central

> IN THESE FILMS THE VIRUS IS OFTEN SEEN AS A PUNISHMENT INFLICTED ON THE PROTAGONISTS AND THEIR FAMILIES FOR THEIR BREACH WITH MIDDLE-CLASS NORMS AND VALUES."

figures are Cal (Richard Thomas), the lover of the deceased Andre, and Andre's mother (Sada Thompson) who still has not accepted her late son's social-sexual identity. The tension of the film is created by Cal's fight for that acceptance from Andre's mother. The events portrayed center on Andre's memorial service. There, for one last time, the characters attest to their attachment to the admired, beloved, almost worshipped friend. The outsider AIDS dimension in this film is illustrated by Andre's mother, who does not understand the releasing of the memorial balloons in Central Park as a symbol of a final "letting go," a ceremony that has become part of many AIDS memorials. Cal's behavior toward her shows the inside perspective of someone who has lived through months of caretaking of a loved one during the illness. His own need for resolution and closure of his anger and pain may explain his demands upon the mother who has remained an outsider to her son's being gay and to his disease.

Cal introduces the final scene when he attempts resolution of that tension by forcing acknowledgement of what caused Andre's death: "Andre died of AIDS." When he cries "I didn't kill him!" and reveals that he is HIV-negative, he hopes to get the mother to accept and share his love for the deceased Andre. In a vehement tirade of anger and tears about the walls of denial—"how many of us . . . don't want to disappoint our mothers?"—he demands her approval. Indeed, her aversion surprisingly turns to hesitant affection (she returns Cal's embrace) and Cal earns her acceptance. In this scene the musical score, "L'amero, Saro Costante" from Mozart's "Il Re Pastore" underscores the theme of loyalty and commitment but also contributes to the stylized ambiance of this film that never manages to convincingly develop the motivation for the title character's change or Cal's obsessive

behavior. In sum, this short film deals with the two main characters resolving tensions: coming to terms with the "other" and making peace with themselves. Again, attitudes about gay men are reflected in the clashing views of two families. Cal's sister and father are shown as accepting Cal's sexuality, although the latter indicates minimal understanding, "a lack of imagination on my part"; Cal's mother and Andre's father are shown as rejecting it. Andre's mother is moving towards acceptance only as the film ends.

. . . Throughout these four films certain messages, images, and stereotypes are presented about AIDS and gay men. As for demographics, two images of the city are presented: one as a refuge for gay men where they can be free, anonymous, and create their lives as gay men, and another as a location of the AIDS infected. On the other hand, in the rural, suburban settings where there are few gay men, the disease is perceived as an alien phenomenon. Naturally, this reinforces the classic American "city" myth. In reality, gay men do live in rural-suburban America and, even when the earliest of these films was released, most rural-suburban areas had their own indigenous AIDS populations. Bigotry, prejudice, and fear of gay men and AIDS have no geographical boundaries. On a medical level, mixed images of medical professionals illustrate the experiences of many AIDS patients. Some doctors (although not portrayed in these films) are still AIDS-phobic, although most others are both concerned and overworked. And, as these films indicate, some rescue squads, nurses, and other staff members have refused to treat AIDS patients, whereas most others have proven to be deeply compassionate in working with their patients.

As to the familial issues of acceptance, we can discern interesting generational and gender combination patterns. The two grandmothers presented in these films (both played by Sylvia Sidney) are accepting characters. In *An Early Frost* she reacts more to the disease issue than to the fact of having a gay grandson. In *Andre's Mother*, it is—ironically—the grandmother who accepts her grandson as he is. She is also a catalyst pushing her daughter to break through the wall of denial. Similarly, the two sisters presented in the movies both know about and accept their brothers being gay, although Michael's pregnant sister (*An Early Frost*) withdraws in fear because of AIDS. The mothers in the films have difficulties accepting their sons as men bonding with other men. Four mothers, two of them on camera, have known about and rejected their sons. However, the stereotypical female gender roles of nurturing and defending ultimately help all of them to overcome their fears. We only hear of cases in which this does not happen, e.g., the family that disowned its son who had AIDS (Victor in *An Early Frost*). That, on the other hand, is used by Michael's mother to reaffirm that this "is not going to happen to our son."

Men tend to have greater difficulties with acceptance than women. Grandfathers and brothers are absent in these films—with one nameless exception in *As Is*. Even Michael's brother-in-law (*An Early Frost*), who knows Michael is gay, is absent after Michael's return to his family and Cal's future brother-in-law (*Andre's Mother*), who is said to be supportive, is off camera. Like their wives, the fathers of the HIV-infected protagonists, as far as they are introduced, reflect minimal variation of the male parent struggling to accept his gay son. Michael's father in *An Early Frost* rejects but shifts towards more acceptance when his son agrees to fight the disease—like a man. In *Andre's Mother*, Cal's father accepts his son although Andre's father turns his back on his son completely. The absence of the other five fathers, for whatever reason, seems to emphasize the difficulties in presenting male parent acceptance of the gay son to viewers. Overall, the parental generation is shown struggling (presumably because of their own unfulfilled wishes for their sons) with acceptance.

Three variations of gay male interaction with the "straight world" occur in these films: there is the son who is open and accepted by his family (Peter, Saul, Cal, James, the lovers of the HIV-infected protagonists); the son who is open but not accepted or discussed (Rich, Andre, and Donald); and the son who lives in hiding from his family (Michael). An interesting pattern is that those gay men who are neither open to nor accepted by their families are the men stricken with AIDS. Those who are open to their families are uninfected and are shown as supportive, nurturing, caretaking, and constant companions who are willing to sacrifice their energies and emotions for their partners. They choose, even insist on remaining with their partners, reaffirming the positive force of parental acceptance

overcoming all stereotypes and fears. These caring characters present an interesting variation on the stereotype of gay men. Their model of personal and social responsibility may be the beginning of a new gay male image in film. On the other hand, however, all of the other characters who are shown as nurturers are women, which may one more time reinforce the general stereotype of gay men not really being "men."

In all the films a certain blame seems to be imputed to the biased parent, who perhaps did not provide sufficient understanding, openness, warmth, and security for the son to breed the right "virtues." Because of this, the parent becomes partly responsible for the son's exodus to a life in an environment harboring "sin" and disease, away and separate from the mainstream, conservative middle-class values. The flight of the sons can be perceived as an escape from these values, from a world in which they are strangers. Their homosexuality and infection contaminates their identities and they become, much like Kafka's Gregor Samsa, estranged, almost metamorphosized (physically in some films) into a socially unacceptable "other." Usually, the family is unable to provide that much needed ultimate support for its sons; this can only be rendered by the respective lover, their "own kind." And, as in Samsa's case, sometimes only their deaths can restore the former identities as respectable sons and citizens.

Although scattered comments in these films mark the HIV virus as blind to gender, race, or sexual orientation, this does not necessarily neutralize the false image of AIDS as a purely homosexual disease. In these films the virus is often seen as a punishment inflicted on the protagonists and their families for their breach with middle-class norms and values. By contrast, it is most striking that if the son's openness is reciprocated by the family's approval, he does not experience HIV infection. The conclusion lies at hand: unflagging adherence to the solid values of parental or companion love and honesty, constancy and exclusiveness in love relationships, or simply, "doing the right thing" precludes contraction. Although this exhortation to middle-class conformism would weaken the otherwise socio-critical and emancipatory impact with regard to the implicated, these values are presented as larger than the issues that make the characters strangers to each other. These values and behaviors are shown to heal the wounds caused by that strangeness. Throughout these movies the terror of the destruction of AIDS leads most of the characters of both worlds to be involved with each other, to resolve tensions about sexuality or fear of rejection, to break the walls between them. Ultimately, however, and despite parental and sibling love overriding stereotypes and fears, the movies seem to suggest that these walls should have never been built.

Source: Frank Pilipp and Charles Shull, "TV Movies of the First Decade of AIDS," in *Journal of Popular Film and Television*, Vol. 21, No. 1, Spring 1993, p. 19.

SOURCES

Abrams, M. H., *A Glossary of Literary Terms*, 7th ed., Harcourt Brace College Publishers, 1999, p. 311.

Clum, John M., "Where We Are Now: *Love! Valour! Compassion!* and Contemporary Gay Drama," in *Terrence McNally: A Casebook*, edited by Toby Silverman Zinman, Garland Publishing, 1997, pp. 95–116.

Drukman, Steven, "You Got to Have Friends: Gay Reception of *Love! Valour! Compassion!*," in *Terrence McNally: A Casebook*, edited by Toby Silverman Zinman, Garland Publishing, 1997, pp. 117–33.

"Fatwa for 'Gay Jesus' Writer," BBC News website, October 29, 1999, http://news.bbc.co.uk/2/hi/uk_news/493436.stm (accessed July 28, 2013).

Frontain, Raymond-Jean, "McNally and Steinbeck," in *ANQ*, Vol. 21, No. 4, Fall 2008, pp. 43–51.

Harmon, William, *A Handbook to Literature*, 9th ed., Prentice Hall, 2003, pp. 305, 352.

Klein, Alvin, "Frankie and Johnny's Uncommon Glow," in *New York Times*, February 4, 1990, p. D4.

Levy, Michael, "Gay Rights Movement," in *Encyclopædia Britannica* online, http://www.britannica.com/EBchecked/topic/766382/gay-rights-movement (accessed July 28, 2013).

McNally, Terrence, *Andre's Mother*, in *Terrence McNally: 15 Short Plays*, Smith and Kraus, 1994, pp. 349–51.

Montgomery, Benilde, "*A Perfect Ganesh:* McNally's Carnival in India," in *Terrence McNally: A Casebook*, edited by Toby Silverman Zinman, Garland Publishing, 1997, pp. 135–45.

Motoike, Kathleen, "McNally, Terrence," in *Continuum Encyclopedia of American Literature*, Continuum International Publishing, 2003, pp. 746–47.

O'Connor, John J., "Accepting the Lover of a Son Dead of AIDS," in *New York Times*, March 7, 1990, http://www.nytimes.com/1990/03/07/arts/review-television-accepting-the-lover-of-a-son-dead-of-aids.html (accessed July 28, 2013).

"Ronald W. Reagan," in *Encyclopædia Britannica* online, 2013, http://library.eb.com/eb/article-9062864 (accessed July 28, 2013).

Salisbury, Joyce E., and Andrew E. Kersten, "Work in Contemporary America," in *Daily Life through History*, ABC-CLIO, 2013.

"Terrence McNally," Kennedy Center website, http://www.kennedy-center.org/explorer/artists/?entity_id=18184&source_type=A (accessed July 28, 2013).

"Timeline: Milestones in the American Gay Rights Movement," PBS website, http://www.pbs.org/wgbh/americanexperience/features/timeline/stonewall/ (accessed July 28, 2013).

"A Timeline of AIDS," AIDS.gov, http://aids.gov/hiv-aids-basics/hiv-aids-101/aids-timeline/ (accessed July 28, 2013).

Zinman, Toby Silverman, ed., "Interview with Terrence McNally," in *Terrence McNally: A Casebook*, Garland Publishing, 1997, pp. 3–15.

———, ed., Introduction to *Terrence McNally: A Casebook*, Garland Publishing, 1997, p. xiii.

Zinoman, Jason, "A Modern, Gay You-Know-Who Superstar," in *New York Times*, October 21, 2008, http://theater.nytimes.com/2008/10/22/theater/reviews/22corp.html (accessed July 28, 2013).

FURTHER READING

Camardella, Michele L., *America in the 1980s*, Facts on File, 2005.

This reference book is written for young adults, but it provides useful information for students of all ages. It examines the political and cultural trends of the decade, including fashion, art, music, and popular culture.

Harden, Victoria A., *AIDS at 30: A History*, Potomac Books, 2012.

Written from a scientific perspective, Harden explores the history of HIV and AIDS. The book, written for a general audience, examines how science and society have approached the disease, discussing both political influence and cultural influence on research.

Rasebotsa, Nobantu, Meg Samuelson, and Kylie Thomas, eds., *Nobody Ever Said AIDS: Poems and Stories from Southern Africa*, Kwela Books, 2007.

This collection of poems and stories is the result of a creative-writing competition from the University of Cape Town. Contributors explore their experience with AIDS and provide a glimpse into the AIDS epidemic in South Africa.

Shilts, Randy, *And the Band Played On: Politics, People, and the AIDS Epidemic*, 20th anniversary ed., St. Martin's Griffin, 2007.

> This influential book was first published in 1987, and it carefully examines the first five years of the AIDS epidemic. Coming from a journalistic perspective, the book examines how social and political reactions to the illness allowed it to become an epidemic.

Sinfield, Alan, *Out on Stage: Lesbian and Gay Theatre in the Twentieth Century*, Yale University Press, 1999.

> Sinfield examines how representations of homosexual characters in the theater have changed over the years. The text follows playwrights from Oscar Wilde to the end of the twentieth century and provides students with awareness of how views of homosexuality changed over the years.

Smith, Jennifer, *The Gay Rights Movement*, Greenhaven Press, 2003.

> Smith examines the history of the gay rights movement. Readers will appreciate the inclusion of primary documents that highlight the struggles within the movement as well as reactions within society.

Wolfe, Peter, *The Theater of Terrence McNally: A Critical Study*, McFarland, 2013.

> This nonfiction text provides a critical overview of McNally's work. The book is useful for anyone interested in attaining a deeper understanding of the playwright's work.

SUGGESTED SEARCH TERMS

Terrence McNally

gay rights movement

gay rights movement AND America

Terrence McNally AND Andre's Mother

Terrence McNally AND criticism

AIDS AND 1980s

AIDS AND history

Terrence McNally AND biography

America AND 1980s

Beauty

JANE MARTIN

2001

No one knows who Jane Martin really is. Various profiles about her indicate that she is from Kentucky and list the many plays she has written but give no other personal information. She has never accepted any of her awards in person. She has never attended the opening of one her plays, nor met with the directors or actors. No one is even certain that she is indeed a "she." The name is a pseudonym—a fake name adopted by a writer who prefers to keep his or her identity a secret. Speculation about who the author might be and the reasons for the secrecy is widespread in the theater world.

Martin's early plays deal mostly with feminist issues, but her later works expand to address other social issues, ranging from child abuse to satire about the theater world. Her play *Beauty* deals with the theme of jealousy and explores the idea of what beauty really is, as well as how people search for happiness. *Beauty* is available in *Jane Martin: Collected Plays*, Vol. 2, *1996–2001* (2001).

AUTHOR BIOGRAPHY

The only straightforward fact that has ever been revealed about Martin is that she is from Kentucky. Jon Jory, who has produced most of Martin's plays and who acts as a kind of spokesman on her behalf, explained in a press release

Bethany finds a magic lamp on the beach. *(© Fer Gregory | Shutterstock.com)*

cited on the Hartnell College website that "Who-ever writes these plays feels that they would be unable to write them if [their identity] was made public knowledge."

There are stories about Martin, though they seem to be more rumor than truth, including about how her first play, *Twirler*, was produced. It is said that Martin put a copy of the play under Jory's door at the Actors Theatre of Louisville. It is also said that there was a contest, for which *Twirler* was an entry. Whatever the circumstances, *Twirler* was staged in 1981 as part of the Humana Festival of New American Plays, an important and prestigious regional theater event founded and managed by Jory. The play garnered much attention and praise.

Since then, over two dozen plays have been published under the Martin pseudonym, including *Talking With . . .* (1982); *Keely and Du* (1993), which was nominated for the Pulitzer Prize; *Middle-Aged White Guys* (1995); *Mr. Bundy* (1998); and *Anton in Show Business* (2000). Martin often tackles controversial social issues, such as abortion and child abuse, but always injects humor into her plays.

There is much speculation in the theater world about Martin's identity. Some believe that Martin's works might be the products of a group of playwrights working together rather than an individual. Jory, so often Martin's representative and the only one to admit to having "met" her, is himself generally thought to be the playwright behind Martin's work, either working on his own or in collaboration with his wife, Marcia Dixey. Jory was a producing director at the Actors Theatre of Louisville for thirty-two years. His close association with the theater and with Martin's work has naturally led many to conclude that he is the true "Jane Martin." Indeed, some publications treat it as an established fact that Jory wrote the plays, but he has always denied it.

PLOT SUMMARY

Beauty begins with a young woman on the stage alone, talking on the phone. The stage directions indicate that there are not a lot of set pieces—perhaps just enough furniture or a backdrop to

MEDIA ADAPTATIONS

- A 2012 production of *Beauty* performed by first-year students at Circle in the Square Theatre School in New York was recorded and posted on YouTube at http://www.youtube.com/watch?v=RZCCrm31Ikc.

suggest an apartment. The woman is named Carla, and she is on the phone with a man she does not remember who is asking her to marry him. Her conversation is interrupted by a knock at the door.

Carla's friend Bethany is at the door. She is carrying an old-fashioned, Middle Eastern lamp. Bethany is very excited and tries to tell Carla what has happened, but Carla does not pay attention, going back to her phone call.

Each woman is focused on her own concerns: Bethany explains how she found the lamp on the beach, while Carla is absorbed in her phone call. Even after she hangs up, she does not listen to Bethany. Carla begins to tell Bethany about the marriage proposal until her attention is caught by the news that a genie came out of the lamp when Bethany opened the lid.

Carla assumes that Bethany is joking and says that she has to meet with fashion designer Ralph Lauren about possible modeling jobs, but Bethany insists that she is telling the truth. The genie offered her wishes, and when she asked for twenty-five thousand dollars, the money fell out of the sky. She takes the bills out of her purse and shows them to Carla as proof. Carla begins to believe Bethany's story.

Carla notes that Bethany has been acting strangely and asks, "Are you dealing?" Carla is implying that Bethany's unusual behavior may be caused by taking illegal drugs, but Bethany answers that she has not even been eating chocolate lately.

Carla wants to see the genie, but Bethany tells the rest of her story. She explains how her

next wish was for the genie to heal her uncle, who had been in the hospital after being run over. The genie said, "Yes, Master." Bethany called the hospital and learned that her uncle came to and walked out of the intensive care unit, feeling fine.

Bethany is not sure what to do with her last wish. Carla asks to see the genie and demands that Bethany must stop joking because of the meeting with Ralph Lauren. Bethany admits that she has always wanted to be like Carla, who is surprised. Carla points out that Bethany makes a good salary and has written short stories and succeeded in getting them published. Carla is frustrated by her lack of success in her modeling career and was driven to get plastic surgery on her nose.

Bethany insists, "I want to be beautiful." Carla says that Bethany has "charm" and "personality" and that she is "pretty," but Bethany draws a clear distinction between "pretty" and "beautiful." She points out that Carla is always the center of attention because of her beauty, that men are attracted to her, and that studies prove that beautiful people earn higher salaries than plainer people. Carla explains that she attracts the wrong kind of men—those only interested in her because of her looks. Therefore she has never had a meaningful long-term relationship. She complains that she gets harassed on the street and that most women do not want to be friends with her.

In spite of the negative aspects of being beautiful that Carla has explained, Bethany is convinced that great physical beauty is "what everybody wants." She is determined to use her last wish to become beautiful herself. Carla tries to talk Bethany out of her decision, explaining how frustrating it is not to have the concentration to read an entire book and not to have enough general knowledge to make good conversation at a dinner party; Carla clearly envies Bethany's intelligence. Bethany, however, is not swayed. She is certain that "beauty makes you the center of the universe."

Bethany picks up the lamp and makes her wish. The stage directions indicate that the lights go out, flicker, and then come back on. Both women are on the floor. Although the stage directions explain that the actresses have changed places, the audience fully realizes the change only as the two characters begin to speak.

Both women feel strange, and as they inspect themselves for possible injury, they realize they have switched bodies. Bethany looks down to see she is wearing Carla's jewelry, nail polish, and dress, and Carla is dismayed to be wearing Bethany's shoes, which are apparently not stylish enough for a meeting with Ralph Lauren.

Bethany decides to go out to find a man, but Carla stops her. Bethany asks Carla to do a math problem, and Carla asks Bethany a question about makeup. When both can answer the questions, which they would not have been able to answer before the switch, they realize that they have switched brains as well as bodies. Carla expresses sympathy for Bethany's now having her less-intelligent brain, but Bethany says she does not care. She insists that they both now have the thing that everyone wants, more than beauty or brains: "Different problems." The lights go down to indicate the end of the play.

CHARACTERS

Bethany

Bethany falls into the stereotype of a woman who is smarter than she is attractive. Carla calls her "pretty," and Bethany does not disagree, but she accepts that she does not have the extraordinary beauty that Carla has. Carla points out Bethany's positive traits: she has "charm" and "personality," and clearly Carla believes Bethany to be intelligent. Bethany is a published author and has a good job as an accountant that she got right after college, in contrast to Carla, who is still struggling to establish her career.

However, Bethany feels like what she has is not enough. She is not content and believes that she would be happier if she were beautiful. Bethany insists that "beauty is the real deal" and that "beauty makes you the center of the universe." She does not believe Carla's protests and descriptions of the problems of being beautiful. Bethany is certain that beautiful people like Carla are lying "to make us feel better because we aren't in your league."

In some ways, Bethany seems like a good person: Carla says that most women are intimidated by her beauty, but Bethany, even though she admits to fierce jealousy of Carla's beauty,

has been able to look past that and become friends with her. In other ways, however, Bethany seems self-centered. She wants Carla to listen to her story, though Carla explains several times that she is late for an important meeting. Perhaps Bethany, who is secure enough in her job to steal a day off, has forgotten that her friend is still struggling to achieve even modest success in her career. Also, Bethany, so sure that she cannot be wrong, does not listen to Carla's warnings and advice.

Bethany's feelings about her uncle also offer conflicting pictures of the kind of person she is. She wishes for the genie to heal her uncle, but only after she has wished for money to buy a new car. It seems like the idea of helping her uncle only occurred to her as an impossible task, useful as a test for the genie, rather than as a gesture of genuine concern. In the first few lines of the play, she uses her uncle's hospitalization as an excuse to miss work when the real reason is that she "just had a beach urge." Later, she laments the fact that she has only one wish left—"although I'm really pleased about my uncle." The fact that she feels the need to explain that she is pleased makes one question whether it is truly important to her.

In the play's final moments, Bethany gracefully accepts that her wish does not bring her exactly what she expected. She at least has achieved a substantial change in her life and perhaps is hopeful that the change will make her happier. However, Bethany's reaction seems to come more from Martin's plan for the play's end—clearly "different problems" is a kind of punch line to the entire play—rather than being a good illustration of a basic element of Bethany's character.

Carla

Like Bethany, Carla is an example of a stereotype. She represents the beautiful woman who is not so intelligent. The play opens with Carla on the phone with a man who is proposing marriage—a man whom Carla does not even remember. This stresses her extraordinary beauty, the kind that attracts men and makes women jealous.

The audience quickly learns, however, that the fact that Carla is beautiful does not mean that she has no problems. She is no more content than Bethany. When Bethany expresses her wish to be more like Carla, Carla begins to explain all of the problems that her beauty has brought her. For example, she has never had a long and meaningful relationship with a man because her beauty attracts shallow men and scares away intelligent men. She feels that her beauty is the reason why Bethany is her only female friend: most women are intimidated or jealous. Carla is surprised by Bethany's jealousy, suggesting, "Half the time you don't even like me." She must feel isolated, thinking that her closest (perhaps only) friend does not truly like her.

Additionally, Carla's beauty is not even enough to ensure her success in a career based on physical appearance. As Bethany arrives and Carla ends her phone call, she is rushing around to prepare for a meeting with Ralph Lauren, which she calls "very possibly my one chance to go from catalogue model to the very, very big time." Unlike Bethany, who landed a secure, well-paying job directly after college, Carla is still struggling to establish her career, "hanging on by her fingernails" in a highly competitive field.

Perhaps Carla, like Bethany, at times comes across as self-centered. She does not always treat people well, as during the phone conversation, when she brushes off the man who claims to be in love with her. Also, Carla does not give Bethany her full attention when she has an exciting story to tell. However, Carla does try to talk Bethany out of making her third wish, seeming to realize that Bethany's strengths, like intelligence and character, are more important than superficial physical beauty. She seems to understand that Bethany would be making a mistake by wishing for beauty and to genuinely want to prevent such a choice. Carla also expresses sympathy for Bethany once they realize that they have switched brains. Perhaps because she has only one true friend, she values the friendship that much more.

THEMES

Beauty

From the title alone, it is obvious that beauty is an important theme of the play. Indeed, Martin manages to explore different kinds of beauty and its effects on people in the very short span of her brief play.

Bethany and Carla have a discussion about the difference between "beautiful" and "pretty."

Bethany thinks that prettiness can be ignored—people only notice it and pay a compliment about it "a couple of times a year," whereas "*beautiful* is twenty-four hours a day." Because it cannot be ignored, beauty makes a person "the center of any moment."

It is Carla who raises the idea of inner versus outer beauty. She brings up Bethany's intelligence, her "charm," and her "personality," pointing out important traits that are not related to physical appearance. Through Carla, Martin raises the idea that a person's personality might affect how she or he is perceived. Bethany, however, seems to scorn inner beauty. She says, "Pretty is what people discover about you after they know you." Instead of being pretty, she wishes she had the kind of beauty that "knocks them out across the room."

It is not only beauty itself that is discussed in the play, but what beauty might bring a person. Bethany wants to dazzle when she walks into a room. She wants to feel important. She wants men to notice her; she does not want to be ignored. "It's what everybody wants," Bethany claims; but Carla does not seem to enjoy her beauty. She sees the very things Bethany mentions as annoying and feels trapped by her physical appearance. Men *only* pay attention to her looks and never try to get to know her. She wishes she had more inner beauty, more intelligence. She wishes she could have a more important and successful career and form a lasting relationship with a man instead of the shallow ones she has had. Even in one of the areas in which physical appearance might bring a person success—modeling—Carla's beauty has not benefited her. Although she is beautiful, she is "hanging on by her fingernails."

Jealousy

Jealousy is one of the main themes in *Beauty*. The most obvious example of this theme is Bethany's jealousy of Carla's beauty. Bethany admits to being "pretty" but feels that "pretty is the minor leagues of beautiful." She wishes she had the kind of beauty that Carla has—beauty that makes "people stare" and "men flock."

It is not difficult to detect this theme in Bethany's feelings, because Martin has Bethany come right out and state it: she freely admits to being controlled by an "unspoken, ferocious, all-consuming urge," motivated by "the ogre of

TOPICS FOR FURTHER STUDY

- Bethany believes that her life will be better if she is beautiful, so she wishes to become her more strikingly attractive friend. Rather than solve her problems, the switch simply gives Bethany different problems. Write a short play in which Bethany wishes for something different—something that might actually improve her life. You might write a monologue and perform it for your class alone, or you could include Carla or other characters and perform the play with classmates.

- Standards of beauty vary from culture to culture. Even within the same culture, different qualities are valued in different time periods. For example, in the United States long ago, women used to carry parasols to shade themselves from the sun because very fair skin was considered the ideal. More recently, tanned skin has become popular, and some people lie in the sun or create an artificial tan by having their skin treated with chemicals. Choose two very different cultures. Using online and print resources, research what each culture finds beautiful. Create a PowerPoint presentation, including photos, that explains the elements of the two cultures' ideas about what is beautiful.

- Playwright Neil LaBute wrote a series called "the Beauty Plays": *The Shape of Things*, *Fat Pig*, and *Reasons to Be Pretty*. The three short plays deal in different ways with the issue of beauty. After reading LaBute's plays, write an essay comparing one of them to *Beauty*. Discuss what each play says about beauty and how people's perceptions of their physical appearances affect how they feel about themselves.

- In Natasha Friend's novel *Perfect* (2004), Isabelle is grieving for her father, who recently died, and struggles to feel comfortable at school. She is jealous of Ashley, the prettiest girl in class. When Isabelle's stress leads to an eating disorder, her mother brings her to group therapy, where Isabelle is shocked to learn that popular Ashley is also bulimic. Write a short story in which *Beauty*'s Bethany meets Isabelle and shares what happened when she changed her physical appearance. What advice would Bethany give? Post your short story on a blog and allow your classmates to comment.

---

jealousy." However, the ways in which Carla illustrates the theme of jealousy are slightly more subtle.

When Bethany says that she is jealous, Carla is very surprised. Immediately, she points out Bethany's well-paying job as an accountant and her published short stories. In the conversation that follows, Carla counters every point Bethany makes. Bethany sees the attention that Carla gets from men, but Carla feels "hassled" by men who like her only for her looks. Carla mentions that she has never had a successful romance with a man, while she points out to Bethany, "You've had three long-term relationships, and you're only twenty-three." Carla tells Bethany that only "male bimbos" are attracted to her. She completes her speech by saying in frustration, "I don't even want to talk about this!" Carla is as jealous of Bethany's brains as Bethany is of Carla's beauty.

In the end, Martin surprises the audience. The play's title encourages viewers to think that beauty is the main subject of the play, and it is indeed an important theme, but the last line of the play shows the real message: the old saying "The grass is always greener on the other side of the fence." It is easy to look at other people's lives and think that they have it better, but in truth, their problems and challenges are just different and simply not noticed by others.

After finding the lamp, Bethany first wishes for $25,000. (© vovan | Shutterstock.com)

STYLE

Stereotypes

For the characters in *Beauty*, Martin relies on stereotypes. A stereotype is a fixed, oversimplified idea of a particular kind of person. The use of stereotypes means that there is not a lot of in-depth characterization in *Beauty*, but in such a short play, there is not a lot of time for that. By presenting stereotypes, Martin lets the audience make certain assumptions so that it can grasp the characters quickly and the action of the play can move forward. It is a kind of shorthand that is useful for a very short play.

The stereotypes Martin uses are not meant to represent actual, realistic people. They are meant to show society's preconceptions. For example, it is highly unlikely that Martin, well known for the feminist slant of her work, truly believes the idea that a very beautiful woman cannot also be very intelligent. Martin uses the stereotypes in part to expose the fact that such prejudices exist.

One-Act Play

A one-act play is, of course, simply a short play. However, the nature of a one-act is different from that of a full-length play—it is not just a shorter version of a longer play. Just as with a full-length play, or any effective story, a one-act must have basic elements of drama: exposition, conflict, climax, and denouement. During the exposition, the situation is explained, and the characters are introduced. The conflict encompasses the main action of the play—a struggle between two people or two ideas or between the characters and their circumstances. The climax is the turning point of the action of the play, and the denouement is the resolution of the conflict, during which the loose ends are wrapped up. In a longer play, the denouement might be several scenes, but in a one-act it is usually extremely brief or may overlap with the climax. This is a lot to accomplish in a single act.

Because of the brevity of one-act plays, they have specific characteristics that set them apart from longer, standard plays. Everything about a

one-act must be concentrated. Anything super-
fluous must be cut out. Even the dialogue must
be brief and communicate only the essential
information. One-act plays usually have a limited number of characters and less development
of each character because there is not sufficient
time for in-depth character study. Also, one-act
plays usually have a tighter focus than longer
works, sometimes only including one scene and
often portraying a particular situation that can
be managed in the brief span of time. This concentrated focus gives one-act plays a unity of
time, space, and action that make them an art
form unto themselves, different from longer
plays.

Southern Gothicism

The only specific piece of biographical information that Jory provides about Martin is that she
is from Kentucky. This one small detail, whether
true or not, of the actual playwright might provide a clue about how Jory would like critics and
audiences to view Martin's work. In her essay
"Pseudonymy and Identity Politics: Exploring
'Jane Martin,'" J. Ellen Gainor speculates,
"Jory's emphasis on Martin's geographical base
may signal his desire to have her work considered within traditions of Southern writing," specifically Southern gothic literature.

Southern gothicism is a style that incorporates grotesque characters and scenes, where
grotesque indicates something distorted in
appearance or character so that it becomes com-
ical or repulsive, or perhaps both. In *Beauty*,
Martin distorts her characters, turning them
into stereotypes, and presents a scene where reality is distorted to the point of absurdity. In
Southern gothicism, this distortion can also
include abnormal psychological states or possibly elements of the supernatural, as shown in the
magic lamp and the genie in *Beauty*.

Another important element of Southern
gothicism is dark humor. The most straightforward example of dark humor in *Beauty* is in
Bethany's description of her uncle's accident:
"he was hit by two trucks." Obviously, when
thought of in realistic terms, there is nothing
humorous about a man being injured by a
truck. By having Bethany's uncle hit by two
trucks rather than just one, Martin turns it
into something funny. It is unrealistic and ridiculous, and therefore the audience has permission
to laugh.

Finally, Southern gothic literature is exemplified by characters who feel alienated from the
world and alienated from each other. They live
with a sense of futility, feeling that they can do
nothing to affect the world. These themes of
alienation and futility are especially significant
to Southern writers and are the characteristic of
Southern gothicism most clearly reflected in
Beauty. Gainor explains: "The fact that each of
Martin's female figures is a misfit particularly
ties her to the Southern literary tradition."
Both Carla and Bethany feel discontent and disconnected. They are friends, but they do not
seem to understand one another all that well.
They feel unhappy and fear that there is little
they can do to improve their situations. Only the
introduction of the supernatural creates great
changes in their lives.

HISTORICAL CONTEXT

Early Twentieth-Century Regional Theater

Many people associate theater with large cities,
especially New York, and for a long time, it was
true that only in very large cities in the United
States did theaters have enough financial support to stage quality productions. After World
War I ended in 1918, however, things began to
change, in both the theater world and America in
general. Soldiers returned from the war shocked
by the brutality they had witnessed. Many were
tired of following orders and wanted more
choice in life, and more fun. In 1920, the Nineteenth Amendment passed, bringing women the
right to vote. It was the Jazz Age, a time of
prosperity, independent thought, and increased
social freedom.

World War I had cut American theaters off
from what was going on in the theater world in
Europe, where stagecraft was becoming more
experimental. During the war, the "little theater"
movement began. In 1912, Boston's Toy Theatre
and the Chicago Little Theatre opened, followed
by many other small, independent theaters. By
1917, there were approximately fifty such theaters scattered across the United States. After the
war, inspired by Europe's bolder independent
theaters, these smaller theaters blossomed.

Large theaters obtained money for their
expensive productions from investors, who of
course would not invest unless the show was

likely to make money. This meant that the plays chosen and the styles of directing and acting were conservative, aimed at pleasing the widest possible audience and therefore selling the highest number of tickets. In contrast, little theaters relied on volunteers and got money from subscribers. Because they did not have the financial pressures facing the larger, traditional theaters, little theaters were able to make their productions more groundbreaking. Little theaters supported the work of younger, unknown playwrights and new experimental methods of acting and production. For example, a completely realistic set, which was expensive, was the norm in big commercial theaters, whereas little theaters might use just enough props to suggest the setting. This style is simpler but in some ways enhances the experience for audiences because it reduces plays to their basic important elements: actors on the stage interpreting the script.

The Great Depression of the 1930s was very difficult for these small theaters. In bad financial times, people are much less likely to buy tickets to a play or volunteer to do unpaid work. Many independent theaters folded. In an effort to support the arts, Congress initiated the Federal Theatre Project. From 1935 to 1939, the project funded free productions of both classics and new plays. These performances boosted public morale and kept actors working. The Federal Theatre Project was also significant in the history of black drama through the establishment of the Negro People's Theatre, which staged productions with all-black casts.

Post–World War II Theater

After World War II, American theater continued in two almost separate tracks. There were the conservative, traditional theaters in one track and the independent, smaller theaters in the other. By the early 1960s, even some of the smaller theater companies began to feel the same financial pressures as the traditional ones. In New York, the more experimental off-Broadway theater companies had started to feel the need to turn a profit to keep themselves going and became somewhat more conservative. In response, the off-off-Broadway movement began, with smaller, more daring productions. At the same time, more regional theaters formed, providing more opportunities for women and minorities. Indeed, whereas in the traditional, conservative world of big commercial theaters

Although Bethany is "pretty," she is jealous of Carla's more spectacular beauty. (© Olga Dmitrieva / Shutterstock.com)

women had difficulty achieving positions of power, in regional theater women were central, getting their plays produced and opening their own theaters.

Because the survival of a small, independent theater was uncertain, efforts were made in the second half of the twentieth century to stabilize regional theaters. One way theaters did this was to form standing companies rather than auditioning actors for roles for each individual play. Many theaters were able to afford to support their standing companies through outside financial support. This money came not from investors as with traditional commercial theaters but from grants. The National Endowment for the Arts, which was founded in 1965, provides financial support to artists in all fields, including theater, but there is sometimes controversy over these grants: some people dislike their tax money being used to fund artwork or stage productions that they find objectionable in some way.

Another source of support is corporate funding: large companies donating money to a specific theater or production. For example, the Humana Festival in Louisville, Kentucky, where Jane Martin got her start, is supported by the Humana Foundation. This festival, which was founded in 1980, represents the longest sponsoring relationship between a corporation and a theater in the United States.

Regional theater is a valuable part of the theater world and of American culture. Regional theaters bring quality productions to people living outside major cites who might otherwise never have a chance to experience seeing a play. These theaters also provide positions for actors—it is estimated that in 1990, for each actor in a Broadway production, there were four actors employed by nonprofit regional companies. Additionally, little-known or unknown playwrights, like Martin, who might not get the chance to have their work produced on Broadway, get their opportunities in regional theaters. Without regional theaters, American theater would be a far less interesting and varied field.

CRITICAL OVERVIEW

There has not been much critical attention paid specifically to *Beauty*, perhaps because it is such a brief play. Martin's work gets lots of notice in general, however, and not just because of the mystery surrounding the playwright's true identity. Indeed, Leah Green, in her profile of Martin in the *Critical Survey of Drama*, states that "the quality of her plays has retained a surprising quality to overshadow the secondary 'identity controversy' that surrounds them." Green points out that Martin is best known for her short plays: "she in fact has helped make the ten-minute play a valid form of theatrical expression."

When Martin's first play, *Twirler*, was produced at the Humana Festival in 1981, it generated a lot of buzz. In her essay "Pseudonymy and Identity Politics: Exploring 'Jane Martin,'" J. Ellen Gainor describes how "critics and audiences alike saw in this piece the emergence of a new Southern voice in the theater." In reviewing a volume of Martin's collected work, Howard Miller notes in *Library Journal*, "Martin's plays light up the stage with their heady mixture of savage humor and mayhem." Jack Helbig, in a review in *Booklist*, also appreciates the collection, calling Martin "a powerful chronicler."

Martin's play *Anton in Show Business* (2000) is especially well reviewed, and it received the award for best new play from the American Theatre Critics Association. Patti Hadad, a reviewer for the *Austin Chronicle*, describes *Anton in Show Business* as "delicious" and "refreshing." She also praises the biting satire of the play: "Martin skewers everything in the modern American theatre with a satirical flourish that will have your cheeks sore from laughing." Bruce Weber, in a *New York Times* review, agrees that the satire of the play is extremely well done and effective. "The barbs are insider-specific and most are affectionately applied," Weber writes, "and in the end the message is clear."

Some critics are harsh about Martin's work. In a review of *Flags* (2007) for *Daily Variety*, Steven Suskin points out "some exceedingly fine language" but believes that "the writing is clumsy." Max Sparber reviewed *Mr. Bundy* (1998) for the *Minneapolis City Pages* and calls it "both creaky and badly constructed.... Martin sets scenes together awkwardly and intercuts them with monologues that actors deliver directly to the audience." Although Sparber criticizes the structure of *Mr. Bundy*, he does admit that Martin "could not be more precise in the construction of the near-geometric downward arc of a family in crisis."

The performances of the plays seem to hugely affect how critics and audiences respond. Jory is quoted in the *Chicago Tribune* describing how *Keely and Du* (1993), which was nominated for a Pulitzer Prize, "seems to play very differently for audiences in different venues." G. L. Horton, in an online review of a Boston production of *Jack and Jill* (1995), explains that when he read the play, "it seemed to be a mere patchwork affair—adroit and literate but dismissable; a shallow opus stitched together from skits." When he saw the play on stage, however, it came "across the footlights as a kind of minor masterpiece." Perhaps this is what is important to remember when reading Martin's plays: they were not written to be read in a book. They were intended to be seen on a stage, with actors speaking the words, giving the lines their own unique interpretations and bringing them to life.

CRITICISM

Kristen Sarlin Greenberg

Greenberg is a freelance writer and editor with a background in literature and philosophy. In the following essay, she examines the effect and significance of the Jane Martin pseudonym and how Beauty *reflects the progression of Martin's career.*

After more than twenty years of success in the theater world, the playwright known as Jane Martin has managed to keep his or her identity a secret. Although over two dozen plays by Martin have been produced and reviewed—mostly favorably—the person responsible has not stepped forward to take credit, not even when nominated for a Pulitzer Prize for *Keely and Du.*

There is a story about Martin's first play, *Twirler* (1981), saying that the script was slipped under the door of the office of Jon Jory. It seems that this is indeed just a story, but the fact remains that Jory is the theater figure most closely associated with Martin. He has produced or directed most of her plays, many of which first appeared at the Humana Festival of New American Plays, which Jory founded. Also, Martin is the playwright whose work appears most often at the Actors Theatre of Louisville, where Jory was the producing director for more than thirty years. Jory is often asked whether he is indeed the playwright behind "Jane Martin," and his reaction ranges from mildly irritated to coy. "Oh, I can't tell you that," Jory slyly told *New York Times* critic Bruce Weber in 2000 when asked directly if he penned Martin's plays. A year later, David Schaeffer, who directed a production of Martin's *Talking With...*, told reviewer Scott Vogel, "I think pretty much everyone is convinced that Jane Martin is Jon Jory." It leaves the theater world wondering: why does the playwright use a pseudonym?

One theory to explain the fake name is that it is intended to generate publicity. In a review of *Keely and Du*, Sarah Bryan Miller points out, "The mystery surrounding the playwright's identity has been a steady source of publicity for the plays and the Actors Theatre." Speculation about Martin's identity has kept people talking about her plays since the very first time her work appeared in 1981. A little-known playwright might get buzz for a popular new play, especially at the Humana Festival, which is known for promoting the work of new authors, but the

> IT SEEMS NO ONE CAN DISCUSS MARTIN'S WORK WITHOUT ALSO DISCUSSING THE MYSTERY OF THE PLAYWRIGHT'S TRUE IDENTITY. BUT IS THE PSEUDONYM JUST A GIMMICK?"

secrecy makes the situation even more interesting, almost guaranteeing attention from the press. It seems no one can discuss Martin's work without also discussing the mystery of the playwright's true identity. But is the pseudonym just a gimmick? Just a publicity stunt?

Some believe that the issue is related to gender politics. Critic Nancy Wick explains:

> If Jory is indeed Martin, he may be using the pseudonym to explore his feminine side. Two of the full-length plays (*Talking With* and *Vital Signs*) are essentially a series of monologues by female characters.

In 2001, Scott Vogel, in a review of a production of Martin's play *Talking With...*, pointed out that "critics remain divided on the issue of whether a man could have authored these works." If Jory or another male author indeed wrote Martin's plays, perhaps he believes that anonymity helps people view the plays without prejudice. If audiences and critics knew that Martin's plays were written by a man, they might have certain expectations about the words he would put into his female characters' mouths.

Over and over, since 1981, when Martin's *Twirler* appeared in the Humana Festival, Jory has insisted that he cannot reveal Martin's real name. He explained in a press release cited on the Hartnell College website: "Whoever writes these plays feels that they would be unable to write them" if his or her true identity "was made public knowledge." This supports the idea that Martin is a man who feels his plays on women's issues will not be taken as seriously if audiences and critics knew they were written by a man.

However, when Miller talked with Jory while writing her 1995 review, she asked him directly, "Would the plays have the same impact if it turned out they were written by a man?" He seemed annoyed by the question at first, but he answered after a moment's thought: "I

WHAT DO I READ NEXT?

- *Beauty Queens* (2011), by Printz Award–winning author Libba Bray, sets up a ridiculous situation: a plane full of teen beauty-pageant contestants crashes on a desert island. Although the book is a comedy, Bray tackles notions of beauty and femininity in a way that will provoke thought and stimulate discussion.

- Beth Younger's *Learning Curves: Body Image and Female Sexuality in Young Adult Literature* (2009) examines how young women are portrayed in literature. Younger explores some of the themes that Martin addresses in *Beauty*, such as stereotyping, lack of self-confidence, and social expectations and restrictions.

- In 1997, *Plays in One Act*, edited by Daniel Halpern, was published. The volume collects a wide variety of plays and monologues by important modern playwrights, like David Mamet, Wendy Wasserstein, and Sam Shepard, as well as classics by Arthur Miller, Eudora Welty, Joyce Carol Oates, and many others.

- Martin's play *Anton in Show Business* (2000) portrays a small regional theater staging Anton Chekhov's play *Three Sisters*. From the initial auditions through a seemingly endless progression of directors, the production does not go smoothly, giving Martin

plenty of room to inject her trademark humor. *Anton in Show Business* pokes fun at the process of putting on a play, the people involved, and the state of American theater in general.

- In *The Fold* (2008), Printz Award–winning author An Na tells the story of Joyce, a young Asian American woman who is given the opportunity to get plastic surgery to make her eyes seem more "American." Although Joyce is tired of being compared with her beautiful older sister, she is not sure she wants to go through with the surgery. In setting up this dilemma for Joyce, Na delves into an investigation of the myths of beauty in American society.

- Although it was published over twenty years ago, Naomi Wolf's *The Beauty Myth: How Images of Female Beauty Are Used against Women* (1990) remains a popular and controversial book. Wolf examines the unrealistic standards of beauty that are seen everywhere—in movies and magazines and on television—and how these images feed women's insecurities. With exhaustive research, Wolf presents a convincing argument that women should reject these narrow, impossible ideals and embrace the varied beauty of a diverse population.

---

assume there might at one time have been an impact; who she was was a titillating factor. But I think that ended six or seven years ago." If it were true that hiding the playwright's gender were the only reason for the pseudonym, perhaps the truth would have been announced by now, since Jory seems to think any need for secrecy on that score has passed. Still, for a playwright whose early plays center around women's issues, there might be lingering uncertainty about revealing male authorship.

Freedom from expectation is one possible reason for the use of the fake name, but J. Ellen Gainor, in her essay "Pseudonymy and Identity Politics: Exploring 'Jane Martin,'" believes that the pseudonym is used for the opposite reason. Gainor proposes that Jory hopes to give people specific expectations, to determine how people see Martin's work by only revealing a small amount of information. The only piece of biographical detail that has been provided about Martin is the playwright is from Kentucky.

Gainor explains that "Jory's emphasis on Martin's geographical base may signal his desire to have her work considered within traditions of Southern writing." However, Gainor admits that providing the fact of Martin's Kentucky roots "seems more likely to reflect his interest in reinforcing her regional ties to him and his theater." This returns the argument to the idea that the pseudonym might be for the sake of publicity.

The secrecy around Martin's identity has created an almost impossible puzzle, and the mystery surrounding the pseudonym will remain until the real playwright chooses to reveal the truth. It is likely that the mystery will be discussed with every review of every production of any play by Jane Martin. However, once the issue of the pseudonym is explained and Jory is mentioned as the prime suspect, critics spend more time and energy discussing the work itself. This seems to be part of Jory's plan. Leah Green, in the *Critical Survey of Drama*, writes that Jory "consistently encourages reporters to focus on the plays themselves, rather than the identity of their playwright." Also, Green believes that "the quality of her plays has retained a surprising quality to overshadow the secondary 'identity controversy' that surrounds them."

Perhaps Jory is right that the secrecy frees Martin from expectations: it has given Martin a surprising degree of freedom regarding the subject matter of her plays. Martin was at first considered, according to Green, "a feminist dramatist intent on examining women and gender and the role women play in society." However, her later works, such as *Anton in Show Business* and *Keely and Du*, prove Martin to be "a playwright with a wide range of social issues at hand and with specific aims in tackling them."

With this progression of Martin's career in mind, it is interesting to examine *Beauty*, which, in a way, reflects Martin's development as a playwright. At the start of *Beauty*, it seems as though the play will discuss feminist issues: Why does society define women by their appearances? What constitutes true beauty? What can women do when they feel trapped by their beauty, or their lack of it?

However, the end of the play generalizes Carla's and Bethany's discontent and jealousy from what are often thought of as specifically women's issues to a statement about the human condition. It seems to be human nature for

Carla believes her beauty is the only thing worthwhile about her. (© Subbotina Anna / Shutterstock.com)

people to imagine that other people's lives are better than their own. *Beauty*, at its heart, is not just about a young woman who wishes to be more beautiful. It is also about how people try to find happiness, even if their attempts are misguided. It is about how people form their self-image. The final line of the play comes off as a joke, and it is a bit of a surprise. Perhaps because the true identity of the playwright behind the work of "Jane Martin" is not known, the audience is more able to be surprised by her punch-line ending, which seems to be exactly what Martin—as well as Jory, whether he is in fact the playwright or simply her best advocate—wants.

Source: Kristen Sarlin Greenberg, Critical Essay on *Beauty*, in *Drama for Students*, Gale, Cengage Learning, 2014.

Linda Rohrer Paige

In the following excerpt, Paige analyzes Martin as a specifically Southern and feminist playwright.

. . . For playwrights Henley, Norman, and Gilman, a would-be biographer might easily refer to their personal histories; however, with Jane Martin, biographers must be content to record merely that the playwright hails from Kentucky. Though one may refer to a long list

> **THESE FOUR PLAYWRIGHTS UNDERSTAND THE SOUTHERN WORLD, MAKING THEM OUTSPOKEN REPRESENTATIVES OF THEIR REGION AS WELL AS SPOKESWOMEN FOR LARGER THEMATIC CONCERNS."**

of awards and successful plays by Martin, including the American Theatre Critics' Award in 1993 for the year's best play, not to mention the nomination of *Keely and Du* for the Pulitzer, the issue of anonymity raises as much critical response as do the plays themselves. Most people in theatre circles nowadays accept the notion that Jane Martin is Jon Jory (who currently directs at the Guthrie Theatre, and quite noticeably takes the premieres of Jane Martin's new plays along with him). Nevertheless, years of speculation as to Jane Martin's identity have tantalized theatre critics. In my co-edited volume with Robert L. McDonald, *Southern Women Playwrights: New Essays in Literary History and Criticism*, J. Ellen Gainor finds fault with the issue of pseudonym and Jane Martin: "When I sent a letter of inquiry to the theater [Actors Theatre of Louisville]...I was shocked to receive an early morning telephone call from Mr. Jory himself, who cordially, but firmly, informed me that Jane Martin actively discourages scholarly explorations of her work" (2002).

Though Jane Martin continues to mask "her" identity, the playwright unmasks society's ills, unveiling its myths and secrets. An early play by Martin, *Coup/Clucks* (1984), provides a sort of Southern extravaganza of farce, satirically pushing the Southern envelope of tradition, ideals, and prejudices: the idea of the Southern Lady and landed gentry, the lost paradise of *Gone With the Wind*, and the camaraderie of the Ku Klux Klan. In *Coup*, the first part of the play, the white inhabitants of Brine, Alabama, prepare for the annual *Gone With the Wind* parade, under the direction of 60-year-old Miss Zifty, who plays Scarlett O'Hara. Everything goes wrong as the redneck taking the part of Rhett refuses and Dr. Kennedy, the local black dentist, "inherits" the role. Aghast, the offended Miss Zifty resigns in disgust and Don Savannah,

the old lady's flamboyant, gay hairdresser, dons the dress of Scarlett, though ultimately relinquishing it to the black maid, Beulah. *Clucks*, the second part of Martin's farce, presents the aftermath of the parade. A dispirited rally of indignant Klansmen, filled with bravado (yet clearly under the thumbs of their women) and incensed at the "desecration" of their parade, retaliate with a "ride" on the dentist's home, where the cast of Mitchell's classic has gathered. Carting a "dynamite sandwich" and an 11-foot cross, the half-hooded remnants of the Invisible Empire huddle curiously, arguing, outside in the dentist's front yard:

> *Travis*: Ryman, gimme that hand-gun.... Pritch, I'm forty years old, been laid off six months, my wife's turned colored on me, m' oldest boy ran over m' neighbor's blue-ribbon Pekinese on his motorbike, I can only git it up oncet a week an' I'm goin' t' light that cross lyin' down.... (*Gives pistol to Pritchard and goes to the cross. Searches in pocket for matches, finds nothing.*) Somebody give me a light. (*A pause. They look at each other.*) Gimme a match. (*They look in their pockets.*) Gimme a lighter! (*They look at him.*) Gimme two goddamn sticks! (*Bobby Joe does. Travis breaks them and throws them at him.*) Colored, hell. We oughta run *ourselves* outta' Alabama.

Taking a serious subject, racial hatred, Martin transforms it into a comedic uproar, turning tragedy into farce. By the end of the play, the redneck Travis reluctantly learns a new song from his wife: the "Ode to Joy" theme of Beethoven's *Ninth*, which he proclaims to be "nigger music."

Martin's better-known play, *Keely and Du* (first performed in 1993), examines another serious subject: abortion rights. Kidnapped by religious extremists, Keely, a young woman pregnant as a result of a rape, gradually develops an unexpected alliance with one of her abductors, an older woman named Du. Set not in the South but somewhere near Cincinnati, the play introduces another variation of a "mother-daughter" relationship. Unlike Walter, the pastor who masterminded the kidnapping, Du talks to Keely in personal terms, telling her about her own religious awakening, artfully embellished by its sexual overtones:

> *Du*: The fact is he [her husband] was an uninteresting man, but he got into the storage business and turned out a good provider. Now, listen close here, we went along 'til he bored me perfectly silent, if you can imagine, and

God found us pretty late when the kids were gone or near gone, and when God found that man he turned him into a firebrand and an orator and a beacon to others, and I fell in love with him and that bed turned into a lake of flame and I was, so help me, bored no more, and that's a testament.

Keely's marital experience has differed considerably: she has been raped by her ex-husband. Despite herself, Du begins to side with Keely against Walter, the ex-spouse, and in one scene of kindness, tries to cheer up her captive, bringing her a change of dress from the nightgown she previously wore. Left alone for a moment, Keely, in a frenzy of disgust after a visit from her now "reformed" ex-husband, uses the dress-hanger to abort herself. In the last scene of the play, Martin reverses the situations of the characters: Keely is now free from both the baby and her imprisonment, and Du serves time in prison for kidnapping. Having suffered a stroke in the interim, Du can hardly speak. Keely calms her, exposing a depth of friendship and also indicating a hint of regret for her lost baby. In *Keely and Du*, the "mother-daughter" relationship congeals with Keely's abortion as Keely describes to Du a concert that she has recently attended with personal affection and inferences:

> *Keely*: I went to a Judd concert. You know the one that sings without her mother now . . . (*She stops.*) . . . without her mother now . . . There was this guy next to me . . . had a little girl on his lap, maybe two.

Another subject as topical as abortion rights emerges with *Mr. Bundy*, premiering five years after *Keely and Du*. Here, Martin explores another current subject: how to treat a convicted pedophile after his release from prison. Mr. Bundy, a retired school teacher in his sixties, has recently moved next door to Cathryn and Robert Ferreby and their 8-year-old daughter, Cassidy, with whom he makes friends. Another couple, a trucker named Jimmy Ray and his unappealing wife Tianna (a pure Southern stereotype, part "spa-day girl," part hell-fire preacher), warn the Ferrebys that Mr. Bundy has recently been in prison for molesting teenage boys. Robert and Cathryn are repelled by this couple, who are vulgar and ignorant (Jimmy Ray insists that Mr. Bundy "turn[ed]" his victims homosexual), but the news, nonetheless, alarms them. A child psychologist, Cathryn wants Mr. Bundy to have a second chance, but Robert, outraged, ultimately attacks his neighbor physically, pummeling him to the floor with groin and face kicks. Shocked by her husband's brutality, Cathryn then leaves, taking Cassidy with her. Mr. Bundy leaves as well. The play begins and ends with Cassidy's rhyme about the "oogey-boogey," but Martin leaves the audience in doubt quite who the "oogey-boogey" really is. As with *Keely and Du*, the playwright challenges audience assumptions. Never appearing as anything but a harmless, gentle old man, Mr. Bundy, nonetheless, inspires fear in Robert because of the potential danger he represents. But the play queries, when is one's debt to society paid? Though at times actions of the characters seem contrived, they demonstrate that the playwright tackles difficult societal problems and refuses to settle for easy solutions. Even the unappealing Jimmy and Tianna deserve a degree of sympathy, Martin insinuates, having lost their own child to a murderous pedophile. Martin, like Henley, Norman, and Gilman, is unafraid to examine topical issues. These four playwrights understand the Southern world, making them outspoken representatives of their region as well as spokeswomen for larger thematic concerns.

Source: Linda Rohrer Paige, "'Off the Porch and into the Scene': Southern Women Playwrights Beth Henley, Marsha Norman, Rebecca Gilman, and Jane Martin," in *A Companion to Twentieth-Century American Drama*, edited by David Krasner, Blackwell Publishing, 2005, pp. 401–404.

Howard Miller

In the following review, Miller describes Martin's plays as insightfully uproarious.

Martin's plays light up the stage with their heady mixture of savage humor and mayhem, as she probes the often dark side of American politics and culture and takes a sharp look at the interpersonal relationships of her characters. Martin has won several awards, including the American Theatre Critics Association New Play Award in 1994 for her full-length work *Keely and Du*. The ten plays in this collection include "Middle-Aged White Guys," a satire on the lost American dream set in a garbage dump and featuring a visit by an angelic Elvis. "Mr. Bundy" is a shocking examination of the dangers of self-righteous retribution, while "Flaming Guns of the Purple Sage" is a hilarious, Grand Guignol takeoff of B Westerns and slasher movies. This work makes a nice addition to Martin's other collections, *Vital Signs* and *What Mama*

Don't Know. Recommended for contemporary theater arts collections in public and academic libraries.

Source: Howard Miller, Review of *Jane Martin: Collected Plays*, Vol. 2, *1996–2001*, in *Library Journal*, Vol. 127, No. 8, May 1, 2002, p. 102.

Jack Helbig

In the following review, Helbig considers Martin a "powerful chronicler."

Jane Martin is today's most famous and prolific pseudonymous dramatist, who nearly every year has a new play in the Humana Festival—a seriocomical take on a hot topic, such as white male backlash, the culture wars, the persecution of former sex offenders; or a poke at pop culture, professional wrestling, contemporary relationships, or the state of modern American theater. Martin's plays from 1996–2001, a period noted more for its bubble economy and poisonous partisan bickering than for depth of ideas, reflect on their time's shallow mendacity. *Middle-Aged White Guys* wittily limns three small-time businessmen who have made a quick buck filling their town with toxic waste and now must pay the price. In a serious mood, *Mr. Bundy* lays out the ramifications of the so-called Megan laws, which pass a virtual life sentence of fleeing fearful, angry citizens on sex offenders. Even whether Martin is one person or more is unknown, that Martin is a powerful chronicler of a peaceful, silly era in American history is certain.

Source: Jack Helbig, Review of *Jane Martin: Collected Plays*, Vol. 2, *1996–2001*, in *Booklist*, Vol. 98, No. 16, April 15, 2002, p. 1376.

SOURCES

"About the Humana Festival of New American Plays," Actors Theatre of Louisville website, http://actorsthea tre.org/humana-festival-of-new-american-plays/history/ (accessed July 30, 2013).

Boyd, Molly, "Gothicism," in *The Companion to Southern Literature: Themes, Genres, Places, People, Movements, and Motifs*, edited by Joseph M. Flora and Lucinda H. MacKethan, Louisiana State University Press, 2002, pp. 311–16.

Gainor, J. Ellen, "Pseudonymy and Identity Politics: Exploring 'Jane Martin,'" in *Southern Women Playwrights: New Essays in Literary History and Criticism*, edited by Robert L. McDonald and Linda Rohrer Paige, University of Alabama Press, 2002, pp. 139–51.

Green, Leah, "Jane Martin," in *Critical Survey of Drama*, 2nd rev. ed., Vol. 5, edited by Carl Rollyson and Frank N. Magill, Salem Press, 2003, pp. 2245–48.

Hadad, Patti, Review of *Anton in Show Business*, in *Austin Chronicle*, April 27, 2007, http://www.austinchroni cle.com/arts/2007-04-27/469103/ (accessed August 2, 2013).

Helbig, Jack, Review of *Jane Martin: Collected Plays*, Vol. 2, *1996–2001*, in *Booklist*, Vol. 98, No. 16, April 15, 2001, p. 1376.

Horton, G. L., Review of *Jack and Jill*, in *Aisle Say*, June 1998, http://www.stagepage.info/reviews/j&jill.html (accessed July 6, 2013).

"Jon Jory," Santa Fe University of Art and Design website, http://www.santafeuniversity.edu/Program sOfStudy/PerformingArts/Faculty.aspx (accessed July 30, 2013).

Lewis, Benjamin Roland, *The Technique of the One-Act Play: A Study in Dramatic Construction*, John W. Luce, 1918, pp. 9–26.

Martin, Jane, *Beauty*, in *Jane Martin: Collected Plays*, Vol. 2, *1996–2001*, edited by Michael Bigelow Dixon, Smith and Kraus, 2001, pp. 251–56.

Miller, Howard, Review of *Jane Martin: Collected Plays*, Vol. 2, *1996–2001*, in *Library Journal*, Vol. 127, No. 8, May 1, 2002, p. 102.

Miller, Sarah Bryan, "The Connection Question: Pseudonymous *Keely and Du* Personalizes Abortion Politics," in *Chicago Tribune*, February 19, 1995.

Paige, Linda Rohrer, "'Off the Porch and into the Scene': Southern Women Playwrights Beth Henley, Marsha Norman, Rebecca Gilman, and Jane Martin," in *A Companion to Twentieth-Century American Drama*, edited by David Krasner, Blackwell Publishing, 2005, pp. 401–404.

Sparber, Max, "Staged Sex," in *Minneapolis City Pages*, March 13, 2002, http://www.citypages.com/2002-03-13/ arts/staged-sex/ (accessed August 2, 2013).

Suskin, Steven, Review of *Flags*, in *Daily Variety*, Vol. 296, No. 58, September 21, 2007, p. 15.

"Theater and Musical Theater," in *Encyclopedia of American Social History*, edited by Mary Kupiec Cayton, Elliott J. Gorn, and Peter W. Williams, Charles Scribner's Sons, 1993.

"A Two Decade Old Mystery: Who Is Jane Martin?," Hartnell College website, http://www.hartnell.cc.ca.us/ westernstage/press_releases/Anton/antonarticle.htm (accessed July 6, 2013).

Weber, Bruce, "Critic's Notebook: When Theatre Sends Up Itself to Save Itself," in *New York Times*, April 4, 2000, http://www.nytimes.com/2000/04/04/the ater/critic-s-notebook-when-theater-sends-up-itself-to-save-itself.html?n = Top%2fReference%2fTimes%20To-pics%2fPeople%2fW%2fWeber%2c%20Bruce (accessed August 2, 2013).

Wick, Nancy, "The Mystery of Jane Martin," in *Columns: The University of Washington Alumni Magazine*, https://www.washington.edu/alumni/columns/march02/jory_martin.html (accessed July 28, 2013).

FURTHER READING

Cassady, Marsh, *An Introduction to the Art of Theatre: A Comprehensive Text—Past, Present, and Future*, Meriwether Publishing, 2007.

> Readers interested in the world of theater will find an in-depth, approachable overview in Cassady's book, which addresses all aspects of theater production, from directing, staging, and acting to business and management.

Hornbacher, Marya, *Wasted: A Memoir of Anorexia and Bulimia*, Harper Perennial, 2006.

> When Hornbacher was in college, her weight dropped to fifty-two pounds. She admits that she fell for the myth that if she lost weight and looked a certain way, she would have a better life and be happy. For years, she alternately binged and starved herself. While it tackles an emotionally difficult topic, Hornbacher's memoir is compelling.

Martin, Jane, *Talking With . . .*, Samuel French, 2011.

> In 1982, *Talking With . . .* won the American Theatre Critics Association Award for best regional play and was praised by critics for its originality and humor. It is a collection of eleven monologues rather than a single story. Each speech is delivered by a different character, from a baton twirler to an actress to a former rodeo rider.

Vaught, Susan, *Big Fat Manifesto*, Bloomsbury USA Children's Books, 2007.

> Vaught's comic but thoughtful novel draws on the author's training as a psychotherapist, as well as her own experiences with losing weight. Protagonist Jamie, an overweight high-school senior, writes a weekly newspaper column describing her hopes and fears as she tries to find her place in the world and struggles with her first real romance.

Volansky, Michele, and Michael Bigelow Dixon, eds., *Twenty One-Act Plays from Twenty Years of the Humana Festival: 1975–1995*, Smith and Kraus, 1995.

> Martin is closely associated with the Humana Festival, where many of her plays were first produced. Volansky and Dixon's volume presents a selection of other popular and critically acclaimed plays from the festival. Works by major playwrights are included, as well as plays by lesser-known writers.

SUGGESTED SEARCH TERMS

Jane Martin AND pseudonym

Jane Martin AND Jon Jory

Jane Martin AND Humana Festival

Jane Martin AND Beauty

Jane Martin AND feminism

Southern gothic literature

regional theater

one-act plays

Hell-Bent fer Heaven

HATCHER HUGHES

1924

Hell-Bent fer Heaven, Hatcher Hughes's best-known work, opened on January 4, 1924, at the Klaw Theatre in New York, New York. After receiving rave reviews, the production was moved to the Frazee Theatre (also in New York), and its run continued until May 11, 1924. The following day, *Hell-Bent fer Heaven* was awarded the Pulitzer Prize. The play was subsequently published by Harper and Brothers the same year, though the original edition has long since gone out of print. The play is not widely available. As of 2013, an undated copy, released by Samuel French as *Hell Bent for Heaven*, can be ordered on the publisher's website.

Hell-Bent fer Heaven is set in the Carolina mountains, on the Hunt family homestead over the course of a single afternoon, just after the end of World War I and the start of Prohibition. While these historical markers influence the plot in small ways, *Hell-Bent fer Heaven* is a play about faith, religion, and their use, misuse, and abuse. In this manner, the play is somewhat timeless, and its themes still resonate today. Love, jealousy, loyalty, and family ties also drive the story.

AUTHOR BIOGRAPHY

Harvey Hatcher Hughes was born on February 12, 1881, in Polkville, North Carolina, the tenth of eleven children born to Martha Gold Hughes

Hell Bent fer Heaven *is set in the Carolina mountains.* (© Dave Allen Photography | Shutterstock.com)

and Andrew Jackson Hughes. The playwright enrolled at the University of North Carolina, Chapel Hill, in 1901. He often took breaks from college to earn money, writing for local newspapers and eventually teaching at the university during his senior year. Hughes received his undergraduate degree in 1907 and continued to teach there while completing his master's degree. He next moved to New York to attend Columbia University as a doctoral candidate, but he became an English lecturer and never finished his PhD.

Hughes devoted himself to teaching and writing, and he remained on the Columbia faculty for the rest of his life. He took a sabbatical from 1917 to 1920 to serve as an army captain during World War I but returned to the university immediately after completing his service. He was promoted from lecturer to assistant professor in 1928 and retained the post until 1945, specializing in playwriting and serving as founder of the Morningside Players of Columbia.

Hughes's first play, *A Marriage Made in Heaven*, was completed in 1918 but was never staged or published. A revised version,

performed as *Honeymooning* or *Honeymooning on High*, was produced in 1927. His first produced play, *Wake Up, Jonathan*, was written with Elmer Rice, published in 1920, and performed at New York's Henry Miller's Theatre in 1921. The play features a bored wife, her boring husband, and the appearance of an exciting former suitor. The 1924 play *Hell-Bent fer Heaven* expands on the love-triangle theme, adding a family feud and religious zealotry. The play won the 1924 Pulitzer Prize for Drama and is considered Hughes's best work.

His next play, *Ruint*, was produced in New York at the Provincetown Playhouse in 1925 and published the same year. It is almost as well regarded as *Hell-Bent fer Heaven*. Both plays are set in the Carolina mountains and written in dialect, but unlike its predecessor, *Ruint* focuses on social expectations. The play features a rich boy who kisses a local girl, but the townspeople believe that the boy and girl have slept together.

It's a Grand Life, Hughes's fourth play, premiered at New York's Cort Theatre in 1930, and Hughes married actress Janet Cool Ranney the same year. The couple had a daughter, Ann, in

1935. Hughes also served as director of his 1934 play *The Lord Blesses the Bishop*, produced in New York at the Adelphi Theatre. He split his time between teaching, writing, and directing in New York and farming on his family's land in West Cornwall, Connecticut. Hughes left a rehearsal at Columbia on October 18, 1945, and he died shortly afterward of coronary thrombosis at his home in New York. His popularity has waned over time, and Hughes's work is not often studied or restaged. Nevertheless, he offers a distinct and singular voice, providing rare glimpses of life in the rural Carolinas during the early twentieth century.

MEDIA ADAPTATIONS

- *Hell-Bent fer Heaven* was adapted as a film of the same title by Marian Constance Blackton. The movie, starring Patsy Ruth Miller and John Harron, was produced and distributed by Warner Brothers in 1926.

PLOT SUMMARY

Hell-Bent fer Heaven takes place over the course of a single afternoon on the Hunt homestead in the Carolina mountains. The house is rough-hewn and filled with old, handmade furniture. Mountain and valley views, a rose-covered trellis, and blue mist surround the house. A barn and the family store are nearby.

Act 1
David Hunt, the family patriarch, comes inside and stows his rifle on the well-stocked gun rack. Meg Hunt, his daughter-in-law, comes in from the kitchen and shells peas. They comment on the warm, stormy summer. Another storm appears to be on its way. Meg's son, Sid, is due home soon, and he is returning a war hero. Meg hopes Sid read the Bible while he was overseas, and she wonders if the war has changed him. David thinks Sid will eventually settle down, like him. Meg says that David has confused getting old with settling down. She implies that David's soul has not been saved by religion.

Sid sneaks in from the kitchen and surprises them. David praises Sid as a war hero. David fought for the Confederacy during the Civil War, and they tease each other about their bravery and service. Rufe Pryor appears on the stairs and listens as David tells Sid that Meg wanted him to come home weak and in need of mothering. Meg points out that Jesus Christ puts the sick and needy first. Rufe comes downstairs and says that Meg has been like a mother to him since his own died when he was very young. Rufe has been helping out around the store while Sid was

away, and he tells Sid that the army would not take him because he has a bad stomach. David does not believe Rufe, but Meg defends him. Rufe admits that the army lowered its entrance standards at the end of the war, but he did not see the point in joining a fight that was nearly over.

Sid's father, Matt Hunt, comes inside carrying some of Sid's belongings. David mentions Jude Lowry, Sid's sweetheart from before the war. Rufe seems upset. David notices and begins to tease him, but Rufe says all women are the same. David tells Sid to marry Jude. Rufe is even more upset by this suggestion, and Matt asks him to go outside to bring in the rest of Sid's things. Rufe agrees, but not before complaining that they hired him to work in the store, not as an errand boy. Matt and Rufe bicker, and Meg defends Rufe. She continues to defend him after he is outside, but David and Matt think he is a lazy good-for-nothing. Matt says Rufe has only gotten worse since "he got that camp-meetin' brand o' religion. I've never seed a man so hell-bent fer heaven as he is!"

When Rufe comes back inside, Matt fires him and tells him to move out. He was hired to replace Sid, and now that Sid is back they do not need him. Rufe has known for a month that Sid was coming back and knew he would be let go, but he has done nothing to search for a new job. Rufe admits this is true but counters that he has been saved and Matt has not, and he will always love his enemy as a good Christian should. Meg sides with Rufe. Rufe goes upstairs to pack his things, and Sid tells his family that he wants Rufe to stay on a little longer so he can have some time off before he starts working on the farm.

Andy Lowry, Sid's best friend and Jude's brother, comes by the house to deliver the mail. He is happy and surprised to see Sid, and he mentions all the newspaper articles about Sid's heroics. Sid remains humble, and Andy tells him he wanted to fight very badly, but his parents would not let him. He seems more sincere than Rufe did. Rufe comes downstairs with his things, and Sid tells him he can stay for another month. Andy mentions that he needs ammunition for his gun, and Sid shows Andy the automatic pistol he took from a German soldier. Meg is upset by the knowledge that Sid has killed a man, and she says, "Thou shalt not kill!" Andy replies, "Ner git killed if you can help it!" Rufe says Sid survived and the other man did not because God willed it. Sid thinks God usually protects the man with the best aim.

Sid and Andy want to try out their guns, but Rufe says they should not because they might rekindle the old feud between the Hunts and the Lowrys. Matt is angry at Rufe for bringing the feud up, but Rufe claims he is trying to help. Andy and Sid trust their friendship and are not worried about the old feud. Then they make fun of religion, but David stops them and says Christianity is not something that deserves ridicule. Rufe and David begin to debate theology, and David says Rufe only became religious to get his exemption from serving in the army.

Meg reminds David that he promised to harvest some honey, and she goes with him to help. Matt heads outside to bring the hay in before it starts to rain. Andy has been drinking, and he shows Sid a bottle of contraband liquor. Rufe tells him he has a barrel, but he has not had anything to drink since he found his faith. He offers to sell it to Andy and Sid. Andy sees Jude from the window and tells Sid that she has been recently saved. She does not drink and yells at Andy when he does, so he hides upstairs. Sid tells Rufe to go upstairs so he can be alone with Jude. They bicker, but Rufe agrees in the end. Sid surprises Jude and kisses her. They tease each other, and Rufe overhears them as he comes downstairs with Andy. Sid takes her over to the store, leaving Andy and Rufe behind. After they leave, Rufe reminds Andy about the old feud again. He implies that Sid called Andy a coward, effectively rekindling the feud and turning Andy against his friend.

Act 2

Andy waits for Sid and Jude to return. He prays over his gun as if it were a Bible, asking it to help him "love his enemies." Jude and Sid come back from the store. Jude asks Andy to walk home with her, but he wants to have a word with Sid. Jude waits for him in the kitchen. Sid gives Andy the bullets he wanted. Andy insists on paying with cash, telling him "I don't want no Hunt... to say 'at I killed him on a credit!"

When the Lowrys and Hunts last feuded, three more Lowrys were killed than Hunts, and Andy intends to settle the score and then some. Sid remains calm and asks how he can make things right. Andy says the Hunts made his grandfather dance before they shot him. He points his gun at Sid and tells him to dance. Sid begins to dance toward the door, but Andy cuts him off. Rufe screams in terror. Jude comes in from the kitchen and rushes toward her brother as Sid grabs Andy's gun. Rufe praises God, and Jude begs Sid not to kill Andy.

Sid does not want to kill his friend. Meg and David return, and Sid explains that Andy wants to kill six Hunts in retaliation for the old family feud. Meg is terrified, and David thinks that Rufe is to blame. Sid defends Rufe. He puts Andy's pistol in his pocket and tells Andy to go home. Jude says she will go with him, but Sid asks her to stay so they can talk.

Sid and David take Andy outside, and Meg goes into the kitchen. Rufe says he wishes everyone would be at peace but implies that the feud may be God's will. He also suggests that Andy and Sid are equally to blame for the situation, and he says Sid "can be mighty overbearin'." When Jude asks Rufe to explain himself, he says she will understand once she marries Sid. Jude says she cannot see how they can wed given what has just happened. Rufe declares his love for Jude and says God will decide whom she should marry. He explains that God told him to love her, and that is how he found religion.

Sid comes back in and laughs at Rufe's declaration. Rufe mentions that Sid had a French girlfriend during the war, which upsets Jude. Sid replies: "I dunno whether you're a trouble breeder or whether you're jist teched in the head with religion." Then he says he and Jude are going to get married. Jude points out that she has not said yes yet, and Rufe says it is up to Jude to decide if she wants to marry a heathen. Rufe leaves the house.

Sid tells Jude that Andy may be her brother, but he is her future husband. The Bible says man and wife must put each other first, and he believes that to be true, even if he is not as religious as Rufe. Jude starts to cry because she wants to be his wife, and she agrees to marry him and stand by him, no matter how painful it will be to go against her family. Sid tells her not to worry. He is confident he can stop the feud from progressing. David and Matt enter the house, and Sid tells them that he and Jude are getting married. They are happy about the news, but worried about Andy and the feud.

Rufe comes inside and tells them Andy has sobered up and is ready to go home. Jude and Sid go outside to talk to him. David notes that the river is high and a storm is coming. Rufe worries about the dam holding, but David thinks only dynamite can crack it. Rufe leaves as Sid, Jude, and Andy come back inside. Andy apologizes for his behavior. Sid forgives him and returns his gun. Andy and Jude get ready to leave, and Sid offers to get the horses ready and ride with them. Sid goes to the barn. Jude and David leave to look for Meg. Rufe comes back in, and Andy tells him that the feud is settled and that Sid and Jude are getting married. As soon as Rufe hears the news, he tells Andy that Matt and Sid are plotting to kill him.

Rufe tells Andy to attack Sid before Sid can attack him. Jude, Sid, David, and Meg come inside. They assure Andy that all is forgiven. Jude decides to stay and wait out the storm. Andy and Sid ride out without her. Rufe tells Meg not to worry, and Meg begins to start a fire, but David insists on doing it. A lively debate about gender relations ensues. The discussion turns to power, and Rufe says power should be maintained by any means, including trickery. David says only the weak use trickery.

Two shots ring out in the distance. Jude and Meg worry about Sid and Andy, and David and Rufe try to calm them. They hear horse hoofs approaching. Meg runs outside to find that Sid's horse has returned without him. She is certain Andy has killed her son. David claims the horse could have been startled and thrown him. Matt comes in and grabs a shotgun. He says Sid's horse has never startled before. David grabs a rifle and insists on coming with Matt. He wants to learn what happened rather than jump to conclusions.

Matt wants revenge, and Rufe says, "Vengeance is mine, saith the Lord." David remarks that God needs an "instrument to work through." Then he leaves with Matt. Meg questions a God who would allow such tragedies to happen, but Rufe says God is always right. He starts to go upstairs, stopping to eavesdrop on Jude and Meg as Jude swears to kill Sid's murderer, even if it is her own brother. Jude and Meg leave the house. Rufe comes back downstairs and says he cannot marry a murderer. He asks God to stop her.

Sid comes in and tells Rufe that Andy shot at him and missed. He asks where his family is. Rufe lies, saying they are in the barn. Sid asks Rufe why Andy wants to kill him, and Rufe feigns innocence. Sid says he will ask Andy instead, and Rufe claims that Andy will lie and blame him. Sid asks if his horse came back, but Rufe claims he does not know. Sid asks if his family went to look for Andy, and Rufe repeats the same lie. Sid sees the guns missing from the rack. He realizes that Rufe wants his family to kill Andy and stop him from revealing that Rufe is to blame for the entire situation.

Sid thinks he can stop his family if he gets to the telephone beneath the dam. After he leaves, Rufe prays for guidance, asking God if he should kill Sid by blowing up the dam. Wind, lightning, and thunder shake the house, and Rufe interprets this as God's voice, telling him to proceed.

Act 3

Matt and David enter the house, holding Andy at gunpoint. Andy tells them he shot at Sid and missed, but Matt does not believe him. David reminds Matt that Sid could be in the woods, and Matt checks the barn for Sid's horse. Andy tries to make David angry, but David remains calm. Rufe returns and says he has not seen Sid. Rufe is afraid that Andy will tell David that he started the feud. Matt returns, and David goes to find a rope so they can tie Andy up.

A large explosion goes off in the distance. Rufe says it must be thunder and leaves the house. Jude and Meg return, and Andy explains what happened. Jude thinks he is lying and tries to take Matt's gun so she can shoot him. Andy says Matt is a better shot, and he would prefer to be killed by him. Andy refuses to beg for mercy, even inviting them to get it over with. David comes back inside with the ropes, and he and Matt tie Andy to a chair. Matt and David are about to leave when they hear rushing water. Rufe enters and tells them the river has flooded. He says Judgment Day has arrived, and he has been out doing God's bidding.

Everyone goes outside to watch the rising waters, leaving Andy and Rufe behind. Andy has not told anyone that Rufe is to blame and promises not to tell if Rufe helps him escape. Rufe offers to pray for Andy instead, and Andy swears he will take Rufe to hell with him. Everyone comes back inside, and Matt goes out to pen the cows on higher ground. Jude worries about the rising water, but David says that even in the worst floods, only the cellar gets wet. Andy, David, Rufe, and Meg start to bicker, and David realizes that Rufe is hiding something. Meg defends Rufe, as does Jude to a lesser degree.

Rufe does not care what David and Andy think of him because they will go to hell and he will not. Rufe tells them he has had a vision and speaks like a possessed man, spouting images of apocalypse as Meg and Jude praise God. Andy threatens to tell the truth, and Rufe sings a loud hymn to keep him from speaking. Andy says, "I dunno what the devil 'll do 'ith you, Rufe . . . they ain't no place in hell hot enough fer you!" Rufe says they should put Andy in the cellar. Andy believes Rufe has finally decided to help him escape. David and Meg carry him downstairs and notice that there is already some water coming in. Upstairs, Rufe watches the rising water and smiles.

David and Meg head to the barn to check on the animals, and Jude goes out to watch the flood on the porch. Rufe calls down to Andy, who says Rufe needs to free him soon, but Rufe lies that he hears Matt coming. Jude comes back inside, worried about Sid. Rufe tells her to trust in God's plan, and they pray together. Rufe kisses her. Jude pulls away, but he explains that the kiss was only spiritual. They begin to pray again. Meg enters and asks Jude to help her move the turkeys from the coops. Rufe offers to get Andy out of the cellar so he does not drown.

Alone, Rufe calls down to Andy and says he will help him, but only if he promises not to say anything. Andy is so fed up with Rufe that he refuses. Rufe closes the cellar door, grabs a shotgun, and tells God he will only kill Andy if it is his will. Sid comes inside, muddy and bruised, but Rufe does not notice. Sid speaks in a deep voice, and Rufe thinks that he is listening to God. He says he is Sid's ghost, and he has come to haunt Rufe until he finds out who killed him. Rufe explains that God killed him, and he was acting only as God's instrument.

Andy shouts from the cellar, and Sid decides to find out why Andy tried to kill him. Rufe claims that Andy will lie. When Sid goes downstairs, Rufe grabs a bag of clothes and tries to leave, but the house is surrounded by water. Meg, Jude, Matt, and David return to the house. Rufe tells them he saw Sid's ghost. Andy comes out of the cellar and tries to attack Rufe, but David and Matt stop him. Andy jokes that Sid's ghost freed him, Sid comes out of the cellar, and Jude and Meg cry tears of joy to see him alive.

Sid forgives Andy for trying to kill him, and they reveal that Rufe is to blame. Meg and Jude defend Rufe, but Sid explains that Rufe blew up the dam and tried to drown him. Rufe says, "I swear on a stack o' Bibles I didn't." Meg and Jude believe him at first. However, when he says he was acting as God's instrument, the women finally turn on him. Matt and Andy try to kill Rufe, who runs into the cellar. He locks the door behind him and prays for God's help. Meg, Matt, and Andy decide to tear the door down, but David stops them and says God will punish him. God has kept them safe despite Rufe's scheming. Meg and Sid agree with David.

Sid says that all of the dams upstream have been breached, and the flood will likely swallow the house. He brought a boat back from the dam so they can escape. Rufe does not want to drown, but Andy tells him that only God can save him. Andy, Sid, Jude, Meg, David, and Matt all head for the boat. Rufe emerges into the empty house and prays for help. When nothing happens, he curses God and decides that God does not exist. Then he realizes he has committed "the unpardonable sin"—denying God—and he collapses. He calls for help, but his fate is sealed. He dies in the flood he caused.

Notably, before the premier production run of *Hell-Bent fer Heaven* was complete, the ending was changed, with Rufe surviving. In the published version, the original conclusion remains.

CHARACTERS

David Hunt

David Hunt, the family patriarch, is a weathered but robust old man in his eighties. He is often the voice of reason, able to see through Rufe's actions, gently tease his grandson Sid, and stop his son Matt from making rash decisions. He frequently reminds Matt that he is jumping to conclusions without any evidence. When Andy tries to goad David into killing him, David refuses to do so. Meg also wants David to kill Andy, and he refuses again. Although Meg and Rufe do not believe that David is a religious man, he proves his faith on more than one occasion. He believes that strength is more powerful than trickery, he does not believe in killing recklessly, and he does not pretend to know what God wants or what God thinks. This last trait puts David in direct opposition to Rufe, who loudly and often proclaims that he is intimately acquainted with God's will.

David thinks that this tendency is blasphemous, while Rufe thinks the same thing of David's beliefs. Although David is perhaps the most reasonable and thoughtful character in *Hell-Bent fer Heaven*, he is not without his flaws. The most notable is his evident sexism. When Meg attempts to build a fire, he insists on doing it for her because he sees it as a man's job and not a woman's. In the end, however, David proves to be the play's most enlightened character. He points out that God has been watching over and protecting them even as Rufe has plotted against Sid, telling his family, "I hain't lost my belief in the Lord on Rufe's account. Fact is, I ain't so shore but what I believe in Him more 'n ever." Because David is always in opposition to Rufe, the play's antagonist, one could argue that David, not Sid, is the protagonist.

Matt Hunt

Matt Hunt, David's son and Sid's father, is a quiet man in his forties. He is not especially religious, but Meg does not accuse him of being a heathen the way she accuses David. Matt, however, is the most vengeful character in *Hell-Bent fer Heaven*. Matt tries to kill Andy at every opportunity, but David stops him. Matt does not put up too much of a fight when David restrains him, and it is possible that Matt does not truly want to become a murderer. When Andy is freed from the cellar, Matt and David

stop him from attacking Rufe, but then Matt joins Andy in the attempt when he learns that Rufe rekindled the feud and blew up the dam. Again, David stays his hand.

Matt is the least talkative character in the play, but he is very vocal about his dislike for Rufe. Matt is eager to fire Rufe and thinks he is a lazy good-for-nothing who has only gotten worse since "he got that camp-meetin' brand o' religion." Meg sides with Rufe against her own husband, but the largely unassuming man is tasked with the quote that shapes the play's guiding theme and its title, as he tells Meg, "I've never seed a man so hell-bent fer heaven as he is!"

Meg Hunt

Meg Hunt is a middle-aged woman, Matt's husband and Sid's mother. After Rufe, she is the most devout character in the play, accusing David of being a heathen and worrying about the Bible she gave to Sid when he left for the war. Meg points out that Jesus Christ puts the sick and needy first, and Rufe says that Meg has been like a mother to him since his own died when he was very young. At times, she seems more affectionate toward Rufe than toward her own son, possibly because he is weak and Sid is not.

Meg is also very naive. She chastises Sid for killing soldiers in the midst of the war, quoting scripture without considering that her son's survival, and her joy that he has returned, stem from his ability to defend himself. When Rufe says that he has had a vision, Meg believes him and falls into a religious trance. When he tells her he has seen Sid's ghost, she wants to know if Sid went to heaven or hell.

Meg defends Rufe, siding with him against her husband and the rest of her family, until she learns that he blew up the dam. Then, like Matt, Andy, and Jude, she wants him to die. Her extreme faith, like Rufe's, is prone to doubt. Meg questions a God who would allow her son to be killed, and she questions God again when Rufe's evil actions are revealed.

Sid Hunt

Sid Hunt appears to be the protagonist of the play. He is a humble war hero, he survives all attempts to kill him, he forgives the people who try to harm him, and he gets the girl. Like his grandfather, Sid is often the voice of reason. He is good-natured and calm, even when Andy is pointing a gun at him. When Andy says he plans to kill six Hunts, Sid tells him to sleep on it. He also offers to let Andy kill six Hunts who are not good people. Sid often sees through Rufe and is able to sense when he is being lied to.

Sid is certain that Jude will marry him, so certain that he does not ask her and assumes that she will. He even ignores her comments that she has not agreed to marry him. Sid appears to be one of the least religious characters in the play, claiming that his Bible was stolen during the war and making fun of Rufe's overzealous proclamations. However, he exhibits many Christian traits, forgiveness chief among them. He also tells Jude that he believes what the Bible says about man and wife, that they must put each other first, no matter the cost. After Jude tearfully agrees to side with him against her own family and become his wife, he comforts her and tells her not to worry because he is sure that he can put the feud to rest.

Sid resorts to violence only once in the play, when Rufe tries to stop him from finding his family and telling them not to kill Andy. Sid throws Rufe across the room in an effort to get by him. Sid later uses cunning to trick Rufe into confessing that he blew up the dam. He also thinks ahead and brings the boat that will allow him and his loved ones to escape the flood.

Andy Lowry

Andy Lowry is Sid's best friend and Jude's brother. He works as a mailman, and he was unable to enlist in the war because his parents made him take an exception. Andy regrets having been unable to fight like Sid, and his regret seems more genuine than Rufe's.

Andy is easily manipulated. Rufe mentions the Hunt-Lowry feud a few times and says that Sid has been making fun of him. Rather than question Rufe's motives and rely on the relationship he has with Sid, Andy believes Rufe and decides to kill his best friend.

However, Andy is also brave and sincere. The first time he tries to kill Sid, he is sincerely apologetic and remorseful. The second time he tries to kill Sid, Andy shows his bravery by refusing to beg for his life. He even tries to goad David and Matt into killing him so he can face death instead of sitting around helplessly, waiting for it to arrive. When Andy finally realizes that Rufe will not take responsibility for his role in Sid's attempted murder and that he has been

lying to him and everyone else, Andy vows to take Rufe to hell with him.

Jude Lowry

Jude Lowry is Sid's sweetheart and Andy's sister. She has a romantic past with Sid, but at first their future together is uncertain. Sid assumes they will be married, but Jude points out that he has not asked her and she has not said yes. When they finally decide to get engaged, Jude pledges her loyalty to Sid, even if that means being disloyal to her own family. She agrees to Sid's demands, and this is a sign that Jude values romantic love over familial love.

Jude, like Meg, is very religious, but she seems less zealous and more reasonable. At times, she questions Rufe's motives. She has a strong personality and stands up for herself when David makes sexist comments. In a moment of weakness, Jude prays for Sid's life, and Rufe almost succeeds in seducing her. In the end, she remains loyal to Sid.

Rufe Pryor

Rufe Pryor is a religious zealot who works for the Hunt family. He is petty, jealous, and murderous, but he masks his faults by aligning God's will with his own, and he truly believes that God's desires reflect his. Rufe is in love with Jude, and he wants Sid to die so he can marry her. At first, he tries to persuade Jude by pointing out that Sid is not religious. Then he manipulates Andy by telling him about the old family feud and implying that Sid thinks Andy is a coward. When Andy fails to kill his friend, Rufe takes the thunder during a rainstorm as a sign that God wants him to blow up the dam and drown Sid.

Rufe is a coward who uses Andy and then God to try to kill Sid. He runs and hides in the cellar when his treachery is finally revealed. Rufe is self-pitying, noting that his mother died when he was young, that he is sickly, and that everyone always blames him when things go wrong. He uses his religious faith to hide behind Meg and lies constantly. Rufe also uses his faith to woo Jude, inviting her to pray and then kissing her when she is at her most vulnerable. When confronted with his attempt to kill Sid, he lies and says, "I swear on a stack o' Bibles I didn't." When Rufe is left to die in the flood that he caused, he prays for help. When help does not arrive, he declares that God does not exist. For Rufe, faith is only useful if it serves his interests.

THEMES

Christianity

Christianity, as well as its use and abuse, is the prevailing theme in *Hell-Bent fer Heaven*. The subject is mentioned in the play's first pages as Meg wonders whether her son read the Bible while he was at war. Meg is clearly devout, and she deems David a lost cause. From this beginning, Christianity and each character's relation to it drive the plot. Meg defends Rufe because he is as religious as she is. Rufe is able to kiss Jude while they are praying. He equates his love for Jude with his spiritual awakening and believes that God told him to love her.

Even Sid, one of the least religious characters, quotes the Bible when he and Jude discuss their impending nuptials. He tells her the Bible says that man and wife must remain loyal to each other above all others. David, who does not appear to be religious, is constantly affronted by Rufe's zealotry and religious fervor. In the end, David's faith is confirmed, and even strengthened, by Rufe's failure to kill Sid. Rufe, on the other hand, loses his faith for precisely the same reason. All along he is sure that God's will is aligned with his own, but the moment he realizes this is not the case, he declares that God does not exist. Rufe still believes in God, however; he collapses in fear and despair, aware that he has committed an "unpardonable sin" and condemned himself to hell by denying God's existence.

Heaven and hell, the eternal reward and punishment of the Christian religion, are discussed at length, usually as the characters claim that they are going to heaven while everyone else is going to hell. Andy, however, is sure that he is going to hell, and he wants to be in charge of how he gets there. He tries to get David and Matt to kill him, and when he realizes that Rufe will not help him, Andy decides to take Rufe to hell with him.

Blasphemy

Of the multiple religious and theological concepts that run throughout *Hell-Bent fer Heaven*, blasphemy, insulting or speaking against God, is the most prominent. In a sense, it serves as a

TOPICS FOR FURTHER STUDY

- The events in *Hell-Bent fer Heaven* are put into motion by an old family feud, while the events in Katori Hall's young-adult play *Children of Killers* (available in the anthology *National Theatre Connections 2011: Plays for Young People*) are caused by the aftermath of the Rwandan genocide. Write an essay comparing and contrasting the two plays.

- Religion, namely Christianity, plays an important role in *Hell-Bent fer Heaven*. Do you think religion plays an important role in everyday life? Write a paper or stage a class debate on the topic.

- Use the Internet to research the Carolina mountains and their topography. Draw on available maps and atlases to create a model of the backdrop for *Hell-Bent fer Heaven*. You may use whatever format you prefer, including electronic media.

- Sid served in World War I, and David served in the Civil War. Both have killed in order to survive, but they are the only characters who do not want to kill Andy or Rufe. Is this a typical response to wartime violence? Research the firsthand experiences of soldiers in both wars and present your findings to the class.

contrast to the theme of Christianity, and often when characters disagree, they accuse one another of blasphemy. The final lines of the play focus on Rufe's blasphemy, on his denial of God. The antagonist has no moral awakening, no understanding that his own actions have led to his certain death in the flood he caused. Instead, Rufe is only concerned with his blasphemy, and the play ends as he grapples with his despair.

Meg accuses Andy of blasphemy for rejecting Rufe's religious notions, but David thinks that Rufe is far more blasphemous than Andy.

Sid returns home after serving in World War I.
(© johnbraid / Shutterstock.com)

Rufe claims he knows the will of God, and David tells Meg that God's "will's too big a thing fer any one man to git a strangle hold on it. . . . Fer all we know, God hisself may consider *that* more blasphemous 'n what Andy's a-doin'."

Revenge

Revenge is another theme in *Hell-Bent fer Heaven*, and it also has religious connotations. Andy wants revenge for the long-ago feud between the Hunts and Lowrys. He plans to get that revenge by killing six Hunts, double the number of Lowrys who were murdered during the initial feud. When Meg finally realizes that Rufe is responsible for attempting to murder her son, she wants revenge as well. Matt believes that Andy has killed Sid, and he wants revenge. He tries to kill Andy several times but is stopped by David, who prefers to leave the vengeance to God, or at least wait until he is sure that Sid is dead. Yet David acknowledges that God's vengeance can be worked through human hands: when Rufe observes, "Vengeance is mine, saith the Lord! I will repay!" David dryly responds, "He has to have a instrument to work through! Even God cain't smite evildoers 'thout a fist!"

STYLE

Dialect

Hughes's play's characters speak in dialect, using regional slang, abbreviations, and other forms of nonstandard English. While dialect is often associated with ignorance or lack of education, the characters in *Hell-Bent fer Heaven* are highly intelligent. Their rural lifestyle is ruled largely by religion and their interpretation of the Bible, and they engage in lively debates on religion and gender roles. Furthermore, because *Hell-Bent fer Heaven* is an example of American mountain literature, the use of dialect is essential. It adds authenticity and local color and becomes part of the play's setting, as integral to the plot as the Hunts' remote mountain homestead.

Foreshadowing

There are several examples of foreshadowing in *Hell-Bent fer Heaven*, particularly in regards to the plot's main turning points (the flood and Rufe's role in causing it). One of Meg's first lines in the play references the rainy summer, with more rain to come. In the second act, as the storm approaches, David notes that the river is high and may flood the banks. When Rufe worries about the dam that is still under construction, David comments that it will hold, and only dynamite could crack it. David also points out that Rufe has access to dynamite, and he has detonated it in the river before as an easy alternative to fishing.

Foil

A *foil* is a character with traits that contrast with, and thus emphasize, another character's qualities. Foils often exist in contrast to the protagonist, but in *Hell-Bent fer Heaven*, David, rather than Sid, serves as a foil to Rufe (the play's antagonist). Throughout the play, David and Rufe exist in direct opposition to one another. Where Rufe is sure that he knows what God wants, David is unsure. Where Rufe is certain that he is going to heaven, David is not. David even points out that Rufe's certainty is a form of blasphemy, and Rufe responds by accusing David of the same sin. Rufe is willing to accept thunder as a sign that he should kill Sid, but David demands undeniable proof of Sid's death before allowing Matt to kill Andy in retaliation. In the end, David's faith in God grows stronger, and Rufe's faith weakens to the point that it vanishes entirely.

COMPARE & CONTRAST

- **1920s:** Evangelical religion is increasingly popular, but Protestant Christians remain in the majority. Roman Catholics are the second-largest Christian population. Regardless of denomination, Christianity is socially and culturally dominant.

  Today: Protestants make up only 51 percent of the religious population in America, and religious diversity is the norm. Some 16 percent of Americans do not claim any religious affiliation at all.

- **1920s:** Farming is in decline as a significant economic sector in the United States, but it still provides families like the Hunts with sustainable income. Farming is also becoming increasingly mechanized with the introduction of industrial tractors and other modern farm equipment.

Today: In many areas, family farms are largely extinct, replaced by industrialized factory farms owned and operated by corporations. Smaller farms devoted to organic or sustainable farming practices struggle to compete outside of niche markets.

- **1920s:** Women are granted the right to vote in 1920 with the passage of the Nineteenth Amendment. It is the first major achievement of the women's movement in the United States.

Today: Women have since gained almost the same legal rights as men. However, as of 2007, per person they earned seventy-seven cents for every dollar that was paid to men. This gender-wage gap is not expected to close until 2057.

HISTORICAL CONTEXT

Pulitzer Prize Controversy

In 1924, the Pulitzer Prize jury recommended George Kelly's play *The Show Off* for the drama award. *The Show Off* received one first vote and two second votes, while *Hell-Bent fer Heaven* only received one first vote. The jury's final recommendation was sent to the Pulitzer board, but Columbia University professor Brander Matthews, one of Hatcher Hughes's colleagues, intervened. Matthews was not on the Pulitzer board or jury, but he wrote a letter to the board decrying Kelly's nomination and suggesting that *Hell-Bent fer Heaven* was a more deserving candidate.

It is unclear why the board chose to honor Matthews's arguments over the recommendation of its own jury, especially given the obvious favoritism that doing so implied. Juror member Owen Johnson, a novelist who recommended Kelly's play, made the jury's initial recommendation public and resigned his position to protest the board's reversal. Yale University professor William Lyon Phelps backed Johnson's claims, but he did not resign. Clayton Hamilton, the third member of the jury and another Columbia University professor, did not comment on the controversy at all. He was the juror who offered his vote in favor of *Hell-Bent fer Heaven* to begin with. Regardless of the controversy, *Hell-Bent fer Heaven* remained popular with audiences and critics alike.

World War I

The action in *Hell-Bent fer Heaven* begins as Sid returns from fighting in World War I. When he arrives, David comments that it is impossible to know the real reasons the war began. Historically, World War I was caused by poor diplomatic relations, waning imperialism, and rampant nationalism. Tensions between the United Kingdom, Italy, France, Germany, Russia, and Austria-Hungary had been building since around 1870, fueled by fading colonialism and territory disputes in the Balkans. Conflicts

Rufe attempts to get rid of Sid by blowing up a dam. (© Lee Morriss | Shutterstock.com)

regarding the Balkans occurred between Austria-Hungary, Serbia, and Russia, and their various allies (e.g., Germany, France, and the United Kingdom) were drawn into the dispute. A diplomatic quagmire ensued, and strained relations were further damaged by nationalist loyalties, an unchecked arms race, and economic instability.

The tipping point occurred in 1914 when the Archduke of Austria-Hungary, Franz Ferdinand, and his wife, Sophie, were assassinated. Their killer, Gavrilo Princip, was a member of the Serbian terrorist group known as the Black Hand. By the time the war ended in November 1918, civilian casualties were estimated to be around seven million, and almost ten million soldiers had been killed.

CRITICAL OVERVIEW

As Laura Grace Pattillo reports in the *Dictionary of Literary Biography*, initial critical reaction to the original production of *Hell-Bent fer Heaven* was positive. She quotes John Corbin's *New York Times* article of January 5, 1924, stating that Corbin calls the play "one of the most

original and vividly colored pieces in the contemporary drama." Pattillo also cites Carl Van Doren's *Nation* assessment of January 16, 1924, noting that he calls Hughes "a satirist, bringing to bear upon his theme a shrewd and humane intelligence," and a playwright who has "succeeded in telling a story thoroughly suited to the popular stage...making its intellectual implications unmistakable."

Since its first release, however, *Hell-Bent fer Heaven* has fallen into relative obscurity. When it is discussed, it is called an example of period folk drama or an example of religious themes in drama. Commenting on the latter topic in 1983's *Drama and Religion*, Thomas P. Adler calls the play "a study in how the evangelical spirit... can, like any good, be perverted by an excess of zeal." Christopher Brooks Bell, writing in the 2010 edition of *The Facts on File Companion to American Drama*, explains, "Hughes's drama is a classic example of folk drama, a subset of the realistic melodrama that dominated the period." Bell observes that this style has long since gone out of fashion and suggests that *Hell-Bent fer Heaven* "is not particularly distinguishable from the countless other melodramatic works of the time."

CRITICISM

Leah Tieger

Tieger is a freelance writer and editor. In the following essay, she argues that David is the protagonist of Hell-Bent fer Heaven *and then explores the nature of true faith and false faith as they are expressed through the characters of David Hunt and Rufe Pryor.*

Sid Hunt is the obvious protagonist in Hatcher Hughes's *Hell-Bent fer Heaven*. He is a war hero who returns to his loving family, best friend, and girlfriend. He remains calm and forgiving when Andy attempts to kill him. He wants all of his loved ones to get along and puts his life in danger when he attempts to stop his family from killing Andy. Sid is not just a war hero; he is his family's hero as well. Sid knows that the floodwaters will overtake the Hunt farm, and he brings a boat that allows everyone (except Rufe) to escape with their lives. Sid seems to be the play's protagonist largely because Rufe, the antagonist, is obsessed with killing him.

Rufe and Sid appear to be in constant opposition, but this opposition is one-sided. Sid hardly notices Rufe. He is not threatened by Rufe's crush on Jude or by Rufe's close relationship with Meg. When he realizes that Rufe is responsible for convincing Andy to kill him, Sid does not want revenge; he only wants Rufe to get out of his way so he can save Andy from the rest of his family. Sid nearly drowns after Rufe blows up the dam, but he does not try to hurt Rufe. He simply uses cunning to trick Rufe into confessing what he has done. He does not care about Rufe or what happens to him. After the family realizes what Rufe has done, Meg, Andy, Matt, and David discuss revenge. Meg wants revenge. Matt grabs his gun. Andy stops Matt and insists that he is the one who should shoot him. David stops both of them and points out that they should leave Rufe's punishment to God. Sid is noticeably absent from the conversation.

The relationship between the antagonist Rufe and the protagonist Sid lacks opposition, but the relationship between Rufe and David does not. Thematically, David Hunt is the protagonist in *Hell-Bent fer Heaven*. If the play is about the use and abuse of religion, then Rufe abuses religion for his own ends while David does not. Rufe believes that God wants what he

> THEMATICALLY, DAVID HUNT IS THE PROTAGONIST IN *HELL-BENT FER HEAVEN*. IF THE PLAY IS ABOUT THE USE AND ABUSE OF RELIGION, THEN RUFE ABUSES RELIGION FOR HIS OWN ENDS WHILE DAVID DOES NOT."

himself wants. David believes that no one can know what God wants.

There are several clues in the play supporting the idea that David is the protagonist. David is the first character who appears in the play, and the stage directions include a lengthy description of David and his demeanor. He has a "peculiar radiance," a serenity that is emphasized by the sunlight shining on "a personality that is rich, humorous, and mellow without a touch of sentimentality." When Sid appears onstage a few pages later, he is described briefly, in far less detail, and the description offers no insight into his character. It only addresses his appearance.

Although Meg and Rufe think David is a heathen, David proves again and again that he is the most principled and Christian character in the play. This puts him in direct opposition with Rufe, who is the least principled and least Christian character in the play (even though Meg and Jude believe otherwise). Rufe claims to know God's will, and David not only claims the opposite but also points out that Rufe's beliefs may be more blasphemous than Andy's disdain for God. After David and Matt capture Andy, Meg gets tired of Andy's blasphemy and tells David to shut him up. David will not harm Andy, however, until he has proof that Sid is dead. David also stops Matt from killing Andy (multiple times) for the same reason. He realizes he cannot know God's will, and Rufe's certainty that he does know it may be more blasphemous than Andy's jokes. David tells Meg that God's "will's too big a thing fer any one man to git a strangle hold on it. . . . Fer all we know, God hisself may consider *that* more blasphemous 'n what Andy's a-doin'."

Rufe believes this statement to be blasphemous, and Meg does too. She says Rufe

WHAT DO I READ NEXT?

- *Ruint*, Hughes's most famous play after *Hell-Bent fer Heaven*, was released in 1925. Like its predecessor, the play is set in the Carolina mountains. It explores the social expectations of the region's inhabitants.

- For more insight into the area where Hughes set his best plays, read Danny Bernstein's 2013 guidebook *The Mountains-to-Sea Trail across North Carolina: Walking a Thousand Miles through Wildness, Culture and History*. More than a guidebook, Bernstein's volume explores the history of the Smoky Mountains, Jockey's Ridge State Park, Revolutionary War sites, historic monuments, and cemeteries.

- In *Hell-Bent fer Heaven*, the characters are constantly discussing their interpretations of Christianity. To put these discussions in context, read Diarmaid MacCulloch's 2011 title *Christianity: The First Three Thousand Years*. This straightforward history follows the inception of Christianity and its many iterations over three millennia.

- Eugene O'Neill's play *Desire under the Elms* premiered in 1924, the same year as *Hell-Bent fer Heaven*. Like Hughes's play, *Desire under the Elms* is set in a farmhouse and features the loves and jealousies that tear a family apart. It is also written in dialect.

- The 1996 anthology *Teatro! Hispanic Plays for Young People*, edited by Angel Vigil, features fourteen plays that draw on Hispanic holidays, religious practices, folktales, and fables. Aimed at young-adult readers and actors, the plays offer a different take on dramatic renderings of religious and cultural issues.

- In the 2008 young-adult novel *Does My Head Look Big in This?*, Randa Abdel-Fattah presents the challenges faced by a Muslim girl named Amal. The protagonist, like Rufe, is extremely devout, and when she decides to wear the hijab, her less-religious friends and relatives struggle to understand her decision.

is a true believer because he comforts her, but David thinks that if comfort were the measure of religion, then alcohol would be more effective than God. He also thinks that Rufe is drunk, from either alcohol or religion. Andy comments, "One's jist as dangerous as t'other when it gits into a cracked head." The statement nicely sums up the difference between David and Rufe, as well as the play's overarching themes.

David has faith. He trusts in God's decisions and does not pretend to understand them. Whenever Rufe claims to know what God is thinking, David makes fun of him. He asks Rufe, "Have you been up to heaven to git the latest news?" In the play's opening act, Rufe tells David, "I'm satisfied 'ith my religion!" and David responds, "That's a shore sign God ain't." Rufe's faith, as David implies, is vanity in disguise. Rufe, David posits, found religion in order to avoid being drafted. Rufe does not agree with this assessment, but when he confesses his love for Jude, he tells her he found God when he found her. He believes that his feelings for Jude have been ordained by God. He also believes that his desire to kill Sid is endorsed by God—thunder during a rainstorm is all it takes for Rufe to decide that the Lord is on his side. When Rufe realizes that Andy will not protect him, he asks God for permission to kill his enemy. Rufe believes that God's desires will align with his own once more, but Rufe is interrupted by Sid's ghost before God can "answer" him.

When the characters plot their revenge against Rufe at the end of the play, David points out that God has been watching over and protecting them even as Rufe has conspired against them. He tells his family, "I hain't lost my belief in the Lord on Rufe's account. Fact is, I ain't so shore but what I believe in Him more 'n ever." Here, David is in direct opposition to Rufe. The events of the day have strengthened David's faith, but they have weakened Rufe's. The antagonist denies God's existence as soon as he feels that God's will does not match his. He rails against God for failing to strike down his enemies and failing to save him, for leaving him to die in the flood that he caused while operating under the belief that God wanted him to cause it.

Rufe believes that God's desires reflect his.
(© Duncan Andison | Shutterstock.com)

The play's inevitable flood calls the biblical story of Noah's ark to mind, and David compares Meg to Noah's wife as she worries about whether or not her turkeys will drown. In the story of Noah, the flood is sent to rid the wicked from the earth, and in *Hell-Bent fer Heaven*, Rufe is left to drown while the Hunts and Lowrys escape on the ark (boat) that Sid has brought them. Rufe is abandoned after David stops the others from killing him by explaining that they should leave Rufe's punishment to God.

Commenting on David's argument in *Drama and Religion*, Thomas P. Adler finds that the character is not as morally exalted as he appears. Adler suggests that "Hughes places an onerous burden on the audience if he expects them to sympathize with David's insistence that no one interfere with God's 'chance' to inflict punishment." Adler feels that this decision on David's part is disgraceful, and he condemns the Hunts and Lowrys for leaving Rufe to die. Adler writes, "Hughes intends that the close of

his play function on a mythic as well as a literal level. Here, however, the Remnant who are saved seem hardly better than the evil one washed off the face of the earth."

If Adler is correct, the play has no protagonists, only antagonists. However, David makes his belief about God and vengeance clear long before he persuades the other characters to leave Rufe to die. In the second act, when Matt wants revenge against Andy, Rufe tells Matt, "Vengeance is mine, saith the Lord!" David remarks that God needs an "instrument to work through. Even God cain't smite evildoers 'thout a fist!" In *Hell-Bent fer Heaven*, Rufe believes that he is that instrument and that fist, but in the end, it is David who assumes the role.

Source: Leah Tieger, Critical Essay on *Hell-Bent fer Heaven*, in *Drama for Students*, Gale, Cengage Learning, 2014.

SOURCES

Adler, Thomas P., "'The Mystery of Things': The Varieties of Religious Experience in Modern American Drama," in *Drama and Religion*, edited by James Redmond, Cambridge University Press, 1983, pp. 139–58.

Auger, Peter, *The Anthem Dictionary of Literary Terms and Theory*, Anthem Press, 2010, p. 114.

Bell, Christopher Brooks, "*Hell-Bent fer Heaven*," in *The Facts on File Companion to American Drama*, 2nd ed., edited by Jackson R. Bryer and Mary C. Hartig, Facts on File, 2010, p. 227.

Bhattacharjee, Riya, "50 Years after Equal Pay Act's Passage, Gender Wage Gap Still Persists," *MSN News*, June 10, 2013, http://news.msn.com/us/50-years-after-equal-pay-acts-passage-gender-wage-gap-still-persists (accessed July 16, 2013).

Conkin, Paul K., *A Revolution down on the Farm: The Transformation of American Agriculture since 1929*, University Press of Kentucky, 2008, pp. 31–50.

Fischer, Heinz-Dietrich, "1924 Award for Hatcher Hughes," in *Outstanding Broadway Dramas and Comedies: Pulitzer Prize Winning Theater Productions*, Lit Verlag, 2013, p. 18.

Harper, Douglas, *Changing Works: Visions of a Lost Agriculture*, University of Chicago Press, 2001, pp. 61–84, 247–78.

"Hatcher Hughes," in *Who's Who of Pulitzer Prize Winners*, edited by Elizabeth A. Brennan and Elizabeth C. Clarage, Oryx Press, 1999, p. 96.

Henig, Ruth, *The Origins of the First World War*, 3rd ed., Routledge, 2001, pp. 1–24.

Hughes, Hatcher, *Hell-Bent fer Heaven*, Harper and Brothers, 1924.

Joannou, Maroula, and June Purvis, eds., *The Women's Suffrage Movement: New Feminist Perspectives*, Manchester University Press, 1998, pp. 140–56.

Lieven, D. C. B., *Russia and the Origins of the First World War*, St. Martin's Press, 1983, pp. 30–53.

Link, Arthur Stanley, *The Impact of World War I*, HarperCollins, 1969, pp. 8–51.

Marwick, Arthur, *The Impact of World War I: Total War and Social Change; Europe, 1914–1945*, Open University Worldwide, 2001, pp. 1–35.

"The 1920s: Religion: Overview," *Encyclopedia.com*, 2001, http://www.encyclopedia.com/doc/1G2-3468300972.html (accessed July 16, 2013).

Pattillo, Laura Grace, "Hatcher Hughes," in *Dictionary of Literary Biography*, Vol. 249, *Twentieth-Century American Dramatists, Third Series*, edited by Christopher Wheatley, The Gale Group, 2001, pp. 160–66.

"Timeline: Faith in America," PBS website, 2009, http://www.pbs.org/godinamerica/timeline/ (accessed July 16, 2013).

FURTHER READING

Hemeyer, Julia Corbett, *Religion in America*, 6th ed., Pearson, 2009.
  Hell-Bent fer Heaven examines rural religious values in 1924, and Hemeyer's overview places these values in historical and cultural context.

McLoughlin, William G., *Revivals, Awakenings, and Reform*, University of Chicago Press, 1980.
  This religious history focuses on the camp revivals that David and Rufe reference in *Hell-Bent fer Heaven*. The book explores the social, anthropological, and psychological impact of these revivals.

Valenti, Jessica, *Full Frontal Feminism: A Young Woman's Guide to Why Feminism Matters*, Seal Press, 2007.
  Although feminism is a minor subject in *Hell-Bent fer Heaven*, it offers an interesting counterpoint to the play's religious concerns, as well as insight into gender roles in the 1920s. Valenti's accessible exploration of feminism offers a modern perspective.

Williams, Tennessee, *A Streetcar Named Desire*, New Directions, 1947.
  Both Hughes and Williams are adept at capturing regional culture. Like *Hell-Bent fer Heaven*, Williams's *A Streetcar Named Desire* offers a claustrophobic domestic drama that presents a distinct segment of Americana.

SUGGESTED SEARCH TERMS

Hatcher Hughes

Hell-Bent fer Heaven

Hell-Bent fer Heaven AND Hughes

Hell-Bent fer Heaven AND religion

World War I

Prohibition

Christianity

1924 Pulitzer Prize for Drama

Ruint AND Hughes

How to Succeed in Business without Really Trying

FRANK LOESSER
ABE BURROWS
JACK WEINSTOCK
WILLIE GILBERT

1961

How to Succeed in Business without Really Trying is a musical that opened on October 14, 1961, at the 46th Street Theatre in New York City, where it ran for over three years. After 1,417 performances, the show closed in March 1965. The music and lyrics were written by Frank Loesser. The book of the musical play was written by Abe Burrows in collaboration with Jack Weinstock and Willie Gilbert. Burrows also directed the show. The origins of *How to Succeed in Business without Really Trying* lie in a satirical book of that title by Shepherd Mead, himself a business executive. Weinstock and Gilbert adapted the book for the theater, but their play sans music was not produced.

The musical *How to Succeed in Business without Really Trying* won the Pulitzer Prize for Drama and seven Tony Awards, including Best Musical and Best Book. It was revived on Broadway in 1995, in a highly successful production starring Matthew Broderick at the Richard Rodgers Theatre. In 2011, a fiftieth-anniversary revival was produced, starring Daniel Radcliffe, at the Al Hirschfeld Theatre. The show is also often produced by amateur and student drama groups. Although aspects of the story now seem rooted in the 1950s and early 1960s and therefore outdated, the songs remain entertaining, and the satire about corporate life still has the ability to amuse a twenty-first-century audience.

Frank Loesser (© CSU Archives / Everett Collection / Alamy)

The book of the play, published in 1965, has long been out of print and is difficult to obtain. The vocal score, however, is available, published by Frank Music Corp., as are audio CDs of the major productions. The song lyrics are available at the Internet Archive, http://web.archive.org/web/20070807011417/http://libretto.musicals.ru/text.php?textid = 165&language = 1.

AUTHOR BIOGRAPHY

Composer and lyricist Frank Henry Loesser was born in New York City on June 29, 1910, the son of Henry and Julia Ehrlich Loesser. Although his family was a musical one, his father being a teacher of classical piano, Loesser never had any formal musical training but as a teenager taught himself to play the harmonica and the piano. He attended City College of New York in 1926 but dropped out after a year following the death of his father. He then worked a series of jobs, including selling classified ads and becoming city editor for the *New Rochelle News*. His main

interest was in popular music, and he wrote songs and sketches.

In the mid-1930s, writing with Irving Actman, he contributed five songs to a short-lived Broadway show, *The Illustrator's Show*, which won him a Hollywood contract with Universal followed by another with Paramount. He wrote lyrics for nearly sixty films, and his career as a composer began in 1939, when he wrote the music as well as the lyrics for the title song of the film *Seventeen*. His first major success came in 1948, when he wrote the score for the hit Broadway musical *Where's Charley?* Further success came in the 1950s, with the musicals *Guys and Dolls* (1950) and *The Most Happy Fella* (1956). *Greenwillow* (1960) was less successful, but beginning on October 24, 1961, *How to Succeed in Business without Really Trying*, for which he wrote the music and lyrics, was a huge hit. It ran for over three years on Broadway and won the Pulitzer Prize for Drama and seven Tony Awards, including Best Musical.

Loesser married actress Lynn Garland in 1936. The couple had two children and divorced in 1957. Two years later, Loesser married Jo Sullivan, who had played a leading role in *The Most Happy Fella*. They also had two children. Loesser died of lung cancer at the age of fifty-nine on July 26, 1969, in New York City.

Abe Burrows, who collaborated with Willie Gilbert and Jack Weinstock on the libretto for *How to Succeed in Business without Really Trying* and also directed the Broadway production, was born on December 18, 1910, in New York City. He was educated at City College of New York and New York University and made his career as a songwriter, composer, writer, singer, and director. He wrote the libretto for *Guys and Dolls* and directed such shows as *Two on the Aisle* (1951), *Can-Can* (1954), *Silk Stockings* (1955), *Happy Hunting* (1956), *Say, Darling* (1958), *First Impressions* (1959), *What Makes Sammy Run?* (1964), and others. Burrows wrote the screenplay for the 1956 film *The Solid Gold Cadillac* and produced the television series *The Big Party* (1959). Burrows married twice and had two children. He died in New York City on May 10, 1985, of Alzheimer's disease.

Willie Gilbert was born William Gomberg on February 24, 1916, in Cleveland, Ohio. He earned a bachelor of science degree and moved to New York City, where he collaborated with Jack Weinstock on comedy sketches. In addition to *How to Succeed in Business without Really Trying*, Gilbert collaborated with Weinstock on several other plays and also wrote for television. He died on December 2, 1980, in New York City.

Jack Weinstock, who was by training a physician, collaborated with Gilbert on many plays, including *Catch Me If You Can*. He also wrote the book for the musical *Hot Spot*. Weinstock died on May 23, 1969, in New York City.

PLOT SUMMARY

Act 1

As the show opens, J. Pierrepont Finch is washing the windows of the World Wide Wicket Company in New York City. He shows more interest, however, in the book he is reading, titled *How to Succeed in Business without Really Trying*. The book outlines some simple steps by which anyone can ascend the corporate ladder, whether they have talent or not.

When Finch enters the building, he immediately bumps into J. B. Biggley, the company president, who is indignant that Finch bothers him with an inquiry about a job. Although rebuffed by Biggley, Finch is noticed by Rosemary, a secretary, who immediately falls for him. Finch then encounters the personnel manager, Mr. Bratt, who hires him because he gets the wrong impression that Finch has been recommended by Biggley.

Finch begins work in the mail room. Biggley's nephew, Bud Frump, who does not take kindly to having a competitor, also works there. Finch flatters Miss Jones, Biggley's formidable middle-aged secretary, who introduces him to Mr. Milton Gatch, the head of the Plans and Systems Department.

When the long-serving head of the mail room, Mr. Twimble, is promoted to another position, Finch turns down the offer of his job. He knows from the book that if he wishes to rise in the company, the mail room is not the place to linger. Instead, the job goes, at Finch's recommendation, to the obnoxious Frump, who is content to trade on his connection to the company president. Meanwhile Finch, having impressed his superiors, finds himself promoted to junior executive under Gatch.

Meanwhile, Biggley arranges for his mistress, the sexy Hedy LaRue, to be hired as a

MEDIA ADAPTATIONS

- The musical was adapted into the film *How to Succeed in Business without Really Trying* in 1967, directed by David Swift, with a screenplay also by Swift. Robert Morse stars as Finch, as he did in the stage version.

- Audio CDs are available of the musical, both of the original cast (Sony Masterworks, 2010) and the 2011 Broadway revival (Verve, 2011),

secretary. When the executives meet her, they all want her as their secretary. However, Mr. Bratt, in spite of the fact that he likes to pursue the ladies himself, warns that a secretary is a vital part of the company organization and must not be treated as a toy.

At the end of the workday, Rosemary's friend and fellow secretary Smitty helps her and Finch arrange a dinner date. Frump sees Biggley and Hedy together and guesses what their secret relationship is, and he uses this information to blackmail Biggley into promoting him.

Finch is ready to plot his ascent in the company. He finds out that Biggley will be coming into the office on Saturday morning to pick up his golf clubs. Finch deliberately puts some empty coffee cups on his own desk and makes sure the desk is untidily covered in papers. He makes himself look disheveled, and then just before the boss comes in, he puts his head on the desk and pretends to be asleep. He wants Biggley to think he is so conscientious he has been working all night. Biggley falls for the ruse. Finch then starts to hum the fight song from Biggley's old college—Miss Jones told him what college it was—and Biggley starts to sing it. He is mightily impressed, thinking that Finch is an alumnus of the same college. He does not notice that Finch does not really know the words of the song. Keen to give Finch a helping hand, Biggley gives him his own small office and assigns Hedy as his secretary.

With the help of the book that is his guide, Finch soon discovers that Hedy has no secretarial skills and guesses that she is only there because of her relationship with Biggley. He sends her on an errand to Mr. Gatch, knowing that Gatch will make a pass at her, which he does. Gatch is then quickly transferred to a branch office in Venezuela, and Finch takes his place as head of the department.

Rosemary, having had one date with Finch, is keen to advance her chances with him. She has been invited to a reception for the new advertising manager, Benjamin Burton Daniel Ovington, whose secretary she is. She hopes to impress Finch with her new dress, which she thinks is an exclusive original design from Paris. Unfortunately for her, all the women arrive wearing the same dress.

Meanwhile, Frump is plotting to get rid of Finch, whom he regards as a rival. He sends Finch into Biggley's office when he knows Hedy is in there. He hopes to arrange for Biggley to catch Finch in the act of kissing Hedy. In the office, Hedy virtually forces Finch to kiss her, but in doing so he realizes that he is in fact in love with Rosemary. Hedy leaves and Rosemary enters, followed after a while by Hedy's reappearance wearing only a towel, since she has just had a shower. Finch manages to convince an indignant Rosemary that it is she whom he loves. As the couple embraces, Biggley enters the office, but he does not react too severely to what he sees.

Ovington is forced to resign after it is revealed (thanks to Finch, who knows exactly what he is doing) that he is a graduate of Northern State, which is a fierce rival of Biggley's college, Old Ivy. Biggley appoints Finch as vice president in charge of advertising. He asks him to prepare a presentation in which he will explain his creative ideas. After Biggley leaves, Rosemary returns, and Finch says he will appoint her as his secretary. Rosemary is not excited by the prospect but relents when Finch tenderly says that he needs her. She is even less pleased when she sees that Finch is more excited by his job promotion than by her. Frump, meanwhile, having been outwitted by Finch, plots his revenge.

Act 2

Rosemary, still dissatisfied with being subordinated to Finch's career ambitions, resigns, but Smitty persuades her to stay on. The book Finch is relying on informs him that being head of advertising is a good position to be in. He must think up a great idea. Frump, faking friendship and making what he pretends is a helpful suggestion, offers the idea of a treasure hunt in which the company hides a thousand-dollar savings bond somewhere and every week on television gives out clues as to where it is. Frump happens to know that Biggley dislikes this kind of thing. After Frump leaves, Rosemary and Finch rekindle their affection for each other. Finch develops Frump's idea, deciding that in the treasure hunt, the company will give away stock.

Hedy decides to quit, saying she is going to Los Angeles, where she says she has an exciting job prospect. Biggley protests and tries to talk her out of it. She relents and offers to become his secretary. When Biggley is less than thrilled by this prospect, Hedy gives him twenty-four hours to find her another position in the company that is not a secretarial job.

Before a meeting, the company executives convene in the executive washroom. They dislike Finch because of his rapid ascent and fear for their own jobs. They want to devise a way to stop him. Finch, meanwhile, looks into the mirror in the washroom and likes what he sees. He believes in himself and his abilities.

At the meeting with Biggley and the other executives, Finch presents his idea. It is to hide five thousand shares of company stock in each of ten company buildings around the country and give the television audience clues each week as to where they can be located. Predictably, Biggley hates the idea of a giveaway show, but Finch persuades him with the idea of a sexy Treasure Girl who will appear on the show, giving out the clues. Finch brings Hedy on just to demonstrate how this might work, intending that the real job go to a big star. Biggley immediately sees this a way out of his problem with Hedy and offers her the job as a response to her earlier ultimatum.

However, things do not go according to plan. Officially, only Biggley and Finch know where the treasure is located, but on the first television show Hedy is asked to swear on a Bible that she does not know any of these locations. Unwilling to tell a lie, she describes the ten locations. As a result of this disclosure, hundreds of company employees and other television viewers ransack the company offices looking for the treasure. At the company headquarters,

Finch gets the blame, which is good news for Frump and the other executives. Finch tells Rosemary he will resign and become a window washer again, but Rosemary tries to talk him out of it.

Finch is summoned to a meeting in Biggley's office, and Biggley demands that he resign and accept all the blame for the fiasco. Finch accepts this calmly, saying he plans to return to washing windows. This gets the attention of Wally Womper, the company chairman, who is present at the meeting. It turns out that Womper used to be a window washer too, so he is sympathetic to Finch. As they talk, Finch reveals that the television giveaway was actually Frump's idea. He also mentions that Frump is the boss's nephew, which angers Womper. He is about to take some drastic action when Finch steps in and saves the day for everyone. He reminds the chairman that they are all members of the brotherhood of man and asks him to consider that before firing anyone.

In the end, only Frump is fired, but there is a big company shake up. Womper retires, marries Hedy, and is about to take her on a trip around the world. Finch becomes company chairman, accepting the position only after consultation with Rosemary, who has become his wife. A chance remark by Rosemary inspires Finch to conceive an ambition of becoming president of the United States. Meanwhile, Frump has become a window washer, clutching a copy of the book *How to Succeed in Business without Really Trying*.

CHARACTERS

J. B. Biggley

J. B. Biggley is the president of the World Wide Wicket Company. He is a ruthless businessman who does not suffer fools gladly. He has his weaknesses, however. He arranges for his mistress, Hedy LaRue, to get a job at the company, even though her secretarial skills are close to zero. He also hires his nephew, Frump, even though Frump has few abilities. Biggley takes a liking to Finch and promotes him, although later he blames Finch for the fiasco with the television giveaway and demands that he resign.

Book Voice

The Book Voice reads *How To Succeed in Business without Really Trying* and is heard from time to time during the show as Finch consults the book.

Bert Bratt

Mr. Bert Bratt is the company's personnel manager. He is a yes man who knows that his job is safe as long as he always agrees with the boss.

J. Pierrepont Finch

J. Pierrepont Finch is an ambitious young man who becomes very successful in business. When the play begins, he is working in a more humble capacity, washing windows at the World Wide Wicket Company building. He becomes inspired by the book he is reading titled *How to Succeed in Business without Really Trying*, and he successfully applies for a job at the company. He begins working in the mail room, but he does not remain there for long. Following the advice in the book, making use of good luck, cunning, and an instinct for making the right move at the right time, he quickly climbs the corporate ladder, ending up as chairman of the company. Finch also finds success in love, marrying the secretary Rosemary Pilkington, who admired him as soon as she first laid eyes on him.

Bud Frump

Bud Frump is a company employee who is also the nephew of J. B. Biggley. Frump is arrogant because of his connection to the company president, but he is neither smart nor competent, and no one seems to like him. Frump develops a dislike for Finch and tries to plot his downfall, but the plot backfires and it is Frump who gets fired. He ends up like Finch was at the beginning, washing windows and reading *How to Succeed in Business without Really Trying*.

Milton Gatch

Mr. Milton Gatch is head of the Plans and Systems Department. Finch becomes a junior executive in the department and soon observes Gatch's weakness and successfully exploits it. Gatch cannot resist chasing the ladies, but when he targets Hedy LaRue, who unbeknownst to him is the boss's mistress, he is soon shunted off to a branch office in Venezuela.

Miss Jones

Miss Jones is Biggley's formidable, middle-aged secretary. Finch finds a way of charming her as a means of acquiring useful information about her boss.

Miss Krumholtz

Miss Krumholtz is a secretary, assigned at first to Mr. Gatch, then to Finch. She turns up at the reception for the new advertising manager wearing a dress that is identical to Rosemary's—to their mutual annoyance.

Hedy LaRue

Hedy LaRue is Biggley's secret mistress, and he arranges for her to get a job at the company. Although she is attractive and sexy, she is not very clever and has almost no secretarial skills. She also proves to be a disruptive influence. She makes an unsuccessful play for Finch and is subject to the amorous attentions of Gatch, which costs Gatch his job. Dissatisfied with her lot, Hedy tells Biggley she is going to leave her job and head for Los Angeles, but she is persuaded to stay on, if Biggley gets her a nonsecretarial job. She is eventually selected as Treasure Girl on the television show, but her first and only appearance is a disaster, since she reveals the location of the ten prizes. However, Hedy lands on her feet, marrying Mr. Womper, who takes her on a world trip for their honeymoon.

Benjamin Burton Daniel Ovington

Mr. Benjamin Burton Daniel Ovington is selected to be the new head of the advertising department. When Biggley learns, through Finch, that Ovington is a graduate of Northern State, he asks for his resignation. Northern State is the archrival of Biggley's college, Old Ivy, and Biggley cannot bear to employ a Northern State alumnus.

Rosemary Pilkington

Rosemary Pilkington is a secretary at the World Wide Wicket Company. She falls in love with Finch as soon as she sees him and entertains daydreams of their life together when they are married. After a few bumps along the road— Rosemary's brief and misguided jealousy of Hedy and her frustration with Finch's apparent greater interest in his career than in her—she and Finch are married.

Smitty

Smitty, also known as Miss Smith, is a secretary at the World Wide Wicket Company. She is friends with Rosemary and helps her set up her first date with Finch. Smitty continues to give Rosemary support and good advice throughout the play.

Mr. Twimble

Mr. Twimble is the head of the mail room. He has worked in the mail room for twenty-five years. He is not ambitious and always plays it safe. Whatever the company decides is fine by him. He has no ideas of his own and does not want any. While others lose their jobs by trying to be too creative, Mr. Twimble is certain that he will keep his. Early in the musical, Mr. Twimble finally gets a promotion, moving to the shipping department.

Wally Womper

Mr. Wally Womper is chairman of the World Wide Wicket Company. Like Finch, he started out as a window washer, and also like Finch, he followed the guidance of a book, in his case, a book of betting records that he used to place bets for all the other window washers. Because of their shared background, he takes a liking to Finch, and this saves Finch from being fired over the disaster of the television program. Womper decides to retire and marries Hedy LaRue.

THEMES

American Dream

Hiding behind the humor and the satire in the play is something that the audience may easily recognize: the realization of the American dream. The American dream refers to the notion, widely believed in American culture, that anyone who works hard and has talent can rise to the top and become wealthy and successful. Americans have always viewed their society as a meritocracy rather than one divided along rigid class lines in which wealth and success are inherited. In the play, Finch rises from humble status to become chairman of the company; it is also revealed late in the play that Wally Womper began in the same low-status job as Finch. The satirical reversal, of course, is that Finch achieves his goal not

TOPICS FOR FURTHER STUDY

- Write a satirical essay or short story about how to succeed in school. For inspiration, you may read the play by Jonathan Rand titled *How to Succeed in High School without Really Trying.*

- Research the progress women have made in achieving high positions in business over the last fifty years or so. Give a PowerPoint presentation to your class in which you show how women may now aspire to be CEOs rather than secretaries. Do women still face discrimination regarding promotion to top executive positions? What is the "glass ceiling"? Is it holding women back from achieving the highest positions in business?

- The cast of *13*, the successful Broadway musical that ran from 2008 to 2009, was made up entirely of teenagers. Consult *13: The Complete Book and Lyrics of the Broadway Musical* (2011), by Dan Elish, Robert Horn, and Jason Robert Brown, and also listen to an audio CD of the show. Write an essay in which you discuss the themes of the musical and how they are presented. Is the musical comic or serious? Is it true to life? How would you compare the music to the songs in *How to Succeed in Business without Really Trying*?

- Research how a musical is developed and produced. What stages does it go through? How is it financed? Are musicals driven solely by commerce, the need to make a profit, or are artistic concerns most important? Consult John Kenrick's article "How Broadway Musicals Are Made," at http://www.musicals101.com/makemusi.htm. Give a class presentation in which you discuss your research.

through hard work but just by following the simple rules that are explained in the book that he uses as his guide.

Ambition

Finch is as ambitious as any seeker after the American dream is likely to be. He wants to rise in the company, and he will do whatever it takes to advance. In his own way he is as ruthless as any seeker after success. He has no qualms about lying, and he is quite prepared to exploit the weaknesses of others, for example, as when he sends Hedy along to Mr. Gatch, knowing that Gatch will likely make a pass at her and that this will cost him his job. Finch shows ruthlessness again when he takes Frump's idea, develops it, and presents it as his own, but then tries to blame Frump when the outcome is bad. (Frump, of course, deliberately gave Finch the idea, knowing Biggley would hate it, to stop Finch's rise in the company—something that all the executives, who are also driven by ambition, are equally concerned about.) Finch is supremely confident in his own abilities, as the song "I Believe in You," which he sings while looking at his reflection in the mirror, demonstrates. He is not presented as a naïf who merely stumbles his way to success. He also wants the trappings that success brings, leaving instructions when he is promoted that he wants his name to appear in gold leaf on his office door. Frump shows ambition too, but in contrast to Finch has no idea of how to fulfill it other than by trading on the fact that he is the nephew of the chairman.

Nepotism

Nepotism is favoritism shown to relatives, usually in business or politics, regardless of merit. Bud Frump is hired by Biggley just because he is a relative. Frump is a mediocre employee, but he tries to exploit his connection to the boss. He does this indirectly. Whenever he wants some favor or advancement, he calls his mother, who calls her sister, who is Biggley's wife, who passes on the message to Biggley. When Wally Womper, near the end of the play, expresses his disapproval of how Biggley hired his nephew, Biggley protests, saying that he has never shown Frump any favoritism and in fact dislikes him.

Romantic Love

Although it is not the major theme, love has a role in the play, as Finch and Rosemary start to date. They are obviously made for each other, and there is little doubt that they will end up getting married, since this is a comedy and is unlikely to end in any other way. Finch does

New York Mayor Michael Bloomberg with Beau Bridges and Nick Jonas, who starred in a 2012 Broadway production of How to Succeed In Business without Really Trying. *(© Neilson Barnard | WireImage | Getty Images)*

need a little prod, however, before he realizes what his feelings really are. This comes when Hedy kisses him, and he realizes that it is Rosemary whom he loves. "There is wonderful music in the very sound of your name," he sings in the song "Rosemary."

After that there are two small incidents that briefly threaten to obstruct the happy conclusion: Rosemary's initial jealousy, until she understands the situation, of Hedy, and her frustration when Finch appears to be more interested in his career than in her. It appears that they are set for a conventional marriage in which he earns the money and she stays at home cooking and doing the housework. When Smitty suggests, early in the play, that as the wife of a business tycoon, Rosemary might face some lonely nights at home, Rosemary responds, in the song "New Rochelle," that she will be "happy to keep his dinner warm" until he comes home.

The ideal love of Rosemary and Finch is contrasted with the more practical arrangement in the extramarital relationship of Biggley and

Hedy: Biggley, a married man in a powerful position in business, gets the attentions of a much younger woman, and Hedy secures a job for herself.

STYLE

Satire

Finch's rise from window washer to chairman of a large company is presented in a satirical manner. A satire pokes fun at or ridicules the foolishness, vices, or shortcomings of people or institutions. The satirical intent of this play is clear from the beginning, as the Book Voice explains: "If you have education, intelligence, and ability, so much the better. But remember that thousands have reached the top without them. You, too, can be among the lucky few." (This line from the play is an exact quotation from the original book by Shepherd Mead.) The book says that the aspiring executive should select a large company to join: "In fact, the bigger the better. It should be big enough so that nobody knows *exactly* what anyone else is doing." The target of the satire, then, is the large American company and corporate life. Examples are not difficult to find.

In the first scene, a company executive says that they are sending out too many memos, and it must stop. A secretary responds that she will send out a memo about that. The song "Coffee Break" satirizes the routine of office life and the dependence of the employees on their daily coffee breaks. If they do not get this break, they all sing, "something within me dies."

The character Mr. Twimble is a satire of the unimaginative employee who always plays it safe, never steps out of line, and does things "the company way" because he wants to make sure he hangs on to his job. The result is that he has been stuck in the mail room for twenty-five years, even though the mail room, according to the Book Voice, is a place a man needs to get out of as soon as possible if he is going to advance.

Biggley's attachment to his alma mater, his erroneous belief (carefully encouraged by Finch) that Finch also attended the same college, and his refusal to hire someone who graduated from a rival college, is a satire of what is sometimes called the "old boy network." The old boy network refers to the practice of powerful men in business or other professions showing friendship and assistance to those who attended the same school.

Another example of satire is Finch's need for a big idea that will help him advance. He is following the advice of the book. In Shepherd Mead's original text, he refers to the advantages of being known as "an Idea Man" and continues, "You may say, 'But I've never had an idea in my life!' This may be true, but do not be discouraged! Men like you head many of our nation's greatest businesses." The way to succeed, Mead writes, is to take one of your assistant's ideas and develop it just a little and then claim it as your own. Finch follows this plan exactly when he takes Frump's idea about the television giveaway, adapts it, and hopes to receive the exclusive credit for it.

Musical

A musical is a dramatic stage work that features many songs or "numbers," as well as spoken dialogue, although some musicals are through-composed, which means that the entire play is set to music. In the twentieth century, musicals evolved from operetta and other musical entertainments such as burlesque and vaudeville. Musicals are often categorized as either musical comedy or musical play. Those in the former category, which includes *How to Succeed in Business without Really Trying*, are usually light-hearted, often featuring song and dance routines, and have relatively simple plots. The latter are more serious works, with more demanding plots and subjects and more complex integration of lyrics and music. Examples of musical plays include the works of Stephen Sondheim.

HISTORICAL CONTEXT

Broadway Musicals from the 1940s to the 1960s

One of the most successful of writing teams for Broadway musicals in the post–World War II era was Richard Rodgers (1902–1979) and Oscar Hammerstein II (1895–1960), who together created a string of hits, many of which are still performed in the twenty-first century. The first of these was *Oklahoma!* (1943). Not only was this an extremely successful show, running on Broadway for over five years, but it also, according to Raymond Knapp in *The American Musical and the Formation of National Identity*, "ushered in the age of the 'integrated musical,' in which all the elements involved in a musical—music, drama, song, dance, scenery, costumes, etc.—contribute to a single integrated whole."

The team had another success with *South Pacific* (1949), which won ten Tony Awards and was also notable for dealing constructively with the issue of racial prejudice. Other Rodgers and Hammerstein hits include *The King and I* (1951) and *The Sound of Music* (1959). John Kenrick, on his website *Musicals101.com: The Cyber Encyclopedia of Musical Theatre, TV and Film*, refers to the 1950s as witnessing the "golden decade" of the Broadway musical, which extended also into the 1960s. Kenrick writes,

> In the 1950s, Broadway musicals were a major part of American popular culture. Every season saw new stage musicals send songs to the top of the charts. Public demand, a booming economy and abundant creative talent kept Broadway hopping.

The most successful of these musicals, Kenrick writes, "integrated every element, offering recognizable characters singing in stories told

COMPARE
&
CONTRAST

- **1960s:** Women have fewer career paths open to them than men. Women are expected to be content with roles as wives and mothers. The publication of Betty Friedan's *The Feminine Mystique* in 1963 launches second-wave feminism, in which women begin to challenge the limitations of traditional gender roles.

  Today: Many jobs and careers that were traditionally open to men only are now open to women. However, women still earn less than men and often in business and other professions face the "glass ceiling," an invisible barrier that prevents them from reaching the highest positions and amounts to gender discrimination.

- **1960s:** In the early 1960s, the biggest US companies are manufacturing firms, such as General Motors, Chrysler, and U.S. Steel.

  Today: The US economy has shifted over recent decades, resulting in the service industry becoming bigger than the manufacturing industry. Service companies provide services but do not manufacture goods. Examples include government, banking, insurance, health care, financial services, and retail services. Some of the biggest firms are retailers such as Wal-Mart and Target. Technology companies, such as Dell and Google, are also among the country's largest.

- **1960s:** Notable musical comedies of the early 1960s are *The Fantasticks*, which begins in 1960 and runs for over seventeen thousand performances, *Bye Bye Birdie* (1960), *Carnival* (1961), and *Hello Dolly* (1964).

  Today: *Kinky Boots*, with music and lyrics by Cyndi Lauper, wins six Tony Awards including Best Musical, after opening on Broadway in April 2013. A revival of Stephen Schwartz's 1972 show *Pippin* wins four Tony Awards in 2013. *Matilda the Musical*, based on the children's novel by Roald Dahl, wins seven 2012 Olivier Awards after a run on London's West End and debuts on Broadway in 2013.

---

with wit and genuine heart." Kenrick refers to this recipe for success as "the Rodgers & Hammerstein formula."

Other successful Broadway musicals of the 1950s include *My Fair Lady* (1956), an adaptation of Bernard Shaw's 1912 play *Pygmalion*, with book and lyrics by Alan Jay Lerner and music by Frederick Loewe. In 1960, that writing team produced another big success with *Camelot*, based on the King Arthur legend. *The Music Man* (1957) by Meredith Wilson, and *West Side Story*, inspired by William Shakespeare's *Romeo and Juliet*, with book by Arthur Laurents, music by Leonard Bernstein, and lyrics by Stephen Sondheim, were two other hits in this decade. Frank Loesser succeeded with the music and lyrics for *Guys and Dolls* (1950) and *Most*

Happy Fella (1956) and so had mastered the formula for success by the time he wrote the music and lyrics for *How to Succeed in Business without Really Trying*.

Kenrick notes in "1960s II: Long Running Hits" that from 1964 to 1966, six musicals opened on Broadway that each ran for more than one thousand performances. These were *Hello Dolly* (1964), *Funny Girl* (1964), *Fiddler on the Roof* (1964), *Man of La Mancha* (1965), *Mame* (1966), and *Cabaret* (1966). Times were changing, however. "The late 1960s," Kenrick states, "marked a time of cultural upheaval. Young Americans were rocking to a different beat, and the Broadway musical was about to be dragged into a new, uncertain era." That change was embodied in the musical *Hair*.

Rose Hemingway, Daniel Radcliffe, and John Larroquette during the curtain call of the opening night of a 2011 Broadway production of How To Succeed In Business Without Really Trying *at the Al Hirschfeld Theatre in New York City* (© Jim Spellman / WireImage / Getty Images)

Hair began off-Broadway in 1967 and moved to Broadway in 1968. It was a revolutionary musical because, according to Knapp, it

> marked a deliberate attempt to create a viable alternative to the musicals of the older generation, grounded in a documentary-like approach to life as it is actually lived, and steeped in the emergent political issues, alternative life-styles, iconoclastic manner of appearances—and of course the music—of the younger generation.

Hair was controversial for its sexually explicit language, its depiction of drug use, and a brief nude ensemble scene. Coming only a few years after *How to Succeed in Business without Really Trying*, a musical that offended no one and provided no serious challenge to the cultural beliefs of the audience, *Hair* definitely marked a new departure for the Broadway musical.

CRITICAL OVERVIEW

Over the half century or so since it was first performed, *How to Succeed in Business without Really Trying* has proved its staying power. The show received generous and enthusiastic reviews

during its first run on Broadway from 1961 to 1965, and critics were still responding favorably in 1995, when the show was revived first at the Kennedy Center in Washington, DC, and later on Broadway. J. Wynn Rousuck, for the *Baltimore Sun*, writes that director Des McAnuff dealt with the "politically incorrect, chauvinist aspects of the script by adhering firmly to the 1961 setting, pumping up the satire . . . and adding a feminist fillip to 'A Secretary Is Not a Toy.'" Rousuck concludes, however, that perhaps the musical "may not be dated at all. . . . In these newly Republican-dominated times, this musical about big business is likely to be a show whose time has come—again."

Critical opinion of the Broadway revival that ran from March 2011 to May 2012 was mixed. For *Los Angeles Times* critic Charles McNulty, "it's not easy to turn back the clock. . . . Nothing ages faster than comedy, and the show's episodic structure now seems as belabored as a sitcom plucked from a rusty time capsule." McNulty concedes that "the satirical perspective on corporate personnel is certainly as pertinent as ever. . . . But all the romantic brouhaha with moony secretaries is beyond retro." Elysa Gardner, however, in the *USA*

Today, describes the show as a "thoroughly charming revival." Gardner has particularly positive words for Daniel Radcliffe, who played Finch: "This young Finch speaks rapidly and purposefully, so that we always see the wheels spinning behind his schoolboy smile." Gardner adds, "He also reveals, in the musical numbers, a serviceable tenor and sufficient rhythmic savvy to handle Loesser's jaunty, jazz-tinged score."

Ben Brantley in the *New York Times* took a different view, however. He comments that the show's book writers "failed to give Ponty [Finch] any defining traits beyond all-consuming ambition. It was left to whoever played him to provide the extras, like a personality." In that respect, according to Brantley, Radcliffe did not succeed:

> He purg[es] Ponty of any individualizing quirks. He's a tabula rasa who absorbs his professional bible's lessons on whom to stroke and how. This blank-slate aspect is unconditionally supported by the prevailing blankness of Mr. Radcliffe's face.

Brantley does believe that "Loesser's songs are wonderful, of course, top-of-the-line models of tuneful wit and economy. But they aren't rendered here with the conviction that might make them ring new."

CRITICISM

Bryan Aubrey

Aubrey holds a PhD in English. In the following essay, he discusses How to Succeed in Business without Really Trying *in the context of Shepherd Mead's book of the same title which inspired it.*

A Broadway musical is a highly collaborative venture that takes many people—writer, composer, lyricist, producer, director, choreographer, musical director, conductor—and sometimes quite a long period of time to come to fruition. The seeds of *How to Succeed in Business without Really Trying* go back to the 1952 best-selling book of that title by an advertising executive, Shepherd Mead. The book is a satirical take on American corporate life in the format of a self-help manual for a young man just starting out on his career.

The theme of the book is that anyone can succeed in rising to the top of the company ladder as long as he learns a few basic rules about how corporations function. Success is not a matter of talent or ability or even hard work; none of those things matter. The only thing that does

> THE REVOLUTION IN GENDER ROLES THAT HAS TAKEN PLACE SINCE THE MUSICAL'S DEBUT IN 1961 IS NOWHERE MORE APPARENT THAN IN ONE OF ITS PROMINENT THEMES: A SECRETARY WILL ALWAYS BE OUT TO SNAG A HUSBAND."

matter is understanding how a large company really operates and using that knowledge to one's own advantage. Mead introduces a fictional character named J. Pierrepont Finch, as well as a company chairman named J. B. Biggley, and creates a number of fictional scenarios for them, complete with dialogue.

The book is actually a satire of Mead's own twenty-year rise from mail-room clerk at an advertising agency to vice president of the company. In the book, however, he emphasizes that the aspiring business executive should join a large company that manufactures something ("any company with a factory will do"), not a company in the service industry, like an advertising agency. Mead's fictional corporation manufactures wickets.

Three years after Mead's book was published, playwrights Willie Gilbert and Jack Weinstock saw the dramatic potential in it and adapted it as a play. However, the play was never produced. Then, in 1960, the play came to the attention of a theatrical agent, Abe Newborn, who showed it to producers Cy Feuer and Ernest Martin, who thought it could be successful as a musical. They brought in Abe Burrows to write the book and Frank Loesser to write the music and lyrics, and the result one year later was the Pulitzer Prize–winning *How to Succeed in Business without Really Trying*.

Although the musical had a lengthy evolution, Mead's 1952 book is still very much recognizable in it. One of his first pieces of advice to the aspiring business executive is to start in the mail room but get out of it as quickly as possible, and of course this is one of the notions that the Book Voice in the musical explains to Finch. It is important to get noticed by the higher-ups. Finch in the musical achieves this by making himself known to Miss Jones, J. B. Biggley's

WHAT DO I READ NEXT?

- *Great Songs from Musicals for Teens* (2001) compiled by Louise Lerch, is a collection of music from a variety of musicals, including *South Pacific*, Loesser's *Guys and Dolls*, *Camelot*, *My Fair Lady*, and *Big River*. The book comes with a CD of recordings by young singers and an accompaniment track for each song. There are two editions of the book, a Young Men's edition and a Young Women's edition.

- *A Most Remarkable Fella: Frank Loesser and the Guys and Dolls in His Life; A Portrait by His Daughter* (2000), by Susan Loesser, is a biography of Loesser by his daughter, who draws on her own memories and those of others who knew him. The book includes photos, drawings, and lyrics.

- Scott Adams is the creator of the popular comic strip Dilbert. In *The Dilbert Principle: A Cubicle's Eye View of Bosses, Meetings, Management Fads & Other Workplace Afflictions* (1996), Adams turns a satiric eye on corporate America, with some sage and amusing advice to the office worker about how best to survive a rather crazy environment.

- *The Peter Principle: Why Things Always Go Wrong* (2011) is a reprint of the 1969 edition of this classic book by Laurence J. Peter, in which he put forward his now famous Peter Principle to explain why, in any organization, incompetence rules. It is because everyone will inevitably rise to the level of their own incompetence. In other words, people will go on getting promoted from jobs they can do until they end up in one that they cannot do, which is where they stay.

- *Broadway Musicals: The 101 Greatest Shows of All Time* (revised and updated edition, 2010), by Ken Bloom and Frank Vlastnik, is an illustrated celebration of over one hundred of the best-loved Broadway shows, including *How to Succeed in Business without Really Trying*. The book includes commentary, plot synopses, cast and song lists, production details, and anecdotes.

- *Black Musical Theatre: From Coontown to Dreamgirls* (1989), by Allen L. Woll, is an account of African American musical theater from the end of the nineteenth century until the 1980s. Woll discusses many performers and analyzes many shows, including *A Trip to Coontown*, *Porgy and Bess*, *Ain't Misbehavin'*, and *Dreamgirls*.

---

secretary, and flattering her. That gets him the attention he needs.

The scenario that follows in Mead's book is that an employee likely to succeed may be offered a promotion to head of the mail room, but he would be advised to turn it down with the modest comment that he does not deserve the promotion and recommend someone else to fill the position. This is exactly what Finch does in the musical. He says that Frump is better qualified and has been there longer, and he recommends Frump for the job. (Frump himself has been lobbying for the job and does not appear to know that this is likely a bad career move.) As a result of his apparent generosity and concern for the welfare of the

company, Finch gets offered a position as junior executive—exactly as Mead promises in his book.

The mail-room scene proves to be an excellent vehicle for Loesser's satirical lyrics. The longtime head of the mail room, Mr. Twimble, is an example of what happens if you do not know the rules of how to succeed. Mr. Twimble actually tries very hard, but he has not had the advantage of reading the book that Finch has been lucky enough to get his hands on. Twimble started as a "brash young man" but told himself not to "get any ideas."

In a clever twist on this perfectly reasonable notion of making sure one does not make unwarranted assumptions about one's own abilities, the next line of the satirical song "The Company Way" reveals that he stuck to his plan so well that he has not had an idea for years. He has allowed himself to be brainwashed by the company and goes along with whatever the company wants, making sure he says all the right things whenever he encounters a company executive. He even lets his superior win every time they play gin rummy. "The Company Way" recalls the song "When I Was a Lad" from the W. S. Gilbert and Arthur Sullivan operetta *H.M.S. Pinafore* (1878), in which the First Lord of the Admiralty tells of how he started out as an office boy but eventually got sent to Parliament, where

> I always voted at my party's call / And I never thought of thinking for myself at all. / I thought so little, they rewarded me / By making me the Ruler of the Queen's Navee!

"The Company Way" is actually a satirical reversal of this, in which not thinking for oneself is rewarded not by a dizzying series of promotions but by stagnation in a lower-level position.

The section in Mead's book titled "The Old School Tie" provided the writers of the musical with another opportunity to plumb the satire. "You are fortunate indeed if the Old Man is a loyal alumnus," writes Mead. He advises the aspiring junior executive to do a little research, acquire the relevant "school rings, ties, pins, pennants, and old footballs painted with historic scores," and then seize an appropriate time to give the boss the impression—even by outright lying—that they are alumni of the same college. It is this scenario that inspired the scene in the musical in which Finch easily convinces Biggley that he is an alumnus of Old Ivy. So slick is Finch that he does not even have to bother with accumulating the college paraphernalia.

The original book also provided the inspiration for the song "A Secretary Is Not a Toy." Indeed, Mead even supplied the title of the song and the gist of the lyrics:

> A Secretary is NOT a Toy. She will be a girl selected for her ability, at one thing or another, and she will only too often be skillful with the typewriter, and perhaps even shorthand. She will be entrusted to your care as a helpmate *in your work*, and should not be used for pleasure, except in emergencies.

Loesser turned this into the witty lines of the song:

> She's a highly specialized key component / Of operation unity, / A fine and sensitive mechanism / To serve the office community.

And also:

> Her pad is to write in / And not spend the night in.

It is in reference to female roles that Mead's book, as well as the musical that it is based on, has become outdated, as at least one reviewer of the 2011 Broadway revival noted. Using native cunning and an amoral approach to life to outsmart competitors may well be as effective—at least for the purposes of satire—today as it was fifty years ago, but gender roles have evolved to the point where they are almost unrecognizable from what they were in the 1950s and early 1960s. As Stanley Bing points out in his introduction to the 2011 edition of Mead's *How to Succeed in Business without Really Trying*, "You may not call a woman a girl.... You may not even call a secretary a secretary, any more than you can call a firefighter a fireman or a flight attendant a stewardess."

The revolution in gender roles that has taken place since the musical's debut in 1961 is nowhere more apparent than in one of its prominent themes: a secretary will always be out to snag a husband. One of those secretaries, Rosemary Pilkington, is even presented as a Cinderella figure who gets her Prince Charming—the rising young business executive who happens to have just become her boss, and who will sweep her off to a new and better life of "glorified unemployment." It is a dream that all the other secretaries have, as the song "Cinderella, Darling" makes clear, but it smacks of a bygone time when women did not have the opportunities that they have in the twenty-first century for careers other than housewife and mother.

Loesser, of course, as is to be expected in this satirical musical, has some fun with the limitations of Rosemary's ambition and how she is willing to embrace a role that leaves her keeping her husband's dinner warm as he works late at the office. Social change came so rapidly during the 1960s that a mere decade or so later, the Rosemary Pilkingtons of America had become a rapidly diminishing breed. It is probably this sea change that Stanley Bing has in mind when he facetiously refers to Mead's book as "a seminal work from the late corporate stone age." Of course, the fact that certain aspects of a musical no longer reflect today's realities is no reason not to enjoy the show, as the continuing parade of Broadway revivals of earlier musicals (such as

J. Pierrepont Finch starts as a window washer but works his way up to become chairman of the board. (© ostill | Shutterstock.com)

that quintessential embodiment of the 1960s counterculture, *Hair*) demonstrates.

Source: Bryan Aubrey, Critical Essay on *How to Succeed in Business without Really Trying*, in *Drama for Students*, Gale, Cengage Learning, 2014.

Thomas L. Riis

In the following excerpt, Riis provides an in-depth analysis of the music in How to Succeed in Business without Really Trying.

. . . THE MUSIC

The music of *How to Succeed* follows the familiar Broadway model of the period, with more songs in the first act than the second and a liberal number of reprises throughout to ensure continuity. The published piano-vocal score includes twenty numbers in the first act with nine principal songs, and seventeen numbers in the second act with four major songs plus an extended dance number. Each of the fourteen major pieces has its own personality, yet all contribute to the plot and action in a distinctive manner. The other musical numbers for the most part consist of music for scene changes,

> SINCE THEN, *HOW TO SUCCEED* HAS TRAVELED AROUND THE WORLD; IT WAS SUCCESSFULLY MOUNTED IN LONDON, MELBOURNE, SYDNEY, PARIS, AND VIENNA (ADAPTED), EVEN BEFORE THE END OF THE ORIGINAL NEW YORK RUN IN MARCH 1965."

background, or fanfares. *How to Succeed*, while not needing the reflective, emotion-laden recitatives or poignant melodic outcries indispensable to musical dramas, nevertheless was crafted to fit the action in microscopic detail. This was the essence of its novelty.

Loesser's return to a simpler, more traditional Broadway song sequence should not be understood as a retreat to formula, but rather as an attempt to maintain continuity while neither overwhelming the action nor slowing its pace. Comedy relies more than drama on quick, efficient pacing. Extended breaks in the action for reflection or expansive emotional statement would have doomed the effort.

Each of the show's major songs falls into one of three musical categories, defined by what could be called "rhythmic attitude." The first of these attitudes consists of a steady beat and meter, a strict tempo, a continuous line of melody notes, and a straightforward optimism in the lyric. "Happy to Keep His Dinner Warm," "A Secretary Is Not a Toy," and "Grand Old Ivy" clearly fit into this category. One almost irresistibly wants to move to the beat of these songs. They are dance numbers in spirit, if not in fact. ("Happy to Keep His Dinner Warm," while not choreographed, is marked with a dance tempo.)

The second attitude reflects a more jazz-inspired edginess. They are also dance-oriented, but the beats and rhythm patterns here are casually syncopated (that is, musical accents often land in unexpected places). More rests interrupt the flow in the melodic lines, and steady foundational bass-note patterns (ostinatos) impart a driving feeling. "Been a Long Day," "Coffee Break," "The Company Way," and "Brotherhood of Man" belong in this category.

The third attitude can be characterized as broadly romantic, but also tinged with overdone nostalgia. The melodies of this type employ a relaxed tempo, have fewer and longer notes, and, because their rhythms are less busy, they induce a release of tension. The type was an early Loesser specialty. "Rosemary," "Paris Original," "Love from a Heart of Gold," and "Cinderella, Darling" share these qualities. Gayle Seaton suggests that "Love from a Heart of Gold" "adopts the style of a 1940s movie-musical love song." "Rosemary," with its false authority owed to an obviously borrowed classical quotation, enhances the singers' and audience's imagination of ideal love. Finch's lyric in the final section of the song, "Rosemary, just imagine if we kissed / What a crescendo . . ." is followed by nine measures of Grieg's A-Minor Piano Concerto before he completes the rhyming couplet with the words, "not to be missed." Such a sudden and dramatic extension rings true with the general thrust of the show, calling attention to Finch's comic egocentrism and grandiosity.

The centerpiece song, "I Believe in You," exhibits traits from all of these attitudes, but its overall vocabulary is closely related to the other ballads. By employing this family-resemblance method of songwriting, Loesser avoided the need to invoke explicit melodic quotations, transformations, or leitmotifs as we have seen in *The Most Happy Fella*. His approach was validated by observations from the opening-night reviewers, such as Richard Watts Jr., who declared in the *New York Post* that "it is possible that Frank Loesser's score lacks any outstanding hit song, but it is invariably gay, charming and tuneful, and it has the enormous virtue of fitting in perfectly with the spirit and style of the book's satire. In his lyrics, Mr. Loesser is characteristically bright and ingenious, and in the right mood. It is this *fitting together* [emphasis added] of all of the parts, from the brisk imaginative dance numbers to the excellent settings, that is the distinguishing feature of 'How [to Succeed in Business],' and gives it such a comforting feeling of all being well."

As with the songs for *Guys and Dolls* and *The Most Happy Fella*, Loesser built his melodies in *How to Succeed* on the normal speech accents of the most important words. For example, "Happy to Keep His Dinner Warm," Rosemary's first solo in the show, a hymn to self-sacrifice at the altar of domesticity, presents a commonplace line of English text with the musical stresses matched precisely to the way in which the line might be spoken in direct conversation.

The biggest musical difference between *How to Succeed* and *The Most Happy Fella* is represented by the far jazzier idiom of the more recent show. Jazz elements had not loomed large in 1940s or early '50s Broadway musicals, but much had changed by 1961. Through the efforts of figures such as Dizzy Gillespie, Charlie Parker, and Dave Brubeck, jazz was being reconfigured in the mainstream American public consciousness as a progressive idiom, appealing to wider audiences than its earlier manifestations as a marginalized black cultural product (for instance, in the New Orleans-style improvisations of Louis Armstrong or Bessie Smith's searing blues) and as a dance phenomenon (expressed in the swing craze of the mid-1930s, spearheaded by Benny Goodman). The highly successful marketing of the long-playing 33 rpm vinyl disc also had increased audiophiles' opportunities to hear extended improvisational passages on home sound systems, since the new format allowed a single recording to last more than twenty minutes.

In other words, contemporary jazz in the late 1950s was becoming "hip," "cool," and widely accessible. A small but growing group of middle-class whites began to savor the technical complexities of black bebop and became at least superficially familiar with the racial argot of big-city black neighborhoods. The musical codes of jazz signaled not just urbanity but sophistication, and they began to appear in record stores, at the movies, and on the radio. In an era when rock 'n' roll was a mere infant, jazz—or at least a jazz-flavored popular style—represented the height of fashion and could boast cultivated aficionados who welcomed its strains into their living rooms, private clubs, and even concert halls.

Leonard Bernstein's *West Side Story* burst on the Broadway scene in 1957, followed by a popular movie version in 1961, many regional and international productions, and substantial sales of the original cast recording. Bernstein's use of several syncopated and Latin elements expanded audiences' ideas of what the urban soundscape was like. The show confirmed both the danger and the vitality of the big city by providing an energetic and rhythmic sonic backdrop for Tony, Maria, Anita, and the other Sharks and Jets.

That elements of jazz expression should appear in a satire about American urban business life seems logical in retrospect, especially coming from a composer who had so smoothly worked to assimilate many earlier musical idioms into his shows. Even before the overture to *How to Succeed* is concluded—with its last fifty measures marked "Fast Swing in 4"—any alert listener will suspect that syncopated tunes and jagged offbeats are going to be actively shaping the musical textures to come. Moreover, it serves multiple purposes in the show. Jazz is both background for the bustle of city business life and also a sly counterpoint to the stodgy and rigid old regime doomed to give way before the ingenious younger generation epitomized by J. Pierrepont Finch.

The play's musical vocabulary also suggests several other musical markers, whether jazz-inflected or not, denoting the urban setting: a higher density of dissonant clashing chords, chords formed with stacks of fourths rather than thirds (stacks of fourths were also assuming more prominence in jazz chord voicings at the time), more twists and turns in melodies to include notes not in the major scale, and the frequent presence of ostinatos. The beginning of the title song features such an ostinato of a sort often found in Latin dance numbers (with 3 + 3 + 2 eighth-note groups in the bass).

The importance of dance movement and rhythm is reflected elsewhere in the score for *How to Succeed*, with expressive terms borrowed directly from dance tempos: "Happy to Keep His Dinner Warm" is an "Easy Schottische," an old-fashioned round dance that bespeaks a traditional sentiment; "Coffee Break" is directed to be done in an "Ominous Cha-Cha Tempo"; and "A Secretary Is Not a Toy" was famously converted into a compound meter (12/8)—four moderately paced triplets per measure—for a "Soft Shoe Tempo," suggested by Bob Fosse to go with a production number for all the secretaries in the office. A "light swing" tempo backed by another ostinato and orchestrated with modern jazz instrumental colors is invoked for "Been a Long Day."

"The Company Way" also seems to be marked by a breezy rhythmic swagger. The basic pattern of the song emphasizes two moderately quick beats per measure, but with so much flexibility and syncopation on the shorter notes within the measures that it gives the impression of being made up on the spot. We might wonder whether it was based on a loose set of general directions, rather than being sung precisely "as written." A listener cannot tell at first by ear alone—and that casualness may be the root of its attractiveness and function. "The Company Way" fundamentally represents the subject of its lyric, the fawning flexibility of World Wide Wickets employees (Twimble, Frump, and chorus) and their conformity to shifting corporate demands. The music itself is also pliant, which is to say easily altered or modified. Indeed, as a musical metaphor it is the perfect parodic tune.

The final second-act number, "Brotherhood of Man," with a similarly flexible rhythmic line, meter, and speed, exhibits a parallel vein of aroused good feeling. Less snide than "The Company Way" (in which a duo sings, "Your brain is a company brain. / The company washed it, and now I can't complain"), "Brotherhood of Man" invokes a religious phrase in its title to justify the good old boys' pecking order. The insincerity of its claim is not hard to ferret out. After all, the chorus sings, despite our different clubs (Elks, Shriners, and Diners), we are all members of "a benevolent brotherhood.... Your lifelong membership is free.... Oh, aren't you proud to be / in that fraternity?" Loesser knew the theatrical effect of this kind of delivery, having previously used such intensified quasi-religious metaphors with great success for "Make a Miracle" (*Where's Charley?*) and "Sit Down, You're Rockin' the Boat" (*Guys and Dolls*).

The hit song of the show, "I Believe in You," can be performed in as many different moods, attitudes, and settings as singers can muster, and, what is more, it makes perfect sense outside of the play. Apart from the immediate theatrical context of *How to Succeed*, "I Believe in You" is an attractive number, a solid example among the many happy songs of encouragement lodged in Broadway shows....

THE PULITZER PRIZE IN DRAMA...FOR A MUSICAL COMEDY

How to Succeed picked up the 1962 Tony Award for best musical, Morse won the same award for best actor in a musical, and the show's team garnered six other Tonys. So much was easy to predict from the critics' raves. But to win the Pulitzer Prize was something else again. First presenting the award to a drama in 1918, the judges took another fourteen years before a musical comedy script pleased them enough to win amid an assortment of straight plays. After *Of Thee I Sing* (1931), for which the composer George Gershwin received no prize (since Pulitzers were not then being given to musicians), only *South Pacific* (1949) and *Fiorello* (1959) among musicals had succeeded in picking up this honor. Burrows and Loesser (despite Frank's joke name, the "Putziller") were deeply gratified, and the original run continued through May 1965, totaling 1,417 performances, more than *Guys and Dolls* had achieved in its initial run and more than any other show of the 1950s except *My Fair Lady* (1956) and *The Sound of Music* (1959).

Subsequent critical recognition echoed the general praise at the premiere. Signaling their impatience with Broadway sentimentality, critics latched on to the book's charming effrontery. Walter Kerr happily declared the script "deadpan and deadly." Morse was seen to be a brilliant compound of Horatio Alger and Machiavelli (Kerr). Rudy Vallee (whose frayed and aging ego tried the patience of the producers, especially Loesser) was "merely magnificent." The newcomer Charles Nelson Reilly, in the role of the president's nephew Frump, "turned in a most hilarious and artful performance...like Mephistopheles on needles," "a major achievement in hilarious exaggeration" (Nadel). "No one could suffer as exquisitely as he does" (McClain). The critics found few faults and excused the paucity of blockbuster songs, pointing to the brilliant lyrics and the skill with which music knit the whole show together. Loesser's love of in-jokes and classical allusion were not lost on the critics, who duly noted and lauded his "romantic" quotation of Grieg's piano concerto during "Rosemary," when Finch and his girlfriend come to the clinch.

After a year in office, President Kennedy chose *How to Succeed* for his first theatrical outing to New York in January 1962. The *New York Daily News*'s front page captured the moment with a photo of the president's arrival underneath the neighboring Imperial Theatre's marquee. The caption: JFK LEARNS: HOW TO SUCCEED. According to Abe Burrows, the president liked the show so much that he recommended it in a cabinet meeting. Burrows even

recalled that a contingent of the original American Mercury program astronauts, led by John Glenn and Alan Shepard, attended the show. Since then, *How to Succeed* has traveled around the world; it was successfully mounted in London, Melbourne, Sydney, Paris, and Vienna (adapted), even before the end of the original New York run in March 1965. The film version appeared in 1967, trimmed of five original songs ("Cinderella, Darling," "Heart of Gold," "Happy to Keep His Dinner Warm," and the Pirate ballet number, "Yo Ho Ho"; "Paris Original" was used only as underscoring). Directed by David Swift, the movie retained much of the original stage show, including the performances of Morse, Vallee, Ruth Kobart (as Biggley's prim secretary, Miss Jones), and the second Rosemary in the Broadway production, Michele Lee.

Revivals since the premiere have been less frequent, but the 1995 production, featuring Matthew Broderick as Finch, achieved substantial plaudits. Some changes were made in the direction of political correctness (the original bimbo Hedy LaRue was now played as a wilier and more calculating character, for example), ticket sales were excellent, and the critics were divided. A reprise of "The Company Way" sung by aspiring women executives replaced "Cinderella, Darling," but most of the original songs were retained, albeit with new orchestrations (by Danny Troob) that at least one listener likened to an assault on the ears. The choreography and sets were updated, and the stage action made even more busy than the original had been, leading to charges of heavy-handedness on the director's part. The *Wall Street Journal*'s Donald Lyons blamed director Des McAnuff for misjudging the show's underlying motivation. Lyons deplored the production's "mindless lack of irony," which celebrated what in his view Loesser and Burrows had intended to satirize: conformity, hypocrisy, and sexual mischief in the workplace. The flat office spaces of 1961, he observed, had been replaced by flashy movable sets. The intentionally insincere "Brotherhood of Man" was treated as a straight-up rock gospel number (and brought the house down). The originally crisp caricatures were gone from a show now encrusted with too much staginess and too much noise; to Lyons, this *How to Succeed* represented the loss of "charm, intimacy, and humanity," washed away in a torrent of technology.

Still, almost all the critics professed to like the show, with *Variety* declaring it "as good as it gets." Apparently, office politics turned out to be a hardier perennial theme than Loesser and Burrows could have imagined in 1961, satire or not.

Source: Thomas L. Riis, "How to Succeed in Business without Really Trying," in *Frank Loesser*, edited by Geoffrey Block, Yale University Press, 2008, pp. 179–85, 188–191.

SOURCES

"Abe Burrows," Internet Movie Database, http://www.imdb.com/name/nm0123242/bio (accessed June 7, 2013).

Bing, Stanley, "How to Succeed in Business without Really Trying 2.0," Introduction to *How to Succeed in Business without Really Trying*, by Shepherd Mead, 2011, p. xii.

Brantley, Ben, "Wizard of Corporate Climbing," in *New York Times*, March 27, 2011, http://theater.nytimes.com/2011/03/28/theater/reviews/how-to-succeed-in-business-with-daniel-radcliffe-review.html?_r=0 (accessed July 7, 2013).

"Frank Loesser Biography," Frank Loesser website, http://www.frankloesser.com/life_biography (accessed June 7, 2013).

Gardner, Elysa, "Daniel Radcliffe Succeeds in 'Business,'" in *USA Today*, March 28, 2011, http://usatoday30.usatoday.com/life/theater/reviews/2011-03-28-succeed28_ST_N.htm (accessed July 7, 2013).

"Jack Weinstock," Redirectify.com, http://www.redirectify.com/people/jack-weinstock.html (accessed June 7, 2013).

Kenrick, John, "1950s I: When Broadway Ruled," Musicals101.com, http://www.musicals101.com/1950bway.htm (accessed July 10, 2013).

———, "1960s II: Long Running Hits," Musicals101.com, http://www.musicals101.com/1960bway2.htm (accessed July 10, 2013).

Knapp, Raymond, *The American Musical and the Formation of National Identity*, Princeton University Press, 2005, pp. 123, 154.

Loesser, Frank, *How to Succeed in Business without Really Trying*, Internet Archive, http://web.archive.org/web/20070807011417/http://libretto.musicals.ru/text.php?textid=165&language=1 (accessed July 6, 2013).

McNulty, Charles, "Theater Review: 'How to Succeed in Business without Really Trying' on Broadway," in *Los Angeles Times* online, March 27, 2011, http://latimesblogs.latimes.com/culturemonster/2011/03/theater-review-how-to-succeed-in-business-without-really-trying-on-broadway.html (accessed July 7, 2013).

Mead, Shepherd, *How to Succeed in Business without Really Trying*, Simon and Schuster, 2011.

Rousuck, J. Wynn, "Broderick Is Cute, Not Commanding, in Revived 'How to Succeed in Business,'" in *Baltimore Sun*, February 6, 1995, http://articles.baltimoresun.com/1995-02-06/features/1995037130_1_matthew-broderick-megan-mullally-finch (accessed September 17, 2013).

"Theater: How to Succeed in Business without Really Trying (1961)," Frank Loesser website, http://www.frankloesser.com/work_theater/6 (accessed July 10, 2013).

"When I Was a Lad Lyrics," AllTheLyrics.com, http://www.allthelyrics.com/lyrics/gilbert_and_sullivan/when_i_was_a_lad-lyrics-446448.html (accessed July 10, 2013).

"Willie Gilbert," Internet Movie Database, http://www.imdb.com/name/nm0318276/ (accessed June 7, 2013).

FURTHER READING

Jones, John Bush, *Our Musicals, Ourselves: A Social History of the American Musical Theater*, Brandeis University Press, 2004.
  Jones discusses musicals from the late nineteenth century to the early twenty-first century that deal with politics and culture.

Morden, Ethan, *Anything Goes: A History of American Musical Theatre*, Oxford University Press, 2013.
  Morden examines Broadway musicals from the 1920s to the 1970s.

Riis, Thomas L., *Frank Loesser*, Yale University Press, 2008.
  This is a well-researched critical biography of Loesser by a professor of music who specializes in musical theater. Riis thoroughly covers Loesser's life and career.

Scott, James, *Satire: From Horace to Yesterday's Comic Strips*, Prestwick House, 2005.
  This is an introduction to satire from the ancient world to the modern era. It covers poetry, journalism, and fiction as well as cartoons and television.

SUGGESTED SEARCH TERMS

How to Succeed in Business without Really Trying

Frank Loesser

Abe Burrows

Shepherd Mead

Broadway musical

musical theater

women's liberation movement

satire

Icebound

OWEN DAVIS
1923

Icebound is a play by twentieth-century American dramatist Owen Davis. It was awarded the Pulitzer Prize for the best American play of the 1922–1923 season. The play was produced at the Harris Theatre in New York City beginning on February 10, 1923, and ran until June 1, for a total of 145 performances. The play portrays a dour, unhappy middle-class family in rural Maine in the early 1920s. The family matriarch is dying, and the family has gathered at the homestead. Three siblings are expecting to receive a substantial inheritance, but the situation is complicated by the arrival of a younger brother, the black sheep of the family, and the presence of Jane, a distant relative. When the contents of the old woman's will are disclosed, everyone gets a shock. As the drama proceeds, jealousy and resentment fester, while in the end love blooms unexpectedly.

Icebound is an example of the realism that was popular in American theater in the first few decades of the twentieth century. Although there have been no recent revivals of the play, it remains interesting not only for its rather grim portrait of rural New England folk but for its quietly developed theme of change and redemption. The play was published in 1923 and has long been out of print, but it is available in many libraries.

Owen Davis *(© Conde Nast Archive | Corbis)*

AUTHOR BIOGRAPHY

Owen Gould Davis was born in Portland, Maine, on January 29, 1874, one of eight children of Owen Warren Davis, an iron manufacturer, and Abigail Augusta Gould Davis. Davis grew up in Bangor, Maine, until the family moved to southern Kentucky when he was in his early teens. He enrolled in the University of Tennessee in 1888 and studied there for one year before transferring to Harvard University. He studied geology but left Harvard without obtaining a degree. Returning to Kentucky, he worked as a mining engineer, but in 1895 he moved to New York City in order to pursue a career as a dramatist. He had long had an interest in drama and later claimed to have written his first play at the age of nine. He also wrote several plays while at Harvard.

In New York, Davis joined an acting company and appeared in several small roles before penning the first of his works that would be produced, a formulaic melodrama titled *Through the Breakers.* The play was performed at New York's Star Theatre in 1899 and was taken on tour for several years. Davis had found his niche as a playwright, and over the next decade he wrote over one hundred

melodramas. These were popular entertainments featuring characters who were either very good or very bad; the hero always triumphed over the villain, and the heroine was always (eventually) rescued from the series of dire situations in which she was placed.

In 1901, Davis married Elizabeth Drury Breyer, an actress. They had two sons, Donald and Owen Jr. During this decade, Davis decided to stop writing sensational melodramas and write for the Broadway stage. It took him a while to establish himself, but in 1913 his play *The Family Cupboard* had a Broadway run of 140 performances. Davis achieved lasting success when he turned to realism. His play *The Detour,* which was performed in 1921, impressed critics although it ran for only forty-eight performances. Davis followed this with *Icebound,* which ran for 145 performances at the Sam H. Harris Theatre in 1923. The play was published in the same year and won the Pulitzer Prize for Drama. Davis continued to write plays throughout the 1920s and 1930s.

In 1927, Davis began writing screenplays for Paramount Pictures. Among them were *They Had to See Paris* and *So This Is London,* both of which starred Will Rogers. Davis adapted his own play *Jezebel* (1933) for the screen, with Bette Davis playing the leading role in the 1938 film.

Over the course of his career, Davis wrote up to three hundred plays, although the exact number is not known. His last play was *No Way Out,* in 1944. In addition to writing plays, Davis wrote two autobiographies, *I'd Like to Do It Again* (1931) and *My First Fifty Years in the Theatre: The Plays, the Players, the Theatrical Managers and the Theatre Itself as One Man Saw Them in the Fifty Years between 1897 and 1947* (1950). Davis died in New York City on October 14, 1956.

PLOT SUMMARY

Act 1

Icebound begins in late October 1922 in the parlor of the Jordan homestead in Veazie, Maine. A group of relatives has gathered to await the imminent death of old Mrs. Jordan, the family matriarch, who is lying in an upstairs bedroom. Mrs. Jordan is the mother of Henry Jordan and his younger sisters, Ella and Sadie. The family members have little affection for one another,

MEDIA ADAPTATIONS

Icebound was made into a silent movie in 1924, directed by William C. DeMille, the older brother of the famous film director and producer Cecil B. DeMille.

and old Mrs. Jordan has no respect for them either. The old woman is being attended by Doctor Curtis and Jane Crosby, a distant relative whom she befriended some years earlier. The rest of the family does not like Jane and plans to ask her to leave when the old woman dies and leaves them her property in her will. Ella hopes that the will will divide the property equally among the three of them. Henry is hoping for more than a third, to help him with his struggling business. They are all certain that their mother will leave nothing to the fourth child, Ben. Ben is the black sheep of the family. He drinks too much and has been indicted for a criminal offense. He would be in prison had he not run away, Henry says.

Judge Bradford, who is Mrs. Jordan's lawyer, enters. Henry quizzes him about the contents of his mother's will, but Bradford will reveal nothing. Then Ben arrives unexpectedly from Bangor. Jane told him to come, he says, and gave him money so he could make the trip. It is clear that Ben is not welcome. Henry says he will be arrested when news gets out that he has come, adding that he will not bail him out. Jane invited him because she thought his mother would want to see him, even though the old woman said she did not. Jane thought otherwise because she believes Ben is the only child old Mrs. Jordan actually wanted to have.

Ben wants to go upstairs to see his mother, but Henry will not let him. Jane goes instead. Soon she returns with the news that Mrs. Jordan has died. The doctor leaves. Egged on by his sisters, Henry tells Jane that there is no longer any point in her staying with them. Jane says she hates them all and will be glad to get away. Then

the judge tells them that Jane has inherited Mrs. Jordan's entire estate. Everyone is stunned at the news. The judge explains that Mrs. Jordan thought that Jane would handle the money better than anyone else. He adds that the three siblings will inherit a very small sum—one hundred dollars each. They all complain loudly and leave the room, leaving Ben, Jane, and the judge alone.

Judge Bradford tells Ben he cannot stay; he is wanted for arson. Ben does not seem to care and goes upstairs to view his mother's body. The judge tells Jane, who does not know why she inherited the estate, that he has a sealed letter for her in his strongbox that will explain why the old woman acted as she did.

Jim Jay, the sheriff, arrives and is ready to arrest Ben. But Jane intervenes, saying she will post bail for him on the condition that Ben, who has been speaking to her in a hostile manner, agree to do exactly what she says. The only reason Ben returned home was the hope that he would inherit some money, but now he accepts Jane's offer as a way of staying out of prison, at least until his trial comes up the following spring. Jane tells Ben that he must stay at the house and work the family farm. Ben reluctantly agrees.

Act 2

Two months have passed. In the Jordan sitting room, Ella and Sadie, who is visiting, make remarks that show their resentment of Jane. Orin and Nettie are also present. Ella, who is sitting at a sewing machine making towels, complains that Jane makes them work too hard. Even Ben is working hard.

Sadie plans to ask Jane for money. Henry has already borrowed money from Jane, but his business is still doing poorly. Ella says Jane will not lend any more money; she herself has already been refused. Nettie remarks that Ben is good-looking, but Sadie, her step-aunt, warns her to stay away from him. She explains why Ben is facing trial: he got drunk and was beaten up by two men in a fight, after which he went at night to the men's barn and burned it down. Ella agrees that Ben is bad.

Ben enters with some firewood. It is clear that he does not like the hard work he is having to do on the farm. Nettie talks sympathetically to him by the fire. He says it will almost be a relief for him to go to prison.

Henry and Emma enter. They tell Nettie not to talk to Ben. Emma makes her resentment of Jane clear, and Sadie says she needs money to pay the rent. Nettie says she must have a new dress. Ella wants money so she can set up a dressmaking business with a friend. Henry still needs money. They think that Jane ought to help them financially.

Ben says they should earn some money themselves. They all react badly to that and insult Ben, telling him that in the village, everyone laughs at him for being Jane's slave.

Jane enters and says that one of the horses is sick. Ben goes off to tend to the horse, while Jane insists to her relatives that she will not lend them any more money.

When Jane is alone with Hannah, she says it is her birthday and asks Hannah to prepare a special meal, just for herself, Ben, and Ella.

Ben reports that the horse is better. It turns out that Ben likes animals. Jane also gets him to talk about the pleasant time he had in France. After he was wounded in battle, he was billeted with a French family for nearly a month, and he remembers that time fondly. He remembers the oldest daughter, who wore a blue dress. After Ben exits, Jane takes a blue dress out of a cardboard box, holds it up over the dress she is wearing, and smiles as she looks at her reflection in the mirror. The dress is her birthday present to herself.

The judge enters. Jane asks him to have the charges against Ben dropped. She suggests offering to pay the man whose barn was burned down. The judge is reluctant at first but then suggests that it might be possible to bring charges against the two men who beat Ben up. Then the men's father could be approached and informed that he would receive payment for the barn and asking him, in return for the withdrawal of charges against his sons, to withdraw the charges against Ben.

The judge then blurts out that he loves Jane and says he wants to marry her. Jane is not interested, but she does read to the judge the letter old Mrs. Jordan wrote to her a short while before she died. In the letter, Mrs. Jordan explains that the only person she cares about is Ben. But she cannot leave him any money because she knows he will squander it. Instead, she is leaving the money to Jane because she knows Jane loves Ben and

thinks that when Ben knows she has the money, he will want to marry her.

Hearing this, the judge is angry and disappointed, but he agrees that he will still help Ben. They exit together, as Jane wants to buy a ribbon at the store.

Nettie and Ella enter. Nettie saw the judge and Jane together and thinks they are romantically involved. Ella spots the box with the dress in it and opens it out of curiosity. Both she and Nettie are envious. There is a ring at the front door. Ella puts the dress back in the box, and Nettie exits, taking the box with her.

Orin enters with a note from his mother, Sadie, for Jane. After Jane reads the note, she immediately writes a check to Sadie and gives it to Orin to take to her. Then Jane writes a check for two hundred dollars to Ella so she can start her dressmaking business. She explains to the astonished Ella that it is her birthday.

After Ella exits, Jane and Ben talk. It transpires that Ben partly knows why his mother left the money to Jane: he has guessed that his mother considered him irresponsible. But he resents the way Jane has controlled his life. Jane encourages Ben to take more responsibility in making the farm successful. Then she tells him she has a surprise for him and goes to the dining room.

While she is out of the room, Nettie enters, wearing Jane's new blue dress. She has been waiting in the hall. She looks pretty, and it is the first time Ben has really noticed her. He takes her in his arms and kisses her ardently. At that moment Jane enters. Behind her, the birthday meal has been spread out. Ben speaks to her angrily, saying he is not interested in farmwork. He has found what he wants. Nettie apologizes for wearing Jane's dress and says she will take it off. Jane says there is no need; she does not want it anymore. She calls out to Ella that supper is ready.

Act 3

Two months have passed. The family is again assembled in the parlor of the Jordan homestead. Jane has asked them all to come. Sadie lets out the secret that Nettie and Ben have been seeing each other. Henry and Emma are angered by this news, but Ben says it is over between them. Nettie did not want to be known as the girlfriend of a man who would soon be in prison.

Judge Bradford enters, followed by Jane, who says she has summoned them to inform them that their mother did not want her to have all the Jordan money. The judge explains that at Jane's request he has drawn up a deed of gift that transfers the property to Ben. Jane confirms that old Mrs. Jordan actually wanted Ben to receive the money eventually. She also says that Ben will not be going to prison; Judge Bradford's plan has succeeded, and charges against Ben have been withdrawn.

Henry makes it clear that he expects Ben to lend him some money, but Ben is unwilling. He reminds Henry how uncharitable he has been to him in the past. Ben also says that he is turning everyone out of what is now his house. Just before Henry and Emma leave, Ben relents a little and says he will endorse a note for Henry that will enable him to have access to some funds at the bank.

Jane indicates that she is renting a place elsewhere and will leave, but this disappoints Ben. He is planning on ordering new farm machinery and wants her to stay. Ben says he is grateful to the judge for what he has done to keep him out of prison, but the judge replies that it is Jane to whom he should be grateful. It is she who has done everything for him.

After the judge exits, Jane comes downstairs dressed to depart. Ben wants to know why she has done so much for him. Jane says it was because she loved his mother, and his mother asked her to promise to help him if ever she could. Ben asks if she will stay. He needs her. Jane shows him his mother's letter to her; he reads that he is the only person she cares about even though he has not been kind to her. Ben is moved by this and breaks down in sobs. He says he did love his mother, more than he was ever able to tell her. He also says he loves Jane, but he does not trust himself to behave well. Jane says she will stay if he wants her and really does love her. Hannah enters to remind Jane not to miss her train, but Jane says she is never leaving, and Ben says they will marry.

CHARACTERS

Judge John Bradford

Judge John Bradford is about thirty-five years old. He is a local judge with a reputation for being the best lawyer in town. It is he who draws up old Mrs. Jordan's will. Also, at Jane's request, he helps to arrange for the charges against Ben to be dropped. The judge develops an affection for

Jane and wants to marry her, but Jane does not return his affection.

Jane Crosby

Jane Crosby is a distant relative of the Jordan family, a stepcousin once removed. She is twenty-four years old and quiet. She is not very articulate and appears cold in her manner. Jane sits with old Mrs. Jordan during her final illness. Mrs. Jordan liked Jane more than she did her immediate family, and Jane has been living at the Jordan home for eight years. The other family members do not like her and plan to tell her to leave when they inherit the property. But it is Jane who inherits everything. She continues to live at the house with Ella, and also with Ben, whom she puts to work on the farm.

Jane refuses requests by the Jordans for loans, and they continue to resent her. Her aim is to reform Ben by making him work hard, which she hopes will turn him into a responsible individual. She does everything she can to help him even though he does not appreciate it. Eventually, Jane turns over ownership of the property to Ben because she knows that this is what old Mrs. Jordan had in mind. Jane is also in love with Ben, although she does not tell him so. She is determined to leave the home, but Ben, finally realizing her value, persuades her to stay, and they agree to marry.

Doctor Curtis

Doctor Curtis is an elderly country doctor who attends old Mrs. Jordan in her final illness.

Orin Fellows

Orin is Sadie Fellows's son. He is ten years old and wears large spectacles.

Sadie Fellows

Sadie Fellows, sister of Henry, Ella, and Ben Jordan, is a forty-year-old widow, tall and thin. She is known as a gossip and keeps close watch on all the activities of people in the village. Her husband did not leave her much money, so she is not in comfortable circumstances. She complains about always having to work and save and, like the other Jordans, expects her mother to leave her a considerable amount of money. When she and her siblings receive only a pittance, she says they should contest the will, but nothing comes of it. Sadie tries to borrow money from Jane in order to pay the rent, but Jane is unwilling to help her. Sadie also seems to dislike

Nettie and often makes remarks implying that Nettie has loose morals.

Hannah

Hannah is a middle-aged servant in the Jordan home. She looks after old Mrs. Jordan until her death, and she prepares the special meal for Jane's birthday.

Jim Jay

Jim Jay is the sheriff who comes to arrest Ben. He is described as a kindly middle-aged man.

Ben Jordan

Ben Jordan is the youngest of the four children of old Mrs. Jordan. Much younger than the others, he has not done well in life. He is described as "wild, selfish, arrogant…handsome but sulky and defiant." The best period in his life was when he served two years in the army during World War I. He recalls with pleasure how, after being wounded, he was billeted with a French family near Nancy.

When he returned from France, he tried to straighten out his life, but it did not work. He got drunk and got in a fight with two men and later burned down the barn of the men he had quarreled with. For this reason he has been criminally indicted and is facing a prison sentence. Jane gives Ben a chance to turn his life around by getting him to work on the farm. She also successfully works with Judge Bradford to have the criminal charges against Ben withdrawn. Ben, however, does not at first like working on the farm and resents the control Jane has over him. He eventually learns from a letter that his mother wrote to Jane that he was the child his mother loved best. This softens his heart. He claims that he loved his mother and that he also loves Jane. This provides the emotional breakthrough Jane had been hoping for but had given up on, and the couple finally get together and agree to marry.

Ella Jordan

Ella Jordan is the sister of Henry, Sadie, and Ben. She is thirty-six years old, unmarried, and dissatisfied with her life. She feels bitter toward Jane, believing that Jane supplanted her in her mother's affections. Ella has plans to set up a dressmaking business with a friend, and she asks Jane to lend her two hundred dollars to get started. Jane refuses, and Ella gives up hope of ever getting anything she wants in life. On Jane's birthday, however, Jane relents and gives Ella the money.

Emma Jordan

Emma Jordan is Henry Jordan's wife. She is ten years younger than he is and carries "a look of chronic displeasure." Henry is her second husband. She married him a year after her first husband died. She has a daughter, Nettie, from her first marriage. Like the other family members she dislikes Jane, but she has no love for Ella or Sadie, her sisters-in-law, either. In addition, she hates Ben and wants him to stay away from Nettie.

Henry Jordan

Henry Jordan is married to Emma. He is the eldest son of Mrs. Jordan; his siblings are Ella, Sadie, and Ben. Henry is described as "a heavy set man of fifty, worn by his business cares into a dull sort of hopeless resignation." Henry owns a grocery store that is not doing well. He hopes to save the business by inheriting at least one-third of his mother's estate. His hopes are dashed, however, and Jane, the new property owner, will not even endorse a note for him that would enable him to get funds from the bank. Henry hates Ben, believing that his younger brother has disgraced the family name, and refuses to help him. When the property passes to Ben, Henry thinks it is the final straw; he can barely believe the turn events have taken and is ready to give up. He hopes that Ben will help him, but Ben despises Henry because his brother offered him no help at all when he needed it. However, Ben does agree to endorse the note for Henry that Jane had refused, although he says it is only because it would not help his own cause if his brother had to go the poorhouse.

Mrs. Jordan

Mrs. Jordan does not actually appear in the play. She dies early in the first act. She was the mother of Henry, Ella, Sadie, and Ben, and her will, in which she leaves all her property to Jane, a distant relative, creates ill feeling and misunderstanding among her children. Mrs. Jordan was a lonely old woman who did not know how to show affection to her children.

Nettie

Nettie is Emma Jordan's daughter by a previous marriage. She is described as "a vain and shallow little rustic beauty." She also develops a reputation, according to Sadie, as a flirt, so it is little surprise when she takes up for a while with Ben. But their relationship soon ends because Nettie thinks that Ben will be going to prison and that she will become a laughingstock in the village by being associated with him.

THEMES

Family Relationships

All the major characters in the play, with the exception of Judge Bradford, are members of the same family. This includes even Jane, the distant cousin. But this is not a happy family. Indeed, the Jordan family is united only by their general unhappiness and their acute dislike for one another. (The one exception is Jane's fondness for Ben, which she keeps well disguised until nearly the end.) It appears to have been this way for a very long time, although the playwright chose not to give any details about how everything went wrong. Mrs. Jordan, the dying mother of the four siblings, has, it seems, been widowed for many years. She says in her letter to Jane that the three older children had "forgotten how to love" her for years before her youngest child, Ben, was born. Why that should have been the case is unstated, but the old woman died alone and unloved, despite the pious sentiments of grief uttered by the three eldest siblings in act 1.

Emma Jordan, who married into the family, has a low opinion of her in-laws, and not one of the three older siblings has much to be happy about: Henry's grocery store is failing; Sadie is a gossip with a harsh tongue who is widowed and poor; and Ella has failed to find a husband or anything else that she has wanted in life. The fact that their mother leaves her money to Jane, whom they also dislike, merely exacerbates their difficulties in life and their frostiness with each other. Not for nothing is the play called *Icebound*; these people are locked into their negative emotions about each other and about life in general. They cannot break out of this long-entrenched pattern. There is no warmth at all in their lives. After their mother wills her entire estate to Jane, the distant cousin takes the brunt of their negativity. They cannot understand how their mother could have preferred this young woman over her own flesh and blood. Blaming Jane for their situation in life soon becomes a habit. They reserve their

TOPICS FOR FURTHER STUDY

- Write a letter to a local theater company, amateur or professional, encouraging it to put on a production of *Icebound*. Tell what the play is about and why you think it would be successful. What sort of audiences would enjoy it, and what resources would the company need to stage it?

- With a group of classmates, present a dramatic reading of act 3 of *Icebound*. You need no costumes or props and do not have to memorize the text or make any movements. Just speak the character's words, interpreting how each character would speak in the situation he or she is in. Allocate a part to each person, and perform the act with the rest of the class as your audience. Performing plays in this manner is called readers' theater.

- Go to Glogster.com and create a "glog" (*glog* is short for "graphic log" and is a kind of poster) that could be used to advertise a new production of *Icebound*. Through your blog, share your glog with your classmates.

- Read *I Don't Want to Talk about It*, by Bradley Hayward, which is a series of monologues for teens, including teens who have issues in dealing with parents. The play is available from Playscripts, at http://www.playscripts.com. Additionally, you can go to AceYourAudition.com at http://www.ace-your-audition.com/free-monologues.html and select a free monologue to consult. Then write and perform for your classmates a monologue for either Nettie or Orin, the two young people in *Icebound*.

special venom, however, for Ben, who is an outsider in his own family, and Ben returns their hatred in full measure. Ben had fallen out with his siblings long before the death of their mother, and he appears to have made a

Icebound is set in a small town outside of Bangor, Maine. (© Don Landwehrle / Shutterstock.com)

spectacular mess of his life—one more member of the Jordan family who cannot seem to find happiness, love, or security. In short, then, the family relationships depicted in the play are a toxic brew of anger, jealousy, resentment, envy, and spite, often hiding behind a thin veneer of dour resignation. Like the bleak countryside and the gray days of fall and winter in which the play is set, this family cannot seem to find the ray of light that would ease their shared pain.

Redemption

The four months that the play covers are depressing times for the Jordan family, and it seems as if nothing good can come out of their situation. Even Jane, who is not quite so closely involved in the negative dynamic that is part of the Jordans' world, is a taciturn, humorless young woman who has no joy in her life. Her attempts to straighten out the wayward Ben seem at first to be fruitless and barely worth the effort.

And yet the dramatist has in mind a carefully worked-out scheme of redemption. There is a seed of love in this family, and it does flower in the end. It was planted by old Mrs. Jordan, who,

even if she did not love her other offspring, genuinely loved Ben. For reasons unknown, it appears that Ben was not able to respond to her, which meant that her love had to go into hiding. As she nears death, she knows that she cannot simply leave her estate to Ben, because she is under no illusions about Ben's nature. "Ben's a bad son, and a bad man," she writes in her letter to Jane, and she knows he would squander the money. But she still has a plan to save him. She guesses that Jane loves him and decides that she will leave the money to a woman "who'd work, and pray, and live for him, until as age comes on, and maybe he gets a little tired, he'll turn to her." It might seem a far-fetched scheme, and from what the reader or audience member has seen of Ben in the first two acts, it does not seem likely to bear much fruit. Ben is stubborn and resentful of Jane and unwilling to change. Just as old Mrs. Jordan knew he would, and wrote in the letter, Ben "trample[s]" on the woman who "hold[s] out her heart to him." But in the final act of the play, old Mrs. Jordan's wisdom becomes plain, and the outcome she sought comes true much sooner than she expected. Ben is in effect redeemed by the love of Jane, and he finally learns to value her and accept her. While the rest of the family seem unlikely ever to gain much happiness, Ben, the black sheep, appears to have found his way to something better.

STYLE

Realism

Realism is a literary movement that began in the nineteenth century and became a characteristic of American drama in the first two decades of the twentieth century. A realistic play is an attempt to present life truthfully, as it really is. Realistic plays from this period often dealt with serious issues, quite unlike the popular melodramas that had held the stage in earlier years. These were marked by exaggerated stock characters and formulaic plots that relied on action rather than motivation and always showed a superficial struggle between good and evil. Davis himself had much commercial success with melodrama before he turned to the greater artistic demands of realism.

Realism often involves greater naturalness in dialogue, with characters talking the way people talk in real life rather than in the more literary language that had been fashionable in an earlier period of American drama. In *Icebound*, for example, the characters frequently speak ungrammatical English (sometimes referred to as nonstandard English) that was typical of the way people in small-town Maine at that time spoke. Davis knew this kind of speech well because he was a native of Maine. In the play, Henry says this, for example, to Jane: "We was thinkin' now that mother's dead, that there wasn't much use in your stayin' on here." He uses "was" instead of the grammatically correct form of the verb *to be* ("were"), and drops the *g* at the end of the present participles *thinking* and *staying*. Other characters speak in similar fashion.

Dour New England Setting

The *setting* of a play is the place and time in which the drama takes place. The setting forms the background to the action and may also create an atmosphere or mood for the entire play. The lifeless, frozen setting in *Icebound* is a reflection of the inner lives of the characters, who are unable to show any warmth to one another. The stage directions at the beginning of the play describe a bleak late-October day in New England, which can be seen through two windows at the back of the stage: "the grass brown and lifeless, and the bare limbs of the trees silhouetted against a gray sky." Inside, the room is "dull and . . . drab" with "no sign of either comfort or beauty," which suggests that the characters' lives are as bleak as the countryside. This continues in the stage directions for act 2, in which a window looks out "on to the farm yard, now deep in midwinter snow." Another window overlooks "a snowbound countryside." In act 3, which takes place in late winter or early spring, the window reveals "partly melted snow drifts," suggesting the partial thawing of the central characters' emotions that takes place in this final act.

HISTORICAL CONTEXT

American Drama in the 1920s

It was not until the 1920s that American drama began to establish itself as a serious, independent art form. Before that time, the plays performed in the theatrical district known as Broadway, in New York City, where the industry was concentrated, were based on English models. This was true of tragedy, melodrama, and comedy, including farce. It was in this environment that Davis first made a name for himself, writing the kind of popular sensational melodrama that did not require original thought or creativity and was not intended to be a vehicle for serious ideas and themes. According to the introduction to the section "American Literature between the Wars, 1914–1945" in the *Norton Anthology of American Literature*, at the turn of the century, "Broadway managers emphasized spectacle, machinery, and conventionalized, bombastic, star-oriented acting."

One important engine of change in American drama was the formation of two theatrical production companies in the 1910s. One of these was the Provincetown Players of Provincetown, Massachusetts, in 1915. The company set itself the task of producing serious plays on which Broadway theaters would not take a chance. The following year, the company rented premises in New York's Greenwich Village and produced plays well into the 1920s. These were almost entirely American plays, including the earliest works of Eugene O'Neill (1888–1953), such as the one-act

COMPARE & CONTRAST

- **1920s:** Veazie, a small town in Penobscot County, Maine, was prosperous in the nineteenth century because of its sawmills, but in the early twentieth century the mills close and the workers move to other towns in Maine. The population of Veazie declines steadily. In 1920, the population reaches its lowest point, numbering only 504 people.

  Today: According to the 2010 census, the population of Veazie is 1,917, an increase of about 10 percent from the previous decade.

- **1920s:** American drama flourishes as never before. The number of productions on Broadway reaches record levels. In the 1927–1928 season, there are 264 new productions on Broadway, more than three times the number in the 1899–1900 season.

  Today: Broadway continues to flourish as a venue for plays and musicals, although more musicals than plays are produced. Leading American dramatists include Tony

Kushner, author of *The Intelligent Homosexual's Guide to Capitalism and Socialism with a Key to the Scriptures* (2009); David Mamet, author of *November* (2007) and *Race* (2009); and John Patrick Shanley, author of *Doubt: A Parable* (2004) and *Sailor's Song* (2004).

- **1920s:** After the carnage of World War I and the disillusionment that followed it, a number of plays in this decade depict the miserable lives of ex-soldiers who survived the war. These characters include Ben Jordan in *Icebound* and Oswald Lane in Gilbert Emery's play *The Hero* (1921).

  Today: Dramatists continue to write plays about war or the aftermath of war. *Black Watch* (2006), by Gregory Burke, is about British soldiers in the Iraq War, which began in 2003. *The Whipping Man* (2009), by Matthew Lopez, is set in the aftermath of the American Civil War.

---

play *Ile* (1917), a character study of the captain of a whaler. The Provincetown Players also produced some of the plays of Susan Glaspell (1876–1948), including her one-act play *Trifles* (1916), which is still highly regarded a century after it was first performed. By 1925, the Provincetown Players had produced ninety-three new plays by forty-seven playwrights and had helped launch American drama into the new, modernist era. The company was disbanded in 1929.

The second vanguard theatrical company was the Washington Square Players, who also produced plays in Greenwich Village beginning in 1915. Unlike the Provincetown Players, this company was a vehicle not only for new American plays, such as O'Neill's one-act play *In the Zone* (1917), but also for foreign plays in translation, such as works by Irish playwright George Bernard Shaw

(1856–1950), Russia's Anton Chekhov (1860–1904), and the Norwegian Henrik Ibsen (1828–1906). Introducing these playwrights to American audiences helped to create a literary climate in which plays with a more serious purpose than providing superficial formulaic entertainment became an accepted part of the scene.

According to literary historian Arthur Hobson Quinn in *A History of the American Drama from the Civil War to the Present Day*, "The most significant tendency in the American drama since 1920 has been the attempt to deal sincerely with character." By this Quinn means that dramatists began to create in-depth portrayals of their characters and were no longer content with presenting character types that lacked individuality. This greater attention to character was part of the trend toward realism

The Jordan siblings gather to say goodbye to their mother on her deathbed and then hear a reading of her will. *(© SteveWoods / Shutterstock.com)*

in drama. Davis credited his study of Ibsen, a pioneer in realism on the stage, with his new interest in writing serious drama. Davis was also inspired by the work of O'Neill, who in the early 1920s was establishing himself as the leading American playwright of the period. Indeed, it was O'Neill's play *Beyond the Horizon,* which won the Pulitzer Prize in 1920, that prompted Davis to write his first serious realist play, *The Detour* (1921).

CRITICAL OVERVIEW

During its run of performances in 1923, *Icebound* was a success with audiences and critics. According to James Fisher and Felicia Hardison Londré in *The A to Z of Modern Theater: Modernism,* "Critics applauded Davis's skill at imbuing *Icebound* with a richly textured atmosphere and depth of character." The *Facts on File Companion to American Drama,* edited by Jackson R. Bryer and Mary C. Hartig, notes that when Davis was awarded the Pulitzer Prize for

the play, "his transition from sensational, moneymaking lowbrow melodramas to playwright for the legitimate stage was complete." The reference book also notes that "some critics at the time objected that there were better plays that season, one that included the now classic, *The Adding Machine,* by Elmer Rice." Burns Mantle, in his introduction to *The Best Plays of 1922–23,* also notes that the success of *Icebound* marked a major transition in Davis's career, describing the play as "a study of the coldly calculating home folk of his native Maine, who are 'icebound within and without' the better part of their lives." Mantle further observes of *Icebound* that "though it plays better than it reads, it is a fine and honest native drama." Later in this volume Mantle writes of *Icebound,* "It was not one of the big popular successes, but it was promptly accepted as a human and worthy drama that enriched the repertoire of the native theatre." *Icebound* was revived several times during the 1930s and 1940s, but unlike some other plays of the 1920s, such as Sidney Howard's *They Knew What They Wanted* (which won the Pulitzer Prize in 1925), it has had no recent revivals.

CRITICISM

Bryan Aubrey

Aubrey holds a PhD in English. In the following essay, he discusses Icebound *in the context of realism in American drama in the 1920s and the theme of redemption.*

The 1920s were an extraordinarily productive period for American drama, and by the middle of the decade, realism was firmly established as the preferred mode of contemporary playwrights. Many dramatists were interested in presenting more realistic settings for their plays than had been the practice in the nineteenth century and the early years of the twentieth century. Owen Davis's *Icebound*, set in snowbound Maine, provides an instructive example. As Brenda Murphy notes in *American Realism and American Drama, 1880–1940*, "Owen Davis had a special gift for showing the relation between character and milieu." Commenting on Davis's plays *The Detour* (1921) and *Icebound*, Murphy writes, "The characters and their conflicts are inseparable from the milieux that produce them." She notes in connection with the play's central metaphor that "the characters have grown 'icebound' in response to the natural setting, and they have in turn created the interior setting that reflects it." Murphy highlights Ben's speech in act 2, in which he tells Jane of his view of the Jordan family, carrying the theme of the play and also making the underlying metaphor explicit:

> Just a few folks together, day after day, and every little thing you don't like about the other raspin' on your nerves 'til it almost drives you crazy! Most folks quiet, because they've said all the things they've got to say a hundred times. Other folks, talkin', talkin', talkin' about nothing. Sometimes somebody sort of laughs and it scares you; seems like laughter needs the sun, same as flowers do. Icebound, that's what we are all of us inside and out.

No one who has read the play would dispute that in the last sentence in particular, Ben has well described the family from which he has tried hard to escape but that has made its mark on him. Ben is likely the only member of the family who is able to articulate this dismal view of his own kin. As the youngest by far of the four siblings, he chose to make himself an outsider; he is a man who has escaped the claustrophobia of the family home, although he has not found any success in life. Indeed, since Ben is facing a criminal indictment, and Henry accuses him in his absence of bringing

THE PICTURE THAT EMERGES OF THE JOR-
DANS IN THE FIRST ACT OF THE PLAY IS THAT OF A
DISAPPOINTED, BITTERLY DIVIDED FAMILY. THEY ARE
WORN DOWN BY LIFE, WHICH HAS NOT PRODUCED ANY
HAPPINESS FOR THEM."

disgrace to the Jordans, he is in the eyes of society less acceptable than the other family members, who are no doubt regarded in their village as dour but respectable folk.

Davis seems to have prided himself on the skill with which he created the Jordan family. A joyless example of small-mindedness and selfishness they may be, but Davis believed he had rendered them accurately from life. He wrote in his foreword to the play that the characters in it were "my own people, the people of northern New England," adding, "I have at least tried to draw a true picture of these people, and I am of their blood, born of generations of Northern Maine, small-town folk, and brought up among them." Their faults and virtues, Davis writes, "are the direct result of their own heritage and environment." That last comment shows that Davis regarded his characters with some sympathy. They may not be admirable, but they have been made the way they are by the somewhat repressive, Puritan-influenced culture in which they grew up. Davis was thus able to write a play in which he was prepared to grant these stunted characters, at the last, a measure of redemption. But that redemption will not come easily, and it will not touch all of them.

The picture that emerges of the Jordans in the first act of the play is that of a disappointed, bitterly divided family. They are worn down by life, which has not produced any happiness for them. It seems that they have not had much luck, although why they are so estranged from their mother, and from one another, is never explained in any detail. Perhaps it is simply a matter of a family in which there is a long tradition of not expressing their deep feelings, a situation in which the seeds of misunderstanding and emotional distance would easily be sown. Henry's comment "This family don't ever agree

WHAT DO I READ NEXT?

- *Beyond the Horizon*, by Eugene O'Neill, was the dramatist's first full-length play, winning the Pulitzer Prize in 1920. Set in eastern Massachusetts in 1907, the play is a domestic drama about two brothers who fall in love with the same woman, a farm girl who lives next door. It is still in print.

- *Fierce and True: Plays for Teen Audiences* (2010), edited by Peter Brosius and Elissa Adams, contains four plays that have been staged by the Children's Theatre Company of Minneapolis. These plays are aimed at audiences age twelve to eighteen. They are *Anon(ymous)*, by Naomi Iizuka; *The Lost Boys of Sudan*, by Lonnie Carter; *Five Fingers of Funk*, by Will Power; and *Prom*, by Whit MacLaughlin and New Paradise Laboratories.

- *Lost Plays of the Harlem Renaissance, 1920–1940* (1996), edited by James Vernon Hatch and Leo Hamalian, contains sixteen plays written during the Harlem Renaissance. Playwrights represented include Langston Hughes, George S. Schuyler, Francis Hall Johnson, and Shirley Graham. Hatch's introduction puts the plays in historical context.

- *Trifles* (1916), by Susan Glaspell, is a one-act play by one of the leading American playwrights of the early twentieth century. Glaspell, who cofounded the Provincetown Players, is recognized today as the first important American female dramatist. In *Trifles*, the wife of a murdered farmer is arrested on suspicion of having committed the crime. An edition of the play was published in 2010.

- *The Adding Machine*, a play by Elmer Rice, was first performed in 1923, the same year as *Icebound*. The protagonist is Mr. Zero, who works for a company as an accountant for twenty-five years but then falls victim to new technology in the form of an adding machine. Angered, he kills his boss and is tried for murder. Unlike *Icebound*, which belongs to the category of realism, this is an expressionistic, nonrealistic play. The play still arouses interest today and is available in a modern edition published in 2011.

- The humdrum lives of the characters in *Icebound* do not give any sign that things have changed much in their rural Maine location for many years, or that there will be any big changes in the future. However, in the United States as a whole, the decade of the 1920s was a time of great change. *America in the 1920s* (2010), by Edmund Lindop, which is aimed at a young-adult readership, explores all aspects of the 1920s, including politics, technology, economy, social changes, literature, drama, art, music, sports, and games.

on nothin' but just to differ" seems like an apt statement of how they interact with each other, and their resigned acceptance of it.

The leading traits of each character are created by the dramatist with a few deft touches at the beginning of the play. Henry cannot stop himself from worrying about his struggling grocery business. To come to his dying mother's home he has had to leave the store in the hands of a couple of young assistants, and he is not sure he can trust them to cope. Both his sisters quickly find a way of reproaching him for his concern, which they see as inappropriate under the circumstances. The situation turns almost grimly comic when Henry makes an inquiry of the doctor—which he is too embarrassed to actually complete—about whether he has time, at four o'clock in the afternoon, to go to the store and still get back before his mother dies. Henry is actually a religious man who makes a number of references to God, although it is a stern, cheerless God he has in mind. Henry is concerned with observing the proprieties. He does not want to do anything wrong, but one has the impression that he is not so much worried about behaving badly as he is about appearing to do so.

The others, too, are a sad bunch. Ella is the disappointed spinster who at the age of thirty-six is bitter about what she sees as her wasted life. "I've never had a chance," she moans early in the play; "I've been stuck here till I'm most forty, worse than if I was dead, fifty times worse!" She and Sadie, an impoverished widow whose main interest in life is neighborhood gossip, launch barbed remarks at each other right from the beginning. Jane, while not immediate family, has some of the characteristic Jordan qualities, being joyless and possessing a cold manner. "I hate you, the whole raft of you," she says venomously when Henry informs her that after the funeral the family will expect her to leave the house where she has spent eight years caring for Mrs. Jordan. When Ben arrives unexpectedly, he is roundly attacked by all of them. Angry and belligerent, estranged from his siblings, and facing the prospect of a prison sentence, Ben seems to have no more chance of finding happiness than do any of the others. Finally, there is Emma, Henry's wife, who is under no illusions about the kind of family she has married into and joins in the backbiting as if she were born to it.

These are the unpromising ingredients out of which, the dramatist has decided, some kind of healing and love must ultimately emerge. To accomplish this end, he tracks the hidden path by which a mother's love eventually reaches her estranged, delinquent son. The device by which he accomplishes this is the letter that the dying Mrs. Jordan leaves for the eyes of Jane only. Jane is told about the letter in the first act, but it is not until near the end of act 2 that the contents—Mrs. Jordan's hope that she can save Ben by leaving Jane her money—are disclosed to the audience.

This marks the turn in the play from a prevailing life-negating tone to one that affirms life and, to an extent, even holds out the possibility for joy. In fact, this turn has already started a few minutes before that, when Jane unpacks her light-blue lace dress and holds it up to herself in the mirror. It is a sudden and unexpected flash of color and adornment, of pride in personal appearance, which reveals all of Jane's pent-up longings and dreams. It also shows that Jane is ready to make a leap beyond the drab Puritanism that has up to now dominated her environment. The Puritanism of this New England setting is clear from the stage directions at the beginning of acts 1 and 2, describing the Jordans' parlor and sitting room. The parlor, for example, shows "no sign of either comfort or beauty, both of which are looked upon with suspicion as being signposts on the road to perdition." And the "stern faith of the Puritan" is responsible for the plainness and lack of imagination in the sitting-room furnishings.

At the end of act 2, the dramatist creates a coup de théâtre when it is Nettie, not Jane, who suddenly appears to Ben in the beautiful blue dress—Nettie has temporarily filched it—but this only delays the destined conclusion. Jane overcomes her disappointment at the spoiling of the birthday party she planned, and two months later, in the events shown in act 3, she makes over the property to Ben, and Ben finally realizes that he needs her. Shortly before this, Jane has revealed that she loved Mrs. Jordan, and her devotion to fulfilling the old woman's wishes has finally paid off: the seeds of love that were planted in this forbidding snowbound landscape—both interior and exterior—shoot up above ground just as spring approaches. That this happens is largely due to Jane's doggedness; she is the long-suffering conduit for the long-suppressed love of Mrs. Jordan to finally reach her youngest child. It is hardly due to Ben, who lacks belief in his power to overcome his past: "Can a feller change—Just 'cause he wants to?" he asks, but all Jane asks of anyone is that they should try. This is her recipe for life. She has said as much to Ben before, in act 2:

> Icebound, you said. Maybe it don't have to be like that. Sometimes, just lately, it's seemed to me that if folks would try, things needn't be so bad. All of 'em try, I mean, for themselves, and for everybody else.

This plain wisdom is neither dramatic and visionary, nor emotional and romantic, and in that respect it fits the character of the culture and region where Jane has lived all her life. Anything other than that, as the dramatist well knew, would have been out of keeping with the tenor of the play. And it pays off for Jane and, through her, for Ben, allowing this rather grim play to end on a note of optimism and even love.

Jane's property inheritance from Mrs. Jordan creates misunderstanding and frustration among Henry, Ella, Sadie, and Ben. *(© eelnosiva | Shutterstock.com)*

Source: Bryan Aubrey, Critical Essay on *Icebound*, in *Drama for Students*, Gale, Cengage Learning, 2014.

Owen Davis

In the following excerpt, Davis explains his formula for writing the melodramatic and violent plays for which he was best known, as well as his reasons for leaving that genre behind.

. . . The plays that we produced were written largely by rule. In fact the actual writing of one of these sensational melodramas I had reduced to a formula, about as follows:

TITLE (at least fifty per cent of success)

PLOT: Brief story of the play.

CAST: *Leading Man*, very (even painfully) virtuous.
Leading Woman, in love with him.
Comedy Man, always faithful friend of *Hero*.
Soubrette, very worthy person (poor but honest) and always in love with *Comedian*.
Heavy Man, a villain, not for any special reason, but, like "Topsy," "born bad."
Heavy Woman,—here I had a wider choice, his lady being allowed to fasten her affections upon either *Hero* or *Villain* (sometimes both) but never happily.
Father (or *Mother*), to provide sentiment.
Fill in as desired with character parts.

ACT I—Start the trouble.

ACT II—Here things look bad. The lady having left home, is quite at the mercy of *Villain*.

ACT III—The lady is saved by the help of the Stage Carpenter. (The big scenic and mechanical effects were always in Act III.).

ACT IV—The lovers are united and the villains are punished.

I suppose that I have been responsible for as many executions as the Queen in "Alice in Wonderland." I am honest enough to admit my cold-blooded attitude; but apply this chart to many plays of authors who consider their work inspired, and see if it fits.

These plays depended very greatly upon scenic effect, sensational dramatic title, and enormously melodramatic pictorial display on the bill boards. I think we touched upon every theme known to man, and every location. We limited ourselves, however, to American subjects. We always had a clear and dominant love interest, which we crossed with an element of danger, usually furnished by a rather impossible villain or adventuress. The themes of some of these plays were absolutely legitimate and the stories in many cases, with different dressing, would have done for a Broadway theater of the present day. But we had to, or fancied we had to, have such an over-abundance of climactic material that our plays resulted in an undigested mass of unprepared situations. Where one carefully prepared and well-developed episode would really have been of far greater dramatic value, we made a rule of dividing our plays into no less than fifteen scenes, the end of each being a moment of perilous suspense or terrifying danger. This gave the playwright rather less than seven minutes to instruct his audience, to prepare his climaxes, to plant the seed for the next scene, and to *reach* his climaxes, which of course was absurdly impossible and resulted, I feel sure, in a form of entertainment which was only too ready to yield to the encroachment of the cheap vaudeville and moving pictures. . . .

Source: Owen Davis, "Why I Quit Writing Melodrama," in *Discussions of Modern American Drama*, edited by Walter J. Meserve, D. C. Heath, 1966, pp. 128–129.

Lewin Goff

In the following excerpt, Goff divides Davis's melodramas into three distinct categories: comedy dramas, Western thrillers, and "sexy" plays.

It might be said, with reasonable certainty, that the popular-priced melodrama (some fifty years ago) was not intended for placement in the archives of classical literature. As one playwright said:

> My dear fellow, just let literary quality and all the rest of that sort of nonsense take care of itself. What is plays written fer, anyhow, I'd like to know! They ain't written ter read; they're written ter act!

The dealers in popular-priced melodrama "ter act" had their greatest day in the first decade of the Twentieth Century. The lurid advertisements of the period suggest exciting competition on the Stair and Havlin circuit among such play proprietors as P. H. Sullivan, Spencer and Aborn, Jacob Litt, Sam Harris, T. L. Veronee, and Al Woods who produced the works of such melodramatists as Theodore Kremer, Charles A. Blaney, Hal Reid, Charles A. Taylor, and Owen Davis. This competition demanded speed in construction, and speed demanded a formula. When, in 1905, the two who were giants in their respective fields (Al Woods and Owen Davis) united forces, the popular-priced theatre world

> PART OF THE FORMULA POSSIBLY UNIQUE TO THIS 'FACTORY' WAS WOODS' GENIUS FOR SELECTING TERRIFYING TITLES AND ORDERING COLORFUL LITHOGRAPHS AND DAVIS'S ABILITY TO WRITE A PLAY TO FIT BOTH TITLE AND LITHOGRAPH."

saw the production of the formula play reach factory proportions. Indeed, the success of the Davis-Woods factory may very well be one of the chief reasons the popular-priced melodrama lasted as long as it did.

Pulitzer-prize winner Owen Davis had an early start as a melodramatist. He records that when he was nine years old he wrote a play called "Diamond Cut Diamond; or, the Rival Detectives," which had five acts and eleven characters. In the fifth act only two of the eleven characters remained alive, a record, he says, ". . . which I have since been unable to beat." After graduating from Harvard, and before teaming with Woods, Davis learned the popular-priced theatre business all the way from box-office man to stage director. In 1897 he turned out the first in a long series of sensational productions, *Through the Breakers*. This play ran some five years in the popular-priced houses and was produced in England, South Africa, and Australia. Davis firmly established himself as a melodramatist of note in these "pre-Woods" years with such successes as *Lost in the Desert, Under Two Flags, The Lighthouse by the Sea* and *Her Marriage Vow*.

Al Woods gained his theatrical experience much as had Davis, by doing any and everything around the theatre. Davis said that Woods gained considerable experience as an advance agent for a sensational melodrama, and ". . . was known as the best man in the show business to draw a big opening to a bad play." Sidney Skolsky says he started out as a billposter, an experience that fitted him peculiarly for his later success as a proprietor of melodrama. Skolsky says that Woods' real entry into show business was when he took a piece of lithograph paper to Theodore Kremer and commissioned him to write a play about it. The picture was of the Bowery. Kremer had the measles at the time and was resting in a darkened apartment to protect his eyes. The combination of lithograph and darkened apartment resulted in *The Bowery After Dark*, one of the most famous of sensational pieces.

In 1905 Davis and Woods entered into a truly remarkable legal contract. It stipulated that for the succeeding five years Davis could write plays for no other proprietor and that Woods could produce plays for no other author. Woods was to produce at least four new Davis plays each year, and, after the first year, not less than four of his old ones. After the first year there were to be at least eight Davis plays on the popular-priced circuits at the same time, each playing a season of not less than thirty weeks. Skolsky says that Davis wrote fifty-eight melodramas for Woods, or almost a play a month for the next five years. Davis estimated that he addressed each season an audience numbering upward of seven million people, and that at one time eighteen of his plays were touring the popular-priced houses.

The formula used by the "factory" was not unlike that used by other playwrights and proprietors of the period. . . .

The "factory" placed great emphasis upon the sensational scene in the third act. There can be no estimation of the number of explosions, battles, earthquakes, fires, and murders of assorted variety that were produced under the banner "Al Woods Presents." Davis himself admitted that "I suppose that I have been responsible for as many executions as the Queen in 'Alice in Wonderland.' I am honest enough to admit my cold-blooded attitude." Franklin P. Adams remarked:

> "If all the blood spilled in the one hundred and seventeen Davidramas were put into one caldron, it would equal the average rainfall for Asia, Rhode Island, and Tasmania. The blank cartridges shot off in those same plays would supply the Bulgarian army for 1342 years, 7 months, and 12 days."

Part of the formula possibly unique to this "factory" was Woods' genius for selecting terrifying titles and ordering colorful lithographs and Davis's ability to write a play to fit both title and lithograph. Many of their successes seem to have begun with Woods shouting to Davis "I have a title for you!" Completely inspired, Davis set to writing the play which apparently did not take a great deal of his time:

> An itemized account of the time spent . . . would be about three days thinking out general outline of play, three days on the first act, about two days on each of the three succeeding act . . .

The teamwork employed in choosing titles wisely and in writing dialogue rapidly was of no small importance to the successful venture of the two partners.

The output of this "factory" reached such proportions that it became a regular practice for names other than "Owen Davis" to appear as author on the advertisements of the plays. Davis says he followed this practice of using assumed names to ". . . hide my evil deeds." He went on to elaborate, however, that this was done for the very good reason that the plays were so closely syndicated. Considering the number of plays he had on the road at any one time, had he used his own name on all of them ". . . there would have been about ten or fifteen weeks booked with plays following one another and all bearing my name." Davis says he was abused by the dramatic critics under six different names—names which Al Woods happily borrowed from his office clerks and supplied to the advertisements. The advertisements reveal that the names of some of Mr. Woods' clerks evidently were John Oliver, Walter Lawrence, Arthur J. Lamb, Martin Hurley, and Robert Wayne. Each of these men had a sudden taste of popular-priced fame before 1910 as the author of at least one of Owen Davis's plays. John Oliver came very near usurping some of Davis's popularity, for Davis records that a Pittsburgh critic in reviewing *Convict 999* stated: "Here at last is a fine melodrama and heaven be praised. Here, in the person of John Oliver, a new writer, we have at last a man who knows more about how to write a play of this kind than the irrepressible Owen Davis ever knew."

Davis has divided his products into three groups: the "New York comedy drama," the "Western thrillers," and the "sexy" play. Highlights of a few of the more popular plays in each of these groups might serve to show the application of the formula of this fabulous "factory."

Of the three groups the "New York" is probably the largest. Scenes representing "big city" people were much in demand on the popular-priced circuits. *Convict 999; or, From Society and Riches to Prison and Shame* was the third play written under the Davis-Woods contract. It was written by the famous "John Oliver" in four acts and fifteen scenes and carried thirteen different "massive settings." The thirteen "massive settings" included the Waldorf Astoria Hotel; the criminal court room; "Sing Sing Prison in 3 Scenes"; a "Ruined Red Stone Mill Transformed into a Field of Waving Corn"; a "Ball in a Regimental Armory"; a "Sensational Jail Delivery," which featured the famous "Zouaves" in their "Marvelous Feats of Wall Scaling and Ladder Climbing"; and a "Wedding in a Magnificent Church."

. . . The same mold served all three groups of plays with equal success. And, until the end came in 1910, these plays and many like them made the "Davis-Woods Melodrama Factory" a really big business enterprise. According to Davis, he and Woods were profiting some 20,000 dollars a year on each of their successful productions. He went on to say that it was their effort to increase profits by producing "Super-Special" shows that were in large measure responsible for the collapse of the popular-priced theatre business. They had decided to increase the average weekly business of 3,500, ". . . by putting out a show so much bigger than any of the others that we can safely count on over-capacity business to pay our increased expense and yield us a greater than average profit." Their first experiment was a success. *Nellie, the Beautiful Cloak Model* played for a year, averaging over 4,000 dollars a week. In succeeding years they sent more of the "Super-Specials" on the road and were able to allow an increase in the cost of operation. Other proprietors began the same practice, and the competition soon sent the costs of operation beyond the capacity of the popular-priced business."

By 1910 Davis foresaw the fate of the popular-priced field and, realizing there would soon be no market for his plays, broke with "factory" methods of play construction and began ". . . trimming my sails to suit the new wind." But he goes on to suggest that there were other reasons for his break:

> My paramount reason for ceasing to write sensational melodramas was that they began to appeal too strongly to my sense of humor. This, with the fact that my wife was constantly declaring that she would rather share in two thousand dollars a year legitimately earned than share in the results of my "iniquity," made me decide to free myself from a line of work that had earned for me money, ridicule, and censure in almost equal quantities.

Davis's transition from the popular-priced play to quality plays was made with some difficulty; not because he was unable to throw off the pattern of construction he had worked with for so long, but primarily because his name had become so closely associated with a particular brand of melodrama that the managers could not conceive his writing anything else.

> My name, as the author of literally hundreds of bloodthirsty melodramas, was a thing of scorn to the highbrows of the theatre, used as a horrible example to young authors and to frighten bad children. The very thought of my being allowed to produce a play in a Broadway theatre was quite absurd, as my friends all assured me.

Davis rose from his "Queens," "Nellies," and "Gamblers" of the Al Woods days to plays like *The Family Cupboard, Sinners,* and *Forever After*, and finally to his real triumphs in *The Detour* and *Icebound.*

Al Woods, too, had been preparing for this future as early as 1910. In April of that year he became a partner with Harry H. Frazee and George Lederer for the extravagant production of *Madame Sherry*. In the years immediately following, Woods continued with "Super-Specials" (this time in the expensive houses) such as *The Fascinating Widow, Gypsy Love,* and *The Littlest Rebel*. Woods was a partner in the building of the "Julian Eltinge Theatre," acquired the "Woods Theatre" in Chicago, and by 1929 was rated a millionaire.

As the partnership was dissolved and each member of the "factory" became successful in new ventures, Davis managed to conceal the early sensational pieces in a bank vault and from the eyes of a critical public. This has, perhaps, afforded him more opportunity to reflect upon this part of his career with a sort of nostalgic fondness:

> Years ago I decided to stop all production of my old melodramas, not that I was in the least ashamed of them but because the actors of today don't know how to play them and the directors don't know how to put them on. I have in a bank vault one copy of some hundred odd of these old plays and, as far as I know no one else has any of them. "Nellie, the Beautiful Cloak Model" has always been the one supposed to be the extreme example of old fashioned blood and thunder melodrama and it has always been selected by historians of the theatre and by little theatre groups to be a "horrible example"—but so far it never has been as I decided long ago to let it rest in peace and I absolutely refuse to take it out of that bank vault—because if I did I might read it myself and I am sure I wouldn't understand a word of it. Plays like "Nellie, The Beautiful Cloak

Model" were meant only for young people with courage and faith and sympathy—and at my age I am lacking . . .

Source: Lewin Goff, "The Owen Davis-Al Woods Melodrama Factory," in *Educational Theatre Journal*, Vol. 11, No. 3, October 1959, pp. 200–207.

Owen Davis

In his foreword to Icebound, *Davis explains his inspiration for the play.*

With the production of "The Detour," about a year ago, I managed to secure some measure of success in drawing a simple picture of life as it is lived on a Long Island farm; encouraged by this, I am now turning toward my own people, the people of northern New England, whose folklore, up to the present time, has been quite neglected in our theatre. I mean, of course, that few serious attempts have been made in the direction of a genre comedy of this locality. Here I have at least tried to draw a true picture of these people, and I am of their blood, born of generations of Northern Maine, small-town folk, and brought up among them. In my memory of them is little of the "Rube" caricature of the conventional theatre; they are neither buffoons nor sentimentalists, and at least neither their faults nor their virtues are borrowed from the melting pot but are the direct result of their own heritage and environment.

Source: Owen Davis, Foreword to *Icebound: A Play*, Little, Brown, 1923.

SOURCES

"American FactFinder," US Census Bureau website, http://factfinder2.census.gov/faces/nav/jsf/pages/index.xhtml### (accessed June 17, 2013).

Baym, Nina, Ronald Gottesman, Laurence B. Holland, Francis Murphy, Hershel Parker, William H. Pritchard, and David Kalstone, eds., "Introduction: American Literature between the Wars, 1914–1945," in *The Norton Anthology of American Literature*, 2nd ed., W. W. Norton, 1985, p. 872.

Bryer, Jackson R., and Mary C. Hartig, eds., *Facts on File Companion to American Drama*, 2nd ed., Facts on File, 2010, p. 261.

Curry, J. K., "Owen Davis," in *Dictionary of Literary Biography*, Vol. 249, *Twentieth-Century American Dramatists, Third Series*, edited by Christopher Wheatley, The Gale Group, 2002, pp. 75–84.

Davis, Owen, *Icebound: A Play*, Little, Brown, 1923.

Fisher, James, and Felicia Hardison Londré, *The A to Z of Modern Theater: Modernism*, Scarecrow Press, 2008, p. 239.

Hamilton, Jean, "History of Veazie, Maine," Veazie, Maine, website, http://www.veazie.net/public_documents/index (accessed June 17, 2013).

Mantle, Burns, ed., Introduction to *The Best Plays of 1922–23*, Maynard, 1923, p. ix, http://www.archive.org/stream/cu31924107204475/cu31924107204475_djvu.txt (accessed June 12, 2013).

Mantle, Burns, ed., Introduction to *Icebound*, in *The Best Plays of 1922–23*, Maynard, 1923, p. 141, http://www.archive.org/stream/cu31924107204475/cu31924107204475_djvu.txt (accessed June 12, 2013).

Murphy, Brenda, *American Realism and American Drama, 1880–1940*, Cambridge University Press, 1987, pp. 138, 143.

Quinn, Arthur Hobson, in *A History of the American Drama from the Civil War to the Present Day*, F. S. Crofts, 1936, p. 208.

Teachout, Terry, "Why Straight Plays Can't Make It on Broadway," in *Wall Street Journal*, March 29, 2012, http://online.wsj.com/article/SB10001424052702303816504577309663296504788.html (accessed September 10, 2013).

FURTHER READING

Demastes, William W., ed., *Realism and the American Dramatic Tradition*, University of Alabama Press, 1996.
This is a collection of sixteen essays that examine the development of realism in American drama.

Gewirtz, Arthur, and James Kolb, eds., *Art, Glitter, and Glitz: Mainstream Playwrights and Popular Theatre in 1920s America*, Praeger, 2004.
This collection of twenty-two essays covers all aspects of American drama during the 1920s.

Murphy, Brenda, *The Provincetown Players and the Culture of Modernity*, Cambridge University Press, 2005.
Murphy describes the work of the Provincetown Players, the experimental theater group that existed from 1916 to 1922, in the context of American culture of the time, particularly modernism.

Shiach, Don, *American Drama, 1900–1990*, Cambridge University Press, 2000.
This is a concise introduction to twentieth-century American drama, from Eugene O'Neill to David Mamet.

SUGGESTED SEARCH TERMS

Owen Davis

Icebound

realism

American drama AND realism

American drama AND 1920s

Provincetown Players

Pulitzer Prize for Drama

melodrama AND Owen Davis

The Importance
of Being Earnest

2002

The Importance of Being Earnest, first produced in 1895, is recognized as Oscar Wilde's greatest comedy, and it is generally considered one of the funniest stage plays ever written. Oliver Parker, who wrote and directed the 2002 film adaptation of the play—which is subtitled *A Trivial Comedy for Serious People*—had honed his understanding of Wilde with his adaptation of the Irish playwright's *An Ideal Husband* in 1999. His experience brought him to a strikingly original approach to the material: while he retained most of Wilde's dialogue (along with a few minor controversial additions to help open the story to the minds of modern audiences), he set that dialogue in a rich visual world of London and the British countryside.

The story plays off of clichés familiar to Wilde's audience of the Victorian era. It weaves together such fanciful elements as society gentlemen who make up imaginary ill friends as an excuse to go off nightclubbing, not one but two young women who have such detailed dreams of their perfect lovers that they refuse to marry any man not named "Ernest," and that most familiar standard of Victorian literature, a man who was abandoned as an infant finding out who his real parents were. Lead actors Rupert Everett, Colin Firth, Reese Witherspoon, Frances O'Connor, and Dame Judi Dench bring these unlikely characters alive with the light touch that Wilde's plotline requires. Although other film adaptations of

The 2002 film stars Frances O'Connor, Colin Firth, Rupert Everett, and Reese Witherspoon. (© Paul Chedlow, Miramax / Dimension Films / The Kobal Collectiton)

Wilde's play have been considered more faithful to their source material, Parker's is considered the one that makes Wilde's humor most accessible to modern audiences.

PLOT SUMMARY

The film begins with Algernon Moncrieff ("Algy") being pursued through alleys of London by two men. Algy's cape and the men's bowler hats indicate that it is set in the late 1800s or early 1900s. To elude them, Algy jumps into a woman's carriage. With a charming smile, he offers her a cigarette, presumably from Jack's cigarette case, which will be integral to the plot later. He jumps out as the carriage passes his house, leaving her sighing, smitten.

Inside his apartment, in a smoking jacket, Algy plays jazzy ragtime music on the piano as his butler, Lane, enters. This is the first scene of Wilde's play, and, like most of the movie, it uses Wilde's dialogue. Algy looks over the mail that Lane has brought in and is bothered by the

number of overdue bills, including, as Lane calmly points out, the wages due to the butler himself.

The scene changes to Jack Worthing's estate in the country, called the Manor House by Oscar Wilde, who uses a simple generic description as the house's formal title. Jack is wearing glasses and sternly giving orders to his own butler as he walks out the door for his carriage. He waves goodbye to his ward (a younger person of whom he has guardianship), Cecily Cardew, and gives instructions to her tutor, Miss Prism. Quietly, he asks the butler whether he has found a cigarette case he lost.

On a crowded, bustling London street, Jack looks different, with jaunty clothes, no glasses, and a cigarette in his smiling mouth. He goes to a dance hall with bawdy dancers and runs into Algy. Algy knows him as "Ernest." He comments on the fact that his friend is always away on weekends, and it becomes clear that Algy does not know exactly where Jack's country house is located.

Algy mentions that his aunt Augusta is coming to tea. Jack associates her name with

FILM TECHNIQUE

- *Cross-cutting* is the technique of showing what is happening at two or more different places at the same time in quick sequential order. Parker uses this technique a few times during the film. When Algy mentions his aunt Augusta, the camera cuts to Lady Bracknell and Gwendolyn participating in an archery tournament, visually introducing them to the audience. Gwendolyn's automobile trip to the country is conveyed in a series of cross cuts, interrupting the action at the Manor House with scenes of her car on the road. When Gwendolyn arrives and has tea with Cecily, the camera cuts to Jack preparing to tell Gwendolyn his real name and Algy escaping from the cart that is taking him away. Giving audiences knowledge of two things happening at once, on a collision course with each other, heightens the sense of comic excitement.

- Throughout the film, Parker uses close-up shots to draw audiences' attention to details in a way that a theatrical performance would not be able to do. For instance, when Algy receives his mail, glances at it, and throws it out, theater audiences must assume that the mail contained bills, but the film can show the red "Final Notice" warnings on the bills. The close-up camera shot is also used to build suspense, as when, during their interview to determine if Jack would be a good suitor for Gwendolyn, the camera focuses on Lady Bracknell's silver bell, making viewers anticipate the moment she will ring it and send him away.

- For much of this film the actors were filmed in a medium shot, from the waist up. This technique allows the camera to capture several characters in one shot, giving the comedy an active, hectic feeling. Sometimes,

such as in the London dance halls or when the staff of the Manor House comes out to welcome Jack home, there are ten or more actors onscreen. This type of shot also allows the film to show the background behind the people, and Parker makes use of the busy London streets, the rolling hills of the country estate, and the tall, decorated walls of Lady Bracknell's mansion to give viewers a strong sense of location throughout the story.

- *Non-diegetic* sound refers to sounds that appear in the movie but are not present in the world that is inhabited by the characters; these are sounds that the characters would not hear. One example of this is Gwendolyn's voiceover as Jack reads her letter, hearing her voice in her head. Most of the film's score is non-diegetic, heard only by the audience, as is the case with most film scores. Even the song "Lady Come Down," which Jack and Algy use to serenade Gwendolyn and Cecily, only begins with diegetic sound, as they play the instruments and sing; later in the scene, they are joined by a full orchestra that is not present with the characters.

- When Jack is trying to find out who might have abandoned him at the train station, the film shows a brief shot, looking up from inside of a suitcase. It is presumably Jack's memory from when he was an infant. This subjective point of view is later repeated, briefly, when Jack finds out that Algy is his older brother, and he remembers seeing an older boy from inside of his carriage. In between Jack's two memories is Miss Prism's memory of the day Jack was put in the handbag: from her point of view, the camera shows a young man—young Algy—standing nearby, watching her.

Gwendolyn, with whom Jack is in love. He tells Algy that he has come to town to propose marriage to Gwendolyn. Algy disapproves—not of

them as a couple, but of marriage in general. He asks who Cecily is, which panics Jack, who had tried to keep his ward's existence a secret. Algy has found out about Cecily from the inscription on the cigarette case that Jack lost. When pressed, Jack explains that she is his aunt, but Algy does not believe him; the person who inscribed the case calls herself "little Cecily" and calls him "dear Uncle Jack." Algy wants to know why she is calling him Jack, not Ernest. Jack explains that he uses one name in town and a different one in the country.

Algy suggests that Jack is a "Bunburyist," like himself. He has made up a friend named Bunbury who is supposedly sick and needs constant attention, giving him an excuse to get out of boring events. He calls his visits to his imaginary friend "Bunburying." Their discussion is interrupted by the creditors from the first scene, causing Algy to run away.

The scene changes to the Manor House, where Miss Prism is boring Cecily with German grammar. Cecily notes that her uncle Jack is too serious, and she wishes that he could be more like his brother Ernest, who Jack tells stories about. As Miss Prism talks, Cecily daydreams about a knight in armor on a steed galloping toward her across the field.

Jack goes to Algy's house to deny being a Bunburyist. Algy, though, has figured out that Jack invented his younger brother, Ernest, in order to come to town for fun.

Lady Bracknell (Algy's aunt Augusta) and Gwendolyn arrive. Lady Bracknell is clear about her dislike for Jack. She invites Algy to a dinner party, but he excuses himself, explaining that he has to visit his sick friend Bunbury. She tells him to ask Bunbury to not be sick next week, when she is having another party, for which she needs Algy to provide the music. He leads her to the next room to show her the music he has prepared for her party, giving Jack some time alone with Gwendolyn.

As Jack works toward proposing, Gwendolyn explains that one reason she likes him is that his name is Ernest: she has felt for a long time she was destined to love a man named Ernest. He tries to change her mind, telling her that he has been thinking of changing his name, but she insists that she will only marry him if his name is Ernest. As he formally proposes to her, Aunt Agatha bursts in and interrupts. She says that she will not let Jack marry her daughter, but that she is willing to discuss it at her house the following morning.

At the Manor House, Miss Prism interrupts Cecily in another daydream about her knight in armor. Explaining why she keeps a diary, Cecily speaks disparagingly about the "three volume novel," a fad of the mid- to late nineteenth century. Miss Prism says that she once wrote one herself, in her youth, showing that she does, or did once, have romantic tendencies. A neighbor, Dr. Chasuble, comes to visit, and Cecily observes that he and Miss Prism are interested in each other.

As Jack enters Lady Bracknell's opulent home the next morning, a servant wishes him luck. Lady Bracknell and two unidentified women question him about matters such as whether he smokes, and whether he thinks he knows everything or nothing, and his income. When he gives his address in town, she identifies it as being on "the unfashionable side" and nearly calls for the butler to usher Jack out, but decides that his address can be changed. Jack explains that he is an orphan, having been found in a suitcase at the Victoria train station, and does not know who his parents were. Lady Bracknell tears up her notes and tells him that she cannot let him marry Gwendolyn if he cannot come up with at least one parent. Jack, panicking, says that he knows where the suitcase is, and that should be enough. She rings for the butler to see Jack out.

At a bar, Jack and Algy discuss Gwendolyn. The room becomes silent as Gwendolyn herself enters: the men surrounding them are shocked to see a woman entering a tavern. She assures Jack that she is still dedicated to him, and asks for his country address so she can write to him. Algy overhears and writes the address on his sleeve, as in Wilde's play.

After a brief scene in a library, with Jack searching old newspapers for clues of his parents, comes a scene of Jack dismantling his town house, taking down pictures. He explains to Algy that he plans to pretend his fictional brother, Ernest, has died and to give up visits to the city. When Jack mentions Cecily, Algy expresses his interest in meeting her, though in the play his interest in meeting her was clear before he took down Jack's address.

Arriving home, Algy sees that his house is being watched by the bill collectors who have been chasing him. He sneaks in a window while his butler Lane practices with a musical quartet.

Algy, with his moustache shaved off, arrives at Jack's Manor House estate by hot-air balloon. Cecily watches him arrive, and then a butler arrives with a business card Algy took from Jack, announcing the arrival of Ernest Worthing—he is taking on the role of Jack's fictional brother. Reading it, Cecily imagines her knight riding to her on his horse.

Meeting him, Cecily refers to him as her "wicked" cousin Ernest and is disappointed when he denies being wicked. She expects Jack to return home on Monday, and Algy says he will be gone by then.

Jack comes home unexpectedly, dressed in his conservative clothes and glasses, and announces that his brother Ernest has died in Paris, showing Dr. Chasuble and Miss Prism an urn that is supposed to contain his ashes. Cecily approaches and tells Jack that his brother Ernest is in the garden. When they find Algy, he is eating breakfast. Jack shows him the telegram from Paris, but Algy, playing Ernest, laughs off the announcement of Ernest's death as a joke he tried to play. At Cecily's urging, Jack shakes the hand that Algy offers.

When they are alone, Algy tells Jack how much he likes Cecily. Jack tells him that he must leave, but Algy pulls out a handkerchief with the initials "E.W."—Ernest Worthing—on it, a veiled threat to reveal Jack's secret life in the city. This infuriates Jack, who strangles him until he sees that they are being watched by Cecily, Miss Prism, and Dr. Chasuble. Then he hugs Algy and pretends that they are friends.

That night, Algy sits at the piano with Cecily. He tries to flirt with her, but Jack hovers nearby. Looking through his personal scrapbook, Jack stares at a photo of Thomas Cardew, who found him in the suitcase as a baby, and at the ticket to Worthing station that he was named for. He has a vague memory, seeing through the handles of the suitcase as he is carried into Victoria station as an infant. He can only hazily see the face of the woman who left him there.

A letter from Gwendolyn arrives in the morning mail. Her words are sweet and proper, but as Jack hears them in his head while reading them, the film shows her going to a tattoo parlor and having the name *Ernest* inscribed on her back. At the end of her note she announces that she is coming to the country house. Subsequent scenes are intercut with images of Gwendolyn nervously driving a rickety open-air automobile down country roads.

Algy rows Cecily and Miss Prism out on the lake while Cecily practices her German grammar. Later, she takes out her diary to record something he said, and he expresses interest in reading it. His romantic words to her are interrupted by Jack's butler, Merriman, who announces that two men have come to see Algy—the bill collectors. Rather than go to jail, he suggests that his "brother," Jack, should pay the bill. Jack agrees, but only if Algy/Ernest will leave the Manor House.

With his belongings packed, Algy stops to ask Cecily to marry him. She explains that they have been engaged for three months. She shows him the letters he has sent to her (she wrote them herself) and her diary chronicling their engagement. A dream of medieval romance, in which he is her knight and she is his lady and they are serenaded by wood nymphs, is shattered by harsh reality when she points out that she must marry him because his name is Ernest, and she has always wanted to love someone named Ernest.

Miss Prism interrupts Dr. Chasuble in his study. Nervously, he leaves the room; in his absence she sees drawings and paintings that he has made of her, depicting her as young and vivacious. This confirms his unstated love for her.

Gwendolyn arrives and introduces herself to Cecily. They immediately become friends, as Jack had guessed they would. As they uncomfortably smoke cigarettes and talk, confusion arises: they both think that they are engaged to Ernest Worthing. Cecily shows her diary, to prove that Ernest proposed to her ten minutes ago, but Gwendolyn produces her own diary to prove that he proposed the day before.

Algy escapes from the cart taking him away and returns to the Manor House while Cecily and Gwendolyn become increasingly angry with each other, each thinking the other is involved with her fiancé. They express their anger through sarcastic remarks and sneaky actions: Gwendolyn mocks the idea that a fashionable person would want sugar in her tea, so Cecily dumps a lot of sugar into hers, and then when Gwendolyn chooses buttered bread instead of cake, Cecily serves her a huge slab of cake.

Algy's approach calms their tension when they realize that the "Ernest" who is engaged to Cecily is not the same man Gwendolyn was thinking of after all. But Cecily finds out, to her horror, that his name is not actually Ernest.

When Jack arrives, Gwendolyn is pleased to announce that he is her fiancé, but immediately saddened to find that his name is not Ernest either. Cecily and Gwendolyn, who were at each other's throats a moment ago, console each other about the deception and declare their sisterly love.

Jack goes to Dr. Chasuble to arrange to be christened (that is, baptized in the Christian faith—though the script downplays this aspect—and given a new name) with the name Ernest. He makes an appointment for 5:30 p.m. Algy goes to Dr. Chasuble and makes an appointment for six o'clock to be christened with the same name. They pick flowers for the girls to win their affection back, but the girls ride past them on horses, splattering them with mud.

Jack and Algy serenade the girls with a song, "Lady Come Down," which is actually based on a poem by Oscar Wilde (Colin Firth and Rupert Everett are both skillful musicians). They follow the ladies around the house, with servants carrying Algy's piano as he plays it. The women forgive the men, but both women announce in unison that they still cannot marry men not named Ernest. Both men announce in unison that they are scheduled to be baptized that afternoon.

Lady Bracknell arrives. She tells Jack that he cannot marry Gwendolyn and asks Algy about his friend Bunbury, whom Algy declares dead, as Jack tried to do with his imaginary brother Ernest. When she hears that Cecily has inherited a fortune from her parents, Lady Bracknell recalls her own poverty, working as a showgirl and becoming pregnant by Lord Bracknell. She consents to Cecily's marriage to Algy: Jack, however, has the right as Cecily's guardian to block her marriage until she is thirty-five years old, and he claims that he will block it until Lady Bracknell consents to his own marriage to Gwendolyn.

Lady Bracknell refuses, and she is leaving with Cecily when Dr. Chasuble arrives for the christening. Miss Prism's name comes up. Lady Bracknell recognizes the name and demands to see her immediately, so they all go to the church, where Miss Prism is waiting for Dr. Chasuble.

Lady Bracknell, in a rage, demands to know what Miss Prism did with "the child," causing Miss Prism to faint. Lady Bracknell explains, with visual flashbacks, how Miss Prism took a baby out for a stroll more than thirty years ago and disappeared, and that a three-volume novel was found in the stroller instead of the baby. Miss Prism explains that she became confused that morning, putting her novel in the baby carriage and the baby in the handbag, which she left in the cloakroom at Victoria Station. Jack briefly thinks this means that Miss Prism is his mother. It is revealed that the baby in the handbag—Jack—was the child of Lady Bracknell's sister, who was Algernon's mother.

Jack is delighted to discover his identity and to find that he has a brother, Algy. Lady Bracknell accepts him into her family and agrees to let him marry Gwendolyn. Miss Prism resigns her position as Cecily's teacher and starts leaving in shame, but Dr. Chasuble proposes marriage to her.

Jack asks Lady Bracknell his real name. She can only remember that he is named after his father. Knowing that his father was an army general, Jack goes to a book in his library that lists all military generals of the time and announces that his father was named Ernest, so this is therefore his own name. Everyone is happy and in love.

In Wilde's play, the discovery of General Moncrieff's name reminds Lady Bracknell that he was, in fact, sometimes called Ernest. In the film, however, she looks at the book that Jack has read from and sees that the general's name was really John, which would mean that Jack's name was really Jack all along. She sternly accuses Jack of showing signs of "triviality," which provides him the opportunity to end the film with the same line that ends the play: "I've realized for the first time in my life the vital importance of being earnest." She breaks into a laugh and throws the book aside, accepting the silliness of the situation.

As the credits roll, the characters assemble for a somber funeral around the tombstone for "Bunbury." The scene then changes to Jack holding Gwendolyn's hand as he has her name tattooed on his behind, matching her Ernest tattoo.

CHARACTERS

Aunt Augusta

See Lady Bracknell

Lady Bracknell

Lady Bracknell is played by Dame Judi Dench, one of Britain's most respected and recognized actresses. She stands in the film, as in the play, as a standard-bearer for old society. She grudgingly accepts her nephew Algernon but rejects Jack Worthing, even though he is more stable and balanced in his worldview, because he does not have a clearly defined ancestry. Lady Bracknell conducts formal interviews of a series of possible suitors for her daughter, Gwendolyn, making the young men sit and answer a series of questions while she and several other unnamed society women listen in judgment.

Although Lady Bracknell appears to uphold the moral standards of society, she turns out to be a hypocrite, acting against her own stated beliefs. She disapproves of Cecily as a match for Algernon until she finds out that Cecily is wealthy. She is unable to remember the name of her own sister's husband, General Moncrieff.

In the end, though, Lady Bracknell proves to be a good sport: she knows that Jack has lied about his real name being Ernest, but she laughs and lets it go.

Cecily Cardew

Cecily is Jack Worthing's ward. They are not related, but because he is older and connected with her family (her grandfather found the infant Jack, long before she was born), she calls him "Uncle Jack." In the film, Cecily says that she is eighteen years old. She is played by American actress Reese Witherspoon, who was twenty-six when the film was made.

Wilde shows Cecily's girlish nature when she shows her scrapbook to Algernon, whom she thinks is named Ernest, and explains to him, with all seriousness, that they have been engaged for months and that he has written love letters to her (though she had to write them herself). Oliver Parker's script supplements this impression of her by adding fantasies of Cecily dressed as a medieval damsel being rescued by a knight with his visor down: after she meets Algy, he is the knight in armor in her dreams.

Like Gwendolyn Fairfax, Cecily insists that the man she is going to love must be named Ernest. In the end, though, when Ernest ends up being the name of Algy's brother, she drops that insistence, happy to have her man.

Dr. Frederick Chasuble

Chasuble is played by Tom Wilkinson, a popular character actor. He resides near Jack's Manor House in Hertfordshire. He serves two functions in this play. First, being a minister, he is able to baptize people, and he therefore offers both Jack and Algy the opportunity to have themselves rechristened with the name "Ernest." In addition, his undeclared love for Miss Prism adds one more romantic couple to the story, increasing the air of fun and frivolity.

The character is generally nervous around Miss Prism; Wilkinson adds a habitual sneeze, which serves to show that he is trying to keep his true emotions bottled up.

Gwendolyn Fairfax

Gwendolyn is played by Frances O'Connor. She is the cousin of Algernon, the daughter of his aunt Augusta Bracknell, and the love interest of Jack Worthing.

In Wilde's play, Gwendolyn is more of an obscure character. She does have the quirky insistence that she will only love a man named Ernest, for reasons that she explains but that seem arbitrary. She accepts her mother's rejection of Jack, but later sneaks away to visit him. When she meets Cecily Cardew, in both the play and the film, she declares her immediate friendship with her, but then, seeing Cecily as a rival for the love of the man they both think of as Ernest, she becomes bitter and competitive, only to become best of friends again. Wilde's play presents Gwendolyn as having the mind of a fickle, unreasonable girl.

In the film, Gwendolyn is more assertive. She has the name "Ernest" tattooed on her lower back, which is certainly something that would be unthinkable in the early years of the twentieth century. She also undertakes a long journey in a rickety automobile that she does not seem to know how to operate in order to reunite with the man she loves. She still insists that Jack should change his name to Ernest, and she is pleased when told that that was actually the name he was born with.

Lane

Lane, Algernon's butler, is played by Edward Fox, a British film star whose career dates back to the 1960s. In Wilde's play, his bantering with Algernon in the first scene sets the lighthearted tone for what is to come. In the film, though, Lane appears in only a few scenes near the beginning, his best lines overshadowed by the film's earlier introduction of Algy. One scene added to the film—in which Lane plays the tuba with a few other musicians in Algy's apartment while Algy is out, with champagne glasses on the table—alludes to a discussion that Lane and Algy have in the play about why servants drink champagne when they serve in the houses of bachelors, but not in the houses of married men.

Merriman

Merriman is the butler in Jack's Manor House. He serves the same basic function that Lane serves in Algy's apartment in London, but he does not have witty banter with his employer. Instead, he raises an eyebrow now and then to show that he knows how ridiculous the events he observes are.

Algernon "Algy" Moncrieff

Algy, played by Rupert Everett, is the character who most strongly embodies the sort of wit and casual attitude that readers associate with Oscar Wilde's writing. He is the sort of person who will make up an ill friend so that he can avoid social engagements whenever he wants to, who claims that the proof that he did not run up a large restaurant bill is that he never signs the check at restaurants, who eats most of the sandwiches he bought for his aunt's visit but then slaps the hand of a friend who tries to take one. Algy enjoys life as a carefree man-about-town, living beyond his means with no concern about how to pay for his extravagant lifestyle.

The change that overcomes him when he goes to the country coincides with his decision, while fleeing his creditors, to shave his moustache. His new look fits his new personality in the country: he is no longer the scoundrel but is instead the dashing, romantic figure that Cecily has dreamed of. When he meets Cecily he immediately falls in love, making him vulnerable in a way that he never would have been in London. He arrives at the Manor House with a devious plan to pass himself off as "Ernest Worthing"; the fact that he is contentedly trapped in the role can be seen when he jumps out of the carriage to

run back to Cecily, risking imprisonment because of his emotional ties to her.

Miss Laetitia Prism

Miss Prism starts the play as Cecily Cardew's tutor. She bores her pupil, who would rather dream of romance than study German grammar. When she is out on a boat ride with Cecily and Algernon, listening to Cecily recite her lessons, Miss Prism falls into a deep sleep that allows them to have an intimate conversation. She once wrote a three-volume novel, which is a sign that she was once romantic but in a conventional way.

Throughout most of the film, the only person in whom Miss Prism shows interest is Dr. Chasuble, with whom she flirts girlishly.

When Lady Bracknell arrives at the Manor House, however, Miss Prism becomes an integral part of the film's plot. She is revealed to have been the person who abandoned Jack in the cloakroom of Victoria Station when he was an infant, a revelation that allows him to trace his parentage back to Algy's parents.

Miss Prism is about to leave her job and home in disgrace when Dr. Chasuble admits his love for her. At the end of the film, they are another happy romantic couple.

Ernest Worthing

See Algernon "Algy" Moncrieff *or* John "Jack" Worthing

John "Jack" Worthing

Jack, played by Colin Firth, is a more stable character than his counterpart, Algy. Even when he is in London, where he supposedly goes to escape the strictness of his everyday life at the Manor House, he is the more reserved of the two. Still, he is the character who undergoes the greatest change over the course of the film.

Jack lives a double life. The scenes shown during the opening credits present a man of prim bearing and conservative attire who is responsible for running an old, stodgy English manor. By the time the credits end, however, he has changed into a tuxedo and is living it up in a nightclub, surrounding himself with scantily clad women. In order to live this double life, Jack has two personalities: the somber man in the country is "Jack" and the wild partyer of the city is his imaginary brother, "Ernest."

His one weakness is his love for Algy's cousin Gwendolyn. When she accepts his proposal (even though her mother forbids it), Jack makes plans to kill off his fake brother. He does announce Ernest's death, but his plan is complicated when Algy arrives at the same time and pretends to be Ernest.

Gwendolyn's mother, Lady Bracknell, rejects Jack's proposal to her daughter because he does not know who his parents are. She is eager for her nephew, Algy, to marry Cecily when she finds out that Cecily is wealthy, so Jack uses his position as Cecily's legal guardian to force Lady Bracknell to permit his own marriage.

Once it is realized that Jack is Algy's brother and thus has the same family background, Lady Bracknell accepts him into the family and is willing to allow Jack's marriage to Gwendolyn. Jack is overjoyed to have a brother and not be a mystery anymore. He lies to Gwendolyn about his true name being Ernest. Though Lady Bracknell sees through his lie and is shocked for a moment, she has come to respect him, and so she goes along with his deceit. When she uncovers the ruse, it becomes clear that, even though he is in his country estate, Jack still has some of the devilishness that his made-up brother Ernest had.

THEMES

Hypocrisy

The mood of this film is one of joyous hypocrisy. From the start, Algy is considered a gentleman, a member of the upper class, tended by his butler at home and seen in all of the fashionable places around town, despite the fact that he is a deadbeat about paying his bills and is on the run from creditors. His self-image becomes clear when he explains to Lane, his butler, that he thinks he is a good musician, even though he cannot play accurately, because he believes that playing "with wonderful expression" is the same thing as talent, or even better. Jack, on the other hand, acknowledges his own hypocrisy, presenting himself as a rigid, proper gentleman at the Manor House and as a fun-loving man-about-town when assuming his Ernest identity in London. Although his London persona cavorts with disreputable people, including Algy, Jack is

careful to not expose his ward Cecily to the sort of people whose company he enjoys.

The most hypocritical character, though, is Lady Augusta Bracknell. As a standard-bearer of Victorian morality, she holds strict expectations for men who want to marry her daughter Gwendolyn. She rejects Jack because he does not know who his parents are and therefore might possibly be of a lower social class, and she rejects Cecily as a possible wife for Algernon because of Cecily's connection to Jack. When she finds out that Cecily is going to inherit a fortune, however, she immediately changes her mind and welcomes the girl into her family. A subsequent scene shows that she is not very strict in her morals at all, as she is only a lady of rank because, before marriage, she became pregnant by Lord Bracknell, which encouraged him to marry her.

Illegitimacy

The character who does not know who one or both of his or her parents are, only to find out the truth in a way that dramatically affects the story, was a plot element often used in nineteenth-century British literature. It can be found in some of the century's greatest works, such as Charles Dickens's *Bleak House* and *Great Expectations*, George Eliot's *Silas Marner*, and (to a lesser degree) Jane Austen's *Emma*. It was also used as a mechanical plot device in lesser works of romantic fiction, injecting intrigue into stories that otherwise had none.

It is this tradition that Wilde lampoons in *The Importance of Being Earnest*. The plot thread of Jack having been abandoned at the train station as a child and later finding out that he had been left there by Cecily's tutor, who was employed at the time by Lady Bracknell, is of course impossible to believe, but Wilde and the filmmakers as well were very aware of how impossible it was. This common plot device of Victorian literature is stretched to its extreme to show how unlikely the mysterious parentage idea in literature usually is.

Love

Near the start of the film, Jack Worthing's love for Algernon's cousin Gwendolyn is introduced. It has already developed in the months or years before the story begins. Algy, on the other hand, does not know that he is susceptible to love until he meets Cecily. Almost the moment he meets her, though, he falls deeply and hopelessly in

READ, WATCH, WRITE

- There have been many biographies written about Oscar Wilde, who is considered one of history's funniest writers but died a tragic death. One of the most respected biographies is Richard Ellman's 1988 book *Oscar Wilde*, which won both the National Book Critics Circle Award and the Pulitzer Prize. Read Ellman's biography and write a report about which character, Jack or Algernon, you think was most like the real Wilde.

- Watch Oliver Parker's film adaptation of William Shakespeare's tragedy *Othello*, featuring Lawrence Fishburne and Kenneth Branagh, and read Shakespeare's text of the play. Make a chart of what you deem the five or so most significant changes Parker made in each adaptation (*Othello* and *The Importance of Being Earnest*), and from that write up your conclusion about which one is more successful as an adaptation.

- Author Jaclyn Moriarty matches Oscar Wilde's sense of improbability and irreverence in her novel *The Year of Secret Assignments*, published in 2005. The subject matter, about teen girls given the assignment to correspond with students from another school, is very different from Wilde's, but, as in all great comedies, tension builds as deceptions build. Use that book and this film to support an essay in which you explain the relevance of either humor or wit.

- In 2010, director Guy Ritchie presented a view of Victorian London similar to the one in this film in his revisionist film *Sherlock Holmes*, starring American actor Robert Downey Jr. as one of Britain's greatest

heroes. Examine Ritchie's interpretation of that time period and take note of how his treatment of the times is similar to and different from Parker's treatment. Choose one scene from each film that you think could never possibly have been incorporated into the worldview of the other film, and explain why in a blog post. Allow your classmates to view your post and comment.

- The song "Lady Come Down," written for this film, is adapted from a poem by Oscar Wilde called "Serenade." Choose another of Wilde's poems, possibly from the 1994 edition of *The Collected Poems of Oscar Wilde*, and set it to original music. Explain which scene in the film it could be used in.

- Like most comedies, this one ends at the moment when all good things have come together for its characters. Write a short story about Jack, Algy, Gwendolyn, and Cecily that takes place ten years after this film ends.

- Both Gwendolyn and Cecily believe that having the name "Ernest" is necessary for a man to be a good husband for them. Devise a questionnaire that could help you determine which male and female names are most often associated with stable relationships. Write a report on your findings. In addition to the questions you asked, include the scientific standards you used to test the significance of the information you collected: which characteristics you think qualify as signs of a good relationship, which names you would categorize as being similar, and so forth.

love with her, and he becomes willing at once to give up the bachelor lifestyle he has previously enjoyed.

In Wilde's play, the women are more superficial in their view of love than the men.

Gwendolyn loves Jack, but her love is rooted in her belief that his name is Ernest, which she feels, for no discernible reason, is necessary for lasting love. Cecily adds to the random "Ernest" requirement a fantasy relationship that she

The Importance of Being Earnest *is set amidst the rigid social rules of the wealthier class in Victorian* England. *(© 1000 Words | Shutterstock.com)*

kept up with Jack's imaginary brother Ernest, following the standards that she has seen in books for such relationships: passion, an engagement, a breakup, and a reconciliation. Although the film follows Wilde in framing both romances with these unnecessary difficulties, it leaves no question in the end that Gwendolyn is in love with Jack and Cecily is in love with Algy.

The film and the play contrast the young lovers with the obvious attraction between Dr. Chasuble and Miss Prism. Instead of being kept apart by whimsical self-imposed laws, such as the necessity that a man be named Ernest, they are foiled by something much more realistic: their own shyness. The barrier between them is broken down only when Dr. Chasuble speaks up to prevent Miss Prism from being driven away from the Manor House in shame. Overall, love is presented as a natural state of being that people must nonetheless struggle to achieve.

Decadence

The Importance of Being Ernest is a celebration of decadence over Victorian prudery. Algernon

is the main character in this regard. He cheats his creditors and lies about his sick friend "Bunbury" to avoid responsibilities, and he invades his friend Jack's country estate to satisfy his curiosity, but he does it all with such charm that audiences side with him. Jack lives a respectable life most of the time, but his London persona, Ernest, is Algy's match in decadence. Wilde's play and the film use decadence for comic effect, showing how much fun these two characters are having at the expense of the stuffy social forces that try to suppress them. Lady Bracknell, their principal oppressor, only smiles at the end of the film, after its last line, when she has become decadent herself in accepting Jack's lie about his true name.

STYLE

Opening the Story for Film

Some productions, though very few, adapt a stage play for film by simply training cameras on the stage and capturing the action and dialogue within that specific defined space. When film versions add scenes that go beyond the theater's limitations, scenes set in places that a film crew can reach but a theater audience cannot, it is said to have "opened up" the story for the film.

Writer and director Oliver Parker opens up *The Importance of Being Earnest* from the very first shots, which show Algy being pursued through the streets of turn-of-the-century London. While some films include only a few exterior shots to open up a stage play, Parker continuously moves Wilde's dialogue into settings that are more exciting and more evocative of their time than anything that could be achieved in the confines of a theater. For instance, instead of simply having Lady Bracknell question Jack, the film takes viewers to her expansive mansion, up grand staircases and through doorway after doorway. Dance halls that are referred to in Wilde's play are shown in the film. An automobile trip is shown. The Manor House and its surrounding grounds are covered. In one extreme example of the opening-up process, Algy's arrival at the Manor House, presented onstage with an actor walking through a door, is shown in the film from the sky, with a hot-air balloon sailing down from the clouds.

Romantic Fantasy

Wilde made Cecily's exaggerated imagination real for theater audiences by having her quote passages from her diary. Parker takes this concept further by including scenes in the film of Cecily dressed as a medieval maiden, waiting for rescue by an armored knight. These added scenes tell film audiences that Cecily's imagination is colorful and steeped in romantic tradition. Like her diary, they give a physical presence to the yearning for romance that she has felt is lacking in her boring life at the Manor House. Overall, they help establish the mood of romance and fantasy that readers must feel if this unrealistic story is to work.

Costuming

The costumes worn by the main characters are important for showing the different personas that they wear in the country and in the city. At his country estate, Jack wears tweed and glasses, but when he arrives in London, taking on his "Ernest" character, he wears the evening clothes that are expected of a debonair man-about-town. Algy dresses similarly in London, but the clothes he wears when he arrives at the Manor House are fitting for the sort of dashing romantic hero that Cecily imagines him to be: in particular, his long duster, worn for his aviation voyage in a hot-air balloon, helps to engulf him like a cape in an aura of heroism. In contrast, at this same time Jack returns from London dressed in mourning for his fictitious brother Ernest, looking more drab and somber than ever.

The rakish moustache that Algy wears in London serves to accentuate his costuming, helping to establish him as a scoundrel who cannot be trusted. When he arrives in the country without the moustache, he looks more sincere and trustworthy.

CULTURAL CONTEXT

The Victorian Era

The Importance of Being Earnest was written and produced at the end of the Victorian era in Great Britain, and it is usually viewed as a reaction to the prevailing attitudes of the time.

Queen Victoria ruled Britain and Ireland from 1837 until her death in 1901. She was a woman with a powerful personality who was generally liked by her subjects, and as a result her personality came to define the prevailing attitudes of the last half of the nineteenth century. The common perception, which has defined the Victorian era in the minds of many people since her death, is that she promoted a prudish attitude toward sex and an inflexible attitude about the roles of the various social classes. Some of this was simply a matter of age: Victoria was known to be quite rebellious as a girl, but her decades as the country's leader made her more measured and conservative in her practices, particularly after the death of her beloved husband, Prince Albert, in 1861. Critics believe that the country's reputation for strict morality, which Wilde satirizes in his play and Parker further ridicules in his film, was strongly affected by the forty years the queen spent in mourning.

The class consciousness that is associated with the Victorian era stemmed from the changes in the British social structure throughout the nineteenth century. In part because of the movement against traditional aristocratic rule that had caused, among other notable events,

When Jack travels to London, he claims he is going to see his brother Ernest. (© Morphart Creation / Shutterstock.com)

the American and French revolutions at the end of the previous century, and in part because of the way the Industrial Revolution promoted the rise of cities, Britain developed a substantial middle class during Victoria's reign. In theory, at least, the existence of a middle class ensured that some people born in poverty could rise above their station with hard work and some luck, although historians agree that through the time of Victoria's death at the start of the twentieth century, the upper class still held firmly to its traditions of birth privilege, at least until the beginning of World War I in 1914.

In the play, Lady Bracknell is seen as a defender of the traditional class system, though Parker adds the twist of her having been an impoverished dancer who became a member of the aristocracy by getting impregnated by Lord Bracknell. Her skepticism of Jack because of his unknown parentage may have been a common attitude among the ruling class, but the weakness of such a defensive attitude would have been obvious to Wilde's middle-class audiences.

Anachronisms

Audiences for Oscar Wilde's comedy can assume that it takes place at or around the same time that the play was first performed, in 1895. Oliver Parker's screenplay includes several elements that blur the possible historical setting. Some elements are minor, the kind of inaccuracies that can be expected of any period film, such as the fact that the banjo being played in Algy's apartment is a five-string version, which did not become popular until decades later. Other elements seem to be added to purposely confuse audiences.

The car that Gwendolyn drives out to Jack's Manor House estate, for example, is too technologically advanced: it has a windshield, a steering wheel, and wide rubber tires, giving her a relatively smooth ride down unpaved roads at a time when the first four-wheel automobiles had just been introduced on the market. Similarly, the tattoo that she receives of the name "Ernest" would have been not impossible, but highly unlikely: tattoos were associated with men of lower class, not society women, and the place-ment of the tattoo at the base of the lower back is a strictly modern phenomenon.

Most of the music in the film is ragtime jazz, or something close to it. This includes not only music that is played on the soundtrack, heard by audiences only, but also music played by char-acters within the film, including Algy and his butler, Lane. Ragtime became popular in the southern United States in the 1890s and spread across America after the 1893 World's Fair in Chicago, but it was not common in Europe until well into the twentieth century. The music that is played in the film would have been more likely in the period from 1910 to 1920, when ragtime blended into the rise of jazz music.

It is clear that Parker was not trying to be exact about the time frame of his film, and that he freely adapted elements from different times to give his film a sense of timelessness and irreverence.

CRITICAL OVERVIEW

Critics were generally dismissive of the 2002 release of *The Importance of Being Earnest*. Their indifference in general grew out of their judgments of the changes that Parker, the film's writer and director, made to Wilde's classic play. Jeff Vice, for instance, writing in the *Deseret News* of Salt Lake City, Utah, captures the atti-tude of many critics when he notes that "Oliver Parker has misfired with what would seem to be can't-miss material." To illustrate his problems with the film, Vice draws attention to "the dis-tracting, curious modern-day touches that keep cropping up" and "the uncertain tone of this re-do, which alternates between whimsy and seri-ousness." Jason Best, writing for the BBC, notes that Parker's method of opening up the play for the screen had "mixed results," but his review is generally negative; he declares that "Parker's overheated direction...destroys the poise and rhythm of Wilde's dialogue." He closes his review with the comment that "handled cor-rectly, Wilde's play is a masterpiece of elegant wit and artifice. Here, alas, it collapses like an overcooked soufflé." One of the most overtly negative responses to the film comes from Gabriel Shanks of *Mixed Reviews*, who focuses on Parker's changes in the story and dialogue in a review titled "Why I'd Like to Egg Oliver Parker's House." After eviscerating the film throughout his review, Shanks writes, "As a movie on its own, this film is passably entertain-ing. As an adaptation of the comic masterpiece known as *The Importance of Being Earnest*, Parker should be strung up, drawn and quartered."

The outrage at Parker for changing his source material reaches its peak in the review written by Peter Rainer for *New York* magazine. After noting that Wilde's play "is such a per-fectly conjoined comic creation that it's practi-cally tamperproof," Rainer notes that the best way to adapt the work is "with the utmost seri-ousness," but that Parker's film, by contrast, plays as "a rampaging yukfest." He concludes, in a play on Wilde's own subtitle for his play, that "this movie seems intent on being a trivial comedy for trivial people."

Even positive reviewers pointed out how much Parker's film pales in comparison to its source material. David Ansen, writing in *News-week*'s online publication the *Daily Beast*, cap-tures that mood when he lays the film's problems at the feet of Parker, who, in altering Wilde's work, "just gets in the way, spoiling the rhythm of Wilde's shapely comic scenes with fussy busi-ness," a reference to the images added for the film. Anson at least is willing to acknowledge the positive aspects of the film when he adds, if begrudgingly, "This may be a less than ideal *Earnest*, but it still has delights," including the performances of the actors.

CRITICISM

David Kelly

Kelly is a professor of creative writing and liter-ature. In the following essay, he discusses the requirements for adapting a work to film, and whether the changes Parker made to Wilde's The Importance of Being Earnest *were appropriate and necessary.*

Adapting any kind of artistic work from one medium to another is going to require changes, of course, and making changes is going to annoy fans of the original work. Film, being balanced between art and commerce, is the form where adaptations are most often noticed. It would be impossible to make a play, novel, or other type of work into a successful film without changes. The current trend of adapting comic books or

> THE PHRASE 'GILDING THE LILY' IS NOT USED OFTEN THESE DAYS, BUT THIS IS EXACTLY THE SORT OF SITUATION FOR IT. IT MEANS TAKING SOMETHING RARE AND WONDERFUL, LIKE A LILY, OR WILDE'S CHARACTERIZATION OF CECILY AS A ROMANTIC, AND DESTROYING IT WHILE ATTEMPTING TO SHOW OFF ITS SPLENDOR."

graphic novels offers a good example. They are clearly a film-friendly source, already visual in nature and, with stories that have continued month after month perhaps for decades, offering filmmakers ample plot lines to choose from, as the figures that once could only be captured in an artist's imagination are brought to life. Even so, the movies have had to make alterations. Costumes have been changed to show the faces of high-priced actors instead of hiding secret identities, and the limitations of special effects, though they are loosening, dictate who the heroes can fight, and how.

Fiction adapted to film, meanwhile, cannot help but disappoint. It is the very nature of the two very different media. Text can weave in and out of a character's mind seamlessly in a book, but film is basically external: a voiceover of a character's thoughts can only go on for a short time before audiences start wondering, "Why is this voiceover so long?"

A stage play would seem to be the closest art form to film. Plays tell their stories through things we can see and hear, and their storytelling is trimmed to the approximate amount of time a person can comfortably sit in a theater seat. But moviegoers are accustomed to more variety and spectacle than a story made for a few people in a finite space can give them. Film directors could turn the camera on and let a play run, or they could take a cue from directors of concert films and put cameras all over the stage, to capture views that theater audience members never get. Usually, though, they rewrite a play to make it a screen-worthy story.

This is all to say that Oliver Parker must have felt he had little to lose in adapting Oscar

Wilde's *The Importance of Being Earnest* in 2002. Some segment of the audience was bound to find his work too boring and stagey, and another segment would take any additions or omissions as signs that Parker believed himself to be as important an artist as Wilde himself.

The version of Wilde's play that Parker wrote and directed is interesting for Parker's bold acknowledgment of his responsibility. He certainly gives the play a look that matches the settings Wilde gave his play in 1895: the drawing rooms are all opulent, the grounds of the country estate peaceful and dreamy, and Parker adds crowded dance halls and London streets that evoke an urban, though dated, mood that is appropriate for a sparkling comedy of more than a century past.

Parker's biggest trouble with critics has been the scenes he added. As with any adaptation, there are a few camera shots that any viewer will agree are necessary for projecting a story up on the silver screen. Opinions quickly divide, though, on scenes that supporters, including the film's makers, will argue are perfectly in keeping with how Wilde himself would have told the story if he were making a modern film, but that detractors will find just a pale imitation of Wilde.

First are the sort of things that are useful for opening up a theater space, bringing the story into the world beyond the stage. Modes of transportation are the most conspicuous in this category. A drawing room or a garden can be implied onstage with good set design, but travel is the stage's true enemy. Parker opens the film by showing Algernon Moncrieff racing through the busy London streets: fans who have seen the story on the stage or read it in an English class will be wakened with a jolt. Later, about halfway through the film, the shift from city to country is marked with a hot-air balloon journey. This might be a bit too whimsical for a sour wit like Wilde, but the second half of the play does turn into something of a dreamy romantic reverie, so the cartoonish balloon does make sense: the playwright asked for it.

At about the same time, one character, Gwendolyn, takes a long car drive from the city to the country. Though it has little to do with the reality of either cars or aristocratic young ladies of the late nineteenth century, the drive makes a statement about Gwendolyn's character. It is not a statement that is made about her in the

WHAT DO I SEE NEXT?

- Anthony Asquith directed the first film adaptation of *The Importance of Being Earnest* in 1952. Starring Michael Redgrave, Michael Denison, and Dame Edith Evans, it is a more literal adaptation, hardly changing the settings from what one would see in a theater production. The performances are memorable, and critics consider it hilarious. It is unrated and available on DVD in a Criterion Collection edition, released in 2002.

- Stephen Frye starred in *Wilde*, director Brian Gilbert's 1998 biography of Oscar Wilde, done with lavish sets and costumes. This R-rated film also stars Tom Wilkinson (who plays Dr. Chasuble in *Earnest*), Jude Law, and Vanessa Redgrave. Sony Pictures Home Entertainment released it on DVD in 2002.

- Parker's film's breezy, beautiful settings are reminiscent of the Italian vistas that provide the backdrop for the 1995 romantic comedy *A Month by the Lake*, about a London society woman who vacations near Lake Como in the years before World War II. It stars Vanessa Redgrave, Uma Thurman, and Edward Fox (who plays Lane, the butler, in *Earnest*). The DVD, rated PG, was released by Echo Bridge Home Entertainment in 2011.

- Parker first directed Rupert Everett in another adaptation of a Wilde play, *An Ideal Husband*, in 1999. That film, in which Parker himself played a character named Bunbury, is said to have led to the producers pursuing him for the *Earnest* adaptation. Cate Blanchett, Minnie Driver, and Jeremy Northam also star in the PG-13 rated film, released on DVD by Lionsgate in 1999.

- Parker and Colin Firth also collaborated on *Dorian Gray*, a 2007 adaptation of Wilde's most famous novel, *The Picture of Dorian Gray*. The story is a serious drama about a man whose age and sins never mar his looks; instead, the passing years and his dissipations affect a portrait that he must keep hidden from the world. The film features Ben Barnes in the title role, along with Emilia Fox and Ben Chaplin. It was produced by the same studio, Ealing, that produced *Earnest*. The DVD, rated R, was released by Alliance Films.

- Everett and Firth starred together in the 1984 film *Another Country*. Set in 1932, director Marek Kanievska's adaptation of Julian Mitchell's play features Everett as a young gay upperclassman at a private school and Firth as a classmate who is increasingly interested in Marxism, portraying their struggle against class confinement. The film, rated PG, also stars Kenneth Branagh and Cary Elwes. It is available on DVD from Henstooth Video.

- Wilde is considered an incomparable comic wit. One of the few plays thought to be in the league of *The Importance of Being Earnest* is French playwright Moliere's social satire *Tartuffe; or, The Impostor*, first performed in 1664. The greatest film version of *Tartuffe*, produced in 1925 by legendary German director F. W. Murnau, suffers from being a silent film that lacks Moliere's dialogue. The 1983 version, starring Antony Sher, Nigel Hawthorne, Katy Behean, and Sylvia Coleridge, is considered the most amusing, a production by the Royal Shakespeare Company. The 2005 DVD of this performance is available from RKO Home Video.

- Teens and adults can relate to novelist Jane Austen, shown as a young woman in her first love affair in the 2007 romantic comedy *Becoming Jane* (rated PG), starring Anne Hathaway, James McAvoy, Julie Waters, and Maggie Smith. The film's style and locations evoke the lighthearted mood of *Earnest*. It was released on DVD in 2007 by Lionsgate.

play, where she never shows the kind of courage that such a ride would have required of a woman in her position, but Wilde tended to make his female characters a little too meek for their own good, so there is certainly a case to be made that Parker did everyone a favor by expanding Gwendolyn's rebellious streak. Audiences would find Parker's version of Gwendolyn less whimsical and more relatable.

By the time of the car ride, though, the film has already tinkered enough with Gwendolyn, turning her into a woman with modern sensibilities in a scene that, unfortunately, panders to young audiences but annoys anyone with the slightest historical sense. Parker has Gwendolyn walk into a tattoo parlor and bare her buttocks to have the name *Ernest* tattooed on her lower back, mistakenly thinking that it is the name of the man she loves. It is a low, pointless joke. Her rebelliousness is better established by two scenes that are believable for a Victorian-era woman asserting her independence: the car ride and, later, when she and Cecily smoke cigarettes while they talk. Yes, tattooing occurred at the time, and women sometimes were tattooed, but there is nothing in Gwendolyn's character to make her so bold in breaking social standards. Placing the tattoo where he does makes Parker seem desperate for the approval of younger twenty-first-century audiences, at the expense of historical accuracy (which he is under no obligation to serve) and, even worse, at the expense of the established reality of his film.

Gwendolyn's enhanced character in the film is matched by additions meant to show Cecily, her counterpart, to be a young woman with a huge romantic imagination. Wilde had Cecily chronicle in her diary an imaginary romance with the nonexistent Ernest Worthing. Parker translates this fantasy, expanding on it while dumbing it down, by interspersing into the story wordless shots of Cecily, in her imagination, as a damsel in distress, being rescued by a knight, faceless until Algernon appears in her life and gives a face to her fantasy hero. The phrase "gilding the lily" is not used often these days, but this is exactly the sort of situation for it. It means taking something rare and wonderful, like a lily, or Wilde's characterization of Cecily as a romantic, and destroying it while attempting to show off its splendor. *Gilding* means covering something with gold, which would of course kill a flower, just as the strange bondage fantasies of

Cecily's daydreams in the film smother her romantic imagination and make it less striking, more foolish.

But each of these instances can at least be traced back to character traits Wilde wrote. Parker's most intrusive addition to *The Importance of Being Earnest* takes place onscreen without any words, for just a few seconds, but it changes a major character and alters the story's entire worldview. While Lady Bracknell recites the lines that Wilde wrote about having once been poor herself, before she married Lord Bracknell, Parker shows her as a young chorus dancer, first dancing in a bawdy dance and then sitting on a stuffy old lord's lap, showing him that she is pregnant as the monocle pops from his eye. The implication is that she was once the opposite of what she is now: a fun-loving woman, but also a manipulator, trapping Lord Bracknell into marriage with pregnancy.

As with the other character changes, Parker's overelaboration has some basis in Wilde's original, though not a strong one. Wilde had Lady Bracknell rise from poverty to aristocracy, which makes for plenty of hypocrisy for someone who is so defensive about the possibility of Jack breaching the class system. Making her promiscuous and conniving is just a cheap joke. Parker once again broadens the material, playing up his interpretation of what Wilde only implied, not trusting his viewers to get the implications of these subtleties by themselves. Wilde shows the upper class as being a little shady, but Parker, a century away, shows them as being outright frauds.

All in all, this adaptation of *The Importance of Being Earnest* proves overambitious. It is always necessary for script writers to add material when bringing a story to the screen, but Parker goes too far and adds things that actually change the characters that his film is trying to honor. Despite the misfires, though, the changes that Parker made almost certainly help modern audiences, especially young audiences who do not have a strong background in Victorian social standards, understand and appreciate what is going on in the play. Parker's changes might go beyond what is necessary for a legitimate adaptation, but they are just the thing to ensure that Wilde's play, which amused audiences in the nineteenth and twentieth centuries, will still be funny in the twenty-first.

Source: David Kelly, Critical Essay on *The Importance of Being Earnest*, in *Drama for Students*, Gale, Cengage Learning, 2014.

Source: Paul Connolly, "Movie of the Week," in *Daily Mail* (London, England), February 13, 2010, p. 27.

Paul Connolly

In the following review of Anthony Asquith's 1952 film, Connolly calls Parker's version of The Importance of Being Earnest *"overheated."*

Oscar Wilde's most successful play was last attempted on screen in 2002, when Oliver Parker's overheated version, starring Colin Firth and Reese Witherspoon, sucked all the air from the frothy masterpiece.

Given Anthony Asquith's peerless 1952 adaptation of Wilde's satire on Victorian society, it almost beggars belief that they even tried. His production is perfect in almost every way, from the succinct contraction of some of the scenes of Wilde's 1895 original, through the monumental performance of Dame Edith Evans as Lady Bracknell, to the engorged hues of the Technicolor film process.

Michael Redgrave as Jack Worthing and Michael Denison as Algernon, the two society dandies who both pretend to be called Ernest in order to snaffle their respective fancies (Joan Greenwood's smoky-voiced Gwendolen and Dorothy Tutin's improbably pretty Cecily), share a particularly exuberant chemistry—their rapport seems instinctive. But it's Evans's monstrous Lady Bracknell, the personification of Victorian social hypocrisy, determined to stymie Jack and Algernon's romantic plans, who utterly dominates every scene in which she appears.

THE STORY BEHIND THE FILM

The director of this, the finest movie version of any of the Irish playwright's work, was, as previously mentioned, Anthony Asquith. With an almost impossibly delicious irony, Asquith was the son of H.H. Asquith who, as Home Secretary, brought the criminal charges that led to Wilde's imprisonment for gross indecency (a typically coy Victorian euphemism for homosexual acts) in 1895. It's difficult to decide what kind of reaction Wilde would have had to such a turn of events. Would the playwright have revelled in the preposterousness of his tormentor's son extending and enriching his legacy, or would he have been infuriated at the idea of an Asquith profiting from his work? Given Wilde's well-developed sense of mischief, I'd like to think it would have been the former.

Lloyd Evans

In the following review of a London stage production, Evans calls Wilde's play "flawless" in its structure and asserts "it's the best play ever written."

My favourite play is on its way to the West End and I fully expect to be disappointed. It's not that Peter Gill's production of *The Importance of Being Earnest* hasn't been widely praised. It has. But I prefer to see the play done by amateurs because with the sheen of professionalism stripped away the brilliance of the script becomes all the more evident. *The Importance* has been called the best comedy ever written. I'd say it's the best play ever written. Its structure is flawless. Every theatrical effect it aims for it carries off effortlessly, and there's an integrity to the whole that spreads to every component part. Wilde wrote the play in just three weeks while holidaying in Worthing with his wife and children in 1894. He gave it the subtitle 'A Trivial Comedy for Serious People,' which neatly signals the play's governing motif—paradox.

Everything operates on two levels. The storyline is both perfectly ridiculous and completely sincere. It uses the artifices of sentimental melodrama—a lost heir, mistaken identities, predatory lovers, a faked death, a final reconciliation and three marriages—and deploys them with a degree of panache that is without parallel in the theatrical repertoire.

The play's satirical ethos is itself a brilliant intellectual contradiction. Set amid the Victorian upper classes it mocks all their most cherished values. Its ruthlessness is light-hearted, its cruelty innocent. Jack and Algy are frivolous gadabouts and yet there's genuine depth and sincerity about their approach to life. Their reflections on romance, marriage, education and idleness aren't just superficially amusing, they are also touched with profundity and truth.

All the characters, by some miracle, seem to be both caricatures and real people at once. Lady Bracknell constantly makes daft remarks ('I dislike arguments of any kind. They are always vulgar and often convincing'), and yet she's a recognisable type with serious motives. Finding a rich and well-connected husband for Gwendolen is the gravest responsibility of her life. The delicate balance of opposites appears even in minor narrative twists such as the final disclosure that the moralising spinster Miss Prism (a pun on 'misprision') has a shameful past.

The plot's numerous duplicities are said to be a reflection of Wilde's covert romantic life and his taste for 'feasting with panthers' as trysts with rent boys were called. Those in the know will tell you that the script is studded with secret symbolism. 'Earnest' is a codeword for 'gay.' Cecily means a male prostitute. Silver cigarette cases were used by wealthy homosexuals to pay off their boyfriends. Numerous myths cluster around the word Bunbury. It's supposed to be an in-joke coined by Wilde after he boarded a train at Banbury, met an attractive schoolboy and arranged a further meeting at Sunbury. Others will tell you Bunbury is a well-known Victorian term for a married homosexual. It's equally possible that the notion of a gay code embedded in the text is the fantasy of a later age. According to Donald Sinden the encryption rumours started only in the 1980s. He consulted John Gielgud, an authority on the play, who dismissed the whole idea. 'Absolute nonsense. I would have known.'

Contrary to one well-nurtured myth, the play wasn't universally shunned after Wilde's disgrace and imprisonment. In 1902, just two years after the author's death, the first revival was praised as 'an exhilarating champagne farce.' In 1909 a second revival was planned as a stopgap and ran for eight months. When Charles Laughton took the smallish role of Dr Chasuble in 1934, his 'devastating, brilliant and outrageous lampoon' created the impression that his was the leading part. In 1939 Edith Evans followed suit and upstaged not just the cast but also the entire play with her infamous shrieking delivery of 'a handbag.' Unintentionally, she bequeathed a lasting problem. The scene in which the line appears is perhaps the funniest piece of stage comedy ever written.

Certainly, it contains the best-known joke in the English language, 'To lose one parent may be considered a misfortune, etc.' as well as a handful of other scintillating wisecracks. 'Land has ceased to be either a profit or a pleasure. It gives one position but prevents one from keeping it up.' But the 'handbag' line is neither witty nor funny, and Edith Evans probably felt under

pressure to do something absurd to provoke yet another big laugh. Once her performance had been filmed in 1952, the line passed into legend and it now represents a terrible crash barrier that every new Lady Bracknell must discover some elegant way to negotiate.

I like the play so much that I've now seen it too many times and its best moments have staled with familiarity. Still, there are plenty of under-appreciated lines brimming with humour and psychological truth. A favourite comes in Act Three after Jack has discovered that he's Algy's brother. Lady Bracknell can't remember his real name but suggests that he was probably named after his father, a general. Jack turns to the Army Lists which by some absurd yet perfectly plausible coincidence happen to be on display in his drawing-room. Searching frantically for the right volume he blurts out, 'These delightful records should have been my constant study.' A small but wonderfully silly moment. That a fun-loving aesthete should chastise himself for not poring over the world's most tedious almanac is exquisitely absurd. It's also spot-on psychologically. The secret of his Christian name will determine his future happiness with Gwendolen, so his anxious self-castigation is perfectly in tune with his state of mind.

Another favourite line pops up when Algy is playing the piano off-stage. He enters and asks the butler if he heard what he was playing. 'I didn't think it polite to listen, sir.' This sly dig sounds perfectly deferential and its innocuous tone disguises its subtle sophistication. It draws on a very fine semantic distinction between 'to listen' (intentional action) and 'to hear' (unintentional action). And it's the second line of the play. In fact, now I come to think of it, I can't wait to see the whole thing again. Even done by professionals.

Source: Lloyd Evans, "Why It's Important: Lloyd Evans Believes That Wilde's Comedy Is the Best Play Ever Written," in *Spectator*, January 19, 2008, p. 33.

Jim Kershner

In the following review of a stage production in Spokane, Washington, Kershner considers Wilde's play a precursor to modern dramas that are both silly and smart.

Oscar Wilde's *The Importance of Being Earnest* remains uncommonly popular, considering its lowly genre (the farce) and its advanced age (well over a century): —A West End revival was one of the hottest tickets in London this year. —Rupert Everett, Colin Firth, Reese Witherspoon and Judi Dench starred in a 2002 movie version. —It continues to be a staple at regional theaters. Beginning this weekend, Spokane's professional Actor's Repertory Theatre has chosen the play to kick off its fifth season. Which begs the question: How do you explain the importance of *Importance*? For one thing, it changed the attitude of comedy even into our own time, according to Michael Weaver, who is directing it for ARt. "It's really a subversive play," said Weaver. "It led to the comedies of Kaufman and Hart, to screwball comedies, to Mel Brooks and *American Pie*. It was the first absurdist play in some ways." Weaver paused for a moment to let that absurdity sink in. "So, yes," he said, laughing, "I'd say Oscar Wilde is responsible for *American Pie*." *The Importance of Being Earnest* is that rare creature, a farce both silly and smart. Weaver called it both "really funny" and "one of the great plays of the last 113 years." Here's how *Time* magazine described it, in a 1947 Broadway revival starring John Gielgud: "It is often farce at its most absurd, but it is also farce at its most elegant." The writer called it "insolently monocled in manner" and "killingly high-toned in language." Also, it's strongly identified with a time and place—Edwardian England—yet it somehow seems completely contemporary in its attitudes. Wilde's characters are noted for their irreverence, cynicism, sarcasm and breezy refusal to take anything seriously. This is hardly the stuff of most costume dramas. Wilde himself gave the play the subtitle, "A trivial comedy for serious people." "It's the first example we see of characters saying something, in complete seriousness, that is completely off the wall," said Weaver. And finally, another overriding reason: This is the acknowledged masterpiece of one of the funniest, cleverest and most biting of Irish writers.

"Few comedies of the English stage have such wit, elegance and theatrical dexterity," says the "Oxford Companion to the Theatre."

Nobody could construct a wicked observation like Wilde, and nowhere did he do it better than in this play. Here, for example are some characteristic bits of Wildean wisdom: —"Relations are simply a tedious pack of people, who haven't got the remotest knowledge of how to live, nor the smallest instinct about when to die."—"I never travel without my diary. One should always have something sensational to read in the train." —"The good ended happily, and the bad unhappily. That is what fiction means." Wilde averages about 20 of these killer epigrams in every act of *The Importance of Being Earnest*. The plot is a relatively standard farce involving two separate cases of mistaken identity. Jack needs an excuse to run off to London, so he invents a wicked brother that he has to look after. Algernon wants to see Jack's niece, so he pretends to be the wicked brother. Complications ensue. Yet out of this comes a number of memorable characters—notably Lady Bracknell, who has been played by the most formidable actresses of the 20th (and 21st) century, including at least three certified dames: Dame Edith Evans, Dame Judi Dench and Dame Margaret Rutherford. In the ARt production, Karen Nelsen (fresh from a brilliant role in last year's *Long Day's Journey Into Night*) will sink her teeth into the Lady Bracknell role. Damon Mentzer will play Jack and Jon Lutyens will play Algernon. Patrick Treadway will play the Rev. Chasuble. The rest of the cast includes Caryn Hoaglund-Trivett, Kari McClure, Carolyn Crabtree, Jeremiah Hatch and Brandon Montang.

Source: Jim Kershner, "Utmost 'Importance': ARt Presents Ageless Wilde Classic to Open Fifth Season," in *Spokesman-Review* (Spokane, WA), August 21, 2008.

Pat Nason

In the following review, Nason criticizes Parker's decision to add physical comedy to Wilde's "talky" play.

Actor Colin Firth tried to tell a friend the story behind his new movie, *The Importance of Being Earnest*, but he gave up when he realized the real appeal of Oscar Wilde's comedy masterpiece isn't the story—it's the chance to see people at their most ridiculous.

"You can't pitch this movie," said Firth. "I try to explain it, and I realize there's no point. There's this guy who has a boring life so he pretends to be someone else—as soon as you hear yourself explaining it, you give up and just say, 'Go see it and listen to the way it will make you laugh.'"

Firth—best known to American movie audiences for *Bridget Jones's Diary* (2001) and *Shakespeare in Love* (1998)—said the story is there more or less to provide characters with opportunities to deliver some of the wittiest dialogue Oscar Wilde ever wrote.

"In all of the other Oscar Wilde plays, you can tell a very compelling story," he said. "*A Woman of No Importance* has plot and conflict. You can tell that story without raising a single laugh. *An Ideal Husband, Lady Windermere's Fan*, all could be told as serious dramas."

But try to get serious about *Earnest*, said Firth, and it "flips out of your hands like a bar of soap."

For the record, the story goes like this.

Two young gentlemen in Victorian England decide to twist the truth to make their lives more exciting. Jack Worthing (Firth) has invented a brother, Earnest, whom he uses as a pretext to leave his dull country life and visit the ravishing Gwendolyn Fairfax (Frances O'Connor) in London.

Algernon Montcrieff (Rupert Everett) appropriates the fictitious identity to get somewhere with Worthing's young and beautiful ward, Cecily Cardew (Reese Witherspoon) at the country manor.

When all four young lovers wind up together, Jack and Algernon have some serious explaining to do if they don't want to lose their ladies.

Oliver Parker (*An Ideal Husband*) adapted Wilde's play and directed the movie—adding some physical comedy that some critics have found objectionable. The physicality is intended to transform the piece from a "talky" play to the kind of visual experience that moviegoers expect.

"I think this film definitely plays to a crowd," said Firth, who counts himself as a Wilde fan of long standing.

"I can barely remember a time before I was a fan," he said. "He's just sort of in the air in the English-speaking world. Quotes float about."

Even with Parker's approach, *The Importance of Being Earnest* faces a stiff challenge breaking into a marketplace dominated by movies that appeal to the widest possible audience.

"I'm not even sure I would be rushing out to see it if I didn't know it was good," said Firth. "I am hoping word of mouth will help."

Audiences seemed to respond to the movie in limited early release. Over the Memorial Day holiday weekend, it grossed $470,000 at 38

theaters, for a solid average of $12,368 per theatre. It is scheduled to expand to 40 markets this Friday.

Source: Pat Nason, "Wilde Comedy May Challenge Audiences," in *United Press International*, May 28, 2002.

Ben Walters

In the following review, Walters concludes that the success of the film is due more to the quality of the original play than to the director's interpretation.

London, 1895. Man-about-town Algernon Moncrieff and his friend Jack Worthing discover they are both leading double lives: Algy has invented a friend, 'Bunbury,' whose ill health provides an excuse to avoid unwanted social occasions, while Hertfordshire-based Jack poses as his own feckless, non-existent brother 'Ernest' when in London. Algy's cousin Gwendolen and 'Ernest' are in love, but her imposing mother, Lady Bracknell, vetoes the match on learning that as a baby Jack was found in a handbag at Victoria Station.

Jack returns to his country house to announce the death of his wayward brother, only for Algy to arrive posing as Ernest. He and Jack's young ward Cecily fall in love, to Jack's outrage. When Gwendolen and Cecily, both of whom longed to marry a man named Ernest, discover that neither of the men is genuine, they reject them. The couples are eventually reconciled but Lady Bracknell arrives and maintains her objections to Jack, who in turn refuses to give Cecily permission to marry Algernon. Lady Bracknell recognises Cecily's tutor, Miss Prism; 35 years earlier she left Lady Bracknell's family home with a baby and never returned. Jack turns out to be Lady Bracknell's nephew, Algy's younger brother. The marriages are approved.

The premiere of Oliver Parker's last film *An Ideal Husband* apparently went so well that Harvey Weinstein, whose Miramax was one of the film's backers, suggested a follow-up there and then. If he was after more of the same, then Weinstein got what he wanted. Parker's second Wildean adaptation follows the same recipe as its predecessor: the casting and performances do enjoyable justice to the text, but the rationale behind transferring it to the screen remains unclear.

Anthony Asquith's 1952 film is rightly remembered as stagey and uncinematic, but it's hard to imagine how so consummately theatrical a piece as *The Importance of Being Earnest* could be successfully translated to the screen. Centred on foundling Jack and dandyish Algy, who fall in love with girls who believe they are both called 'Ernest' and must come clean without scaring them off, it is a play about acting and appearance, the dissembling sleights of hand which pass smoothly in society or the theatre but are less well served by the mechanical record of film. Not only does the intimacy of the theatre insist on the audience acknowledging its position in this daisy-chain of deceit, but the unity of action that Wilde employs is the milieu in which such heady concoctions thrive.

Parker's approach of 'opening out' the plays with flashbacks, multiple locations and a weakness for concrete details could therefore be seen as precisely what is not required. He seems determined to remove as many ambiguities as possible, effectively denying the characters their ability to deceive us as well as their foils. For instance, when the play has Algy casually tearing up the morning's letters, we might deduce they are bills but respect his nonchalance: the film, however, provides a close-up of the bottom line and inserts some despairing dialogue to drive the point home. Decisions such as this compromise the spirit of the play without promoting any filmic re-imagining. The guiding principle— also apparent in Parker's *Othello* (1995)— appears to be choosing things simply because they are possible on film but not on stage. This produces a wide variety of results. Some are gimmicky (Algy's arrival at the manor by hot-air balloon), some bizarre (Cecily's fantasies in the form of Pre-Raphaelite tableaux) and some work against the operation of the text: exchanges between Algy and Jack can skip across three or four locations within minutes, breaking the momentum of the dialogue. Others, however, bring far happier results: the exterior shooting in the country scenes, for instance, allows Parker to tap directly into the bucolic tradition Wilde consciously recalls. And, earlier on, the relocation of Lady Bracknell's interrogation of Jack to her home turf suits her domineering self-satisfaction—enthroned in a cathedral of a drawing room, she is flanked by secretaries with the air of courtiers or familiar spirits. As Bracknell, Judi Dench deploys the formidable regal demeanour, with occasional twinkle, familiar from *Mrs Brown* and *Shakespeare in Love*, and delivers the handbag line in a stunned choke.

The performances in general are good enough to ensure the film is consistently entertaining: Dench is nicely balanced by Anna Massey's gormless, birdlike Miss Prism, whose relationship with Tom Wilkinson's Dr Chasuble has been beefed up with material from an early draft of Wilde's. *Ideal Husband* veteran Rupert Everett's suavely disreputable Algy has a touch of Terry-Thomas about him and Frances O'Connor's randy Gwendolen makes a fruity contrast to Joan Greenwood's simpering turn in the 1952 version. The company's lively account of the characters and dialogue should prove attractive enough to keep Weinstein content, yet this is more to the playwright's credit than to Parker's.

Source: Ben Walters, "*The Importance of Being Earnest*," in *Sight and Sound*, Vol. 12, No. 9, 2002, pp. 61–62.

SOURCES

Ansen, David, "Wilde at Heart," in *Daily Beast*, May 26, 2002, http://www.thedailybeast.com/newsweek/2002/05/26/wilde-at-heart.html (accessed June 10, 2013).

Best, Jason, Review of *The Importance of Being Earnest*, BBC website, September 3, 2002, http://www.bbc.co.uk/films/2002/08/21/the_importance_of_being_earnest_2002_review.shtml (accessed June 10, 2013).

Heller, Steven, "The Colorful, Subversive History of Women Getting Tattoos," in *Atlantic*, April 4, 2013 http://www.theatlantic.com/sexes/archive/2013/04/the-colorful-subversive-history-of-women-getting-tattoos/274658/ (accessed July 11, 2013).

"History of Ragtime," in *Performing Arts Encyclopedia*, Library of Congress website, September 29, 2006, http://lcweb2.loc.gov/diglib/ihas/loc.natlib.ihas.200035811/default.html (accessed July 11, 2013).

The Importance of Being Earnest, directed by Oliver Parker, DVD, Lionsgate, 2002.

Loftus, Donna, "The Rise of the Victorian Middle Class," BBC website, http://www.bbc.co.uk/history/british/victorians/middle_classes_01.shtml (accessed July 11, 2013).

"Queen Victoria (1819–1901)," Victorian Station website, http://www.victorianstation.com/queen.html (accessed July 11, 2013).

Rainer, Peter, Review of *The Importance of Being Earnest*, in *New York*, May 27, 2002, http://nymag.com/nymetro/movies/reviews/6033/ (accessed June 10, 2013).

Shanks, Gabriel, "Why I'd Like to Egg Oliver Parker's House: A Rant," in *Mixed Reviews*, 2003, http://

www.mixedreviews.net/maindishes/2002/earnest/ear
nest.shtml (accessed June 13, 2013).

Vice, Jeff, Review of *The Importance of Being Earnest*, in
Deseret News (Salt Lake City, UT), May 31, 2002, http://
movies.deseretnews.com/movies/2000002853/The-Impor
tance-of-Being-Earnest (accessed June 13, 2013).

FURTHER READING

Cohn, Elisha, "Oscar Wilde's Ghost: The Play of Imitation," in *Victorian Studies*, Vol. 54, No. 3, Spring 2012,
pp. 475–85.

> This academic essay starts with a discussion of
> Wilde's appearance during a séance in 1923
> and goes on to discuss his influence on imi-
> tators of his style throughout the twentieth
> century. Other works by Wilde are discussed,
> but Parker's film is not.

Loewenstein, Joseph, "Oscar Wilde and the Evasion of
Principles," in *South Atlantic Quarterly*, Vol. 84, No. 4,
Fall 1985, pp. 392–400.

> This article, which has been reprinted in collec-
> tions about Wilde and on the Internet, captures
> the playwright's wit in explaining the impor-
> tance of this particular work in the history of
> literature.

Mendelsohn, Daniel, "The Two Oscar Wildes," in *New
York Review of Books*, October 10, 2002, p. 18.

> This long, detailed article is a review of Oliver
> Parker's film from a strictly literary perspec-
> tive, showing an intense appreciation of
> Wilde's artistry and the challenges faced by
> the filmmakers.

Robbins, Ruth, *Oscar Wilde*, Continuum, 2011.

> This brief overview of the writer's life is concise
> enough to give students a good idea of his
> importance and is written directly enough to
> evoke a sense of his inimitable style.

SUGGESTED SEARCH TERMS

Oscar Wilde AND The Importance of Being Earnest

Oscar Wilde AND Oliver Parker

Rupert Everett AND Oscar Wilde

Rupert Everett AND Colin Firth

The Importance of Being Earnest AND film adaptation

The Importance of Being Earnest AND Victorian morals

Oscar Wilde AND social satire

The Importance of Being Earnest AND wit

Victorian literature AND parentage

Oscar Wilde AND love

Nine-Ten

WARREN LEIGHT

2001

Warren Leight's *Nine-Ten* is a brief one-act play set on the eve of the terrorist attacks against the United States on September 11, 2001. It was first performed just thirteen days after the attacks and may be the earliest piece of literature to deal with 9/11. Its treatment is ironic, focusing on what seem to be everyday events and only revealing at the end that they take on a wholly different significance because they take place on September 10, the day before the attack. Working within a surprisingly classical dramatic form, Leight deals with many of the issues that were already emerging in American culture as a result of the attacks, such as racial profiling and the intrusion of security measures into the lives of ordinary Americans (which has remained a highly controversial issue). He also explores the clash of cultures between East and West that led to the attack. Though somewhat obscure to the general public, Leight's work has in recent years become more widely known since he is one of the main creators of the *Law & Order* television franchise. *Nine-Ten* is available in *Dark, No Sugar* (2007), a collection of plays by Leight.

AUTHOR BIOGRAPHY

Leight was born in the borough of Queens, New York City, on January 17, 1957, but grew up in another borough, Manhattan. His father was a

Warren Leight *(© Astrid Stawiarz | Getty Images Entertainment |*
Getty Images)

jazz musician, a sideman, meaning that he would
play in recordings and with established bands
when an additional performer was needed. A
great deal of Leight's dramatic work is based
on his father's life. Leight attended Stanford
University on a scholarship and took a degree
in journalism but has principally worked as a
dramatist and especially as a screenwriter for
film and television. His work has been nominated for the Pulitzer Prize and for Tony Awards
several times.

Upon graduation Leight took a series of odd
jobs in an effort to support his parents. His
father's career as a musician, though memorable, had left him constantly on the verge of bank-
ruptcy. Leight's first produced script was for the
low-budget horror movie *Mother's Day* in 1980.
A more important project was the documentary
*Before the Nickelodeon: The Cinema of Edwin
S. Porter* (1982), a history of the very earliest
American cinema based on Leight's screenplay.
He has written numerous scripts and doctored
(edited and rewritten) still more. In 1993, he

directed the romantic comedy *The Night We
Never Met.*

The middle part of Leight's career was anch-
ored in stage drama. His most successful stage
play was the off-Broadway production *Mayor!*
(1985), about the rivalry between Ed Koch,
mayor of New York City in the 1970s and
1980s, and businesswoman Leona Helmsley.
He has written numerous plays about jazzmen
in New York in the 1930s, including *Side Man*
(1998) and *The Glimmer Brothers* (1999).
Although Leight's jazz plays are to a large extent
based on events from his father's life, they are
also notable for achieving a universal appeal
based on themes that resonate with audiences
of his generation. Leight's *Nine-Ten* must be
one of the first artistic responses to the 9/11
terrorist attacks on the World Trade Center in
New York. It premiered on September 24, 2001,
only thirteen days after the twin towers
collapsed.

Leight's greatest success has come in television. He began to write episodes for various
television shows, including *Law & Order: Criminal Intent,* for which in 2006 he became the head
writer and executive producer. He stayed with
the show until 2009. In 2012, he became the head
writer and executive producer for *Law & Order:
Special Victims Unit.* As of 2013, he was attempting to produce a film version of *Side Man.*

PLOT SUMMARY

Nine-Ten is set in the waiting room for the jury
pool in a Manhattan civil court at about 9:00 in
the morning as potential jurors are arriving.
John and Nick are already waiting for the selection process to start.

At the beginning of the play another potential juror, Lyris, enters and asks whether she is in
the right place, known in the technical language
of the court printed on her jury summons as
"Part B." John responds with a pun that alludes
to the first line of the famous soliloquy from
Shakespeare's *Hamlet,* which begins "To be or
not to be, that is the question." Although this is
quite silly, it is not unrealistic small talk, and the
point is that it builds up a human connection
between John and Lyris. John explains that
although their summons say 8:30 a.m., because
many people will arrive late the process of jury
selection won't start until about 9:10. This

strongly suggests to the audience that this time provides the enigmatic title of the play, directing them away from its real significance.

Another juror, Leslie, soon arrives, and Nick engages her in a manner similar to how John did Lyris, answering the question "Part B?" with the rhyming retort, "Must be." But Leslie does not take up the theme. She starts to complain, to no one in particular. First she talks about her failed attempts to get out of jury duty over the phone. Then she starts talking about the difficulties and delays imposed by the elaborate security necessary to enter the courthouse, and how she cannot smoke in the building but cannot leave without going through security again. Nick responds that he intends to get out of jury duty by telling the judge he is a felon. Although no felon would have been sent a summons, he anticipates the judge will believe him because of "racial profiling." Leslie is impressed by the cleverness of this scheme.

John and Lyris have also been chatting, but the audience hears only the end of their discussion. Lyris says, "My brother's in the same building. Security guard. You probably don't know him." She means the same building where John works. Given John's profession as an international bond trader, and the overall context of the play, this can only mean the World Trade Center, although, owing to the elliptical way it is introduced, this might not be apparent on first viewing.

Finally, the last character to arrive is Kearrie. John and Lyris try to revive the Shakespeare pun with her, but she angrily snaps at them, "It's too early for cute." She too wants out of jury duty, since she is scheduled to leave on a business trip the next day.

After a moment's reflection, John recognizes Kearrie. He has to remind her that his name is John McCormack. They had been classmates ten years earlier at the Wharton School (at the University of Pennsylvania) and even worked on class projects together. Kearrie finally recognizes him, too. She did not think much of him then because his grades were inferior to hers, and she thinks even less of him now when she learns he is still stuck in the same job he got when he finished school. Lyris mentions that she attended the same school, but after they left, and explains that she is now working as a sort of New Age guru, healing people through the spiritual energy generated by dance.

Meanwhile, Nick and Leslie complain to each other. Leslie had been spending a long weekend in the Hamptons but cut it short when she remembered her jury summons. They joke, comparing the financial professionals who can afford to live full-time in the exclusive community of the Hamptons to sharks. Leslie complains about the traffic she encountered in the middle of the night, and the difficulties in finding a parking spot near her apartment on returning to the city at a very late hour.

John starts to admire Lyris for her spiritual work, which disgusts Kearrie. She does her own complaining now, about how she has a phone or other electronic device wirelessly connected to the Internet (then a fairly new thing), with a program that would let her make an advantageous business deal then and there, except the wi-fi signal keeps fading in and out, because the courthouse does not have its own wi-fi.

Kearrie eventually gets through on her phone to someone in her office. Meanwhile, Nick and Leslie complain to each other about how they've been inconvenienced by film crews working in their neighborhoods in the past.

Lyris starts to instruct John how to dance in her own spiritual style. Rather than heighten the attention that is being drawn to the scene she is making by demurring, he accepts. But he begs off when he realizes people are staring at him anyway. Nick and Leslie are appalled. "That is sick the way he's flirting with her," Leslie judges.

Finally, the court officer gets things under way. Before hearing people's excuses for getting out of jury duty (the most common reaction to the jury duty summons), he wants to make sure everyone is in the right place, so he specifies the court they are in, Civil Courts Part B. Also, in the last line of the play, he gives the date: "Today is Monday, September 10th . . . Two thousand and one"—the day before the 9/11 attacks. For the audience at the premiere of the play, this was only two weeks in the past.

CHARACTERS

Court Officer

The court officer has the smallest role in the play and appears only at the end, to begin the actual process of jury selection, though he gets no further with that than announcing the date in the last line. The one thing he says that is more than strictly necessary for the duties of his office is to acknowledge that most people in the jury pool actively resents having to do jury service and want to get out of it. This may signal a message from Leight as the playwright that one reason behind what will happen the next day is the failure of Americans to take their duty as citizens seriously enough, or at least that public apathy is partly responsible for responses to the attack such as racial profiling and the surrender of personal liberties to government security measures. The officer's line "Most of you will get to go back to your life in two or three days" also has a larger significance. Although, in fact, most Americans would go on more or less as they did before the 9/11 attacks (the 2008 bursting of the housing bubble, for instance, had a far more devastating effect on the everyday lives of Americans), there was a powerful sense at the time that no American's life would ever be the same, giving the officer's words an ironic meaning.

Leslie

Leslie's single function in the play seems to be to complain. Two of her complaints have a particular significance. The less important of these is her soliloquy about being inconvenienced by film crews shooting television programs or movies in her neighborhood. This must be an in-joke, since Leight is often on the other side of this nuisance as a writer and producer of shows that are shot in the city. More importantly she complains about the security screening she has to go through in order to get into the courthouse. She feels as if she is being treated like a "serial killer." Worse, if she goes outside to smoke a cigarette, she will have to go through all the security screening again. At that time such screenings were rare except in courts and prisons. But after the 9/11 attacks, the first thing that changed in American life was the expansion of security measures, especially surrounding airports. For the first few days, no civilian planes were allowed to fly at all, and when service resumed, the airports were subject to greatly enhanced security screenings that were widely viewed as intrusive and inconvenient, although the greater scrutiny was and is tolerated because of the fears inspired by the 9/11 attacks. In the play, Leslie's complaints foreshadow what the audience quickly came to experience in real life.

John McCormack

John McCormack stands precisely in the middle between the two extremes represented by Kearrie and Lyris. He has ostensibly made the same career choices as Kearrie, but only because this was what was expected of him, not because he felt the same personal drive as she did. He probably makes a better living than most people, but what he wants to do is live his life, not constantly get more money and climb higher in the organization. He tells Lyris directly what gives comfort to his life: "Same office, same view. Married my junior high school sweetheart. We take the same train to work. We have the same lunch. Tuna. On rye. No mayo." He adds, "It's not so bad, once you get used to it," clearly referring to more than the lack of mayonnaise on his sandwich. Because he lacks Kearrie's drive, he is vulnerable to Lyris's seduction. He claims that, although he turned out like Kearrie, he had always wanted to be like Lyris. But when he begins to actually carry out his desire, to dance with her, he soon turns away, unwilling to be singled out for ridicule by his peers.

Nick

Nick plays a smaller role than most of the other characters. Like Kearrie and Leslie, he wants to get out of jury duty, and he has a plan to accomplish this that Leslie thinks clever. He will tell the judge that he cannot serve on a jury because he is a felon. However, if he were a felon, his name would have been excluded from the pool of potential jurors and he would never have been sent a summons in the first place. So he means he is going to lie. But he thinks the judge will nevertheless believe him because of "racial profiling." While the text of the play does not identify the race of any of the characters, Nick certainly means that because he is black, he can rely on the judge's inherent racism to make him believe that any black man is a felon. This use is ironic, but racial profiling is an operative fact in law enforcement in which police presume that certain races or ethnic groups are more likely than others to be associated with certain crimes.

Lyris Touzet

Lyris, as a New Age healer, is an outsider to the mainstream business culture embraced by Kearrie and inhabited by John. When John mentions that he and Kearrie both took MBA degrees from the Wharton School in 1991, Lyris responds that she must have just missed them since she attended the same school somewhat later. She may mean the University of Pennsylvania, of which the Wharton school is a part, or she may have taken a business degree also, since as much business acumen is needed to be an entrepreneur in her field as any other. As a person, she seems far more engaging, and far more happy, than any of the other characters. She is able to draw John out of the private little world he inhabits and immediately relates closely to anyone who gives her a chance. In contrast, when she tries to reach out to Kearrie, she is met with condemnation and angrily barked orders.

Kearrie Whitman

All of the characters in *Nine-Ten* are remarkably flat and uninteresting stereotypes. Before hastening to the judgment that Leight is a playwright lacking in talent, rushing to be the first to write a play dealing with the 9/11 tragedy, a judgment that cannot be sustained by the artfulness of the play, it is worth considering other possible reasons for this style of character presentation. Leight presents his characters as broad stereotypes within an ideological dialectic. Kearrie and Lyris represent the poles of conformity and rebellion, modernity and tradition, and other similar dichotomies. A dialectical process ought to be resolved into a new synthesis. Such a resolution would drive the plot of the play along more typical dramatic lines. But no such development or synthesis takes place. Instead the play ends abruptly, enticing the audience to work through the unspoken climactic events that will take place the next day during the attack. The conflict between Kearrie and Lyris is a microcosm of the larger drama that will then play out. One could imagine, for example, Kearrie's abuse of Lyris leading to her getting slapped in the face. But that explosion of emotion into physical violence would not change anything, as the two characters would remain what they were before and understand what had happened (or rather misunderstand it) from diametrically opposed viewpoints. And that is exactly what will happen on the next day, only writ large. One culture, or rather a tiny, sharp splinter of that culture, that perceives itself as embodying tradition, independence, and virtue, will lash out violently against another culture that it perceives as controlling, hegemonic, bullying and destructive.

Kearrie has only one interest, to advance her career, which means her wealth and power. She is resentful of the jury summons for the same reason she resents being unable to make a good wi-fi connection in the courthouse. It is not merely that these obstacles represent immediate impediments to her plans but that they effectively put controls on her behavior. In her view, she is the one who ought to be controlling other people. She has completely sacrificed her identity to her desire to get ahead. Although she is a woman, she takes on exaggerated masculine mannerisms, such as her constant cursing, not out of some sort of feminist idealism, but because that is the persona that she feels will best advance her career.

THEMES

American Culture

In *Nine-Ten*, Leight presents an image of normative American culture. Most of the characters are middle-class office workers, primarily concerned with upward economic mobility through their work in the financial industry, which is the foundation of the US economy. Several attended the Wharton School, one of the most prominent business institutions of its kind and the origin of a network of connections and patronage which is vital to their careers. In the compressed world of the play, this particular social configuration stands as a symbol for the larger world of middle-class life. They are also exercising one of the principle rights and duties of Americans as citizens of a free society, doing jury duty.

But it is precisely here that this ideal of American life starts to break down. Kearrie, most vocally, has serious objections to this duty, because it interferes with her business affairs. It is evident, on the other hand, that John has no interest in his career, or at least not the kind of interest Kearrie approves of. He is content with his life as it is: "I like things as they are. I've had the same job for ten years." He is happy in his family life and has reduced his job as a bond trader to a comfortable routine. This leaves him safe and secure but with little chance for advancement. To Kearrie, this makes him a "loser," since she is only concerned with advancing her career and with it her wealth and power. They are all agreed, however, that people who have found the kind of success Kearrie aspires to

TOPICS FOR FURTHER STUDY

- The literature of the 9/11 attacks includes a large number of graphic novels, of which by far the most important is Art Spiegelman's *In the Shadow of No Towers* (2004). Already a successful novelist and graphic artist, best known for his *Maus*, an allegory of the Holocaust, Spiegelman lived in lower Manhattan in 2001 and was an eyewitness to the collapse of the World Trade Center towers. Read *In the Shadow of No Towers*, then make your own adaptation of *Nine-Ten* as a graphic novella.

- The 9/11 attacks originated in Afghanistan, and after the US invasion of the country, its society was even more profoundly disrupted and changed than America's. Khaled Hosseini is an Afghan author who writes in English. His novel *A Thousand Splendid Suns* (2008) is set over a period of thirty years, both before and after 2001, and explores the transformation of his country. Write your own short story about how the life of an American family was changed by 9/11, such as by a death or by military service in Afghanistan.

- Blogging was already well developed in 2001. Search the Internet for blogs that dealt with the 9/11 attacks at the time. Also look for photos taken by bystanders on the Manhattan streets and posted to the Internet. These will provide a response to the events even more immediate than Leight's *Nine-Ten*. Write a paper comparing these early responses to a more considered perspective on the attacks that has developed in the intervening time.

- Write a play about the 9/11 attacks that uses *Nine-Ten* as its first act. Explore what happens to one or more of the characters on the next day. With classmates, act out your play and record it. Show your play to the class.

are "sharks," predators who have built their careers at the expense of others. Significantly, they do not necessarily consider this term and

this analogy as a condemnation. John, at least, realizes that there may be something wrong with this way of life and looks on the alternative presented by Lyris's countercultural way of life as seductive. "It's funny, I always wanted to be a spiritual dancer," he tells her. Another factor that is implied, rather than fully explored in the short scope of the play, is the particular kind of work that they do. Two or more work in the World Trade Center, which concentrated the offices of international traders and investors. Though they may play only small roles as individuals, they are part of the international process of globalization that exports American culture to the rest of the world and also exploits developing countries by extracting wealth from them. The World Trade Center was chosen as the target of the 9/11 attacks precisely because of the resentment this activity causes among traditional cultures. Leight is calling the imperialistic nature of American culture into question.

Bohemianism

Lyris stands in contrast to the mainstream culture embraced by the other characters. The counterculture that she represents is still sometimes called *bohemian*, after the era in the nineteenth century when French intellectuals opposed to the official culture of state-run institutions lived in the district of Paris inhabited by poor Bohemian immigrants. Lyris describes herself as a "Spiritual Dancer. And healer." Elaborating she says, "I heal people, through movement. Rhythm. Every person has their own . . . pulse. Below the surface that—." She adds further, "I help them to get in touch with their inner—." Kearrie in particular holds Lyris in complete contempt and reacts to her with scorn and hostility, cursing at her. John, on the other hand, is seduced by the perspective she brings.

Mainstream society operates on the basis of science, but Lyris lives in a world that is defined by magic. Perhaps more importantly, she stands for personal growth, as opposed to the acquisitiveness that is the foundation of the other characters' lives. Like much else in the brief play, Lyris's worldview is not explored in depth but is aligned with traditional culture as it existed before the scientific and capitalist revolutions of the seventeenth century. Thus she has something in common with the traditional cultures of the developing world that are about to strike back at the hegemonic culture of the West through the 9/11 attacks. The government of Saudi Arabia, for instance, still believes in magic and regularly

The action of the play happens in New York on the day before the terrorist attacks on the World Trade Center. (© Northfoto | Shutterstock.com)

prosecutes people for practicing witchcraft, resulting in executions as recently as 2007. And hundreds, perhaps thousands, of people are executed or lynched every year for practicing magic in many parts of the developing world. Lyris's particular beliefs and practices probably do not have extensive contact with any authentic tradition of spiritual practice, though she probably believes that they do. Her kind of New Age spirituality is a manufactured product of Western culture that depends on a kind of spurious or imitative tradition. But the same can be said of the fundamentalist ideology that inspired the 9/11 attacks. They are both symptoms of a desire to return to a lost world of tradition that cannot now be recaptured in preference to the commodified globalized culture.

STYLE

Drama

Aristotle, the first literary critic, defined the literary characteristic of drama based on the work of the Athenian dramatists of the fifth century

BCE. Dramas were performed every year over most of that century in an annual festival, in which twelve plays were presented by three different authors. Of these, about seventy plays survive, all by Aeschylus, Sophocles, and Euripides. According to Aristotle's analysis, the purpose of drama was to imitate life in order to evoke fear and pity in the audience. It achieved its purpose, Aristotle felt, by dealing with the lives of great men and taking a strictly serious approach to its subject matter. At the same time, Athenian culture also supported comedy. This form was similar to drama in having three actors and a singing and dancing chorus, and also had annual dramatic festivals. The greatest comic playwright was Aristophanes, eleven of whose plays survive. According to Aristotle, comedy achieved its unique character by imitating, and exaggerating, the ridiculous parts of life, especially the grotesque. Although Aristophanes's verse is elegant and sophisticated, his subject matter is obscene and politically vicious.

In Aristotle's view, the two genres could, or should, never be mixed. But later dramatists have not always been so scrupulous. Shakespeare's dramas, for instance, all contain lewd and obscene comic relief. Given its brevity, Leight's *Nine-Ten* follows the form of Aristotelian drama quite closely, in terms of eliciting fear and pity from the audience, and following the dramatic unities of time and place by playing out in a single location in real time. But he introduces subversive and comic elements, in his criticism of both establishment culture and counterculture, that Aristotle would have found out of place.

Irony

Irony is a device by which an author says exactly the opposite of what he means, and yet conveys his true meaning to the audience. This is generally achieved by a sarcastic or satirical tone to the ironic statement, to which the reader must be very attentive. It can also be achieved by setting up an expectation that a certain event will turn out one way, then having it suddenly turn out in some unexpected way that changes the meaning of what had gone before. The term *dramatic irony* is used to describe a play whose plot reaches a conclusion that is markedly different from what has been signaled throughout the play. The most notable example of this is the ancient dramatist Sophocles's *Oedipus the King*, in which the title character conducts an investigation into his father's murder, only to find out that he himself is guilty of it. *Nine-Ten* is entirely ironic in this sense. Most of the characters do little but complain about jury duty, but two of them (at least) will be inside the twin towers when the planes hit, unless they are serving on a jury. The play is ostensibly about a group of professionals who wish to avoid jury duty (or are at best resigned to it), but the meaning of the play is only revealed when the audience learns the date of the play. Leight uses misdirection to build up this impression. The characters' jury summons tell them to be at the courthouse at 8:30 a.m., but the selection process is said not to begin until a little later: "around nine ten they start calling names." This would make the audience think that the title of the play refers to 9:10 a.m. and that the action of the play will somehow be resolved in the jury selection process. Another kind of dramatic irony occurs when a character speaks a line that has a double meaning, a line which the audience has been primed to take one way, but which the characters take in another. Leight's play hinges on this kind of irony in the last line when the clerk reads out the date:

"Today is Monday, September 10th . . . Two thousand and one." To the characters this is just another day, but the audience alone knows its significance as the day before the 9/11 attacks.

HISTORICAL CONTEXT

Osama bin Laden and al-Qaeda

On September 11, 2001, operatives of al-Qaeda, an Islamist terrorist network led by Osama bin Laden, hijacked four American airliners. Two of them were flown into the towers of the World Trade Center in New York, causing the buildings to collapse and killing three thousand people who had been working inside. The third plane was flown into the Pentagon, the headquarters of the US Department of Defense in northern Virginia, and the fourth was intended to crash either into the White House or the Capitol, but it crashed in rural Pennsylvania during a struggle in which the passengers tried to regain control of the aircraft. In sum, this was the deadliest terror attack ever made on US soil. Its effects have significantly changed US culture and determined the course of major geopolitical events throughout the world since that time.

Bin Laden, who came from a wealthy Saudi family, first rose to prominence fighting the occupation of Afghanistan by the Soviet Union in the 1970s. He probably did not even understand what Communism was and certainly had no interest in resisting its expansion on ideological grounds as they are understood in the West. He merely wanted to preserve the integrity of the Islamic world as a goal in itself. He certainly had no interest in the competing Western ideology of capitalism, but he built up his terrorist network, which eventually became al-Qaeda, with US support that he accepted on the principle that *my enemy's enemy is my friend*. To bin Laden, the Soviet Union and the United States were in essence indistinguishable. They presented the same threat against his version of Islamic traditionalism (which was based on his own ideological view of history and had very little to do with the facts of the matter). His goal was to purify the Islamic world according to his own interpretation of Islam. As strange as it may seem to an outsider, he viewed the oppressive regime in Saudi Arabia as excessively liberal and Westernized. His ultimate goal was to replace the Saudi government with what he considered an ideologically pure

COMPARE
&
CONTRAST

- **2001:** Before the 9/11 attacks, invasive searches and security checkpoints, with long delays in line while bags are searched and other security measures are taken, are relatively rare. One of the few places they might be encountered is at a courthouse.

  Today: Invasive searches are far more widespread than they were before 9/11. Most notably, security measures at airports are much more extensive than they were before the terrorist attacks.

- **2001:** While cellphones are commonplace, other wireless devices are still rare, usually in the hands of the business elite, and wi-fi areas are practically nonexistent.

  Today: Many people use a variety of wireless devices, and wi-fi areas and other forms of wireless connectivity are commonplace.

- **2001:** Racial profiling is recognized as legal by the Supreme Court but is condemned in practice by the federal government.

  Today: Racial profiling remains both legal and officially disapproved of but is frequently invoked as a panacea against terrorist attacks, especially after the 9/11 attacks, and again after the Boston Marathon bombing in 2013.

---

regime. This had to begin, in his view, with the expulsion of foreign influence from the Islamic world, not because he resented economic and political imperialism per se, but so that he could make it over into a closed society that embodied his own version of Islam. He made it very clear before the attacks that his immediate demand for the United States was that it evacuate US military forces that had been in Saudi Arabia since the Gulf War in 1991. This was not because he feared an abstract concept like globalization, but because he considered US forces in Saudi Arabia to be a threat to the ritual purity of the holy places (Mecca and Medina). Bin Laden succeeded in this goal: within a year of the 9/11 attacks all but a token presence of US forces had left the country.

However, al-Qaeda did not, and does not, rely on radicalized Islamists for its operations. The hijackers were for the most part Westernized, middle-class professionals. They became hostile to the West because of the political corruption fostered by the West in the Arab world. In countries like Egypt, Tunisia, and Saudi Arabia, the West has traditionally supported authoritarian regimes on the understanding that they would work to oppose Soviet (and in the twenty-first century Iranian) influence in the region. These governments have ruled through a network of patronage, and no qualification, even a Western university degree in a field like engineering, could advance the career of someone outside of that patronage network. The hijackers most likely struck back at what they perceived as the source of corruption in their own countries that had affected their own lives. This was the foundation of their alliance with al-Qaeda. Bin Laden would point out that the United States supported Iraqi dictator Saddam Hussein in his war with Iran from 1980 to 1988, including Hussein's use of poison gas, over which it is easy to generate moral outrage. Bin Laden would also mention the US destruction by missile attack of a pharmaceutical plant in Khartoum, Sudan, in 1998. He was thus able to make common cause with those who were also angered by Western influence, even if their view of Islamic culture could not have been more different from his own. Actions by terrorist groups like al-Qaeda inevitably harm the poor and oppressed in the Arab world, not least by attracting Western retaliation. But it is precisely the resulting hostility to the West that the

The characters in Nine-Ten *meet when they are all called for jury duty.* (© bikeriderlondon / Shutterstock.com)

terrorists rely upon for recruiting and expanding their influence.

Invasions of Afghanistan and Iraq

While *Nine-Ten* relies for its effect on the audience's knowledge of the events that immediately follow the play, the attacks themselves led to a catastrophic sequence of events. The initial US response was to invade Afghanistan for the stated purpose of hunting down bin Laden. This certainly had to be done, and the monstrousness of the crimes he committed is not at issue, although the initial effort failed, and he was assassinated, rather than brought to justice, by US forces in 2011. The immediate effect of the invasion was to restore to power in Afghanistan a regime of warlords so brutal and corrupt that they made people accept the Taliban (the radical Islamic movement that sheltered bin Laden) with open arms, and it proved impossible to suppress the radical Islamic elements in the country.

Bin Laden and much of his network fled to Pakistan and Yemen, and both countries were radicalized and destabilized as a result. More exceptionally, the United States invaded Iraq in 2003, claiming that its dictator Saddam Hussein had been complicit in the 9/11 attacks. Additionally, the US government argued Hussein was amassing an arsenal of weapons of mass destruction on evidence that is now recognized to have been fabricated. During its occupation of Iraq, the United States authorized and carried out the torture of prisoners of war to gather intelligence about future terrorist plots. The fabricated evidence for weapons of mass destruction, coupled with the torture, worked together to undermine America's legitimacy in the region. The occupation of Iraq lasted for more than eight years and resulted in the deaths of more than six thousand US soldiers and private contractors.

CRITICAL OVERVIEW

Leight's *Nine-Ten* has not itself received any critical attention. It is, however, one of the first works of literature inspired by the 9/11 terrorist attacks, and these works have collectively received increasing attention, especially in reviews and journal articles published at the tenth anniversary in 2011.

The most important monograph to appear in this wave of criticism, Martin Randall's *9/11 and the Literature of Terror* (2011), is representative of the general critical attitude. For Randall, "it takes some time for 9/11 to appear in literary fiction." His work concentrates on novels dealing with 9/11, starting around 2004 with Frederic Beigbeder's *Windows on the World* (2004). Randall is somewhat dismissive of earlier responses, like Leight's, as found "in short, generally commemorative fiction, in hastily written plays and poems, slowly appearing in graphic novels and commix, as the iconography of, in particular, the burning WTC Towers, began to be assimilated into culture." Randall points out the significance of the quickly agreed-upon convention of referring to the attacks by their date, 9/11: "the adoption of this numerical abbreviation itself [is] an aspect of the posthumous assimilation of the event into history." Leight plays on this element with the title of his play, *Nine-Ten*. A major element of 9/11 that Randall explores is the drama inherent in the attacks, particularly the visual effect of the burning and collapsing World Trade Center towers. Spectacular in themselves, these images took on a life of their own as they played on the television news channels almost continuously for twenty-four hours. But Leight eschews any exploitation of the dramatic elements of the events. He depends rather on allowing the audience to bring this background to their viewing of the play. Although treated in many different ways, Randall points out that this is a feature of 9/11 literature: whatever the author shows the reader evokes other elements that are common to the memories of those who lived through the attacks (even, or especially, those who did so vicariously on television) but that are never directly mentioned.

Samuel Thomas, writing in *Modern Fiction Studies* in 2011, deals with literature that approaches 9/11 as part of a more general conflict between a globalized capitalist economy and particular, traditional cultural identities. This is a theme that Leight exploits in *Nine-Ten*, making several of his characters bond traders or other capitalist agents of globalization, while his character Lyris is a sort of caricature of traditional culture, which is often all that is left over in the wake of globalization and capitalism.

CRITICISM

Rita M. Brown

Brown is an English professor. In the following essay, she analyzes Nine-Ten *in terms of the Aristotelian conception of drama.*

At the very beginning of drama in ancient Greece more than 2,500 years ago, the character Oedipus, in Sophocles's play *Oedipus the King*, asks who is the murderer of Laius, his predecessor as king of the city of Thebes. This comes at the beginning of the play, and the whole development of the plot concerns his investigation into that question. It is perhaps the first detective story, a genre that Leight knows well. When Oedipus asks the question, he does not know the answer. But the audience at that time knew the answer. The story was a familiar one that everyone in Athens would have known. They knew already what Oedipus slowly discovers, that his parents, warned by the oracle of Apollo, had abandoned him on a hillside, where a shepherd found him and took him to the king and queen of Corinth, who raised Oedipus as their foster son. When Oedipus himself learned from Apollo that he was destined to kill his own father and marry his mother, he decided to get as far away from Corinth as possible, believing that his adoptive parents were his real parents. The audience knew that the man who insulted and attacked Oedipus at a crossroads outside Thebes, whom Oedipus killed in self-defense, was his own true father. The audience knew what Oedipus did not, that Oedipus was the man who had killed Laius, the king of Thebes, that Oedipus himself was the man who had killed his own father and then unknowingly married his own mother.

For Oedipus the character, his play is a detective story, but for the audience it is a revelation of horror. They know from the beginning the truth that Oedipus slowly uncovers. The audience feels the fear that Oedipus is too ignorant to feel about deeds that are hardly less monstrous for being unintended, and feel pity for him because he is an ignorant victim of fate. A student reading *Oedipus the King* today might well not know Oedipus's story and not know the answer to the question when Oedipus asks who is the murderer of Laius. That student will watch a detective story unfold, and only come to feel fear and pity at the end, sharing Oedipus's feelings when he makes his discovery. But that was not

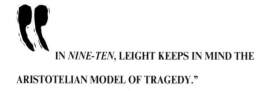

IN *NINE-TEN,* LEIGHT KEEPS IN MIND THE

ARISTOTELIAN MODEL OF TRAGEDY."

the point Sophocles had in mind when he wrote the play.

Drama began in ancient Greece in the sixth century BCE as a competition in which the playwright, acting as poet and composer, would compete in a religious festival retelling a myth in the form of a song sung by a chorus. Eventually one and then three soloists were added (each playing several parts) until the familiar form of telling a story through having actors imitate life on stage was developed. The original effect was probably more like opera than Shakespeare's plays (and indeed, opera was first conceived of as a reconstruction of Greek drama). The philosopher Aristotle, writing his *Poetics* almost a century after the heyday of Greek drama, produced the first literary criticism of drama as a form or genre. He identified the elicitation of fear and pity in the audience as the peculiar characteristic of drama, which distinguished it from all other forms of literature with their different aims. Sophocles plunged his audience into these powerful emotions from the beginning of his *Oedipus the King.* He could do so because they knew how the story turned out, which the characters, of course, could not. This might seem like a drawback to writing about myth, since the dramatist is telling the audience a story they already know. There can be no surprise or thrill of the unexpected. But Sophocles used it to his advantage. He depends not only on the audience's knowledge, but also on its awareness of the characters' ignorance, to create situations that stir up the very emotions of fear and pity. If the viewer knows the answer to the question about who is the murderer of Laius, and knows what Oedipus has done, and further knows that when he discovers what he has done, he will be so overcome with revulsion at himself that he will gouge out his own eyes, the viewer cannot help but feel pity for the ignorant wretch who seems so wise as he pulls back all the layers covering the truth one by one. The viewer wants to shout out, *Stop! Don't do it! You are better off*

not knowing! Sophocles creates his drama on the foundation of the audience's knowledge and his characters' ignorance.

Warren Leight uses precisely the same technique in *Nine-Ten.* The scene of the play is set in a jury pool. The characters have all tried to get out of jury duty, since they consider that they are better off doing their jobs than serving on a random jury. (Incidentally, the practice of selecting jurors at random from citizens also goes back to classical Athens.) They all either work in the World Trade Center or know someone who does. The audience may well sympathize, since the characters' sentiments are widely shared. The court officer who addresses the other characters at the end of the play tries to reconcile the jurors to their duty by offering what they want, suggesting that whatever trial they are assigned to will only keep them for a short time: "On the bright side, most of you will get to go back to your life in two or three days." But they "all groan. Two days is an eternity." The audience is by this time meant to be feeling the characters' frustration. But this vicarious feeling ends with the last line of the play when the court officer gives the date, the day before the attack on the World Trade Center.

The audience is suddenly catapulted into the state of tragic knowledge that the audience of *Oedipus the King* possessed. Now the audience's feelings suddenly become completely different from the characters' self-centered frustration. On the one hand, they will feel relief that the characters will be spared the suffering and trauma endured by everyone in the towers on the eleventh. They will not feel fear for the characters, however, since they know they will be fortunate to be in the courthouse, even if in their ignorance the characters think otherwise. But Leight certainly intends to arouse fear and pity nonetheless, since no one, especially only thirteen days after the attack, could think of it without feeling those emotions for the three thousand people who were victims that day. The point is driven home, on the other hand, by Lyris's mention of her brother who is a security guard in the towers. Given his job, he will almost certainly stay in the building helping others evacuate until it is too late and the whole structure crashes down around him.

In *Nine-Ten,* Leight keeps in mind the Aristotelian model of tragedy. He is scrupulous, for instance, in respecting what Aristotle called the

WHAT
DO I READ
NEXT?

- Moshin Hammid's *The Reluctant Fundamentalist* (2008), a novel short-listed for the Booker Prize, tells the story of a young Pakistani man who manages to take a degree from Princeton and become a successful, completely secularized American businessman, evaluating foreign companies for takeovers by American firms. He is in Manila, the Philippines, on business on September 11, 2001, and as he watches the attacks unfold on the news, he realizes that he sides with the terrorists against American capitalism. Back in the United States, he feels the discrimination widely directed against Muslims at that time. He eventually visits his family in Pakistan and slowly slips into the identity of a radicalized, anti-Western jihadist.

- *Extremely Loud and Incredibly Close* is a 2005 novel by Jonathan Safran Foer (a student of Joyce Carol Oates). It tells the story of a nine-year-old boy whose father was killed in the World Trade Center on 9/11. As the novel unfolds the boy searches throughout New York for a lock that will be opened by a key his father left behind, which he feels is also the key to the mystery of his father's life.

- *The 9/11 Commission Report: Final Report of the National Commission on Terrorist Attacks upon the United States* (2004) is the official government account of the terrorist attacks. It became the basis of a 2006 documentary by Leigh Scott.

- *The 9/11 Commission Report* was adapted as a popular graphic novel of the same title by Sid Jacobson and Ernie Colón in 2005.

- *Tower Stories: The Autobiography of September 11th*, edited by Damon Di Marco in 2004, collects the oral histories of dozens of ordinary New Yorkers who survived or witnessed the attacks on the World Trade Center. Also included is a collection of photographs by amateur photographers.

- Warren Leight has published numerous plays, including the 2004 title *Glimmer, Glimmer & Shine*, about the lives of jazz musicians in New York in the 1930s.

- Alice Walsh's *A Long Way from Home* (2012) is a young-adult novel that tells the story of a Pakistani girl whose family came to the United States in the days following the 9/11 attack.

---

dramatic unities. The drama takes place in one spot and plays out in real time. The viewer sees just what he would if he were watching a videotape of a security camera in the courthouse. In this sense also, Leight achieves a successful imitation of life. Indeed, he imitates it more closely than the Athenian dramatists did, since in *Nine-Ten* there is no artistic form like versified dialogue, fantastic costumes, or singing and dancing. But Aristotle also recognized that tragedy is an action complete in itself. Leight fails in that regard. *Nine-Ten* reaches what might be the climax of a first act, but the idea of the play is not completed. It does not portray the events of the

next day, and the characters' reactions to the event that happens then are not shown. The play might easily have been extended, setting it on the morning of the attack, and showing the disaster unfolding on the television news, which would be like the messenger speech that was traditionally used in tragedy to report events that could not be shown onstage without violating the Aristotelian unities. Instead, Leight depends on the viewer's imagination. Once the revelation of the date is made, everyone in the audience can fill in the rest in his own imagination. Leight's work is in this sense a fragment, but at the same time, its entire power derives from forcibly evoking this imaginative completion from the audience. Also, a longer play would have required a longer preparation, and much of the impact of the play comes from striking while the iron is hot. Premiering the work so soon after the attack allowed the author to play with the audience's real emotions, rather than the imitation emotions usually manufactured by drama.

Source: Rita M. Brown, Critical Essay on *Nine-Ten*, in *Drama for Students*, Gale, Cengage Learning, 2014.

Frank Scheck

In the following review, Scheck writes that Leight made a mistake in writing No Foreigners beyond This Point *as a play rather than as a personal memoir.*

This new play by Warren Leight (*Side Man*) demonstrates the pitfalls of creating dramatic works based on personal experience.

Inspired by the playwright's time spent teaching English in China shortly after the ravages of the Cultural Revolution, *No Foreigners Beyond This Point* reveals an impressive authenticity and depth of knowledge about its subject matter. But it also lacks a compelling dramatic arc, and its attenuated series of vignettes never satisfyingly coalesce.

Presented by the Ma-Yi Theater Company, the play details the adventures of Ean (Andrew Baker) and Abby (Paula Wheaton), two young, inexperienced innocents who show up in Guangdong, China, to teach at a trade school.

While Abby has idealistic notions about her pursuit and Ean, well, wants to be with Abby, they both quickly discover that their plans for cross-cultural communication have to be drastically curtailed.

Aghast at the constraints placed upon both them and the students by the rigidly controlling faculty, the pair gradually find themselves educated as to the true nature of their surroundings.

While some of these revelations border on the trivial—Ean is outraged to discover that his students have never heard of The Beatles—others are far more serious, as students and colleagues describe the brutally repressive conditions they've long had to endure.

While many of these encounters resonate in a quietly powerful fashion, the play ultimately feels more educational than dramatic. How little

> LEIGHT HAS RECEIVED MANY LETTERS AND COMMENTS THAT REFLECT HOW THE PLAY ALLOWS PEOPLE TO OPEN UP EMOTIONALLY."

we care about the central characters is illustrated in a coda depicting their reunion many years later, which has none of the intended poignancy.

Under the sensitive direction of Loy Arcenas, the largely Asian-American cast deliver sterling performances as a variety of students, faculty members and government officials. Still, it's hard to avoid the feeling that the material would have been far better served by a memoir than by this awkward dramatization.

Source: Frank Scheck, "'Beyond' Has Little 'Point,'" in *New York Post*, October 10, 2005, p. 45.

Laura C. Kelley

In the following excerpt, Kelley talks with Leight about winning the Tony Award for Best Play for Side Man.

For what seemed like forever, Warren Leight couldn't find anyone in New York City to produce his play *Side Man*. Except the company Naked Angels, who mounted a reading in a basement for four days in 1996. Producers called the play "old-fashioned." "I didn't understand," Leight recently recalled in a telephone interview from his Manhattan office. "I thought, 'I can't write any better than this right now. And if this can't get a production, I don't know what to do.'"

Critic Mimi Kramer dubbed the play "the best unproduced play in New York." She saw it at New York Stage and Film Company's Powerhouse Theater at Vassar College in Poughkeepsie, which staged the show in the summer of 1996. Audiences there loved it. Many told Leight he would win a Tony for the semi-autobiographical memory play about the declining personal and professional lives of jazz musicians from the fifties through the eighties. Was a New York run so impossible?

Finally, nearly two years after the successful Poughkeepsie production opened, Leight secured an Off Off Broadway run, produced by the Weissberger Theater Group. Five weeks in a small theatre could be the show's final run. Or it could be just the beginning. The stress of uncertainty continued. "Everything hinges on the critics, who come three days after you've moved into the theatre," Leight said. "You don't have that two-week rehearsal in the theatre and fifteen previews. The day the *New York Times* came, we had an actor exit the wrong way; stop, turn, go back halfway; stop in the middle of the stage, frozen; stop and turn three more times, then go off the other way. It was highly professional," he joked. "We all imitate him to this day. That sort of the-deer-in-the-headlights look, you know?"

Side Man seemed stalled once again. "It took me a long time to write *Side Man*," Leight said. "It took me a long time to *start* to write it, and then I spent a lot of time reworking it and reworking it. And the reason it took me a long time to start it was I was writing about things that I had spent most of my life hiding from people. Family, you know, family craziness stuff. And what I've found is so many people are grateful to go see a play that airs that stuff out, that lets them know that things they grew up with they weren't alone in growing up with." Letters from audience members revealed the play's impact, but no one seemed able to move the show. Where was the financial support and trust to match audience enthusiasm?

"One of the producers said, 'Warren, you've had a success, it seems. Congratulations, your next play will have a much better chance.' I said, 'I think this play has a longer run left in it.' And he sort of looked at me and said, you know, 'We always like to think that about our plays.' I only note that it's a year and a half since then." In the meantime, *Side Man* has moved Off Broadway to the Roundabout Theatre, and then to Broadway's John Golden Theatre. It has won the Tony Award for best play, actor Frank Wood won a Tony for his portrayal of father and trumpeter Gene, and the show has received numerous other accolades, including ranking as a Pulitzer Prize finalist. Now, even as the Broadway production is closing and beginning a tour, regional theatres across the country are presenting local premieres of the play.

"There were so few places that had responded to the play in any way," Leight said, "that I thought it would be a courtesy to look out for them if I could." He lobbied producers to permit the play to be licensed to regional theatres despite the uncertainty of touring plans. In September, the first production outside of New York opened at Ensemble Theatre of Cincinnati. That was quickly followed by shows at Chicago's Steppenwolf Theatre and A Contemporary Theatre in Seattle. In January Arizona Theatre Company will perform *Side Man* in Tucson and in February they move the show to Phoenix. The play also appears on the spring 2000 schedules of Denver Center Theatre Company, the Guthrie Theater in Minneapolis, and Philadelphia Theatre Company.

Artistic directors of many of these companies wanted the play even before it won the Tony. D. Lynn Meyers of Ensemble Theatre tried to secure the rights just before it opened in New York. "It's hard for me to believe that this play wouldn't be produced a lot, even if it hadn't won the Tony," Meyers said. "I think the thing that is wonderful about it is that it is such an amazingly honest play. These people are people you come to know very quickly, it's an interesting situation, it's really well-written. And I mean that in the greatest of terms, in that it's what every writer, I think, strives to do, which is create something that is compelling and honest and interesting and humorous and changes its audience."

Side Man celebrates the passion and dedication of musicians who would play and record with big-name jazz players while remaining virtually anonymous. The play also portrays the painful effects that rock'n'roll, television, and other popular entertainment had on the careers of the sidemen.

. . . From calculating how to balance their unemployment checks and work to announcing recent deaths, they maintain camaraderie, complete each other's sentences, and laugh at retold stories. Music infuses the script. Sinatra plays from a wireless recorder, Elvis sounds from a television set, Clifford Brown's final trumpet solo soars from a cassette player.

Paying tribute to the sidemen was important to Leight, whose own father was a trumpet player. (The playwright jokes that his father liked the show only when given the compact disc for the jazz soundtrack.) "Certainly the sidemen are the forgotten artists of the century," Leight said. "There have been how many dozens of plays about painters in America, or about opera singers? Nobody ever writes about these guys. I was always very worried about what musicians would think of the play. First of all, you know they have 'jive detectors,' as they call it. A lot of them have just said, 'Man, thanks for telling our story.'"

Jazz also influenced the play's structure. Scenes shift, covering a period from 1955 to 1985. Leight rejected the potentially dull dioramas of a chronological presentation. He explained, "Jazz is all about being in one moment and quoting a moment from the past and linking up something that's going on. It's almost the opposite of being linear. And so I thought I was entitled to play with chronology.

"I love being able to shift time," Leight continued. "There's a couple of moments where Patsy, the waitress, is talking to Clifford in the bar in 1985. She passes him her old lady glasses and her leather coat, and she walks across the stage to the booth and she's in her waitress outfit, which was under her coat, and she goes, 'I'm off for awhile.' And she sits down with them in 1955. And then Clifford stares and watches her and those guys, thirty years earlier. And that's *only* theatrical. It was [New York director] Michael Mayer figuring out a couple of things, and actually my costume designer saving us on it. And the audience is never lost for a second."

Side Man is both fueled by jazz and transcends it. Donovan Marley, artistic director of Denver Center Theatre Company, said, "I love that the underlying passion of the piece is expressed in music and is outside the text. And I think that because it is, that there is a power that maybe exceeds the kind of power that a text-driven discussion of the same issues might do." David Ira Goldstein, artistic director of Arizona Theatre Company, who saw the New York production, said, "I was so struck by the universality of it. Although I don't come from a family of jazz musicians, I immediately saw people that I knew, in the theatre, or in classical music, or, you know, in everything, computer science. It seems the emotions Clifford goes through and the relationships he has with his family are so universal."

Leight has received many letters and comments that reflect how the play allows people to open up emotionally. "Older guys can go the first time because it's a play about jazz and that era," he said. "I had a seventy-five-year-old guy come up to me at Williamstown, and he said, 'I saw your play and I ended up crying.' And I said, 'Oh, I'm sorry.' He said, 'Well, that was my life

up there.' And I said, 'Were you a musician?' And he said, 'No no no. That was my father in your play.' And he was crying about his childhood from sixty years earlier. And I had completely misinterpreted. And his wife was with him, and she said it was the first time he had ever talked about his childhood with her."

Leight added, "I've been very lucky to write something that seems to have touched people as opposed to just, you know, sold tickets."

Side Man will continue to sell tickets, thanks in part to the Tony Award, which extended the New York run for five months and propelled the show's shift to the regional theatre scene. "I think it assured the life of the show," Leight said, "and a lot of people who had gone out of their way early on to help the show, I think it helped legitimize what they had done. It's a funny thing, the show played much more confidently after it won the award. Audiences didn't come in with a show-me attitude quite so much." . . .

Source: Laura C. Kelley, "'Side Man' out Front: A Play and Its Writer before and after the Tony Award," in *Dramatics*, November 1999, pp. 5–9.

SOURCES

Aristotle, "Poetics," in *The Complete Works of Aristotle*, Vol. 2, edited by Jonathan Barnes, Princeton University Press, 1982, pp. 2316–40.

Chomsky, Noam, *9-11*, Seven Stories Press, 2001, pp. 11–70.

Leight, Warren, "Nine-Ten," in *Dark, No Sugar*, Dramatists Play Service, 2007, pp. 48–51.

"Racial Profiling Fact Sheet," US Department of Justice website, June 17, 2003, http://www.justice.gov/opa/pr/2003/June/racial_profiling_fact_sheet.pdf (accessed June 24, 2013).

Randall, Martin, *9/11 and the Literature of Terror*, Edinburgh University Press, 2011, pp. 1–18.

Thomas, Samuel, "The Means and Ends of Suicide Terror," in *Modern Fiction Studies*, Vol. 57, No. 3, 2011, pp. 425–49.

FURTHER READING

DeLillo, Don, *Falling Man*, Scribner, 2008.
    DeLillo's novel is perhaps the best-known piece

of 9/11 literature. The lives of its characters, which seemed to be going nowhere before 9/11, are transformed by the attack.

Franzen, Jonathan, *The Corrections*, Picador, 2002. Written before the 9/11 attacks, Franzen's novel depicts the American culture of that era as anxious and uncertain, oppressed as much by failure as by a lack of growth, very much the world inhabited by the characters of Leight's *Nine-Ten*.

Leight, Warren, *Stray Cats*, Dramatists Play Service, 1998.
Stray Cats is a collection of nine one-act, one-actor monologues about jazz musicians of Leight's father's generation. Note that the vast majority of Leight's drama, including his television and film scripts, remains unpublished.

Picotto, Richard, and Daniel Paisner, *Last Man Down: A Firefighter's Story of Survival and Escape from the World Trade Center*, Berkley, 2003.
This is a memoir by Picotto, who was in charge of the rescue efforts inside the towers on 9/11. After making the decision to evacuate the north tower following the collapse of the south tower, he stayed behind to help a number of handicapped people inside the tower get out and was caught in the collapse. He was among the survivors rescued from the rubble.

SUGGESTED SEARCH TERMS

Warren Leight

Nine-Ten AND Leight

one-act play

9/11 OR September 11

terrorism

Osama bin Laden

World Trade Center AND 9/11

Aristotle

drama

Passion Play

SARAH RUHL
2010

A "passion play" is a story of the death and resurrection of Christ, originally a part of medieval Catholic liturgy. Sarah Ruhl wrote Part One of her *Passion Play* as an undergraduate thesis at Brown University, telling the story of people who put on this play and its effect on them. She was inspired by a childhood book that told about the famous passion play at Oberammergau in Bavaria. The whole town participates, and parts are traditionally passed down in families for generations. She wondered what it would be like to play the character of Pontius Pilate, for example, year after year. Ruhl's *Passion Play* follows reincarnations of the same players in three different locations and eras—England during the Elizabethan era, Oberammergau in Hitler's Germany, and the Black Hills in the twentieth-century United States. Ruhl's play focuses on the actors playing the main characters, especially the one who plays Pontius Pilate and his obsession with the figure of Christ.

Part One of *Passion Play* was Ruhl's first staged play at Trinity Repertory in Providence, Rhode Island, in 1997. The first two parts of *Passion Play* were put together in London in 2002. The third part was commissioned for a production of the entire cycle at Arena Stage in Washington, DC, in 2005. It was revised in 2007 and published in 2010.

Ruhl has become well known as a feminist playwright on the American stage in the

Sarah Ruhl *(© Bruce Glikas / FilmMagic / Getty Images)*

twenty-first century, having been nominated for the Pulitzer Prize twice and the recipient of many awards. Ruhl likes to return to the roots of theater in ancient storytelling, using myth, fantasy, and Eastern theater techniques to produce a drama, as she points out, not of human psychology, but of the inner life of the soul.

AUTHOR BIOGRAPHY

Ruhl was born to Kathy Kehoe Ruhl and Patrick Ruhl in Wilmette, Illinois, on January 24, 1974. Her mother directed high-school plays and earned a PhD in language, literacy, and rhetoric. Ruhl's father marketed toys before his death. He loved puns and language and history. Her older sister is a psychiatrist. Ruhl was raised as a Catholic but left the church as a teenager because of what she felt was its bias against women.

Ruhl was telling fantasy stories before she could write, dictating them to her mother. She spent time in the theater from childhood when her mother was directing school plays. She began taking classes at the well-known Piven Theatre Workshop in Evanston, Illinois, in fourth grade. This workshop has turned out many famous actors, including John Cusack and Aidan Quinn. It specializes in the improvisational work of Viola Spolin, using stories, myths, fairy tales, folktales, and such authors as Anton Chekhov and Flannery O'Connor, with an emphasis on language and transformation.

Ruhl's father died of cancer when she was twenty, affecting her profoundly. The play *Eurydice* is an expression of her grief. She graduated from Brown University in 1997 with a bachelor's degree in English; she had also spent an undergraduate year at Pembroke College of Oxford University. After teaching in public schools for two years, she returned to Brown for a master of fine arts degree in playwriting in 2001 under her mentor, Pulitzer Prize–winning playwright Paula Vogel. Ruhl married Anthony Charuvastra, a child psychiatrist, in 2005. They had a daughter, Anna, in 2006 and twin daughters in 2010.

After an initial period when no one was interested in her plays, Ruhl became successful in having her work constantly performed while still in her thirties. Using techniques like magic realism, puppets, and nonlinear structure, she deals with issues of gender, race, class, sexuality, politics, and art. She has dominated American stages in the twenty-first century with her most famous plays: *Passion Play* (1997, 2002, 2005); *Eurydice* (2003); *Orlando* (2003); *The Clean House* (2004); *Demeter in the City* (2006); *Dead Man's Cell Phone* (2007); *In the Next Room; or, The Vibrator Play* (2009); *Stage Kiss* (2011); and *Dear Elizabeth* (2012). In 2004, she won the Susan Smith Blackburn Award of $10,000. In 2006, she won the MacArthur Foundation "genius grant" of half a million dollars. The recipient of dozens of other awards, she has also been a Pulitzer finalist twice.

PLOT SUMMARY

Part One

The opening setting of *Passion Play* is a village in northern England in the spring of 1575. The minimal set suggests the seaside.

MEDIA ADAPTATIONS

- Ruhl is interviewed by Howard Sherman for American Downstage Center, from June 16, 2010, about *Passion Play* and other plays on an hour-long audio that can be downloaded in MP3 format at http://americantheatre wing.org/downstagecenter/detail/sarah_ruhl.

PROLOGUE

A chorus sets the play for the audience by reciting a few rhyming lines, as in Shakespeare's prologues. They say the play is set in northern England with the Virgin Queen (Elizabeth I) on the throne, and the Catholics are not in favor now. The chorus tells the audience the play is simple, without fancy props. They must use their imaginations to fill out the rest.

SCENES 1–5

John the Fisherman, the man who is to play Christ, is measured for the cross. The sky turns red, as it ominously does at various moments in the play. John the Fisherman's cousin, Pontius, who plays Pontius Pilate, is jealous of John. He has wanted to play Christ all his life, but he is an ugly, bent-over man, not well liked. Pontius is a fish gutter who once gutted his own hand by mistake.

A visiting friar enters in disguise and sees Pontius speaking aloud about how much he hates his cousin, John. Finally the friar asks Pontius for a drink of water. He wonders if this is the town with the beautiful young man who plays Christ? Pontius says it is his cousin. He, on the other hand, plays Pontius Pilate and Satan. He grimaces to the audience. He invites the stranger to his house for water. The friar is hidden by John the Fisherman since Catholic clerics are outlawed in Protestant England. The friar thinks John is good and kind like Jesus.

The heavenly choir rehearses while the director conducts and the friar watches. The village idiot sits cross-legged playing with a jack-in-the-box. She speaks in a nonsensical way to the jack who pops out, and the director tells her to shut up. She tells the jack he has to go back in the box because there are no parts for them. The director ties her to a stump, and she says she will close her eyes and make the sky turn red. The sky turns red, and the choir stops singing.

While the director and John the Fisherman rehearse the crucifixion with the friar watching, Mary 1 (the Virgin Mary) and Mary 2 (Mary Magdalene) sit apart under a tree talking between scenes. Mary 2 comments that Mary Magdalene was a whore because she pretended, and so she also is a whore because she pretends. (Mary Magdalene was the prostitute who became a devoted disciple of Christ.) Mary 1 is distracted because she sees John the Fisherman's loincloth slipping. She is in love with him. Mary 2 says it is easy to seduce men, you just pretend. Mary 1 and 2 want to switch roles, but the director refuses to let them because he thinks Mary 1 looks holy, and Mary 2 looks more like a prostitute. The friar announces he will hear confession of sins, and Mary 2 says she will meet him after dark.

SCENES 6–10

Mary 2 confesses to the friar her dreams of kissing women. He tells her that it is sinful and that her brain has been addled by playing the role of a whore from a young age. He says only God can tell her why it is sinful to kiss a woman. The sky turns red.

Pontius is cleaning his shoes with a knife, speaking a passionate monologue, explaining to the moon that at birth, his guts were not sewn up properly, and now they are exposed and stink like the dead fish he guts for a living. He closes his eyes, and huge beautiful fish puppets surround and undress him. As he turns to the audience, they leave to drumbeats.

Mary 1 kneels at her bed and begins to recite a prayer. She breaks off and turns to the audience, explaining she hates to sleep alone. When she is cold she finds a man to sleep with by sneaking out of her window, as she does now. John the Fisherman is out walking in the night, speaking a monologue, in a shaft of light. He explains that on nights like this with the beauty of the moon he feels grace and is ready to die. He speaks poetically of the world and other humans. Mary 1 approaches John with a jar and says she is gathering night air for her mother. He offers to help her, climbing on a wagon to capture the spot of air she points to. Meanwhile, she looks at his body from behind. He escorts her offstage.

Pontius has been hiding behind a bush and comes forward, jealous. Meanwhile Mary 1 climbs back in her window, complaining she will be continue to be cold, for John is chaste. John the Fisherman is famous for having played Christ so often he has become like his role.

The director rehearses a scene with Mary 1 as Eve and Pontius as Satan tempting her with a fruit. The director gives directions to Pontius to be bolder and to Mary 1 to bite the fruit so hard the juice dribbles down her chin. Pontius sees Mary 1 out walking at night and begins to woo her. She says he smells of fish, but she pities him and kisses him. He promises not to tell. There are watery noises.

SCENES 11–15

The village idiot wakes up frightened by a prophetic dream that she tells to the jack. She has dreamt of Queen Elizabeth, naked and pregnant in heaven. Her private parts were red. The queen said she had come to stop the passion play (as she actually does in a later scene).

In a forest, Mary 1 and Mary 2 speak in half sentences that imply Mary 1 is pregnant and contemplating an abortion because she could be killed for her crime. She lies, saying John is the father. She wants to keep her part in the play, although she is beginning to show. The two Marys never have to finish the sentences because the audience can perfectly understand what is meant through their hints.

At rehearsal, Mary 1 is told by an angel she will have a child and name him Jesus. Mary says the lines where she tells Joseph she is with child by God. The sky turns red.

While Pontius is gutting fish at work, Mary 1 appears. She tells him she is pregnant, and he begs her to run away and marry him. She claims she wants to keep her part in the play. She wants Christ to love her, and he asks which one, the actor or the real one?

Mary 2 tells Mary 1 she has an idea and whispers it to her.

SCENES 16–20

Mary 1 tells the friar that there has been a miracle. God impregnated her so she could better play the Virgin Mary. In rehearsal, Pontius Pilate gets in trouble for killing Jesus and dies a stage death by stabbing himself with a fake knife. Just then the friar enters and says there has been a miracle: Mary is with child.

As Mary 1 is lying in bed, John kneels and blesses her, praising her holy radiance. He asks her to marry him so that they can raise the child together as Mary and Joseph did. She says, if she only could . . . but she is God's bride now.

A male actor makes lecherous remarks about Mary 1, and another actor fights with him for speaking of God's bride that way. John enters in a loincloth. He tells them to stop fighting; there is a miracle in town. A new Christ is to be born.

The director directs the scourging scene (where Jesus is whipped). He says he will fine Mary 1 for missing rehearsal, but John says she has woman's sickness; she is bearing the new messiah. Mary 2 reads the parts of both Marys. Pontius gives his speech about washing his hands of the blood of Christ. Pontius hints to John that he himself is the baby's father. Mary 1 watches them from a window, her face illuminated.

SCENES 21–27

Mary 1 says she hears people whispering that she is a whore. Mary 2 says not to listen. Mary 2 declares her love for Mary 1 and wants to run off together and raise the child. She will dress as a man. Mary 1 says that where she is going, no one can follow her. The sky turns red as she leaves.

In the town square, the village idiot has her jack-in-the-box and says Mary 1 is not at home. She is floating in the water. The friar enters and tells the director that God wants the play to be stopped. They cannot find Mary. The director says the play must go on because they made a pact with God. The sky is already turning red. The director asks the village idiot to take a part in the play.

The bell rings for the performance. John prays to play his part well, while Pontius wants to kill John. Trumpets sound, and there is a tableau of the Garden of Eden, with the village idiot playing Eve, Pontius playing the snake, and John playing Adam. Adam blames Eve for the fall, and she blames the snake. They cover their nakedness with fig leaves as Queen Elizabeth arrives in a fanfare.

Elizabeth announces that when she dies they will scrape layers of white paint off her face, put there so she would not look old. (As Elizabeth aged, she wore a white powder or makeup all over her face.) She says she will behead any subject impersonating a holy person.

In John's kitchen, the friar says he will go to France. He will join political groups against the queen. John makes a last confession: he enjoyed playing Christ too well. His words imply some regret that he was trying to be too holy, losing his nature as a man. If he had loved Mary in a warm, human way, things might have turned out differently.

In the town square, players hand in their costumes to the director. John the Fisherman enters carrying the body of Mary 1, who drowned herself. Water pours from her body. The sky is red as Pontius, by the body of Mary, holds a knife. He says the last lines of Pontius Pilate in the play, but this time he kills himself for real. Drums beat, and the fish puppets appear to lift his body and take it offstage. The sky turns blue.

Part Two

This part of the play is set in Oberammergau, Bavaria, in 1934. The set suggests a forest.

SCENE 1: PROLOGUE

The chorus hawks the passion play as though selling rides at a carnival. A train whistle is heard.

The Oberammergau passion play began in 1634 in a pact with God to spare them from the plague. It is put on every ten years and continues to this day. The train whistle is an ominous foreshadowing of the Holocaust, when the Nazis transported Jews to concentration camps. Hitler actually came to the passion play in 1934, and he appears later in this play.

SCENES 2–5

A visiting Englishman is writing a letter to his wife in England, telling her about the town and the superstitious Catholics who do not know the relationship of art to life. He has met a remarkable little girl, Violet, who is crying because she does not have a part in the town play. She is an outsider and does not look like one of them. She says they call her the village idiot. She can also make the sky turn red, but no one notices. The Englishman tells her the story of Little Red Riding Hood and makes it turn out happy, with the wolf and Red Riding Hood becoming friends.

At rehearsal, Eric, the actor who plays Jesus, is on the cross. Eric has trouble memorizing his lines, even though his father played this role for twenty years. The director is telling them to play their parts for the new Germany.

Later, Eric speaks to a Nazi foot soldier who has played Pontius Pilate. Eric says he would like to fight in the war too; he is tired of crucifixions. The foot soldier says they will play a game called "would you rather?" He gives a number of riddles. The final riddle is "Would you rather be Christ or Pontius Pilate?" The soldier would rather be Pontius because he does not want the nails and whipping. They flirt, with the foot soldier helping Eric rehearse his lines, and then they go mushroom hunting in the forest together.

The Englishman is interviewing Mary 2. He has come to town to write a book on theater. She says she used to hate the Jews when she saw her father play Jesus over the years. (This alludes to the fact that some Christians blamed the death of Christ on the Jews for their turning Jesus in to the Roman authorities. This became the rationale for violence against Jews over the ages.)

SCENES 6–10

As the Englishman takes pictures, Eric rushes in as Christ sending the money changers from the temple. Violet enacts her own play to compete with the other play. She begins to tell the story of Hansel and Gretel. The director yells at her. The rehearsal moves to the Jewish High Council's debate about how to deliver Jesus to the Romans. This version of the passion play emphasizes the supposed Jewish conspiracy against Jesus and the stereotypical

Jewish obsession with money. The director yelling at the village idiot is a repetition from Part One. Several lines are repeated through all three parts.

Elsa (Mary 1) is looking in a mirror in her dressing room. A German officer enters and begins flirting with her and then grabbing her, forcibly making her his mistress. At home Eric tells his sister, Mary 2, he is leaving home. He wants to be part of something bigger—the new Germany.

The Englishman interviews the director, asking why he enjoys directing, and the director answers that people need directors when they lack vision. He repeats the speech twice, hoping the Englishman is writing it down. He has the same bullying character as in Part One.

At a rehearsal of the Last Supper, Violet hides under the table. Eric rushes into the scene late. He cannot remember his lines, so Violet prompts him. He repeats whatever she says. This scene is very funny but has serious implications, because Violet warns against leaders like Hitler. She finally tells the disciples through Eric to always remember that Jesus is a Jew. At this, the director pulls her out and locks her in an empty birdcage. She threatens to make the sky turn red, but it does not.

SCENES 11–15

Mary 2 asks Eric how he could forget his lines. She thinks he should pray like their father did. Eric asks Mary if she has ever felt the grace of God, such that she did not have to make decisions. Eric is falling victim to Hitler's charisma and comparing it to a religious experience.

Violet is imprisoned in her box. It is night, and Eric lets her out. The German officer appears but is not observed as the foot soldier meets Eric. The foot soldier discusses, what if they changed roles? He does not like the role of Pontius Pilate having to put Christ to death. He would rather take him home and take care of him. Eric says that they cannot change their roles. They embrace.

It is day backstage. The German officer admires and touches Elsa and encourages the foot soldier to do the same. He says that soldiers in the German army who do not appreciate women get in trouble. This scene registers the hypocrisy of the passion play, with the actors in various illicit sexual affairs. The German officer makes it clear that homosexuality is not tolerated by Nazis.

Eric prays to get his lines right for the play. It is the exhortation of Jesus to beware of false prophets. Again, there is a warning about Hitler, but Eric does not understand it.

The foot soldier plays Pontius Pilate in the scene where the crowd chooses Barabbas the thief to be released and Jesus to be crucified. When Pilate says to crucify Jesus, the German officer and Hitler enter.

Hitler turns to the audience and explains that he was once a painter. People seem to fall in love with him, greeting him with "Heil!" Hitler warns them against Jews and praises the passion play for depicting them as evil; Pontius Pilate, on the other hand, is racially superior as a Roman. The Englishman snaps a picture. A train whistle sounds. This important scene connects the Nazis symbolically to the crucifixion. Hitler feels justified in his belief that the Jews are enemies of Christ. Eric falls under his spell.

SCENES 16–18

The Englishman writes a letter to his wife on the train and says that the passion play was glorious, with the young man playing Christ glowing with spirit. He did not like Hitler, however, and prefers staying out of politics to pursue art. This scene points to history: the English prime minister Neville Chamberlain tried to appease Hitler in an effort to preserve peace.

The foot soldier and Eric are in the forest. The foot soldier has orders to leave. They kiss to the sounds of war. The foot soldier names all the countries Hitler has invaded.

Violet sits in the forest and scatters bread crumbs to find her way home. The sky is red. Eric enters wearing a Nazi uniform and tells Violet she is not a native Oberammergauer. She reminds him of Christ's lines in the play about false prophets. She asks for the story of Little Red Riding Hood, and his version ends with the wolf eating the girl. He says he has to take her away. She pleads for her life. He picks her up and starts to take her away to a concentration camp.

EPILOGUE

The cast enters and watches Violet and Eric. There is a sound of a train speeding on the track.

Eric gives Violet a shove forward. The light changes from red to grey, as the play ends in silence.

Part Three

ACT ONE

The first act takes place with a minimal set in the background of a tollbooth and the line of a horizon.

SCENE 1: PROLOGUE

The chorus recites something like a travelogue about Spearfish, South Dakota, where the Black Hills Passion Play takes place. They tell the audience to expect red earth, dead Indian tribes, a corn palace, the Badlands, the site for the Battle of Wounded Knee, and a Harley convention of riders in beards.

SCENES 2–5

It is 1969. J, who plays Jesus, and P, who plays Pontius Pilate, are brothers. They take off their costumes and drink cold sodas because it is hot out. P has to leave soon for Vietnam. P asks J to take care of Mary while he is gone. The cast in costume surprises P with a good farewell party. P gets down on his knees and proposes to Mary 1. Queen Elizabeth enters, says she is married to England, and puts her hand on P's head and blesses him to go forth in battle. He gives a ring to Mary 1 and kisses her.

In a backstage tour, Mary 2 answers questions from the crowd. She plays Mary Magdalene because she believes in the message of the play, which is love. Mary 2 says she has a night job at the tollbooth on highway 16. In their apartment, Mary 1 and P say goodbye, and he goes off to war.

Backstage, Mary 1 and Mary 2 are in bathrobes, putting makeup on each other for the show. Mary 1 plays Eve. Mary 2 reassures her sister that P will be fine. Mary 1 says her feet get cold at night; she does not like sleeping alone. Her sister tells her to get a cat, but Mary 1 is allergic to them. Mary 2 wonders why God made allergies. This leads to the question of where evil comes from, as the actors are ready to play the fall of man in the Garden of Eden. Mary 2 says God must be responsible. This is different from the biblical account that blames Eve for evil.

SCENES 6–9

In her apartment, Mary 1 is alone in her bathrobe. J enters, and she thanks him for coming over because she is afraid. He tells her he is taking acting classes at college. He wants to be a professional actor on TV. He offers Mary some marijuana to help her sleep. Mary smokes it and talks about snakes. They kiss. The sound of a gunshot transitions to the next scene in Vietnam.

P in uniform drags a huge bloody fish across the stage. He holds a gun. The sky is red. He collapses. Queen Elizabeth enters, saying she believes a monarch should be on the battlefield with the soldiers. P mumbles that he killed a fish. Big fish puppets enter. Elizabethan courtiers carry P off the battlefield.

Mary 2 is in her tollbooth alone at night, with headlights shining across her face as cars pass. Mary 1 approaches, needing to talk. They have the same conversation as in Part One. Mary 1 speaking in half sentences indicates she is pregnant. She thinks she should end the pregnancy but waits for a sign. Just then a headlight flashes, and she believes it is a sign. She kneels while Mary 2 takes the toll from the driver.

J and Mary are at rehearsal the next day. J is on the cross. The director is not satisfied with how they are saying their lines. They do not portray anguish because they have just become lovers. J tells Mary he has always loved her. When the cast returns, J performs the ascension scene on a platform moving up to music.

ACT TWO

SCENES 1–4

P is hesitating outside a door. He winces and pulls back. He does not want to be touched. He asks Mary to help him be himself again. Three-year-old Violet enters and calls him daddy. She shows him a picture of a bird she drew, and he picks her up and flies her around the room like a bird. P says he wants to sleep outside the door so he can hear if anything is coming. He is obviously suffering from post-traumatic stress disorder.

P sees that the sky is red. A chorus enters with wind machines and Elizabethan boats as P says he is controlling the wind so the ships can get to shore. Violet comes out and asks him why there are boats in the sky. She can see them, and P tells her he can control the wind. She tells him a memory of being in a war in a former life when she died (Violet dying in the concentration camp in Part Two). They both try to get war out of their heads by jumping up and down on the memories.

The two brothers, J and P, are in the dressing room getting ready for rehearsal. J has now become a well-known actor. He tells P there have been some changes in the play, and there is a new young director. The actors are now professionals. Playing Christ is something of a curiosity for him now.

In the rehearsal, P breaks down as Pontius Pilate when he washes his hands of the guilt of murder. P sees blood instead of water. He questions his lines in which he has to say that he condemns Christ at the desire of the Jewish people. Hitler appears, but only P sees him. P says he wants to change his speech to say that Pontius Pilate is an agent of the state, and it is Pilate who is killing Jesus, not the Jews. The whole Jewish choir cheers his speech.

Mary 1 speaks to the young director, who has an ice pack on his cheek. P hit him during rehearsal, and the director says he will have to fire him. She says he cannot fire a soldier.

SCENES 5–6

The sky is red. P tries to tell Mary about Vietnam. He made a mistake, firing into a forest. He held a little girl Violet's age while she bled to death in his arms, with her brains blown out. He was not able to wash the blood off for months. P says he does not want to be in the play anymore because he does not believe in God.

At a rehearsal, J argues with the director. He wants to have a quiet, realistic dialogue with P instead of big gestures and bombast. The director points out that it is a spectacle for six thousand people. P loses it again: He says if J wants it real, he will make it real. He takes a nail and hammers it through his palm to the cross. The women scream.

SCENES 7–9

It is 1984. P is in a veteran's hospital talking to a psychiatrist. His left hand is limp. He correctly identifies that Ronald Reagan is president. He was hospitalized in 1974 for a suicide attempt. P still believes he can control the wind. P's conversation with the psychiatrist shows that P is cynical but not insane. He just wants to get a pill and go back to South Dakota to play Pontius Pilate the way he is supposed to be played, like a politician who took stupid orders. (P brings up

issues of the war in Vietnam, applying them to his role in the play, hoping to get some healing for his real-life experience.)

In South Dakota, P is drunk, trying to kiss Mary 1, asking for a shower and place to sleep. He wants to get his part back. Mary 1 says another actor has his part now. P thinks the actor does not know what it is like to give orders to kill a man, but he had to kill people for the president. She says there is now a different president, one everyone likes. He answers that a likeable man is no different than an evil man when he sends you to your death.

Mary 1 lets him stay the night, and Violet comes in to give him another bird picture. P remarks that there must be a God when he sees Violet. She kisses his limp hand.

J enters, and it is obvious he is spending the night with Mary, though he says he was just in town and needed a place to stay. P accuses him of sleeping with his wife, and J says he has been supporting this family for the last ten years. The two brothers fight, while Violet tries to stop them.

At the performance, Ronald Reagan is in a spotlight and gives a speech that armageddon (final battle of good and evil) is coming, and he intends to stop it. He says a good leader does not even need to be at the game, citing his radio broadcast days when he made up the plays for baseball games. America is about God, baseball, and intact families like Jesus, Mary, and Joseph.

Mary 1 and J play the scene of farewell when Jesus has to go to Jerusalem. They embrace for a long time, like lovers. Reagan wipes the tears from his eyes. The scene stops while P says he wants to go on stage and say his own lines. P speaks to Reagan, who salutes him and says he never served in the military himself. He asks P if he has a part in the play, and P says no, pulling out a gun. A secret service man leaps for him, and as he points the gun at himself, there is a blackout.

Epilogue: The Present

Light comes up on P and a final monologue. He did not kill the president or himself or Mary or J. He is homeless and sends part of his disability check to Mary. He watches his brother on soap operas. Violet sends him pictures of birds. He believes in God again. He summons the wind. Boats, courtiers, and fish puppets enter. The sky turns white as P gets on a boat and sails off.

CHARACTERS

Part One
Director
The director is dictatorial and yells at the actors to keep them in line.

John the Fisherman
John the Fisherman plays Jesus and Adam. He is strong, handsome, good, and well liked. He is modest, kind, and generous, trying to help others. When Mary becomes pregnant by Pontius and declares it is a miracle from God, John believes her and says he will marry her. He believes she is holy. In the end, he sees that living up to his role may have caused problems.

Machinist
The machinist is an Elizabethan engineer proud of inventing a flying machine that can lift the angel actors of the passion play into the air.

Mary 1
Mary 1 plays the Virgin Mary and Eve. She is a very sexy woman who desires John the Fisherman. She tries to change roles with Mary 2 to become Magdalene, the prostitute. When Mary 1 plays Eve, her character is seduced by Satan, played by Pontius, and then she is really seduced by Pontius the actor and becomes pregnant. She refuses to marry Pontius, however, because she wants to keep her part in the play, and she is in love with John. When she gets the friar to declare her pregnancy a miracle, she still refuses to marry when John proposes, saying she is God's bride, trying to stay in character. She knows Pontius told the truth about her, and people are whispering about her, so she drowns herself in despair.

Mary 2
Mary 2 plays Mary Magdalene, the prostitute of the play, but she is a bookworm who thinks sex is boring. She pretends to like sex with men. She confesses to the friar that she has lesbian dreams, and he tells her it is a sin. She offers to run away with Mary 1 when she is pregnant, promising to dress as a man. Mary 2 comes up with the idea for Mary 1 to declare the pregnancy a miracle.

Pontius the Fish Gutter
Pontius the Fish Gutter plays Pontius Pilate and Satan. He is small, crooked, and not liked by the others. He once gutted his own hand thinking it was a flounder. Jealous of his cousin John, he wants to kill John so he can play Christ. He is in love with Mary 1, who loves John. When John refuses to be seduced, Mary 1 gives in to Pontius and becomes pregnant. He wants to marry her, but she refuses. After she drowns herself, he also commits suicide.

Queen Elizabeth
The text indicates that Queen Elizabeth is preferably played by a man in drag. Her face is completely painted white as she shuts down the passion play.

Village Idiot
The director calls this character the "village idiot" because she is disruptive and provides predictions that seem like nonsense to him. She interrupts the rehearsal with her imaginary dialogue with her jack-in-the-box. She makes the sky turn red when the director ties her to a stump. The village idiot adds a lot of humor by mimicking the lines of the actors and substituting her own words. She replaces Mary 1 as Eve when Mary gets pregnant.

Visiting Friar
The visiting friar is in disguise because Catholic clerics are being put in prison. He is taken in by John the Fisherman. The friar hears the confessions of the players, and he believes and declares Mary's pregnancy a miracle. At the end, he goes to France to plot against the Protestant Queen Elizabeth.

Part Two
Director
The director is played by the same actor who was the director in Part One. He is the same kind of bully but now has a German name.

Elsa
Elsa plays the Virgin Mary in Part Two. She is played by the same actress who was Mary 1 in Part One. Elsa, forced to give in to the sexual advances of the Nazi officer, becomes his mistress and collaborator.

Eric

Eric plays Jesus in this era. He is played by the same actor who was John the Fisherman in Part One. Eric tries to fill his father's shoes in taking over the part of Jesus but is not sure of himself. He cannot remember his lines. He wants to go to war with his friend and lover, the foot soldier. As a Nazi, Eric betrays Violet and sends her to a concentration camp.

Foot Soldier

The foot soldier plays Pontius Pilate in this passion play and also played Pontius the Fish Gutter in Part One. He is drafted into the Nazi army and has to leave the play. He flirts with Eric and has a homosexual relationship with him, eventually getting him to enlist as a soldier too.

German Officer

The actor who played the machinist in Part One plays the German officer in this era. He forces a sexual liaison with Elsa, who plays the Virgin Mary. He warns the foot soldier that taking advantage of women is normal but that homosexuality is not tolerated in the army.

Hitler

Hitler is to be played by the same actor who played Queen Elizabeth in Part One. He points out in his speech how magnetic his personality is. He was once a sensitive painter, but now he feels it is right to kill Jews for what they did to Christ.

Mary 2

Mary 2 plays Mary Magdalene in this era, just as she did in Part One. Mary 2 is Eric's sister. She tries to keep him in line to play the part of Jesus as their father did.

Violet

The actress who plays Violet played the village idiot in Part One. She is now dressed as a normal girl, but she is still an outcast in the town. She cannot take a part in the play because she is a Jew. She seems to have some magic or imagination about her, as she says she can make the sky turn red. While the play is going on, she stages her own play about Hansel and Gretel. She becomes symbolic of all the Jewish victims of the war, sent to a concentration camp by Eric at the end.

Visiting Englishman

The actor who played the visiting friar in Part One plays the visiting Englishman. In Part Two, he writes to his wife in England about the passion play at Oberammergau, glossing over anything bad going on. He tells Violet that little Red Riding Hood and the wolf became friends. She does not think he tells the truth. He is supposedly in town to write a book about the passion play.

Part Three

J

In this passion play, J plays Jesus. He is played by the actor who portrayed John the Fisherman and Eric. J is P's younger brother. He is somewhat pretentious, proud of becoming a professional TV soap-opera actor and getting the director and old actors upgraded to professionals. He is condescending to his brother, P, after he comes home from the war. J is the real father of Violet.

Mary 1

Appearing as Mary 1 and Elsa in the other parts of the play, Mary 1 again plays the Virgin Mary and in this era is a sensuous woman who likes having sex and a man to sleep with. As soon as her husband leaves for the war, she seduces his brother and gets pregnant with Violet, whom she passes off as P's daughter. She divorces P after he comes home.

Mary 2

Mary 2 continues to play the role of Mary Magdalene, as in Parts One and Two. She stays in character, saying she believes in the message of the play: love. She has a job as a tollbooth attendant, seeing herself as a beacon of light, helping strangers. She tells Mary 1 to put herself in God's hands.

Old Director

The old director was the director in Parts One and Two. He is out of tune with modern methods of acting and directing. He seems to be an amateur, expecting the actors to follow orders instead of collaborating on the production. He is replaced by the young director.

P

P plays Pontius Pilate and Satan in this era. The same actor played Pontius the Fish Gutter and the foot soldier. He is drafted into the Vietnam War. After he comes home, he suffers from post-traumatic stress disorder and cannot make human connections except with three-year-old Violet, who pretends with him. He believes that she is his daughter and does not know his brother and wife betrayed him until later. P is the one who undergoes the biggest transformation, taking responsibility for his actions in Vietnam. He changes the lines of Pontius Pilate in rehearsal to say that he is an agent of the state, ordered to kill. He absolves the Jews of guilt.

Queen Elizabeth

The queen makes brief appearances in Part Three to give P her blessing before he goes to Vietnam and then again on the battlefield.

Ronald Reagan

The actor who played Queen Elizabeth and Hitler also plays Ronald Reagan. Reagan is one of the great comic characters of the play, like a stand-up comedian revealing his folksy, likeable manner but showing himself to be somewhat incompetent and flippant for a person with such an important job. Unlike Hitler and Queen Elizabeth, he does not have hands-on contact with his subjects, but he still makes decisions that affect them, without understanding the implications.

VA Psychiatrist

The actor who played the visiting friar and the visiting Englishman in the other two parts plays the veteran's hospital psychiatrist in Part Three. He is a sort of modern priest, taking confession and then prescribing medication for the patient. He does not really help P.

Violet

Violet is Mary 1's child. The actress playing this role was the village idiot in Part One. As an innocent child, Violet is the only one who can reach P after the war. Although she is three years old, they communicate perfectly. Even as she grows up, they continue to love each other and understand one another. She is obsessed with birds, just as P is obsessed with the wind.

Young Director

The young director is played by the actor who had the machinist and officer roles. The young director is savvy and more technically competent than the old director but still runs up against the ego of J, who wants to do the production his way.

THEMES

Art and Life

Passion Play is structured as a play—that is, several plays—within a play. Ruhl inserts the rehearsals so that the play scenes and real-life episodes alternate and comment on each other. In fact, often the line between performance and living is blurred. In Part One, the characters are famed for being as virtuous as the biblical characters. John the Fisherman seems as generous and forgiving as Christ. This becomes a problem when the woman playing the Virgin Mary falls in love with him. He rejects her advances in order to stay in character. She satisfies her urges with Pontius and becomes pregnant. John the Fisherman believes he is living the story he plays, so he treats Mary's pregnancy as a divine miracle.

Church and State

The relationship between church and state is represented in each play when the head of state visits a rehearsal of the passion play, revealing the official state policy towards what is strictly a religious performance. In Part One, Queen Elizabeth comes to stop the play as a vestigial mark of Catholic idolatry in her Protestant reign. Elizabeth's appearance and later that of Hitler show that Christianity, for much of European history, was not a matter of individual conscience but a matter of state policy. There was no separation of church and state.

Ruhl says in her introductory notes that the theme of separation of church and state has become an issue again in the United States, because although it is guaranteed in the Constitution, in contemporary politics, right-wing religion wants to co-opt the state. Reagan exemplifies this approach for her. He uses the passion play as a campaign opportunity. Reagan jokes that he was a radio broadcaster who made up baseball games as though watching them live. Ruhl makes this into a critical metaphor for an untrustworthy statesman.

TOPICS FOR FURTHER STUDY

- One of Ruhl's favorite novels is *The Unbearable Lightness of Being* (1984), by Czech writer Milan Kundera, because of the concept of "lightness," or seeing even terrible events with humor, imagination, and ecstasy. Read Kundera's book, and then apply the concept of lightness to *Passion Play*. Write a short paper comparing the two works in terms of lightness, giving examples.

- Work with a group to find relevant websites on the relationship between Christianity, Judaism, and Islam. Use Delicious.com as your social bookmarking service to share results. What background do these religions share? Create a group presentation showing visually on a large screen sample websites and your conclusions about the history and relationship of these religions.

- Religion was once only discussed in church or in religious works. Now, it can be the topic of a play (*Passion Play*) or be projected in fantasy worlds to be investigated from a different angle. Read C. S. Lewis's *The Lion, the Witch, and the Wardrobe* (1950), and create a class blog to discuss ways in which Lewis has told the Christian story in terms of fantasy. Which character is the Christ figure? Is this a sympathetic treatment of Christianity? How can you tell?

- Read the book by Anne Frank, *The Diary of a Young Girl* (1947). Frank was a Jewish teen in hiding from the Nazis for two years in Amsterdam before she was betrayed in 1944 and sent to her death in a concentration camp. Her diary has become world famous for depicting racial persecution. Compare her to Ruhl's character Violet in *Passion Play*, Part Two. Write a story where Eric the Nazi soldier makes a different choice and saves Violet rather than sending her to her death, or create a different ending for the life of Anne Frank. What could she have done or been after the war?

- Read *Hullabaloo in the Guava Orchard* (1998) Kiran Desai's comic young-adult novel about the Chawla family in India, juxtaposing ancient Hindu attitudes and beliefs with the westernized India of today. When young Sampath runs away from home to live in a tree, the villagers assume he is a holy man and ask his advice. Read the novel as a class and make an online wiki, adding information on Hinduism and how that relates specifically to the book. Include personal responses, Hindu links and artwork, and questions for further investigation. If possible, include interviews with Hindu students about the customs and practices of their religion.

Religious Criticism

Ruhl rejected her Catholic religion when she perceived its bias against the role of women and their lack of participation in church ritual. Ruhl is like many feminist theologians today who critique Christianity and other religions for their denial of female worth. *Passion Play* contains many such feminist points. The two Marys, Mary 1 (also Elsa) and Mary 2, present a sort of character doubling of woman in her two main roles according to Christian stereotypes. Woman is either pure, like the Virgin Mary, untouched by sin and sex, or else a whore like Mary Magdalene. Ruhl subverts these stereotypes. In Part One, Mary 1 has no desire to be a virgin, and Mary 2 hates sex with a man. When they step outside their given roles, they lose their places in society. The actors rehearse the fall of man in the Garden of Eden, traditionally blamed on Eve, who is tempted by the snake, which in part represents sexuality. Christianity is shown to devalue and suppress sex, women, and the body. It has also historically condoned the persecution of other

The cast of Passion Play *takes a curtain call on opening night.* *(© Steve Mack | Getty Images Entertainment | Getty Images)*

races and religious groups, such as the Jews, even though Christ himself was a Jew who preached tolerance and love.

STYLE

Postmodern Theater

Postmodernism is a general term used of the experimentation in art after World War II. Postmodern art is often ironic, showing the impossibility of closure or a final meaning. Ruhl's plays are open-ended. She rejects the classical and rational plot structure of action leading to a central climax, a catharsis or revelation of truth. She favors the fantastic story lines of Ovid, showing small changes for characters all through the play. Ruhl often includes puppets or other elements from Kabuki theater, the stylized Japanese drama.

Postmodern theater exhibits a resistance to realism. Ruhl favors nonlinear storytelling with archetypal images that allow audiences to feel emotion and draw their own meaning. Scenes

are vignettes suggesting the story, weaving random bits of the passion play with the lives of the characters. Intertextuality is another characteristic of postmodern theater. *Intertextuality* means playing off and engaging with other sources. *Passion Play* is full of scenes from other texts, especially the Bible, and it references well-known songs, poems, and fairy tales.

Many of the practices of German playwright Bertolt Brecht (1898–1956) have been adopted by postmodern playwrights, such as "defamiliarization" of material to make people see it in a new way. Another Brechtian technique is breaking the illusion of the play by having actors turn and address the audience directly. American playwrights who have used some of these techniques include Thornton Wilder in *Our Town* (1938) and Tony Kushner in *Angels in America* (1993).

Postmodern critics influencing Ruhl's work are Victor Shklovsky (1893–1984), who insists that artists do not have to copy reality, and Italo Calvino (1923–1985), who expounds on the quality of "lightness" in art in *Six Memos for the Next Millennium* (1993). Ruhl subscribes to lightness as a philosophical and aesthetic technique, allowing her to treat serious and even tragic ideas with a certain humor. *Passion Play* is tragic but also very funny.

Magic Realism

Magic realism became a popular style during the 1960s Latin American boom in literature. Gabriel García Márquez, from Colombia, for instance, is well known for magic realism in *One Hundred Years of Solitude* (1967). Literature written in this style intermixes realism and everyday events with seeming magical or supernormal events without commenting on their juxtaposition. Ruhl is known for using fantastical images to reveal deeper reality and inner states of being. Supernormal perception or alternate realities are accepted without explanation in her scenes. Magical thinking and fairy-tale formulas characterize Ruhl's plays. In *Passion Play*, for example, Violet claims she has the power to turn the sky red; she remembers a former life; and John the Fisherman believes in a modern-day virgin birth.

Feminist Theater

Ruhl began her career at a time when few women playwrights were produced in the United States. Dramatic structure in women's plays tends to be relational or character-based. The traditional dramatic structure leading to an action climax is seen by many feminist writers as masculine and power-based. Paula Vogel, Ruhl's professor and mentor at Brown University, won a Pulitzer Prize for her play *How I Learned to Drive* (1997). Feminist plays emphasize feminist concerns and community over individual action. *Eurydice* (2003) is about Ruhl's father's death. Ruhl discusses women's work in *The Clean House* (2004), in which a Brazilian maid is employed by a woman doctor. Latina playwright Lisa Loomer's *Living Out* (2003) is about two working mothers, a lawyer and the nanny she hires, and explores similar themes. Some feminist playwrights tackle religious questions, as in Ruhl's *Passion Play* and *100 Saints You Should Know*, by Kate Fodor, concerning an ousted priest.

HISTORICAL CONTEXT

Christianity and the Passion Play

The passion play, depicting the trial, suffering, crucifixion, and ascension of Christ, was originally part of medieval Catholic ritual, sung in Latin. It developed as a separate popular play in vernacular languages for large audiences, performed during Lent before Easter to increase devotion.

Christians affirm in their creeds that Jesus is the son of God sent to save humanity from its original sin inherited from Adam and Eve. His coming was prophesied in the Old Testament as the coming of the Christ or the Messiah. He was denounced by the Jewish council and condemned to death alongside common convicts by the Romans who ruled Judea at the time. Although he died and was buried in a tomb, he arose bodily from the dead and ascended directly to heaven to be with God the father. There he will judge humans and give eternal life to those who believe in him. Parts of this story are enacted in Ruhl's play. She is especially interested in the character of Pontius Pilate, who in her versions has a love-hate relationship with Christ.

While historically the Catholic Church blamed the Jews for Christ's death, modern papal letters and revised wording of the liturgy have amended this to absolve the Jews of Christ's death and instead express Christianity's roots in Judaism.

Elizabethan England

The first of Ruhl's *Passion Plays* takes place in England in 1575, at a time when the nation is changing permanently from a Catholic to a Protestant one. Elizabeth I (1533–1603) outlawed passion plays as a form of Catholic idolatry. Elizabeth's Act of Supremacy in 1559 made her the head of the Protestant Church of England, so she was both monarch and head of the Church of England. To keep the peace and her throne, she refused to marry, declaring herself the Virgin Queen, married to her subjects. Ruhl portrays Elizabeth as a consummate actor, painting her face and making herself into a cult figure, almost like the Catholic Virgin Mary. It was the age of Shakespeare, with the blossoming of great secular and professional drama, making the religious and amateur drama of the village obsolete.

Hitler's Germany

The passion play at Oberammergau, Bavaria, began in 1634 and is still put on as a spectacle every ten years, with half the townspeople taking parts. Hitler visited the performance in 1934. His speech in the play praising its anti-Jewish bias is based on his actual speech. Adolf Hitler (1889–1945) believed in a Jewish and Marxist conspiracy against Germany and gave polemic speeches with hypnotic appeal. The Great Depression allowed Hitler to gain power as chancellor of Germany in 1933. In 1938, Neville Chamberlain (1869–1940) of Great Britain signed the Munich Agreement, allowing Hitler to take over part of Czechoslovakia in order to appease him. Chamberlain is satirized in the play as the visiting Englishman who watches what goes on but does nothing. The Holocaust refers to the genocide and mass murders perpetrated by his Nazi regime during World War II. Jews, homosexuals, and all social undesirables were removed to concentration camps for forced labor, and finally, they were sent by trains to extermination camps. The train whistle in the play reminds the audience of those death trains.

Vietnam and Ronald Reagan

Part Three of *Passion Play* covers 1969 to the present. It opens with P going off to fight in Vietnam. The United States' involvement in the Vietnam War (1959–1975) was part of the Cold War between the Soviet Union and the United States, over whether democracy or Communism would predominate in the world. In the end, the Communists won in Vietnam, and Americans were bitter and divided over this unnecessary conflict that took so many lives and resources. The Gulf of Tonkin Resolution of 1964 allowed President Lyndon Johnson to pursue military operations in Vietnam without declaring war. The war escalated until the bloody Tet Offensive by the Viet Cong in 1968 practically proved that the United States could not win the war. In the play, P drags a dead fish across the stage, representing the dead Vietnamese. He comes home, like many Vietnam veterans did, destroyed in mind if not in body. The mass demonstrations against the war at home denounced leaders like Johnson for unilaterally deciding the fate of so many so far away for the sake of some ideology.

By extending this part of the play to Reagan's presidency, Ruhl brings up the point that though times and political processes appear to change, the state still interferes without just cause, capitalizing on religion and using ideology to promote itself. Reagan was known for escalating the Cold War with covert operations in South America, Africa, and Asia. Ruhl uses Reagan symbolically to stand for the recent history of government aligning with right-wing

In the first act of Passion Play*, Queen Elizabeth declares such plays sacrilegious.* (© Georgios Kollidas / Shutterstock.com)

Christian ideas and groups, undoing the separation of church and state. Ronald Reagan (1911–2004) was a popular president who gained the trust of Americans. Ruhl, however, points out the credibility gap with the story that Reagan once broadcast made-up baseball games to the public as real.

CRITICAL OVERVIEW

Ruhl began to emerge as a promising playwright as she studied under her mentor, Pulitzer Prize–winning playwright Paula Vogel, at Brown University. Ruhl wrote and produced over a dozen plays in her first decade out of graduate school. In an interview with Ruhl for *BOMBInterviews* in 2007, after Ruhl became well known in American theater, Vogel mentioned that Ruhl is "one of the most unique minds in theater I've encountered." Vogel says she loves "the scope of [*Passion Play*]. It has an incredible humanity, *heart*, that really grabs me."

Ruhl's first major success was *Eurydice* in 2003, a play about the wife of Orpheus and her descent into the underworld to find her father. The play is one of her most popular. In a *New Yorker* review of a 2007 performance, John Lahr calls it "a luminous retelling" that "frees the stage from the habitual" with a "surreal world, as lush and limpid as a dream."

The *Passion Play* trilogy is recognized as Ruhl's most ambitious work and wins praise for its epic length and depth. A review of the cycle by Celia Wren, in *American Theater* in 2005, says the plays have "a steely lyricism; a pronounced whimsy"; and "metaphysical intensity" with "a quirky, compassionate humor."

Lahr reviewed a 2008 production of *Passion Play* in the *New Yorker*, saying, "Ruhl trades in verbal and visual irony" to "offer the audience illumination, not distraction." In a review for *Books & Culture* in 2009, Lauren F. Winner notes the "self-conscious and captivating theatricality" of *Passion Play* which shows "how performing shapes performers."

Working with a number of different designers to shape the unusual productions requiring items like an elevator that rains water or giant fish puppets and boats in the sky, Ruhl has credited the actors and designers as important collaborators in shaping the final productions. Each production is different and gives her continued insights into her own work. In the twenty-first century, Ruhl's plays are among the most produced plays on American stages (especially *In the Next Room, Eurydice, Dead Man's Cell Phone*, and *The Clean House*). Her prizes and awards have been numerous, including being a finalist twice for the Pulitzer and winning the MacArthur Foundation "genius grant" of half a million dollars, the Whiting Foundation award of $35,000, the Susan Smith Blackburn award of $10,000, and a PEN/Laura Pels International Foundation for Theater Award, all while in her thirties.

CRITICISM

Susan K. Andersen

Andersen holds a PhD in literature. In the following essay, she considers how the plays within a play function in Passion Play *as a metaphor for society and the constraining roles people try to escape by deviating from the script.*

> IN SHOWING HOW LIFE IN SOCIETY IS LIKE A PLAY, RUHL WARNS THAT WE NEED TO BE CONSCIOUS OF THE PARTS WE PLAY AND WHO IS WRITING OR INTERPRETING THE SCRIPT FOR US."

Sarah Ruhl's *Passion Play* does not try to come to a conclusion about Christ or the Christian religion. Ruhl is rather interested in how humans have interpreted and interacted with the symbols of Christianity for personal and political agendas. Critic James Al-Shamma, in his book *Sarah Ruhl: A Critical Study of the Plays*, asserts that *Passion Play* contains many "other counter-narratives to the passion itself." This means that the actors are playing one narrative and each living another.

Christ's passion is a sad but hopeful message about atonement with God. The play's central image of crucifixion, however, is a bloody one that Ruhl juxtaposes with images of personal and historical violence. The passion play is acted by flawed and frustrated individuals; their lives do not bring out the doctrine of atonement but are rather an indictment of human narrowness. No one seems able to live up to the ideal portrayed in the passion, especially since the message has been distorted over time.

In the author's note of the 2010 acting edition of the play, Ruhl explains that the play brings up many questions: "How are we scripted? Where is the line between authentic identity and performance?" In showing how life in society is like a play, Ruhl warns that we need to be conscious of the parts we play and who is writing or interpreting the script for us.

Ruhl demonstrates that the distinction between art and life is not clear for the actors. They get caught up in their roles, thinking they are or have to be their characters in real life. John the Fisherman in Part One thinks he has to be exactly like Christ, without sexual desire. Pontius, who plays the villain Pontius Pilate in Part One, is typecast because of his looks. He longs to play Christ so people will love him, but he does not look the part. Ruhl thus comments on the social injustice that types people and represses

WHAT DO I READ NEXT?

- Jean-Claude Carrière's play and Peter Brook's translation of the Indian epic *The Mahabharata* brought to the stage a religious classic that is longer than the Bible and full of drama and wisdom. This script of the original 1985 nine-hour play that toured the world with an international and racially diverse cast was later reduced in length for the TV miniseries and 1989 film. It was published in paperback in 1989.

- *The Secret Life of Bees* (2003), by Sue Monk Kidd, is a novel exploring feminist theology and racism, like Ruhl's play. She describes a southern black community's worship based on a Black Madonna.

- *Christianity: The First Three Thousand Years* (2011), by Diarmaid MacCulloch, is a history that illustrates how Christianity has always inspired diverse churches, each with its interpretation of who Jesus Christ was. The volume covers Christianity across the globe.

- *Church* (2007) is a play by Korean American playwright Young Jean Lee about growing up in a fundamentalist Evangelical church that she hated. Her play is a challenge to herself to find something redeeming in her church.

- Ann Loades is the editor of *Feminist Theology: A Reader* (1990), with selections of British and American feminist theologians pointing out some of the issues Ruhl

addresses in her play about the place of women in the Bible and Christianity.

- Ruhl's *The Clean House* (2004) is a play about women's work and includes a doctor, her Brazilian housemaid, and her spinster sister. The three women act as caretakers for the mistress of the doctor's husband, who has breast cancer.

- James Shapiro's *Oberammergau: The Troubling Story of the World's Most Famous Passion Play* (2001) explains the beginning of the tradition in 1634 and how it became controversial after Hitler's visit in 1934. The villagers have been forced to revise the play to remove prejudice against Jews for the thousands of world travelers who see it.

- Lowell Swortzell has brought together a young-adult collection of plays, *Around the World in 21 Plays: Theatre for Young Audiences* (1997), with works from diverse cultures. The volume includes plays, both serious and lighthearted, by writers from many different cultural backgrounds, including African American, Latino, German, and Jewish.

- Paula Vogel's play *The Long Christmas Ride Home* (2005) is an emotional takeoff by Ruhl's mentor on Thornton Wilder's *The Long Christmas Dinner*. The play uses magic and Noh theater techniques to tell the story of a family of five and their holiday.

their desires. Mary 1's tragedy in Part One would have been avoidable if she had been allowed to express her sexuality and love freely. The illusory nature of role-playing is pointed out by J in Part Three when he recounts how he had to smell a lemon in acting class though there was no lemon (act 1, scene 6). Similarly, human roles in society are often based on pretending, as Mary 2 points out when she pretends to like men (Part One).

The actors are frustrated by feeling they have the wrong roles. Mary 1, who plays the Virgin Mary, does not want to be a virgin in real life. She finds John the Fisherman sexy in his loincloth. She wants to switch roles with Mary 2, who plays the prostitute, Magdalene. Mary 2 is a lesbian who would rather play the chaste Virgin Mary. The director, however, will not let them switch roles because Mary 1 looks holy and Mary 2 looks sensual, so they are doomed to be misfits.

The play and its script become a metaphor for the tyranny of social convention. Besides actors being constrained by the script, there are marginal or outcast people who cannot even get a part in the play. The village idiot in Part One is a prophetic woman who seems to speak nonsense, but she can make the sky turn red and see the future. She is funny when she puts on her counter-play with her jack-in-the-box while the director is trying to rehearse. The village idiot is finally given the part of Eve, responsible for the fall of man. When women are given parts, they are either impossible (Virgin Mary) or villainous (Eve). The sky turns red as an omen of impending disaster around the marginalized social figures and victims who do not fit in.

Who are the admirable people in this play? They are the ones who perhaps understand something of the spirit of the story they play. They break away from the script to speak their own authentic voices: the village idiot, Violet the Jew, Violet the little girl, and P in Part Three. The village idiot in Part One and Violet in Part Two play the wise fool, making up their own stories and commenting on the action. Violet the little girl in Part Three is the only one P the veteran can relate to when he comes home from Vietnam. They are able to play together with artistic images in a healing way. When Violet draws pictures of birds for P, he says he knows there is a God.

The most complex role is given to P, or Pontius Pilate, in Part Three. He suffers war trauma and is rejected by society when he comes home, but he takes responsibility for his actions and eventually finds himself and his belief in God again. He rushes onstage during rehearsal saying he wants to speak his own lines instead of the script. He has had to play Pontius Pilate, who ceremoniously washes his hands of the blood of Christ. P found that in Vietnam, he was literally unable to wash his hands of the blood and brains of the little girl he accidentally shot. He wants to amend the lines of the play to admit that he (as both Pontius Pilate and himself) was an agent of the state, ordered to kill. P becomes transformed by experience and exercises his free will. Eric, on the other hand, who plays Christ in Part Two, is given a chance to make an ethical choice and declines. As he is ready to

take Violet away to the concentration camp, she begs him to break out of the role: "It's not like being in a play—no one's watching—you could do something different... a man must decide for himself." This idea of moral choice is amplified by P in the epilogue when he says, "It's good to be awake. When you're awake you can fight for what you believe in, no matter what costume you're wearing." Ruhl thus reinforces a message of social responsibility.

Christ's warning in the Bible against following false prophets is repeated in this passion play. Eric ignores the message in order to follow Hitler. He confuses religion and politics, comparing the grace of God to marching with the Nazis. He feels that he is part of something larger and so does not have to make decisions. In Part Three, the prologue alludes to the bloody massacre of Wounded Knee, implying the genocide of the Indian tribes, echoing the genocide of the Jews in the previous part. Once again, the human history of war and politics is intertwined with the passion play, allowing the two lines of action to comment on one another. P points out that whether a leader is nice (like Reagan) or evil (like Hitler), if the leader orders killing, men come home in body bags.

By using magic realism and satiric humor, Ruhl keeps the audience awake and off balance. The village idiot can make the sky turn red and mock seriousness with her jack-in-the-box, while P can control the wind and make boats appear in the sky. Ruhl uses jokes and riddles and fairy tales, genres from oral tradition, as incantations that make things happen in a shamanistic way. Violet tells the tale of Hansel and Gretel, where the evil witch is put in the oven, a hopeful talisman against having to go to the gas chambers. When Eric tells the story of Red Riding Hood to Violet, he emphasizes that the wolf eats up the little girl, a prelude to his sending Violet to the concentration camp.

Ruhl believes that American drama today must exhibit "a kind of primal familiarity wedded to the newness of soaring insight," as she pronounces in her article "Re-runs and Repetition" for *Contemporary Theatre Review*. In *Passion Play*, the audience is familiar with the biblical story and the fairy tales but not the way they are presented on stage. She has taken familiar material and defamiliarized it to produce revelations about our lives.

The second act takes place in Oberammergau, Germany, where the Passion Play began in the Middle Ages. (© Georgios Kollidas / Shutterstock.com)

Source: Susan K. Andersen, Critical Essay on *Passion Play*, in *Drama for Students*, Gale, Cengage Learning, 2014.

James Al-Shamma

In the following excerpt, Al-Shamma examines the imagery in Passion Play.

Ruhl establishes a rich set of images in the first part upon which she draws in the second and third; much of this imagery is derived from biblical and Christian symbology, some of it associated with Revelation and apocalypse. These images include fish, water, the moon, the red sky, birds and air. The fish is an important Christian symbol. In the early church, the Greek word for fish (*ichthus*) was taken to be an acrostic for "Jesus Christ, Son of God, Savior" (*Iesous Christos Theou Huios Soter*) (Speake, 54), and early Christians secretly identified themselves to one another by drawing the symbol of a fish (55). A number of Jesus's followers were fishermen, including the apostle John (Matthew 4: 21), as is the character of the same name in the first part of *Passion Play*. Jesus urges Peter and Andrew to become "fishers of men" (Matthew 4: 19), meaning that they should become savers of souls, and Matthew uses an analogy of the sorting of fish for judgment day, upon which the unworthy will be cast into a furnace as into hell (Matthew 13: 47–50). Jesus performs a number of piscine miracles. On one occasion he feeds 5,000 people with two fish and five loaves of bread (Mark 6: 38–44; Matthew 15: 17–21; Luke 9: 12–17; John 6: 5–13), and on another he feeds 4,000 with a few fish and seven loaves (Matthew 15: 34–39). After the disciples have had an unsuccessful night of fishing, the resurrected, disguised Jesus instructs them to cast the net on the right side of the boat, upon which they draw in 153 fish (John 21: 1–14). Matthew compares the internment and resurrection of Jesus to Jonah's confinement to, and release from, the belly of the whale (Matthew 12: 40), with "whale" appearing as "fish" in early versions of the Bible (Roop, 124).

"

THE SKY COLOR REINFORCES THE BLEAK CONCLUSION, EVOKING AS IT DOES THE SMOKE FROM CONCENTRATION CAMP CREMATORIA."

Lois Drewer analyzes the occurrences of what she terms "fish ponds" in early Christian art in "Fisherman and Fish Pond: From the Sea of Sin to the Living Waters" (1981). She notes, "The fish are usually recognized as symbols of Christian souls, while the fisherman is an image of Christ or the apostles who bring them into a state of salvation." The current alternates, as water conveys contradictory meanings in these images as derived from early Christian writings, both as "the 'living water' in which Christian souls flourish" and as "the sea of this world, or as the bitter sea of sin." The Christian soul is rescued from the sea of sin by the fisherman, but also enjoys eternal life in the living water of baptism. The fish-soul experiences a death to the world, that is the sea of sin, and then a resurrection through the effect of the living waters. Birds sometimes appear in early Christian art alongside fish and other sea creatures. Both fish and birds came into being on the fifth day of creation (Genesis 1: 20–21), and Tertullian associates birds with "the martyrs which essay to mount up to heaven" (qtd. in Drewer, 545). In *The Dent Dictionary of Symbols in Christian Art* (1994), Jennifer Speake notes that "birds may sometimes be symbolic of souls, which inhabit both the physical and the spiritual world as birds inhabit the earth and air." Thus both fish and birds may represent the soul. The dove specifically symbolizes the descending Holy Spirit.

Another biblical image employed by Ruhl is that of the red sky. When asked by the Pharisees and Sadducees for a sign from heaven, Jesus replies:

> When it is evening, you say, "It will be fair weather, for the sky is red." And in the morning, "There will be a storm today, for the sky is red and threatening." Do you know how to discern the appearance of the sky, but cannot discern the signs of the times [Matthew 16: 2–3]?

Whereas in Matthew a red sky serves as a metaphor for changing times, in Acts and Revelation it foretells the apocalypse. In Acts 2: 20, it is prophesized that a sign of the second coming will be the sun going dark and the moon "turning into blood." In Revelation also, the moon becomes "like blood" (6: 12) and is associated with a pregnant figure:

> A great sign appeared in heaven: A woman clothed with the sun, and the moon under her feet, and on her head a crown of twelve stars; and she was with child; and she cried out, being in labor and in pain to give birth [Revelation 12: 1–2].

Deriving from this vision, the crescent moon is associated with Mary in early Christian art according to F. R. Webber in *Church Symbolism*, published in 1938. Webber indicates that the rose also is associated with Mary. Although the moon is not mentioned, the Gospels note that the sky turned dark during three hours of Jesus's crucifixion, from the sixth to the ninth hour (Matthew 27: 45; Mark 15: 33; Luke 23: 44), which is equivalent to the span from 12:00 noon until 3:00 P.M. (Dake).

FISH OF THE SEA

Ruhl associates the Pontius of the first part with fish, those that swim in the sea of the world rather than the living water of grace. He reeks of the fish that he guts for a living. His attractive cousin, John, who plays the Christ, spends his days upon the clean, living waters. Pontius equates the stench of fish with his own unworthiness, particularly in regards to Mary 1, whom he imagines will be repelled by the odor. She offers rose water as an antidote. Through association with the Virgin Mary, the rose connotes purity, and therefore rose water would have a cleansing effect. In the New Testament, Pilate washes his hands of Jesus's blood before releasing him to be crucified (Matthew 27: 24). Ruhl's Pontius is so immersed in the waters of sin that he lacks any means of washing the smell off of him. He begs of Mary 1 that she run off with him to bear her child, couching his plea in terms of the passion with himself in the role of the Christ, promising that she can scourge and crucify him every night. He flounders in a state of generalized primal sin. He expresses joy rather than remorse over Mary 1's out-of-wedlock pregnancy. Like the biblical Pilate, he is unable to wash away his sin.

An incident that Pontius relates from his workday is rife with symbolism:

I gutted a fish today—I thought it was dead—I slit open its belly—and five live fishes squirmed out. They stunk of death. They wriggled and wraggled in the guts of their mother and they died one by one. The last one to go was a real wriggler. He watched everyone go before him—he swam around in their fishy guts—and then I slammed the knife down on his back. I couldn't stand to see one so alone and so alive, so I killed the poor devil to put it out of its misery.

The image of the lone survivor swimming around in "fishy guts" symbolizes, in a general sense, the lost soul floundering in the waters of sin. It may also be read in turn, specifically, as Mary 1, her unborn child, Pontius himself, the historical/biblical Pilate, Christ, and Pontius's cousin John. Pontius may be seen to have killed Mary 1 by impregnating her, causing her to be trapped in a set of circumstances from which she imagines suicide her only escape. The fish also represents Pontius killing himself with a knife over Mary 1's body. His suicide is foreshadowed at rehearsal, during which he stabs himself with a stage knife, miming puncturing his eyes and slitting open his belly as one might a fish. Although the New Testament does not narrate Pilate's death, speculations may be found in various sources. In *Pontius Pilate* (1999), Anne Wroe chronicles some of these, including a version related in the medieval *Golden Legend* in which Pontius preempts a death sentence with suicide. Wroe states that in the Rome of his time, suicide was often "performed for the sake of others," as the wishes of the deceased would be honored and the family's reputation salvaged. Also according to the *Golden Legend*, the emperor ordered Pilate's body thrown into the Tiber, but the river rejected it through the agency of devils that "made the air and water seethe" and attacked the city with storm and flood. Next the body was thrown into Vesuvius, which erupted, and thence into the Rhone, which also became troubled by devils. According to local legend, he was finally thrown into "a flaming pit somewhere in the Alps" where the demons were happy to claim their own (Wroe). The "wriggling and wraggling" of the fish in their mother's guts evokes the seething waters that expelled Pilate's body.

The fish stabbed by Pontius also represents the Christ. In this symbolic murder Pontius comes as close as he ever does to fulfilling his wish to kill his cousin, as expressed in his opening monologue. It is not his wish merely to kill him, he wants to take his place on the cross, to play the role of Christ. He imagines that crucifixion would straighten his twisted spine and sanctify him. It would function as a baptism, a dip in the living waters. His way to the cross would be through his cousin's crucifixion, his own holiness bestowed through punishment for the crime of murder. His yearning finds precedence in the Coptic account of Pilate, who is scourged and crucified as punishment for ordering the Savior's death. However, he is perceived as unworthy to follow in the Savior's path and his blood as defiling the Savior's crucifix, upon which he is hung (Wroe). Since, according to Christian theology, Christ died on the cross to bear the burden of all men's sin, Pontius's following him to atone for his own sin is redundant and even heretical.

Ruhl provides a counter-narrative to the Christian doctrine of salvation. Huge fish puppets appear to Pontius twice like pagan gods. They hint at fulfilling his wish for crucifixion by stripping him as Jesus was stripped before scourging. The fish are his allies and he belongs to them, as they provide his livelihood and he reeks of them. They reappear to carry him off after his suicide. These beautiful fish represent neither lost souls swimming in the sinful waters of the world, nor saved souls swimming in the living water of salvation. As an unrepentant suicide, Pontius's soul leaves the earth in an unclean state, undeserving of Christian grace. The grace that the fish bestow upon Pontius emanates from some other source. Their presence cleanses as signified by the sky turning from red to blue while they carry him off like a king. The fish challenge the primacy of Christ as the unifying symbol. They inhabit Frye's disintegrating element, water, associated as it is with death and the passage to the underworld. Yet they are native to this element, and for them it represents life, not the passage into death. They bear Pontius away as if to ready him for the next act and foreshadow, through association, his ability, as P in part three, to navigate currents, albeit those of the air.

Prior to his death, Pontius reports to Mary 1's corpse that the fish drink his cousin's tears. The author of Psalm 80 refers to the drinking of tears while pleading with God to answer the prayers of the Israelites to restore their good fortune (Psalm 80: 5–6). Drinkers of tears are, in this biblical sense, unfortunates whose prayers go unanswered. Earlier in the play, when John encounters Mary 1 alone at night, he wishes to drink her sorrow. This desire to shoulder Mary 1's troubles aligns him with the Christ. The trope is reversed, however, at the conclusion of the first part, as the fish drink John's tears, absorbing his sorrow. John fishes across from Pontius and Mary 1's body "as if in a dream," silhouetted against the lit backdrop and casting a net, as staged in the Goodman Theater production. The waterlogged corpse of Mary 1 represents one fish that he was unable to catch; Pontius's self-immolated body, another. It is left to the fish to absorb the Christ-figure's sorrow and to honor the sacrifice of Pontius. Rather than emblems of Christianity, they emerge as if from a Jungian collective unconscious. They remove Pontius's body to the beating of drums, as if honoring him in an ancient ceremony, granting him the respect he desired to earn on the cross. The central symbol of the One Man is thus displaced by a school of fish.

"THE SMELL OF THE MOON"

As noted above, the moon symbolized the Virgin Mary in early Christian art. Pontius notes that Mary 1 smells like the moon, and John poetically associates her with it as he treads a nighttime landscape, which he imagines is covered in "moonskin." He expresses a readiness to die coupled with an aversion to breaking the skin, and this evokes Jesus on the night before his crucifixion, anticipating scourging and nails. The moonskin, however, is also associated with Mary 1, whose assumed virginity John cautions himself against breaching. Pontius expresses a complex relationship to the moon. He imagines it sequentially as "a laughing pitchfork" and a bewildered dunce, as a "white wedge" one evening and a full moon the next. The "white wedge" suggests a crescent, as associated with the Virgin Mary and by extension Mary 1. Pontius's perception of a laughing moon projects his fear of rejection by Mary 1. The sudden transformation into full phase foreshadows Mary 1's pregnancy, as the moon becomes as round and full as an expectant mother's belly. Suddenly the moon is no longer laughing; he looks "bewildered and afraid" as will the pregnant Mary 1. Only Mary 1 will witness Pontius's grief as she refuses to flee with him and publicly disavows earthly paternity.

Pontius makes one last reference to the moon before he commits suicide. It is once again in virginal crescent form, and is "cradled by the night" as Mary 1 is cradled in death. The rocking cradle evokes the unborn child, and Pontius assumes the role of child as well, with the prospect of death softened by thoughts of his lover/mother. He vows to swim after her into the beyond. Within the narrative of Ruhl's cycle, he finds her once more in the third part, thereby resisting the disintegrative tendencies of water.

RED SKY

As noted above, in both Revelation and Acts the moon appears as though drenched in blood as a harbinger of the second coming. The sky ominously reddens in the first part of *Passion Play* on several occasions. Pontius notices it first, in the second scene, and complains that everyone is too busy to notice. The Visiting Friar next bears witness to the transformation at two o'clock in the afternoon, which hour falls within the time span of the darkened sky during Jesus's crucifixion. The Village Idiot next wills the sky red when the director ties her to a stump to prevent her from disrupting the rehearsal. She relates to her Jack-in-the-Box as confined in the dark while she does so. She turns the sky red with the power of God the Father and suffers as God the Son trapped in a box, symbolic of Christ in his moment of despair on the cross. The positioning of God the Father as wise fool transgresses Erasmus's formulation, reducing the eternal divine to mere humanity.

When Mary 2 asks the Visiting Friar why her dreams of embracing women are wrong, he defers her question to God the Father. The sky turns red once again, as if in protest of a homophobic, patriarchal god. While rehearsing the annunciation scene, The Village Idiot blasphemously inserts the name Jack into the lines as she mimics Carpenter 1 as the Angel Gabriel. At this juncture, the sky turns red and the harnessed Carpenter 1 crashes to the ground. The fact of Mary 1's terrestrial pregnancy appears to impinge upon the enactment of immaculate conception. The Village Idiot's blasphemous substitution of the name Jack for Biblical names, including Jesus, provokes, if not the wrath, then perhaps at least the ire of a vengeful God. The Village Idiot disrupts Frye's archetype of Christ as the unifying One Man. "Jack" references the Jack-in-the-box, but is also a nickname for John, which designates both the character playing Christ and one of Christ's apostles. It refers to Pontius as well through his association with the Jack-in-the-box. The name Jack, through its many associations, signifies an everyman as opposed to the One Man and thus secularizes the Biblical story.

The sky and moon portend a second coming, one that is aborted. The sky turns blue again when the fish gods carry Pontius away, but Mary 1 fails to give birth to the new fish messiah. Pontius's fish salvation fails to transcend earthly life, as he must return in the following two parts of the cycle in order to reenact the passion play. In both of those parts, he longs for release. As he escapes in a flying ship he transmutes from a fish immersed in the waters of sin to a bird-like Tertullian martyr ascending to heaven. The medieval passion was staged as representative of all time and meant to remind its audience of the impending endpoint, doomsday, and of the redemptive power of the crucifixion and resurrection (Kolve). The repetitive nature of Ruhl's passion cycle however, with actors playing the same parts in successive sections, suggests reincarnation rather than redemption, which is philosophically consistent with Hinduism or Buddhism rather than Christianity. P's plea to be excused from the play brings to mind the cry of the weary soul, in Eastern philosophy, for release from the cycle of death and rebirth with its inevitable, and endlessly repeated, suffering. His escape in a ship, staged as a vertical ascent in the Goodman Theatre production, suggests enlightenment as defined as a release from the earthly, karmic cycle although, as will be explored below, his flight from the earth is not as completely liberating as it may seem.

EARTHBOUND BIRDS

Ruhl sparingly redeploys images from the first part in the second, and delays the reincorporation of fish and air imagery until the third. Characters mention the moon twice in the second part, in the first instance as discussed by Eric and the Footsoldier as they surreptitiously flirt. Stage directions call for an orange moon, described by Eric as a judge, that mirrors the German officer who is observing, and disapproving of, their homosexual flirtatiousness; however, the moon also projects, as judge, the eventual indictment of the Nazi regime at the Nuremberg trials. When the Footsoldier removes his hands from Eric's eyes, the moon appears in gold, conveying a German optimism under Hitler's leadership. The moon is mentioned one more time as Eric rehearses, in a warning about the darkening of the sky that will occur with the emergence of false

Christs and prophets. The passage refers to Hitler in the context of Matthew 24. Revelation also refers to a false prophet who is in league with the devil in three separate verses (16:13, 19:20, 20:10). Hitler referred to the Third Reich as a 1,000-year reign in a secularized millennium, one in which he implicitly assumed the role of messiah. When he is cast as a false prophet, his projected reign is inverted as a millennium celebrating the triumph of sin.

Images of birds and the red sky figure prominently in the second part, the former associated specifically with Violet. The director imprisons her in the basket that houses the doves released during the temple scene. The dove is generally recognized as a symbol of peace and in Christian symbology, particularly when descending, represents the Holy Spirit. The peaceable Violet replaces the doves in the basket in a foreshadowing of her eventual internment in a concentration camp. When Eric expresses a desire to join the army, his sister, Mary 2, relates an incident from their childhood in which he accidentally kills her pet bird. Afterwards, filled with shame, he despairs of anyone ever loving him again. This memory foreshadows the final scene of part two in which Eric, now a soldier, captures Violet. They play a word game in which they challenge each other with horrible dilemmas. The first poses the choice between cruelty to two innocents, the second between self-interest and self-sacrifice. Eric chooses to kill a dog rather than kick a baby, and to poke someone in the eardrum rather than become deaf since, as he explains, "It would be terrible to be deaf. I love music." His decisions fail to correspond to what Jesus would do, in spite of his playing that role in the passion.

Violet disrupts a rehearsal as she tells the story of "Hansel and Gretel," a fairy tale in which hungry birds strand children in the forest. Even though Violet disavows breadcrumbs as trail markers to the Visiting Englishman (85), she finds herself in the position, later on, of using them for that purpose. When a giant bird appears in the forest, she kindly feeds him all of her stock, confident in her sense of direction. The unreliable bird immediately abandons her when she closes her eyes to sleep. In any case, it is too large to fly and therefore unable to provide rapturous transport away from the tribulation, and thus abandons Violet to her fate.

The red sky, which portends the death of Mary 1 and an aborted second coming in the first part, reappears here within a context that suggests a sky reddened by war or the glow from concentration camp crematoria. Violet claims to be turning the sky this color, as does her counterpart in the first part. Violet tells the Visiting Englishman that no one notices when she reddens the sky, and when the Director locks her in the birdcage, she unsuccessfully attempts to do so, which failure demonstrates her impotence within the context of the second part. A red sky overhangs Eric's capture of Violet in the forest. Violet carries with her a white ribbon that, as she has explained to the Visiting Englishman, represents "the white drool of a snake." Through its association with the serpent in the garden of Eden, the ribbon would seem to represent evil or sin. In Nazi Germany, Jews were forced to wear the star of David and homosexuals a pink triangle as means of identification; like these markers, Violet's ribbon flags the immorality of the society that surrounds her. Whereas in the first part the sky turns from red to blue when the giant fish remove Pontius, in the second part it shifts from red to gray as the cast members look out to the audience to the sound of a train "speeding across tracks," suggestive of Violet's journey to Dachau. The sky color reinforces the bleak conclusion, evoking as it does the smoke from concentration camp crematoria. . . .

Source: James Al-Shamma, "Apocalypse Deferred: *Passion Play*," in *Sarah Ruhl: A Critical Study of the Plays*, McFarland, 2011, pp. 121–31.

SOURCES

Al-Shamma, James, *Sarah Ruhl: A Critical Study of the Plays*, McFarland, 2011, pp. 5–11, 38–39, 49–67, 117.

Durham, Leslie Atkins, *Women's Voices on American Stages in the Early Twenty-First Century: Sarah Ruhl and Her Contemporaries*, Palgrave Macmillan, 2013, pp. 1–29, 75–98.

Lahr, John, "Gods and Dolls: *Eurydice*," in *New Yorker*, Vol. 83, No. 18, July 2, 2007, p. 82.

———, "God in the Fun Machine: 'Passion Play' and 'Equus,'" in *New Yorker*, Vol. 84, No. 31, October 6, 2008, p. 92.

MacGregor, Geddes, *The Gospels as a Mandala of Wisdom*, Quest Theosophical Publishing House, 1982, p. 199.

Ruhl, Sarah, Author's Notes to *Passion Play*, Samuel French Acting Edition, 2010.

———, *Passion Play*, Samuel French Acting Edition, 2010.

———, "Re-runs and Repetition," in *Contemporary Theatre Review*, Vol. 16, No. 3, 2006, p. 287.

Vogel, Paula, "Sarah Ruhl: Interview," in *BOMB Interviews*, No. 99, Spring 2007, pp. 54, 58.

Winner, Lauren F., "Pretenders: Church and State in Sarah Ruhl's 'Passion Play,'" in *Books & Culture*, Vol. 15, No. 1, January–February 2009, pp. 44–46.

Wren, Celia, "The Golden Ruhl," in *American Theatre*, Vol. 22, No. 8, October 2005, pp. 30–34.

FURTHER READING

Brecht, Bertolt, *The Caucasian Chalk Circle*, Methuen, 2012.

Brecht's techniques of epic theater have influenced postmodern playwrights like Ruhl. This fable set in Soviet Georgia discusses the question of who is the true parent of a child—the one who loves and sacrifices for it or its biological parent?

Case, Sue-Ellen, *Feminism and Theatre*, Palgrave Macmillan, 2008.

This reissued classic study of feminism and theater has a foreword by UCLA professor Elaine Aston, who explains the influence of this seminal book.

García Márquez, Gabriel, *Love in the Time of Cholera*, Oprah's Book Club, 2007.

This novel is an example of magic realism from one of South America's most famous founders of the style. García Márquez sets his story in Colombia with a historical background. It describes a romance between a couple in their youth that is not consummated until their old age fifty years later.

Meier, Johanna, *Black Hills Passion Play*, Arcadia, 2008.

Johanna Meier is the daughter of Josef Meier, the founder of the American Passion Play in the Black Hills, here telling its history in the Images of America series. She has been in the play all her life and is now codirector with her husband.

Mitchell, John D., *Noh and Kabuki: Staging Japanese Theatre*, Fordham University Press, 1994.

Ruhl uses techniques from Japanese theater. This book has bilingual versions of Japanese plays, in Japanese and English, and discusses how to stage them. Photos, diagrams, and stage directions are included.

Orel, Gwen, "How I Write: Interview with Sarah Ruhl," in *Writer*, Vol. 122, No. 8, August 2009, p. 66.

Ruhl describes her writing habits and gives advice to other writers.

Schmidt, Kersten, *The Theater of Transformation: Postmodernism in American Drama*, Rodopi, 2005.

A look at contemporary experimental

American theater, this book explores the relationship between postmodernism and the theater, taking up such topics as race, gender, textuality, popular culture, and playwrights from the 1960s to the present.

SUGGESTED SEARCH TERMS

Sarah Ruhl

Passion Play

postmodern theater

feminist theater

Black Hills Passion Play

Oberammergau Passion Play

Adolf Hitler

Ronald Reagan

Elizabeth I of England

Vietnam War

magic realism

Rabbit Hole

DAVID LINDSAY-ABAIRE

2006

Rabbit Hole, a play by David Lindsay-Abaire, explores the dark topic of a couple struggling with the accidental death of their only child. Known for his humorous work, Lindsay-Abaire was challenged by a mentor to write about a subject that scared him. The result is a delicate and intimate look into the lives of Becca and Howie as they navigate the unknown waters of grief in a play where the simplest memories and smallest items unleash the strongest emotions. Lindsay-Abaire's hyperrealistic dialogue combines with profound moments of silence to create a play quiet in volume but thunderous in meaning.

Rabbit Hole was commissioned by the South Coast Repertory in Costa Mesa, California, and premiered on Broadway in 2006, receiving Tony nominations for Best Play, Best Direction of a Play, Best Scenic Design of a Play, and Best Featured Actress in a Play. Cynthia Nixon won the 2006 Tony Award for Best Performance by a Leading Actress in a Play for her portrayal of Becca. In 2007, Lindsay-Abaire won the Pulitzer Prize for Drama for *Rabbit Hole*, despite the fact that the play was not actually nominated for the award. *Rabbit Hole* was made available in print in 2006.

AUTHOR BIOGRAPHY

Lindsay-Abaire was born in Boston, Massachusetts, on November 30, 1969. Growing up in the

David Lindsay-Abaire (© AP Images / Mary Altaffer)

subject. As a father of a young son, Lindsay-Abaire chose the death of a young child for *Rabbit Hole*, an atypically somber play that is, however, not lacking in humor. *Rabbit Hole* was nominated for five Tony Awards in 2006 and won for Best Performance by a Leading Actress (Cynthia Nixon). Lindsay-Abaire's plays have been produced by the Soho Rep, Mammoth Theatre Company, Minetta Lane Theatre, the Arts Theatre on London's West End, the South Coast Repertory—which first commissioned *Rabbit Hole*—and the Manhattan Theatre Club, which first produced the play on Broadway at the Biltmore Theatre.

Lindsay-Abaire is a talented lyricist, having written the lyrics and book for *Shrek: The Musical* and the book for *High Fidelity*. In addition to the Pulitzer Prize he was awarded for *Rabbit Hole* in 2007, he won the Ed Kleban Award in 2008, naming him America's most promising theater lyricist. Lindsay-Abaire is also a screenwriter, having adapted *Rabbit Hole* to film and with screenwriter credits for *Oz: The Great and Powerful*, *Inkheart*, *Robots*, and *Guardians of Childhood*. He is a member of the Writers Guild of America, the New Dramatists, and the Dramatists Guild Council. As of 2013, he was living in Brooklyn, New York, with his wife and children.

PLOT SUMMARY

Act 1

SCENE 1

The play is set in a comfortable home in the suburbs of New York City. In the kitchen, Becca, a reserved woman in her thirties, folds a child's clothes while listening to her younger sister, Izzy, tell a story as she pours herself a glass of orange juice. Izzy tells the story of a woman who approached her in a bar while she was hanging out with her friend Reema. The woman got in Izzy's face, screaming that Izzy had stolen her boyfriend. Izzy, who is indeed with the woman's boyfriend—a man named Auggie—but did not know about this woman's involvement, punched her. Hearing this, Becca is beside herself with disapproval. She frequently interrupts the story with matronly concern over her younger sister's actions. Izzy says she is still in mourning—over whom is not stated—but Becca sternly tells her not to use *him* as an excuse. Tensions are high in the kitchen, as

neighborhood of South Boston, Lindsay-Abaire developed the eclectic sense of humor for which his work is known. In an interview with the Huntington Theatre Company he explained: "My sense of humor is *very* Southie—dark and inappropriate. Laughter in the face of hardship." In the seventh grade he received a scholarship to Milton Academy in the suburbs of Boston. Traveling by train between his working-class neighborhood and the affluent private school, Lindsay-Abaire lost his Boston accent but not his rich sense of humor or his love for his hometown. He attended Sarah Lawrence College, where he studied theater, graduating in 1992. In 1996 he was accepted into the Juilliard School as a member of the Lila Acheson Wallace American Playwrights Program.

His plays include *FuddyMeers*, *Kimberly Akimbo*, *Wonder of the World*, *A Devil Inside*, and *Good People*. Marsha Norman, a former teacher at Juilliard, encouraged Lindsay-Abaire to write a play about a frightening, personal

MEDIA ADAPTATIONS

- *Rabbit Hole*, adapted as a film by David Lindsay-Abaire and starring Nicole Kidman as Becca, was directed by John Cameron Mitchell, produced by Nicole Kidman, and distributed by Lionsgate in 2010.

Becca seems too acutely critical to find any humor in Izzy's wild behavior. Becca accuses Izzy of being drunk the night of the fight, but Izzy contends that she was not drinking because she is pregnant with Auggie's baby. This is a heavy blow to Becca, and Izzy apologizes for the discomfort it may cause. Izzy thinks the baby will give her a sense of clarity and interrupts Becca's attempt to correct her by asking her to refrain from lecturing. Becca reluctantly hugs her sister and tells her that instead of giving the child's clothes she has been folding to goodwill, she will give them to Izzy for her baby. Izzy refuses. Becca insists she take the clothes. Izzy says it would be too strange to see her child in Danny's clothes. It is then the audience realizes that Becca had a child who died, whose name was Danny, and that the clothes she was folding are his. Izzy apologizes again for her pregnancy, acknowledging how hard it must be for Becca.

SCENE 2

Becca and her husband, Howie, sit in the living room, talking about Izzy's pregnancy. Becca still believes that Izzy was drunk at the bar, endangering her baby. Howie tells her to relax, pouring her a glass of wine and dimming the lights. Becca wonders if she should buy baby stuff for Izzy's upcoming birthday, but Howie suggests that she wait for the baby shower. Becca decides to buy Izzy a bathroom set because her bathroom is sparsely decorated. Howie seems amused by this choice of such a practical present but backs down once Becca becomes defensive. Howie mentions Debbie and Rick, a couple with a child the same age as Danny was. Howie encourages Becca to call Debbie to catch up,

but Becca still harbors resentment against her because she acted distant following Danny's death. Becca gets worked up thinking about Debbie, but again Howie encourages her to relax, turning on music and giving her a back massage. He suggests that they go on a vacation, and he kisses her neck. She rejects him, getting up to bag Danny's clothes. Howie cannot believe that she is still uninterested in intimacy. He turns off the music. They begin to argue. Howie encourages Becca to come back to group therapy, which Howie still attends, but Becca instead suggests that they sell the house and move. Howie loves the house because it reminds him of Danny, but that is precisely why Becca wants to sell. She goes upstairs to bed. Howie stays up watching a home video of Danny playing with their dog, Taz. From the top of the staircase, Becca briefly listens to the video before returning to bed.

SCENE 3

At Izzy's birthday party, Nat—Izzy and Becca's mother—leads the celebration. Howie hands Nat a printout she asked for: a time line of deaths in the Kennedy family. There is a rumor that the Kennedy family is cursed, but Nat argues that in reality it is their money and recklessness that doom them to die young. She is a little tipsy on wine. Izzy opens presents. Nat's present is a gift card for maternity clothes, which upsets Becca. She explains that she thought they would wait until the shower for baby-themed presents, but Nat waves off her displeasure. Becca is immediately defensive of the shower set, trying to pry it from Izzy's hands to return it over Izzy's protests that she likes the gift. Howie asks after their dog, Taz, whom Nat is watching. Taz has gotten fat, making Howie upset that Nat has not been feeding him the more expensive dog food. Nat gets back on the topic of the Kennedy curse, saying people need someone or something to blame to make a death in the family make sense. Becca argues with her mother, thinking Nat is making a point about her own grief, while Izzy pleads with them that it is her birthday party. Nat encourages Becca to go to the support group. After Nat's son Arthur died, she found group therapy helpful. Becca lashes out at her, saying her thirty-year-old son committing suicide because of a drug addiction is different from a four-year-old being hit by a car after chasing his dog into the street. Becca storms upstairs. Nat is upset that her personal grief has been rendered inadequate and asks why Becca is so cruel. Howie mentions that they received a letter from Jason, the young man who hit Danny with his car.

SCENE 4

Becca sits in Danny's room—preserved from the time of the accident—reading the letter from Jason, a seventeen-year-old. He apologizes for the accident eight months ago and hopes his letter does not make them feel bad. He has been struggling in school since the accident and hoped writing Becca and Howie would help. He has written a short story in Danny's memory that will be published in his high-school magazine. He asks permission to dedicate the story to Danny. Jason would like to meet them in person.

In the living room, Howie puts the tape into the VCR to watch the home video of Danny again, but finds to his horror that it has been taped over. Frantic, he calls Becca into the room. She apologizes, saying it was an accident, but Howie is suspicious. He points out she has been removing all signs of Danny from the house, "You're trying to get rid of him. . . . Every day it's something else. It feels like you're trying to get rid of any evidence he was ever here." This includes the dog, Taz. Howie wants Taz back, just as he wants to keep the house. Becca says it makes it easier on her mind to erase Danny's presence around the house. She thinks Howie is judging her for grieving in a different way. They agree that the differences between them are becoming too hard to overcome.

Act 2

SCENE 1

Izzy helps Howie hold an open house, but they fail to attract any potential buyers. Taz is in the yard. Izzy asks Howie if Becca is mad at her because of the pregnancy, but Howie tells her to ask Becca these questions. She continues to ask until Howie loses patience with her. Izzy mentions that her friend Reema saw Howie at a restaurant holding hands with another woman. Howie gets upset, explaining that the woman is from the support group and had recently lost her son, but Izzy replies that even if he and Becca are having troubles, he should be honest. She leaves for the kitchen while Howie reels from being caught. Nat and Becca arrive home. There was an incident at the grocery store when Becca saw a mom refusing to buy her young son fruit roll-

ups. The son reminded Becca of Danny, and when his mom began to ignore him, she intervened. The mom, trying to get away from Becca, ran over her foot with her shopping cart by accident, and Becca slapped her. Nat got Becca into the car and tried to explain Becca's situation to the woman. Becca notices Howie's shocked expression, but before they can talk any further, Taz begins to bark, which Becca cannot stand. When Howie goes to see to Taz, they all find that Jason has walked into their midst, seeing the open house sign out front. Howie tells him it is not a good time. He is very abrupt and callous with Jason—blaming him directly for their son's death. Becca is more forgiving, but not before Howie makes Jason leave, telling him to show some respect.

SCENE 2

A week later, Nat helps Becca clean out Danny's room. As they toss items into a keep or throw away pile, Nat comes across a tiny sneaker of Danny's and freezes. Becca quickly takes the sneaker from her and puts it in the toss pile, telling Nat that if she succumbs to emotions they will never get the job finished. Becca mentions that she is taking a continuing-education class in another town, where no one recognizes her or knows about her tragedy. She seems much happier and more stable, even getting laughs out of her mother. Nat starts to tell a story about how her friends acted after her son Arthur's death but stops abruptly and apologizes. Becca tells her to keep talking. Nat says that while Becca's friend Debbie will not talk to her, the opposite can be worse. After Arthur's death Nat had a friend who would not stop coming over until one day Nat snapped at her. Becca tells Nat that she can talk about Arthur if she wants to, just that it is difficult for her when he is compared to Danny. Nat finds Jason's short story, called "Rabbit Hole," which Becca explains is a science-fiction story about portals to other worlds. She likes the story and has decided to meet with Jason. Howie appears briefly in the doorway to Danny's room, but things seem more strained than ever between the couple. Alone again, Becca asks her mother if the grief ever goes away. Nat says no, but that the grief changes with time until, "not that you *like* it exactly, but it's what you have instead of your son, so you don't wanna let go of it either. So you carry it around."

SCENE 3

Jason and Becca sit on the couch. She tries to get him to eat lemon squares and drink a glass of milk, which he does after much prodding and only out of a sense of obligation. They make small talk. Becca assures him that she and Howie do not resent him, though Jason believes that Howie is still mad. Jason guiltily admits that he may have been going three miles over the speed limit the day he hit Danny. Becca asks him about senior prom, tearing up as he describes it. Jason apologizes when he sees her crying, but she does not seem to mind. She tells him she liked his story, especially when the main character travels to parallel universes. Jason explains that in infinite space all parallel universes are possible. Becca says that means that there is a version of them where everything goes well and that this reality is just the sad version of them. She takes this to heart.

SCENE 4

Nat comes into the kitchen to give Izzy a box of Danny's toys and books for her baby. Becca joins them, teasing Izzy about her cooking. Everyone seems cheerful. Howie comes home early—he has decided not only to skip group but to stop going altogether. Izzy, happy to see them getting along, makes Nat leave early to take her to Lamaze class, over Nat's protests. Howie asks after Jason, but would still rather not meet him in person. Becca asks Howie if he wants to go to a cookout at Debbie and Rick's house. She called Debbie to catch up, and Debbie apologized to Becca in tears. Howie is impressed, but the couple realize how hard it will be to see young kids Danny's age running around at the cookout. They decide to wait on selling the house since there are no interested buyers. They talk about what they will do at the cookout, step by step, but seem a little scared. They hold hands. The lights fade.

CHARACTERS

Arthur

Arthur was Nat's son and Becca and Izzy's brother. He died before the events of the novel. He was a drug addict and committed suicide when he was thirty-one years old. Nat is very much affected by her grief for Arthur and believes that her experiences losing Arthur could help Becca mourn, but Becca will not let her speak of him in comparison to Danny.

Auggie

Auggie is the father of Izzy's child, a working musician who is thrilled to be having a baby with Izzy. Though he is never seen on the stage, Auggie is heard about through Izzy. When Izzy unwittingly went to a bar where Auggie and his girlfriend were drinking, Auggie confessed to his girlfriend about the baby he will be having with Izzy, sparking the argument that ended with Izzy punching the woman, whom she claims she did not know about. Izzy's answers to Becca about Auggie and the other woman are somewhat vague, making their exact relationship up until the time of the bar fight (as well as the extent of Izzy's knowledge of their relationship) ambiguous.

Becca

Becca, a stay-at-home mom in her late thirties, lost her only child, Danny. Still unemployed eight months after Danny's death, Becca has begun to remove all evidence of her son from the house, including giving the family dog to her mother. She and her husband, Howie, have grown distant. She rejects his attempts to relax her, instead suggesting they sell their house and move away. Becca is cold but functioning in her grief. She treats her sister, Izzy, like a child, and her mother, Nat, as if Nat does not understand her pain. News that Izzy is pregnant greatly disturbs her. Throughout the play Becca bakes intricate desserts for her family. When she sees a woman at the grocery store ignoring her son, she confronts the woman and slaps her. Nat must take Becca away and explain her situation to the shocked woman. Becca asks her mother for help with her grief, finally allowing Nat to talk about her own son's death. After meeting with Jason, the teenager who hit Danny with his car, Becca—who does not blame Jason—begins to improve in mood. Becca calls her estranged friend Debbie, letting go of an old grudge, and accepts Debbie's apologies for not being there for Becca. She and Howie reconnect—holding hands silently as they sit on the couch after deciding not to sell the house.

Danny

Danny was Becca and Howie's four-year-old son who died. An only child, he ran into the road after his dog, Taz, and was struck by a car.

Danny's memory is everywhere in Becca and Howie's house: in his toys, his drawings, his room, his fingerprints on the walls. Danny's loss weighs heavily on each member of the family he left behind, and all are grieving deeply when the play begins eight months after his death.

Debbie

Debbie and Rick are a married couple with children the same age as Danny. Though they were once close to the couple, Debbie distanced herself from Becca after Danny's death, causing Becca to disown Debbie as a friend. Howie still plays squash with Rick and Debbie, but Becca will not speak to the couple, feeling it is their job to call on her in order to break the ice. Becca thinks that Debbie must see Danny's death as contagious, but Howie attempts to convince her that Debbie only feels awkward and does not know what to say to her mourning friend. In the final scene, Becca finally calls Debbie. After Debbie apologizes and weeps over the phone, she invites Becca and Howie to a cookout. The couple decide to go, taking a step toward socializing again after Danny's death.

Howie

Howie, Becca's husband, lost his only child at the age of four. While his wife would rather hide all evidence of Danny, Howie finds comfort in the toys, fingerprints, home videos, and books his son left behind when he died. Howie especially loves the family dog, Taz, bringing him back to their house after Becca gave Taz away to her mother. Howie works during the day, plays squash with friends, and attends support-group sessions for parents who have lost young children. He encourages Becca to come to group therapy meetings, to forgive Debbie, and to take it easy on Izzy, but Becca is unmoved by his attempts to help her. Though he seems more relaxed, friendly, and caring than Becca, he is still in deep pain from Danny's death. Reema catches him holding hands with another woman at a restaurant, causing Izzy to confront him about his fidelity to Becca. Though he claims he was comforting the woman—she is a member of his support group—Howie is clearly shaken up after Izzy's confrontation. Howie cannot stand the sight of Jason, struggling not to hit the boy when he walks into the house uninvited. Howie quits the support group and comes home to Becca. They decide to attend Rick and Debbie's cookout but seem frightened at the idea of socializing. Still, the play ends as they hold hands.

Izzy

Izzy is Becca's flighty younger sister. Pregnant in her early thirties, Izzy tiptoes around Becca's emotions. Reckless and carefree, Izzy gets under Becca's skin with her irresponsible behavior. When an argument between Becca and Nat breaks out at Izzy's birthday party, Izzy tries and fails to bring the focus back to her birthday. Though she generally keeps a happy face, she is aware of Becca and Howie's feelings toward her pregnancy. Izzy tells Howie, "I resent the feeling I get from her, and you too sometimes, honestly, that I don't *deserve* the baby. Or that I'm not mature enough, or smart enough or something, to take care of it." Though Becca picks at her for mistakes small (eating a dessert before its ready) and large (getting fired from her job), Izzy supports her sister. When she finds out from Reema that Howie was at a restaurant holding hands with another woman, Izzy confronts Howie directly.

Jason

Jason is the seventeen-year-old who hit Danny with his car accidentally, killing him. Jason writes a letter to Becca and Howie apologizing for his role in the accident and asking to meet them in person. He is a high-school senior heading to college to pursue his interest in fiction writing. He wrote a short story in honor of Danny that features travel between parallel universes. When he walks in on the family unannounced during the open house, Howie rejects him harshly. While Howie still blames Jason and cannot face him, Becca feels more compassion for the young man and agrees to meet him. She enjoys his story and finds comfort in his belief in parallel universes, especially a universe in which they are all happy instead of grief stricken. When Jason describes his senior prom to Becca, she weeps openly. Jason is mild mannered and quiet around the family. He has been having trouble in school since the accident. He confesses to Becca that he may have been just over the speed limit when he hit Danny.

Nat

Nat is Becca and Izzy's mother. Like Becca, she lost a son to an early death, in his thirties. Nat is kindhearted and funny, with a sense of humor Becca finds inappropriate. When she tries to reminisce about her own son, Arthur, Becca stops her, angered by the comparison to Danny. Though Nat loves Becca dearly, she cannot fully understand Becca's anger toward her, remarking, "You don't need to strike out at me, Becca. I know you're still in a bad place but I'm trying to help you.... I wish someone had sat me down when Arthur died. I wish someone gave me a little advice." Despite Becca's sometimes cruel treatment of her mother, Nat stays patiently by her side. When Becca finally asks her mother for advice with coping, Nat's answer is simply that grief changes over time. Becca, like Nat, will learn to live with her grief.

Reema

Reema, Izzy's friend, is mentioned in Izzy's stories but never seen in the play. Reema was there the night Izzy punched Auggie's girlfriend at the bar. Reema told Izzy about waiting on Howie and an unfamiliar woman at the restaurant where she works. Reema saw the two holding hands. Neither Howie nor Becca remember meeting Reema, though Izzy insists they have met her at a party.

Rick

Rick, not appearing onstage, is Debbie's husband.

Taz

Taz is the family dog. The day Danny died, he was chasing after Taz into the street, and Jason, swerving to avoid Taz, struck Danny. Becca, who dislikes Taz, gave her to Nat to look after. Howie, who loves Taz but forgets to take care of him, wants and eventually gets Taz back to their house, objecting to Nat's care of the dog on the grounds that she is making him fat. Taz's bark cuts through Becca—a reminder of the events leading up to Danny's death.

THEMES

Family

Becca, Howie, Izzy, and Nat must band together as a family to overcome the loss of the family's youngest member, Danny. The play begins when the family is at its most distant. Howie spends most of his time away from the house. Becca, resentful of Izzy's pregnancy and of Nat's attempts to console her, pushes her loved ones

away. Arguments break out at Izzy's disastrous birthday party; Becca leaves in a huff, Nat's feelings are hurt, and Izzy is left cynical about what her birthday next year might bring.

The family is broken over Danny's death, and at the center of its dysfunction is Becca's inconsolable grief, which she believes no one can understand. Nat's interest in the Kennedy family is not far from the mark—her family has suffered the loss of two sons. Becca and Izzy's father is nowhere to be found, and Howie is left alone as the only remaining male. Of course, some family members are born and others chosen: once Howie has the family dog, Taz, back, the house seems fuller (and noisier). Next, Becca invites Jason into her home to accept his apology and treat him like a son. Plying him with milk and lemon squares, fussing over his comfort, crying as he talks about prom, Becca takes a step forward in her recovery as a result of spending time with Jason. When Becca finally asks for her mother's advice—calling her "mom" for the first time in the play—Becca begins to find comfort for the loss of her son in the mother and sister who have stayed by her side. They stayed through the nit-picking and insults simply because they love her. Howie, too, comes home to Becca, giving up his group therapy sessions to be with his wife. By the end of the play, the characters can face their grief as a united family.

Grief

Rabbit Hole is primarily a lesson in grieving. Such a terrible loss—that of a young child—is an earth-shattering experience for those involved. The play begins in medias res eight months after Danny's death, when the characters have settled into their mourning. The day of the accident is far behind them. The funeral has come and gone, leaving Becca and Howie alone to piece their lives back together. The couple is not lost, not blinded with their own tears, but instead are living life as best they can: unhappy but willing to keep on living, to get out of bed each day and try again. For Becca grief is something to work through—she bakes, she cleans, she organizes the house. She is efficient and swift in her actions, comparing throwing Danny's belongings away to ripping off a Band-Aid—the faster the better.

Once she begins sweeping evidence of Danny away, however, Howie becomes alarmed.

TOPICS FOR FURTHER STUDY

- Watch the film *Rabbit Hole* (2010). Take notes on the differences between the play and the film as you watch. Afterwards, discuss the differences you found in small groups. Why do you think these alterations to the plot, characters, dialogue, etc., were made? What do the changes add or take away from the story? Answer these questions in your small group to prepare for a class discussion comparing the play and the film.

- Read *Alice's Adventures in Wonderland* (1865), by Lewis Carroll. What does this young-adult novel have in common with *Rabbit Hole*? Write an essay in which you make connections between the novel and the play. For example, why is the play named after a feature of the novel? What is the significance of naming this particular play after a children's book?

- Write a science-fiction story inspired by the short story Jason writes in *Rabbit Hole*, using portals to other worlds as an element of your plot. Who are your characters and how do they discover the portals? What do these portals look like and where will they take your characters? Use your imagination, and remember that anything is possible in an alternate universe.

- How is the Pulitzer Prize awarded? Research online to learn more about the Pulitzer Prize. First, research the history and categories of the Pulitzer Prize. Then, choose a category to research further, and write an explanation of who can qualify and the process of selecting a winner for this category. Finally, write a brief description of the past five winners and the works for which they won. For example, if you choose the Pulitzer Prize in Poetry, you will write a description of what poems are eligible in a given year, how a winning poem is chosen, and a paragraph on each of the last five poets to win. Remember to cite your online sources.

- Support your local theater by attending a play. Write a review of the play you watched, relating what you thought of the play—writing, acting, set design, costuming, etc. Were you familiar with the play before going or was it a new experience? Would you recommend the play to a friend?

- Chose a scene from *Rabbit Hole* to explore in depth. Lindsay-Abaire's dialogue subtly reveals the characters' inner feelings. Try to read into the dialogue of the scene to find what lies beneath. Write a summary of the scene focusing on what is not said but is implied about the characters' emotions. Use specific examples to illustrate how Lindsay-Abaire creates emotional depth without having his characters come out and say how they feel.

Becca would rather not be confronted with Danny's memory in every room, but Howie feels just the opposite. Howie, like Becca, remains active and functional in his mourning. He goes to work, exercises, and attends group therapy meetings. At home, Howie watches home videos of Danny almost obsessively, wanting to keep the memory of his child as close as he can. Howie may seem friendlier, and Becca more cold, but both have developed questionable habits as a result of their grief. Becca strikes out at her husband, at Izzy, and especially at Nat, over perceived insults to her choices, to Danny, or to her motherhood. Howie, as much as he claims to love the house, stays away from it—busying himself with activities after work, including a secret date with a woman from his support group.

Lindsay-Abaire's title brings to mind the bizarre trip down the rabbit hole in Alice in Wonderland.
(© Elena Schweitzer | Shutterstock.com)

Becca and Howie's grieving styles could not be more different, but this is ultimately Lindsay-Abaire's point. Everyone grieves in different ways and must be allowed to do so. Becca is not wrong for being short-tempered. Howie is not right because he attends group therapy. There is simply no right and wrong to grieving. Howie's anger is seen when he blows up at Jason. Becca's lighthearted side is seen when she teases Izzy about her cooking. Each day of grief as severe as that of Becca and Howie can bring with it any combination of feelings. Izzy and Nat are also grieving for Danny, though Becca attempts to discourage them from expressing their feelings. Nat lost a grandchild, Izzy a nephew. One of Becca's greatest accomplishments in the play is simply to ask her mother for her advice on grief. Until that point, Becca had treated her family as if grief were a competition and Becca the undisputed winner, but Nat and Izzy need to be allowed to express their sadness over Danny's death, and once Becca allows that, she takes a step forward toward healing. Of course, the healing will never be complete, but it will be easier after enough time has passed. Each small step is a step closer to a day when Becca and Howie can be happy.

STYLE

In Medias Res

Lindsay-Abaire begins *Rabbit Hole* in medias res, meaning in the middle of the story. *In medias res* is a Latin term roughly translated as "in the middle of things," used to describe any narrative that begins in the middle of the action. This allows an author to jump into the narrative without first explaining the backstory—what led the characters to their current situation. Instead, the audience must wait until later in the plot to fully understand the characters' behaviors.

There are several levels on which *Rabbit Hole* begins in medias res. The first is Danny's death, which occurred eight months before the play's scenes take place. Though the loss of Danny is the driving force behind much of *Rabbit Hole*'s plot, the audience is told of the actual event in snippets and hints—the accident is not experienced in real time. Not until the end of the first scene does Lindsay-Abaire reveal the death of Becca's child. Details of what happened trickle out slowly through the scenes that follow. The audience finds the characters in the middle of grieving: Becca and Howie already distant, their marriage struggling, Izzy and Nat already accustomed to speaking carefully around Becca so as not to upset her, Taz living at Nat's home.

Rabbit Hole also begins quite literally in medias res, as Izzy is in the middle of telling a story when the play starts: "And then I see her across the bar, coming at me with this *look*, you know." The first words of the play—"and then"—foreshadow the coming mystery of Danny's accident. The audience must piece the tragedy together using context clues and clipped dialogue from characters all too painfully familiar with the time line of events. The child's laundry, which Becca is in the middle of washing, drying, and folding (there is the sound of a dryer buzzing in act 1, scene 1, indicating that the clothes Becca folds are not the last of the pile, nor are they the first—she has neat stacks formed around her), offers the first clue to what has happened to the family. Soon Becca scolds Izzy for using *him* as an excuse (with no clues for the audience as to who *he* is), and then Izzy's embarrassed refusal when Becca offers Izzy the clothes awakens the audience to the situation: they have stumbled into the middle of a very tragic story about the death of a child.

Audience

The audience of a work is the group of people for whom the work was made. For example, a short story could be aimed at an audience of women, or a novel could be written for young adults. Though a work of literature can be read and enjoyed by anyone, certain stories will affect some groups of people more than others. *Rabbit Hole* is a moving story for any audience member, but parents—especially those of young children—are especially susceptible to the play's heartbreaking accident and Becca and Howie's struggles to move on after Danny dies. Zachary Pincus-Roth, in his article "David Lindsay-Abaire's *Rabbit Hole* Wins Pulitzer Prize for Drama," recounts Lindsay-Abaire's experiences with the play's first audiences: "According to the writer, other parents who had attended performances at Manhattan Theatre Club's Biltmore Theatre approached him after seeing the play. . . . 'It really affected parents more than anything,' he said."

A parent of a young child himself at the time, Lindsay-Abaire carefully considered the potentially overwhelming power of Danny's tragedy over his audience. He wrote clear instructions to those who would produce *Rabbit Hole* on how to manage the audience's emotions. Unlike the audience for a novel—readers who take in the work privately, using their imaginations to visualize the work—the live audience for a play is a large gathering of people watching actors on a stage who must suspend their sense of disbelief in order to enjoy the story. Lindsay-Abaire, in his author's note to *Rabbit Hole*, warns against any melodrama on the part of the actors: "Tears: if the stage directions don't mention tears, please resist adding them. . . . Laughter: there are, I hope, many funny parts in the play. They are important. Especially to the audience. Without the laughs, the play becomes pretty much unbearable." Through the delicate balance of tears and laughter, the audience can make it through the play to see Becca and Howie take their first steps toward healing.

HISTORICAL CONTEXT

The Kennedy Curse

At Izzy's birthday party, Nat discusses the curse on the Kennedy family after asking Howie to print her a time line of their deaths. The

Danny's death puts a huge strain on his parents' marriage. (© Steve Cukrov | Shutterstock.com)

Kennedy curse—a media-created explanation for a string of family tragedies—is a folktale claiming that the actions of an early patriarch in the Kennedy family resulted in a curse dooming his relatives to unnatural deaths. Notable Kennedy family members who have passed away include President John F. Kennedy in 1963 and his brother, presidential candidate Robert F. Kennedy, in 1968, both assassinated. Other members of the family have died in plane and car crashes, in a skiing accident, and of a drug overdose.

In reality, Nat argues, the Kennedy lifestyle of power, money, and privilege has led them into danger: "Too much money, that's their curse. And too much time on their hands." The unblinking eye of the media, too, has contributed to the overreporting of the influential family's personal troubles: Nat says, "You know what it is, really? Hype. Perpetuating the myth." Despite her irreverent tone toward the rest of the Kennedy family, Nat sympathizes with the matriarch, Rose, who lived to be 104 while so many in her family—her children and grandchildren—died prematurely. Not unlike Rose, Nat has experienced the terrible losses of

both her son in his thirties and her grandson at only four years old. Like the Kennedy family, Becca, Howie, Izzy, and Nat must overcome devastating consecutive losses, but unlike the Kennedys, they are an average American family left alone in their grief.

Alice's Adventures in Wonderland

Rabbit Hole takes its name from Lewis Carroll's children's book *Alice's Adventures in Wonderland*, first published in 1865 but still wildly popular and well known. In the novel's first chapter, titled "Down the Rabbit Hole," Alice, a bored young girl, chases a talking white rabbit down a rabbit hole—emerging into a bizarre new world: "She ran across the field after it, and was just in time to see it pop down a large rabbit-hole. . . . In another moment down went Alice after it, never once considering how in the world she was to get out again." Lindsay-Abaire ties the last moments of Danny's life to Alice's adventure as she chases the white rabbit. Danny, like Alice, was taken away from known reality the day he chased Taz into the street. Jason's short story, also called "Rabbit Hole," features travel to other dimensions where possibilities are endless, as he explains to Becca: "So even the most unlikely events have to take place *somewhere*, including other universes with versions of us leading different lives, or maybe the same lives with a couple things changed." Becca finally begins her healing process after hearing Jason speak of these other alternate universes: "Well that's a nice thought. That somewhere out there I'm having a good time." After her conversation with Jason, Becca seems more relaxed—letting her mother speak about her own lost son, joking with Izzy, and calling her estranged friend Debbie. She is no longer frozen in sorrow. Danny's disappearance down the rabbit hole brought the entire family into the overwhelming world of grief. The path is not clear, but it is up to them to find their own ways out.

CRITICAL OVERVIEW

Rabbit Hole was nominated for five Tony Awards in 2006, including Best Play. Cynthia Nixon won Best Performance by a Leading Actress in a Play for her portrayal of Becca.

Though *Rabbit Hole* did not receive a nomination from the Pulitzer Prize jury, the play was chosen as the 2007 winner of the Pulitzer Prize. In this rare instance, instead of picking from the three nominated plays that year, the Pulitzer Prize Board chose a play that, though not nominated by the jury, had fared well in their reviews of the eligible plays.

Ben Brantley, one of the jurors for the 2007 prize, wrote in his review "Mourning a Child in a Silence That's Unbearably Loud," for the *New York Times*: "The Biltmore Theatre [site of the play's Broadway premier] had better be paid up on its flood insurance. *Rabbit Hole*, the wrenching new play . . . inspires such copious weeping among its audience that you wonder early on if you should have taken a life jacket." He elaborates: "The sad, sweet release of Rabbit Hole lies precisely in the access it allows to the pain of others, in its meticulously mapped empathy."

In "Couple Trouble," Anthony Lane's *New Yorker* review of the film version of *Rabbit Hole*, also written by Lindsay-Abaire, Lane pinpoints the surprising emotional arc of Becca and Howie's story: "Against all expectations, you approach *Rabbit Hole* with a heavy heart and leave with a lighter one." As the characters work through their grief, the audience too can find relief from their terrible situation.

Charles McNulty, in his review "Down a *Rabbit Hole* for Reflections on Grief," for the *Los Angeles Times*, writes:

> If the story of a husband and wife struggling . . . . after the accidental death of their four-year-old son seems too much to bear, rest assured that the work is infused with more humorous life than the majority of carefree comedies clamoring on our stages and screens these days.

Many reviewers have touched on the comedic elements of the play, without which the sadness of the characters would be too difficult to watch.

Somewhat to the contrary, Michael Kuchwara writes in his review "'Rabbit Hole' Startling, Heartfelt": "While there are some laughs in *Rabbit Hole* and things are definitely off-kilter, the situation in this Manhattan Theatre Club production is somber and severe." Kuchwara goes on to discuss the drastic difference between this and other plays by Lindsay-Abaire: "In his past, more comic plays, Lindsay-Abaire has often been accused of overdosing on aggressive cuteness and whimsy. . . . That charge can't be made against *Rabbit Hole*, a remarkably affecting redirection of his considerable talent."

Stephen Wells writes in his review "Sounds of Silence and Anguish" for the *New York Times*: "This is honest playwriting with no platitudes or tidy resolutions to placate either the audience or the play's emotionally drained 30-something parents, Becca and Howie."

A quiet play with a small set and few characters, *Rabbit Hole*'s powerful emotional force has continued to impress critics and audiences who cry and laugh along with Lindsay-Abaire's fragile Becca and Howie. McNulty writes:

> *Rabbit Hole* has been criticized for being less theatrically ambitious than Lindsay-Abaire's previous efforts. But if creating drama this beautifully observed is a step backward, then it's one that more playwrights should consider taking in their zigzag to maturity.

CRITICISM

Amy Lynn Miller

Miller is a graduate of the University of Cincinnati and currently resides in New Orleans, Louisiana. In the following essay, she examines the

WHAT DO I READ NEXT?

- *Me and Earl and the Dying Girl* (2012), by Jesse Andrews, is a young-adult novel about two best friends in high school who are forced by their parents to befriend Rachel, a girl who has recently been diagnosed with leukemia. When Greg and Earl decide to make a film for Rachel, the result has a wide-ranging impact on all of their lives.

- *Fuddy Meers* (1999), a comedic play by Lindsay-Abaire, tells the story of a woman stricken with amnesia who must have her husband and son reexplain the world and her life each day when she wakes up. More typical of Lindsay-Abaire's style than the tear-inducing *Rabbit Hole*, *Fuddy Meers* is a freewheeling romp through a wacky world.

- August Wilson's *The Piano Lesson* (1990) involves a family in conflict over a piano passed down from their ancestors. Winner of the 1990 Pulitzer Prize for Drama, *The Piano Lesson* pits relatives against each other in a fight to decide how their family legacy will be remembered.

- *Six Characters in Search of an Author* (1921), by Italian playwright Luigi Pirandello, is a shockingly experimental play featuring a family of characters waiting on stage for the appearance of their author. Like that in *Rabbit Hole*, the family is in disarray, but this metafictional work lacks an author to properly organize the plot.

- *The Play That Changed My Life: America's Foremost Playwrights on the Plays That Influenced Them* (2009), edited by Ben Hodges and presented by the American Theatre Wing (founder of the Tony Awards), is a collection of essays by prominent playwrights about their most memorable experience in the theater. Regina Taylor, Doug Wright, Nilo Cruz, Tina Howe, and many others contribute their thoughts on a play that inspired them to pursue a career in drama.

- *Wit* (1999), also known as *W;t*, by Margaret Edson, won the 1999 Pulitzer Prize for Drama for its remarkable examination of life and death through the eyes of a woman dying of cancer.

- In *Bleak House* (1853), by Charles Dickens, a prolonged court battle over several wills affects the life of Ester Summerson, a woman separated from her birth mother and raised in an adopted family. Ester's mother, Lady Dedlock, believes her daughter is dead. In *Rabbit Hole*, Becca attends a continuing-education class in which the students read *Bleak House*, much to Becca's amusement. The novel is one of Dickens's most respected works, especially for its pointed criticism of the broken court system in England at the time.

---

effects of Becca's behavior after the death of Danny on those closest to her and how Lindsay-Abaire creates this tension between his main characters in Rabbit Hole.

Rabbit Hole, for all its darkness, grief, and pain, is a play about the love of a family and that love's redeeming power over the distraught main character. Becca, the center of her family's attention, must learn to accept them—their consolations, their imperfections, their own feelings about the death of her son—in order to progress through her grief to a happier mental state. This proves difficult, for, without a son to protect, Becca is protective of her grief, defending her own sorrow against comparisons, slights, and insults, however small and often unintentional. David Lindsay-Abaire creates tension between Becca and her family in the characters' dialogue, which often reveals more than what is said, as well as in stage directions that frequently call for "beats": moments of silence after a character has finished speaking to allow the implications of their words to sink in. Though quick to attack those around her, Becca is not the play's villain. Instead, the characters battle their own grief, finding love to be the best weapon. By the end of *Rabbit Hole* love is extended not only between family members but outside the family as well—to Jason and Debbie in the form of Becca's forgiveness. Nat teaches Becca that her grief will never go away, but she can and does take a firm step toward healing before the curtain falls.

The audience is the last to learn that Danny has died, but once it is revealed that the child's clothes Becca folds do not belong to a living child, the effect is immediate, as Ben Brantley writes: "Every action, big and small, and every word that follows are informed by our awareness of the characters' awareness of Danny's death." Indeed, like Becca, who complains of thinking about Danny constantly, the audience too enters a world where every detail of the scenery, every conversation calls back to the fact that he is gone. The family members have lived in this world of loss for eight months and dance around Becca's feelings as best they can. But Nat and Izzy, both with personalities that are a bit messier than that of the uptight Becca, stumble into thorny conversations with her with discouraging regularity. Howie, who desperately wants Becca to unwind, has sought comfort with another woman. Brantley writes, "Grief has obviously not brought the members of Becca's family... closer together. Sorrow isolates them. Anything that anyone says is almost guaranteed to be the wrong thing." Lindsay-Abaire accomplishes this unique pressure on the family to avoid triggering Becca's short fuse through dialogue that implies

meaning rather than coming out and saying what is meant. Consider this exchange between Izzy and Becca:

> Izzy: Hey, I'm still coping, too, Becca. I know it's not the same, but it's still hard. Okay?
> (Beat.)
> Becca: Don't do that.
> Izzy: Do what?
> Becca: Give me a break.
> Izzy: What? I'm not allowed to be *upset* anymore?
> Becca: No, you're not allowed to *use* him.

On the surface, Izzy says she acted irresponsibly because she is still upset over Danny's death. Becca replies that she cannot use Danny's death as an excuse for her own actions. But more is implied by this brief exchange between the sisters. Becca expects Izzy to know not to mention Danny in this manner, her sarcastic "Give me a break" expressing a level of exasperated disappointment. She also effectively negates any real feelings about Danny's death that Izzy has been dealing with. It is possible that Izzy has truly been struggling to get her life together after the sudden loss of her nephew, but Becca firmly denies this possibility—placing the blame on Izzy for being so naively selfish as to use Danny's death as an excuse. For her part, Izzy feigns a level of innocence about why Becca is suddenly offended, but she is aware of what she said to make Becca mad—supplying it in her response, "I'm not allowed to be *upset* anymore," before Becca has a chance to call her out specifically. Also worth noting is the language of the family when speaking to Becca. Izzy asks if she's "not allowed" to feel bad, and later Nat pleads that she does not know Becca's rules. Becca has made herself into the authority on Danny's death—to be consulted for the rules of what is and is not allowed to be said during the family's grieving. For example, comparisons of Danny with Nat's deceased son, Arthur, are strictly not allowed. Brantley writes of the tense exchanges with Becca: "Jokes and cute anecdotes only wound; kindly advice is received as if it were a slap in the face. Family conversations are shaped by a spastic pattern of recrimination and apology, of irritation and misdirected comfort."

Though Becca pushes them away, her family will not let her succeed in isolating herself entirely. They mourn for Danny as well, and Becca is their leader. If she were to fall under the weight of her grief, they would consider themselves responsible. This sentiment, too, goes unspoken in the play. Stephen Wells writes: "In writing *Rabbit Hole* ... Lindsay-Abaire was obviously aware that what his characters didn't say had to be even more revealing than what they did." Significantly, Howie's relationship with the woman from his support group is one such silent issue. Neither Howie nor Izzy mentions this indiscretion to Becca. In fact, the topic is never broached in her presence. Instead, Izzy snuggles closer to Becca on the couch after confronting Howie—showing him her solidarity with her sister. Howie later quits the support group to join Becca at home. That the relationship with the other woman is over goes without saying, because Lindsay-Abaire shows us through Howie's decision to work through his grief by Becca's side instead of at group therapy.

Charles McNulty writes, "Heartbreaking as it can be, the play is never grim. It's too truthful, too spirited, too wise to be depressing." One of Becca's most surprising traits is her acceptance of Jason, which neither Howie nor Nat understands. But for Becca, Jason is the son Danny would have become. This is why, as Jason tells her about his prom, she weeps openly for the first and only time in *Rabbit Hole*. Though she has her anger issues, she does not direct that anger at Jason, as Howie does. She forgives his mistake and enjoys his company, recognizing his grief as legitimate and identifying with his feelings of guilt as well. After speaking with Jason, Becca decides to forgive her old friend Debbie. Typically of Becca, she takes this step in her own time, surprising and impressing Howie with the news when he comes home from work. The now-united couple sit together on the couch holding hands, but the specter of Rick and Debbie's cookout silences their conversation. Lindsay-Abaire writes, in his author's note to *Rabbit Hole*:

> There can and should be moments of hope and genuine connection between these characters, but I don't ever want a moment (not even the very end) where the audience sighs and says, "Oh good, they're gonna be okay now." *Rabbit Hole* is not a tidy play. Resist smoothing out its edges.

Rabbit Hole narrowly avoids both corny sentimentality and terrifying depression through Lindsay-Abaire's steady hand—balancing between extremes to create an exceedingly tender work of art.

What lesson can be taken from *Rabbit Hole*? Wells writes, "That grief takes on many guises and manifestations, and affects survivors' relationship in different ways. Each of the play's five characters has created his or her own reality in order to deal with the personal tragedy." They do their best not to interrupt each other's realities, but they cannot help but run into trouble. Nat, a victim of two losses, wants to help Becca using the knowledge she gained from the loss of her own son. Izzy wants to bring new life into the world, to give her a purpose and gain the family's respect and attention. Jason wants to apologize, to know he is not hated by the family he hurt beyond anything his seventeen years have taught him of pain. Howie wants a new child, wants Becca to be close to him again, and wants to honor Danny's memory instead of hiding it away. Becca's reality is well known by all in the family, and it is to her grief that they defer. Though all are hurting, they put Becca's feelings first. Because they help her, Becca begins to open up, giving Nat a chance to talk about her experience of losing Arthur, giving Izzy baby toys, accepting Jason's apology, and deciding to keep the house while holding Howie's hand. McNulty writes: "A study of the subterranean passageways of grief, [*Rabbit Hole*] serves to remind that loss, even of the most shattering kind, can move us incrementally toward a deeper appreciation of what remains." The family is rewarded for their efforts with Becca's love, and Becca's reward is realizing how deeply her family loves her and wants her to be okay.

Source: Amy Lynn Miller, Critical Essay on *Rabbit Hole*, in *Drama for Students*, Gale, Cengage Learning, 2014.

James MacKillop

In the following review, MacKillop praises Lindsay-Abaire's dialogue as having deep meaning hidden in deceptively simple conversations.

The origins of this production of David Lindsay-Abaire's *Rabbit Hole* reach back two to three years, back when John Nara's Simply New Theater was riding high with stylish productions of Martin McDonagh's *Pillow Man* and Shaun Davey's *James Joyce's The Dead*. For *Rabbit Hole*, a Pulitzer winner, Nara wanted to cast Shannon Tompkins in the lead role of Becca, a Tony-winning part for Cynthia Nixon. But Nara left town a year ago, and the project foundered, until now, when his instincts are proven sound.

Becca and Howie disagree over whether to get rid of their son's things or to keep them. (© Steve Cukrov /
Shutterstock.com)

Rabbit Hole appears under the ad-hoc aegis of DCS Full Circle Theater at the little-used St. Clare Gardens at Assumption Church on the city's North Side, but the whole venture has a pedigree. "DCS" comes from the family name in plural, DeCooks, which includes director Jenn DeCook and husband Todd, the latter having built a set to evoke an affluent household in Larchmont, N.Y. Jenn DeCook has her own street cred, starting with an association with Nara going back to Simply New's first manifestation two decades ago, as well as with Salt City Center for the Performing Arts. She directed the much-acclaimed world premiere of Garrett Heater's *Lizzie Borden Took an Axe* in 2010.

Reducing the plot to a Twitter line, *Rabbit Hole* can easily be misunderstood. A professional-class household of diverse characters reacts to the death of a small boy named Danny in a traffic accident, eight months before the beginning of the action. It sounds like a TV movie

promising lots of tears and recrimination, and film director John Cameron Mitchell's dreary art house version in 2010 choked off what makes the play compelling. Not only is there unexpected humor in the stage script and resonant silent patches, but how characters react to one another—sometimes hearing them, sometimes not—is how we get to a conclusion. Most of the dialogue in *Rabbit Hole* is conversational and workaday, with meanings all flowing under the surface. The timing of live performance lets us perceive that more readily.

Becca was once a working professional and is now a stay-at-home mom for a boy no longer there. She's married to Howie (David T. Walker), who commutes to the city for what looks like a well-paying job. Despite the decline in their sex life (her complaint), they have a passably good marriage, and neither partner is a predator nor troublemaker. They both are grieving Danny in their own ways, but Howie reveals an unwelcome vein of suspicion. When Becca accidentally tapes over footage of the boy (the action is set in the VHS era), Howie heatedly and hurtfully accuses her of doing it on purpose.

The exchange does not make Howie a bully or Becca an unfeeling deceiver, but rather reveals that under the stress of unrelieved grief we express emotions that otherwise would never get out, and also inflict wounds on people we care about. Audience members know this, because figuring out what to say to a loving survivor is damned difficult. How we live with and then pull out of this torment is much of what *Rabbit Hole* is about.

Tension and pain sound like poor premises for comedy, which is just why we need it. Enter Becca's family, her expansive, free-speaking mother Nat (Nora O'Dea) and her less-than-domestic sister Izzy (Sara Caliva). O'Dea plays Nat as possibly a little blowsier than what would go in tony Larchmont, but not so much as to undercut her tabloidish fascination with the Kennedy "curse." In an error of catastrophic unprepossession, Nat commiserates with her daughter, reminded that she too lost a son, Arthur, before his time. "Yeah, he was a heroin addict who hanged himself," responds Becca.

Darker and foxier, Izzy hardly looks like Becca's sister at all. A lively party girl, Izzy finds herself pregnant by an unseen boyfriend, Auggie. Izzy's aggressive manner is one thing, but Becca's learning that a new life is growing within her sister becomes a strident reminder of loss.

Another player unexpectedly appears in the first act. DeCook has him stand up in the audience and begin speaking. He's Jason (Nick Ziobro), and at first we don't know what he's about. Responding to a sign that Howie and Becca's house is for sale, he knocks on the door and tries to enter, only to be sternly rebuffed by Howie. Becca knows who he is, however: He's the teen whose driving is complicit in Danny's death.

Against Howie's wishes, Becca meets further with Jason. Even without tears, Jason cares deeply about the family his actions have hurt. He speaks of parallel universes and introduces the rabbit hole metaphor of the title, an allusion to Lewis Carroll's *Alice in Wonderland* books. In her program notes, director DeCook cites that the play is linked to Elizabeth Kubler-Ross' five stages of grief, with the five characters speaking for each one. Maybe so. In a play so festooned with literary allusions, many to Dickens' *Bleak House*, an obvious if ancient model seems likely. Consider the reconciliation between grieving parent Priam and killer Achilles that Homer places at the end of *The Iliad*.

For a start-up company DCS Full Circle has credibility as well as pedigree. Director DeCook draws polished performances from experienced players. David T. Walker has played this kind of character before, but his gruffness is appropriately threatening and he can produce tears on cue. Nick Ziobro is beguiling as Jason, both courageous and tender. Experienced pro Nora O'Dea will not be upstaged for laughs. And Sara Caliva makes sexiness feel aggressive, even threatening.

Playwright Lindsay-Abaire, previously neglected locally, will have three works produced here within a year. The Syracuse University Drama Department produced his early absurdist comedy *Fuddy Mears* in November, and Syracuse Stage will give us his *Good People* next season. Putting aside invidious comparison between professional and non-professional company, *Rabbit Hole* might be the best literary property of the three.

Source: James MacKillop, "David Lindsay-Abaire's *Rabbit Hole*," in *Syracuse (NY) New Times*, April 25, 2012.

Les Spindle

In the following review, Spindle praises both the script and the performances in the film adaptation of Rabbit Hole.

Film adaptations of plays have a spotty success record, due to the vastly different sensibilities of the two mediums—the poetic fragility of stage imagery versus the literalness and immediacy captured by the film lens. Screenwriter David Lindsay-Abaire's celluloid version of his play *Rabbit Hole*, brilliantly directed by John Cameron Mitchell, offers a surprisingly fresh take on the writer's compelling drama, punctuated with wry humor. It loses none of the play's power and resonance, remaining an eloquently understated portrait of grief and emotional resilience experienced by an affluent married couple coping with a nearly unspeakable tragedy—the accidental death of their 4-year-old son.

Faithful to his narrative and characters, but thankfully not slavishly so, Lindsay-Abaire has opened up the action to myriad locations and added characters, expanding his artistic canvas without compromising the intimacy and stark truthfulness that drove the play. The script smartly captures the humor that we use as an escape mechanism when coping with despair, while illuminating the wide range of emotions we travel through while learning to accept life's calamities.

Nicole Kidman delivers one of her most memorable performances as the sardonic and ostensibly thick-skinned Becca Corbett, mother of the deceased child. The tightly wound Becca is working toward cherishing life anew—sometimes awkwardly, yet always determinedly. The wit and authenticity of her multilayered portrayal is best exemplified in the scene in which Becca and her husband, Howie (Aaron Eckhart), reluctantly attend a grief support group session. When a grieving mother remarks that God needed another angel so he took her daughter, the bemused Becca firmly challenges what she clearly considers a ridiculous notion. Her retort is that if he's God, he doesn't need to take someone's child to make an angel; he can make a new one. Though Kidman's portrayal is tastefully restrained, her depiction of the character is far from stoic. The anguish and challenges of moving past such a tragedy are seamlessly conveyed in Kidman's subtle yet devastatingly moving line readings, facial expressions, and body language.

Kidman and Eckhardt share a splendid chemistry. Though Howie appears to be a bit closer to emotional renewal than his wife, his pain is also palpable in Eckhardt's finely nuanced characterization. His effort to dull the suffering by dabbling in an extramarital affair with a woman (Sandra Oh) he meets at the support group rings true. Dianne Wiest is warm and winsome as Becca's compassionate mother, and Miles Teller is deeply affecting as the young man involved in the accident, who befriends Becca, aiding in her healing. Tammy Blanchard offers sublime comic relief as Becca's reckless sister, Izzy, an unmarried party girl who reveals she's pregnant. The journey that the free-spirited Izzy takes tellingly contrasts with the road to rebirth that her more responsible sister faces.

Mitchell, noted for his work in the iconoclastic and dicey films *Hedwig and the Angry Inch*

and *Shortbus*, makes a triumphant creative segue to the tender sensibilities of this hard-hitting slice-of-life film. *Rabbit Hole* is a career high point for all of its gifted collaborators.

Source: Les Spindle, Review of *Rabbit Hole*, in *Back Stage*, national edition, Vol. 51, No. 50, December 16, 2010, p. 19.

Bob Verini

In the following review, Verini praises Rabbit Hole *but is disappointed in a particular production of it.*

David Lindsay-Abaire's *Rabbit Hole* is a play tailor-made for people who, as a rule, don't care for plays—who find the theater too rarefied, artificial or remote from their everyday existence. Script's precise and tactful exploration of a family's grief when 4-year-old son Danny is killed in a traffic accident resonates with verbal and emotional truth, generating enormous empathy. Even in the disappointingly under-nourished West Coast premiere production at the Geffen Playhouse, play's themes are durable and its appeal strong.

Rabbit Hole was an unexpected Manhattan Theater Club triumph earlier this year for Lindsay-Abaire, known in Gotham for a string of hysterical, hyperrealistic farces in which desperate characters are seen as if in carnival funny mirrors (or *Fuddy Meers*, title of scribe's best known work). That rep, plus Lewis Carroll-ish title, promised something knockabout and otherworldly, as if toddler's ghost might pop in at any moment in a bunny suit.

But Lindsay-Abaire surprised everyone with his slice-of-life naturalism and characters drawn straight and true, especially the boy's mother, Becca, whose heartbreaking struggle to regain equilibrium is the piece's central action. Play dramatizes the vain efforts of other family members to help Becca return to normalcy.

As in any family, most of the talk centers on mundane issues: the so-called Kennedy curse, birthday gifts, baking, a bar fight. But whenever the topic seems furthest away from poor Danny, of course we need to feel that's just a ploy and that in fact everyone is thinking of Danny and nothing else.

In this respect, new production is woefully weak. While Broadway helmer Dan Sullivan orchestrated tension like chamber music, playing Danny's death as a wound that could—and did—reopen at any moment, Carolyn Cantor directs her actors on the most superficial level: Comfortable and easy with each other when the lines are casual, cast suddenly ratchets up the anger when the lines say to do so. Scenes that should crackle with conflict just drift by. For long stretches we lose sight of Danny altogether, which couldn't be further from playwright's intention.

Most serious casualty of directorial approach is the Becca of Amy Ryan, a gifted actress with a wide smile far too much in evidence on the Geffen stage. She is so naturally relaxed, and her manner so forgiving, that it becomes easy to forget her supposedly ever-present grief. Sister Izzy (Missy Yager) wonders, "Why is Becca so mad at me?," but we haven't seen that anger, just some gentle scolding.

By contrast, Cynthia Nixon's award-winning Becca was a woman turned to stone. She loomed over the other characters like one of those heads on Easter Island, and her refusal to even consider any offer of comfort was her particular hubris that turned her melodrama into true tragedy. Any great role is open to multiple interpretations, of course, but Ryan's never suggests why someone playing this part might be worth consideration for a Tony.

Rest of cast falls victim to directorial laxness, with only Tate Donovan, as husband Howie, suggesting the depth and texture that might have pervaded. He alone seems to be preoccupied and troubled at all times, though like the others, he is occasionally directed to shout in a way that seems underprepared for.

Cantor's blocking, too, does the piece a disservice. Again and again she has characters confronting each other while standing apart and in profile, as if at a gunfight, and the navigation around Alexander Dodge's set is awkward and often unmotivated. When the youthful driver who hit Danny arrives to make amends, Becca is placed on a downstage sofa with her back to us; we have to take another character's word for her reaction to the visitor.

Setting initially impresses by presenting an impeccable suburban living room from which all traces of a child's influence have been painstakingly eliminated. But once play begins, a huge downstage-left dinner table and chairs act as an implacable barrier that cramps movement and swallows up all the action in the upstage kitchen.

Instead of using the Broadway revolve to bring on Danny's bedroom, designer Dodge places it on the upper level, masked until the first scene there. Once the masking is removed, it might have been effective to leave the room revealed. But the set designer, like the rest of those behind this production, sees no need to give us constant reminders of the victim's existence.

Source: Bob Verini, Review of *Rabbit Hole*, in *Variety*, September 14, 2006.

Celia Wren

In the following excerpt, Wren praises Rabbit Hole *as both heart-wrenching and funny.*

Don't look for *Alice in Wonderland* in *Rabbit Hole*, the profound and heartbreaking new play by David Lindsay-Abaire. The title may hint at Lewis Carroll—and, indeed, a certain Mad Hatter absurdity is what you might expect from this ingenious dramatist, whose previous works featured quirky happenings and far-fetched situations. But Lindsay-Abaire's first Broadway outing turns out to be a beautifully controlled piece of realism that tells a harrowing story about loss and healing. There may be a looking-glass reality here, but it's the reality of grief.

Earlier this year, the Manhattan Theater Club production received substantial media attention for its casting coup: the show stars Cynthia Nixon, best known for portraying the lawyer Miranda on HBO's *Sex and the City*. In *Rabbit Hole*, she plays Becca, a suburbanite who's struggling to recover, along with her yuppie husband Howie (John Slattery), from the accidental death of the couple's four-year-old son. As she drifts through a house still rife with painful reminders—baby clothes, toys, even the family dog—Becca finds herself alienated from Howie, trapped in her own isolating sorrow. Meanwhile, despite good intentions, Becca's loud-mouthed mother Nat (Tyne Daly) and ditzy sister Izzy (Mary Catherine Garrison) only make the situation more agonizing.

Lindsay-Abaire's earlier plays also showcased beleaguered female characters. *Fuddy Meers*, his zany breakout piece, revolved around a woman who woke each morning with a brand-new case of amnesia. The comedy *Kimberly Akimbo* centered on a teenager with a rare aging disease, and *Wonder of the World* sent its heroine fleeing through a grotesque landscape to Niagara Falls. In *Rabbit Hole*, it's as if all that madcap energy has been funneled into a stream-lined form—a wrenching story that's seeded with funny lines, and ultimately speaks about human resilience.

Gracefully directed by Daniel Sullivan, *Rabbit Hole* reminds us how loss can give cozy details a harrowing edge. One of the play's most wrenching moments occurs when Becca fetches a glass of milk for Jason (John Gallagher Jr.), the local teenager responsible for the tragedy, whose guilt forces him to stop by several months after the accident. As both actors quietly let the moment resound—like all the show's performers, these two are riveting—the action seems all the more terrible because it is so simple. In other scenes, too, tokens of domesticity (a stuffed Curious George doll, a cup of creme caramel, a basket of laundry) turn into measures of tragedy.

But the play also moves past the material world to touch on metaphysics. "People want things to make sense," Nat says as she urges her daughter to grasp some kind—any kind—of philosophical comfort. But Becca is convinced that her loss does not, in fact, make sense, and she particularly hates the way the forlorn parents in her support group have turned to religion. Ultimately, she herself finds solace not in religion or philosophy but in a notion from a science-fiction story: the "rabbit hole" of the title refers to the idea that there are innumerable parallel universes, each accessible through a "rabbit hole" entry point, and each presenting a variation on our own world. In some of those alternate universes, Becca reflects, she is happy. The concept seems to offer another kind of faith. . . .

Source: Celia Wren, "Crime & Punishment: *Rabbit Hole & Sweeney Todd*," in *Commonweal*, Vol. 133, No. 5, March 10, 2006, p. 18.

SOURCES

Brantley, Ben, "Mourning a Child in a Silence That's Unbearably Loud," in *New York Times*, February 3, 2006, http://theater.nytimes.com/2006/02/03/theater/reviews/03rabb.html?pagewanted = all (accessed July 9, 2013).

Carroll, Lewis, *Alice's Adventures in Wonderland & Through the Looking-Glass*, Signet Classic, 1960, pp. 19–20.

"David Lindsay Abaire," American Theatre Wing website, April 2011, http://americantheatrewing.org/biography/detail/david_lindsay_abaire (accessed July 9, 2013).

Gans, Andrew, "Lindsay-Abaire Snags Kleban Award for Lyrics; Harrington, Solly and Ward Also Honored," in *Playbill*, May 1, 2008, http://www.playbill.com/news/article/117311-Lindsay-Abaire-Snags-Kleban-Award-for-Lyrics-Harrington-Solly-and-Ward-Also-Honored (accessed July 19, 2013).

Haugland, Charles, "An Interview with David Lindsay-Abaire," Huntington Theatre Company website, http://www.huntingtontheatre.org/articles/Good-People/An-Interview-with-David-Lindsay-Abaire/ (accessed July 19, 2013).

Henderson, Kathy, "What's Up, David Lindsay-Abaire? The *Good People* Scribe on Nicole Kidman, South Boston's Mystique, and More," Broadway.com, February 11, 2011, http://www.broadway.com/buzz/155184/whats-up-david-lindsay-abaire-the-good-people-scribe-on-nicole-kidman-south-bostons-mystique-more/ (accessed July 19, 2013).

Kuchwara, Michael, "Review: 'Rabbit Hole' Startling, Heartfelt," Associated Press website, February 2, 2006, http://www.apnewsarchive.com/2006/REVIEW-Rabbit-Hole-Startling-Heartfelt/id-4b12bbc5dd5ae77093acdc3d62e4c627 (accessed July 19, 2013).

Lane, Anthony, "Couple Trouble," in *New Yorker*, January 3, 2011, http://www.newyorker.com/arts/critics/cinema/2011/01/03/110103crci_cinema_lane (accessed July 17, 2013).

Lindsay-Abaire, David, Author's Note to *Rabbit Hole*, Theatre Communications Group, 2013, pp. 159–60.

———, *Rabbit Hole*, Theatre Communications Group, 2013.

McGrory, Brian, "Family Overshadowed by a Litany of Tragedy," in *Boston Globe*, July 18, 1999, http://www.boston.com/news/packages/jfkjr/mcgrory.htm (accessed July 17, 2013).

McNulty, Charles, "Down a *Rabbit Hole* for Reflections on Grief," in *Los Angeles Times*, September 15, 2006, http://articles.latimes.com/2006/sep/15/entertainment/et-rabbit15 (accessed July 19, 2013).

Pincus-Roth, Zachary, and Robert Simonson, "David Lindsay-Abaire's *Rabbit Hole* Wins Pulitzer Prize for Drama," in *Playbill*, April 16, 2007, http://www.playbill.com/news/article/107364-David-Lindsay-Abaires-Rabbit-Hole-Wins-Pulitzer-Prize-for-Drama (accessed July 17, 2013).

Wells, Stephen, "Sounds of Silence and Anguish," in *New York Times*, September 14, 2008, http://www.nytimes.com/2008/09/14/nyregion/nyregionspecial2/14theatnj.html?_r = 0 (accessed July 9, 2013).

FURTHER READING

Hayman, Ronald, *How to Read a Play*, 2nd ed., Grove Press, 1999.

> Hayman's guide to reading drama addresses several important issues that arise when reading a play versus seeing the play performed, encouraging readers to use their imagination to the fullest: visualizing the costumes and scenery, acting out the dialogue as opposed to scanning over it, and reading into the silent moments to find what is being said without words. The 1999 revised and updated edition includes advice for reading screenplays.

Lindsay-Abaire, David, *Good People*, Dramatist's Play Service, 2012.

> Lindsay-Abaire's *Good People* premiered in 2011 in New York, produced by the Manhattan Theatre Club. The play, about a hardworking but down-on-her-luck woman living in South Boston (where Lindsay-Abaire grew up), was nominated for two Tony Awards, including Best Play. Frances McDormand won the 2011 Tony Award for Best Performance by a Leading Actress for her portrayal of Margie.

Marasco, Ron, and Brian Shuff, *About Grief: Insights, Setbacks, Grace Notes, Taboos*, Ivan R. Dee, 2010.

> Shuff and Marasco's beautifully written guide to grief stands out among books on coping and loss for its simplicity and truth. Acknowledging that every person grieves in a different way, the authors offer helpful lessons on taking it one day at a time after an emotional loss.

Taraborrelli, J. Randy, *After Camelot: A Personal History of the Kennedy Family—1968 to the Present*, Grand Central Publishing, 2012.

> Taraborrelli follows the lives of the Kennedy family beginning in 1968, after the tragic loss of John F. Kennedy and Robert F. Kennedy to assassin's bullets, to the present day, chronicling the family's struggles and triumphs as they navigate the American dream.

SUGGESTED SEARCH TERMS

David Lindsay-Abaire AND Rabbit Hole

Rabbit Hole AND drama

Rabbit Hole AND Pulitzer Prize

David Lindsay-Abaire AND Pulitzer Prize

South Coast Repertory AND Rabbit Hole

Manhattan Theatre Club AND Rabbit Hole

2006 AND Rabbit Hole

Becca AND Rabbit Hole

Howie AND Rabbit Hole

Romeo and Juliet

1968

Franco Zeffirelli's 1968 film *Romeo and Juliet* is a tragedy adapted from the stage play of the same name. William Shakespeare wrote *Romeo and Juliet* around 1595, and this film reinforces the timelessness of the tragic love story, first envisioned so many centuries earlier. In addition to directing it, Zeffirelli contributed to the screenplay adaptation, along with writers Franco Brusalti and Masolino D'Amico. The film was nominated for several Academy Awards, including Best Director (Zeffirelli) and Best Picture, and it received Academy Awards for Cinematography (Pasqualino De Santis) and Best Costume Design (Danilo Donati). The prologue and epilogue are narrated by Sir Laurence Olivier.

As in Shakespeare's play, this film version of *Romeo and Juliet* focuses on the tragedy that ensues when the only children of two feuding families fall in love and marry in secret. Shakespeare's themes of fate, youth, and undue haste are reproduced in Zeffirelli's film. Zeffirelli chose two relatively unknown teenage actors to play the roles of Romeo and Juliet, which helped to make the film popular with teenage audiences. It was filmed in Italy at several locations, including Rome and Pienza. The box office gross for this Paramount production was estimated to be $50 million, for a film that cost less than $2 million to produce. Zeffirelli's *Romeo and Juliet* has continued to be a popular film with audiences, especially for classroom use, and is readily available on DVD.

The 1968 film stars Olivia Hussey and Leonard Whiting. *(© Paramount | The Kobal Collection)*

PLOT SUMMARY

Romeo and Juliet opens with a shot of Verona shrouded in fog, as the narrator speaks the prologue to Shakespeare's play. The next scene shows members of the Capulet and Montague families on the street. Each group speaks insulting words to the other group, leading to a sword fight. The initial exchange is almost comic, but with the sword fight things become much more serious. It becomes clear that this feud between two families is disruptive to the other townspeople, who must dodge the fighting. The fighting between the Capulet and Montague groups brings a halt to commerce, as well. The prince rides into the middle of the fray and complains about the frequent fighting. He reminds the townspeople, especially the Capulets and Montagues, that fighting is illegal and that both families will be severely punished if it continues.

In the next scene, Montague's wife asks about Romeo, who was not involved in the fighting. She is told that Romeo is elsewhere and has been observed to be deep in thought. When Romeo enters, he explains that he is in love with Rosaline, who is cold to him. The scene quickly shifts to a young man named Paris, who is also in love. Paris asks Capulet, Juliet's father, for Juliet's hand in marriage. Capulet explains that Juliet is too young to marry, but that Paris has time to begin courting her so that she can marry him willingly.

In the next scene, Capulet's wife asks the nurse to call Juliet. In this scene, the audience sees that the nurse is both a servant of the household and something of a friend and counselor for Capulet's wife, who is unsure how to approach the subject of the proposed marriage with Juliet. The nurse, with her many crude comments about marriage, is a bawd—that is, a morally loose or untethered woman. The nurse is excited about a possible suitor for Juliet, but Juliet is not pleased by this honor, which she says she has not sought. Soon Juliet and her mother are called to dinner, as their guests for the evening's festivities are arriving.

In the next scene, the Montague men are dressed for the Capulet masquerade ball, to which they are not invited. As they walk along the way, Romeo's friend Mercutio stops the merriment to tell his companions about his dream. Mercutio delivers a lengthy monologue about a fairy named Queen Mab, who visits men and women in their sleep. This speech is heavy with sexual references, but it is also gloomy and scares the revelers enough that it quickly brings a halt to the celebratory air of the men. Mercutio is so manic that Romeo must calm him down. As the men move off, Romeo expresses concerns about bad omens for his future.

When he arrives at the ball, Romeo watches the many beautiful women, searching for Rosaline, but then he sees Juliet dancing and is unable to pull his gaze away from her. As he watches Juliet and then speaks of his admiration for her beauty, Tybalt, a Capulet, sees Romeo and identifies him as a Montague. Tybalt demands that Romeo be thrown out of the party, but since Romeo is behaving with proper decorum, Capulet can see no reason to force Romeo to leave. When Romeo joins in the dancing, Tybalt watches and again complains to Capulet, who is now visibly angry that Tybalt appears to be assuming the authority of the host. Capulet's wife must calm both men. The dancing is halted when a young man begins to sing, "What Is a Youth?" This song about the journey of two lovers serves as a backdrop as both Juliet and

FILM TECHNIQUE

- Opening shots help to set the mood of a film. The initial scene of *Romeo and Juliet*, in which Olivier gives the prologue, shows a dark and gloomy Verona engulfed in fog. This opening scene immediately marks the film as tragic, but when the prologue ends the scene shifts to a colorful scene of street action, where street people are laughing and mild insults can lead to sword fights. The juxtaposition of these two scenes (that is, their placement next to each other) suggests that there is a dark undercurrent behind the brilliant sunshine of Verona's town square.

- Fast camera movements are used for scenes of chaos. At the initial masquerade ball, for example, the camera moves so quickly that the scene begins to blur. The fast camera movements also successfully capture the chaos of street fighting.

- A variety of camera techniques are used, such as wide-lens, close-up, and tracking shots in several scenes. In the film's opening sequence, which uses a wide lens, the camera pans across the town of Verona. Within moments, the camera lingers on individual characters as they speak. In the sword-fighting scenes, the camera tracks individual fighters as they move along the town streets. The shifting of camera shots from wide lens to close-up to tracking is accomplished smoothly and makes the audience feel present for the events taking place.

- Close-up shots also reveal emotion and work to focus the audience's attention on the romance. For example, as Friar Laurence tells Juliet of his plan to bring Romeo back into Verona and reunite the couple, the camera moves in closely to focus on Juliet's face and captures her immediate joy, as well as her extreme youth. The audience is again reminded that Juliet is only a child, not yet fourteen.

- Film editing is often invisible to the viewer of a film. If it is done correctly, the film moves smoothly without any visible breaks between the action, the actor's movements, and the narration. For instance, in the scene following Romeo and Juliet's wedding night, the camera initially focuses on the couple as they sleep, quickly moves to Romeo as he rises and prepares to leave, and then moves back to Juliet as she awakens. Within a few minutes the camera action has also captured the couple's good-bye kisses, the nurse's announcement that Juliet's mother is approaching, and Romeo's final exit from Juliet's window. Because of careful film editing, the shifts in the scene are smooth and convey multiple scenes and groups of people without disruption.

- Handheld cameras can make the audience members feel that they are up on the screen with the actors. The handheld camera is often closer to the action and can catch a scene from almost any angle. Handheld cameras increase the intensity of the shot for the audience. With a handheld camera there can be fewer problems with continuity and editing, since the camera does not have to be set up and moved constantly to capture the action. Zeffirelli used handheld cameras in several scenes, but one of the clearest and best examples is during the sword fight between Romeo and Tybalt. The actors are in constant movement as they battle in the square and alleys, but the director does not need to stop the action so that a camera can be moved. Instead, the camera is right in the action, creating an immediacy of involvement for the viewer.

Romeo begin moving through the crowd seeking one another. Their movements are watched by Tybalt. Romeo moves behind a curtain and is hidden from Juliet's sight when he takes her hand and begins to pull her toward him. They exchange words and touch hands. Romeo is insistent in his expressions of love; he kisses Juliet, who welcomes his kiss. After the singer finishes his song, the nurse comes seeking Juliet. It is the nurse who tells Romeo that Juliet is a Capulet. He immediately understands the difficulty of his situation. When Juliet finds out (also through the nurse) who Romeo is, she understands it too: they have both fallen in love with a member of their enemy's family.

As his friends leave the masquerade ball, Romeo stays behind to try and see Juliet. Standing outside, he sees her in her window. She is sitting on the window ledge high above him, where he can hear her speaking. She is speaking about Romeo and how she wishes his name was different. After listening for several minutes, Romeo finally speaks and says he would tear his name from himself if it were possible. This is the famous balcony scene, in which Romeo and Juliet pledge their love. Juliet is sensible and warns Romeo not to speak words of love unless he means it. She then admits her love for him. In response, Romeo swears his love for Juliet, who tells him not to swear by the moon or anything but himself. After many exchanges of kisses and words of love, Juliet and Romeo finally part as a rooster crows in the distance. They part with promises to meet and get married later that same day. As Romeo leaves, he is euphoric in his joy.

The next scene begins with Friar Laurence picking herbs just outside the church. Romeo arrives and explains that he and Juliet want to get married that very day. Friar Laurence is shocked and says it is too soon and too fast. He recalls Romeo's recent affection for another young woman named Rosaline. But then, Friar Laurence begins to consider that this wedding might finally bring an end to the long-standing feud between the two families, and he agrees to marry them that afternoon.

The scene shifts to Mercutio and Benvolio talking. Mercutio is wondering where Romeo has been, since he has not been seen since the previous evening. They soon see Romeo on the street, and the joking continues among several young men who have joined them. The nurse approaches, looking for Romeo. Mercutio taunts her, becoming rather cruel, but finally Romeo intervenes and Mercutio leaves. The nurse tells Romeo that his intentions had better be honorable (that is, his love should lead toward marriage), and he directs her to send Juliet to Friar Laurence's home that afternoon, where they will be married.

Juliet waits anxiously for the nurse's return. When the nurse arrives, she plays games, delaying her news until an increasingly impatient Juliet demands to learn what Romeo said. When she learns she is to be married that afternoon, Juliet is filled with joy. Soon both young people meet with Friar Laurence, who marries them.

The scene shifts. Benvolio keeps trying to get Mercutio to come out of the streets, where they are likely to meet with the Capulets. It is the heat of the afternoon, and as Mercutio cools himself in the fountain in the square, Tybalt arrives, looking for Romeo. When Mercutio and Tybalt begin to bicker, Benvolio tries to separate them and calm things, but then Tybalt sees Romeo approaching and challenges him to a fight. Romeo declines, but soon Tybalt insults Mercutio, who has wanted to fight all along. A duel begins, which draws a crowd. Initially there is much joking and laughing and the fight does not seem serious, but then further insults are exchanged, and Romeo rushes to break up the fight. Romeo's intrusion results in Tybalt's sword hitting Mercutio and killing him. As he ails, he curses both the Montague and Capulet families. Everyone laughs as Mercutio struggles to walk away. They do not realize that he is mortally wounded until he falls to the ground dead.

Romeo is angry and wants to avenge his cousin's death against Tybalt, who has left the scene with the other Capulets. Romeo chases after Tybalt and quickly catches up to him. Soon both Romeo and Tybalt have drawn swords, and a duel to the death begins. Romeo kills Tybalt, and it is only when Tybalt is dead that Romeo's anger is dissolved. He realizes that in killing Tybalt, he has killed his chance to be with Juliet.

The nurse cries out her grief at Tybalt's death, but Juliet will not hear of Romeo being blamed. She will defend her husband, but knows that there will be a demand for Romeo's blood. And indeed, the prince must soon break up a mob, where Capulet's wife demands that Romeo be killed. The prince notes that although Romeo killed Tybalt, Tybalt had killed Mercutio. Therefore, Romeo is to be banished but not executed.

Romeo is grief-stricken and weeps in Friar Laurence's room. The nurse seeks to calm him; she reminds him of his wife. Romeo asks whether Juliet hates him. He is mad with grief and speaks of wanting to kill himself. Friar Laurence immediately calms things and sends Romeo to Juliet. The next scene is the following morning, when Romeo and Juliet awaken after having spent their wedding night together. Romeo begins to get dressed; Juliet, not wanting to lose his company, argues that it cannot be morning yet and he must not leave. They are both torn, but they both finally realize that if Romeo is to live, he must not be found there and must leave. Their parting is bittersweet, and they exchange many words of love.

Juliet's mother asks to speak with Juliet, who weeps not for Tybalt but for Romeo, who has just left. When Juliet refuses to marry Paris in two days' time, Capulet is so angry he can scarcely control himself. He threatens to throw Juliet out into the streets, but she responds only with more tears. She begs her mother to help her postpone the wedding to Paris. The nurse tells Juliet that she should marry Paris, since Romeo has been banished and no one will ever know they were married. Juliet is dumbstruck at the nurse's suggestion, but she finally stops crying. Juliet tells the nurse that she will go to Friar Laurence to make confession (a religious ritual in which sins are confessed and forgiven) since she has displeased her father, and the nurse believes her.

Juliet arrives at Friar Laurence's to find Paris, there arranging his upcoming wedding to Juliet. When Paris leaves, Juliet collapses in grief and demands that Friar Laurence find a solution to prevent the marriage. Friar Laurence explains his plan: Juliet will take a potion to make her appear dead for two days. She will be thought dead and then taken to the family tomb for her funeral, where Romeo will awaken her. Back at her home, Juliet apologizes to her father for her disobedience and then, when alone in her room, drinks the potion. Friar Laurence sends a letter to Romeo to alert him to the plan. In Shakespeare's play, Juliet has a soliloquy (words spoken aloud but not to another character) in which she must decide whether she trusts Friar

Laurence; she wonders if he wanted to poison her to hide his crime of having married two young people without their parents' knowledge. Zeffirelli's film, however, leaves out this scene.

Zeffirelli also omits the wedding preparations that are taking place as the Capulets prepare for Juliet to marry Paris. Instead, there is upheaval in the palace as Juliet is discovered apparently dead in her bed. Her funeral takes place very soon. Balthasar, Romeo's servant, weeps as he tells Romeo of Juliet's death and her funeral. Zeffirelli shows Balthasar on the road, passing by the person who was sent with Friar Laurence's letter. Romeo quickly races to Verona, and on his way, he also passes the messenger, making it clear that he does not receive Friar Laurence's explanation that Juliet is not really dead. At the tomb, Romeo says good-bye to Balthasar. His intent to die is obvious.

Romeo enters the tomb and sees, as he thinks, Juliet lying dead. He addresses her as his love and his wife, and tells her of his love for her. Romeo also addresses the corpse of Tybalt and asks for his forgiveness. When Romeo returns to Juliet's body, he says that she still appears as alive in death, as she did when last he saw her. He kisses her and weeps over her body, and then drinks the poison that he brought. He kisses her hand and dies. Outside the tomb, Friar Laurence appears, and Balthasar, who had been keeping watch for Romeo, leaves. Friar Laurence finds Romeo and begins to weep over his body. Juliet awakens and is happy to find Friar Laurence with her. She immediately asks for Romeo. Friar Laurence tries to convince her to leave, but she sees Romeo's body. Friar Laurence panics because he hears the watch (a security force, similar to police) approaching. He runs away, leaving Juliet with Romeo's body. She kneels next to him and finds in his hand the bottle that had held the poison. She kisses him, hoping to absorb some of the poison, and collapses over his body in grief. Her weeping is halted when she hears the watch approaching. She grabs Romeo's dagger and stabs herself. Juliet dies on top of Romeo's body.

The final scene is of the two biers with Romeo's and Juliet's bodies being carried toward their funerals. Their families walk behind as they approach the steps, where the prince stands. He addresses the Capulets and Montagues and tells them that it is their hatred that has killed their children, who loved one another. The prince also takes some of the blame for having tolerated their feud. The prince says that everyone has been punished enough. An epilogue, consisting of a voice-over by Olivier, closes the story.

Although Zeffirelli cut many of Shakespeare's lines in adapting the play to film, most of the larger scene cuts occur at the end of the film, in the play's final act. In Shakespeare's play, all the events occur over a space of four days. In the film, this time line appears to be compressed, and the events from Juliet's burial to Romeo's arrival at her tomb are covered in only a few moments. The scene at the beginning of act 5 when Romeo visits an apothecary to buy poison is eliminated from the film, as is the scene in which Friar Laurence learns that his message to Romeo was not delivered. (The play explains this by saying that the messenger was quarantined in a house where plague had been detected, while the film shows Balthasar passing the messenger on the road.) In the third scene of the final act, Paris is at Juliet's tomb mourning her death when Romeo arrives. Paris thinks Romeo is there to vandalize Juliet's tomb; the two fight, and Paris is killed. The film eliminates this scene entirely. Also left out is Friar Laurence's lengthy explanation of how he married Romeo and Juliet and how he concocted an elaborate plan for them to be together after Romeo was banished. Finally, Montague's and Capulet's final lines, in which they vow to honor their children's love and to end their feud, are left out of the film.

CHARACTERS

Balthasar

Balthasar, played by Keith Skinner, is Romeo's servant. This is a small role but an important one, since it is Balthasar who tells Romeo of Juliet's death.

Benvolio

Benvolio, who is Montague's nephew, is played by Bruce Robinson. His role is primarily that of a genial friend to Romeo, and in fact his name, related to *benevolent*, means "good will." As a cousin to Romeo, Benvolio is a member of the Montague household. He wants only to maintain peace and tries to calm Mercutio and the others who would fight. Benvolio is the only one

of the younger generation of the Montague family to survive the feud.

Capulet

Capulet, the patriarch or head of the Capulet family, is played by Paul Hardwick. He is milder than his wife, but when Juliet refuses to marry Paris, he is driven to rare anger against his daughter. Capulet thinks that he has a right to rule Juliet's actions, and her disobedience is an affront to his honor. As a result, he threatens to lock Juliet away or throw her out into the streets.

Capulet's Wife

Capulet's wife—Juliet's mother—is played by Natasha Parry as a proper woman of the household, managing the servants and her daughter's care. Initially she is so proper that she is not even comfortable discussing Juliet's possible marriage to Paris. She was fourteen when Juliet was born, and her husband is many years older. The Capulets are not happily married, which Zeffirelli's camera work establishes quite clearly. It is Capulet's wife who urges that Romeo be put to death for killing Tybalt. When a hysterical Juliet refuses to marry Paris, her mother rejects her daughter, with whom she is angry for refusing the planned betrothal. In thrusting aside her daughter's pleas, Lady Capulet helps to set in motion the final desperate plot.

Escalus
See The Prince

Juliet

Juliet is played by Olivia Hussey, who was awarded a Golden Globe for her performance as Juliet. Juliet is a Capulet—part of a family that is sworn to hate the Montagues. Juliet is impetuous but also capable of thinking clearly about what falling in love with Romeo will mean to her and their respective families. She understands immediately that there is great risk in falling in love with Romeo. Like Romeo, Juliet is very much in love. She can scarcely stop kissing him on the occasions when they are together. Juliet is not even fourteen years old, but in many ways, she is mature beyond her years. She is capable of great love and passion, and she is willing to defy her father and her family name to marry the man she loves. She agrees to Friar Laurence's plot because she sees it as the only possible way to succeed, even though it means she will awaken in a crypt filled with many generations of dead family members. Juliet is brave, but she is young enough that she sometimes acts in too much haste.

Friar Laurence

Friar Laurence is played by Milo O'Shea. Friar Laurence is of dubious moral character. He chooses to marry an underage couple without their parents' permission. He then concocts an elaborate plan to make it appear that Juliet has died, and when he encounters Juliet and a dead Romeo in the family crypt, he runs away, leaving Juliet alone. He thinks first of himself and of absolving himself of any responsibility for the tragedy that unfolds.

Mercutio

Mercutio is played by John McEnery, who captures the quick and witty speech that is characteristic of Mercutio. Mercutio, a kinsman of the prince and Paris, is moody and quick to love and anger. Mercutio's behavior is often manic, uncontrolled, and irreverent. He is devoted to Romeo, who seems not to be aware of how deeply Mercutio loves his friend. Yet Mercutio's actions lead to tragedy: he cannot pass an opportunity to fight with the Capulets. When Mercutio takes offense at Tybalt's insults, he throws himself into a sword fight that results in death for himself and Tybalt and an intensification of the feud between their two families. Mercutio's name is derived from that of the Greek god Mercury, who is fast and quick-witted, and Mercutio shares these characteristics. His speeches are brilliant conversations that are largely one-sided. He requires only an audience, not a dialogue.

Montague

Montague, Romeo's father, is played by Antonio Pierfederici, but his heavily accented voice is dubbed by Sir Laurence Olivier. Montague is the elderly patriarch of the Montague family and is a sworn enemy of the Capulet family. Montague has very little dialogue, however, and often is simply present in a scene.

Montague's Wife

Montague's wife is played by Esmeralda Ruspoli. This role is very small, and she scarcely has any dialogue.

The Nurse

The nurse—not a nurse in the modern, medical sense, but a nanny or caretaker—is played by Pat Heywood. The nurse has raised Juliet from infancy, ever since her own baby died. Although she is a servant, her position as Juliet's nurse gives her added stature and very nearly makes her a member of the family. In keeping with the Shakespeare play, Heywood plays her as a bawd (a woman of loose morals). The nurse's first words are about sexual matters. She is a master of innuendo and delivers many of her lines with great humor and a dash of slapstick. Her words are sometimes crude and offend Capulet's wife, who tries to quiet the nurse. In one scene, she grabs a retreating Romeo and pulls him into her lap as he tries to escape. The nurse is easily identified by her cackling laughter and her crude comments. Along with Friar Laurence, the nurse participates in the plot to help Romeo and Juliet marry. Although Friar Laurence agrees to the marriage as a way to make peace between the two families, the nurse is a romantic and simply wants to ease the way of true love.

Paris

Paris, who is related to the prince, is played by Robert Bisacco. He wants to marry Juliet and is impatient to do so, although he is initially put off by Capulet. Later, Paris pressures Capulet to push the wedding forward. He thinks that marrying him will ease Juliet's grief after Tybalt is killed. He does not understand that Juliet is grieving Romeo's banishment, not Tybalt's death. Paris's demand for a quicker wedding is one element of the tragedy that results in Romeo's and Juliet's deaths. Paris's name is taken from a Trojan prince, made famous in Homer's *Iliad*, who kidnaps the wife of a Greek king and sparks the Trojan War. Where that Paris was responsible for the many deaths in the war, this Paris is partially responsible for the deaths of the two young lovers. Although Paris's death scene is left out of Zeffirelli's film, in Shakespeare's play, Romeo finds Paris at Juliet's tomb and is forced to kill him when he will not allow Romeo to enter the tomb.

The Prince

The prince—named Escalus, but referred to only by his title in the film—is played by Robert Stephens. *Escalus* means "scales," which are a symbol of judgment and justice; administering justice is part of the prince's role. He tries to halt the feud between the Capulets and Montagues by making fighting in the street punishable by death. He appears only three times in the play and film, the first two times to render judgment on a sword fight. The first time, he warns the families not to continue their feud. The second time, he pronounces a sentence of banishment on Romeo following the deaths of Mercutio and Tybalt. In the final scene, as the bodies of Romeo and Juliet are brought before him, the prince renders judgment on these two families who cared more for their hatred than for their children.

Romeo

Romeo is played by Leonard Whiting. Romeo is a Montague, one of the sworn enemies of the Capulet family. Initially Romeo is a romantic who falls in love with every beautiful woman he sees. Then he sees Juliet and finally understands that real love is all-consuming passion. He needs to be with Juliet every moment and cannot wait to marry her. When they are together, he seems compelled to keep kissing and touching her. Romeo arranges the wedding for the day after their initial meeting. Between the moment of the marriage and his wedding night, though, Romeo gives in to his temper and slays Tybalt in revenge for Mercutio's death. It is a reminder that Romeo is very young, still a teenager, and can act without thinking things through. The moment that Tybalt is dead, Romeo's anger disappears and he becomes capable of rational thought again. Similarly, in Juliet's tomb, he notes how lifelike Juliet is in death, but he is so quick to join her that he swallows the poison without pausing to think through what his words mean. The name Romeo has become synonymous with the persona of the passionate and idealistic young lover, or more generally a romantic man.

Tybalt

Tybalt is played by Michael York. It is Tybalt who recognizes Romeo at the Capulet masquerade ball. He insists that Romeo should be thrown out, and even when Capulet tries to reason with him, Tybalt wants to fight. Tybalt's name is associated with a mythical prince of cats; Mercutio refers to this fable when he insults Tybalt. Tybalt is vengeful, agile, swift, quick to take offense, predatory, territorial, and sometimes sneaky. In the sword fight with Mercutio,

the duel begins almost playfully. Tybalt is laughing, but like some cats, he is crafty and moody, and the tone shifts quickly. However, when he kills Mercutio, Tybalt is shocked; the death was an accident.

THEMES

Fate

Fate is one of the central themes in *Romeo and Juliet*. The feud itself suggests that a Capulet daughter and a Montague son cannot find lasting happiness together. Several times, Romeo blames fate or destiny for the obstacles that he and Juliet face. However, they were never fated to be together, and thus, their union is at odds with what the stars—that is, fate, as believed to be revealed through astrological workings—had decreed. In fact, the prologue describes them as "star-crossed lovers." Destiny has placed them apart and not together. Romeo, in particular, believes in the stars' ability to predict his destiny. After Mercutio's Queen Mab speech in act 1, as Romeo and his friends prepare to attend the masquerade ball, Romeo says he is concerned about "some consequence yet hanging in the stars." Upon first seeing Juliet, he says of her beauty that it is "for earth too dear" (that is, too expensive)—more suited to being found in heaven, among the stars. Similarly, when Romeo waits for Juliet to arrive and Friar Laurence to marry them, he says that even if "love-devouring death" takes them, that if Juliet is only his for a moment, it will be worth it. He clearly understands that there is a significant risk to their love and that death is a possibility.

When Mercutio dies, he curses both the Capulet and Montague households, with "a plague [on] both your houses." This curse foretells Romeo and Juliet's fate. This is the weight of their cursed destiny. After he kills Tybalt in a duel, Romeo says that "he is fortune's fool." This film and play ask the audience to consider whether fate or destiny can be escaped. When Friar Laurence's messenger fails to reach Romeo before he hears of Juliet's death, is that fate? For Shakespeare's audience, which believed in fate or destiny as a controlling factor in life, it would have been clear that the lovers could never have escaped their fate, which was to die to end a feud so old that no one even remembered how or why it began.

READ, WATCH, WRITE

- Read Shakespeare's *Romeo and Juliet*. After reading the play and watching the film, choose one scene that you think is especially important in revealing something critical about the characters' personalities, actions, and choices. Adapt the scene using modern language, and ask your friends to take on key roles in the scene and act it out. Videotape the performance and show it to your classmates. Discuss with your classmates what they learned from seeing this scene updated for a modern setting.

- Research the re-created Globe Theatre in London, where *Romeo and Juliet* was performed in the summer of 2004. Create a PowerPoint presentation showing diagrams of the theater, including the stage area and seating for the audience. Include information about the costuming and staging of plays at the Globe, both in Shakespeare's time and in the present day.

- Although the play is set in Verona, Italy, the behavior of Shakespeare's characters is based on English customs and moral codes. Research courtship in Renaissance England and write a paper in which you explain how these customs are portrayed in *Romeo and Juliet*. Also discuss ways in which the behavior shown in this play deviates from customary courtship rituals of the time.

- To understand how a theatrical production is changed when it is filmed, it is first necessary to understand the kinds of film techniques that Zeffirelli used. Working in small groups with two or three classmates, create a glossary of film and camera terms. Some terms to consider include point of view; montage; dissolve; high angle; short, medium, and long shots; wide tracking shots; panning; and close-up shots. In your glossary, define each term and then provide an example of how it is used in this film and why. In addition to creating a written film glossary, prepare a video of examples to illustrate your glossary terms. If a film technique that you discuss in your glossary is not used in filming *Romeo and Juliet*, provide an example from a different film. Organize the film clips into a computer presentation and show it to your classmates.

- Read Alice Hoffman's novel *Incantation* (2006), in which a young girl living in sixteenth-century Spain learns that she is a hidden Jew. There is also an unlikely romance in this young-adult novel. Compare the male and female protagonists in Hoffman's novel with Romeo and Juliet. In what ways are the characters and the depictions of romance similar? How are they different? The threat of death hangs over both couples in the novel and the film. What did you notice about how the two different couples handle the pressures that they face to keep part of their lives hidden? In a class presentation, read relevant sections from *Incantation* and compare those scenes to complementary scenes from *Romeo and Juliet*. Ask your classmates to tell you what they learned about living in the sixteenth century and the dangers faced by young men and women who chose to defy the customs of their world.

Romantic Love

At the opening of *Romeo and Juliet*, the audience learns that Romeo has thought himself in love with a young woman who is cold to him. When his mother asks where he is, the camera shows him walking along, seemingly melancholic, as he holds flowers and longs for a young woman who has rejected him. Montague reports having seen Romeo with tears in his eyes. When asked, Romeo replies in clichés about the fair Rosaline, with whom he thinks himself in love. Romeo explains his love as a kind of madness, a

Zefferelli's background in stage operas shows in the drama of the film's scenes. *(© Paramount / The Kobal Collection)*

passionate fire, a love that causes grief and that is easily extinguished by the woman's coldness. As he walks along with his friends, Romeo talks about love using these familiar clichés, filled with much sighing. The supposed rejection by Rosaline, who may not even know that Romeo exists, lies heavy on his chest, which he explains Cupid has pierced with a painful arrow. Both Shakespeare and Zeffirelli want to contrast Romeo's earlier unrequited love with the passionate love he will feel for Juliet.

When Romeo first sees Juliet, he no longer has eyes for any other woman. Although Rosaline is also present at the ball, once Romeo sees Juliet, he can see only her and no one else. His love for her is passionate and overwhelming. Juliet's instant love for Romeo is similarly intense. Zeffirelli captures this on film by blurring the faces of the other dancers while showing Romeo and Juliet clearly. When they speak to one another, both at the masquerade ball and

later in the balcony scene, their dialogue is filled with words of love, but without the clichés that Romeo had used earlier. At the ball, Romeo explains his immediate love for Juliet as a religious experience, and Juliet responds similarly. Later, both compare their love to wealth or other riches. Romeo's passion for Juliet is so great that he cannot focus on anyone or anything but her. When Romeo's friends leave the ball, they search all over for him, but he ignores them and instead lingers outside Juliet's home, hoping to see her one more time. In the Elizabethan world, love at first sight was often considered to be the most authentic kind of love, and thus Shakespeare's audience would have immediately recognized that Romeo and Juliet were, indeed, passionately and deeply in love.

Because so many people die in *Romeo and Juliet*, it is necessary to discuss the role of love in the ensuing violence and death that permeate the film and play. Romeo rejects Tybalt's challenge to fight: his honor is at stake, but Romeo's love for Juliet means that he cannot fight her kinsman. Mercutio's fight with Tybalt, then, is undertaken to salvage Romeo's honor. Thus both Mercutio and Tybalt die because Romeo and Juliet fall in love. Of course, it is not fair to blame Romeo and Juliet for the culture of sword fighting or the feud that their families have perpetuated, but it is Romeo's desire to stop Tybalt and Mercutio from fighting that directly results in Mercutio's death. If not for Juliet, Romeo would not have been put in that position. Romeo and Juliet also threaten suicide. Romeo makes the threat after killing Tybalt, and Juliet makes the threat when faced with an imminent marriage to Paris. Their suicides at the end of the film are the most striking outcomes of a love so intense that it is defined by both its passion and its violence.

STYLE

Costuming

The film's colorful costumes, with their lavish use of velvet, satin, and silk, earned costume designer Danilo Donati an Academy Award. The women's costumes are well displayed during the masquerade ball, in the elaborate gowns covered with ribbons and ruffles and trimmed with pearls and gemstones. Many of the gowns are noted for their vibrant colors, such as Juliet's crimson velvet ball gown. Romeo wears a fine gray-blue jacket of luxurious materials. The two rival families wear distinctly different clothing: the Capulets wear more colorful clothing of reds and golds, while the Montagues wear mostly blues and greens. The men wear fitted tights and ruffled shirts, with their family emblem on their sleeve. The costumes appear authentic and help evoke the film's setting in Renaissance Italy.

Music

The music for *Romeo and Juliet* was created by Nino Rota. The music is most often a background accompaniment that sets the tone. Soaring violin passages help the audience participate in the sadness and grief of the tragedy. In the end, the Capulet and Montague families have suffered the loss of their only children, besides other young relatives. The city of Verona is the poorer because of the duel, and the music helps to capture the sorrow that so much death brings.

One specific musical number became especially well known when the film was released. At the masquerade ball, the song "What Is a Youth?" is sung as part of the entertainment. The song focuses on the journey that two lovers take as their courtship progresses. When the song was released as a love song, separately from the film, it was called "A Time for Us," with different lyrics that more directly speak of lovers who are separated and must overcome obstacles to be together.

Setting

Shakespeare set *Romeo and Juliet* in Verona, which was a city-state during the sixteenth century. In filming the play, Zeffirelli used several different locations in Italy. The balcony scene was filmed in a sixteenth-century palace, Palazzo Borghese, which is located in Rome. The church and tomb scenes were filmed in Tuscania (about sixty miles north of Rome), including at the Church of Saint Peter (San Pietro), which was built in the eighth century and renovated in the eleventh and twelfth centuries. The Palazzo Piccolomini in Pienza was used for the home of the Capulet family. This palazzo was built in the fifteenth century as a summer home for Pope Pius II. Pienza, a small town north of Rome, was also used for filming street scenes, but the sword fights were filmed in the town of Gubbio. In choosing to film in locations in central and northern Italy, Zeffirelli did not stray far from Shakespeare's location of Verona, which is located in the northern part of the country. The antiquity of the locations also helps to add authenticity to the film.

CULTURAL CONTEXT

Feuds

In sixteenth-century England, Queen Elizabeth I outlawed the kinds of sword fights that are featured in *Romeo and Juliet*. As a result, Shakespeare's audience was enthusiastic about watching sword fights onstage. The world of sword fighting was different in Renaissance Italy, where the violence of feuds and sword fights was common, as were the attempts by local governments to contain the violence. *Romeo and Juliet* captures the disruption to commerce and daily life that accompanied feuds. Italy was not a unified country at this time, and each city government enacted its own laws. If the government was ineffective, people sought to avenge crimes against them by taking action themselves. As is the case in *Romeo and Juliet*, the origin of feuds was not always known, since they might have begun decades earlier and the originators might have been dead. Feuds often extended beyond the immediate individuals to include multiple generations and extended families, servants, and neighbors. To control feuding, some governments tried mediation to solve disputes, often with local clergy helping to resolve differences. Friar Laurence's supposition that by marrying Romeo and Juliet he might bring about the end of the feud would not have been completely unexpected.

If a feud was finally resolved, it was common to have a public celebration in recognition of the end of the feud. The participants would quite literally kiss and make up. However, such reconciliations did not always occur. Eventually governments began to develop policing by magistrates, and where that did not occur, a more military form of policing was used. Often, though, these efforts were no more successful than mediation. The judicial system occasionally proved successful in ending feuds through prosecution, but kinship groups and a natural inclination to view those with whom one did not agree as enemies meant that feuds were easier to begin than to end.

Rebellion

In Shakespeare's England, the deaths of Romeo and Juliet would have been judged as the natural outcome of young people marrying too quickly or attempting to control their own destinies. Although the prince's final lines in *Romeo and Juliet* make clear that the parents' hatred of one another has claimed the lives of their children, there were enough other contributing factors present in the play to dilute the parental blame, including fate, the lovers' extreme youth, and the interference of the nurse and the friar.

Although youthful rebellion was not unheard of in Renaissance Italy, or even in England, where Shakespeare was writing, it would have been a much more familiar theme for audiences of the film in 1968. Those audiences would likely have blamed the lovers' deaths not on their disobedience but rather on Juliet's parents, whose insistence that she immediately marry Paris leads to her desperate attempt to fake her

death. Teenage rebellion was a normal part of the growing generation gap that defined the 1960s. Zeffirelli embraced that generation gap and crafted a story of two teenagers who fall in love and choose to ignore the wishes of an older generation.

In *Romeo and Juliet*, the parents are not directly involved in perpetuating the feud; instead, it is youthful rebellion that keeps the feud alive. The fathers do not fight in the street. It is Tybalt, Mercutio, Romeo, and their young relatives and servants who continue to feed the feud. This kind of rebellion was much more common in the turbulent years that permeated the decade from the mid-1960s through the mid-1970s. Youthful rebellion against a prevailing culture that subordinated women and people of color marked this decade. The Vietnam War further stoked the fires of rebellion. Young people felt that the older generation cared more about the military supremacy of the United States than about basic human rights. The younger generation often viewed older generations as self-serving and more interested in accumulating wealth than in social justice.

The rebellion of the 1960s began with young college students. The free-speech movement at the University of California at Berkeley in 1964 is often considered the era's first major rebellion. Students refused to obey an administration edict regarding the distribution of protest writings, and in the process they occupied several buildings on campus. It did not take long for such protests to spread to other university campuses. By March 1965, the first of many antiwar protests was staged by students at the University of Michigan. By 1967 and 1968, antiwar protests and demands that the United States withdraw from Vietnam were becoming increasingly common, both on and off college campuses. Rebellion against the establishment—whether family, university, work, or society—moved like wildfire across the country. Martin Luther King Jr. and Robert F. Kennedy were assassinated in 1968, and the streets of America erupted with an upheaval that threatened centuries of well-established traditions of obedience to authority. *Romeo and Juliet*, with its two young protagonists rebelling against their society and their families, was the perfect story for 1968.

Romeo and Juliet *is set in Verona, Italy.* *(© Igor Plotnikov / Shutterstock.com)*

CRITICAL OVERVIEW

Zeffirelli's *Romeo and Juliet* earned positive reviews when it was released, and it has held up well in the decades since. Reviewing it for the *New York Times*, Renata Adler celebrated the many strengths of Zeffirelli's film and the choices he made in casting the two young leads. She calls it "a lovely, sensitive, friendly popularization of the play" and says the actors playing Romeo and Juliet are "as young and full of life as they ought to be." She does criticize the movie's handling of Shakespeare's language, which sometimes sounds "more like *West Side Story* than perhaps it ought to." However, Adler praises it as "the sweetest, the most contemporary romance on film this year." For Adler, Zeffirelli proves that the timelessness of Shakespeare can speak to modern audiences in the right director's hands.

The review of *Romeo and Juliet* that appeared in *Time* magazine is just as complimentary of the director's talent. This reviewer notes that "Zeffirelli has managed to make the play alive and wholly contemporary without having had to transfer the action to a modern setting." Much of the credit, this reviewer suggests,

belongs to the two young leads, who are, "believably, agonized teenagers." They happen to live in Verona in the sixteenth century, but they might just as easily have been living in a more recent time. Both young actors "look their parts and read their lines with a sensitivity far beyond the limitations of their age."

One of the most enthusiastic reviews is that provided by Roger Ebert, writing for the *Chicago Sun-Times*, who first begins by lamenting the pedantic and often boring way that Shakespeare is taught in the American education system. Perhaps that background accounts for why Ebert writes, "I believe Franco Zeffirelli's *Romeo and Juliet* is the most exciting film of Shakespeare ever made." This film, he says, "has the passion, the sweat, the violence, the poetry, the love and the tragedy" that make Shakespeare great. It may lack the grand drama or cinematic excellence of some other films made from Shakespeare's plays, but it "is a deeply moving piece of entertainment, and that is possibly what Shakespeare would have preferred." Like other reviewers, Ebert praises the work of the two young lead actors, and he comments favorably on the camera work and use of colors. He also writes that this production is able to give a freshness to even the most familiar lines.

CRITICISM

Sheri Karmiol

Karmiol is a lecturer in interdisciplinary studies at the University of New Mexico. In the following essay, she discusses how Romeo and Juliet's youth and the manipulations of the nurse and Friar Laurence contribute to the tragic ending of Zeffirelli's Romeo and Juliet.

Shakespeare's *Romeo and Juliet* is filled with moments of great joy and even greater tragedy. The saddest moments in both the play and Zeffirelli's film occur in the tomb, where first Romeo thinks Juliet is dead and then Juliet finds Romeo dead. Even the most hardened member of the audience must feel grief at the deaths of these two teenagers, barely out of childhood, who were so in love and whose suicides cost their families so dearly. Underlying both Shakespeare's play and Zeffirelli's film is the breach between the older generation and the younger generation. Each group represents different values and traditions, depicted through the ongoing feud and through Romeo and Juliet's decision to marry. The feud and their own hot tempers kill Mercutio and Tybalt. The Capulets bear much of the responsibility for Romeo and Juliet's deaths, since both deaths occur after Juliet is given a deadline that would have forced her to marry Paris (committing bigamy, though her parents do not know this). But more than the feud, and more than parental interference, there are two characters who assume the role of confidants and who more directly bring about the final tragedy. Only the nurse and Friar Laurence bridge the gap between generations, and ultimately, these two make possible the events that lead to the tragic deaths of Romeo and Juliet.

Why do Romeo and Juliet have to die? Up until the end, the story itself shares many of the characteristics of Shakespeare's romantic comedies. There are fools and villains, misunderstandings and missed messages, and comic characters, but *Romeo and Juliet* ends with death and not a wedding. What might have been a romantic comedy becomes tragedy. Why? The answer might be found by returning briefly to Shakespeare's source, Arthur Brooke's

ONLY THE NURSE AND FRIAR LAURENCE BRIDGE THE GAP BETWEEN GENERATIONS, AND ULTIMATELY, THESE TWO MAKE POSSIBLE THE EVENTS THAT LEAD TO THE TRAGIC DEATHS OF ROMEO AND JULIET."

The Tragicall Historye of Romeus and Juliet. Brooke's translation of an Italian novel was the first version of this story in English. In an opening comment "To the Reader," Brooke writes that his work will describe

> a couple of unfortunate lovers, thralling themselves to unhonest desire; neglecting the authority and advice of parents and friends; conferring their principal counsels with drunken gossips and superstitious friars (the naturally fit instruments of unchastity); attempting all adventures of peril for th' attaining of their wished lust; using auricular confession the key of whoredom and treason, for furtherance of their purpose; abusing the honourable name of lawful marriage to cloak the shame of stolen contracts; finally by all means of unhonest life hasting to most unhappy death.

Brooke's judgment of Romeo and Juliet is harsh, and it includes a condemnation of the couple's poor choices and their willingness to flout local customs and traditions, such as in their failure to bow to parental authority and the laws of the land. Brooke never suggests that the feud is responsible. He does, however, suggest that the nurse, who is seen sneaking drinks at the masquerade ball, and the friar, who deceives the couple's parents, are partly responsible for the deaths. Certainly Romeo and Juliet are inexperienced and naive, and they do make many poor choices, but ultimately they rely upon the advice of two adults whom they trust. It is this trust that results in their deaths.

Although at the end of Shakespeare's version, the prince blames the feud for the many deaths, the feud actually bears little responsibility, at least for the deaths of Romeo and Juliet. Although the feud is old and its origin is now shrouded in mystery, the elders of the Capulet and Montague families are not dueling in the

WHAT DO I SEE NEXT?

- *Shakespeare, the Animated Tales* is a BBC series that ran from 1992 to 1994. The series' entire set of twelve plays (with a total running time of five hours) was released on DVD by Ambrose Video. These animated films are unrated.

- *William Shakespeare's Romeo + Juliet* (1996), directed by Baz Luhrmann, stars Claire Danes and Leonardo DiCaprio. This film is a modern retelling of Shakespeare's play, with gang warfare in place of the Capulet and Montague family feud, but with the original dialogue boldly preserved. This two-hour film was released by Twentieth Century Fox and is rated PG-13.

- One of the earliest filmed versions of *Romeo and Juliet* was made in 1936; it was directed by George Cukor and stars Norma Shearer and Leslie Howard. This film is unrated. One notable problem is that Leslie Howard was 43 when he played Romeo, but the film is well done, and all of the actors were highly regarded for their work in it. This film was distributed by Metro-Goldwyn-Mayer and is available on DVD.

- A 2005 version of *Romeo and Juliet*, produced as part of the Thames Shakespeare Collection, presents the complete play, with a running time of about three hours. This well-regarded production stars Christopher Neame and Ann Hasson as the leads and is not rated.

- An animated version in Spanish, *Romeo y Julieta: Sellado con Beso*, was produced in 2007. This short film (just over an hour) was directed by Phil Nibbelink. Reviews are generally positive, though they suggest that audiences find it light or even silly. This film is not rated.

- A 1994 Royal Opera production, *Romeo et Juliette*, is considered to be one of the better stagings of this play as an opera. The production was directed by Brian Large, with Roberto Alagna and Leontina Vaduva singing the lead roles. This film was made available by Kultar and is not rated.

- *West Side Story* (1961) is a modern retelling of *Romeo and Juliet* in the form of a musical, set around the Puerto Rican immigrant community in New York City. The feuding families are replaced with rival gangs. The film stars Natalie Wood and George Chakiris. It was choreographed by Jerome Robbins and directed by Robert Wise. This film, which is 152 minutes long and is unrated, won ten Academy Awards.

- *A Fond Kiss* is a multicultural retelling of *Romeo and Juliet* in a modern setting. The film focuses on a young Pakistani Muslim man (Atta Yaqub) who falls in love with a young Irish Catholic woman (Eva Birthistle). Both the community and their families are opposed to this romance. This 2005 film, which was directed by Ken Loach and distributed by Icon Films, is not rated.

- *Shakespeare in Love* (1998) is a fictional account about how *Romeo and Juliet* might have first been written, cast, and staged in Shakespeare's London. It is a clever merging of *Romeo and Juliet* and *Twelfth Night*, a Shakespearean comedy. The film won seven Academy Awards and stars Gwyneth Paltrow and Joseph Fiennes. The film was directed by John Madden and distributed by Miramax, and it is rated R.

streets. The feud is kept alive by the young. It is the next generation, with their youth and rebellious nature, who continue to fight. In a chapter from *Shakespeare on Film* that examines Zeffirelli's *Romeo and Juliet*, Jack J. Jorgens focuses on youthful rebellion as a cause of the tragedy.

He claims that Shakespeare blends "the impulses of the young toward rebellion . . . [with] hot tempers and the need to prove their maturity, which keeps the feud alive when the old are ready to let it die." Tybalt and Mercutio clearly keep the feud alive, but they are not alone. Early in the film, Romeo watches as two wounded Montague men, presumably victims of the feud, are carried past on stretchers. Then at the masquerade ball, Romeo and his friends attend a Capulet ball to which they were not invited, thus dishonoring the Capulet name, or so Tybalt claims. Both Romeo and Juliet choose to ignore the past and the feud that governs their lives, in favor of forging a future that they know will be denied to them. By becoming lovers and marrying when they know very well that it would be forbidden, Romeo and Juliet both further the feud, just as their deaths bring it to an end. Jorgens argues that Romeo and Juliet remain naive children at the end of the play, and that "they never see what a corrupt and flawed world it is that they are leaving, never give any indication that they know how they contributed to their own downfall, and never understand that love of such intensity not only cannot last but is self-destructive."

Romeo and Juliet do not see a corrupt world or their own complicity in the tragedy that threatens their love because they see only each other. Zeffirelli captures this complete focus the first time Romeo and Juliet meet. As each catches a glimpse of the other, the camera focuses on their respective faces, as they slowly begin to be more aware of the other. Eventually the faces of the other guests are blurred, and Romeo and Juliet only see the face of their beloved.

Keeping true to Shakespeare's play, Zeffirelli stresses the extreme youth of the players. When filming began, the actors playing the lead roles were fifteen and sixteen years old, very close to their ages in the play. In most stagings of the play and most film versions, the two young lovers are played by actors who are twenty or thirty years old. Zeffirelli's casting of unknown actors for the parts further emphasizes their youth and, in a sense, absolves them of adult responsibility for their actions. Romeo and Juliet are not much more than children, and as teenagers, they rebel against the wishes of an older generation. They also fall in love quickly. As audiences take note of Romeo and Juliet's youth, so clearly projected on film, they need only recall the dialogue from the beginning of the play, when the audience learns that Juliet is not yet fourteen years old. Zeffirelli's Juliet not only looks young, she *is* young.

Shakespeare gives the couple words of love to speak, but she and Romeo lack complexity and depth. They simply see one another and fall in love the first time their hands touch. They need something more for the audience to feel real grief at their deaths. Shakespeare gives Juliet some beautifully memorable verse, but because Hussey and Whiting are not experienced Shakespearean actors, Zeffirelli eliminates many of Shakespeare's lines and replaces them with action and with loving gazes. Instead of words, they must convey much of what they feel through passionate kisses and longing glances. As a result, the audience sees two characters who are never static. Jorgens notes that "what Romeo and Juliet lack in depth of character they make up in energy, beautiful innocence, and spontaneity." It is their energy, innocence, and impulsiveness that are captured on-screen through Zeffirelli's direction.

Juliet is young and innocent, which the nurse surely knows. In the balcony scene, it is Juliet who instructs Romeo about love, and she is the one who promises to send word to him the next day that they can be married. She sends him away but then calls him back for more embraces. Juliet's ability to laugh at herself and Romeo and her obvious passion for him play out in front of Zeffirelli's camera. The couple spends so much time embracing that audiences can hear a rooster crowing as dawn approaches. Juliet's plan is to send the nurse to find Romeo to confirm that the arrangements for their wedding have been made. The nurse has cared for Juliet all her life, but she is employed by the Capulets. Her willingness to deceive her employers and do something that she certainly knows would not be approved is the first of her errors. Acting as a go-between for Juliet and Romeo is part of the nurse's romantic fantasy about love. She never expresses the slightest misgiving about either Juliet's young age or her parents' certain disapproval. The nurse pretends to be outraged when Mercutio calls her a bawd, a common name for a procurer or panderer, who deals in sexual trade. The word is not a compliment, but the nurse is far less offended than might be expected. After all, in arranging a meeting between Juliet and Romeo, she is fulfilling the functions of a bawd. In Zeffirelli's film, the nurse is excited to learn that Juliet and Romeo are to marry. She laughs and crosses herself with great joy. She is so excited that she pulls Romeo onto her lap. Later she will make it possible for Juliet and Romeo to consummate their marriage, when she allows Romeo to spend the night in Juliet's room. She does this even though Romeo has killed Tybalt and is exiled from Verona.

Both the nurse and her parents ultimately abandon Juliet to an unwanted marriage to Paris. In response, Juliet must depend only on her own efforts to extract herself from this untenable position. In desperation, she chooses to trust Friar Laurence, who tells her that he has a potion that will cause her to sleep for two days, after which time she will awake and be free to run away with Romeo, who will be waiting in the tomb for her to awaken. Zeffirelli deletes Juliet's soliloquy in act 4, in which she considers whether to trust Friar Laurence. Juliet's willingness to drink Friar Laurence's potion and her willingness to agree to two days interred in the family crypt is a factor of her extreme youth. Whereas the Juliet in Brooke's poem is sixteen years old, Shakespeare makes her even younger. This change reinforces Juliet's extreme youth and naiveté. As Romeo enters the tomb, Zeffirelli has the camera linger on the decomposing bodies. When Juliet awakens, Friar Laurence is with her, instead of the promised Romeo. She refuses to leave, and Friar Laurence runs away, frightened of being caught in the tomb and blamed for all that has happened. Instead of accepting responsibility, Friar Laurence blames "a greater power" that has thwarted their plans. In the play, he says, "I dare no longer stay," but in the film, he repeats this line four times as he flees in panic. This change emphasizes both Friar Laurence's guilt and his fear of being caught. In fact, Shakespeare does have Friar Laurence step forward and accept blame for his actions. Zeffirelli's omission of Friar Laurence's long explanation of his role makes him a coward and not just a corrupt clergyman.

In the end, Juliet is betrayed both by her nurse and by Friar Laurence. The nurse tells Juliet that she should marry Paris. She makes the bed that Romeo and Juliet have just vacated and tells Juliet to simply pretend that the marriage, which the nurse has facilitated, never happened. The second betrayal occurs in the tomb

when Friar Laurence abandons an obviously distraught Juliet to grieve alone over Romeo's dead body. The nurse ignores her responsibility to the Capulet family that employs her, and Friar Laurence ignores his responsibility to the church to which he owes allegiance.

Why do Romeo and Juliet die? In Shakespeare's source, Brooke's *The Tragicall Historye of Romeus and Juliet*, it is clear that Romeo and Juliet die because they are disobedient and too lustful. Their cohorts perpetuate the feud through foolish actions and hot tempers. Romeo's and Juliet's extreme youth and consequent lack of experience in the real world lead them to make foolish choices. But also contributing to the tragedy are Juliet's nurse and her parents, who trade in her sexuality—the nurse because she thinks all love, even an inappropriate love, is romantic, and her parents because they seek an advantageous marriage for their only child. Finally, Friar Laurence contributes to the tragedy by deceiving everyone, deliberately or accidentally. Zeffirelli follows Shakespeare in placing the blame on youth and hasty actions. In choosing to cast two very young actors, Zeffirelli emphasized the lovers' youth and inexperience. By the film's conclusion, Zeffirelli's *Romeo and Juliet* has reminded viewers that death was always too close to Romeo and Juliet. Their deaths bring loss not just to their families but to the viewers as well, who fell in love with the love and passion they saw on screen.

Source: Sheri Karmiol, Critical Essay on *Romeo and Juliet*, in *Drama for Students*, Gale, Cengage Learning, 2014.

Courtney Lehmann
In the following excerpt, Lehmann discusses the varied critical reaction to Zeffirelli's film.

. . . Nevertheless, for all its success at the box office and beyond, the release of Zeffirelli's *Romeo and Juliet* spawned a heated debate—not just among film critics writing in the sixties, but also between present-day scholars—as the place of this adaptation in the Shakespearean film canon remains the subject of dispute. Dividing the principal combatants into two 'rival households,' Ace Pilkington observes that

> if the war between scholars and directors seems to be over, the peace terms have not yet been agreed, and there is a large no-man's-land into

> INDEED, ZEFFIRELLI IS OFTEN CRITICISED FOR THE OVER-SENTIMENTALITY AND MELODRAMA THAT CHARACTERISES HIS FILMS, WHICH MOST CRITICS ATTRIBUTE TO HIS BACKGROUND AS AN ACCLAIMED OPERA DIRECTOR."

which film-makers wander at their peril. The principal combatants in this guerrilla conflict might perhaps be called the purists and the popularizers, and no modern director has a better claim to the dangerous title of popularizer-in-chief than Franco Zeffirelli.

Indeed, among leftist critics at the time, Zeffirelli's *Romeo and Juliet* was 'simply cashing in on one of the "softer" versions of radicalism'; for as Russell Jackson explains, Zeffirelli and his cohort were accused of conflating the youth culture that the film celebrates with real innovation and social change. Drawing a parallel between the Zeffirelli's 'Capulets and Montagues' and the British invasion's 'mods and rockers,' Nina Hibbins' comment in a Communist publication, the *Daily Worker*, exemplifies this position, complaining that Zeffirelli's film failed to expose the underlying causes of the youth generation's angst: 'mods and rockers, or Jets and Sharks, are products of working class conditions in an advanced industrial age.' In other words, in order to live up to its billing as 'the thing for young people to see,' Zeffirelli's film—set in an exclusively aristocratic society—could not possibly offer a meaningful investigation of the lived reality of social class antagonisms that fuelled so many of the youth movements of the sixties.

Yet, if, for some 'popularisers' Zeffirelli did not go far enough, then for the conservative 'purists' his *Romeo and Juliet* wandered too far afield from Shakespeare's sacrosanct verse. As Jackson points out, *Variety*'s comment on the release of the film in London says it all in its subheading: '"Inexperienced leads, or Franco Zeffirelli's brash casting experiment, hampers classic tale of love. Kids don't understand meaning of their lines. A tough sell."' On the subject of the proper articulation of these all-important lines, Harold Hobson epitomises the class

snobbery that preoccupied the purists; citing Robert Stephens' noble portrayal of the Prince as the film's only redeeming feature, Hobson observes that the others—clearly lacking classical, 'Oxbridge' training, let alone an education in 'Received Pronunciation' (RP)—lazily 'trail around with them the flat vowels of red-brick universities.' Even Renata Adler, who raved about the film following its opening in New York's Paris Theater, contends that the verse 'suffers a bit, sounding more like "West Side Story" than it ought to. In the classic speeches, one begins to worry about diction and wish the modern would recede and let Shakespeare play through.'

Adler's reference to *West Side Story* is significant, as movie ads from 1968 indicate that this musical film was revived in theatres in order to capitalise on the popular success (not to be confused with critical acclaim) of Zeffirelli's film in America and around the world. In a *New York Times* ad from 4 October 1968, *Playboy* magazine brings both films together in an explicit pitch for Zeffirelli's adaptation: 'The entire film is a poem of youth, love, and violence . . . a Renaissance recapitulation of "West Side Story" played with pure 1968 passion!' Indeed, the cultural relevance of Zeffirelli's film is suggested by the *New York Times* ad, which encourages audiences to attend the 'Swinging Youth Premiere': 'Come on down and meet OLIVIA HUSSEY and LEONARD WHITING, the fabulous teenage stars of "Romeo & Juliet" as well as your favorite deejays from WNEW-FM and a host of rock stars . . . IT'S YOUR NIGHT . . . COME DOWN AND MAKE IT YOUR SCENE.' And in the end, it wasn't just teenage girls with their long, straight hair in centre-partings—in imitation of Hussey's look—who left the cinema in tears. For as Kenneth Rothwell pointed out in 1973, even 'the harsher critics, the professional Shakespeareans, admitted they had wept despite themselves.'

Ultimately, critics and scholars remain divided at best in their assessment of whether the film is, in fact, 'a poem' or a sacrilege. If Adler and Hobson critique the principals' enunciation of the lines, then others, like Kenneth Rothwell, defend the pair: 'Hussey and Whiting, while very young and inexperienced, have nevertheless been coached to within an inch of their lives to read selected passages with cogency and fidelity.' In a directors' symposium, Zeffirelli himself confirms the rigor of the rehearsals to which he subjected the young actors:

> I've experienced the full range of actors and actresses playing in my films, from the two little 'green' actors playing Romeo and Juliet—he was a Cockney boy and she was fourteen—but I pulled out of them what I was looking for—youth, innocence, and passion. The words were conquered practically one by one, through the painstaking efforts of voice coaches and the actors themselves.

The critical reception of the film's other major actors has similarly assumed a rather schizophrenic path. For many, Pat Heywood's robust Nurse was a revelation—at last sufficiently risqué, in both dialogue and demeanour, to bring the role to life—whereas for others, her portrayal 'seems too bawdy, cold and almost terrifying—in the way that characters in Disney movies suddenly become uncanny, and haunt children's dreams.' The same contradiction affected reviews of Michael O'Shea's Friar Laurence, who is either a peace-loving academic—in Renata Adler's description—'a modern, radical-understanding Dean,' or the far shadier character of the early Italian novellas. Indeed, many critics have commented on the excision of the Friar's final speech (and appearance) from Zeffirelli's film, a decision that leaves the audience questioning his moral fortitude at the very least, and, at the worst, his motives. Not even John McEnery's Mercutio has been spared a divided reception. Kenneth Rothwell contends that '[t]he only Mercutio who could possibly rival Barrymore's [from Cukor's 1936 film] is John McEnery's . . . [But] comparisons are misleading because the actors' conceptions of the role were so different: Barrymore was the master craftsman; McEnery, the exponent of an emerging youth culture and lifestyle.' Chastely suggesting what this 'lifestyle' might be, Adler observes that 'a lot [is] made of the relationship between Romeo and Mercutio, beautifully played by John McEnery.' Yet John Russell Taylor referred to McEnery's performance as '"an exercise in gutter camp,"' while Anderegg more scathingly describes McEnery as 'an inveterate clown,' whose individual scenes drag on to become 'merely another set piece, existing for its own sake.'

More controversial than the acting is the music. For Rothwell, the score, has much to do with his singularly amusing observation that 'quite possibly Volpone in even his most orgiastic dreams could not have conceived of the box office fortune the film yielded,' for the 'saccharine strains of the pseudo-Elizabethan "What is a Youth?" took the cinematic public, especially the youth audience . . . by storm and overnight generated an unparalleled interest in Shakespearean film.' Page Cook sees the merits of the music even without considering the box-office returns, arguing that Nino Rota's score is not only 'cogent' and 'eloquent,' but also 'a major contribution to film-music' in its own right. Assuming quite the opposite tone, Michael Anderegg observes that '[p]articularly unfortunate is the inserted song, "What is a Youth?" a pseudo-Renaissance ballad . . . that accompanies the meeting of Romeo and Juliet, its banal lyrics and sentimental orchestration taking away from, rather than contributing to, the coming together of the lovers.' Indeed, Zeffirelli is often criticised for the over-sentimentality and melodrama that characterises his films, which most critics attribute to his background as an acclaimed opera director. In this context, as Rothwell notes, Nino Rota's score alone makes Zeffirelli's *Romeo and Juliet* more akin to Paul Czinner's filmed ballet (1966) than to the 1954 adaptation by Renato Castellani, principally because 'it draws heavily on an operatic sensibility,' resulting 'in a film unusually sensitive to the interplay between words and music.' Deborah Cartmell describes the director's entire oeuvre as 'shar[ing] an unmistakable operatic conception,' while Anderegg adds: 'The Capulet ball demonstrates how much Zeffirelli is in love with spectacle . . . Zeffirelli's background in opera is here fully in evidence.' . . .

Source: Courtney Lehmann, "Zeffirelli's *Romeo and Juliet*: Then and Now," in *Screen Adaptations: Shakespeare's "Romeo and Juliet"; The Relationship between Text and Film*, Methuen Drama, 2010, pp. 222–29.

Lindsey Scott

In the following excerpt, Scott discusses how Zeffirelli's film focuses specifically on Juliet.

Given each director's decision to adapt and popularize Shakespeare's *Romeo and Juliet* for a teenage audience, it is hardly surprising that many critics have highlighted the similarities between the film adaptations of Franco Zeffirelli (1968) and Baz Luhrmann (1996). Critical discussions of Luhrmann's *William Shakespeare's Romeo + Juliet* often speculate on how much influence Zeffirelli's earlier film had on

Luhrmann's approach: James N. Loehlin comments that Luhrmann's frequent borrowings from Zeffirelli tend to be "simple replications rather than pointed reworkings"; Samuel Crowl describes how it was directors such as Zeffirelli who "nudged the Shakespeare film from the art house to the Cineplex," paving the way for the likes of Luhrmann to find success with an international teenage market. Both directors make large cuts to the play-text in order to make its contents more "accessible" for audiences and, as a result, their treatment of Shakespeare has been likened to Shakespeare's treatment of his own sources (Walker). Like Zeffirelli before him, Luhrmann cast young, attractive actors in the roles of Romeo and Juliet and, as Elsie Walker comments, this reflects how each director saw "the ability of a wide audience to identify with their protagonists as crucial." However, despite the many noted similarities, these Shakespeare films offer radically different representations of Juliet for their respective audiences.

What is perhaps most unexpected, given the cultural climate of Luhrmann's film and "the pressure put on cinema by an increasingly educated, increasingly sexually confident, and increasingly salaried female audience" of the nineties (Daileader), is that, in terms of desire and agency, Claire Danes's Juliet resides at the opposite end of the spectrum to Olivia Hussey's. While critics such as Peter S. Donaldson observe how Zeffirelli's film underscores "Shakespeare's treatment of Juliet as an active, desiring subject," notably less has been said about the agency of Danes's Juliet under Luhrmann's direction. Danes's lack of agency in the film becomes most apparent through a consideration of the body's representation, an analytical framework that demonstrates, as Aebischer observes, how "Shakespearean performance studies have benefited from a lively dialogue with film theory and gender studies." This essay looks at the bodily and *spatial* representations of Juliet on film in order to explore the differences between each director's handling of her role as "desiring subject." By focusing on a comparative reading of the tomb scene, my argument will consider how the directorial choices of Zeffirelli and Luhrmann either promote or repress the sexual agency of Shakespeare's heroine.

The spatial strategies of Franco Zeffirelli's *Romeo and Juliet* emphasize Juliet's sexual awareness and her open expressions of desire.

> I WOULD ALSO SUGGEST THAT, IN THIS PARTICULAR SEQUENCE, THE PERSPECTIVE OF ZEFFIRELLI'S CAMERA TRANSGRESSES THE CONVENTIONS OF THE TRADITIONAL CINEMATIC MALE GAZE, VISUALLY CODING JULIET AS BEARER OF THE LOOK AND PROVIDING A UNIQUE SPACE FOR A 'FEMININE' GAZE."

Despite the fact that Shakespeare's heroine "hath not seen the change of fourteen years" (1.2.9), critics observe how Juliet's use of language would have allowed an Elizabethan audience to "grasp her sexual knowledge and her consciousness of carnal desire" (Bly 99). Zeffirelli's film visualizes this aspect of her characterization by associating images of ripeness, growth, and sexual awakening with Olivia Hussey's Juliet. While the "Gallop apace" speech (3.2.1–31) is omitted from Zeffirelli's script, its verbalization of Juliet's sexual longing is mediated through the film's gendered spaces that mark the awakening of carnal desire. The colorful visual excess of Zeffirelli's ball scene creates a space for Juliet's sexual awakening and her self-progression from adolescence to womanhood: lavish displays of fruit and wine; warmly lit archways; rich fabrics, and Juliet's red dress as central focus, all connote a feminine softness that alludes to the "ripeness" of Juliet's impending sexuality.

Critics such as Celia Daileader note how Shakespeare's play "has always been, to some degree, about *Juliet*" (188), and Zeffirelli's interpretation strengthens such viewpoints by privileging Juliet's first experience of desire, rather than Romeo's. In the dance sequence, the alternating camera shots of the lovers are carefully balanced to connote reciprocal feelings and a sense of harmony in their first meeting. However, elsewhere in this scene, Zeffirelli's camera favors Juliet's responses. As Romeo begins the line, "My lips, two blushing pilgrims, ready stand" (1.5.94), the camera cuts to a close-up shot of Juliet's face; her eyes close slowly, and the "ineffable, almost drugged quality of her gaze" connotes awakened desire and "the surprise of adolescent sexual discovery" (Dai-leader 188). The intense close-up marks the attachment of the viewer's gaze and Juliet's internal thoughts: it is not Romeo who is looking at Juliet and registering her desiring look at this point, but the spectator, as Romeo is shown to be standing behind her in the previous shot.

Ultimately, we are not encouraged to share in Romeo's experience of this first meeting as intimately as we are with Juliet's, and the shots that follow indicate a gaze that initiates from Juliet's perspective—a gaze that Romeo recipro-cates—as she turns to face him behind the cur-tain. The alignments of the gaze seem to suggest a balance between gender roles in terms of object and bearer of the look; as Donaldson observes, Zeffirelli's camera addresses us as "watchers of male as well as female beauty." However, I would also suggest that, in this particular sequence, the perspective of Zeffirelli's camera transgresses the conventions of the traditional cinematic male gaze, visually coding Juliet as bearer of the look and providing a unique space for a "feminine" gaze. While the film's opportunities for a female gaze may not be fre-quent enough to indicate a reversal of cinema's conventional patriarchal structures of seeing (as Donaldson suggests), a denial of these unique spaces seems equally inadequate in light of Zef-firelli's treatment of Juliet as the film's active subject, and the audience's intended identifica-tion with her desiring look.

The film's spatial and bodily signifiers of Juliet's agency extend beyond the ball scene. Images of Juliet's body (and body parts) are used to connote her strength, growth, and sexual maturity. Close-ups of hands are first used to symbolize the meeting of the lovers, as in Shake-speare's play-text (1.5.92–106), but elsewhere in the film, the image of the hand most frequently belongs to Hussey's Juliet: she moves her hand to her lips in remembrance of Romeo's kiss; she once again initiates the joining of hands in the balcony scene to signal her return of "love's faithful vow" (2.2.127); and the film's final and most significant hand gesture, filmed in a tight close-up, is reserved for her waking in the tomb.

Hussey's use of hand gestures suggests Juliet's ability to *internalize* emotion, and thus control it. In contrast to this suggestion of control, Romeo's emotions are frequently sig-naled to the viewer, not through the immediate use of the body, but with external objects that

symbolize feeling. First shown carrying a flower to indicate his romantic and melancholy mood, and later taking up the blood-stained handker-chief to express his anger over Mercutio's death and his own "reputation stained" (3.1.102), Leo-nard Whiting's Romeo does not express himself in the same internal fashion as Hussey's Juliet. Whether it is a mask to hide behind, or a phallic sword with which to assert his masculinity and thus remove his "effeminate" weakness, Romeo's display of emotion remains externally displayed through objects rather than the body. As a result of this, the "internal" signifiers of Juliet's self-development are pitched against the "external" signifiers of Romeo's perpetual state of adolescence. Although Irving Ribner notes that, "to demonstrate the particular progress of the human life journey, Shakespeare concen-trates upon Romeo," Zeffirelli's representations of the body overturn such arguments to promote Juliet as the major character who grows and develops through her experiences.

In the tomb scene, Zeffirelli constructs a space that holds Juliet's unconscious body as its central focus, despite Romeo's mobility and her rigidity. The centrality of her body is sig-naled to the viewer by the camera remaining on her face, while Romeo repeatedly speaks his lines out of shot. When he delivers his final speech, the camera alternates between shots of Romeo and close-up shots of Juliet, as if a conversation were taking place between them. A further image implies a subjective camera shot from Romeo's perspective: he stands at her feet and looks up at the entire length of her body from what appears to be a submissive viewpoint, due to the camera's low position. Spatially, the tomb's domain is inherently female: an early shot of Romeo and Balthasar arriving outside the church is domi-nated by the dark arches of the entrance gates and the tomb's arched doorway; a statue of a mother holding her child guards its entrance and is frequently in shot as Romeo breaks open the doors. After Romeo "descends" into the vault, with its pillars and dark passages, he stands over Juliet's body in long-shot, and the ominous arch-way that looms behind her body fills the space of the frame and draws the viewer's eye toward another female statue at the center of its dark tunnel. The tomb's interior is not unlike Romeo's metaphor of the "womb of death" (5.3.45–48); however, Zeffirelli's "womblike vault surrounded with pillars" (Cartmell 44) is a gendered space that simultaneously removes the abhorrence of female sexuality that can be found in the language of Shakespeare's play-text. . . .

Source: Lindsey Scott, "'Closed in a Dead Man's Tomb': Juliet, Space, and the Body in Franco Zeffirelli's and Baz Lurhmann's Films of *Romeo and Juliet*," in *Literature/Film Quarterly*, Vol. 36, No. 2, 2008, pp. 137–40.

Kenneth S. Rothwell

In the following excerpt, Rothwell looks at the difficulties of adapting Shakespeare's play to film.

. . . The question of "capturing Shakespeare" or performing "Shakespeare himself" is always an ambiguous one because the truth is that no one, not even the wisest and best informed among us, can be entirely certain of exactly what Shakespeare intended. Suffice it to say that Zeffirelli hatched his *Romeo* in the context of at least three other *Romeo* films—Cukor's, Antonelli's, and RADA's, and in addition he had the notable example of Wise's 1962 *West Side Story*, which was of course a deliberate adaptation of the Shakespearean story to modern realities. Of all the makers of cinematic *Romeo and Juliet*'s, Zeffirelli best succeeded in integrating the disparate elements that make up the film experience. Cukor, as we have seen, yearned for success with spectacle (*opsis*, to use Aristotle's term) but was strangled by the limitations of black and white. He did succeed, however, in reproducing the text with great fidelity, losing only a few lines. The little known, educational film made by RADA simply photographs a stage performance on a pseudo-Elizabethan stage and, in relying only on the word without making any innovative use of the camera, makes the experience seem patently redundant or unnecessary. Why not go to see the original on stage for a more satisfactory experience? Antonelli, whose love for camerawork exceeded his concern for Shakespeare's language, used *Romeo* as an excuse for constructing a Technicolor museum piece about the Italian Renaissance. It was a brilliant idea, hugely sensuous to watch and enjoy, but disastrously weak, except for the minor characters noted above, as a dramatic vehicle.

Zeffirelli's version manages to perpetuate the Cukor-Antonelli desire for the High Renaissance set against an Italian backdrop of authentic settings. At the same time, his use of decisive theme music (*melos*) to support the

theme (*dianoia*) of youthful, rebellious love, adds a new dimension. The result, while extravagant, nevertheless brings about a plausibility, an energy, lacking in previous cinematic treatments. Put it this way. Hussey and Whiting, while very young and inexperienced, have nevertheless been coached to within an inch of their lives to read selected passages with cogency and fidelity. Film production allows opportunity for infinite pains in rehearsal and retake which can cover blemishes that would reduce a stage performance to shambles. Film, properly used, allows modern directors an opportunity to use very young actors successfully in the roles of Romeo and Juliet. They do not need the ability to sustain a lengthy part; only the talent to reenact bits and fragments, one at a time. The audience, spared the details of their rehearsal, sees only a finished product. It is, of course, for an actor a lesser achievement, but the end result may appear superficially more attractive to hypnotized audiences in the dark womb of the movie theatre. Add to that the seductiveness of the memorable theme music, and the results are indeed mesmerising. Finally consider the way in which Zeffirelli deliberately employed the theme to "West Side Story" to make "Shakespeare Contemporary" at a time when the word "relevance" had become the touchstone of youth culture, and further reasons for the success of the film are apparent.

Finally the question remains unanswered: is there really any continuity in the experience of reading a Shakespearean play and then viewing several film versions of it? Have the reading of the play and the viewing of the films been separate and discrete experiences? Is the play really no more than source for the film, and the film something entirely different? I don't think so. I think the overall impact of this many creative minds attempting to capture on celluloid the essence of the deepest and most pervasive of human rituals—the tension between the forces of springtime and winter as embodied in the youthful and older generations of Montagues and Capulets—leaves an indelible impression. The myth of Romeo and Juliet, we are assured, continues not only on the printed page, not only irregularly on the stage, but alive and full-fleshed on the film print, stored away and available for instant replay at our leisure.

Howard, Harvey, Whiting as Romeo; Shearer, Shentall, Hussey as Juliet; Oliver,

Robson, Heywood as Nurse; Barrymore, Zollo, McEnery as Mercutio; Smith, Cabot, Hardwick as Capulet; Rathbone, Fiermonte, York as Tybalt; Kolker, Johns, O'Shea as Friar Laurence. The richness and variety of this cluster of acting talent bring us into an even more intimate relationship with Shakespeare's genius than we could have known merely through the printed word or the staged production. The printed word and the stage serve their very important function. No doubt about that. But film offers a capacity for close definition, for minute delineation of character. The human eye is an imperfect lens harnessed to a will that must stray and wander; but the camera lens carries the built-in discipline to focus on the actors whether they move to stage center, left, or right. The camera, by linking vision with discipline, provides a monitor for concentration. The series of *Romeo* films may then be seen as preliminary monitorings of Shakespeare's text on film. As the backlog of our experience with film grows, we grow closer to ideal cinematic versions of *Romeo*. I look forward to fresher versions that will go a step further in conception, that will make the dream that is film an even livelier experience, that will indeed convert Prospero's "insubstantial pageant" into one that by its magical capacity for perpetual reinvocation will become remarkably like a "substantial pageant." And Hollywood's early contributions to this unfolding process should not be ignored as trivial.

Source: Kenneth S. Rothwell, "Hollywood and Some Versions of *Romeo and Juliet*: Toward a 'Substantial Pageant,'" in *Literature/Film Quarterly*, Vol. 1, No. 4, 1973, pp. 349–51.

SOURCES

Adler, Renata, Review of *Romeo and Juliet*, in *New York Times*, October 9, 1968, http://movies.nytimes.com/movie/review?_r=1&res=EE05E7DF173EE571BC4153DFB6678383679EDE (accessed July 8, 2013).

Brooke, Arthur, *The Tragicall Historye of Romeus and Juliet*, 1562, http://www.canadianshakespeares.ca/folio/Sources/romeusandjuliet.pdf (accessed July 15, 2013).

Cartmell, Deborah, "Shakespeare, Film and Sexuality: Politically Correct Sexuality in Film Adaptations of *Romeo and Juliet* and *Much Ado about Nothing*," in *Interpreting Shakespeare on Screen*, St. Martin's Press, 2000, p. 44.

Cohen, Elizabeth Storr, and Thomas Vance Cohen, *Daily Life in Renaissance Italy*, Greenwood, 2001, pp. 55, 65, 115.

Crowl, Samuel, "Close-Up Major Directors," in *Shakespeare on Film*, W. W. Norton, 2008, pp. 53–57.

Ebert, Roger, Review of *Romeo and Juliet*, October 15, 1968, http://www.rogerebert.com/reviews/romeo-and-juliet-1968 (accessed July 8, 2013).

Gurr, Andrew, "Citizen Staples and Juliet's Rebellion, 1588–1605," in *Playgoing in Shakespeare's London*, Cambridge University Press, 1996, pp. 119–58.

Jorgens, Jack J., *Shakespeare on Film*, Indiana University Press, 1977, pp. 79–91.

Mabry, Donald J., "Student Rebellion in the Sixties," Historical Text Archive, http://historicaltextarchive.com/sections.php?action=read&artid=313 (accessed July 14, 2013).

McDonald, Russ, "Men and Women: Gender, Family, Society," in *The Bedford Companion to Shakespeare*, Bedford/St. Martin's, 2001, pp. 253–77.

Molarsky, Mona, "Costumes from Zeffirelli's *Romeo and Juliet* Visit New York," Examiner.com, May 28, 2009, http://www.examiner.com/article/costumes-from-zeffirelli-s-romeo-and-juliet-visit-new-york (accessed July 9, 2013).

Palazzo Borghese website, http://www.palazzoborghese.it/en/english.html (accessed July 9, 2013).

Palazzo Piccolomini website, http://www.palazzopiccolominipienza.it/en/ (accessed July 9, 2013).

Romeo and Juliet, directed by Franco Zeffirelli, Paramount, 1968, DVD.

Shakespeare, William, *Romeo and Juliet*, in *The Norton Shakespeare*, edited by Stephen Greenblatt, W. W. Norton, 1997, pp. 865–941.

"Tuscania: The Town," A Rome Art Lover's Web Page, http://www.romeartlover.it/Tuscania.html (accessed July 9, 2013).

"Virtuoso in Verona," in *Time*, October 11, 1968, http://www.time.com/time/subscriber/article/0,33009,902414,00.html (accessed July 8, 2013).

FURTHER READING

Cressy, David, *Birth, Marriage, and Death: Ritual, Religion, and the Life Cycle in Tudor and Stuart England*, Oxford University Press, 1999.
    The author creates a picture of what it was like to live in England during the sixteenth and early seventeenth centuries. Of particular interest is the discussion of social and culture changes during Shakespeare's life and the influence those changes had on his work.

Friedman, Lise, and Ceil Friedman, *Letters to Juliet: Celebrating Shakespeare's Greatest Heroine, the Magical City of Verona, and the Power of Love*, Stewart, Tabori & Chang, 2010.

This book indicates how important Verona has become to lovers as the city in which Romeo and Juliet fell in love. Many people mail letters addressed to Juliet in Verona, in which they write about lost love or love found. Volunteers have been answering these letters for more than seventy years, and the book includes many samples of these letters.

Greenblatt, Stephen, *Will in the World: How Shakespeare Became Shakespeare*, W. W. Norton, 2005.

In this biography of Shakespeare, Greenblatt uses historical documents, as well as Shakespeare's texts, to create a picture of the man and his work within the historical context in which he lived.

Kastan, David Scott, ed., *A Companion to Shakespeare*, Blackwell, 1999.

Kastan has assembled a collection of twenty-eight scholarly essays about Shakespeare's world and his work. Each essay offers a focused examination of only one aspect of the playwright's world. Individual essays focus on politics, religion, playwriting, economics of theater life, censorship, and printing.

O'Hara, Diana, *Courtship and Constraint: Rethinking the Making of Marriage in Tudor England*, Manchester University Press, 2002.

This text provides a study of courtship in sixteenth-century England. Much of O'Hara's source material is taken from church records and from legal documents and wills. This book is an interesting source of information about social customs and the economics of courtship.

Pritchard, R. E., ed., *Shakespeare's England: Life in Elizabethan and Jacobean Times*, Sutton, 1999.

Pritchard has collected a large selection of documents written during Shakespeare's time. These firsthand reports provide a glimpse of what it was like to live in England at this time. Pritchard includes excerpts from letters, diaries, pamphlets, plays, and poetry to reveal what writers had to say about the time in which they lived.

Wells, Stanley, *Shakespeare for All Time*, Oxford University Press, 2003.

This is an illustrated and easy-to-read narrative of Shakespeare's life and his legacy. Wells includes a thoroughly researched biography of Shakespeare, as well as many interesting details about the plays and their reception in the four hundred years since Shakespeare wrote them.

SUGGESTED SEARCH TERMS

Romeo and Juliet AND Shakespeare

Romeo and Juliet AND Zeffirelli

Romeo and Juliet AND Olivia Hussey

Romeo and Juliet AND Leonard Whiting

Romeo and Juliet AND tragedy

Romeo and Juliet AND suicide

Zeffirelli AND Shakespeare

Shakespeare AND tragedy

Romeo and Juliet AND romantic love

When I Was a Little Girl and My Mother Didn't Want Me

Joyce Carol Oates is one of the most prominent living American novelists, often considered a candidate for the Nobel Prize in Literature. Even while pursuing a full-time career as a literature teacher, she has written at an incredibly prolific pace, producing forty-two literary novels, series of mystery novels, and numerous collections of dramas, short stories, poetry, and essays, in addition to books for young adults and children. Like many American authors, she has explored her family's experience in an immigrant community (Hungarian in her case), in novels like *A Garden of Earthly Delights* (1967). *When I Was a Little Girl and My Mother Didn't Want Me* is a 1997 play that explores this same territory. Expanding on themes in the 1967 novel, Oates in this play depicts the devastation of a character based closely on her own mother, Carolina, as her family is torn apart by violence and poverty. The play can be found in the Oates collections *New Plays* (1998) and *Dr. Magic: Six One Act Plays* (2004).

JOYCE CAROL OATES

1997

AUTHOR BIOGRAPHY

Oates was born on June 6, 1938, in Lockport, a suburb of Buffalo, New York. Her family was working-class, and she was the first member of it to graduate from high school. About the time of her graduation, her parents had a second

Joyce Carol Oates *(© Stefania D'Alessandro / Getty Images Entertainment / Getty Images)*

daughter, Lynn Ann, who was severely autistic. Oates recalls her childhood as being remarkably stable and happy. Only as an adult did she find out that one of her grandfathers had committed suicide and the other had been murdered. Oates attended Syracuse University on a scholarship and took a degree in English, graduating as valedictorian in 1960. She earned a master's degree in English from the University of Wisconsin and there met her husband, Raymond Smith. Both became English professors. Oates taught for many years at the University of Windsor, in Ontario, Canada, and moved to Princeton in 1978, where she planned to retire in 2014. She and Smith founded the *Ontario Review* and its associated press.

Oates received Lewis Carroll's *Alice's Adventures in Wonderland* as a gift from her grandmother while in grade school and counts this work as her most profound literary influence. She read classic literature such as Faulkner, Kafka, and Dostoyevsky voraciously while she was in high school and began writing novels, although she would throw each work away as soon as she finished it. Her first publication was a short story that won a writing contest in the popular magazine *Mademoiselle*.

In 1963, she began publishing seriously, mainly short stories and novels but also drama and essays. In total, she has written over forty books. Perhaps her best-known work is the short story "Where Are You Going, Where Have You Been?," from 1966, about a child murderer. Her work often deals with violence and conflict. Related themes are racism and race relations, as in her novel *them*, which won the National Book Award. She has been nominated for the Pulitzer Prize many times, winning in 1993 for her novel *Black Water* and again in 2001 for her novelistic exploration of Marilyn Monroe's psyche, *Blonde*. She is often suggested as a likely candidate for the Nobel Prize in Literature.

In the 1980s, Oates experimented with gothic themes and magic realism in novels including *Bellefleur* (1980) and *A Bloodsmoor Romance* (1982). In the 1990s, she began publishing mystery novels under the pen names Rosamond Smith and Lauren Kelly. Oates also writes extensively for popular magazines and in the late 1990s was working on an assignment in which prominent women writers would interview and write about their mothers. She never published that article, but the interview led to her play *When I Was a Little Girl and My Mother Didn't Want Me*, which was published in 1998.

Oates was devastated by the death of her husband Smith in 2008 and quickly remarried. Her productivity has not flagged, and she has published one or two novels a year since then, including *The Accursed* in 2013.

PLOT SUMMARY

When I Was a Little Girl and My Mother Didn't Want Me begins with a simple statement of the dramatic facts of the play:

My father was killed and I never knew why.

Then, I was given away. By my mother.
I was so little . . . six months.
There were too many of us, nine of us,
My mother gave me away.
When I was old enough to know . . . I cried
    a lot.

The speaker goes on to lament again that she does not know why her father died. She knows how—he died in a fight in a tavern when he was forty-four years old—but this knowledge does not give any meaning to her. She observes that now she is eighty-one years old and could have a son the age her father was when he died. Then she focuses on her girlhood. She emphasizes her childhood as the most important part of her life: "I was a little girl for so long."

She describes the circumstances of her poverty-ridden childhood in the Black Rock section of Buffalo on the waterfront of the Niagara River, and in particular the bigotry that immigrants (she is Hungarian) faced there. However, this discussion is cut off by stage directions indicating that she pauses, having decided not to discuss this.

The speaker's mother gave her daughter to her sister, the speaker's aunt Lena, and her husband, John, who had no children of their own. The speaker talks about her relationship with her new parents. She believes that she loved them and that they loved her, but she is clearly unsure. She later found out that such informal adoptions were common in the immigrant community.

The speaker turns to deal more directly with her parents. She takes pride in the fact that when they were young they were unusually good-looking. However, her father was an alcoholic. He had a vicious temper while drunk and had a history of getting into fights in bars. In the last fight, his opponent took up a poker and beat him to death. She finds it deeply unsatisfying that "this was how my life was decided."

The speaker notes that she never learned the identity of the man who killed her father (but in real life, Oates's grandmother at least knew, since she won a wrongful-death judgment against him, the money from which was the main support of the family for many years). The speaker compares the moment of her father's death to the moment of conception or the moment of birth—events that decide one's life but which one plays no part in.

The speaker returns to her own childhood and mentions that she frequently walked the few miles to visit her birth mother. She describes how she was met with resentment. Her mother and aunt, meanwhile, rarely visited each other. She emphasizes how short the distance was that her mother would have had to walk to visit her, and how close the sisters ought to have been since they were the only ones in their family living in America. She concludes that her mother's aloofness was a sure sign that he she did not want her, but she does not really consider the demanding household duties that her mother had to manage: "That was how women were in the old days."

The speaker turns now to her relationship with her birth mother. She is able to say unequivocally, "I loved my mother." She once again praises her mother's looks, emphasizing this time how much her mother looked like her. When people pointed out the resemblance, the speaker as a little girl would cry. She now attempts to leave no uncertainty that her birth mother did not love her, recounting a scolding she received in Hungarian:

Go away, go home where you belong. You
    have a home.
Your home is not here.

The speaker then turns to her siblings, whose rejection of her she has already described. "I loved my big brothers and sisters," she says quite matter-of-factly. She then lists their names and briefly describes them.

The speaker's oldest sibling was her brother Leslie. After her father's death, he became the main breadwinner for the family. She also had a sister Mary whom she never knew well. These children had been born into the family in Hungary before they came to America. The other children were born in America. The next oldest was Steve, who had suffered a brain injury when he was trampled by a horse. (To judge by Oates's real-life uncle, he was an invalid who was bedridden. The constant care he required would, of course, have been very difficult to provide while also raising a six-month-old baby.)

Next in age were Elsie and Frank, whom the speaker refers to as her "'big sister'" and "'big brother'"; the scare quotes are there in the original text of the play, leaving these relationships ambiguous. One interpretation is that although these siblings were not the oldest, they may have been the closest to her in her family. Younger than these were Johnny and Edith. Finally the youngest, except for herself, were George and Joseph, to whom she was not very close. The speaker mentions that all of her siblings have died before her and offers a philosophical meditation on her life:

> Sometimes I think: The soul is just a burning match!
> It burns awhile and then . . .
> And then that's all.

The play ends with another repetition of the lines:

> It's a long time ago now, but I remember hiding away to cry.
> When I was a little girl and my mother didn't want me.

CHARACTERS

Speaker

There is a single character in *When I Was a Little Girl and My Mother Didn't Want Me*, the speaker, who is modeled after Oates's own mother, Carolina Oates. While any actress chosen to play her would certainly have to resemble an eighty-one-year-old, white-haired woman, the play gives no specifics about her physical appearance. She does describe her appearance as a little girl, but tellingly only in relation to her resemblance to her own birth mother:

> My Mother Elizabeth was so pretty.
> Curly hair like mine.

And again:

> She was a short, plump woman.
> Curly brown hair like mine.
> People would say, "You look just like your momma!"

The play is about the inner conflict the speaker feels because of events in her childhood. After her father was killed in a bar fight when she was six months old, her mother, who was overburdened by eight other children including an invalid, gave the baby to her aunt Lena and uncle John. Yet the girl never lost contact with her original family and knew the circumstances of her adoption as she was growing up. She cannot help but interpret her birth mother's

actions as abandonment, and her consequent resentment colors all her relationships. Although she has no complaint about her adoptive parents' treatment of her, she has to do hard linguistic labor to justify to herself the idea that there was not something profoundly wrong with the arrangement:

> I don't know if I loved them . . . I think I loved them.
> I think . . . I think they loved me.
> They wanted children but couldn't have them, so it was right, I think, that my mother gave me to them. . . .
> It was a, a good thing, it was a . . .
> Necessary thing.

Every statement that one would expect to be made by a child about her parents is qualified with doubt. She struggles to say the words, and therefore the passage is filled with stuttering, verbal stumbling, and pauses (the ellipses). Although she wants the adoption to have been a good thing, she must finally settle on it having been a necessary thing.

The speaker also describes her relationship with her birth family as strained and even hostile. One may doubt the simple objectivity of this account (as one may always do in Oates's writing) because she supplies a psychological explanation for it: "They didn't want me, I guess I was a reminder of . . . something." What she means is that her presence was a reminder of what she conceived of as their crime against her, abandoning her. However, the speaker is the one who feels emotional injury. It may well be that she is projecting onto them her own emotional hostility which came into existence because she felt abandoned. She claims that her birth family refused to call her by her name, Carolina, and cannot recall if they called her anything at all. This was certainly a savage rejection of her identity, it seems, but given the tricks of memory, it could just as well be an expression of her own sense of being rejected.

Conversely, the speaker attests to her absolute love for her mother and her birth family. This is presented as a heroic struggle that she kept up despite the supposed rejection and cruelty she suffered from them. The fact that her persistence on this point presents her in an almost saintly light makes it suspect. Is she covering her own hostility which she felt in return for being rejected, or is the rejection exaggerated?

The speaker's most damning statement about her birth mother also demands more careful consideration. She reports her mother telling her as a little girl:

> Go away, go home where you belong. You
>   have a home.
> Your home is not here.

This indeed sounds like a rejection, but it must be borne in mind that this statement is entirely mediated through the speaker. Perhaps it sounded like a cruel rebuff to a little girl's ears, but how does the reader know the mother was not conflicted? Perhaps she said these words because she believed they were in the best interest of her daughter, even if she had to sacrifice the pleasure of raising the girl herself. The hostility could well be a disguised expression of her own anguish. When the speaker says, "And there were too many of us to feed, and my mother . . . gave me away," the situation seems less like an act of indifferent cruelty and more like an act to ensure the daughter's well-being.

The play is also a quest to find an answer to the speaker's question of *why*. She considers the whole course of her life to have been derailed from its proper path by her father's death, but she can never find an answer that addresses her desire to make sense of it all. She provides more and more detail about his death and eventually reveals what at least may be called the effective cause of her father's death—he was an alcoholic who liked to pick fights in bars—but never finds the final cause that would explain to her *why* things happened as they did.

The speaker's speculations rise to the level of the philosophical on two occasions. She seems over the years to have justified the tragedy of her childhood as having been caused by random chance, just like moments of conception or birth, over which one has no control. This compromise clearly does not satisfy her. Finally, unable to find the answer that she wants, she seems to accept, with the metaphor of the burning match for the soul which she develops at the end of the play, that there is no answer and that she will die without the void of meaning in her life being filled.

THEMES

Family

Family is the central theme of *When I Was a Little Girl and My Mother Didn't Want Me*. The speaker of the play explores the discrepancies between the family that she wished she had had and the one she actually had. Her conventional, happy family life, as she imagines it, came randomly to an end with her father's death, which necessitated her transference to her adoptive family. She might have considered it a rescue when her aunt took her in, because her own mother had neither the time nor the means to care for an infant, but instead the speaker counted it as a grievance and source of simmering resentment for the rest of her life against people whom she ought, but could not quite bring herself, to have loved.

The speaker could have had no understanding of what was happening to her at the age of six months, and her disappointment must have arisen during her childhood, as she learned of the American model of the nuclear family and discovered she was not quite part of one. However, she never considers what her life might have been like if she had stayed in her mother's household, where inevitably her older sisters would have become her caretakers. Still less does she consider what her life would have been like if her father had not been killed when he was. Would the girl have been happy in a household dominated by a violent alcoholic? These questions are certainly implicit in the text, but Oates leaves the readers to discover them on their own.

Psychoanalysis

Oates is a great exponent of both psychoanalysis and its rival analytical psychology (or Jungian analysis). She keeps a dream journal and often turns to it to find material for her writing. The memory that she used as the basis for *When I Was a Little Girl and My Mother Didn't Want Me* is one that her biographer has to refer to somewhat apologetically as "repressed," a concept from the early days of psychoanalysis that has less currency today. In short, Oates has based at least three literary works on the circumstances of her grandfather's death, and each time claimed she was

TOPICS FOR FURTHER STUDY

- Although they are not prominent in *When I Was a Little Girl and My Mother Didn't Want Me*, dreams, fantasy, and folklore are often important elements in Oates's work. The giving away of infant children (leading to confused identities or the like) is a common theme in folklore, such as the corpus of sagas published in English by John Colarusso as *Nart Sagas from the Caucasus* (2002). Drawing further inspiration from folkloric texts like this, write a fairy tale that addresses the themes of Oates's play.

- *When I Was a Little Girl and My Mother Didn't Want Me* found its genesis in an interview with her mother that Oates was commissioned to conduct. This kind of family history interview is becoming an increasingly popular way for Americans to explore their history. One venue for this is the Story Corps project, which allows interviews by one family member of another (typically by a young person of a grandparent or other relative of a previous generation) to be recorded and posted online. Many of them are played on NPR programs. Go to the Story Corps website (http://storycorps.org/), which provides helpful tips and suggestions, and set up an interview with one of your family members. Create an audio or video recording of your interview and present it to your class.

- Oates has dealt with the story of her family, in particular with the story of her mother's adoption, in many different formats and styles. Her mother's account could easily be treated as a short story. Look at Oates's 2007 young-adult collection *Small Avalanches and Other Stories* for inspiration and a guide for style, and then write your own short story based on *When I Was a Little Girl and My Mother Didn't Want Me*.

- Write a paper exploring the theme of Oates's grandfather's death and her mother's adoption as she treats it in *A Garden of Earthly Delights*, *Marya: A Life*, and *When I Was a Little Girl and My Mother Didn't Want Me*.

---

inspired to write because she remembered, or learned of them, for the first time. Be that as it may, Oates uses the psychoanalytical concepts of projection and aggression to give her play great psychological depth.

There is a conflict in the narrative between a simple, straightforward reading and what can be gleaned by a more thoughtful examination. The speaker presents herself as a saintly victim, treated heartlessly by her mother and siblings, but the mere fact that her martyr complex, her belief that she has been sacrificed, is so perfect suggests that it is a psychological construct that the speaker has created to give meaning to her own inner life. Therefore it may not correspond to reality. She claims to be a child abandoned by her family who feels no resentment against them, but only unconditional love, while they repeatedly rejected her. However, an abandoned child, especially considering her emotional immaturity, is likely to be the one to feel hostility over rejection. Is it not likely that the hostility she represents as coming from her family is her own against them? She likely projects it onto them, so that she can say "I love my mother" and "I love my big brothers and sisters" without the guilt that would be occasioned if she admitted she felt resentment against them. Also, the speaker's attribution of hostility to her own family might come from their processing, or rather their failing to properly process, their guilt over abandoning her.

Oates's play features a single character, an elderly woman looking back at her childhood. *(© ollyy /*
Shutterstock.com)

STYLE

Dramatic Monologue

When I Was a Little Girl and My Mother Didn't Want Me is a dramatic monologue. This means that there is a single speaker and no other characters. One quality of this particular monologue is its highly conversational nature, as if the speaker is not performing but simply talking to the members of the audience. No doubt this relates to the play's origin in a phone conversation between Oates and her mother. Because it is a dramatic monologue, the few times the play has been performed it has been not fully staged but given a performance more like a poetry reading in a large library room.

Modern Verse

When I Was a Little Girl and My Mother Didn't Want Me must be judged to be written in verse, albeit a highly modern style of verse. In the late nineteenth century, poets began to realize that the formal trappings of traditional poetry, such as rhyme and meter, were not the defining characteristics of poetry and so concentrated on elements of meaning and structure that they considered more definitive. The most obvious poetic feature of the text is a traditional one that Oates preserved: offset printing.

For prose, the text is usually arranged on the page based on the size of the font and dimensions of the page. For offset printing, rather than the length of each line being arbitrarily decided by a typesetter (or now by a computer program), the author decides where each line will end. This preserves the poet's control of the flow of the text. This control can be further emphasized by capitalizing the beginning of each line.

Poetry, which in its origins had to be composed and memorized without the aid of writing, has always favored repetition, and this feature is represented in the play. The title of the play and the first line are repeated verbatim several times to suggest a new perspective that is going to be revealed. Other lines are repeated with transformations, such that "There were too many of us, nine of us" is later developed into "There were nine children. I was the baby." This allows Oates to develop themes and variation as the play turns to new subject matter.

Conversational Tone

Despite the poetic character of the play's text, the tone of the dialogue is a remarkably faithful transcription of the way people actually speak. The text of *When I Was a Little Girl and My Mother Didn't Want Me* is filled with ellipses, almost to the same degree that Oates's private

COMPARE
&
CONTRAST

- **1910s:** The United States welcomes immigrants with almost no limits as a strategy for building up the national economy.

  1990s: Immigration is tightly controlled. Essentially only highly productive workers and political refugees are allowed into the country. However, there is also illegal immigration, especially from Latin America.

  Today: Immigration is perceived as a political crisis because of the tens of millions of immigrants who have entered the United States without proper documentation.

- **1910s:** No reliable form of birth control exists.

  1990s: Many kinds of birth control exist and are freely available to help keep poor families from growing beyond their means.

  Today: The availability of family planning services is an increasingly politically divisive issue at the federal and state levels, owing largely to contrasting religious and practical concerns.

- **1910s:** No state institutions exist to provide any kind of financial assistance or medical services to help families stricken by poverty and accident.

  1990s: An indigent woman with several children, one of whom needs constant medical care, would receive many kinds of state aid, ranging from various kinds of income support to free in-home or institutional medical care.

  Today: The social safety net established in the 1960s through programs such as Medicaid, food stamps, and other assistance for the poor has recently become the subject of political controversy.

---

journals are. These represent sentences that the speaker cannot find a way to end or continue without a dramatic restructuring. Such sentences are very common in transcripts of speech (in fact, transcripts of interviews in magazines and newspapers are almost universally edited to eliminate them) but rare in formal writing. Here the imitation of speech is privileged over the polished presentation of prose.

Similarly, there are many *anacolutha*, which are sentences that begin with one structure or meaning and end with another; the speaker loses track of her thought in the middle of the sentence, which is then finished in a completely different way. There are many examples of this in *When I Was a Little Girl and My Mother Didn't Want Me*, such as: "They didn't want me, I guess I was a reminder . . . of something." The first part of this line, "They didn't want me, I guess," is a logical sentence; it expresses its idea and then qualifies it with uncertainty. Likewise, "I guess I was a reminder of . . . something" is a logical construction. But the words "I guess" cannot do duty in both clauses simultaneously. The speaker finished the first sentence, realized that the second sentence would also begin with "I guess," and joined them together. This is a highly conversational trait, since on first hearing (and that is all one gets in a conversation), the lack of repetition seems less awkward. Also, Oates marks lines of particular emotional intensity with stutters, as if to suggest the tremendous mental effort required to make the statement, as in: "It was a, a good thing, it was a . . . necessary thing."

HISTORICAL CONTEXT

Immigration

All Americans are immigrants. Even Native Americans, so called, came to this continent starting less than twenty thousand years ago, not long in the history of the human species. The United States has been shaped by

The old woman remembers moving from a Buffalo neighborhood to a farm way out in the country.
(© MaxyM | Shutterstock.com)

immigration from Europe in particular. Europeans started coming to the Atlantic seaboard in the seventeenth century, many seeking economic advancement and often political freedom as well. Some, however, like the Dissenters from the Church of England (known in America as Pilgrims), wanted isolation, so as to enforce their own strict social controls.

The largest wave of immigrants from Europe began in the 1880s and continued until World War I. The great attraction was land that they could own and farm as freeholds, without paying rent to an aristocratic class, although many immigrants instead were swept up as workers in the industrialization of America. Oates's great-grandparents, originally from Hungary, arrived during the period generally known as second-wave immigration. Many Hungarian immigrants in this era settled in upstate New York, like Oates's family, and in a belt stretching through the small industrial towns of western Pennsylvania and Ohio. The dream of upward mobility that fueled this immigration was derailed by World War I, because many immigrants (such as

Hungarians) originally came from countries that were now the enemy and thus suffered discrimination. The Great Depression also slowed immigration, as there were far fewer opportunities.

Through the hardships of immigrant life, the family farm often acted as an anchor. For many immigrants, the farm and family functioned together. The income from the farm was the means of maintaining the continuity of family tradition. While Oates's grandparents made their living from semiskilled trades like blacksmithing (fast dying out at the time as cars replaced horses), they also worked to hold on to a farm not only as an economic necessity but further as a means of preserving tradition and family. Many immigrant families to the United States only found the success they dreamed of to the extent that their children and grandchildren Americanized, adopting English instead of their native language and abandoning their traditional culture for American mass culture.

Oates, the great-granddaughter of immigrants, fits this profile. She was the first in her family to make real economic gains (to say nothing of her academic and artistic success), but to do so she embraced the form of American culture to be found through higher education. She makes a point in many places that she rediscovered her Hungarian roots only after returning to her family's native country on a book tour. She purposefully cut herself off from her family history and had to constantly rediscover that too as an adult. *When I Was a Little Girl and My Mother Didn't Want Me* is one of the products of this ongoing rediscovery.

CRITICAL OVERVIEW

General assessments of Oates, such as Gavin Cologne-Brooks's *Dark Eyes on America* (2005), see two main themes in Oates's work: a growing feminist consciousness and the elevation of her life story. More relevant to *When I Was a Little Girl and My Mother Didn't Want Me* is the latter, the story of Oates's American family, which serves as a larger picture of the family story of America. An important element that Cologne-Brooks sees in this transcendence is the seamless fusion Oates seems to make between the smaller and the larger subject matter. When Oates is telling her story, it becomes America's story.

Oates's *When I Was a Little Girl and My Mother Didn't Want Me* has not directly received any critical attention, but it is especially fertile ground for teasing out the relationship between fiction and history in Oates's work. It is easy to overlook this brief play among the huge volume of Oates's literary output, which extends to over seventy books, including novels, short stories, children's literature, and lengthier drama. Oates's biographer Greg Johnson has explored the thematic context of the play in Oates's life and work, although his biography, *Invisible Writer*, was written and published before he could have read *When I Was a Little Girl and My Mother Didn't Want Me*. Johnson makes clear that Oates's play did not spring from some sudden revelation:

> As she grew older,...Joyce's expressions of nostalgia for her family heritage appeared often in her private journal, and by the 1990s her parents' and her own recollections became the focus of several autobiographical essays.

The history of her family had become an increasing concern in Oates's literary work, and she was exploring it systematically. "She had become particularly obsessed with the early lives of her parents," Johnson adds. He focuses on one event of particular interest in Oates's creative work: "Joyce's maternal grandfather, Stephen Bush, . . . met a violent end: he was murdered in a tavern brawl." Johnson notes that "in 1986, when Joyce Carol Oates published *Marya: A Life*, she described the novel as a blending of her mother's early life and her own." In particular, Johnson observes, "In *Marya*, the emotional matrix of Marya's childhood is virtually identical to Carolina's." Johnson stresses the fact that Marya's father was killed in a bar fight, and she was subsequently given away by her mother to other relatives to be raised, the exact circumstances faced by Oates's mother, Carolina.

This interests Johnson because he notes that in her lecture "Beginnings," Oates talked of discovering the parallel between Marya's and Carolina's childhoods only after she had completed the first draft of the novel. Johnson believes that this is inconsistent with the fact that Oates had already used the same plot element in her 1967 novel, *A Garden of Earthly Delights*. He rather glibly explains the contradiction in Freudian terms, suggesting that a "note of surprised discovery has often characterized Joyce's reflections upon the details of her family history. Some of these recollections, previously denied or repressed, have struck her with the force of revelation." The facts of Oates's life that contribute to the plot of *When I Was a Little Girl and My Mother Didn't Want Me* were already well known to her biographer, using no informant other than Oates's own writings, before they were supposedly revealed dramatically to Oates by her mother.

Just as *When I Was a Little Girl and My Mother Didn't Want Me* addresses and clarifies questions Johnson raises, it also bears on unanswered questions posed by Sam Tanenhaus in his review of *Marya: A Life*. In his generally favorable notice, he notes: "There is one problem....As we near the conclusion loose ends dangle....Why, having gone years without giving her missing mother a thought, is Marya consumed in the last chapter with tracking her down?" We see that this, too, is a reflection of Oates's own life.

CRITICISM

Bradley A. Skeen

Skeen is a classicist. In the following essay, he explores the nature of memory in Oates's play When I Was a Little Girl and My Mother Didn't Want Me *and related works.*

Joyce Carol Oates's 1998 play about being an unwanted girl tells a simple but dramatic story. An old woman is alone on stage recounting an event that shaped her life. Her father was killed in a bar fight when she was six months old. Her mother, overburdened with caring for eight other children, one of whom was an invalid, gave the baby away to her sister, who was in a childless marriage. The girl's life thereafter did not play out in the "normal" way, in her own family, but in a new, adoptive family. She could never again be part of what she considered her *real* family but was never separated from them either, because she still lived near them and visited them often.

In an article that Oates originally published in *O, the Oprah Magazine* and later reprinted in her own *Ontario Review*, she explains the genesis of the story of *When I Was a Little Girl and My Mother Didn't Want Me* within her own family. Oates had been commissioned to write a story based on an interview with her mother, Carolina, to show how the relationship between mother and daughter had influenced her writing. After putting the project off for several months, one night in 1997 Oates telephoned her mother and started the interview. Their conversation immediately took on an emotionally intense character Oates had not anticipated.

At the very beginning of the interview, Carolina surprised Oates by blurting out the statement "Well, you know Joyce—my mother didn't want me. When I was a baby. My mother gave me away. I used to cry a lot, I was so ashamed. My mother didn't want me." Oates says she was stunned by what she a considered a revelation. As they continued to talk,

> the story emerged: my mother's father was killed at the age of 44 in a tavern fight and because there were nine children in the family, my mother, six months old, was "given away?" by her desperate mother.

This account seems straightforward enough: Oates is writing the nearly unaltered history of her own mother as drama. However, difficulties arise from this story of the play's creation that

> FOR OATES, MEMORY DOES NOT SEEM TO FUNCTION AS IT DOES FOR OTHER PEOPLE, OR EVEN AS IT DOES FOR OTHER WRITERS."

Oates decided to publish in the media. Had she really suddenly and unexpectedly uncovered a deep, dark family secret that had been kept from her for her whole life?

The Hopwood Lecture is an annual talk given by a distinguished writer at the University of Michigan. In 1987, Oates was invited to give the lecture, and her composition is titled "Beginnings." She spoke about the process of literary creativity and gave specific examples from her recently completed *Marya: A Life*. In that novel, the shape of the title character's life had been largely determined when she was eight years old, when her father was killed in a fight in a bar; she was subsequently given away by her mother to other relatives to raise. Oates talked about how memory and her family history had informed the creation of that novel:

> It wasn't until I had finished a first draft of the novel that I learned, by chance, that the story I believed I had invented recapitulated an incident in my mother's early life. Not my father, of course, but her father had been murdered; not I, but my mother, had been "given away" after her father's death, to be brought up by relatives.

There seems to be something very strange going on here. Oates attributes her creative impulse to two dramatic revelations of memory, but they are the same memory. Moreover, at the beginning of her 1967 novel *A Garden of Earthly Delights* (her second published book), the main character Clara feels abandoned by her mother's death, and then her father kills a man in a bar fight—another variation on a now familiar theme. So far from being a revelation dredged up from the secret history of her family, the main elements of the plot of *When I Was a Little Girl and My Mother Didn't Want Me* seem to be perennial themes in Oates's work, stretching back to the very beginning of her career. How can Oates keep remembering anew the same story over and over?

WHAT DO I READ NEXT?

- *Joyce Carol Oates: Conversations, 1970–2006*, published in 2006 and edited by Greg Johnson, is a collection of interviews with Oates gathered from all periods of her career.

- Oates's 2000 novel *Blonde*, for which she won the Pulitzer Prize, examines the interior life of American icon Marilyn Monroe.

- Oates was inspired to write her 2003 young-adult novel *Freaky Green Eyes* by the collision of media celebrity and domestic violence that came to the public's attention in the O. J. Simpson trial.

- Shilpi Somaya Godwa's 2001 novel *Secret Daughter* follows an Indian family from the slums of Bombay whom poverty forces to give up their daughter for adoption. Alternating chapters portray the professional Indian American family that adopts the little girl as she grows to adulthood.

- The young-adult book *Small Strangers: The Experiences of Immigrant Children in America, 1880–1925*, written by Melissa R. Klapper in 2007, is a study of this often-neglected group of immigrants.

- *Dr. Magic: Six One Act Plays*, published in 2004, is a collection of Oates's more recent drama.

- In *The Accursed* (2013), one of Oates's most recent works, she returns to the themes of gothic literature. In this novel, the faculty of Princeton one hundred years ago is threatened by a mysterious supernatural creature.

Oates's own writings offer some clues to help understand this paradox. In the 1970s, Oates began keeping a typewritten journal, the first years of which were published in 2007. In the entry for August 6, 1979, Oates writes, "Having lived away from home for so many years now, 'breaking away' at the age of eighteen, I have to nudge myself to remember, to recall, that

I am a daughter as well as an individual." This seems prosaic enough. Written by another writer, it might only mean that the life of the child seems alien to the adult. However, Oates's imagination is not so simple. She made her autobiographical character Marya, after all, into a small girl with the inner life of an adult. For Oates, memory does not seem to function as it does for other people, or even as it does for other writers. It may be that Oates means that her own memories are not alive to her unless she is vividly experiencing them through recollection.

In her journal entry for April 6, 1976, Oates writes, "I can't remember my childhood. It is lost." She clarifies this rather sweeping statement: "Memories come back spottily, disjointed, confused in time. I don't remember so much as *see*. Images, scenes without people, intensely-felt sights. . . ." This strengthens the hypothesis that Oates counts her memories as present only while she is actively thinking about them. As with most people, she does not constantly relive the events of her childhood, but when she does, they come alive to her and seem new in a way that is also unique to her.

In her journal entry for March 27, 1979, Oates writes: "The continual raking and reraking of the past doesn't interest me in itself but . . . but I halfway think it should . . . for I lose myself daily . . . hourly . . . it simply flows away. . . ." Oates put the ellipses in the original text to suggest the disjointed character of her thought. It really seems as though when Oates is not actively remembering them, her memories do not exist for her. In her own perception, she can recall something she has known for a long time but feel that she is remembering it for the first time.

Pondering her 1997 interview with her mother, Oates says of her recollection:

> Though I suppose . . . I should not have been surprised. For always there had always been vague rumors about my mother's background; she had been 'adopted' by her mother's younger sister, who had been unable to have children; the only grandparents I knew were my adoptive grandparents, on whose farm in Millersport, New York, my family lived.

So, in fact, Oates had always known the whole story, no doubt learning it piece by piece while she was growing up, as children usually learn of their parents' history. One must resist the temptation to explain these facts in Freudian terms, as Oates's biographer does in *Invisible*

Writer, suggesting that these memories were suppressed from her conscious recollection, but nevertheless active in her unconscious as a source of inspiration. That is, at best, a caricature of Freud's early theories and certainly does not reflect how memory operates. In any case, even if the memories of her grandfather's death and her mother's abandonment proved too traumatic for Oates to consciously recall, it seems unlikely she could have repressed them a second time between her 1987 lecture and her 1997 interview with her mother, Carolina.

Oates admits that she knew growing up that her mother had been raised by her great aunt, and no doubt knew why, but the dormant memory meant nothing to her until the process of creativity brought it to life for her. That is her revelation, or better, her inspiration. There was no true dramatic revelation after Oates finished the first draft of *Marya: A Life*, that she had by some miracle written her mother's life story without knowing it. There was no true dramatic revelation of her mother's life story over a long-distance line as she interviewed Carolina for her never-to-be-published article. What did happen, to use Oates's own terminology, was that she reraked the coals of her own memories. Each time she must have seen the sights of her grandfather dying and her mother being adopted away from her grandmother through new eyes, giving them new meaning. Both times, remembering the same memory resulted in a new work of art: first *Marya: A Life* and then *When I Was a Little Girl and My Mother Didn't Want Me*.

Source: Bradley Skeen, Critical Essay on *When I Was a Little Girl and My Mother Didn't Want Me*, in *Drama for Students*, Gale, Cengage Learning, 2014.

Michael Schumacher

In the following interview excerpt, Schumacher asks Oates about her writing process.

. . . *JCO*: The appeal of writing—of any kind of *artistic* activity—is primarily the investigation of mystery. Somehow, by employing a deliberate speech-rhythm, or by unlocking it, one is able to follow a course into the psyche that reveals different facets of the self. *The Poisoned Kiss* is a "poetic" record of an extreme experience of my own along these lines: Actually, I gave to the *voice* of the stories the adjective "Portuguese" because I knew only that it was foreign, yet not familiarly foreign. Beyond this, it is difficult to speak.

Oates compares the soul to a burning match to highlight the fleeting nature of life. (© Robnroll / Shutterstock.com)

I should stress, though, that the *voice* of these tales was firmly joined to a fairly naturalistic setting by way of subsequent research and conversations with friends who knew Portugal well. And the tales were rigorously written and rewritten.

WD: Could you talk a little about revision? I understand that you spend a great deal of time reworking your novels and stories.

JCO: I revise endlessly, tirelessly—chapters, scenes, paragraphs . . . I don't like to push forward with a story or novel unless it seems to me that the prose is strong enough to be permanent, even though I know very well that once the work is finished I will want to rewrite it. The pleasure *is* the rewriting: The first sentence can't be written until the final sentence is written. This is a koan-like statement, and I don't mean to sound needlessly obscure or mysterious, but it's simply true. The completion of any work automatically necessitates its revisioning. The same is true with reading, of course—at least of a solid, serious, meticulously written work.

WD: How does a novice writer perfect revision skills?

JCO: Since we are all quite different, I can't presume to say. Rereading, with an objective eye, is a necessity—trying to *see* one's work as if it were the work of another, setting aside involvements of the ego.... Revision is in itself a kind of artwork, a process of discipline and refinement that has to be experienced. It cannot really be taught. But my students are amazed and excited by what they learn by revising; they're usually very grateful that they are "strongly encouraged" to do so.

WD: Is it possible to revise too much? Can one be too much of a perfectionist—such as the painter who keeps adding brush strokes to a canvas until the original picture and its inspiration are painted over or altered beyond recognition?

JCO: Certainly. Some people think that, on some pages at least, *Ulysses* is over-polished, its slender narrative heavily burdened with various layers of significance, symbol-motifs, allusions. I am temperamentally hostile to the weighting down of a natural and spontaneous story with self-conscious Significance: to me, the hard part of writing *is* the story. The gifts of a Thomas Hardy, for instance, are far more remarkable than the gifts of a writer like Malcolm Lowry, who so painfully and doggedly and willfully created a novel of symbols/ideas/Significance.

I admire Joyce immensely, of course; I've written a good deal about him. But he had the true Jesuitical mind—as he himself noted—plotting, calculating, outlining, dissecting: In *Portrait of the Artist as a Young Man*, Stephen experiences the "seven deadly sins" in a programmatic way, for instance; once one knows the key, the story seems willed, artificial, slightly tainted by the author's intention. It's ideal fiction for teaching, however.

WD: Where does your writing fit in?

JCO: Temperamentally, I may be more akin to Virginia Woolf, who worked very hard, as she noted in her diary, to achieve a surface of "fluidity, breathlessness, spontaneity." One wants the reader to read swiftly and with pleasure, perhaps even with some sense of suspense; one hardly wants the reader to pause and admire a symbol. In my genre novels, I had to use conspicuously

big words since, to me, that is part of the quaint humor of 19th-century fiction—its humor and its power—but these are not my words, they are those of my narrators.

At the present time, I am writing a novel, set in the years 1947–1956, called *The Green Island*. My hope is to create a colloquial, fluid, swiftly moving prose that sounds, in places—when certain characters are on stage, for instance—rather rough, sheerly spontaneous. Yet I write and rewrite to achieve this "roughness." My prose tends to be more polished, to a degree, in its first state—at least more systematic and grammatical. To find the right voice for this novel, I have had to break down my own voice.

WD: You've drawn a distinction between ideal fiction for reading and ideal fiction for teaching. Have you, through your mainstream and experimental fiction, been seeking a compromise between the two?

JCO: Yes, I believe every writer wants to be read by as many people as possible—with the stress on *possible*. That is, one doesn't want at all to modify his or her standards; there is the hope that readers will make an effort, sympathize, try just a little harder, reread, reconsider—the effort that is routinely made with Modernists like Joyce and Yeats. Since I work so particularly hard on rewriting, and can do a dozen versions of an opening section after I've completed a novel to get it right or in harmony and proportion with the rest of the book, it would seem that my opening sections should be reread, too. Yet I doubt that many—any?—reviewers trouble to make the effort. However, I do keep trying. I must be incurably optimistic.

WD: Did you ever find yourself beginning a story or novel which was difficult or impossible to execute?

JCO: I have never begun a novel that hasn't been *impossible* for the first six or more weeks. Seriously! The outset of a novel is sheer hell and I dread beginning. But it must be done.... I've written 100 pages or more to be thrown away in despair, but with the understanding that the pages had to be written in order that the first halfway-good page might come forth. When I tell my students this, they stare at me in pity and terror. When I tell them that my published work is perhaps one half of the total work I've done—counting apprentice work, for instance—they turn rather pale. They can't seem to imagine such effort and, in retrospect, I must confess that I can't, either. If I had to do it all over again, I'm not sure that I could.

WD: Much of your prose has a rhythmic and lyrical quality about it that approaches poetry. Do you consciously write for the mind's ear? Do you ever read passages aloud to hear what they sound like?

JCO: Absolutely, all the time. It's a practice I am totally dependent on, and have grown to love, though I don't usually read the passages out loud. *Silently out loud*, if that makes sense. . . .

Source: Michael Schumacher, "Joyce Carol Oates and the Hardest Part of Writing," in *Joyce Carol Oates: Conversations, 1970–2006*, edited by Greg Johnson, Ontario Review Press, 2006, pp. 134–37.

Joanne V. Creighton
In the following excerpt, the varied critical reaction to Oates's work is addressed.

Through over 25 years of sustained productivity, Joyce Carol Oates has created an impressive and variegated body of work. "She certainly tried" is the epitaph she wryly suggests for her tombstone. She is a writer seriously and obsessively dedicated to her craft; it is, she says simply, her "life's commitment." Her name is well known in literate circles in the United States and Europe. At a reception at the Soviet Embassy in December 1987, Raisa Gorbachev singled her out as an American writer "much read" and "much admired" by Soviets, including the first lady herself. Oates has for several years been shortlisted for the Nobel Prize. She was elected a member of the American Academy and Institute of Arts and Letters in 1978. In 1970 she received the National Book Award for her novel *them*, and she is the recipient of several other awards from the Guggenheim Foundation, the National Institute of Arts and Letters, and the Lotus Club, among others; she is also a three-time winner of the Continuing Achievement Award in the O. Henry Prize Stories series.

Yet in spite of this public and professional recognition, and in spite of her literal and figurative residence in academia, Oates's corpus was for many years treated with indifference by much of the academic community. To be sure, this is changing. She is the subject of a growing number of dissertations and books. Her archive is now housed at Syracuse University. Recently taken up by feminist critics and studied in

> FINDING US AT THE END OF AN ERA, OATES ARGUES IN THESE ESSAYS THAT THE GRADUAL TRANSFORMATION OF WESTERN CONSCIOUSNESS IS TAKING PLACE, THAT THE MYTH OF THE UNIQUE, PROUD, ISOLATED ENTITY OF THE SELF IS BEING OVERTHROWN."

modern literature courses on many campuses, she has also been invited to many universities in the last few years, including Stanford, Yale, Duke, Wisconsin, Louisiana State, Skidmore, New York University, Columbia, Michigan, the University of California at Los Angeles, Texas, North Carolina, Virginia, Iowa, Oregon, Washington, and Wesleyan. Her work is regularly reviewed, and she herself is prominent as a reviewer, essayist, and commentator on American life and letters.

Nonetheless, Oates is not easily placed within critical contexts or among similar writers. She is not recognized for postmodernist perspectives and technical innovation as are Nabokov, Barth, Pynchon, Gass, Barthelme, and Vonnegut; not beloved and avidly read as are other women writers, such as Atwood, Morrison, Walker, Tyler, Didion, and Godwin; not accorded the respect given a host of male Jewish intellectual novelists, including Roth, Mailer, Singer, Bellow, and Doctorow; not seen within identifiable regional traditions as are Welry, Styron, Taylor, and Penn Warren; not as consistently popular with mass audiences as are King, Vidal, Heller, Kesey, Wolfe, Irving, Salinger, and Updike.

She is unique, alone, one of a kind—although her work is absolutely enriched by American experience, American culture, American intellectual and literary traditions. While exceedingly erudite and a formidable intellectual in her own right, Oates is most often categorized and dismissed as a popular writer with a penchant for the sensational and for the seamy side of life.

A serious critic of Oates's work is still a pioneer, charting one of the first maps of a largely unknown, unexplored, spacious, and expanding territory. In many ways the dialogue of Oatesian scholars takes place within a marginalized, sparsely populated corner of academia; our discourse is protracted over time and seldom interactive. Our subject is elusive, protean, moving off ahead of us into new territory. Not only is it hard to place Oates now; it is also hard to predict the turns her work might take. To be sure, many in the academy believe that it is premature to attempt to place a living author at all, that efforts to do so are doomed to failure, that the critical perspective of time is lacking. Be that as it may, I think we should try to understand the phenomenon of Joyce Carol Oates. I agree with Anne Tyler that "a hundred years from now people will laugh at us for sort of taking her for granted" (McCombs, C11).

The four book-length studies of Oates published at the end of the seventies (by Grant, Waller, Friedman, and Creighton) were each written separately, in isolation from one another, and so did not profit from dialogue and exchange: each picked up a different strand of Oates's work, and each established somewhat different and sometimes contradictory critical frameworks for discussion of it.

In the conclusion of my 1979 book I suggested that sometimes the subject and the form, as well as the emotional and the intellectual levels, of Oates's work seem disjunctive, and this blurs the implicit rhetoric. Readers of *them* (1969) don't know, for example, how to read the language of spiritual rebirth surrounding Jules Wendall's role in the Detroit riot; is his violent liberation treated positively or ironically or both? Similarly, are the compulsive sexual relationships of Oates's fiction potentially liberating experiences, sharing affinities with Lawrence's baptism of fire in passion, or are they more appropriately viewed as "a delirium and a pathological condition" making "of the lover a crazed man; his blood leaps with bacteria that shoots the temperature up toward death" (*T*)? How should we view the pervasive violence, obsession, emotional duress of Oates's characters? Are these troubled, neurotic, violent, restless, antisocial characters deluded dreamers beating against intractable limitations, or are they ripe for liberation, struggling to grow?

As if to validate my concerns about ambiguities of affect on readers of Oates's work, two other studies—G. F. Waller's *Dreaming*

America: Obsession and Transcendence in the Fiction of Joyce Carol Oates (1979) and Ellen Friedman's *Joyce Carol Oates* (1980)—articulate antithetical critical positions on this matter. Both place Oates's work within the same context—"the pervasive idealism of American culture, the romance tradition of classic American literature, and the quintessential American notion of freedom and self-sufficiency." Both see at the heart of Oates's work "the hunger to overcome limitations," to break out of confinements—to in some manner achieve the American dream of a renewed, better, fuller, or higher life. What is startling is how sharply these studies seem to differ on what Oates's work implies about this quest.

Whereas Waller argues that Oates's work is about the possibilities of transcendence, Friedman insisted it is about the necessity of limitations. Whereas Waller characterizes "Oates's aesthetic, in so far as we can talk of one, [as] . . . so clearly a neo-romantic celebration and evocation of flux and the human potential of unpredictability," Friedman characterizes Oates as an "inveterate antiromantic" whose fiction centers on the deflation of deluded Faustian overreachers, solipsistic dreamers, and the American Dream itself: "For Oates the American Dream is a false dream of conquest, control, ownership, and finally an impossible dream of overcoming mutability" (Friedman, 177).

Yet another voice in this implicit debate, this dialogue taking place in separate volumes, is Mary Kathryn Grant's, whose book *The Tragic Vision of Joyce Carol Oates* (1978) brings into play a somewhat different framework. Looking at Oates's extensive critical commentary on tragedy, Grant insists that Oates is "firmly rooted in the tradition of tragedy, in the belief in the self which struggles to achieve personality and identity and to transcend." Essentially, Grant's position is somewhere between Waller's and Friedman's. She believes that Oates shows the limitations of "unheroic human beings" in a "leveled" world, yet that her intent is to articulate a vision of transcendence. Oates portrays "the hope of a hope" that "more than merely 'getting through,' more than just holding together the thousand pieces of one's life, her promised vision will point the way, for those who possess a tragic vision, toward finding a shape for so much pain" (Grant, 125). The vision of transcendence, in other words, will be supplied by the author rather than achieved by her "tragically diminished" characters.

All four of these early critical studies find Oates's essays revealing indexes to her fiction. Waller aptly calls Oates's first two volumes of essays, *The Edge of Impossibility: Tragic Forms in Literature* (1972) and *New Heaven, New Earth: The Visionary Experience in Literature* (1974), "prophetic" and notes her strong affinities with D. H. Lawrence. Relatively early in her career, Oates makes boldly prophetic statements about the state of our culture; she places the human personality in expansive historical and cultural contexts.

Finding us at the end of an era, Oates argues in these essays that the gradual transformation of Western consciousness is taking place, that the myth of the unique, proud, isolated entity of the self is being overthrown. Oates locates the "myth of the isolated self" in the I and not-I dualism that has dominated Western thought for centuries. This myth, rooted in the Renaissance's elevation of noble man over nature, continued in the romantic period with the exaltation of the subjective consciousness and is present in modern-day existentialism, in which man creates himself out of his own consciousness in an indifferent, hostile, or absurd universe. Oates argues that Freudian psychology has perpetuated this myth in the dialectics of the id and the ego and the equation of mental health with the ego's dominion over the id.

A key essay in the articulation of Oates's position is "The Death Throes of Romanticism: The Poetry of Sylvia Plath." Oates portrays Plath as "one of the last romantics," clinging with "gradually accelerating hysteria" to the "once-vital Renaissance ideal of subject/object antagonism." She claims that "Sylvia Plath acted out in her poetry and in her private life the deathliness of an old consciousness, the old corrupting hell of the Renaissance ideal and its 'I'-ness, separate and distinct from all other fields of consciousness."

While both Friedman and Waller stress Oates's repudiation of conquering, masculine "I"-ness, Friedman seems to imply that Oates repudiates intelligence, consciousness, and the quest for meaning as well. On the contrary, Oates argues that Sylvia Plath, in portraying only the darkness of her own personality, only her ego's dissolution, tragically diminished her own superior intellect and failed to see "that the

'I' of the poet belongs as naturally in the universe as any other aspect of its fluid totality, above all that this 'I' exists in a field of living spirit of which it is one aspect" ("Plath," 140).

Friedman is quite right in noting that Oates frequently portrays narcissistic or Faustian overreachers, characters who with bloated egos try to incorporate the world into their selves, to manipulate, to control, to substitute themselves for the world. This kind of hubris attaches itself potently to the American dream of aspiration and self-actualization. American dreamers, Oates contends, are particularly susceptible to "the erecting of gigantic paranoid-delusion systems that are self-enclosed and self-destructing." They are self-destructing because they presume that the human ego is "the supreme form of consciousness in the universe" and fail to account for the "otherness" they exclude: the nonrational side of personality, other people, an implacable, indifferent natural world. . . .

Source: Joanne V. Creighton, "Critical Contexts and Contradictions," in *Joyce Carol Oates*, edited by Warren French, Twayne Publishers, 1992, pp. 105–109.

Ellen G. Friedman
In the following excerpt, Friedman discusses violence in Oates's work.

. . . Characteristically, Oates's novels begin nearly as paradigms of American history. As America loosed its bonds from England, Oates's protagonists find themselves by a variety of routes free from the strictures of family, place, and history. Yet when they attempt to follow the imperatives of the self, they inevitably confront chaos, madness, or death. In the romance tradition of American fiction, many of Oates's characters strain to escape the world in which they find themselves, but they are repeatedly defeated. To survive, they are forced to acknowledge the world and respect its limits. *Wonderland*, for instance, begins with Jesse Harte's escape from his father's murderous gunfire. Orphaned because his father has committed suicide after murdering his family, Jesse undergoes a series of experiences, each representing a period or aspect of American history and culture, that cause him to withdraw further and further into himself, to depend solely on the sufficiency of the self. In the end, however, he comes to full, human consciousness by virtue of an act of rescue and love. The overflow of the self

> HER CHARACTERS NAVIGATE THROUGH A WORLD THAT IS FABULOUS, BUT IT IS A WORLD THAT IS RECOGNIZABLY OUR OWN. HER CHARACTERS ARE LOCKED IN HISTORY AND TIME; THEY EXIST IN AND ARE VULNERABLE TO AMERICAN CULTURE."

to the world, implied by his act of rescue and love, is made a condition of his awakening from the solipsistic nightmare of his freedom.

In Oates, we are always made aware of our otherness. In her *Psychology Today* essay, "The Myth of the Isolated Artist," Oates writes, "In surrendering one's isolation, one does not surrender his own uniqueness; he only surrenders his isolation." In Oates's vision, freedom, in the sense of being above the restrictions of family, place, and society, is synonymous with isolation. She has made her artistic purposes very clear: "The novelist's obligation is to do no less than attempt the sanctification of the world!"

Oates has D. H. Lawrence's suspicions about academic classifications of "high art." In an essay on Lawrence, she complains of R. P. Blackmur's judgment that Lawrence the "craftsman" did not often enough silence Lawrence the "demon of personal outburst." Her artistic alliance is, indeed, with writers like Lawrence rather than with more self-conscious artists like James and Woolf. In a revealing analysis of these two writers she says, "But in the end we are somehow dissatisfied. We recognize the wonder of their aesthetic achievements, yet we must admit that the melodrama of Dostoyevsky and Stendhal has the power to move us more deeply." She disparages their "stubbornly monastic... vision," asserting that "after James and Woolf, after the experiment of the mind's dissection of itself and its dissociation from the body, perhaps we are ready to *rediscover the world*" (emphasis mine). She argues against the strictures of New Criticism, which considers historical and cultural contexts as irrelevant to literary criticism, agreeing with Lawrence that "no poetry, not even the best, should be judged as if it existed in the absolute.... Even the best poetry...needs the penumbra of its own time and place and

circumstance to make it full and whole." With Oates's work, American fiction has abandoned its raft, its forest, its whaling ship—what Poirier has termed its "world elsewhere"—to reenter time and history.

Indeed in Oates's fiction, the sense of place and history is essential. A reviewer has spoken of her ability to "capture the spirit of a society at a crucial point in history." Yet despite her portraits of man in society, her affinities with the American Naturalists are minimal. Naturalism proposed that "natural law and socio-economic influences are more powerful than the human will." It was preoccupied with social and biological inequity and lamented the downtrodden's impotence in the face of materialistic, sociological, and biological forces.

Oates differs from the naturalists on philosophic grounds. It is not indignation against the malevolent forces of heredity and environment that vitalizes her art. Rather, heredity and environment are simply the irrevocable conditions of our being in the world. If we rise above the immediate circumstances of our birth, as Clara, the heroine of *A Garden of Earthly Delights*, does, there is always an external world which must be negotiated. Perhaps the most radical departure of her fiction from that of the naturalists is in her depiction of the will. In naturalistic fiction the human will is powerless against external circumstances, while in Oates's fiction the destructive power of the will becomes one of the author's primary targets.

Our romantic writers view the heroic stance, in which the protagonist asserts his will against the external world, as a liberating stance. For Oates this stance is nihilistic, not heroic or liberating. In her essay, "Melville and the Tragedy of Nihilism," Oates states that "the nightmare of *Moby Dick* ...is not without redemption for us because we are made to understand continually that the quest, whether literal or metaphysical, *need not be taken*" (emphasis mine). Later in the same essay, she argues that Melville dramatized "the plight of the Adamic man who loses his innocence and is precipitated to an immediate Faustian hubris and audacity." These statements reveal Oates's inveterate antiromanticism, a position she continually clarifies in her criticism and repeatedly dramatizes in her fiction. She characterizes Sylvia Plath's poetry as the "death throes of romanticism," and in that same essay she asks, "Why does it never occur to romantic poets that they exist as much by right in the universe as any other creature...?"

Oates views the obsessive drive for absolute freedom, for absolute control as symptomatic of narcissism or megalomania, as an instance of Faustian overreaching, which she regards as a tragic exercise in nihilism. To cite the example of *Expensive People*: matricide is the solution of the child-hero, Richard, to his mother's narcissistic assertion of freedom that denies him her love and recognition. Oates portrays suburbia, the setting of the novel, as an antithetical paradise into whose hallowed terrain one is admitted by virtue of one's greed. The dominant metaphor of the novel is, in fact, gluttony, which stands not only for excessive material acquisition, but more to the point, for an inflated sense of self that leads to a denial of the world, even as is the case with Richard's mother, Nada, a denial of one's children. Indeed, gluttony, obesity, and greed are the metaphors with which Oates repeatedly describes the excesses of will, the excesses of the isolated ego. In Oates, the efforts of the will are rewarded with a perverse form of liberation—with estrangement and alienation.

In *them*, based on the life story of one of her students, Oates describes the struggles of two poor urban adolescents to escape an environment that repeatedly erupts in violence. They attempt to live up to the American ideal of freedom, but inevitably, Jules and Maureen Wendall come up short against the unpredictable. Yet the unpredictable, in the form of beatings, murder, and race riots, is portrayed not so much as a result of sociological upheavals, as an insistent and pervasive rhythm of life. In a universe of caprice and chance, insists Oates, the individual who longs for freedom, for autonomy, is the most vulnerable. In the novel, the effort for freedom is slowly converted into an effort for association, connectedness, and roots. In the last scene of *them*, Maureen is married and pregnant, and her brother, Jules, hopes to find a job and get married. Marriage, pregnancy, jobs—the means by which the individual compromises his freedom and autonomy—are, in Oates, also the means by which the individual constructs barriers against a chaotic and threatening environment.

We can sympathize somewhat with reviewers who gloat over the violence in Oates. Her fiction does alarm and repel, but finally we must admit that what Oates does describe is an oppressive and insistent rhythm of American life. In answer to a question about the violence in her fiction, she said, "These things do not have to be contrived. This is America." It is an America of race riots, migrant labor camps, suburban greed, motorcycle and race-car jocks, mail-order rifles, violent sex, volatile and hyperbolic adolescence, political assassination, family violence, self-proclaimed prophets preaching death and drugs—the America screaming from the headlines of our daily presses. And Oates often sets this "headline" picture of American life against the larger canvas of American history. Her novels, which often begin in the Thirties, give a sense of the movement of American history. Behind the gripping close-up of her characters' lives move the Great Depression, World War II, the Civil Rights Movement, the Vietnam War, and John Kennedy's assassination.

Some writers have expressed a sense of defeat when confronting the monster of American life. Norman Mailer confesses that "The nature of existence cannot be felt any more. As novelists, we cannot locate our center of values." Over two decades ago, Philip Roth complained of the impossibility of realistically portraying American life: "The American writer in the middle of the twentieth century has his hands full in trying to understand, and then make *credible* much of the American reality. It stupefies, it sickens, it infuriates, and finally it is even a kind of embarrassment to one's meager imagination. The actuality is continually outdoing our talents and the culture tosses up figures almost daily that are the envy of any novelist."

Indeed as Raymond M. Olderman has noted, many writers have met the challenge of current American life by writing "fabulous" fictions. That is, "Because experience tumbles fact and fiction, fidelity to some concept of 'ordinary' experience seems close to impossible. All ordinary experience recedes into the fabulous...." Verisimilitude yields to the broader, more exaggerated contours of the fable. Along with the fabulators, Oates recognizes the fabulous quality in American life, but in her writing she makes an extraordinary peace with the reality of this life. Instead of writing fictions that are more fabulous than the headlines, she uses these headline events to form the plots of her stories. Her characters navigate through a world that is fabulous, but it is a world that is recognizably our own. Her characters are locked in history and time; they exist in and are vulnerable to American culture.

Although violence is a dominant mode of contemporary fiction, many contemporary writers, especially the fabulators, objectify the violent and absurd aspects of their culture. John Hawkes's *The Lime Twig*, for instance, competes with Oates's novels in the number and type of violent events it portrays, but it is a metaphorical violence, a projection of psychic images rather than of reality. Although these writers may not be conscious that they are subduing the beast of contemporary life by taking it out of real settings—indeed it is distinctly not the point for them—it is nevertheless an effect of their work. Oates, however, is usually meticulous in drawing her realistic settings so that when a fabulous event invades ordinary circumstances, it is jarring and disturbing because it is made part of the ordinary flow of time; it is not isolated by the imagination from life. It is less an aesthetic image projected by the imagination than it is an imitation, albeit melodramatic, of life. When in *Wonderland*, Monk, a psychotic guru-poet and ex-medical student, reveals to Jesse and his wife that he has stolen a uterus from a cadaver room, taken it home, broiled it, and eaten it, we are justifiably horrified. Our feeling stems from the fact that, given the circumstances, the event does not trespass the limits of possibility. . . .

Source: Ellen G. Friedman, "Variation on an American Hymn," in *Joyce Carol Oates*, Frederick Ungar Publishing, 1980, pp. 4–10.

SOURCES

Cologne-Brooks, Gavin, *Dark Eyes on America: The Novels of Joyce Carol Oates*, Louisiana State University Press, 2005, pp. 1–19.

Johnson, Greg, *Invisible Writer: A Biography of Joyce Carol Oates*, Dutton, 1998, pp. 1–11.

Oates, Joyce Carol, "Beginnings," Hopwood Lecture Program website, 1987, http://www.lsa.umich.edu/UMICH/hopwood/Home/Lecturers%20&%20Readers/Hopwood%20Lectures%20PDF/HopwoodLecture-1987%20Joyce%20Carol%20Oates.PDF (accessed June 28, 2013).

———, *A Garden of Earthly Delights*, Vanguard, 1967, pp. 38–39.

———, "Interview with Carolina Oates," http://www.planetbookgroupie.com/MemorybyPhilippeGrimbert.htm (accessed June 28, 2013).

———, *The Journal of Joyce Carol Oates, 1973–1982*, edited by Greg Johnson, HarperCollins, 2007, pp. 101, 310, 321.

———, *Marya: A Life*, E. P. Dutton, 1986, pp. 28–30.

———, *When I Was a Little Girl and My Mother Didn't Want Me*, in *New Plays*, Ontario Review Press, 1998, pp. 279–82.

Salamon, Sonya, *Prairie Patrimony: Family, Farming, and Community in the Midwest*, University of North Carolina Press, 1992, pp. 53, 101.

Tanenhaus, Sam, "'Marya': A Stunning, If Flawed, Fiction from Oates," in *Chicago Tribune*, February 23, 1986, http://articles.chicagotribune.com/1986-02-23/entertainment/8601140390_1_aesthetic-fiction-literary (accessed July 3, 2013).

Vardy, S. B., "Image and Self-Image among Hungarian Americans since the Mid-Nineteenth Century," in *Hungarian Americans in the Currents of History*, edited by S. B. Vardy and A. H. Vardy, Columbia University Press, 2010, pp. 223–61.

FURTHER READING

Huseby-Darvas, Eva, *Hungarians in Michigan*, Michigan State University Press, 2003.

    This is a brief historical study of the history of assimilation in the Hungarian immigrant community in Michigan.

Oates, Joyce Carol, *Bellefleur*, E. P. Dutton, 1980.

    This book deals with Oates's family origin in the Hungarian immigrant community in Buffalo but treats the material in a magic realist or gothic way.

———, *A Garden of Earthly Delights*, Modern Library, 2003.

    In an unusual step, Oates reissued her 1966 novel *A Garden of Earthly Delights* in a highly rewritten form. The text is revised and polished just as if she had sat on the manuscript for some time and then given it a final edit before publishing. Comparison between the 1966 and 2003 versions therefore gives a unique scope for assessing Oates's changes and development as a stylist.

Sinclair, Upton, *The Jungle*, Doubleday, 1906.

    This novel by the journalist Upton Sinclair is a classic treatment of the poverty and oppression suffered by the immigrant community in America in the early twentieth century.

SUGGESTED SEARCH TERMS

Joyce Carol Oates

When I Was a Little Girl and My Mother Didn't Want Me

dramatic monologue

Hungarian Americans

immigration

history of adoption

family history

one-act play

psychological projection

Why Marry?

JESSE LYNCH WILLIAMS

1917

Jesse Lynch Williams, an author of short fiction, novels, and plays, is perhaps best known for being the recipient of the first Pulitzer Prize for Drama, in 1918, for his play *Why Marry?*, which was first produced in 1917. The work was originally published in 1914 as a three-act play titled *And So They Were Married: A Comedy of the New Woman*. In *Why Marry?*, Williams examines contemporary views on marriage, divorce, and gender roles. The character of Helen epitomizes the cultural phenomenon of the late nineteenth and early twentieth centuries known as the "New Woman." The term was used to describe women with feminist ideals who generally frowned on marriage and who sought higher education, professional careers, and financial independence. Williams, through the character of Helen, appears to challenge conventional views on marriage and gender roles, but as the play progresses, the other characters in the play increasingly view Helen's opposition to marriage as something unnatural and strange. By the play's conclusion, Helen's stance on marriage reaches a critical juncture. *Why Marry?* is available in a modern reprint published in 2013.

AUTHOR BIOGRAPHY

Williams was born in Sterling, Illinois, on August 17, 1871, to Meade and Elizabeth Williams. Educated at Princeton University,

Williams received a bachelor's degree in 1892, then a master's degree in 1895, and would be awarded an honorary doctorate of literature in 1919. Williams married Alice Laidlaw in 1898; the couple had three children over the course of their marriage. While he pursued his studies at Princeton, Williams, along with cofounder Booth Tarkington, established a theatrical group known as the Triangle Club, which remains in existence. During his years as a graduate student, Williams wrote a collection of short stories, *Princeton Stories*, which was published in 1895.

After receiving his master's degree, Williams worked as a reporter for the *New York Sun*. He continued to write and publish literary work during his years as a journalist. He based a 1906 play, *The Stolen Story*, on his experiences as a newspaper reporter. Like many of his dramatic works, *The Stolen Story* was an adaptation of an earlier work of fiction, in this case, a short story Williams had published in the 1899 collection *The Stolen Story and Other Newspaper Stories*. His 1917 play *Why Marry?* won the Pulitzer Prize for Drama in 1918. Williams went on to publish *Why Not?*, a play in which he explores the experiences of divorced individuals, in 1922.

Williams also served as a fellow in creative arts at the University of Michigan and was a member of the National Institute of Arts and Letters and of the Authors League of America. He died on September 14, 1929, at the home of a friend in Herkimer, New York.

PLOT SUMMARY

Act I

Why Marry? is a three-act play. As the first act opens, Rex, who is twenty-seven, is chasing Jean, who is twenty-five. The stage direction indicates that the couple is running through a garden and that Jean intends to let Rex catch her. When he does, they quarrel about something that Jean said to him. The tone is light, and they both laugh. Rex holds the struggling Jean to kiss her. She resists, and he insists that she kiss him and tell him she loves him. Upon confirming that Rex loves her as well, Jean asks if he wants to marry her. Rex seems taken off guard and answers her question with one of his own: "What kind of man do you take me for!" he

queries. At that moment, Lucy, Jean's sister-in-law, appears. Jean tells Lucy, who has interrupted the couple's embrace, that she and Rex are engaged. Rex departs, and Jean and Lucy begin to speak frankly to one another about the way Jean followed Lucy's advice and picked a quarrel with Rex and then ran away. The two women acknowledge that the events that followed progressed in precisely the manner Lucy had told Jean they would. Although Jean is unsure of her love for Rex, Lucy assures her that she will learn how to love him. Jean contends that Rex is in love with her sister Helen. Attempting to comfort Jean, Lucy agrees that while Rex may once have loved Helen, he does not now. "Men admire these independent women, but they don't marry them. Nobody wants to marry a sexless freak with a scientific degree," Lucy states.

Helen appears with Rex in tow. Jean gloats, knowing that Rex is now hers, even though he still seems in awe of her sister. Uncomfortable, Rex departs as Jean and Lucy spar with Helen about the fact that Helen has a career. Lucy continues to assert that men do not like independent women with their own opinions. Despite the vigor with which Lucy expresses her disdain for Helen, Jean acknowledges that she would have liked to go to college. Lucy alludes to the fact that Helen's reputation has been tarnished—that she was sent abroad (to Paris, a trip from which she has returned earlier than expected) because she chose to stay out all night with a man and "get herself compromised, talked about." Helen refuses to be ashamed and proudly recalls the night she and her colleague, Dr. Ernest Hamilton, made a major scientific breakthrough. Lucy continues to try and bait Helen by commenting sarcastically about "New Women" and their superior attitudes. She finishes by revealing that Jean is now engaged to Rex. Lucy is then summoned by her husband, John, and she hurries off to him. Helen confronts Jean, attempting to force her to acknowledge that she is not really in love with Rex, but Jean is evasive. The sisters then argue about whether or not a woman should marry in order to receive financial support, regardless of whether or not she is in love. Helen asks Jean about Bob, a young man who attends Harvard Law School, for whom Jean apparently has real feelings. Jean insists that her feelings do not matter because Bob would not be able to marry her for years—he would have to graduate and

MEDIA ADAPTATIONS

- Willams's *Why Marry?* was adapted as a short black-and-white silent film in 1924, as directed by Ward Hayes.

- A dramatic reading of *Why Marry?* was produced in 2011 by LibriVox and is available at http://archive.org/details/whymarry_1112_librivox.

become established in his profession, and for Jean, the wait is too long. Rex appears to escort Jean to his car, while Helen, being informed by Rex that her family is arguing and headed outside, decides to escape into her brother John's home.

After Jean and Rex leave, Lucy and John exit the house, and are followed by Uncle Everett, who is a judge, and Cousin Theodore, a clergyman. They are arguing over the fact that Uncle Everett and his wife, Aunt Julia (who is not present), are getting a divorce. While the discussion continues, Everett receives a telegram from Julia, who amiably describes her trip to Nevada and the other people in the divorce court. Everett explains to John, who is arguing vigorously against divorce, that he and Julia have little in common. They have made endless compromises out of affection for each other, and now, mutually, no longer care to. At the same time, Everett hints, their habit of making concessions for one another is hard to break. Further, Everett's affection for his wife, even if he no longer characterizes it as love, appears to be genuine. Yet he tells his interrogators that he and Julia were bored with one another and insists that what seemed to be a happy home was a sham. The others are offended. Theodore, who is married and has several children, insists upon his love for his home life, as does John. When John glares at his wife, Lucy, she agrees as well.

As Everett continues to argue in favor of divorce, Lucy tells John that they must keep the

judge's views on divorce quiet if Rex returns, as the Baker family does not believe in divorce. The Bakers are wealthy family friends of John's family. Also, John is a trustee at the Baker Institute. Lucy confirms what John has begun to guess, that Jean has "landed" Rex. He gleefully states, "We're marrying into the Baker family!... Why, she'll have more money than any of us!" Lucy then states her desire to get Helen "safely married to some nice man." The family all seems to acknowledge that Helen has feelings for Ernest, and that he reciprocates those feelings. Despite the fact that the Hamilton family is a respectable one, Ernest himself does not earn enough money for John's taste. Ernest, who has been invited to John's home, does not know that Helen has arrived back from Paris.

John attempts to summon Helen for a second time; she has already refused once to come out to talk to him. Theodore implores Everett to convince Helen that she should marry, but Everett alludes to the unhappy nature of Theodore's own marriage. The family's poverty—due to Theodore's low salary as a clergyman—and the ill health of his wife and children become the topic of conversation. Everett goads John into writing a check to Theodore to help pay for his family's medical care. Meanwhile, John devises a plan to keep Helen and Ernest apart. Theodore cautions John, reminding him that Helen and Ernest love one another. Yet when Helen arrives and guesses that they have been discussing the topic of marriage, she informs the group that she has no intention of marrying anyone. John, Theodore, and Lucy are outraged; Everett is surprised and amused.

John, who still believes Helen should marry someone, just not Ernest, whom he considers beneath his sister, reveals his plan to keep Ernest and Helen apart. He informs Helen that the Baker Institute will send Ernest abroad to do research. Undeterred, Helen states that as she is Ernest's assistant, she will accompany him. John refuses to allow it, warning Helen to not "defy" him. She counters by warning him not to "bully" her. Helen has plans to counter all of John's threats and knows that she can and will accompany Ernest to Paris if she so chooses.

When Theodore asks her why she does not simply marry Ernest, Helen explains that Ernest's salary is insufficient to both support her and meet his research and travel expenses. Helen admires Ernest as a professional and fears that his work would suffer if he had to support a wife. She retreats as Ernest's arrival is announced.

When John tells Ernest that the trustees of the Baker Institute wish to send him to Paris, Ernest is thrilled. He believes that Helen is still in Paris and seems anxious to meet her there and begin working. John alludes to the fact that Helen will have returned home by the time Ernest gets to Paris. When he expresses his confusion over not having his assistant available to him, Theodore, John, and Lucy attempt to explain the impropriety of the situation as they perceive it. Ernest rises to Helen's defense and, knowing that the opportunity to work in Paris would advance Helen's career as much as his own, offers to remain home while Helen returns to Paris. John insists that the head of the Baker Institute, Mr. Baker himself, wants Ernest to go. John continues to lie to Ernest, telling him that Helen would prefer to spend the winter at home rather than abroad.

Lucy and Theodore confer privately. They believe that Ernest and Helen love each other and should marry despite John's objections. Helen appears but remains unseen behind a door; she is surprised at Ernest's presence and listens to the conversation. Theodore has asked Ernest if he has ever asked Helen to marry him, and Ernest replies that Helen "hasn't any money." Ernest goes on to explain that his marrying a woman without money would make her feel inferior, and he feels it would be selfish to put Helen in that position. After Ernest insists that he does not believe in marriage, Helen makes her presence known, and she expresses her agreement with Ernest. Helen reveals privately to Ernest that she believes her family thinks she will try and trap Ernest into marriage. They all leave so that she may do just that. When Helen and Ernest are alone, they speak more frankly about their work and, eventually, their feelings.

When Helen is convinced that Ernest is not interested in marrying her, she announces that she will accompany him to Paris for the research project. Ernest now insists, however, that they could not go together and expresses concern about her reputation. Helen, to the contrary, is concerned about her career and does not wish to miss a professional opportunity out of fear of what people might think about an unmarried man and woman traveling together. Ernest then expresses his love for her. Helen is

dismayed. She states that while she loves Ernest, she knows that these feelings complicate their professional relationship. She wants nothing more than for him to continue his work, and she hopes to be at his side to assist him as she has in the past. They argue—Ernest is joyful that his feelings are reciprocated, but Helen can see only the complications. The first act ends with Ernest ardently expressing his love and the couple embracing.

Act II

The second act of the play opens with Theodore and Ernest having breakfast. They discuss love and the role of sexuality in a relationship. Unsurprisingly, the clergyman and the scientist have differing views on the topic of sex. They go on to talk about the significance of marriage and the role of women in marriage. John arrives. He is still trying to keep Ernest and Helen from one another and urges Ernest to leave immediately for his trip to Paris. Instead, Ernest decides to attend church services at which Theodore is officiating. The two depart. John fumes at Lucy, grumbling about Helen and her defiance of him. They argue, and Lucy suggests that she might leave John. He finds the notion hilarious. When Lucy continues to insist that she will leave and expresses her disgust for him, John grabs her. He asserts his authority, reminding her that he is her "lawful husband." Just then Everett enters. He seems determined to go through with his divorce, but his obvious affection for his wife compels him to keep corresponding with her via telegram. John sends for his sisters and tells Everett that he has agreed to the marriage between Rex and Jean.

Alone, Jean and Rex argue when Jean tells Rex that she releases him of any obligation he feels to marry her. She mentions another man she cares for, and Rex grows jealous. His lukewarm desire to marry her intensifies. After Jean confesses to trying to trap him, Rex tells her how much he admires her honesty. With every effort to break things off with Rex, Jean further endears herself to him. They run off and continue their dispute.

Helen and John discuss her relationship with Ernest. As they continue to spar, Helen reveals that she plans to continue to work and to pursue a romantic relationship with Ernest, but to remain unmarried. John is horrified. The rest of the family members appear. Everett is the only one who is not upset.

Helen insists that not marrying will be the only way both she and Ernest may continue their careers in the manner they desire. She also insists that she cannot be separated from Ernest. John determines that despite his objections, Helen's marrying Ernest is better than the alternative she proposes. Lucy is shocked to learn that Ernest has proposed to Helen and that she refused. A greater shock ensues when Helen informs the family that it was her idea, not Ernest's, that they remain romantically and professionally involved but unmarried. She further explains that Ernest does not yet know of her plan.

Now the family members seek to send Ernest off to Paris as quickly as possible, but Everett believes the couple can still be compelled to marry. When Ernest appears, he and Helen discuss their dilemma. Ernest still wishes to marry Helen, despite her objections. When she refuses, Ernest leaves, and Helen's family pounces on her and scolds her for casting off an honorable man. Moments later, Ernest returns, willing to take Helen on any terms. Everett believes he can still get them to agree to marry, but John is prepared to disown Helen. Jean appears and announces that her engagement has been broken. Ernest and Helen depart.

Act III
The final act opens later that afternoon on the terrace, which is decorated as if for a party. Theodore and Lucy are discussing Everett's attempt to intercept Helen and Ernest. They are in a panic as they consider what people will think if they learn that Helen and Ernest have run off together. John appears and states that he found Rex, who had not been seen since Jean broke off her engagement with him. John seems convinced that he can patch up the breach between Jean and Rex, but Lucy fears that once Rex's family learns about Helen, they will not want their son to marry into a "disgraced" family. John insists that no one will hear anything and that his press agent will report that Helen has simply returned to Paris to complete her research. When John notices the decorations, he questions Lucy, who explains that Everett ordered the decorations put up and the whole family summoned. Upon learning that John seeks to compel Jean to marry Rex, Theodore objects. He pleads with John not to force

her to marry someone she does not love. They argue about what makes a good marriage. John asserts that, regardless of Theodore's views, since he is a clergyman, he will marry Jean and Rex, keep his objections to himself, and "get a big, fat fee for it." Jean approaches. John, handing Theodore a check, orders him to call the medical facility where his wife is being treated and settle his debts so that her care may continue. John and Jean argue heatedly about Rex. Jean despairingly laments that she has so few choices in life because she has no financial means to support herself. She must either remain in her brother's care or marry. As Rex approaches, John departs.

Rex expresses his love for Jean and questions her about Bob, the young man for whom she alluded to having feelings. Rex is tormented by the notion that other men might have touched her, kissed her. Jean confirms that they have. Rex is perplexed by her honesty but still wishes to marry her, and Jean agrees but is candid about the fact that she views the marriage as a business arrangement. Theodore and John appear, with Theodore still insisting he will not perform the marriage since he knows Jean does not love Rex. Just then, Everett arrives. He reports that Helen and Ernest have not run off together. The pair parted ways at Helen's apartment and are now returning to John's house. John would now prefer Helen to be Ernest's wife, rather than his mistress, as she seems to intend. Everett launches into a speech about the need to shift society's views on marriage in order to make it less restrictive to women. He then asks John to trust him and to tell Helen she does not have to marry. Everett is convinced that by telling Helen she does not have to marry, she will want to marry.

When Ernest and Helen appear, they state their opposition to marriage, and Everett and John reveal that John will not try to force his sister into any situation that she does not want. Everett then announces that everything is settled, that the two will begin their lives together immediately. The family is throwing a party for them, and then they will leave on a honeymoon of sorts, to Paris. Ernest is confused. Everett is acting as if they are marrying even though he and John have just accepted that Ernest and Helen will not marry. Ernest restates his desire to marry Helen and points out how opposed John has been to it. When John gives his consent,

Ernest becomes furious and argues that John is bluffing. Helen, arguing at this point with all the men, is forced to once again state her objections to marriage. She delineates her points and insists that being mandated by a contract to love and obey is offensive to her; she loves Ernest because she is moved to do so by her heart, and she obeys him because she loves him. Helen feels hypocritical saying the words of the marriage vows, but Ernest insists that people say them as a symbol even if they do not mean them literally.

By the time the invited family members arrive, no one has been able to change the minds of Ernest or Helen; they vow to leave for Paris together, unmarried. Everyone is seated for dinner when Everett receives a telegram from his wife. Julia no longer wishes to divorce and is on her way back to him. Moments later, John announces the engagement of Rex and Jean. Everyone congratulates them except Helen, who urges her sister to speak the truth. John then announces Helen and Ernest's engagement. Ernest halts all of the congratulating and announces that they are not engaged. John interrupts, stating that the pair is not officially engaged for financial reasons. He then announces that the Baker Institute will double Ernest's salary. Ernest still insists that they cannot marry. They rise to leave. John and Theodore protest, but Everett steps in. He describes the way Ernest and Helen have behaved traditionally in their treatment of one another and in their love, even though they eschew the traditional contract of marriage. He suggests that they go through the motions of a marriage ceremony to please the family, if not themselves. Helen turns the tables on her family as Theodore begins to recite the words of the ceremony, his prayer book in his hand. She announces that he is rather about to marry Rex and Jean. Theodore looks to John for clarification, and John does not object to Helen's proclamation. Ernest and Helen are thus horrified that Theodore seems prepared to marry two people he knows to not be in love. They again try to leave despite John's desperate objection. Everett, who has previously expressed his belief that Ernest and Helen have noble and pure feelings toward one another, steps in once again, telling Ernest, "You know that in the eyes of God you are taking this woman to be your wife." Ernest agrees and begins to object, but Everett cuts him off and urges Helen to speak up. She, like Ernest, asserts, "I take Ernest to be my husband in the eyes of God." Like Ernest, she is about to state objections to the marriage vows, when Everett, who is a judge, cuts her off and pronounces them husband and wife. He has just performed a legal civil ceremony in a state where no marriage license is required. The men congratulate one another, and Ernest tells Helen, "A moment ago you were a bad woman. Now . . . behold! she is a good woman. Marriage is wonderful."

CHARACTERS

Rex Baker

Rex is a wealthy associate of John's. Rex's family owns the Baker Institute, the medical research facility that employs Ernest Hamilton and Helen. During the course of the play, Helen, Lucy, and Jean allude to the fact that Rex used to be in love with Helen, who had no interest in him. John also reveals, in discussion with the male characters in the play, that Rex behaved inappropriately with another woman. There are hints that he was involved in a scandal of sorts that was covered up. John takes pains to hide this information from Jean, whom he hopes to marry off to Rex. Rex's feelings for Jean fluctuate throughout the play. He seems interested in pursuing her, is manipulated into becoming engaged to her, and is upset when Jean suggests that they call off the engagement. He grows jealous of other men with whom Jean confesses she has been romantically involved. As he expresses his desire to marry her, his comments suggest that he views marriage to Jean as a victory over these other men and that he regards Jean as a prize or possession.

Bob

Bob does not appear in the play, but he is present in Jean's thoughts. She prefers him to Rex, to whom she is engaged. Bob attends Harvard Law School. Jean estimates that Bob will not be able to marry until he is forty, when his practice is established and he can provide for a wife.

Judge Everett Grey

Everett Grey, or Uncle Everett, is uncle to siblings John, Helen, and Jean. As the play opens, Everett's family members—specifically John, Lucy, and Theodore—question him when he reveals that his wife, Julia, is in Nevada to secure their divorce. The family members are surprised by the amicable nature of the telegrams exchanged between Julia and Everett and point out that they seem to be on such good terms that a divorce is unnecessary. Everett explains his position, noting that their marriage has been a series of compromises they have made out of concern for the other's feelings. They are now both bored and are unwilling to continue to appease the other. As Julia's telegrams and Everett's responses to them reveal, Julia and Everett have so habitually put the other person's interests before his or her own that they feel lost without the other. Julia's last telegram reveals that she is returning to Everett and does not wish to divorce. Everett is ecstatic. Throughout the play, though, he finds Helen's desire to remain unmarried admirable. He sees little wrong with Helen and Ernest's being romantically involved but unmarried. As the play concludes, however, Everett essentially tricks Helen and Ernest into marrying, characterizing the union as an act to appease Helen's family.

Ernest Hamilton

Ernest Hamilton is a scientist employed at the Baker Institute, a medical research facility. Helen is his college-educated assistant, and with her help, he has made a major scientific breakthrough regarding an antitoxin. He and Helen have feelings for one another, which they finally acknowledge during the course of the play. Ernest is in love with Helen and wishes to marry her. Though Helen loves Ernest, she has contemplated all the ways marriage would complicate both their personal and their professional relationships. Though he tries to convince Helen to marry him, Ernest eventually sees that he will lose Helen if he continues to insist on marriage. Her objections are not lost on him, and he consents to her proposal: that they travel together to Paris, continue their romantic relationship, and continue to work together. With Helen, however, he is duped into a civil marriage by Helen's uncle, Judge Everett Grey.

Helen

Helen is John and Jean's sister. A college-educated scientist, she serves as an assistant to Ernest Hamilton at the Baker Institute. As the play opens, Helen has just returned from Paris, where she was sent by her brother, John, to avoid a scandal that he feared would grow from the fact that she remained out of her home all night as she worked with Ernest on the antitoxin

research. During the course of the play, Helen is confronted with the prevailing view of her family that it is the duty of a woman to marry and serve her husband obediently. She urges Jean to be cautious and not rush into marriage with Rex; she notices the way John bullies and condescends to Lucy; she argues with Lucy about women's independence; and she defends her right to make her own choices about what she should do with her life, even in the face of John's manipulation and attempts to control her fate. Helen feels that even though she and Ernest love one another, marriage would shift the balance of power. It would place her in a subservient position to her husband and force Ernest to abandon his research so that he could take a position as a private-practice doctor and adequately provide for his wife. Helen insists that it would be selfish of her to ask Ernest to give up his work. She further feels that marriage conventions would dictate that she run a household instead of having a career, and Helen is convinced that Ernest's work would suffer if she were not present to serve as his assistant. Helen is adamant and risks losing Ernest as a colleague and a mate in her refusal to marry him. But Ernest acquiesces and agrees to her terms. Yet Judge Everett manages to trick Ernest and Helen into repeating the marriage vows of a civil ceremony and, in doing so, marries the couple.

Jean

Jean is a member of a wealthy family. She is the younger sister of John and Helen. In love with a Harvard law student, Jean feels compelled by the urging of her brother and her sister-in-law, Lucy, to attract the interest of Rex Baker, who was once infatuated with Helen. Jean easily convinces Rex that he wishes to marry her but becomes uncomfortable with what she has done. Although she tries to break things off with Rex, John convinces her that she has no other choice due to her economic dependence. She reveals to Rex that she has been romantically involved with other men. Rex is dismayed but seeks to claim her for himself. John announces their engagement, but Theodore, who knows that Jean does not love Rex, refuses to perform the ceremony.

John

John is the husband of Lucy and the brother of Helen and Jean. He is a businessman and a trustee on the board of the Baker Institute. He is characterized as a bully in his treatment of his wife and sisters as he attempts to assert his dominant status with regard to his wife and to control his sisters' marriages and futures. He is primarily concerned with his family's financial and social status and continuously seeks to improve both. Unlike Everett and Theodore, the other married men in the play, John makes few claims regarding the virtues of love in a marriage. He orders his own wife about and complains when she seems unwilling or unable to serve as a diversion when he requires it. John wishes Jean to marry the wealthy, prominent Rex Baker, and he seems pleased when, with Lucy's help, Jean secures Rex's proposal. John trivializes Jean's crisis of conscience; he does not care that she feels as though she has tricked Rex, or that she actually prefers another man. While John, throughout the play, attempts to force Jean to marry Rex, his opinions change regarding Helen and Ernest. Initially, he attempts to keep them apart. While Ernest comes from a respected family, as a research scientist for the Baker Institute, he earns very little. For this reason, John believes that Helen can do better. When Helen makes clear that she will not allow herself to be separated from Ernest, John believes that the only way he can save her reputation is to have her marry Ernest, a plan Ernest is initially eager to put into action. Eventually, however, Ernest sees that he will lose Helen if he insists on marrying her. He agrees to go to Paris with her, as friends, lovers, and colleagues, but not as husband and wife. John is desperate to avoid this and agrees to trust Everett, who eventually succeeds in marrying the couple.

Julia

Julia is the aunt of Helen, Jean, and John, and the wife of Uncle Everett. She is in Nevada, securing the necessary paperwork for her impending divorce. Julia sends telegrams to Everett, in which her continued affection for him is revealed. In the end, she decides that despite their differences, she cannot live without Everett.

Lucy

Lucy is John's wife and the sister-in-law of Helen and Jean. Throughout the play, Lucy is obedient to John. She has moments when she attempts to stand up to him, and at one point in the play she indicates that she wishes to leave him. Yet John is always able to cow her back into submission.

Lucy repeatedly expresses her views that "nice" girls marry and should not attempt to be independent. She regards the notion of sexual relationships outside of marriage as sinful. Despite the fact that she hints at the oppression she feels within the confines of her own marriage, Lucy continues to advocate for Jean's marriage to Rex. She believes at first that Ernest and Helen should be kept apart, until she learns of their love for one another. Then she stands with Theodore against John to advocate for the marriage of Ernest and Helen, as this is the only possible remedy for an otherwise sinful relationship.

Theodore

Theodore is the cousin of John, Helen, and Jean. He is a clergyman with a wife and children. His wife is ill and is receiving treatment at a sanatorium. Earning only a meager salary, Theodore is dependent on John's largesse to keep his children fed and his wife cared for. Theodore opposes the union of Jean and Rex, knowing that Jean does not truly love Rex. He advocates the marriage of Helen and Ernest, knowing that they love each other and that they seem determined to be together. Theodore regards sexual relationships outside of marriage as sinful, and within a marriage as only necessary to produce children. Further, he objects to Helen's view that marriage vows unnecessarily undermine a woman's independence and identity and that her love for Ernest, without the sanctifying cloak of marriage vows, is noble and pure.

THEMES

Marriage

Marriage is the most prominent theme in *Why Marry?* Each character has an opinion on the subject. The judge's arguments against marriage are rooted in the notion of compatibility, yet by the play's end, and with his wife's impending return, the judge changes course and emphasizes companionship and habit as the comforting features of his marriage. To Helen, he suggests that while marriage may seem odious to her, it can be regarded as a way to appease her family and society. John's views on marriage incorporate the idea of the superiority of the male sex and maintain that women are pawns whose marriages are designed to benefit the family in terms of wealth and social standing. Jean wishes

TOPICS FOR FURTHER STUDY

- Williams focuses on the concept of the New Woman in *Why Marry?* Research the emergence of the New Woman at the close of the nineteenth century and the prominence of the New Woman phenomenon through the 1920s. How did the values associated with the New Woman evolve over the years? How did victories such as the passage of the Nineteenth Amendment shape the New Woman agenda? What was the relationship between the New Woman movement and feminism? Prepare a research paper in which you present your findings. Alternatively, create a web-based time line in which you highlight the major events that transpired during the era of the New Woman.

- In the young-adult novel *Shine, Coconut Moon*, by Neesha Meminger, published in 2009, Meminger uses her teenage protagonist to explore issues related to both gender and race. With a small group, read Meminger's novel and consider the ways in which Samar, the Indian American teenager at the center of the novel, is viewed by her friends and family before and after her Sikh uncle arrives. Consider the ways in which Samar, like Helen in *Why Marry?*, is pushed to alter her behavior based on what is expected of her as a female in her family, in her culture, and in American society. How does ignorance about Samar's heritage change the way she is perceived by her friends in the post-9/11 setting of the novel? How does the arrival of her uncle and her family's desire to reconnect with their Sikh heritage shape the expectations her family places upon her as a young woman? Create a blog your group can use as a forum to discuss the themes and characters in the book. Examine your personal responses to the novel as well.

- In *Why Marry?*, Williams explores issues pertinent to the early feminist movement in America. In *Opening the Gates: An Anthology of Arab Feminist Writing*, published in 1990 with a second edition in 2004, the editors Margot Badran and Miriam Cooke present a variety of writings by Arab feminists. Included are poems, short stories, and essays. Survey the pieces presented in this collection and consider the issues that are confronted by women in the Arab-speaking world. Select two or three short pieces and create a presentation in which you analyze the poem, story, or essay and identify its themes. Prepare a poster or PowerPoint presentation in which you identify each work and its author and provide a summary of the work and its themes.

- Williams published *Why Marry?* in 1917, just as the United States was about to enter World War I but before any major US involvement had begun. Research the involvement of the United States in World War I. What European events prompted the United States to send troops overseas? How did life on the home front alter after American soldiers were deployed to Europe? Use your research to either write a report on US involvement in World War I or imagine a scene in *Why Marry?* that takes place one year after the close of the play. Imagine that it is 1918 and the United States has been participating in the war effort for one year. The dialogue should reflect contemporary events, including the news the characters have received about the war in Europe. Which of the characters might have gone to fight as soldiers in the war? How has the war changed the lives of the family members?

---

to marry for love but recognizes that as she is economically dependent on men, she must either continue to live with her brother or marry well.

Marrying well means wedding the wealthy Rex instead of waiting for her law-school love, Bob, to finish school and become established in his

Why Marry? *takes place in a house in the country.* *(© Paula Cobleigh / Shutterstock.com)*

profession. Theodore, as a clergyman, regards marriage as an ideal to which everyone should aspire and sees it as the necessary step in the journey toward a loving couple producing children.

Lucy is vocal in her arguments in favor of marriage in the early part of the play. She tells Helen, "I'm just an old-fashioned wife. Woman's sphere is the home. My husband says so." Lucy constantly defers to John, follows his orders, and regards marriage as "woman's only true career." Stern looks from John produce nervous agreement from Lucy during conversations about marriage. Lucy also agrees with Theodore's views about sex and sin. When Helen implies a sexual relationship with Ernest, Lucy is horrified. Lucy's devotion to her marriage, though, is marked by her fear of her husband, and as the stage directions sometimes indicate, she hides her true feelings from John. Her actions are described in terms of their timidity and cringing nature as she attends to John at breakfast. At one point, the stage directions indicate, "A look

of resentment creeps over Lucy's pretty face, now that he can't see her." Lucy actually gains enough courage to ask John if he would mind if she left him. He insists that she has no grounds for divorce and, further, that she has no money of her own. She may be "sick of this life," but he is not, and she "belongs" to him. Lucy goes on to express the way he revolts her when she must submit to him at all times. Yet the issue is not raised between the two again. As Thomas H. Dickinson states in *Playwrights of the New American Theater*, "No problem play has presented a more terrifying view of marriage than does the author of this play."

Women's Rights

In the late nineteenth and early twentieth centuries, the feminist movement became a powerful force in American politics, with women fighting for the right to vote and for equal access to educational and professional opportunities. In *Why Marry?*, Williams employs the character of Helen as a spokesperson for women's rights.

The other characters in the play—men and women alike—repeatedly deride her for her views regarding women's education and economic independence. Jabs at the notion of equal rights for women are taken by two women—Lucy and Jean—at the beginning of the play. Acting on Lucy's plan to ensnare Rex, Jean picks a fight with Rex. After Rex has agreed to marry Jean and exited the scene, Jean tells Lucy, "I pretended to believe in woman suffrage!" Lucy replies, "Good! They hate that." Although woman suffrage, or the right to vote, is not an issue that takes center stage in the play, it is part of the larger debate regarding the rights of women. As Jean and Lucy discuss Rex's infatuation with Helen, Lucy comforts Jean by telling her, "Men admire these independent women, but they don't marry them. Nobody wants to marry a sexless freak with a scientific degree."

As an educated, working woman, Helen represents the ideal of economic independence, even though she admits she makes very little money. Lucy and Jean both admit, at various points in the play, that marriage is the only means by which they can support themselves. Even the most open-minded of the men, Ernest, expresses some hint of his belief regarding the inferiority of women. Ernest confronts Theodore about his views on the place of women in the domestic sphere when he asks Theodore, "What makes it more 'womanly' [for women] to do menial work for men than intellectual work with them?" Here, he appears to support a woman's right to work outside the home. But Ernest also insists that women make better assistants than men. He tells Helen about the problems with having male assistants—"They are all so confoundedly ambitious to do original work." He then asks her, "Why is it women can stand day after day of monotonous detail better than men?" He implies that women have no desire to do original work of their own but are content to do the menial and monotonous jobs that support the original work of their male colleagues. Helen indignantly replies that women seem suited to these menial tasks because "men always made them tend the home!"

Jean at one point wishes she were more independent, like her sister, but succumbs to her brother's pressure and agrees to marry Rex. Lucy also attempts to stand up to John, telling him he wishes to leave her, but he quickly points out her lack of income and asserts his ownership

of her. Helen, though, refuses to give up what little independence her education and career afford her. Although she insists that marrying Ernest would be selfish of her because it could damage *his* career (in that he would have to quit research and enter private practice in order to support a family), it is her own career with which she is most concerned. She fears she will have to turn her efforts to running a household instead of pursuing her professional aims.

STYLE

American Discussion Play

The discussion play, also known as a problem play, is a dramatic genre popularized by Irish playwright George Bernard Shaw and employed by American playwright Williams in works such as *Why Marry?* and *Why Not?* A discussion play treats intellectual ideas and is rooted in conversation and debate rather than in physical action. Although some scholars feel that the discussion play existed in some form before Shaw began writing, they note that he was the modern innovator of this type of drama. As critic Alan S. Downer comments in *The British Drama: A Handbook and Chronicle*, in Shaw's works, "events exist only for the discussion they may provoke." James Michael Thomas, in *Script Analysis for Actors, Directors, and Designers*, insists that Shaw "originated the discussion play, a kind of idea play in which current social, political, or economic issues are debated as part of the play's action."

In Williams's play, what is repeatedly referred to as "the marriage problem" is debated from the opening of the play to its conclusion. Many of the characters reiterate their views and are constantly attempting to ascertain and then applaud the benefits of marriage, but they repeatedly find flaws in marriage as an institution. Only Helen remains consistently convinced of the pointlessness of marriage. She articulates her views at times sarcastically, and at times with great emotion, but always intelligently. Fiercely opposed by John, Lucy, and Theodore, Helen is repeatedly forced to defend her viewpoint, and even her supporters, Ernest and Everett, eventually capitulate to societal pressures and argue that there are, in fact, benefits to marriage. At times, Williams's characters' debates seem well intentioned and genuine, but as characters continue to argue their own cases, they become further entrenched in their own opinions and are increasingly unable to objectively analyze the views of the others.

Comedy

While Williams discusses serious topics in *Why Marry?*, he does so within the framework of comedic conventions. As Brenda Murphy points out in *American Realism and American Drama, 1880–1940*, Williams's play combines the conventions of the American discussion play with the notion, solidified in the works of George Bernard Shaw, "that serious points about serious issues could be made through witty dialogue and comic, even farcical, dramatic action." Williams in *Why Marry?* gives his wittiest words and observations to Helen, Ernest, and Uncle Everett, all of whom make strong cases against marriage. Helen seems to delight in making the others uncomfortable, with both her intellectual remarks and her unconventional views. For example, when Lucy alludes to the scandal Helen has caused through her close working relationship with Ernest, Helen responds "mischievously" (according to the stage directions), "Ah, that wonderful night! . . . The night we discovered the Hamilton antitoxin. . . . And, just think, I had a hand in it, Lucy, a hand in the unwomanly work of saving children's lives." Helen goes on to sarcastically remark that perhaps she should have behaved like "an old-fashioned spinster" and said, "Excuse me, Dr. Hamilton, but we must now let a year's work go to waste because you are a man and I am a woman, and it's dark outdoors."

Williams additionally incorporates ironic twists in his plot, further underscoring the play's comedic nature. In traditional comedic plays dealing with romantic relationships, lovers are often opposed by their families, and the action is centered around keeping the central pair of lovers apart. Williams infuses his play with irony by reversing this traditional comic structure. Murphy observes that in Williams's play, "Helen's family is trying to get them to marry instead of going off to Europe together." At the same time, the family is trying to force the reluctant Jean to wed Rex. The intellectual nature of the play's witty exchanges further elevates *Why Marry?* from low comedy or humor to high comedy. In *Fifty Years of American Drama, 1900–1950*, Alan S. Downer describes the work as a drama that "appears to be play of manners"

and describes the dialogue as "up-to-date, journalistically and morally." In the end, though, Downer states, the wit and comedy are undercut by the marriage at the play's conclusion.

HISTORICAL CONTEXT

The Era of the New Woman

In *Why Marry?*, the characters make much of the fact that Helen is a "New Woman." The term was first employed by British feminist novelist Sarah Grand in an 1894 essay for the *North American Review*. As Carolyn Christensen Nelson observes in *A New Woman Reader: Fiction, Articles and Drama of the 1890s*, Grand uses the phrase to describe a woman who has identified the problem "with Home-is-the-Woman's-Sphere, and prescribed the remedy." These women sought independence through education and employment and often eschewed conventional notions of female sexuality. The New Woman was associated with feminist views and political agendas. Ann Heilmann and Margaret Beetham, in *New Woman Hybridities: Femininity, Feminism, and International Consumer Culture, 1880–1930*, describe the New Woman as someone who demanded "access to higher education, the vote, and the right to earn a decent living."

The fervor behind New Womanism was fueled in part by the periodical press, that is, by newspapers and magazines that featured activist essays and fiction focused on the New Woman, as Martha Patterson states in *The American New Woman Revisited: A Reader, 1894–1930*. Through print media, the struggles of women around the world were reported. Patterson describes the way "international feminist art, theory, and practice shaped the American concept of the New Woman," citing the way New Women activists were inspired by the work of Norwegian writer Henrik Ibsen, who criticized gender roles in Victorian England, and by American activist Emma Goldman, who traveled to Paris to learn about birth-control methods. Patterson further comments on the way American feminists Alice Paul and Lucy Burns, who founded the National Woman's Party in 1913, incorporated militant techniques borrowed from their British feminist counterparts.

When the United States entered World War I in 1917, new employment opportunities opened

COMPARE
&
CONTRAST

- **1917:** Women's rights advocates continue to fight for the right to vote, a battle they have waged for decades, and additionally have begun to seek greater access to higher education, employment opportunities, and birth control. Women who have fought against societal norms and financial obstacles to receive a college education and pursue a career find that they are paid significantly less than their male counterparts. Studies show that when education, the percentage of women in the labor force, and job tenure are adjusted for, women in 1920 earned on average about 43 percent of what their male counterparts earned.

  Today: Women's rights advocates, having won the right to vote in 1920, continue to fight for such rights as abortion access, legal protection from domestic violence, and equal pay. In the area of wage inequality, women reportedly earn only 77 cents for every dollar earned by their male counterparts. Despite the passage of legislation in each of these areas, gaps remain in laws designed to protect the rights of women. The Equal Rights Amendment, introduced in 1923 as a means of guaranteeing equal treatment for all citizens, was passed in 1972 but still has not been ratified by enough states—thirty-eight—for it to become part of the US Constitution.

- **1917:** The American theatrical scene is becoming increasingly dominated by dramas that realistically portray contemporary American society. A number of playwrights, including Jesse Lynch Williams, Philip Barry, Sidney Howard, S. N. Behrman, and Robert Sherwood, also incorporate comedy into their realistic plays about the lives and problems of everyday Americans.

  Today: Modern theatrical productions are marked by a variety of trends. Critics have noted a rise in the number of ensemble theater productions, which incorporate a number of performers and casts that vary from one production to the next. These types of productions are reminiscent of the performance art of past decades and are now labeled as devised theater. Another contemporary trend is that of the solo production, in which a play features only a single performer.

- **1917:** Divorce is relatively uncommon in the United States at this time. Contemporary fictional sources such as Williams's play *Why Marry?* suggest that one in eleven marriages ends in divorce. Government statistics indicate that the rate of divorce in 1917 is 1.2 per 1,000 people.

  Today: The Centers for Disease Control and Prevention states that the US divorce rate in 2013 is 3.6 of every 1,000 people.

---

up for women, whose efforts were needed in mills and factories. In the immediate aftermath of the war, women were typically expected to cede these positions back to men. In 1919, the Eighteenth Amendment was passed, prohibiting the manufacture, consumption and sale of alcohol. This gave rise to illegal clubs, known as speakeasies, where alcohol was served. As the New Women had been drinking prior to the

passage of the amendment as a form of defiance, as Patterson states, they now became increasingly associated with the "flapper" of the 1920s, fashionable, independent women who attended jazz clubs and drank in speakeasies. New Women and feminists fought for access to birth control and for divorce reform during this time period. In 1920, women's rights activists achieved an enormous victory when women

Williams's play explores what it means to be married and whether or not it is a necessary institution.
(© Ivan Galashchuk / Shutterstock.com)

were granted the right to vote with the passage of the Nineteenth Amendment. While the feminist movement continued to evolve, with the "first wave" of feminism ebbing with the passage of the Nineteenth Amendment and the second wave to gain momentum in the 1960s, the concept of the New Woman gradually faded by the early 1930s.

Comedy and Realism in Early Twentieth-Century American Theater

During the first decades of the twentieth century, American theater was marked by trends toward realism and toward comedy. Williams featured prominently in both of these developments. As Thomas H. Dickinson states in *Playwrights of the New American Theater*, "If comedy means the arrangement of the lines of human motives in graceful and arbitrary contours in order to reflect a coherent criticism of life, Jesse Lynch Williams is undoubtedly the first writer of comedy in America." Dickinson further emphasizes that "the source of his comedy is always an inner essence and not an artificial agglomeration of laugh lines and sure-fire situations." Brenda

Murphy insists, "The presentation in 1918 of the first Pulitzer Prize for drama to Jesse Lynch Williams for his sophisticated discussion play *Why Marry?* was the first clear sign that realism had arrived in the American theater." Murphy goes on to discuss the play's "witty dialogue" and "comic, even farcical dramatic action," in this way yoking Williams's realism and comedy.

By presenting in a comedic fashion the realities of the time period's social issues, Williams's work influenced that of other dramatists. Murphy notes, "The extent of Williams's influence is hard to measure quantitatively, but his presence is ubiquitous in the tone and dramatic structure that American dramatists adopted in the early twenties." Other dramatists who use both comedy and realism in their works include Rachel Crothers, whose *Mary the Third* (1923) employs comedic formal elements in the exploration of women's equality within a marriage. Likewise, Philip Barry and Sidney Howard tackle similar issues by infusing realism with comedy in their respective plays *Paris Bound* (1927) and *Half Gods* (1929). Robert F. Gross, in *Realism and the American Tradition*, observes that in critical discussions of realism in American theater during this period, comedic writers such as Barry, S. N. Behrman, and Robert Sherwood are often overlooked. Yet these dramatists incorporated both realism and comedy, along with idealism "in the form of intellectual abstraction," in their plays, Gross maintains.

CRITICAL OVERVIEW

Why Marry? received what is considered one of the highest honors when it won the first Pulitzer Prize for Drama in 1918. After opening on Broadway at the Astor Theater in December 1917, it had a successful run of 120 performances. Reviewing the play in January 1918 for *Theatre Magazine*, Arthur Hornblow repeatedly refers to the play as "brilliant" and favorably compares Williams to George Bernard Shaw. Hornblow notes that in fact, "Williams has the higher literary quality." Hornblow additionally praises the actors' handling of the material, stating that the "performance was brilliant."

The play has since been examined for its realism, its comedy, and its stance on women's issues. Alan S. Downer, in *Fifty Years of American Drama, 1900–1950*, notes that the play was regarded as "a highly successful comedy" and observes that Williams was considered "more 'literary' than most of his fellow playwrights." At the same time, Downer's assessment of the play focuses on the way the drama's ending undercuts the points it earlier made about women and marriage. "Whatever point the play may have had, whatever purpose the wit may have served, point and wit are abandoned in the teeth of the final curtain," Downer states, frowning upon the way Ernest and Helen are tricked into marriage at the play's ending.

In *Playwrights of the American Theater*, Thomas H. Dickinson focuses his analysis of *Why Marry?* on the nature of Williams's comedy, stating that the play "is a comedy of such clean-cut and diagrammatic situation as to approach in structural respects farce." He goes on to state that it is "a higher type of farce in which the ends are not momentary laughter but deep understanding." Dickinson further underscores that the view of marriage Williams puts forth is "terrifying." Despite the fact that all the couples in the play are discontented with the notion of marriage, Dickinson states, "he

shows them married because he can think of nothing better for them to do, and he can think of nothing better because man in all the ages has thought of nothing better."

Other critics have demonstrated the extent to which Williams is indebted to Shaw. In *American Realism and American Drama, 1880–1940*, Brenda Murphy argues that in *Why Marry?*, "the reversal of the normal comedy plot, the ironic twist in the ending, and the sparkling wit of the discussions clearly show Shaw's influence."

CRITICISM

Catherine Dominic

Dominic is a novelist and a freelance writer and editor. In the following essay, she studies the ways in which the women in Why Marry? *view marriage and the way marriage is used as a means of silencing them.*

In *Why Marry?*, a play in which the dialogue is virtually unbroken by action, and in which characters repeatedly and forcefully present their views on the topics of marriage, divorce, and the independence of women, silences become almost more meaningful than speech. Lucy, Jean, and Helen are all silenced by men whose decisions and actions dominate the fate of the women in the play. An examination of the female characters and their silencing aids in understanding the play's ending, in which Helen is tricked into a marriage she did not want. This marriage may be regarded as Williams's attempt to undercut what seems to be the play's condoning of Helen's unconventional behavior. By forcing the marriage at the play's conclusion, Williams reveals the heart of the play's tensions. As Thomas H. Dickinson observes in *Playwrights of the New American Theater*, "Legalized prostitution, boredom, frustration of will, the dominance of the weak over the strong—all the charges against marriage are faced." Yet the characters are still all pushed in the direction of marriage. In the end, it is the only recourse offered.

The play opens with Jean's duping of Rex into agreeing to marry her. Not long after, when Rex departs and Lucy appears, Jean indicates that Lucy designed this subterfuge. Jean hints that she does not really love Rex, but Lucy does not see this as an obstacle to the match.

" IT MUZZLES WOMEN AND PREVENTS THEM
FROM EXPRESSING THEIR OPINIONS AND BELIEFS. IT
RESTRICTS THEIR MOVEMENT IN SOCIETY, PREVENT-
ING THEM FROM OPERATING IN THE PROFESSIONAL
SPHERES OF MEN."

When Helen appears on the scene, she and Lucy
spar over the appropriate role of women in society. Lucy feels that women should remain in the
domestic sphere, that "going down-town every
day with men,—it seems so unwomanly." She
also insists that men do not like women with
their own opinions. Jean defends her sister
Helen and Helen's right to her viewpoint, stating, "Helen can afford to have independent
views; she has an independent income—she
earns it." Jean further wishes that she, too, had
gone to college and prepared for a career. Lucy
soon runs off when her husband, John, calls for
her. In her absence, Helen reveals her discomfort
with the way John treats Lucy. In this opening
scene, the women reveal much about themselves.
Jean is young and confused and feels the need to
marry, but does not particularly want to marry
Rex. She idolizes her sister. Lucy is dutiful and
fully embraces the notion that women should be
confined to the domestic sphere and should be
deferential to their husbands. Helen is fiercely
independent and has no desire to marry, but
simply wishes to continue her work. These
views are tested as the play progresses.

When Everett and Theodore begin discussing marriage and divorce with Lucy and John,
Everett defends his impending divorce. Lucy
stands with John and Theodore, asserting, "marriages are made in heaven." Lucy is a defender
also of love and sides with Theodore and against
her husband in advocating the marriage of Helen
and Ernest. Lucy acknowledges that she believes
Helen and Ernest love each other, and she further asserts to John that Helen really cannot be
wed to anyone else. She tells John, "think how
she treats all the nice men." After Helen enters
the scene and insists that marriage is nothing
more than a trap that contractually obligates a
man to financially support his wife, Lucy objects

to Helen's unsentimental view of marriage. As
Helen reveals privately, however, her views
about marriage are not as harsh as Lucy and
the others believe. In an aside (in the theater,
an aside is the means by which a character conveys private thoughts to the audience), Helen
indicates that marriage "ought to be the holiest
and most beautiful thing" but that when seen in
the light in which it is understood by her family
members, it becomes "horrible and dishonest."
Up to this point, marriage has been discussed in
terms of the duties involved: the wife must attend
to the home and obey her husband and rescind
her opinions; the husband must above all else
provide for the wife financially. Although Lucy
and Theodore have spoken of love, the economic
dependence of wives upon their husbands cannot be extracted from the notion of marriage.
Helen is not against marriage in theory, but as
she has seen it practiced, it has become distaste-
ful to her.

Throughout the first act of the play, Lucy is
vocal in her defense of marriage. Her arguments are informed by her views on love,
duty, and religion. At the same time, she has
listened to her family debate marriage. She has
heard Helen's objections, as well as Everett's
insistence that he and Julia are divorcing. By
the opening of act 2, after being ordered about
by John in act 1, Lucy begins to see her own
marriage differently. She suggests to John the
possibility of divorce, timidly at first, and then
more forcefully as John dismisses her viewpoint. She tells him she is "sick of this life,"
but he responds that not only is he "not sick
of it," but that Lucy belongs to him. He grabs
hold of her despite the fact that she tells him she
finds him repulsive and wishes he would seek
out other women so that he would leave her
alone. Lucy insists that John does not respect
her, and she tells him she hates him. After this
confrontation, however, Lucy speaks no more
of the matter to John. Rather, she humbly sub-
mits to him as she always has. He has refused
her the opportunity to "escape decently," telling her she would have no money if she left him.
Lucy, feeling as though she has no other
recourse, reverts to the role of the obedient
wife. John effectively silences Lucy. Even
when the stage directions indicate later in the
play that she disagrees with John, as when she
hides behind her hands and shudders, her
words are dutifully agreeable.

WHAT DO I READ NEXT?

- Williams's *Princeton Stories* was published in 1895. The collection of short stories examines the lives of undergraduates at Princeton. A modern reprint of the stories is available in a 2013 edition.

- *The Stolen Story and Other Newspaper Stories* includes short fiction and sketches published by Williams in 1899 based on his work as a newspaper reporter. *The Stolen Story* was later adapted as a play. A modern reprint is available in a 2010 edition.

- Like Williams, Philip Barry wrote realistic comedic plays about contemporary American society. His first plays were published in the early 1920s, with his first major hit, *Holiday*, appearing in 1928. The script for Barry's *Holiday: A Comedy in Three Acts* is available in a 1956 edition.

- Rachel Crothers, a dramatist and contemporary of Williams's, published the play *A Man's World* in 1910. The work features a protagonist who feels the societal pressure to choose between a career and romance. The play is available in a 2007 edition.

- *Ain't I a Woman: Black Women and Feminism*, written by bell hooks and published in 1981, is considered a groundbreaking work that examines the ways in which African American women fighting for racial equality and women's rights were often excluded from the suffragist and burgeoning feminist movement of white women during the nineteenth and twentieth centuries. A more recent edition was published in 1999.

- Charles Way's young-adult play *The Dutiful Daughter*, published in 2006, tells the story of a princess and obedient daughter, Ke Xin, who is forced to confront her society's notions of gender and power when a stranger arrives on her island. Way's play is published in a bilingual edition with English and Mandarin text.

- Janet Staiger's *Bad Women: Regulating Sexuality in Early American Cinema*, published in 1995, explores the ways New Women were portrayed by the burgeoning film industry in the early decades of the twentieth century.

When Jean and Rex next appear, Jean is attempting to candidly tell Rex that she does not love him and cannot marry him. Rex, impressed with her honesty, and imbued with jealousy because Jean seems to prefer another man, wants her more than ever. Jean runs off, and Rex follows. They do not reappear again until Helen has been forced to repeatedly defend her opposition to marriage. As John begins to see that Helen and Ernest are determined to be together whether or not they are married, he realizes that marriage will be the only way he can save his sister's, and hence the family's, reputation. Helen is consistent and clear about her objections, reiterating her view that marriage would hurt the both personal and professional relationship she enjoys with Ernest. She does not

wish to give up her work so she can manage a household, nor does she wish Ernest to give up his research so that he can take a higher-paying position in private practice.

The argument Helen has with the rest of the family continues, while later, Jean and Rex each reappear. He is still trying to convince her to marry him. John presses upon Jean the economic necessity of marriage, pointing out to her that until she marries someone able to take care of her, she will be dependent on him. Jean finally relents and agrees to marry Rex. She is clear and blunt when she informs him of her acceptance. She states, "I am not going to be a dependent old maid. . . . But, first, I want you to know exactly what you're getting for your money. That seems only businesslike." Here, she is referring to her past romantic relationships. Rex "recoils" at this, but he is determined that no one else should have her. From this moment, Jean's true feelings are silenced. She has committed herself to marriage in a businesslike fashion, and for the remainder of the play she does not resist the idea of marriage as a necessity. John announces the engagement, and when Helen urges Jean to speak on her own behalf and to assert her previous objections to marrying Rex, Jean simply states, "Words cannot describe my happiness." She is literally, by her own admission, without words.

Next, Helen and Ernest, who have vowed to leave for Paris together unwed, become the victims of the family's plotting. Everett, who has had a change of heart about his own divorce, is a key figure in the plot, as he is also a judge. When he coerces Ernest and Helen to agree that in theory they adhere to the basic notion of a wedding vow, he succeeds in tricking them into a legally binding marriage. When the feat has been accomplished, Helen says nothing. Ernest observes, "A moment ago you were a bad woman. Now...behold! she is a good woman. Marriage is wonderful." Helen adds nothing to the remaining dialogue in the play. The trick marriage has left her mute.

For Lucy, Jean, and Helen, marriage is revealed to be damaging. It muzzles women and prevents them from expressing their opinions and beliefs. It restricts their movement in society, preventing them from operating in the professional spheres of men. Marriage is depicted as an economic and social necessity to which women must succumb. Given the way Williams is careful to give each of the women an opportunity to express their honest objections to the restrictive nature of marriage—Lucy and Jean get a moment or two, whereas Helen gets most of the play to do so—he demonstrates the ways in which the institution of marriage as it is practiced in his society should be altered. He shows the women, who are forced into marriage or forced into remaining married, as existing in a situation they find disagreeable at best, suffocating and cruel at worst. His insistence on placing them all in this situation at the play's end, instead of letting any one of them out of it, emphasizes the reality of American society and prevailing viewpoints at the time. Further, by subtly demonstrating the ways marriage traps and silences women, Williams's play suggests

what Everett has explicitly stated—that marriage as an institution needs to change. Yet it is Everett who performs the ceremony that traps Ernest and Helen. By putting this reasonable man up to an unreasonable task, Williams seems to be arguing that it is not just the New Woman who should advocate for the rights of women, but that reasonable men need to resist acquiescing to societal norms and advocate reform as well.

Source: Catherine Dominic, Critical Essay on *Why Marry?*, in *Drama for Students*, Gale, Cengage Learning, 2014.

Keith Newlin

In the following excerpt, Newlin discusses the meaning of Why Marry? *and provides some details about the first production of the play.*

... *Why Marry?* is not, as Arthur Hobson Quinn observed, "an attack upon marriage; it is a scrutiny of the institution." Williams presents five couples in various stages of marriage, examines their reasons for marrying, and finds those reasons to be hypocritical, cynical, and destructive. John is a wealthy businessman and a stereotypical chauvinist along the lines of Malcolm Gaskell of *A Man's World*, who believes in economic Darwinism (those with the most money are the fittest), and who treats his wife Lucy as a possession. Lucy wants a divorce but has no grounds for it and no means of supporting herself. John's youngest sister, Jean, pursues the promiscuous playboy Rex, though she doesn't love him because, as a True Woman, she has been raised only to become a wife. Although she is fully aware that she's entering what she refers to as "legalized prostitution," she is determined not "to be a dependent old maid." Her uncle, Judge Everett, is in the midst of a divorce but discovers that, although he no longer loves his wife, he has become habituated to marriage. Their cousin Theodore, a minister, has had to commit his wife to a sanitarium after a lifetime of economic impoverishment, and he voices the conventional religious reasons for marriage. Finally, John's other sister, Helen, a New Woman who is a self-supporting scientist in love with her boss, Ernest Hamilton, has resolved not to marry him because to do so would destroy their careers.

These relationships become the backdrop for an often hilarious exposé of the reasons people marry, the causes of divorce, and the

A bride's white veil has traditionally been a symbol of virginity, so some question whether a woman who has lived with her fiancé before marriage should wear one. (© Tatiana Morozova / Shutterstock.com)

methods by which society enforces its social codes, all centered upon Helen and Ernest's attempt to defy conventional expectations. As Brenda Murphy observes, *Why Marry?* reverses our normal expectations of the typical comedy plot. Rather than serving as blocking figures, preventing the lovers from getting married, Helen's family is trying to overcome her objections to marriage and to prevent her from living with Ernest as an unmarried couple. Helen and Ernest reject marriage because they cannot afford to live on Ernest's pitiful salary, because Helen does not wish to give up her career, because she despises domestic duties, and because the example of their family suggests that marriage destroys love. Although Helen is depicted as a radical New Woman in her advocacy of "free love," the playwright evidently could not conceive of a marriage divorced from conventional gender-specific roles.

Like Rachel Crothers's Frank Ware, Helen is torn between her desire for a rewarding career and her desire to marry the man she loves. For both Ernest and Helen, marriage means sacrifice, not fulfillment: for Ernest, marriage means giving up poorly paid science for a less rewarding but better-paid job to support a home; for Helen, marriage means giving up challenging work for the drudgery of housework. "The right to work, the right to love—those rights are inalienable," Helen says. "No, we'll give up marriage but not each other." When Lucy points out that she'll be ostracized by society, Helen sketches love-without-marriage as an idyllic companionship: "Instead of making a tired husband work for me, I'll have my days free to work with him, like the old-fashioned women you admire! Instead of being an expense, I'll be a help to him; instead of being separated by marriage and divergent interests, we'll be united by love and common peril." Although Williams presents Helen's radical solution to the work-marriage dilemma with impeccable logic, he was not able to resist the conventional comic closure, so he contrives a solution that undercuts that logic. Uncle Everett manipulates the lovers into admitting their love for one another "in the eyes of God," and he quickly announces a civil marriage. And so they were married, despite their wishes. Williams dissects a social problem but

MUCH OF THE APPEAL OF *WHY MARRY?* STEMS FROM ITS WITTY PRONOUNCEMENTS ON MARRIAGE, MANY OF WHICH STILL RESONATE TODAY."

offers no solution. As Uncle Everett, the play's raisonneur, declaims, "Respectability has triumphed this time, but let Society take warning and beware! beware! beware!"

Much of the appeal of *Why Marry?* stems from its witty pronouncements on marriage, many of which still resonate today. "What does the modern home amount to?" asks the Judge. "Merely a place to leave your wife." "It's curious," Ernest remarks, "but when working with women of ability one learns to respect them so much that one quite loses the habit of insulting them." Or this exchange:

JOHN: True women enjoy sacrificing themselves.

JUDGE: Yes, that's what we tell them. Well, we ought to know. We make 'em do it.

In addition, the actor playing Uncle Everett was Nat Goodwin, who had achieved considerable notoriety for his five marriages and five divorces, as well as for a 1914 book he entitled *Nat Goodwin's Book* (which one biographer referred to as *Why Beautiful Women Marry Nat Goodwin*), and his appearance in the play was a considerable draw. As the reviewer for the *New York Times* wryly remarked, "His strictures on the marital relation are a source of incessant laughter; and it was only in part due to the fact that they emanated from an actor whose authority on the subject is recognized."

Why Marry? had a circuitous route to fame as a Pulitzer Prize winner. Williams began the play as a story but soon decided on a dramatic treatment, publishing it in 1914 under the title "*And So They Were Married.*" Williams was unable to interest Broadway managers because, as he explained in a letter to Arthur Hobson Quinn, "It was written ahead of its time—i.e., ahead of the public's time for such treatment of such ideas." Students at the American Academy of Dramatic Art asked for permission to stage

the play at their annual graduation exercise, and when they did so (on January 3, 1917), demonstrating its comic appeal, three "well-known managers opened negotiations" for rights to the play, all three of whom had refused the play in manuscript. The play received its professional debut under the title *Why Marry?* on November 1, 1917, in Columbus, Ohio, where it ran for 10 weeks before moving to New York. After its 120-performance run it went on the road, but the death of Nat Goodwin (who had become identified with the play) on February 1, 1919, caused managers to cancel bookings.

The play opened to good reviews, with the *New York Times* calling it "perhaps the most intelligent and searching satire on social institutions ever written by an American." The reviewer noted its tendency "to hammer away at current standards in conduct and to underline ideas," but believed that "Short of Shaw, no one has ventilated such a subject with such telling satire and explosive humor. And there are certain respects in which, as it seemed, the play surpasses even Shaw."

Lawrence Gilman, however, writing for the *North American Review*, ridiculed Williams's sophomoric depiction of sentiment (by quoting speeches about love from Helen and Ernest), and pointed particularly to the closing line of the *New York Times* review: "If he had been as scrupulous and vigilant in his expression of feeling as he is shrewd and delightful in his manipulation of comedy," Gilman declared, "Mr. Williams might have given us, if not (as we have been told) 'the most intelligent and searching satire on social institutions ever written by an American,' at least a satire of uncommon point and distinction." Indeed there is some justice to Gilman's remark, for the love talk between Helen and Ernest is conventionally sentimental stuff. Yet as Gilman acknowledges, the play's "surgical wit" redeems it.

Williams proved to be a contentious playwright. John Corbin, the *New York Times* drama editor, praised him for "the keen intelligence of his economic disquisitions and the brilliancy of his dialogue." But Corbin also ridiculed Williams for his sleight-of-hand in contriving the play's ending, called him a propagandist for "free love," and claimed that Ernest Hamilton's salary ($2,000) was too little to be plausible—thus undermining Williams's point about the economic disadvantage of marriage. The next week Williams published a lengthy defense of his play in which he argued, albeit unconvincingly, for his play's economic and social theses: "I thought I was writing comedy, not propaganda, and that my moral was not immoral at all. In fact, I should say that my message is a warning against, not an argument for, what is usually meant by 'Free Love.'" Williams noted that his intent was to show why society makes it difficult to stay married and insisted that marriage is "the most sacred and important relationship in life.... So it really looks as though society would have to reform the rules and regulations of marriage if it expects its young people keep on playing the game for it." He concluded his letter by offering a vision of his heroine as a "true woman" who has become "radical in order to conserve woman's ancient share of the work of the world, ready to seem ridiculous, or even wrong, in order to serve and protect those whom she loves."

Corbin's reply to *this* response must have infuriated Williams. He repeated his charges, castigating Williams for not respecting "the 'logical conclusion' of his own premises and preachments," and concluded that the play was "eloquent in declamation against modern marriage, but ending in matrimony" nonetheless. Williams evidently had enough of this journalistic quibble. In his next play he turned his satire to divorce, ridiculing divorce laws that prevented unsuited couples from separating and entitling the result simply *Why Not?* (1992)....

Source: Keith Newlin, Introduction to *American Plays of the New Woman: Six Plays from the Early Twentieth Century about the "Proper" Role of Women,* Ivan R. Dee, 2000, pp. 24–28.

Thomas H. Dickinson

In the following excerpt, Dickinson analyzes the comedic aspects of Williams's work and compares it to that of Langdon Mitchell.

... When Jesse Lynch Williams started to write comedy, he undertook a task somewhat similar to that of Mitchell, but he based it upon a slightly different convention. With Mitchell the convention had been "manner." Any conception that was realized had to be "put over" the barriers of an artificial and largely arbitrary standard of decorum. These characters were not interested in their own fates, in their characters or predicaments. They were bored, and they

> HE SHOWS THEM MARRIED BECAUSE HE CAN THINK OF NOTHING BETTER FOR THEM TO DO, AND HE CAN THINK OF NOTHING BETTER BECAUSE MAN IN ALL THE AGES HAS THOUGHT OF NOTHING BETTER."

covered their boredom with epigrams. Jesse Lynch Williams created a new and more timely convention. His characters were interested in themselves as specimens. Their destiny was in their hands, and while they were going to pursue their destiny with a certain regard for appearances, they were honestly concerned in getting down to the truth of the dilemmas in which they found themselves caught, in talking them over and coming to conclusions. Manifestly this form of comedy, while closely related to the former, is much more in accord with the canons of responsibility and free will.

Williams does not provide a new style of comedy. He only provides a new motive power for the old comedy. Like the personages of Mitchell's play, his characters have only one outlet of escape, and this is through a trickle of words. But he has done much in supplying these words a new energy. While in Mitchell speech had been at best a game, and like all games a bore, in Williams speech became an adjunct to "straight thinking." Within the narrow limits set up by their understandings, these characters are determined to think through. They are determined, also, to express their thoughts without fear or too much self-consciousness. They live in a time that is very much concerned with its own processes, that tells itself that it is re-valuing values. All of this is a great aid to an author who must bring his play to pass on the tongues of his characters and must in so doing maintain a level of niceness and grave good humor.

Jesse Lynch Williams was born in Stirling, Illinois, August 17, 1871. He was graduated from Princeton in 1892. He has written comparatively little, but what he has written has been marked by standards of elevated taste and a transparent honesty of conception. He first attracted attention with his short stories, and published two collections entitled *Princeton*

Stories (1895), and *The Stolen Story* (1899). An interest akin to that of Meredith in the more delicate features of the relations between men and women culminated in the long novel, *The Married Life of the Frederick Carrolls* (1910). His comedy, *Why Marry?* on the same general theme was begun as fiction but was developed into a stage play, first entitled, *And So They Were Married*. First produced at the American Academy of Dramatic Arts, this play after its subsequent professional production in 1917 ran for two years.

If comedy means the arrangement of the lines of human motives in graceful and arbitrary contours in order to reflect a coherent criticism of life, Jesse Lynch Williams is undoubtedly the first writer of comedy in America. While he is keenly regardful of the design of his composition, the source of his comedy is always an inner essence and not an artificial agglomeration of laugh lines and surefire situations. In many respects Williams is like Meredith. He is a comedian of fine flavors. But there is an important difference which refers more to his environment than to his own method. He was reared in a country in which the quiet, almost unsmiling comedy of the deeper essence is practically unknown. Whatever poise he has achieved has been at the expense of tremendously hard work. His plays are the products of frequent re-writings, each one representing a deeper stage in his understanding of his characters and their situations. He has not been able entirely to clear his plays of the evidences of hard work. Angularities and forced postures appear here and there. Like Meredith, Williams is not content to permit his works simply to develop a situation and there rest. He seeks outside the work and beyond it a conceptual value. He is more interested in what his play implies than in what it displays. More than this, he seeks by the careful choosing of his characters and the arrangement of his action to cover all aspects of the theme. He is very anxious not to be charged with special pleading, nor with disregarding anything important to the understanding of the problem. Nor can he be so charged. But his plays pay the price of his detachment and his catholicity. They appear to be scaled to a symposium rather than to the action of a play. Revealed truth becomes more important than the revelation of truth.

Why Marry is a comedy of such clean-cut and diagrammatic situation as to approach in structural respects to farce. It is, in fact, a higher type of farce in which the ends are not momentary laughter but deep understanding. Farce calls for the moving of men and women as puppets across the stage to get effects of laughter and surprise. This play calls for the moving of men and women as puppets across the stage to get effects of sympathy and insight. In spite of everything that can be said for Williams' characters, I insist that they are puppets. The ordinary good play takes upon itself meaning by the humanity of its characters. These characters take upon themselves humanity by their meanings. The author is interested first of all in presenting a picture of marriage as an institution, not any particular marriage, but marriage in general. And the picture the author presents is sufficiently devastating. The cross currents of opposition to marriage are all represented. Legalized prostitution, boredom, frustration of will, the dominance of the weak over the strong—all the charges against marriage are faced. No problem play has presented a more terrifying view of marriage than does the author of this play. He literally says not one word for the institution. All the couples represent some phase of fundamental discontent. The author spares no pains, and softens no blow. And his courage is well advised. After saying and implying everything that can be charged against marriage, there comes the final question: What then? What have we to offer instead of marriage? Everything that can be said against marriage can be said against life. Yet few of us choose not to live. The greatest castigators of marriage, of woman, have been the much-married men like Strindberg. Is there comedy in that? There is unless you wish to take it tragically. Williams chooses to take it in a spirit of comedy. He shows at the end of the play all the couples who have been in one way or another tugging at the leash safely united in dis-union. He shows them married because he can think of nothing better for them to do, and he can think of nothing better because man in all the ages has thought of nothing better. Rex does not want to get married because he wants to go on with his affairs, but marries nevertheless; Jean loves another, but lacking him, marries anyway; Lucy is weary to death of a husband with a mind of the Pleiocene age, but cannot leave him because neither of them has "sinned"; Uncle Everett believes in divorce in theory but has become used to his wife and cannot give up his bad habits; the clergyman brother reconciles himself and his wife to their hard lot by reference to the sacredness of sacrifice in marriage; Helen and Ernest want above all things to work together without intrusions of sex, but they are not allowed to do so and so they are married. For all of these marriage is the only outlet, the only "practicable" thing.

I think such a play as this cannot be judged by the ordinary standards of comedy. The situations are forced into line. The characters are abstractions. No one could seriously claim that such an imbroglio as this could realize itself in the talk of any group of people, however sophisticated. John, who is in many respects the key character—for he it is who starts the action moving and keeps it going by his dictatorial pig-headedness—is unbelievable either in himself or in relation to the other characters of the play. No character is so all-of-a-piece as John, so consistent in his attitudes. He represents the hidden spring of everything wrong that the author sees in marriage or in human institutions. Any man acting as he acts would be thrown out of doors on his head by some one before the end of the first act. As we cannot accept the play on the score of verisimilitude, we must find some score upon which it can be accepted. For it must be accepted. It is a drama of abstract forces identified with personalities, so arranged and thought through that the impact of the forces takes on a dramatic character. With Shaw and Barker, Williams is the exponent of the brilliant idea in drama. Less adroit than Barker in burying his theme deep under the action he is more entertaining than Barker. And he is more consistent in pointing a situation and seeing it through than Shaw. With a little of Shaw's brilliancy he has more ability to discard what does not belong to his theme; and unlike Shaw he has no disposition himself to come before the curtain and dance. *Why Marry* was awarded in 1917 the first Pulitzer Prize as the best American play of the year.

Williams' second play, *Why Not?* was made from a novelette, "Remating Time," which had been published in 1916. It was produced by Equity Players with success at the end of 1922. The play serves the same underlying philosophy of the earlier play with less force and originality. . . .

Source: Thomas H. Dickinson, "On Our American Comedy: Langdon Mitchell; Jesse Lynch Williams," in *Playwrights of the New American Theater*, Books for Libraries Press, 1925, pp. 230–36.

SOURCES

Brennan, Elizabeth A., and Elizabeth C. Clarage, eds., "Jesse Lynch Williams," in *Who's Who of Pulitzer Prize Winners*, Oryx Press, 1999, p. 168.

Coates, Tyler, "2013 Tony Nominations: The Theatre World Takes Broadway Back from Hollywood," in *FlavorWire*, May 1, 2013, http://flavorwire.com/388624/2013-tony-nominations-the-theatre-world-takes-broadway-back-from-hollywood (accessed July 28, 2013).

Cordell, Kathryn Coe, and William H. Cordell, eds., "*Why Marry?*, Jesse Lynch Williams," in *The Pulitzer Prize Plays*, Random House, 1935, pp. 1–52.

Dickinson, Thomas H., "On Our American Comedy," in *Playwrights of the New American Theater*, Macmillan, 1925, pp. 219–69.

"Did You Know That Women Are Still Paid Less Than Men?," White House website, http://www.whitehouse.gov/equal-pay/career (accessed July 28, 2013).

Downer, Alan Seymour, "American Comedy," in *Fifty Years of American Drama, 1900–1950*, Regnery, 1951, pp. 111–33.

———, "The Revival of the Drama," in *The British Drama: A Handbook and Brief Chronicle*, Appleton-Century-Crofts, 1950, pp. 299–334.

Gross, Robert F., "Servant of Three Masters: Realism, Idealism, and 'Hokum' in American High Comedy," in *Realism and the American Dramatic Tradition*, edited by William W. Demastes, University of Alabama Press, 1996, pp. 71–90.

Heilmann, Ann, and Margaret Beetham, eds., Introduction to *New Woman Hybridities: Femininity, Feminism, and International Consumer Culture, 1880–1930*, Routledge, 2004, pp. 1–14.

Hornblow, Arthur, Review of *Why Marry?*, in *Theatre Magazine*, January 1918, p. 85.

"Marriage and Divorce," National Center for Health Statistics, Centers for Disease Control and Prevention website, April 24, 2013, http://www.cdc.gov/nchs/fastats/divorce.htm (accessed July 28, 2013).

Morris, Steven Leigh, "Group Think," in *American Theatre*, March 2013, Theatre Communications Group website, http://www.tcg.org/publications/at/issue/featuredstory.cfm?story=1&indexID=27 (accessed July 28, 2013).

Murphy, Brenda, "The Final Integration: Innovations in Realistic Thought and Structure, 1916–1940," in *American Realism and American Drama, 1880–1940*, Cambridge University Press, 1987, pp. 162–94.

Nelson, Carolyn Christensen, ed., Introduction to *A New Woman Reader: Fiction, Articles, and Drama of the 1890s*, Broadview Press, 2001, pp. ix–xiv.

"100 Years of Marriage and Divorce Statistics: United States, 1867–1967," US Department of Health, Education, and Welfare: Data from the National Vital Statistics System, Series 21, No. 24, December 1973, p. 22, http://www.cdc.gov/nchs/data/series/sr_21/sr21_024.pdf (accessed July 28, 2013).

Patterson, Martha, ed., Introduction to *The American New Woman Revisited: A Reader, 1894–1930*, Rutgers University Press, 2008, pp. 1–28.

Francis, Roberta W., *The Equal Rights Amendment: Simple Justice—Long Overdue*, National Council of Women's Organizations, November 2013, http://www.equalrightsamendment.org/misc/ERA_presentation.pdf (accessed July 28, 2013).

"That Male-Female Pay Gap Is Narrowing," in *Christian Science Monitor*, 1984, http://www.csmonitor.com/1984/1031/103119.html/(page)/3 (accessed July 28, 2011).

Thomas, James, "Idea," in *Script Analysis for Actors, Directors, and Designers*, Focal Press, 2009, pp. 200–28.

Williams, Jesse Lynch, *Why Marry?*, CreateSpace Independent Publishing Platform, 2013.

FURTHER READING

Barlow, Judith E., ed., *Plays by American Women: 1900–1930*, Applause, 2001.

> Barlow's collection features a range of plays written by American women during the era of the New Woman. The works all feature characters representing the new modern American woman and the challenges she faced in American society.

Fleming, Thomas, *The Illusion of Victory: Americans in World War I*, Basic Books, 2003.

> Fleming examines America's involvement in World War I and describes the political and cultural environment prior to, during, and just after the war.

Heilmann, Ann, *New Woman Fiction: Women Writing First-Wave Feminism*, St. Martin's, 2000.

> Heilmann examines social constructions of feminine identity during the era of the New Woman and studies the influence of feminist literature and the first wave of the feminist movement on social culture during the late nineteenth and early twentieth centuries.

Lowy, Dina, *The Japanese "New Woman": Images of Gender and Modernity*, Rutgers University Press, 2007.

> Lowy traces the New Woman movement in Japan, which paralleled the American New Woman movement. Lowy analyzes the differences in approaches to feminist thought advocated by the rival feminist organizations in Japan during the 1910s.

McDonnell, Patricia, ed., *On the Edge of Your Seat: Popular Theater and Film in Early Twentieth-Century American Art*, Yale University Press, 2002.

> McDonnell's volume includes images from theater and film along with a series of essays by various contributors examining films and plays from the 1890s through 1930. The focus of the work is on the popular entertainment of this era and how visual art in America was transformed during this time period.

SUGGESTED SEARCH TERMS

Jesse Lynch Williams AND Why Marry?

Jesse Lynch Willams AND feminism

New Woman movement

early twentieth-century feminism

American suffragist movement

early twentieth-century American theater

Jesse Lynch Williams AND comedy

Jesse Lynch Williams AND realism

marriage AND divorce AND early twentieth century

Glossary of Literary Terms

A

Abstract: Used as a noun, the term refers to a short summary or outline of a longer work. As an adjective applied to writing or literary works, abstract refers to words or phrases that name things not knowable through the five senses. Examples of abstracts include the *Cliffs Notes* summaries of major literary works. Examples of abstract terms or concepts include "idea," "guilt" "honesty," and "loyalty."

Absurd, Theater of the: See *Theater of the Absurd*

Absurdism: See *Theater of the Absurd*

Act: A major section of a play. Acts are divided into varying numbers of shorter scenes. From ancient times to the nineteenth century plays were generally constructed of five acts, but modern works typically consist of one, two, or three acts. Examples of five-act plays include the works of Sophocles and Shakespeare, while the plays of Arthur Miller commonly have a three-act structure.

Acto: A one-act Chicano theater piece developed out of collective improvisation. *Actos* were performed by members of Luis Valdez's Teatro Campesino in California during the mid-1960s.

Aestheticism: A literary and artistic movement of the nineteenth century. Followers of the movement believed that art should not be mixed with social, political, or moral teaching. The statement "art for art's sake" is a good summary of aestheticism. The movement had its roots in France, but it gained widespread importance in England in the last half of the nineteenth century, where it helped change the Victorian practice of including moral lessons in literature. Oscar Wilde is one of the best-known "aesthetes" of the late nineteenth century.

Age of Johnson: The period in English literature between 1750 and 1798, named after the most prominent literary figure of the age, Samuel Johnson. Works written during this time are noted for their emphasis on "sensibility," or emotional quality. These works formed a transition between the rational works of the Age of Reason, or Neoclassical period, and the emphasis on individual feelings and responses of the Romantic period. Significant writers during the Age of Johnson included the novelists Ann Radcliffe and Henry Mackenzie, dramatists Richard Sheridan and Oliver Goldsmith, and poets William Collins and Thomas Gray. Also known as Age of Sensibility

Age of Reason: See *Neoclassicism*

Age of Sensibility: See *Age of Johnson*

Alexandrine Meter: See *Meter*

Allegory: A narrative technique in which characters representing things or abstract ideas are used to convey a message or teach a lesson. Allegory is typically used to teach moral, ethical, or religious lessons but is sometimes used for satiric or political purposes. Examples of allegorical works include Edmund Spenser's *The Faerie Queene* and John Bunyan's *The Pilgrim's Progress.*

Allusion: A reference to a familiar literary or historical person or event, used to make an idea more easily understood. For example, describing someone as a "Romeo" makes an allusion to William Shakespeare's famous young lover in *Romeo and Juliet.*

Amerind Literature: The writing and oral traditions of Native Americans. Native American literature was originally passed on by word of mouth, so it consisted largely of stories and events that were easily memorized. Amerind prose is often rhythmic like poetry because it was recited to the beat of a ceremonial drum. Examples of Amerind literature include the autobiographical *Black Elk Speaks,* the works of N. Scott Momaday, James Welch, and Craig Lee Strete, and the poetry of Luci Tapahonso.

Analogy: A comparison of two things made to explain something unfamiliar through its similarities to something familiar, or to prove one point based on the acceptedness of another. Similes and metaphors are types of analogies. Analogies often take the form of an extended simile, as in William Blake's aphorism: "As the caterpillar chooses the fairest leaves to lay her eggs on, so the priest lays his curse on the fairest joys."

Angry Young Men: A group of British writers of the 1950s whose work expressed bitterness and disillusionment with society. Common to their work is an anti-hero who rebels against a corrupt social order and strives for personal integrity. The term has been used to describe Kingsley Amis, John Osborne, Colin Wilson, John Wain, and others.

Antagonist: The major character in a narrative or drama who works against the hero or protagonist. An example of an evil antagonist is Richard Lovelace in Samuel Richardson's *Clarissa,* while a virtuous antagonist is Macduff in William Shakespeare's *Macbeth.*

Anthropomorphism: The presentation of animals or objects in human shape or with human characteristics. The term is derived from the Greek word for "human form." The fables of Aesop, the animated films of Walt Disney, and Richard Adams's *Watership Down* feature anthropomorphic characters.

Anti-hero: A central character in a work of literature who lacks traditional heroic qualities such as courage, physical prowess, and fortitude. Anti-heros typically distrust conventional values and are unable to commit themselves to any ideals. They generally feel helpless in a world over which they have no control. Anti-heroes usually accept, and often celebrate, their positions as social outcasts. A well-known anti-hero is Yossarian in Joseph Heller's novel *Catch-22.*

Antimasque: See *Masque*

Antithesis: The antithesis of something is its direct opposite. In literature, the use of antithesis as a figure of speech results in two statements that show a contrast through the balancing of two opposite ideas. Technically, it is the second portion of the statement that is defined as the "antithesis"; the first portion is the "thesis." An example of antithesis is found in the following portion of Abraham Lincoln's "Gettysburg Address"; notice the opposition between the verbs "remember" and "forget" and the phrases "what we say" and "what they did": "The world will little note nor long remember what we say here, but it can never forget what they did here."

Apocrypha: Writings tentatively attributed to an author but not proven or universally accepted to be their works. The term was originally applied to certain books of the Bible that were not considered inspired and so were not included in the "sacred canon." Geoffrey Chaucer, William Shakespeare, Thomas Kyd, Thomas Middleton, and John Marston all have apocrypha. Apocryphal books of the Bible include the Old Testament's Book of Enoch and New Testament's Gospel of Peter.

Apollonian and Dionysian: The two impulses believed to guide authors of dramatic tragedy. The Apollonian impulse is named after Apollo, the Greek god of light and beauty and the symbol of intellectual order. The Dionysian impulse is named after Dionysus, the Greek god of wine and the symbol of the unrestrained forces of nature. The Apollonian impulse is to create a rational, harmonious world, while the

Dionysian is to express the irrational forces of personality. Friedrich Nietzche uses these terms in *The Birth of Tragedy* to designate contrasting elements in Greek tragedy.

Apostrophe: A statement, question, or request addressed to an inanimate object or concept or to a nonexistent or absent person. Requests for inspiration from the muses in poetry are examples of apostrophe, as is Marc Antony's address to Caesar's corpse in William Shakespeare's *Julius Caesar*: "O, pardon me, thou bleeding piece of earth, That I am meek and gentle with these butchers!... Woe to the hand that shed this costly blood!..."

Archetype: The word archetype is commonly used to describe an original pattern or model from which all other things of the same kind are made. This term was introduced to literary criticism from the psychology of Carl Jung. It expresses Jung's theory that behind every person's "unconscious," or repressed memories of the past, lies the "collective unconscious" of the human race: memories of the countless typical experiences of our ancestors. These memories are said to prompt illogical associations that trigger powerful emotions in the reader. Often, the emotional process is primitive, even primordial. Archetypes are the literary images that grow out of the "collective unconscious." They appear in literature as incidents and plots that repeat basic patterns of life. They may also appear as stereotyped characters. Examples of literary archetypes include themes such as birth and death and characters such as the Earth Mother.

Argument: The argument of a work is the author's subject matter or principal idea. Examples of defined "argument" portions of works include John Milton's *Arguments* to each of the books of *Paradise Lost* and the "Argument" to Robert Herrick's *Hesperides*.

Aristotelian Criticism: Specifically, the method of evaluating and analyzing tragedy formulated by the Greek philosopher Aristotle in his *Poetics*. More generally, the term indicates any form of criticism that follows Aristotle's views. Aristotelian criticism focuses on the form and logical structure of a work, apart from its historical or social context, in contrast to "Platonic Criticism," which

stresses the usefulness of art. Adherents of New Criticism including John Crowe Ransom and Cleanth Brooks utilize and value the basic ideas of Aristotelian criticism for textual analysis.

Art for Art's Sake: See *Aestheticism*

Aside: A comment made by a stage performer that is intended to be heard by the audience but supposedly not by other characters. Eugene O'Neill's *Strange Interlude* is an extended use of the aside in modern theater.

Audience: The people for whom a piece of literature is written. Authors usually write with a certain audience in mind, for example, children, members of a religious or ethnic group, or colleagues in a professional field. The term "audience" also applies to the people who gather to see or hear any performance, including plays, poetry readings, speeches, and concerts. Jane Austen's parody of the gothic novel, *Northanger Abbey*, was originally intended for (and also pokes fun at) an audience of young and avid female gothic novel readers.

Avant-garde: A French term meaning "vanguard." It is used in literary criticism to describe new writing that rejects traditional approaches to literature in favor of innovations in style or content. Twentieth-century examples of the literary *avant-garde* include the Black Mountain School of poets, the Bloomsbury Group, and the Beat Movement.

B

Ballad: A short poem that tells a simple story and has a repeated refrain. Ballads were originally intended to be sung. Early ballads, known as folk ballads, were passed down through generations, so their authors are often unknown. Later ballads composed by known authors are called literary ballads. An example of an anonymous folk ballad is "Edward," which dates from the Middle Ages. Samuel Taylor Coleridge's "The Rime of the Ancient Mariner" and John Keats's "La Belle Dame sans Merci" are examples of literary ballads.

Baroque: A term used in literary criticism to describe literature that is complex or ornate in style or diction. Baroque works typically express tension, anxiety, and violent emotion.

The term "Baroque Age" designates a period in Western European literature beginning in the late sixteenth century and ending about one hundred years later. Works of this period often mirror the qualities of works more generally associated with the label "baroque" and sometimes feature elaborate conceits. Examples of Baroque works include John Lyly's *Euphues: The Anatomy of Wit,* Luis de Gongora's *Soledads,* and William Shakespeare's *As You Like It.*

Baroque Age: See *Baroque*

Baroque Period: See *Baroque*

Beat Generation: See *Beat Movement*

Beat Movement: A period featuring a group of American poets and novelists of the 1950s and 1960s—including Jack Kerouac, Allen Ginsberg, Gregory Corso, William S. Burroughs, and Lawrence Ferlinghetti—who rejected established social and literary values. Using such techniques as stream of consciousness writing and jazz-influenced free verse and focusing on unusual or abnormal states of mind—generated by religious ecstasy or the use of drugs—the Beat writers aimed to create works that were unconventional in both form and subject matter. Kerouac's *On the Road* is perhaps the best-known example of a Beat Generation novel, and Ginsberg's *Howl* is a famous collection of Beat poetry.

Black Aesthetic Movement: A period of artistic and literary development among African Americans in the 1960s and early 1970s. This was the first major African-American artistic movement since the Harlem Renaissance and was closely paralleled by the civil rights and black power movements. The black aesthetic writers attempted to produce works of art that would be meaningful to the black masses. Key figures in black aesthetics included one of its founders, poet and playwright Amiri Baraka, formerly known as LeRoi Jones; poet and essayist Haki R. Madhubuti, formerly Don L. Lee; poet and playwright Sonia Sanchez; and dramatist Ed Bullins. Works representative of the Black Aesthetic Movement include Amiri Baraka's play *Dutchman,* a 1964 Obie award-winner; *Black Fire: An Anthology of Afro-American Writing,* edited by Baraka and playwright Larry Neal and published in 1968; and Sonia Sanchez's poetry collection

We a BaddDDD People, published in 1970. Also known as Black Arts Movement.

Black Arts Movement: See *Black Aesthetic Movement*

Black Comedy: See *Black Humor*

Black Humor: Writing that places grotesque elements side by side with humorous ones in an attempt to shock the reader, forcing him or her to laugh at the horrifying reality of a disordered world. Joseph Heller's novel *Catch-22* is considered a superb example of the use of black humor. Other well-known authors who use black humor include Kurt Vonnegut, Edward Albee, Eugene Ionesco, and Harold Pinter. Also known as Black Comedy.

Blank Verse: Loosely, any unrhymed poetry, but more generally, unrhymed iambic pentameter verse (composed of lines of five two-syllable feet with the first syllable accented, the second unaccented). Blank verse has been used by poets since the Renaissance for its flexibility and its graceful, dignified tone. John Milton's *Paradise Lost* is in blank verse, as are most of William Shakespeare's plays.

Bloomsbury Group: A group of English writers, artists, and intellectuals who held informal artistic and philosophical discussions in Bloomsbury, a district of London, from around 1907 to the early 1930s. The Bloomsbury Group held no uniform philosophical beliefs but did commonly express an aversion to moral prudery and a desire for greater social tolerance. At various times the circle included Virginia Woolf, E. M. Forster, Clive Bell, Lytton Strachey, and John Maynard Keynes.

Bon Mot: A French term meaning "good word." A *bon mot* is a witty remark or clever observation. Charles Lamb and Oscar Wilde are celebrated for their witty *bon mots.* Two examples by Oscar Wilde stand out: (1) "All women become their mothers. That is their tragedy. No man does. That's his." (2) "A man cannot be too careful in the choice of his enemies."

Breath Verse: See *Projective Verse*

Burlesque: Any literary work that uses exaggeration to make its subject appear ridiculous, either by treating a trivial subject with profound seriousness or by treating a dignified subject frivolously. The word "burlesque" may also be used as an adjective, as in "burlesque show," to mean "striptease act." Examples of literary burlesque include the comedies of Aristophanes, Miguel de Cervantes's *Don Quixote*, Samuel Butler's poem "Hudibras," and John Gay's play *The Beggar's Opera*.

C

Cadence: The natural rhythm of language caused by the alternation of accented and unaccented syllables. Much modern poetry—notably free verse—deliberately manipulates cadence to create complex rhythmic effects. James Macpherson's "Ossian poems" are richly cadenced, as is the poetry of the Symbolists, Walt Whitman, and Amy Lowell.

Caesura: A pause in a line of poetry, usually occurring near the middle. It typically corresponds to a break in the natural rhythm or sense of the line but is sometimes shifted to create special meanings or rhythmic effects. The opening line of Edgar Allan Poe's "The Raven" contains a caesura following "dreary": "Once upon a midnight dreary, while I pondered weak and weary...."

Canzone: A short Italian or Provencal lyric poem, commonly about love and often set to music. The *canzone* has no set form but typically contains five or six stanzas made up of seven to twenty lines of eleven syllables each. A shorter, five- to ten-line "envoy," or concluding stanza, completes the poem. Masters of the *canzone* form include Petrarch, Dante Alighieri, Torquato Tasso, and Guido Cavalcanti.

Carpe Diem: A Latin term meaning "seize the day." This is a traditional theme of poetry, especially lyrics. A *carpe diem* poem advises the reader or the person it addresses to live for today and enjoy the pleasures of the moment. Two celebrated *carpe diem* poems are Andrew Marvell's "To His Coy Mistress" and Robert Herrick's poem beginning "Gather ye rosebuds while ye may...."

Catharsis: The release or purging of unwanted emotions—specifically fear and pity—brought about by exposure to art. The term was first used by the Greek philosopher Aristotle in his *Poetics* to refer to the desired effect of tragedy on spectators. A famous example of catharsis is realized in Sophocles's *Oedipus Rex,* when Oedipus discovers that his wife, Jacosta, is his own mother and that the stranger he killed on the road was his own father.

Celtic Renaissance: A period of Irish literary and cultural history at the end of the nineteenth century. Followers of the movement aimed to create a romantic vision of Celtic myth and legend. The most significant works of the Celtic Renaissance typically present a dreamy, unreal world, usually in reaction against the reality of contemporary problems. William Butler Yeats's *The Wanderings of Oisin* is among the most significant works of the Celtic Renaissance. Also known as Celtic Twilight.

Celtic Twilight: See *Celtic Renaissance*

Character: Broadly speaking, a person in a literary work. The actions of characters are what constitute the plot of a story, novel, or poem. There are numerous types of characters, ranging from simple, stereotypical figures to intricate, multifaceted ones. In the techniques of anthropomorphism and personification, animals—and even places or things—can assume aspects of character. "Characterization" is the process by which an author creates vivid, believable characters in a work of art. This may be done in a variety of ways, including (1) direct description of the character by the narrator; (2) the direct presentation of the speech, thoughts, or actions of the character; and (3) the responses of other characters to the character. The term "character" also refers to a form originated by the ancient Greek writer Theophrastus that later became popular in the seventeenth and eighteenth centuries. It is a short essay or sketch of a person who prominently displays a specific attribute or quality, such as miserliness or ambition. Notable characters in literature include Oedipus Rex, Don Quixote de la Mancha, Macbeth, Candide, Hester Prynne, Ebenezer Scrooge, Huckleberry Finn, Jay Gatsby, Scarlett O'Hara, James Bond, and Kunta Kinte.

Characterization: See *Character*

Chorus: In ancient Greek drama, a group of actors who commented on and interpreted the unfolding action on the stage. Initially the chorus was a major component of the presentation, but over time it became less significant, with its numbers reduced and its role eventually limited to commentary between acts. By the sixteenth century the chorus—if employed at all—was typically a single person who provided a prologue and an epilogue and occasionally appeared between acts to introduce or underscore an important event. The chorus in William Shakespeare's *Henry V* functions in this way. Modern dramas rarely feature a chorus, but T. S. Eliot's *Murder in the Cathedral* and Arthur Miller's *A View from the Bridge* are notable exceptions. The Stage Manager in Thornton Wilder's *Our Town* performs a role similar to that of the chorus.

Chronicle: A record of events presented in chronological order. Although the scope and level of detail provided varies greatly among the chronicles surviving from ancient times, some, such as the *Anglo-Saxon Chronicle,* feature vivid descriptions and a lively recounting of events. During the Elizabethan Age, many dramas—appropriately called "chronicle plays"—were based on material from chronicles. Many of William Shakespeare's dramas of English history as well as Christopher Marlowe's *Edward II* are based in part on Raphael Holinshead's *Chronicles of England, Scotland, and Ireland.*

Classical: In its strictest definition in literary criticism, classicism refers to works of ancient Greek or Roman literature. The term may also be used to describe a literary work of recognized importance (a "classic") from any time period or literature that exhibits the traits of classicism. Classical authors from ancient Greek and Roman times include Juvenal and Homer. Examples of later works and authors now described as classical include French literature of the seventeenth century, Western novels of the nineteenth century, and American fiction of the mid-nineteenth century such as that written by James Fenimore Cooper and Mark Twain.

Classicism: A term used in literary criticism to describe critical doctrines that have their roots in ancient Greek and Roman literature, philosophy, and art. Works associated with classicism typically exhibit restraint on the part of the author, unity of design and purpose, clarity, simplicity, logical organi-

zation, and respect for tradition. Examples of literary classicism include Cicero's prose, the dramas of Pierre Corneille and Jean Racine, the poetry of John Dryden and Alexander Pope, and the writings of J. W. von Goethe, G. E. Lessing, and T. S. Eliot.

Climax: The turning point in a narrative, the moment when the conflict is at its most intense. Typically, the structure of stories, novels, and plays is one of rising action, in which tension builds to the climax, followed by falling action, in which tension lessens as the story moves to its conclusion. The climax in James Fenimore Cooper's *The Last of the Mohicans* occurs when Magua and his captive Cora are pursued to the edge of a cliff by Uncas. Magua kills Uncas but is subsequently killed by Hawkeye.

Colloquialism: A word, phrase, or form of pronunciation that is acceptable in casual conversation but not in formal, written communication. It is considered more acceptable than slang. An example of colloquialism can be found in Rudyard Kipling's *Barrack-room Ballads:* When 'Omer smote 'is bloomin' lyre He'd 'eard men sing by land and sea; An' what he thought 'e might require 'E went an' took—the same as me!

Comedy: One of two major types of drama, the other being tragedy. Its aim is to amuse, and it typically ends happily. Comedy assumes many forms, such as farce and burlesque, and uses a variety of techniques, from parody to satire. In a restricted sense the term comedy refers only to dramatic presentations, but in general usage it is commonly applied to nondramatic works as well. Examples of comedies range from the plays of Aristophanes, Terrence, and Plautus, Dante Alighieri's *The Divine Comedy,* Francois Rabelais's *Pantagruel* and *Gargantua,* and some of Geoffrey Chaucer's tales and William Shakespeare's plays to Noel Coward's play *Private Lives* and James Thurber's short story "The Secret Life of Walter Mitty."

Comedy of Manners: A play about the manners and conventions of an aristocratic, highly sophisticated society. The characters are usually types rather than individualized personalities, and plot is less important than atmosphere. Such plays were an important aspect of late seventeenth-century English comedy. The comedy of manners was revived in the eighteenth century by Oliver Goldsmith and Richard Brinsley Sheridan, enjoyed a second revival in the late nineteenth century, and has endured into the twentieth century. Examples of comedies of manners include William Congreve's *The Way of the World* in the late seventeenth century, Oliver Goldsmith's *She Stoops to Conquer* and Richard Brinsley Sheridan's *The School for Scandal* in the eighteenth century, Oscar Wilde's *The Importance of Being Earnest* in the nineteenth century, and W. Somerset Maugham's *The Circle* in the twentieth century.

Comic Relief: The use of humor to lighten the mood of a serious or tragic story, especially in plays. The technique is very common in Elizabethan works, and can be an integral part of the plot or simply a brief event designed to break the tension of the scene. The Gravediggers' scene in William Shakespeare's *Hamlet* is a frequently cited example of comic relief.

Commedia dell'arte: An Italian term meaning "the comedy of guilds" or "the comedy of professional actors." This form of dramatic comedy was popular in Italy during the sixteenth century. Actors were assigned stock roles (such as Pulcinella, the stupid servant, or Pantalone, the old merchant) and given a basic plot to follow, but all dialogue was improvised. The roles were rigidly typed and the plots were formulaic, usually revolving around young lovers who thwarted their elders and attained wealth and happiness. A rigid convention of the *commedia dell'arte* is the periodic intrusion of Harlequin, who interrupts the play with low buffoonery. Peppino de Filippo's *Metamorphoses of a Wandering Minstrel* gave modern audiences an idea of what *commedia dell'arte* may have been like. Various scenarios for *commedia dell'arte* were compiled in Petraccone's *La commedia dell'arte, storia, technica, scenari,* published in 1927.

Complaint: A lyric poem, popular in the Renaissance, in which the speaker expresses sorrow about his or her condition. Typically, the speaker's sadness is caused by an unresponsive lover, but some complaints cite other sources of unhappiness, such as poverty or fate. A commonly cited example is "A Complaint by Night of the Lover Not Beloved" by Henry Howard, Earl of Surrey. Thomas Sackville's "Complaint of Henry, Duke of Buckingham" traces the duke's unhappiness to his ruthless ambition.

Conceit: A clever and fanciful metaphor, usually expressed through elaborate and extended comparison, that presents a striking parallel between two seemingly dissimilar things—for example, elaborately comparing a beautiful woman to an object like a garden or the sun. The conceit was a popular device throughout the Elizabethan Age and Baroque Age and was the principal technique of the seventeenth-century English metaphysical poets. This usage of the word conceit is unrelated to the best-known definition of conceit as an arrogant attitude or behavior. The conceit figures prominently in the works of John Donne, Emily Dickinson, and T. S. Eliot.

Concrete: Concrete is the opposite of abstract, and refers to a thing that actually exists or a description that allows the reader to experience an object or concept with the senses. Henry David Thoreau's *Walden* contains much concrete description of nature and wildlife.

Concrete Poetry: Poetry in which visual elements play a large part in the poetic effect. Punctuation marks, letters, or words are arranged on a page to form a visual design: a cross, for example, or a bumblebee. Max Bill and Eugene Gomringer were among the early practitioners of concrete poetry; Haroldo de Campos and Augusto de Campos are among contemporary authors of concrete poetry.

Confessional Poetry: A form of poetry in which the poet reveals very personal, intimate, sometimes shocking information about himself or herself. Anne Sexton, Sylvia Plath, Robert Lowell, and John Berryman wrote poetry in the confessional vein.

Conflict: The conflict in a work of fiction is the issue to be resolved in the story. It usually occurs between two characters, the protagonist and the antagonist, or between the protagonist and society or the protagonist and himself or herself. Conflict in Theodore Dreiser's novel *Sister Carrie* comes as a result of urban society, while Jack London's short story "To Build a Fire" concerns the protagonist's battle against the cold and himself.

Connotation: The impression that a word gives beyond its defined meaning. Connotations may be universally understood or may be significant only to a certain group. Both "horse" and "steed" denote the same animal, but "steed" has a different connotation, deriving from the chivalrous or romantic narratives in which the word was once often used.

Consonance: Consonance occurs in poetry when words appearing at the ends of two or more verses have similar final consonant sounds but have final vowel sounds that differ, as with "stuff" and "off." Consonance is found in "The curfew tolls the knells of parting day" from Thomas Grey's "An Elegy Written in a Country Church Yard." Also known as Half Rhyme or Slant Rhyme.

Convention: Any widely accepted literary device, style, or form. A soliloquy, in which a character reveals to the audience his or her private thoughts, is an example of a dramatic convention.

Corrido: A Mexican ballad. Examples of *corridos* include "Muerte del afamado Bilito," "La voz de mi conciencia," "Lucio Perez," "La juida," and "Los presos."

Couplet: Two lines of poetry with the same rhyme and meter, often expressing a complete and self-contained thought. The following couplet is from Alexander Pope's "Elegy to the Memory of an Unfortunate Lady": 'Tis Use alone that sanctifies Expense, And Splendour borrows all her rays from Sense.

Criticism: The systematic study and evaluation of literary works, usually based on a specific method or set of principles. An important part of literary studies since ancient times, the practice of criticism has given rise to numerous theories, methods, and "schools," sometimes producing conflicting, even contradictory, interpretations of literature in general as well as of individual works. Even such basic issues as what constitutes a poem or a novel have been the subject of much criticism over the centuries. Seminal texts of literary criticism include Plato's *Republic,* Aristotle's *Poetics,* Sir Philip Sidney's *The Defence of Poesie,* John Dryden's *Of Dramatic Poesie,* and William Wordsworth's "Preface" to the second edition of his *Lyrical Ballads.* Contemporary schools of criticism include deconstruction, feminist, psychoanalytic, poststructuralist, new historicist, postcolonialist, and reader-response.

D

Dactyl: See *Foot*

Dadaism: A protest movement in art and literature founded by Tristan Tzara in 1916. Followers of the movement expressed their outrage at the destruction brought about by World War I by revolting against numerous forms of social convention. The Dadaists presented works marked by calculated madness and flamboyant nonsense. They stressed total freedom of expression, commonly through primitive displays of emotion and illogical, often senseless, poetry. The movement ended shortly after the war, when it was replaced by surrealism. Proponents of Dadaism include Andre Breton, Louis Aragon, Philippe Soupault, and Paul Eluard.

Decadent: See *Decadents*

Decadents: The followers of a nineteenth-century literary movement that had its beginnings in French aestheticism. Decadent literature displays a fascination with perverse and morbid states; a search for novelty and sensation—the "new thrill"; a preoccupation with mysticism; and a belief in the senselessness of human existence. The movement is closely associated with the doctrine Art for Art's Sake. The term "decadence" is sometimes used to denote a decline in the quality of art or literature following a period of greatness. Major French decadents are Charles Baudelaire and Arthur Rimbaud. English decadents include Oscar Wilde, Ernest Dowson, and Frank Harris.

Deconstruction: A method of literary criticism developed by Jacques Derrida and characterized by multiple conflicting interpretations of a given work. Deconstructionists consider the impact of the language of a work and suggest that the true meaning of the work is not necessarily the meaning that the author intended. Jacques Derrida's *De la grammatologie* is the seminal text on deconstructive strategies; among American practitioners of this method of criticism are Paul de Man and J. Hillis Miller.

Deduction: The process of reaching a conclusion through reasoning from general premises to a specific premise. An example of deduction is present in the following syllogism: Premise: All mammals are animals. Premise: All whales are mammals. Conclusion: Therefore, all whales are animals.

Denotation: The definition of a word, apart from the impressions or feelings it creates in the reader. The word "apartheid" denotes a political and economic policy of segregation by race, but its connotations—oppression, slavery, inequality—are numerous.

Denouement: A French word meaning "the unknotting." In literary criticism, it denotes the resolution of conflict in fiction or drama. The *denouement* follows the climax and provides an outcome to the primary plot situation as well as an explanation of secondary plot complications. The *denouement* often involves a character's recognition of his or her state of mind or moral condition. A well-known example of *denouement* is the last scene of the play *As You Like It* by William Shakespeare, in which couples are married, an evildoer repents, the identities of two disguised characters are revealed, and a ruler is restored to power. Also known as Falling Action.

Description: Descriptive writing is intended to allow a reader to picture the scene or setting in which the action of a story takes place. The form this description takes often evokes an intended emotional response—a dark, spooky graveyard will evoke fear, and a peaceful, sunny meadow will evoke calmness. An example of a descriptive story is Edgar Allan Poe's *Landor's Cottage,* which offers a detailed depiction of a New York country estate.

Detective Story: A narrative about the solution of a mystery or the identification of a criminal. The conventions of the detective story include the detective's scrupulous use of logic in solving the mystery; incompetent or ineffectual police; a suspect who appears guilty at first but is later proved innocent; and the detective's friend or confidant—often the narrator—whose slowness in interpreting clues emphasizes by contrast the detective's brilliance. Edgar Allan Poe's "Murders in the Rue Morgue" is commonly regarded as the earliest example of this type

of story. With this work, Poe established many of the conventions of the detective story genre, which are still in practice. Other practitioners of this vast and extremely popular genre include Arthur Conan Doyle, Dashiell Hammett, and Agatha Christie.

Deus ex machina: A Latin term meaning "god out of a machine." In Greek drama, a god was often lowered onto the stage by a mechanism of some kind to rescue the hero or untangle the plot. By extension, the term refers to any artificial device or coincidence used to bring about a convenient and simple solution to a plot. This is a common device in melodramas and includes such fortunate circumstances as the sudden receipt of a legacy to save the family farm or a last-minute stay of execution. The *deus ex machina* invariably rewards the virtuous and punishes evildoers. Examples of *deus ex machina* include King Louis XIV in Jean-Baptiste Moliere's *Tartuffe* and Queen Victoria in *The Pirates of Penzance* by William Gilbert and Arthur Sullivan. Bertolt Brecht parodies the abuse of such devices in the conclusion of his *Threepenny Opera.*

Dialogue: In its widest sense, dialogue is simply conversation between people in a literary work; in its most restricted sense, it refers specifically to the speech of characters in a drama. As a specific literary genre, a "dialogue" is a composition in which characters debate an issue or idea. The Greek philosopher Plato frequently expounded his theories in the form of dialogues.

Diction: The selection and arrangement of words in a literary work. Either or both may vary depending on the desired effect. There are four general types of diction: "formal," used in scholarly or lofty writing; "informal," used in relaxed but educated conversation; "colloquial," used in everyday speech; and "slang," containing newly coined words and other terms not accepted in formal usage.

Didactic: A term used to describe works of literature that aim to teach some moral, religious, political, or practical lesson. Although didactic elements are often found in artistically pleasing works, the term "didactic" usually refers to literature in which the message is more important than the form. The term may also be used to criticize a work that the critic finds "overly didactic," that is, heavy-handed in its delivery of a lesson. Examples of didactic literature include John Bunyan's *Pilgrim's Progress,* Alexander Pope's *Essay on Criticism,* Jean-Jacques Rousseau's *Emile,* and Elizabeth Inchbald's *Simple Story.*

Dimeter: See *Meter*

Dionysian: See *Apollonian and Dionysian*

Discordia concours: A Latin phrase meaning "discord in harmony." The term was coined by the eighteenth-century English writer Samuel Johnson to describe "a combination of dissimilar images or discovery of occult resemblances in things apparently unlike." Johnson created the expression by reversing a phrase by the Latin poet Horace. The metaphysical poetry of John Donne, Richard Crashaw, Abraham Cowley, George Herbert, and Edward Taylor among others, contains many examples of *discordia concours.* In Donne's "A Valediction: Forbidding Mourning," the poet compares the union of himself with his lover to a draftsman's compass: If they be two, they are two so, As stiff twin compasses are two: Thy soul, the fixed foot, makes no show To move, but doth, if the other do; And though it in the center sit, Yet when the other far doth roam, It leans, and hearkens after it, And grows erect, as that comes home.

Dissonance: A combination of harsh or jarring sounds, especially in poetry. Although such combinations may be accidental, poets sometimes intentionally make them to achieve particular effects. Dissonance is also sometimes used to refer to close but not identical rhymes. When this is the case, the word functions as a synonym for consonance. Robert Browning, Gerard Manley Hopkins, and many other poets have made deliberate use of dissonance.

Doppelganger: A literary technique by which a character is duplicated (usually in the form of an alter ego, though sometimes as a ghostly counterpart) or divided into two distinct, usually opposite personalities. The use of this character device is widespread in nineteenth- and twentieth- century literature, and indicates a growing awareness among authors that the "self" is really a composite of many "selves." A well-known story containing a *doppelganger* character is Robert Louis Stevenson's *Dr. Jekyll and Mr. Hyde,* which dramatizes an internal struggle between good and evil. Also known as The Double.

Double Entendre: A corruption of a French phrase meaning "double meaning." The term is used to indicate a word or phrase that is deliberately ambiguous, especially when one of the meanings is risque or improper. An example of a *double entendre* is the Elizabethan usage of the verb "die," which refers both to death and to orgasm.

Double, The: See *Doppelganger*

Draft: Any preliminary version of a written work. An author may write dozens of drafts which are revised to form the final work, or he or she may write only one, with few or no revisions. Dorothy Parker's observation that "I can't write five words but that I change seven" humorously indicates the purpose of the draft.

Drama: In its widest sense, a drama is any work designed to be presented by actors on a stage. Similarly, "drama" denotes a broad literary genre that includes a variety of forms, from pageant and spectacle to tragedy and comedy, as well as countless types and subtypes. More commonly in modern usage, however, a drama is a work that treats serious subjects and themes but does not aim at the grandeur of tragedy. This use of the term originated with the eighteenth-century French writer Denis Diderot, who used the word *drame* to designate his plays about middle- class life; thus "drama" typically features characters of a less exalted stature than those of tragedy. Examples of classical dramas include Menander's comedy *Dyscolus* and Sophocles' tragedy *Oedipus Rex.* Contemporary dramas include Eugene O'Neill's *The Iceman Cometh,* Lillian Hellman's *Little Foxes,* and August Wilson's *Ma Rainey's Black Bottom.*

Dramatic Irony: Occurs when the audience of a play or the reader of a work of literature knows something that a character in the work itself does not know. The irony is in the contrast between the intended meaning of the statements or actions of a character and the additional information understood by the audience. A celebrated example of dramatic irony is in Act V of William Shakespeare's *Romeo and Juliet,* where two young lovers meet their end as a result of a tragic misunderstanding. Here, the audience has full knowledge that Juliet's apparent "death" is merely temporary; she will regain her senses when the mysterious "sleeping potion" she has taken wears off. But Romeo, mistaking Juliet's drug-induced trance for true death, kills himself in grief. Upon awakening, Juliet discovers Romeo's corpse and, in despair, slays herself.

Dramatic Monologue: See *Monologue*

Dramatic Poetry: Any lyric work that employs elements of drama such as dialogue, conflict, or characterization, but excluding works that are intended for stage presentation. A monologue is a form of dramatic poetry.

Dramatis Personae: The characters in a work of literature, particularly a drama. The list of characters printed before the main text of a play or in the program is the *dramatis personae.*

Dream Allegory: See *Dream Vision*

Dream Vision: A literary convention, chiefly of the Middle Ages. In a dream vision a story is presented as a literal dream of the narrator. This device was commonly used to teach moral and religious lessons. Important works of this type are *The Divine Comedy* by Dante Alighieri, *Piers Plowman* by William Langland, and *The Pilgrim's Progress* by John Bunyan. Also known as Dream Allegory.

Dystopia: An imaginary place in a work of fiction where the characters lead dehumanized, fearful lives. Jack London's *The Iron Heel,* Yevgeny Zamyatin's *My,* Aldous Huxley's *Brave New World,* George Orwell's *Nineteen Eighty-four,* and Margaret Atwood's *Handmaid's Tale* portray versions of dystopia.

E

Eclogue: In classical literature, a poem featuring rural themes and structured as a dialogue among shepherds. Eclogues often took specific poetic forms, such as elegies or love poems. Some were written as the soliloquy of a shepherd. In later centuries, "eclogue" came to refer to any poem that was in the pastoral tradition or that had a dialogue or

monologue structure. A classical example of an eclogue is Virgil's *Eclogues,* also known as *Bucolics.* Giovanni Boccaccio, Edmund Spenser, Andrew Marvell, Jonathan Swift, and Louis MacNeice also wrote eclogues.

Edwardian: Describes cultural conventions identified with the period of the reign of Edward VII of England (1901-1910). Writers of the Edwardian Age typically displayed a strong reaction against the propriety and conservatism of the Victorian Age. Their work often exhibits distrust of authority in religion, politics, and art and expresses strong doubts about the soundness of conventional values. Writers of this era include George Bernard Shaw, H. G. Wells, and Joseph Conrad.

Edwardian Age: See *Edwardian*

Electra Complex: A daughter's amorous obsession with her father. The term Electra complex comes from the plays of Euripides and Sophocles entitled *Electra,* in which the character Electra drives her brother Orestes to kill their mother and her lover in revenge for the murder of their father.

Elegy: A lyric poem that laments the death of a person or the eventual death of all people. In a conventional elegy, set in a classical world, the poet and subject are spoken of as shepherds. In modern criticism, the word elegy is often used to refer to a poem that is melancholy or mournfully contemplative. John Milton's "Lycidas" and Percy Bysshe Shelley's "Adonais" are two examples of this form.

Elizabethan Age: A period of great economic growth, religious controversy, and nationalism closely associated with the reign of Elizabeth I of England (1558-1603). The Elizabethan Age is considered a part of the general renaissance—that is, the flowering of arts and literature—that took place in Europe during the fourteenth through sixteenth centuries. The era is considered the golden age of English literature. The most important dramas in English and a great deal of lyric poetry were produced during this period, and modern English criticism began around this time. The notable authors of the period—Philip Sidney, Edmund Spenser, Christopher Marlowe, William Shakespeare, Ben Jonson, Francis Bacon, and John Donne—are among the best in all of English literature.

Elizabethan Drama: English comic and tragic plays produced during the Renaissance, or more narrowly, those plays written during the last years of and few years after Queen Elizabeth's reign. William Shakespeare is considered an Elizabethan dramatist in the broader sense, although most of his work was produced during the reign of James I. Examples of Elizabethan comedies include John Lyly's *The Woman in the Moone*, Thomas Dekker's *The Roaring Girl, or, Moll Cut Purse*, and William Shakespeare's *Twelfth Night*. Examples of Elizabethan tragedies include William Shakespeare's *Antony and Cleopatra*, Thomas Kyd's *The Spanish Tragedy*, and John Webster's *The Tragedy of the Duchess of Malfi*.

Empathy: A sense of shared experience, including emotional and physical feelings, with someone or something other than oneself. Empathy is often used to describe the response of a reader to a literary character. An example of an empathic passage is William Shakespeare's description in his narrative poem *Venus and Adonis* of: the snail, whose tender horns being hit, Shrinks backward in his shelly cave with pain. Readers of Gerard Manley Hopkins's *The Windhover* may experience some of the physical sensations evoked in the description of the movement of the falcon.

English Sonnet: See *Sonnet*

Enjambment: The running over of the sense and structure of a line of verse or a couplet into the following verse or couplet. Andrew Marvell's "To His Coy Mistress" is structured as a series of enjambments, as in lines 11-12: "My vegetable love should grow/Vaster than empires and more slow."

Enlightenment, The: An eighteenth-century philosophical movement. It began in France but had a wide impact throughout Europe and America. Thinkers of the Enlightenment valued reason and believed that both the individual and society could achieve a state of perfection. Corresponding to this essentially humanist vision was a resistance to religious authority. Important figures of the Enlightenment were Denis Diderot and Voltaire in France, Edward Gibbon and David Hume in England, and Thomas Paine and Thomas Jefferson in the United States.

Epic: A long narrative poem about the adventures of a hero of great historic or legendary importance. The setting is vast and the action is often given cosmic significance through the intervention of supernatural forces such as gods, angels, or demons. Epics are typically written in a classical style of grand simplicity with elaborate metaphors and allusions that enhance the symbolic importance of a hero's adventures. Some well-known epics are Homer's *Iliad* and *Odyssey*, Virgil's *Aeneid*, and John Milton's *Paradise Lost*.

Epic Simile: See *Homeric Simile*

Epic Theater: A theory of theatrical presentation developed by twentieth-century German playwright Bertolt Brecht. Brecht created a type of drama that the audience could view with complete detachment. He used what he termed "alienation effects" to create an emotional distance between the audience and the action on stage. Among these effects are: short, self-contained scenes that keep the play from building to a cathartic climax; songs that comment on the action; and techniques of acting that prevent the actor from developing an emotional identity with his role. Besides the plays of Bertolt Brecht, other plays that utilize epic theater conventions include those of Georg Buchner, Frank Wedekind, Erwin Piscator, and Leopold Jessner.

Epigram: A saying that makes the speaker's point quickly and concisely. Samuel Taylor Coleridge wrote an epigram that neatly sums up the form: What is an Epigram? A Dwarfish whole, Its body brevity, and wit its soul.

Epilogue: A concluding statement or section of a literary work. In dramas, particularly those of the seventeenth and eighteenth centuries, the epilogue is a closing speech, often in verse, delivered by an actor at the end of a play and spoken directly to the audience. A famous epilogue is Puck's speech at the end of William Shakespeare's *A Midsummer Night's Dream*.

Epiphany: A sudden revelation of truth inspired by a seemingly trivial incident. The term was widely used by James Joyce in his critical writings, and the stories in Joyce's *Dubliners* are commonly called "epiphanies."

Episode: An incident that forms part of a story and is significantly related to it. Episodes may be either self-contained narratives or events that depend on a larger context for their sense and importance. Examples of episodes include the founding of Wilmington, Delaware in Charles Reade's *The Disinherited Heir* and the individual events comprising the picaresque novels and medieval romances.

Episodic Plot: See *Plot*

Epitaph: An inscription on a tomb or tombstone, or a verse written on the occasion of a person's death. Epitaphs may be serious or humorous. Dorothy Parker's epitaph reads, "I told you I was sick."

Epithalamion: A song or poem written to honor and commemorate a marriage ceremony. Famous examples include Edmund Spenser's "Epithalamion" and e. e. cummings's "Epithalamion." Also spelled Epithalamium.

Epithalamium: See *Epithalamion*

Epithet: A word or phrase, often disparaging or abusive, that expresses a character trait of someone or something. "The Napoleon of crime" is an epithet applied to Professor Moriarty, arch-rival of Sherlock Holmes in Arthur Conan Doyle's series of detective stories.

Exempla: See *Exemplum*

Exemplum: A tale with a moral message. This form of literary sermonizing flourished during the Middle Ages, when *exempla* appeared in collections known as "example-books." The works of Geoffrey Chaucer are full of *exempla*.

Existentialism: A predominantly twentieth-century philosophy concerned with the nature and perception of human existence. There are two major strains of existentialist thought: atheistic and Christian. Followers of atheistic existentialism believe that the individual is alone in a godless universe and that the basic human condition is one of suffering and loneliness. Nevertheless, because there are no fixed values, individuals can create their own characters—indeed, they can shape themselves—through the exercise of free will. The atheistic strain culminates in and is popularly associated with the works of Jean-Paul Sartre. The Christian existentialists, on the other hand, believe that only in God may people find freedom from life's anguish. The two strains hold certain beliefs in common: that existence cannot be fully understood or described through empirical effort; that anguish is a universal element of life; that individuals must bear responsibility for their actions; and that there is no common standard of behavior or perception for religious and ethical matters. Existentialist thought figures prominently in the works of such authors as Eugene Ionesco, Franz Kafka, Fyodor Dostoyevsky, Simone de Beauvoir, Samuel Beckett, and Albert Camus.

Expatriates: See *Expatriatism*

Expatriatism: The practice of leaving one's country to live for an extended period in another country. Literary expatriates include English poets Percy Bysshe Shelley and John Keats in Italy, Polish novelist Joseph Conrad in England, American writers Richard Wright, James Baldwin, Gertrude Stein, and Ernest Hemingway in France, and Trinidadian author Neil Bissondath in Canada.

Exposition: Writing intended to explain the nature of an idea, thing, or theme. Expository writing is often combined with description, narration, or argument. In dramatic writing, the exposition is the introductory material which presents the characters, setting, and tone of the play. An example of dramatic exposition occurs in many nineteenth-century drawing-room comedies in which the butler and the maid open the play with relevant talk about their master and mistress; in composition, exposition relays factual information, as in encyclopedia entries.

Expressionism: An indistinct literary term, originally used to describe an early twentieth-century school of German painting. The term applies to almost any mode of unconventional, highly subjective writing that distorts reality in some way. Advocates of Expressionism include dramatists George Kaiser, Ernst Toller, Luigi Pirandello, Federico Garcia Lorca, Eugene O'Neill, and Elmer Rice; poets George Heym, Ernst Stadler, August Stramm, Gottfried Benn, and Georg Trakl; and novelists Franz Kafka and James Joyce.

Extended Monologue: See *Monologue*

F

Fable: A prose or verse narrative intended to convey a moral. Animals or inanimate objects with human characteristics often serve as characters in fables. A famous fable is Aesop's "The Tortoise and the Hare."

Fairy Tales: Short narratives featuring mythical beings such as fairies, elves, and sprites. These tales originally belonged to the folklore of a particular nation or region, such as those collected in Germany by Jacob and Wilhelm Grimm. Two other celebrated writers of fairy tales are Hans Christian Andersen and Rudyard Kipling.

Falling Action: See *Denouement*

Fantasy: A literary form related to mythology and folklore. Fantasy literature is typically set in non-existent realms and features supernatural beings. Notable examples of fantasy literature are *The Lord of the Rings* by J. R. R. Tolkien and the Gormenghast trilogy by Mervyn Peake.

Farce: A type of comedy characterized by broad humor, outlandish incidents, and often vulgar subject matter. Much of the "comedy" in film and television could more accurately be described as farce.

Feet: See *Foot*

Feminine Rhyme: See *Rhyme*

Femme fatale: A French phrase with the literal translation "fatal woman." A *femme fatale* is a sensuous, alluring woman who often leads men into danger or trouble. A classic example of the *femme fatale* is the nameless character in Billy Wilder's *The Seven Year Itch,* portrayed by Marilyn Monroe in the film adaptation.

Fiction: Any story that is the product of imagination rather than a documentation of fact. characters and events in such narratives may be based in real life but their ultimate form and configuration is a creation of the author. Geoffrey Chaucer's *The Canterbury Tales,* Laurence Sterne's *Tristram Shandy,* and Margaret Mitchell's *Gone with the Wind* are examples of fiction.

Figurative Language: A technique in writing in which the author temporarily interrupts the order, construction, or meaning of the writing for a particular effect. This interruption takes the form of one or more figures of speech such as hyperbole, irony, or simile.

Figurative language is the opposite of literal language, in which every word is truthful, accurate, and free of exaggeration or embellishment. Examples of figurative language are tropes such as metaphor and rhetorical figures such as apostrophe.

Figures of Speech: Writing that differs from customary conventions for construction, meaning, order, or significance for the purpose of a special meaning or effect. There are two major types of figures of speech: rhetorical figures, which do not make changes in the meaning of the words, and tropes, which do. Types of figures of speech include simile, hyperbole, alliteration, and pun, among many others.

Fin de siecle: A French term meaning "end of the century." The term is used to denote the last decade of the nineteenth century, a transition period when writers and other artists abandoned old conventions and looked for new techniques and objectives. Two writers commonly associated with the *fin de siecle* mindset are Oscar Wilde and George Bernard Shaw.

First Person: See *Point of View*

Flashback: A device used in literature to present action that occurred before the beginning of the story. Flashbacks are often introduced as the dreams or recollections of one or more characters. Flashback techniques are often used in films, where they are typically set off by a gradual changing of one picture to another.

Foil: A character in a work of literature whose physical or psychological qualities contrast strongly with, and therefore highlight, the corresponding qualities of another character. In his Sherlock Holmes stories, Arthur Conan Doyle portrayed Dr. Watson as a man of normal habits and intelligence, making him a foil for the eccentric and wonderfully perceptive Sherlock Holmes.

Folk Ballad: See *Ballad*

Folklore: Traditions and myths preserved in a culture or group of people. Typically, these are passed on by word of mouth in various forms—such as legends, songs, and proverbs—or preserved in customs and ceremonies. This term was first used by W. J. Thoms in 1846. Sir James Frazer's *The Golden Bough* is the record of English folklore; myths about the frontier and the Old South exemplify American folklore.

Folktale: A story originating in oral tradition. Folktales fall into a variety of categories, including legends, ghost stories, fairy tales, fables, and anecdotes based on historical figures and events. Examples of folktales include Giambattista Basile's *The Pentamerone,* which contains the tales of Puss in Boots, Rapunzel, Cinderella, and Beauty and the Beast, and Joel Chandler Harris's Uncle Remus stories, which represent transplanted African folktales and American tales about the characters Mike Fink, Johnny Appleseed, Paul Bunyan, and Pecos Bill.

Foot: The smallest unit of rhythm in a line of poetry. In English-language poetry, a foot is typically one accented syllable combined with one or two unaccented syllables. There are many different types of feet. When the accent is on the second syllable of a two syllable word (con-*tort*), the foot is an "iamb"; the reverse accentual pattern (*tor* -ture) is a "trochee." Other feet that commonly occur in poetry in English are "anapest," two unaccented syllables followed by an accented syllable as in in-ter-*cept*, and "dactyl," an accented syllable followed by two unaccented syllables as in *su*-i-cide.

Foreshadowing: A device used in literature to create expectation or to set up an explanation of later developments. In Charles Dickens's *Great Expectations,* the graveyard encounter at the beginning of the novel between Pip and the escaped convict Magwitch foreshadows the baleful atmosphere and events that comprise much of the narrative.

Form: The pattern or construction of a work which identifies its genre and distinguishes it from other genres. Examples of forms include the different genres, such as the lyric form or the short story form, and various patterns for poetry, such as the verse form or the stanza form.

Formalism: In literary criticism, the belief that literature should follow prescribed rules of construction, such as those that govern the sonnet form. Examples of formalism are found in the work of the New Critics and structuralists.

Fourteener Meter: See *Meter*

Free Verse: Poetry that lacks regular metrical and rhyme patterns but that tries to capture the cadences of everyday speech. The form allows a poet to exploit a variety of rhythmical effects within a single poem. Free-verse techniques have been widely used in the twentieth century by such writers as Ezra Pound, T. S. Eliot, Carl Sandburg, and William Carlos Williams. Also known as *Vers libre.*

Futurism: A flamboyant literary and artistic movement that developed in France, Italy, and Russia from 1908 through the 1920s. Futurist theater and poetry abandoned traditional literary forms. In their place, followers of the movement attempted to achieve total freedom of expression through bizarre imagery and deformed or newly invented words. The Futurists were self-consciously modern artists who attempted to incorporate the appearances and sounds of modern life into their work. Futurist writers include Filippo Tommaso Marinetti, Wyndham Lewis, Guillaume Apollinaire, Velimir Khlebnikov, and Vladimir Mayakovsky.

G

Genre: A category of literary work. In critical theory, genre may refer to both the content of a given work—tragedy, comedy, pastoral—and to its form, such as poetry, novel, or drama. This term also refers to types of popular literature, as in the genres of science fiction or the detective story.

Genteel Tradition: A term coined by critic George Santayana to describe the literary practice of certain late nineteenth-century American writers, especially New Englanders. Followers of the Genteel Tradition emphasized conventionality in social, religious, moral, and literary standards. Some of the best-known writers of the Genteel Tradition are R. H. Stoddard and Bayard Taylor.

Gilded Age: A period in American history during the 1870s characterized by political corruption and materialism. A number of important novels of social and political criticism were written during this time. Examples of Gilded Age literature include Henry Adams's *Democracy* and F. Marion Crawford's *An American Politician.*

Gothic: See *Gothicism*

Gothicism: In literary criticism, works characterized by a taste for the medieval or morbidly attractive. A gothic novel prominently features elements of horror, the supernatural, gloom, and violence: clanking chains, terror, charnel houses, ghosts, medieval castles, and mysteriously slamming doors. The term "gothic novel" is also applied to novels that lack elements of the traditional Gothic setting but that create a similar atmosphere of terror or dread. Mary Shelley's *Frankenstein* is perhaps the best-known English work of this kind.

Gothic Novel: See *Gothicism*

Great Chain of Being: The belief that all things and creatures in nature are organized in a hierarchy from inanimate objects at the bottom to God at the top. This system of belief was popular in the seventeenth and eighteenth centuries. A summary of the concept of the great chain of being can be found in the first epistle of Alexander Pope's *An Essay on Man,* and more recently in Arthur O. Lovejoy's *The Great Chain of Being: A Study of the History of an Idea.*

Grotesque: In literary criticism, the subject matter of a work or a style of expression characterized by exaggeration, deformity, freakishness, and disorder. The grotesque often includes an element of comic absurdity. Early examples of literary grotesque include Francois Rabelais's *Pantagruel* and *Gargantua* and Thomas Nashe's *The Unfortunate Traveller,* while more recent examples can be found in the works of Edgar Allan Poe, Evelyn Waugh, Eudora Welty, Flannery O'Connor, Eugene Ionesco, Gunter Grass, Thomas Mann, Mervyn Peake, and Joseph Heller, among many others.

H

Haiku: The shortest form of Japanese poetry, constructed in three lines of five, seven, and five syllables respectively. The message of a *haiku* poem usually centers on some aspect of spirituality and provokes an emotional response in the reader. Early masters of *haiku* include Basho, Buson, Kobayashi Issa, and Masaoka Shiki. English writers of *haiku* include the Imagists, notably Ezra Pound, H. D., Amy Lowell, Carl Sandburg, and William Carlos Williams. Also known as *Hokku.*

Half Rhyme: See *Consonance*

Hamartia: In tragedy, the event or act that leads to the hero's or heroine's downfall. This term is often incorrectly used as a synonym for tragic flaw. In Richard Wright's *Native Son,* the act that seals Bigger Thomas's fate is his first impulsive murder.

Harlem Renaissance: The Harlem Renaissance of the 1920s is generally considered the first significant movement of black writers and artists in the United States. During this period, new and established black writers published more fiction and poetry than ever before, the first influential black literary journals were established, and black authors and artists received their first widespread recognition and serious critical appraisal. Among the major writers associated with this period are Claude McKay, Jean Toomer, Countee Cullen, Langston Hughes, Arna Bontemps, Nella Larsen, and Zora Neale Hurston. Works representative of the Harlem Renaissance include Arna Bontemps's poems "The Return" and "Golgotha Is a Mountain," Claude McKay's novel *Home to Harlem,* Nella Larsen's novel *Passing,* Langston Hughes's poem "The Negro Speaks of Rivers," and the journals *Crisis* and *Opportunity,* both founded during this period. Also known as Negro Renaissance and New Negro Movement.

Harlequin: A stock character of the *commedia dell'arte* who occasionally interrupted the action with silly antics. Harlequin first appeared on the English stage in John Day's *The Travailes of the Three English Brothers.* The San Francisco Mime Troupe is one of the few modern groups to adapt Harlequin to the needs of contemporary satire.

Hellenism: Imitation of ancient Greek thought or styles. Also, an approach to life that focuses on the growth and development of the intellect. "Hellenism" is sometimes used to refer to the belief that reason can be applied to examine all human experience. A cogent discussion of Hellenism can be found in Matthew Arnold's *Culture and Anarchy.*

Heptameter: See *Meter*

Hero/Heroine: The principal sympathetic character (male or female) in a literary work. Heroes and heroines typically exhibit admirable traits: idealism, courage, and integrity, for example. Famous heroes and heroines include Pip in Charles Dickens's *Great Expectations,* the anonymous narrator in Ralph Ellison's *Invisible Man,* and Sethe in Toni Morrison's *Beloved.*

Heroic Couplet: A rhyming couplet written in iambic pentameter (a verse with five iambic feet). The following lines by Alexander Pope are an example: "Truth guards the Poet, sanctifies the line,/ And makes Immortal, Verse as mean as mine."

Heroic Line: The meter and length of a line of verse in epic or heroic poetry. This varies by language and time period. For example, in English poetry, the heroic line is iambic pentameter (a verse with five iambic feet); in French, the alexandrine (a verse with six iambic feet); in classical literature, dactylic hexameter (a verse with six dactylic feet).

Heroine: See *Hero/Heroine*

Hexameter: See *Meter*

Historical Criticism: The study of a work based on its impact on the world of the time period in which it was written. Examples of postmodern historical criticism can be found in the work of Michel Foucault, Hayden White, Stephen Greenblatt, and Jonathan Goldberg.

Hokku: See *Haiku*

Holocaust: See *Holocaust Literature*

Holocaust Literature: Literature influenced by or written about the Holocaust of World War II. Such literature includes true stories of survival in concentration camps, escape, and life after the war, as well as fictional works and poetry. Representative works of Holocaust literature include Saul Bellow's *Mr. Sammler's Planet,* Anne Frank's *The Diary of a Young Girl,* Jerzy Kosinski's *The Painted Bird,* Arthur Miller's *Incident at Vichy,* Czeslaw Milosz's *Collected Poems,* William Styron's *Sophie's Choice,* and Art Spiegelman's *Maus.*

Homeric Simile: An elaborate, detailed comparison written as a simile many lines in length. An example of an epic simile from John Milton's *Paradise Lost* follows: Angel Forms, who lay entranced Thick as autumnal leaves that strow the brooks In Vallombrosa, where the Etrurian shades High over-arched embower; or scattered sedge Afloat, when with fierce winds Orion armed Hath vexed the Red-Sea coast, whose waves o'erthrew Busiris and his Memphian chivalry, While with perfidious hatred they pursued The sojourners of Goshen, who beheld From the safe shore their floating carcasses And broken chariot-wheels. Also known as Epic Simile.

Horatian Satire: See *Satire*

Humanism: A philosophy that places faith in the dignity of humankind and rejects the medieval perception of the individual as a weak, fallen creature. "Humanists" typically believe in the perfectibility of human nature and view reason and education as the means to that end. Humanist thought is represented in the works of Marsilio Ficino, Ludovico Castelvetro, Edmund Spenser, John Milton, Dean John Colet, Desiderius Erasmus, John Dryden, Alexander Pope, Matthew Arnold, and Irving Babbitt.

Humors: Mentions of the humors refer to the ancient Greek theory that a person's health and personality were determined by the balance of four basic fluids in the body: blood, phlegm, yellow bile, and black bile. A dominance of any fluid would cause extremes in behavior. An excess of blood created a sanguine person who was joyful, aggressive, and passionate; a phlegmatic person was shy, fearful, and sluggish; too much yellow bile led to a choleric temperament characterized by impatience, anger, bitterness, and stubbornness; and excessive black bile created melancholy, a state of laziness, gluttony, and lack of motivation. Literary treatment of the humors is exemplified by several characters in Ben Jonson's plays *Every Man in His Humour* and *Every Man out of His Humour.* Also spelled Humours.

Humours: See *Humors*

Hyperbole: In literary criticism, deliberate exaggeration used to achieve an effect. In William Shakespeare's *Macbeth,* Lady Macbeth hyperbolizes when she says, "All the perfumes of Arabia could not sweeten this little hand."

I

Iamb: See *Foot*

Idiom: A word construction or verbal expression closely associated with a given language. For example, in colloquial English the construction "how come" can be used instead of "why" to introduce a question. Similarly, "a piece of cake" is sometimes used to describe a task that is easily done.

Image: A concrete representation of an object or sensory experience. Typically, such a representation helps evoke the feelings associated with the object or experience itself. Images are either "literal" or "figurative." Literal images are especially concrete and involve little or no extension of the obvious meaning of the words used to express them. Figurative images do not follow the literal meaning of the words exactly. Images in literature are usually visual, but the term "image" can also refer to the representation of any sensory experience. In his poem "The Shepherd's Hour," Paul Verlaine presents the following image: "The Moon is red through horizon's fog;/ In a dancing mist the hazy meadow sleeps." The first line is broadly literal, while the second line involves turns of meaning associated with dancing and sleeping.

Imagery: The array of images in a literary work. Also, figurative language. William Butler Yeats's "The Second Coming" offers a powerful image of encroaching anarchy: Turning and turning in the widening gyre The falcon cannot hear the falconer; Things fall apart....

Imagism: An English and American poetry movement that flourished between 1908 and 1917. The Imagists used precise, clearly presented images in their works. They also used common, everyday speech and aimed for conciseness, concrete imagery, and the creation of new rhythms. Participants in the Imagist movement included Ezra Pound, H. D. (Hilda Doolittle), and Amy Lowell, among others.

In medias res: A Latin term meaning "in the middle of things." It refers to the technique of beginning a story at its midpoint and then using various flashback devices to reveal previous action. This technique originated in such epics as Virgil's *Aeneid.*

Induction: The process of reaching a conclusion by reasoning from specific premises to form a general premise. Also, an introductory portion of a work of literature, especially a play. Geoffrey Chaucer's "Prologue" to the *Canterbury Tales,* Thomas Sackville's "Induction" to *The Mirror of Magistrates,* and the opening scene in William Shakespeare's *The Taming of the Shrew* are examples of inductions to literary works.

Intentional Fallacy: The belief that judgments of a literary work based solely on an author's stated or implied intentions are false and misleading. Critics who believe in the concept of the intentional fallacy typically argue that the work itself is sufficient matter for interpretation, even though they may concede that an author's statement of purpose can be useful. Analysis of William Wordsworth's *Lyrical Ballads* based on the observations about poetry he makes in his "Preface" to the second edition of that work is an example of the intentional fallacy.

Interior Monologue: A narrative technique in which characters' thoughts are revealed in a way that appears to be uncontrolled by the author. The interior monologue typically aims to reveal the inner self of a character. It portrays emotional experiences as they occur at both a conscious and unconscious level. images are often used to represent sensations or emotions. One of the best-known interior monologues in English is the Molly Bloom section at the close of James Joyce's *Ulysses.* The interior monologue is also common in the works of Virginia Woolf.

Internal Rhyme: Rhyme that occurs within a single line of verse. An example is in the opening line of Edgar Allan Poe's "The Raven": "Once upon a midnight dreary, while I pondered weak and weary." Here, "dreary" and "weary" make an internal rhyme.

Irish Literary Renaissance: A late nineteenth- and early twentieth-century movement in Irish literature. Members of the movement aimed to reduce the influence of British culture in Ireland and create an Irish national literature. William Butler Yeats, George Moore, and Sean O'Casey are three of the best-known figures of the movement.

Irony: In literary criticism, the effect of language in which the intended meaning is the opposite of what is stated. The title of Jonathan Swift's "A Modest Proposal" is ironic because what Swift proposes in this essay is cannibalism—hardly "modest."

Italian Sonnet: See *Sonnet*

J

Jacobean Age: The period of the reign of James I of England (1603-1625). The early literature of this period reflected the worldview of the Elizabethan Age, but a darker, more cynical attitude steadily grew in the art and literature of the Jacobean Age. This was an important time for English drama and poetry. Milestones include William Shakespeare's tragedies, tragi-comedies, and sonnets; Ben Jonson's various dramas; and John Donne's metaphysical poetry.

Jargon: Language that is used or understood only by a select group of people. Jargon may refer to terminology used in a certain profession, such as computer jargon, or it may refer to any nonsensical language that is not understood by most people. Literary examples of jargon are Francois Villon's *Ballades en jargon,* which is composed in the secret language of the *coquillards,* and Anthony Burgess's *A Clockwork Orange,* narrated in the fictional characters' language of "Nadsat."

Juvenalian Satire: See *Satire*

K

Knickerbocker Group: A somewhat indistinct group of New York writers of the first half of the nineteenth century. Members of the group were linked only by location and a common theme: New York life. Two famous members of the Knickerbocker Group were Washington Irving and William Cullen Bryant. The group's name derives from Irving's *Knickerbocker's History of New York.*

L

Lais: See *Lay*

Lay: A song or simple narrative poem. The form originated in medieval France. Early French *lais* were often based on the Celtic legends and other tales sung by Breton minstrels—thus the name of the "Breton lay." In fourteenth-century England, the term "lay" was used to describe short narratives written in imitation of the Breton lays. The most notable of these is Geoffrey Chaucer's "The Minstrel's Tale."

Leitmotiv: See *Motif*

Literal Language: An author uses literal language when he or she writes without exaggerating or embellishing the subject matter and without any tools of figurative language. To say "He ran very quickly down the street" is to use literal language, whereas to say "He ran like a hare down the street" would be using figurative language.

Literary Ballad: See *Ballad*

Literature: Literature is broadly defined as any written or spoken material, but the term most often refers to creative works. Literature includes poetry, drama, fiction, and many kinds of nonfiction writing, as well as oral, dramatic, and broadcast compositions not necessarily preserved in a written format, such as films and television programs.

Lost Generation: A term first used by Gertrude Stein to describe the post-World War I generation of American writers: men and women haunted by a sense of betrayal and emptiness brought about by the destructiveness of the war. The term is commonly applied to Hart Crane, Ernest Hemingway, F. Scott Fitzgerald, and others.

Lyric Poetry: A poem expressing the subjective feelings and personal emotions of the poet. Such poetry is melodic, since it was originally accompanied by a lyre in recitals. Most Western poetry in the twentieth century may be classified as lyrical. Examples of lyric poetry include A. E. Housman's elegy "To an Athlete Dying Young," the odes of Pindar and Horace, Thomas Gray and William Collins, the sonnets of Sir Thomas Wyatt and Sir Philip Sidney, Elizabeth Barrett Browning and Rainer Maria Rilke, and a host of other forms in the poetry of William Blake and Christina Rossetti, among many others.

M

Mannerism: Exaggerated, artificial adherence to a literary manner or style. Also, a popular style of the visual arts of late sixteenth-century Europe that was marked by elongation of the human form and by intentional spatial distortion. Literary works that are self-consciously high-toned and artistic are often said to be "mannered." Authors of such works include Henry James and Gertrude Stein.

Masculine Rhyme: See *Rhyme*

Masque: A lavish and elaborate form of entertainment, often performed in royal courts, that emphasizes song, dance, and costumery. The Renaissance form of the masque grew out of the spectacles of masked figures common in medieval England and Europe. The masque reached its peak of popularity and development in seventeenth-century England, during the reigns of James I and, especially, of Charles I. Ben Jonson, the most significant masque writer, also created the "antimasque," which incorporates elements of humor and the grotesque into the traditional masque and achieved greater dramatic quality. Masque-like interludes appear in Edmund Spenser's *The Faerie Queene* and in William Shakespeare's *The Tempest.* One of the best-known English masques is John Milton's *Comus.*

Measure: The foot, verse, or time sequence used in a literary work, especially a poem. Measure is often used somewhat incorrectly as a synonym for meter.

Melodrama: A play in which the typical plot is a conflict between characters who personify extreme good and evil. Melodramas usually end happily and emphasize sensationalism. Other literary forms that use the same techniques are often labeled "melodramatic." The term was formerly used to describe a combination of drama and music; as such, it was synonymous with "opera." Augustin Daly's *Under the Gaslight* and Dion Boucicault's *The Octoroon, The Colleen Bawn,* and *The Poor of New York* are examples of melodramas. The most popular media for twentieth-century melodramas are motion pictures and television.

Metaphor: A figure of speech that expresses an idea through the image of another object. Metaphors suggest the essence of the first object by identifying it with certain qualities of the second object. An example is "But soft, what light through yonder window breaks?/ It is the east, and Juliet is the sun" in William Shakespeare's *Romeo and Juliet.*

Here, Juliet, the first object, is identified with qualities of the second object, the sun.

Metaphysical Conceit: See *Conceit*

Metaphysical Poetry: The body of poetry produced by a group of seventeenth-century English writers called the "Metaphysical Poets." The group includes John Donne and Andrew Marvell. The Metaphysical Poets made use of everyday speech, intellectual analysis, and unique imagery. They aimed to portray the ordinary conflicts and contradictions of life. Their poems often took the form of an argument, and many of them emphasize physical and religious love as well as the fleeting nature of life. Elaborate conceits are typical in metaphysical poetry. Marvell's "To His Coy Mistress" is a well-known example of a metaphysical poem.

Metaphysical Poets: See *Metaphysical Poetry*

Meter: In literary criticism, the repetition of sound patterns that creates a rhythm in poetry. The patterns are based on the number of syllables and the presence and absence of accents. The unit of rhythm in a line is called a foot. Types of meter are classified according to the number of feet in a line. These are the standard English lines: Monometer, one foot; Dimeter, two feet; Trimeter, three feet; Tetrameter, four feet; Pentameter, five feet; Hexameter, six feet (also called the Alexandrine); Heptameter, seven feet (also called the "Fourteener" when the feet are iambic). The most common English meter is the iambic pentameter, in which each line contains ten syllables, or five iambic feet, which individually are composed of an unstressed syllable followed by an accented syllable. Both of the following lines from Alfred, Lord Tennyson's "Ulysses" are written in iambic pentameter: Made weak by time and fate, but strong in will To strive, to seek, to find, and not to yield.

Mise en scene: The costumes, scenery, and other properties of a drama. Herbert Beerbohm Tree was renowned for the elaborate *mises en scene* of his lavish Shakespearean productions at His Majesty's Theatre between 1897 and 1915.

Modernism: Modern literary practices. Also, the principles of a literary school that lasted from roughly the beginning of the twentieth century until the end of World War II. Modernism is defined by its rejection of the literary conventions of the nineteenth century and by its opposition to conventional morality, taste, traditions, and economic values. Many writers are associated with the concepts of Modernism, including Albert Camus, Marcel Proust, D. H. Lawrence, W. H. Auden, Ernest Hemingway, William Faulkner, William Butler Yeats, Thomas Mann, Tennessee Williams, Eugene O'Neill, and James Joyce.

Monologue: A composition, written or oral, by a single individual. More specifically, a speech given by a single individual in a drama or other public entertainment. It has no set length, although it is usually several or more lines long. An example of an "extended monologue"—that is, a monologue of great length and seriousness—occurs in the one-act, one-character play *The Stronger* by August Strindberg.

Monometer: See *Meter*

Mood: The prevailing emotions of a work or of the author in his or her creation of the work. The mood of a work is not always what might be expected based on its subject matter. The poem "Dover Beach" by Matthew Arnold offers examples of two different moods originating from the same experience: watching the ocean at night. The mood of the first three lines—The sea is calm tonight The tide is full, the moon lies fair Upon the straights.... is in sharp contrast to the mood of the last three lines—And we are here as on a darkling plain Swept with confused alarms of struggle and flight, Where ignorant armies clash by night.

Motif: A theme, character type, image, metaphor, or other verbal element that recurs throughout a single work of literature or occurs in a number of different works over a period of time. For example, the various manifestations of the color white in Herman Melville's *Moby Dick* is a "specific" *motif,* while the trials of star-crossed lovers is a "conventional" *motif* from the literature of all periods. Also known as *Motiv* or *Leitmotiv.*

Motiv: See *Motif*

Muckrakers: An early twentieth-century group of American writers. Typically, their works

exposed the wrongdoings of big business and government in the United States. Upton Sinclair's *The Jungle* exemplifies the muckraking novel.

Muses: Nine Greek mythological goddesses, the daughters of Zeus and Mnemosyne (Memory). Each muse patronized a specific area of the liberal arts and sciences. Calliope presided over epic poetry, Clio over history, Erato over love poetry, Euterpe over music or lyric poetry, Melpomene over tragedy, Polyhymnia over hymns to the gods, Terpsichore over dance, Thalia over comedy, and Urania over astronomy. Poets and writers traditionally made appeals to the Muses for inspiration in their work. John Milton invokes the aid of a muse at the beginning of the first book of his *Paradise Lost:* Of Man's First disobedience, and the Fruit of the Forbidden Tree, whose mortal taste Brought Death into the World, and all our woe, With loss of Eden, till one greater Man Restore us, and regain the blissful Seat, Sing Heav'nly Muse, that on the secret top of Oreb, or of Sinai, didst inspire That Shepherd, who first taught the chosen Seed, In the Beginning how the Heav'ns and Earth Rose out of Chaos....

Mystery: See *Suspense*

Myth: An anonymous tale emerging from the traditional beliefs of a culture or social unit. Myths use supernatural explanations for natural phenomena. They may also explain cosmic issues like creation and death. Collections of myths, known as mythologies, are common to all cultures and nations, but the best-known myths belong to the Norse, Roman, and Greek mythologies. A famous myth is the story of Arachne, an arrogant young girl who challenged a goddess, Athena, to a weaving contest; when the girl won, Athena was enraged and turned Arachne into a spider, thus explaining the existence of spiders.

N

Narration: The telling of a series of events, real or invented. A narration may be either a simple narrative, in which the events are recounted chronologically, or a narrative with a plot, in which the account is given in a style reflecting the author's artistic concept of the story. Narration is sometimes used as a synonym for "storyline." The recounting of scary stories around a campfire is a form of narration.

Narrative: A verse or prose accounting of an event or sequence of events, real or invented. The term is also used as an adjective in the sense "method of narration." For example, in literary criticism, the expression "narrative technique" usually refers to the way the author structures and presents his or her story. Narratives range from the shortest accounts of events, as in Julius Caesar's remark, "I came, I saw, I conquered," to the longest historical or biographical works, as in Edward Gibbon's *The Decline and Fall of the Roman Empire,* as well as diaries, travelogues, novels, ballads, epics, short stories, and other fictional forms.

Narrative Poetry: A nondramatic poem in which the author tells a story. Such poems may be of any length or level of complexity. Epics such as *Beowulf* and ballads are forms of narrative poetry.

Narrator: The teller of a story. The narrator may be the author or a character in the story through whom the author speaks. Huckleberry Finn is the narrator of Mark Twain's *The Adventures of Huckleberry Finn.*

Naturalism: A literary movement of the late nineteenth and early twentieth centuries. The movement's major theorist, French novelist Emile Zola, envisioned a type of fiction that would examine human life with the objectivity of scientific inquiry. The Naturalists typically viewed human beings as either the products of "biological determinism," ruled by hereditary instincts and engaged in an endless struggle for survival, or as the products of "socioeconomic determinism," ruled by social and economic forces beyond their control. In their works, the Naturalists generally ignored the highest levels of society and focused on degradation: poverty, alcoholism, prostitution, insanity, and disease. Naturalism influenced authors throughout the world, including Henrik Ibsen and Thomas Hardy. In the United States, in particular, Naturalism had a profound impact. Among the authors who embraced its principles are Theodore Dreiser, Eugene O'Neill, Stephen Crane, Jack London, and Frank Norris.

Negritude: A literary movement based on the concept of a shared cultural bond on the part of black Africans, wherever they may be in the world. It traces its origins to the former French colonies of Africa and the Caribbean. Negritude poets, novelists, and essayists generally stress four points in their writings: One, black alienation from traditional African culture can lead to feelings of inferiority. Two, European colonialism and Western education should be resisted. Three, black Africans should seek to affirm and define their own identity. Four, African culture can and should be reclaimed. Many Negritude writers also claim that blacks can make unique contributions to the world, based on a heightened appreciation of nature, rhythm, and human emotions—aspects of life they say are not so highly valued in the materialistic and rationalistic West. Examples of Negritude literature include the poetry of both Senegalese Leopold Senghor in *Hosties noires* and Martiniquais Aime-Fernand Cesaire in *Return to My Native Land.*

Negro Renaissance: See *Harlem Renaissance*

Neoclassical Period: See *Neoclassicism*

Neoclassicism: In literary criticism, this term refers to the revival of the attitudes and styles of expression of classical literature. It is generally used to describe a period in European history beginning in the late seventeenth century and lasting until about 1800. In its purest form, Neoclassicism marked a return to order, proportion, restraint, logic, accuracy, and decorum. In England, where Neoclassicism perhaps was most popular, it reflected the influence of seventeenth- century French writers, especially dramatists. Neoclassical writers typically reacted against the intensity and enthusiasm of the Renaissance period. They wrote works that appealed to the intellect, using elevated language and classical literary forms such as satire and the ode. Neoclassical works were often governed by the classical goal of instruction. English neoclassicists included Alexander Pope, Jonathan Swift, Joseph Addison, Sir Richard Steele, John Gay, and Matthew Prior; French neoclassicists included Pierre Corneille and Jean-Baptiste Moliere. Also known as Age of Reason.

Neoclassicists: See *Neoclassicism*

New Criticism: A movement in literary criticism, dating from the late 1920s, that stressed close textual analysis in the interpretation of works of literature. The New Critics saw little merit in historical and biographical analysis. Rather, they aimed to examine the text alone, free from the question of how external events—biographical or otherwise—may have helped shape it. This predominantly American school was named "New Criticism" by one of its practitioners, John Crowe Ransom. Other important New Critics included Allen Tate, R. P. Blackmur, Robert Penn Warren, and Cleanth Brooks.

New Negro Movement: See *Harlem Renaissance*

Noble Savage: The idea that primitive man is noble and good but becomes evil and corrupted as he becomes civilized. The concept of the noble savage originated in the Renaissance period but is more closely identified with such later writers as Jean-Jacques Rousseau and Aphra Behn. First described in John Dryden's play *The Conquest of Granada,* the noble savage is portrayed by the various Native Americans in James Fenimore Cooper's "Leatherstocking Tales," by Queequeg, Daggoo, and Tashtego in Herman Melville's *Moby Dick,* and by John the Savage in Aldous Huxley's *Brave New World.*

O

Objective Correlative: An outward set of objects, a situation, or a chain of events corresponding to an inward experience and evoking this experience in the reader. The term frequently appears in modern criticism in discussions of authors' intended effects on the emotional responses of readers. This term was originally used by T. S. Eliot in his 1919 essay "Hamlet."

Objectivity: A quality in writing characterized by the absence of the author's opinion or feeling about the subject matter. Objectivity is an important factor in criticism. The novels of Henry James and, to a certain extent, the poems of John Larkin demonstrate objectivity, and it is central to John Keats's concept of "negative capability." Critical and journalistic writing usually are or attempt to be objective.

Occasional Verse: poetry written on the occasion of a significant historical or personal event.

Vers de societe is sometimes called occasional verse although it is of a less serious nature. Famous examples of occasional verse include Andrew Marvell's "Horatian Ode upon Cromwell's Return from England," Walt Whitman's "When Lilacs Last in the Dooryard Bloom'd"—written upon the death of Abraham Lincoln—and Edmund Spenser's commemoration of his wedding, "Epithalamion."

Octave: A poem or stanza composed of eight lines. The term octave most often represents the first eight lines of a Petrarchan sonnet. An example of an octave is taken from a translation of a Petrarchan sonnet by Sir Thomas Wyatt: The pillar perisht is whereto I leant, The strongest stay of mine unquiet mind; The like of it no man again can find, From East to West Still seeking though he went. To mind unhap! for hap away hath rent Of all my joy the very bark and rind; And I, alas, by chance am thus assigned Daily to mourn till death do it relent.

Ode: Name given to an extended lyric poem characterized by exalted emotion and dignified style. An ode usually concerns a single, serious theme. Most odes, but not all, are addressed to an object or individual. Odes are distinguished from other lyric poetic forms by their complex rhythmic and stanzaic patterns. An example of this form is John Keats's "Ode to a Nightingale."

Oedipus Complex: A son's amorous obsession with his mother. The phrase is derived from the story of the ancient Theban hero Oedipus, who unknowingly killed his father and married his mother. Literary occurrences of the Oedipus complex include Andre Gide's *Oedipe* and Jean Cocteau's *La Machine infernale,* as well as the most famous, Sophocles' *Oedipus Rex.*

Omniscience: See *Point of View*

Onomatopoeia: The use of words whose sounds express or suggest their meaning. In its simplest sense, onomatopoeia may be represented by words that mimic the sounds they denote such as "hiss" or "meow." At a more subtle level, the pattern and rhythm of sounds and rhymes of a line or poem may be onomatopoeic. A celebrated example of onomatopoeia is the repetition of the word "bells" in Edgar Allan Poe's poem "The Bells."

Opera: A type of stage performance, usually a drama, in which the dialogue is sung. Classic examples of opera include Giuseppi Verdi's *La traviata,* Giacomo Puccini's *La Boheme,* and Richard Wagner's *Tristan und Isolde.* Major twentieth-century contributors to the form include Richard Strauss and Alban Berg.

Operetta: A usually romantic comic opera. John Gay's *The Beggar's Opera,* Richard Sheridan's *The Duenna,* and numerous works by William Gilbert and Arthur Sullivan are examples of operettas.

Oral Tradition: See *Oral Transmission*

Oral Transmission: A process by which songs, ballads, folklore, and other material are transmitted by word of mouth. The tradition of oral transmission predates the written record systems of literate society. Oral transmission preserves material sometimes over generations, although often with variations. Memory plays a large part in the recitation and preservation of orally transmitted material. Breton lays, French *fabliaux,* national epics (including the Anglo-Saxon *Beowulf,* the Spanish *El Cid,* and the Finnish *Kalevala*), Native American myths and legends, and African folktales told by plantation slaves are examples of orally transmitted literature.

Oration: Formal speaking intended to motivate the listeners to some action or feeling. Such public speaking was much more common before the development of timely printed communication such as newspapers. Famous examples of oration include Abraham Lincoln's "Gettysburg Address" and Dr. Martin Luther King Jr.'s "I Have a Dream" speech.

Ottava Rima: An eight-line stanza of poetry composed in iambic pentameter (a five-foot line in which each foot consists of an unaccented syllable followed by an accented syllable), following the abababcc rhyme scheme. This form has been prominently used by such important English writers as Lord Byron, Henry Wadsworth Longfellow, and W. B. Yeats.

Oxymoron: A phrase combining two contradictory terms. Oxymorons may be intentional or unintentional. The following speech from William Shakespeare's *Romeo and Juliet* uses several oxymorons: Why, then, O brawling love! O loving hate! O anything, of nothing first create! O heavy lightness! serious vanity! Mis-shapen chaos of well-seeming forms! Feather of lead, bright smoke, cold fire, sick health! This love feel I, that feel no love in this.

P

Pantheism: The idea that all things are both a manifestation or revelation of God and a part of God at the same time. Pantheism was a common attitude in the early societies of Egypt, India, and Greece—the term derives from the Greek *pan* meaning "all" and *theos* meaning "deity." It later became a significant part of the Christian faith. William Wordsworth and Ralph Waldo Emerson are among the many writers who have expressed the pantheistic attitude in their works.

Parable: A story intended to teach a moral lesson or answer an ethical question. In the West, the best examples of parables are those of Jesus Christ in the New Testament, notably "The Prodigal Son," but parables also are used in Sufism, rabbinic literature, Hasidism, and Zen Buddhism.

Paradox: A statement that appears illogical or contradictory at first, but may actually point to an underlying truth. "Less is more" is an example of a paradox. Literary examples include Francis Bacon's statement, "The most corrected copies are commonly the least correct," and "All animals are equal, but some animals are more equal than others" from George Orwell's *Animal Farm.*

Parallelism: A method of comparison of two ideas in which each is developed in the same grammatical structure. Ralph Waldo Emerson's "Civilization" contains this example of parallelism: Raphael paints wisdom; Handel sings it, Phidias carves it, Shakespeare writes it, Wren builds it, Columbus sails it, Luther preaches it, Washington arms it, Watt mechanizes it.

Parnassianism: A mid nineteenth-century movement in French literature. Followers of the movement stressed adherence to well-defined artistic forms as a reaction against the often chaotic expression of the artist's ego that dominated the work of the

Romantics. The Parnassians also rejected the moral, ethical, and social themes exhibited in the works of French Romantics such as Victor Hugo. The aesthetic doctrines of the Parnassians strongly influenced the later symbolist and decadent movements. Members of the Parnassian school include Leconte de Lisle, Sully Prudhomme, Albert Glatigny, Francois Coppee, and Theodore de Banville.

Parody: In literary criticism, this term refers to an imitation of a serious literary work or the signature style of a particular author in a ridiculous manner. A typical parody adopts the style of the original and applies it to an inappropriate subject for humorous effect. Parody is a form of satire and could be considered the literary equivalent of a caricature or cartoon. Henry Fielding's *Shamela* is a parody of Samuel Richardson's *Pamela*.

Pastoral: A term derived from the Latin word "pastor," meaning shepherd. A pastoral is a literary composition on a rural theme. The conventions of the pastoral were originated by the third-century Greek poet Theocritus, who wrote about the experiences, love affairs, and pastimes of Sicilian shepherds. In a pastoral, characters and language of a courtly nature are often placed in a simple setting. The term pastoral is also used to classify dramas, elegies, and lyrics that exhibit the use of country settings and shepherd characters. Percy Bysshe Shelley's "Adonais" and John Milton's "Lycidas" are two famous examples of pastorals.

Pastorela: The Spanish name for the shepherds play, a folk drama reenacted during the Christmas season. Examples of *pastorelas* include Gomez Manrique's *Representacion del nacimiento* and the dramas of Lucas Fernandez and Juan del Encina.

Pathetic Fallacy: A term coined by English critic John Ruskin to identify writing that falsely endows nonhuman things with human intentions and feelings, such as "angry clouds" and "sad trees." The pathetic fallacy is a required convention in the classical poetic form of the pastoral elegy, and it is used in the modern poetry of T. S. Eliot, Ezra Pound, and the Imagists. Also known as Poetic Fallacy.

Pelado: Literally the "skinned one" or shirtless one, he was the stock underdog, sharp-witted picaresque character of Mexican vaudeville and tent shows. The *pelado* is found in such works as Don Catarino's *Los effectos de la crisis* and *Regreso a mi tierra*.

Pen Name: See *Pseudonym*

Pentameter: See *Meter*

Persona: A Latin term meaning "mask." *Personae* are the characters in a fictional work of literature. The *persona* generally functions as a mask through which the author tells a story in a voice other than his or her own. A *persona* is usually either a character in a story who acts as a narrator or an "implied author," a voice created by the author to act as the narrator for himself or herself. *Personae* include the narrator of Geoffrey Chaucer's *Canterbury Tales* and Marlow in Joseph Conrad's *Heart of Darkness*.

Personae: See *Persona*

Personal Point of View: See *Point of View*

Personification: A figure of speech that gives human qualities to abstract ideas, animals, and inanimate objects. William Shakespeare used personification in *Romeo and Juliet* in the lines "Arise, fair sun, and kill the envious moon,/ Who is already sick and pale with grief." Here, the moon is portrayed as being envious, sick, and pale with grief—all markedly human qualities. Also known as *Prosopopoeia*.

Petrarchan Sonnet: See *Sonnet*

Phenomenology: A method of literary criticism based on the belief that things have no existence outside of human consciousness or awareness. Proponents of this theory believe that art is a process that takes place in the mind of the observer as he or she contemplates an object rather than a quality of the object itself. Among phenomenological critics are Edmund Husserl, George Poulet, Marcel Raymond, and Roman Ingarden.

Picaresque Novel: Episodic fiction depicting the adventures of a roguish central character ("picaro" is Spanish for "rogue"). The picaresque hero is commonly a low-born but clever individual who wanders into and out of various affairs of love, danger, and farcical intrigue. These involvements may take place at all social levels and typically present a humorous and wide-ranging satire of a given society. Prominent examples of the picaresque novel are *Don Quixote* by Miguel de Cervantes, *Tom Jones* by Henry Fielding, and *Moll Flanders* by Daniel Defoe.

Plagiarism: Claiming another person's written material as one's own. Plagiarism can take the form of direct, word-for-word copying or the theft of the substance or idea of the work. A student who copies an encyclopedia entry and turns it in as a report for school is guilty of plagiarism.

Platonic Criticism: A form of criticism that stresses an artistic work's usefulness as an agent of social engineering rather than any quality or value of the work itself. Platonic criticism takes as its starting point the ancient Greek philosopher Plato's comments on art in his *Republic*.

Platonism: The embracing of the doctrines of the philosopher Plato, popular among the poets of the Renaissance and the Romantic period. Platonism is more flexible than Aristotelian Criticism and places more emphasis on the supernatural and unknown aspects of life. Platonism is expressed in the love poetry of the Renaissance, the fourth book of Baldassare Castiglione's *The Book of the Courtier,* and the poetry of William Blake, William Wordsworth, Percy Bysshe Shelley, Friedrich Holderlin, William Butler Yeats, and Wallace Stevens.

Play: See *Drama*

Plot: In literary criticism, this term refers to the pattern of events in a narrative or drama. In its simplest sense, the plot guides the author in composing the work and helps the reader follow the work. Typically, plots exhibit causality and unity and have a beginning, a middle, and an end. Sometimes, however, a plot may consist of a series of disconnected events, in which case it is known as an "episodic plot." In his *Aspects of the Novel,* E. M. Forster distinguishes between a story, defined as a "narrative of events arranged in their time- sequence," and plot, which organizes the events to a "sense of causality." This definition closely mirrors Aristotle's discussion of plot in his *Poetics.*

Poem: In its broadest sense, a composition utilizing rhyme, meter, concrete detail, and expressive language to create a literary experience with emotional and aesthetic appeal. Typical poems include sonnets, odes, elegies, *haiku,* ballads, and free verse.

Poet: An author who writes poetry or verse. The term is also used to refer to an artist or writer who has an exceptional gift for expression, imagination, and energy in the making of art in any form. Well-known poets include Horace, Basho, Sir Philip Sidney, Sir Edmund Spenser, John Donne, Andrew Marvell, Alexander Pope, Jonathan Swift, George Gordon, Lord Byron, John Keats, Christina Rossetti, W. H. Auden, Stevie Smith, and Sylvia Plath.

Poetic Fallacy: See *Pathetic Fallacy*

Poetic Justice: An outcome in a literary work, not necessarily a poem, in which the good are rewarded and the evil are punished, especially in ways that particularly fit their virtues or crimes. For example, a murderer may himself be murdered, or a thief will find himself penniless.

Poetic License: Distortions of fact and literary convention made by a writer—not always a poet—for the sake of the effect gained. Poetic license is closely related to the concept of "artistic freedom." An author exercises poetic license by saying that a pile of money "reaches as high as a mountain" when the pile is actually only a foot or two high.

Poetics: This term has two closely related meanings. It denotes (1) an aesthetic theory in literary criticism about the essence of poetry or (2) rules prescribing the proper methods, content, style, or diction of poetry. The term poetics may also refer to theories about literature in general, not just poetry.

Poetry: In its broadest sense, writing that aims to present ideas and evoke an emotional experience in the reader through the use of meter, imagery, connotative and concrete words, and a carefully constructed structure based on rhythmic patterns. Poetry typically relies on words and expressions that have several layers of meaning. It also makes use of the effects of regular rhythm on the ear and may make a strong appeal to the senses through the use of imagery. Edgar Allan Poe's "Annabel Lee" and Walt Whitman's *Leaves of Grass* are famous examples of poetry.

Point of View: The narrative perspective from which a literary work is presented to the reader. There are four traditional points of view. The "third person omniscient" gives the reader a "godlike" perspective, unrestricted by time or place, from which to see actions and look into the minds of characters. This allows the author to comment openly on characters and events in the work. The "third person" point of view presents the events of the story from outside of any single character's perception, much like the omniscient point of view, but the reader must understand the action as it takes place and without any special insight into characters' minds or motivations. The "first person" or "personal" point of view relates events as they are perceived by a single character. The main character "tells" the story and may offer opinions about the action and characters which differ from those of the author. Much less common than omniscient, third person, and first person is the "second person" point of view, wherein the author tells the story as if it is happening to the reader. James Thurber employs the omniscient point of view in his short story "The Secret Life of Walter Mitty." Ernest Hemingway's "A Clean, Well-Lighted Place" is a short story told from the third person point of view. Mark Twain's novel *Huck Finn* is presented from the first person viewpoint. Jay McInerney's *Bright Lights, Big City* is an example of a novel which uses the second person point of view.

Polemic: A work in which the author takes a stand on a controversial subject, such as abortion or religion. Such works are often extremely argumentative or provocative. Classic examples of polemics include John Milton's *Aeropagitica* and Thomas Paine's *The American Crisis.*

Pornography: Writing intended to provoke feelings of lust in the reader. Such works are often condemned by critics and teachers, but those which can be shown to have literary value are viewed less harshly. Literary works that have been described as pornographic include Ovid's *The Art of Love,* Margaret of Angouleme's *Heptameron,* John Cleland's *Memoirs of a Woman of Pleasure; or, the Life of Fanny Hill,* the anonymous *My Secret Life,* D. H. Lawrence's *Lady Chatterley's Lover,* and Vladimir Nabokov's *Lolita.*

Post-Aesthetic Movement: An artistic response made by African Americans to the black aesthetic movement of the 1960s and early '70s. Writers since that time have adopted a somewhat different tone in their work, with less emphasis placed on the disparity between black and white in the United States. In the words of post-aesthetic authors such as Toni Morrison, John Edgar Wideman, and Kristin Hunter, African Americans are portrayed as looking inward for answers to their own questions, rather than always looking to the outside world. Two well-known examples of works produced as part of the post-aesthetic movement are the Pulitzer Prize-winning novels *The Color Purple* by Alice Walker and *Beloved* by Toni Morrison.

Postmodernism: Writing from the 1960s forward characterized by experimentation and continuing to apply some of the fundamentals of modernism, which included existentialism and alienation. Postmodernists have gone a step further in the rejection of tradition begun with the modernists by also rejecting traditional forms, preferring the anti-novel over the novel and the anti-hero over the hero. Postmodern writers include Alain Robbe-Grillet, Thomas Pynchon, Margaret Drabble, John Fowles, Adolfo Bioy-Casares, and Gabriel Garcia Marquez.

Pre-Raphaelites: A circle of writers and artists in mid nineteenth-century England. Valuing the pre-Renaissance artistic qualities of religious symbolism, lavish pictorialism, and natural sensuousness, the Pre-Raphaelites cultivated a sense of mystery and melancholy that influenced later writers associated with the Symbolist and Decadent movements. The major members of the group include Dante Gabriel Rossetti, Christina Rossetti, Algernon Swinburne, and Walter Pater.

Primitivism: The belief that primitive peoples were nobler and less flawed than civilized peoples because they had not been subjected to the tainting influence of society. Examples of literature espousing primitivism include Aphra Behn's *Oroonoko: Or, The History of the Royal Slave,* Jean-Jacques Rousseau's *Julie ou la Nouvelle Heloise,* Oliver Goldsmith's *The Deserted Village,* the poems of Robert Burns, Herman Melville's stories *Typee, Omoo,* and *Mardi,* many poems of William Butler Yeats and Robert Frost, and William Golding's novel *Lord of the Flies.*

Projective Verse: A form of free verse in which the poet's breathing pattern determines the lines of the poem. Poets who advocate projective verse are against all formal structures in writing, including meter and form. Besides its creators, Robert Creeley, Robert Duncan, and Charles Olson, two other well-known projective verse poets are Denise Levertov and LeRoi Jones (Amiri Baraka). Also known as Breath Verse.

Prologue: An introductory section of a literary work. It often contains information establishing the situation of the characters or presents information about the setting, time period, or action. In drama, the prologue is spoken by a chorus or by one of the principal characters. In the "General Prologue" of *The Canterbury Tales,* Geoffrey Chaucer describes the main characters and establishes the setting and purpose of the work.

Prose: A literary medium that attempts to mirror the language of everyday speech. It is distinguished from poetry by its use of unmetered, unrhymed language consisting of logically related sentences. Prose is usually grouped into paragraphs that form a cohesive whole such as an essay or a novel. Recognized masters of English prose writing include Sir Thomas Malory, William Caxton, Raphael Holinshed, Joseph Addison, Mark Twain, and Ernest Hemingway.

Prosopopoeia: See *Personification*

Protagonist: The central character of a story who serves as a focus for its themes and incidents and as the principal rationale for its development. The protagonist is sometimes referred to in discussions of modern literature as the hero or anti-hero. Well-known protagonists are Hamlet in William Shakespeare's *Hamlet* and Jay Gatsby in F. Scott Fitzgerald's *The Great Gatsby.*

Protest Fiction: Protest fiction has as its primary purpose the protesting of some social injustice, such as racism or discrimination. One example of protest fiction is a series of five novels by Chester Himes, beginning in 1945 with *If He Hollers Let Him Go* and ending in 1955 with *The Primitive.* These works depict the destructive effects of race and gender stereotyping in the context of interracial relationships. Another African American author whose works often revolve around themes of social protest is John Oliver Killens. James Baldwin's essay "Everybody's Protest Novel" generated controversy by attacking the authors of protest fiction.

Proverb: A brief, sage saying that expresses a truth about life in a striking manner. "They are not all cooks who carry long knives" is an example of a proverb.

Pseudonym: A name assumed by a writer, most often intended to prevent his or her identification as the author of a work. Two or more authors may work together under one pseudonym, or an author may use a different name for each genre he or she publishes in. Some publishing companies maintain "house pseudonyms," under which any number of authors may write installments in a series. Some authors also choose a pseudonym over their real names the way an actor may use a stage name. Examples of pseudonyms (with the author's real name in parentheses) include Voltaire (Francois-Marie Arouet), Novalis (Friedrich von Hardenberg), Currer Bell (Charlotte Bronte), Ellis Bell (Emily Bronte), George Eliot (Maryann Evans), Honorio Bustos Donmecq (Adolfo Bioy-Casares and Jorge Luis Borges), and Richard Bachman (Stephen King).

Pun: A play on words that have similar sounds but different meanings. A serious example of the pun is from John Donne's "A Hymne to God the Father": Sweare by thyself, that at my death thy sonne Shall shine as he shines now, and hereto fore; And, having done that, Thou haste done; I fear no more.

Pure Poetry: poetry written without instructional intent or moral purpose that aims only to please a reader by its imagery or musical flow. The term pure poetry is used as the antonym of the term "didacticism." The poetry of Edgar Allan Poe, Stephane Mallarme, Paul Verlaine, Paul Valery, Juan Ramoz Jimenez, and Jorge Guillen offer examples of pure poetry.

Q

Quatrain: A four-line stanza of a poem or an entire poem consisting of four lines. The following quatrain is from Robert Herrick's

"To Live Merrily, and to Trust to Good Verses": Round, round, the root do's run; And being ravisht thus, Come, I will drink a Tun To my *Propertius*.

R

Raisonneur: A character in a drama who functions as a spokesperson for the dramatist's views. The *raisonneur* typically observes the play without becoming central to its action. *Raisonneurs* were very common in plays of the nineteenth century.

Realism: A nineteenth-century European literary movement that sought to portray familiar characters, situations, and settings in a realistic manner. This was done primarily by using an objective narrative point of view and through the buildup of accurate detail. The standard for success of any realistic work depends on how faithfully it transfers common experience into fictional forms. The realistic method may be altered or extended, as in stream of consciousness writing, to record highly subjective experience. Seminal authors in the tradition of Realism include Honore de Balzac, Gustave Flaubert, and Henry James.

Refrain: A phrase repeated at intervals throughout a poem. A refrain may appear at the end of each stanza or at less regular intervals. It may be altered slightly at each appearance. Some refrains are nonsense expressions—as with "Nevermore" in Edgar Allan Poe's "The Raven"—that seem to take on a different significance with each use.

Renaissance: The period in European history that marked the end of the Middle Ages. It began in Italy in the late fourteenth century. In broad terms, it is usually seen as spanning the fourteenth, fifteenth, and sixteenth centuries, although it did not reach Great Britain, for example, until the 1480s or so. The Renaissance saw an awakening in almost every sphere of human activity, especially science, philosophy, and the arts. The period is best defined by the emergence of a general philosophy that emphasized the importance of the intellect, the individual, and world affairs. It contrasts strongly with the medieval worldview, characterized by the dominant concerns of faith, the social collective, and spiritual salvation. Prominent writers during the Renaissance include Niccolo Machiavelli and Baldassare Castiglione in Italy, Miguel de Cervantes and Lope de Vega in Spain, Jean Froissart and Francois Rabelais in France, Sir Thomas More and Sir Philip Sidney in England, and Desiderius Erasmus in Holland.

Repartee: Conversation featuring snappy retorts and witticisms. Masters of *repartee* include Sydney Smith, Charles Lamb, and Oscar Wilde. An example is recorded in the meeting of "Beau" Nash and John Wesley: Nash said, "I never make way for a fool," to which Wesley responded, "Don't you? I always do," and stepped aside.

Resolution: The portion of a story following the climax, in which the conflict is resolved. The resolution of Jane Austen's *Northanger Abbey* is neatly summed up in the following sentence: "Henry and Catherine were married, the bells rang and every body smiled."

Restoration: See *Restoration Age*

Restoration Age: A period in English literature beginning with the crowning of Charles II in 1660 and running to about 1700. The era, which was characterized by a reaction against Puritanism, was the first great age of the comedy of manners. The finest literature of the era is typically witty and urbane, and often lewd. Prominent Restoration Age writers include William Congreve, Samuel Pepys, John Dryden, and John Milton.

Revenge Tragedy: A dramatic form popular during the Elizabethan Age, in which the protagonist, directed by the ghost of his murdered father or son, inflicts retaliation upon a powerful villain. Notable features of the revenge tragedy include violence, bizarre criminal acts, intrigue, insanity, a hesitant protagonist, and the use of soliloquy. Thomas Kyd's *Spanish Tragedy* is the first example of revenge tragedy in English, and William Shakespeare's *Hamlet* is perhaps the best. Extreme examples of revenge tragedy, such as John Webster's *The Duchess of Malfi*, are labeled "tragedies of blood." Also known as Tragedy of Blood.

Revista: The Spanish term for a vaudeville musical revue. Examples of *revistas* include Antonio Guzman Aguilera's *Mexico para los mexicanos*, Daniel Vanegas's *Maldito jazz*, and Don Catarino's *Whiskey, morfina y marihuana* and *El desterrado*.

Rhetoric: In literary criticism, this term denotes the art of ethical persuasion. In its strictest sense, rhetoric adheres to various principles developed since classical times for arranging facts and ideas in a clear, persuasive, appealing manner. The term is also used to refer to effective prose in general and theories of or methods for composing effective prose. Classical examples of rhetorics include *The Rhetoric of Aristotle,* Quintillian's *Institutio Oratoria,* and Cicero's *Ad Herennium.*

Rhetorical Question: A question intended to provoke thought, but not an expressed answer, in the reader. It is most commonly used in oratory and other persuasive genres. The following lines from Thomas Gray's "Elegy Written in a Country Churchyard" ask rhetorical questions: Can storied urn or animated bust Back to its mansion call the fleeting breath? Can Honour's voice provoke the silent dust, Or Flattery soothe the dull cold ear of Death?

Rhyme: When used as a noun in literary criticism, this term generally refers to a poem in which words sound identical or very similar and appear in parallel positions in two or more lines. Rhymes are classified into different types according to where they fall in a line or stanza or according to the degree of similarity they exhibit in their spellings and sounds. Some major types of rhyme are "masculine" rhyme, "feminine" rhyme, and "triple" rhyme. In a masculine rhyme, the rhyming sound falls in a single accented syllable, as with "heat" and "eat." Feminine rhyme is a rhyme of two syllables, one stressed and one unstressed, as with "merry" and "tarry." Triple rhyme matches the sound of the accented syllable and the two unaccented syllables that follow: "narrative" and "declarative." Robert Browning alternates feminine and masculine rhymes in his "Soliloquy of the Spanish Cloister": Gr-r-r—there go, my heart's abhorrence! Water your damned flower-pots, do! If hate killed men, Brother Lawrence, God's blood, would not mine kill you! What? Your myrtle-bush wants trimming? Oh, that rose has prior claims— Needs its leaden vase filled brimming? Hell dry you up with flames! Triple rhymes can be found in Thomas Hood's "Bridge of Sighs," George

Gordon Byron's satirical verse, and Ogden Nash's comic poems.

Rhyme Royal: A stanza of seven lines composed in iambic pentameter and rhymed *ababbcc.* The name is said to be a tribute to King James I of Scotland, who made much use of the form in his poetry. Examples of rhyme royal include Geoffrey Chaucer's *The Parlement of Foules,* William Shakespeare's *The Rape of Lucrece,* William Morris's *The Early Paradise,* and John Masefield's *The Widow in the Bye Street.*

Rhyme Scheme: See *Rhyme*

Rhythm: A regular pattern of sound, time intervals, or events occurring in writing, most often and most discernably in poetry. Regular, reliable rhythm is known to be soothing to humans, while interrupted, unpredictable, or rapidly changing rhythm is disturbing. These effects are known to authors, who use them to produce a desired reaction in the reader. An example of a form of irregular rhythm is sprung rhythm poetry; quantitative verse, on the other hand, is very regular in its rhythm.

Rising Action: The part of a drama where the plot becomes increasingly complicated. Rising action leads up to the climax, or turning point, of a drama. The final "chase scene" of an action film is generally the rising action which culminates in the film's climax.

Rococo: A style of European architecture that flourished in the eighteenth century, especially in France. The most notable features of *rococo* are its extensive use of ornamentation and its themes of lightness, gaiety, and intimacy. In literary criticism, the term is often used disparagingly to refer to a decadent or over-ornamental style. Alexander Pope's "The Rape of the Lock" is an example of literary *rococo.*

Roman à clef: A French phrase meaning "novel with a key." It refers to a narrative in which real persons are portrayed under fictitious names. Jack Kerouac, for example, portrayed various real-life beat generation figures under fictitious names in his *On the Road.*

Romance: A broad term, usually denoting a narrative with exotic, exaggerated, often idealized characters, scenes, and themes.

Nathaniel Hawthorne called his *The House of the Seven Gables* and *The Marble Faun* romances in order to distinguish them from clearly realistic works.

Romantic Age: See *Romanticism*

Romanticism: This term has two widely accepted meanings. In historical criticism, it refers to a European intellectual and artistic movement of the late eighteenth and early nineteenth centuries that sought greater freedom of personal expression than that allowed by the strict rules of literary form and logic of the eighteenth-century neoclassicists. The Romantics preferred emotional and imaginative expression to rational analysis. They considered the individual to be at the center of all experience and so placed him or her at the center of their art. The Romantics believed that the creative imagination reveals nobler truths—unique feelings and attitudes—than those that could be discovered by logic or by scientific examination. Both the natural world and the state of childhood were important sources for revelations of "eternal truths." "Romanticism" is also used as a general term to refer to a type of sensibility found in all periods of literary history and usually considered to be in opposition to the principles of classicism. In this sense, Romanticism signifies any work or philosophy in which the exotic or dreamlike figure strongly, or that is devoted to individualistic expression, self-analysis, or a pursuit of a higher realm of knowledge than can be discovered by human reason. Prominent Romantics include Jean-Jacques Rousseau, William Wordsworth, John Keats, Lord Byron, and Johann Wolfgang von Goethe.

Romantics: See *Romanticism*

Russian Symbolism: A Russian poetic movement, derived from French symbolism, that flourished between 1894 and 1910. While some Russian Symbolists continued in the French tradition, stressing aestheticism and the importance of suggestion above didactic intent, others saw their craft as a form of mystical worship, and themselves as mediators between the supernatural and the mundane. Russian symbolists include Aleksandr Blok, Vyacheslav Ivanovich Ivanov, Fyodor Sologub, Andrey Bely, Nikolay Gumilyov, and Vladimir Sergeyevich Solovyov.

S

Satire: A work that uses ridicule, humor, and wit to criticize and provoke change in human nature and institutions. There are two major types of satire: "formal" or "direct" satire speaks directly to the reader or to a character in the work; "indirect" satire relies upon the ridiculous behavior of its characters to make its point. Formal satire is further divided into two manners: the "Horatian," which ridicules gently, and the "Juvenalian," which derides its subjects harshly and bitterly. Voltaire's novella *Candide* is an indirect satire. Jonathan Swift's essay "A Modest Proposal" is a Juvenalian satire.

Scansion: The analysis or "scanning" of a poem to determine its meter and often its rhyme scheme. The most common system of scansion uses accents (slanted lines drawn above syllables) to show stressed syllables, breves (curved lines drawn above syllables) to show unstressed syllables, and vertical lines to separate each foot. In the first line of John Keats's *Endymion*, "A thing of beauty is a joy forever:" the word "thing," the first syllable of "beauty," the word "joy," and the second syllable of "forever" are stressed, while the words "A" and "of," the second syllable of "beauty," the word "a," and the first and third syllables of "forever" are unstressed. In the second line: "Its loveliness increases; it will never" a pair of vertical lines separate the foot ending with "increases" and the one beginning with "it."

Scene: A subdivision of an act of a drama, consisting of continuous action taking place at a single time and in a single location. The beginnings and endings of scenes may be indicated by clearing the stage of actors and props or by the entrances and exits of important characters. The first act of William Shakespeare's *Winter's Tale* is comprised of two scenes.

Science Fiction: A type of narrative about or based upon real or imagined scientific theories and technology. Science fiction is often peopled with alien creatures and set on other planets or in different dimensions. Karel Capek's *R.U.R.* is a major work of science fiction.

Second Person: See *Point of View*

Semiotics: The study of how literary forms and conventions affect the meaning of language. Semioticians include Ferdinand de Saussure, Charles Sanders Pierce, Claude Levi-Strauss, Jacques Lacan, Michel Foucault, Jacques Derrida, Roland Barthes, and Julia Kristeva.

Sestet: Any six-line poem or stanza. Examples of the sestet include the last six lines of the Petrarchan sonnet form, the stanza form of Robert Burns's "A Poet's Welcome to his love-begotten Daughter," and the sestina form in W. H. Auden's "Paysage Moralise."

Setting: The time, place, and culture in which the action of a narrative takes place. The elements of setting may include geographic location, characters' physical and mental environments, prevailing cultural attitudes, or the historical time in which the action takes place. Examples of settings include the romanticized Scotland in Sir Walter Scott's "Waverley" novels, the French provincial setting in Gustave Flaubert's *Madame Bovary*, the fictional Wessex country of Thomas Hardy's novels, and the small towns of southern Ontario in Alice Munro's short stories.

Shakespearean Sonnet: See *Sonnet*

Signifying Monkey: A popular trickster figure in black folklore, with hundreds of tales about this character documented since the 19th century. Henry Louis Gates Jr. examines the history of the signifying monkey in *The Signifying Monkey: Towards a Theory of Afro-American Literary Criticism*, published in 1988.

Simile: A comparison, usually using "like" or "as," of two essentially dissimilar things, as in "coffee as cold as ice" or "He sounded like a broken record." The title of Ernest Hemingway's "Hills Like White Elephants" contains a simile.

Slang: A type of informal verbal communication that is generally unacceptable for formal writing. Slang words and phrases are often colorful exaggerations used to emphasize the speaker's point; they may also be shortened versions of an often-used word or phrase. Examples of American slang from the 1990s include "yuppie" (an acronym for Young Urban Professional), "awesome"

(for "excellent"), wired (for "nervous" or "excited"), and "chill out" (for relax).

Slant Rhyme: See *Consonance*

Slave Narrative: Autobiographical accounts of American slave life as told by escaped slaves. These works first appeared during the abolition movement of the 1830s through the 1850s. Olaudah Equiano's *The Interesting Narrative of Olaudah Equiano, or Gustavus Vassa, The African* and Harriet Ann Jacobs's *Incidents in the Life of a Slave Girl* are examples of the slave narrative.

Social Realism: See *Socialist Realism*

Socialist Realism: The Socialist Realism school of literary theory was proposed by Maxim Gorky and established as a dogma by the first Soviet Congress of Writers. It demanded adherence to a communist worldview in works of literature. Its doctrines required an objective viewpoint comprehensible to the working classes and themes of social struggle featuring strong proletarian heroes. A successful work of socialist realism is Nikolay Ostrovsky's *Kak zakalyalas stal (How the Steel Was Tempered)*. Also known as Social Realism.

Soliloquy: A monologue in a drama used to give the audience information and to develop the speaker's character. It is typically a projection of the speaker's innermost thoughts. Usually delivered while the speaker is alone on stage, a soliloquy is intended to present an illusion of unspoken reflection. A celebrated soliloquy is Hamlet's "To be or not to be" speech in William Shakespeare's *Hamlet*.

Sonnet: A fourteen-line poem, usually composed in iambic pentameter, employing one of several rhyme schemes. There are three major types of sonnets, upon which all other variations of the form are based: the "Petrarchan" or "Italian" sonnet, the "Shakespearean" or "English" sonnet, and the "Spenserian" sonnet. A Petrarchan sonnet consists of an octave rhymed *abbaabba* and a "sestet" rhymed either *cdecde, cdccdc,* or *cdedce*. The octave poses a question or problem, relates a narrative, or puts forth a proposition; the sestet presents a solution to the problem, comments upon the narrative, or applies the proposition put forth in the octave. The Shakespearean sonnet is divided into three quatrains and a couplet rhymed *abab cdcd efef gg.* The couplet provides an epigrammatic comment on the narrative or problem put forth in the quatrains. The Spenserian sonnet uses three quatrains and a couplet like the Shakespearean, but links their three rhyme schemes in this way: *abab bcbc cdcd ee.* The Spenserian sonnet develops its theme in two parts like the Petrarchan, its final six lines resolving a problem, analyzing a narrative, or applying a proposition put forth in its first eight lines. Examples of sonnets can be found in Petrarch's *Canzoniere,* Edmund Spenser's *Amoretti,* Elizabeth Barrett Browning's *Sonnets from the Portuguese,* Rainer Maria Rilke's *Sonnets to Orpheus,* and Adrienne Rich's poem "The Insusceptibles."

Spenserian Sonnet: See *Sonnet*

Spenserian Stanza: A nine-line stanza having eight verses in iambic pentameter, its ninth verse in iambic hexameter, and the rhyme scheme ababbcbcc. This stanza form was first used by Edmund Spenser in his allegorical poem *The Faerie Queene.*

Spondee: In poetry meter, a foot consisting of two long or stressed syllables occurring together. This form is quite rare in English verse, and is usually composed of two monosyllabic words. The first foot in the following line from Robert Burns's "Green Grow the Rashes" is an example of a spondee: Green grow the rashes, O.

Sprung Rhythm: Versification using a specific number of accented syllables per line but disregarding the number of unaccented syllables that fall in each line, producing an irregular rhythm in the poem. Gerard Manley Hopkins, who coined the term "sprung rhythm," is the most notable practitioner of this technique.

Stanza: A subdivision of a poem consisting of lines grouped together, often in recurring patterns of rhyme, line length, and meter. Stanzas may also serve as units of thought in a poem much like paragraphs in prose. Examples of stanza forms include the quatrain, *terza rima, ottava rima,* Spenserian, and the so-called *In Memoriam* stanza from Alfred, Lord Tennyson's poem by that title. The following is an example of the latter form: Love is and was my lord and king, And in his presence I attend To hear the tidings of my friend, Which every hour his couriers bring.

Stereotype: A stereotype was originally the name for a duplication made during the printing process; this led to its modern definition as a person or thing that is (or is assumed to be) the same as all others of its type. Common stereotypical characters include the absentminded professor, the nagging wife, the troublemaking teenager, and the kindhearted grandmother.

Stream of Consciousness: A narrative technique for rendering the inward experience of a character. This technique is designed to give the impression of an ever-changing series of thoughts, emotions, images, and memories in the spontaneous and seemingly illogical order that they occur in life. The textbook example of stream of consciousness is the last section of James Joyce's *Ulysses.*

Structuralism: A twentieth-century movement in literary criticism that examines how literary texts arrive at their meanings, rather than the meanings themselves. There are two major types of structuralist analysis: one examines the way patterns of linguistic structures unify a specific text and emphasize certain elements of that text, and the other interprets the way literary forms and conventions affect the meaning of language itself. Prominent structuralists include Michel Foucault, Roman Jakobson, and Roland Barthes.

Structure: The form taken by a piece of literature. The structure may be made obvious for ease of understanding, as in nonfiction works, or may obscured for artistic purposes, as in some poetry or seemingly "unstructured" prose. Examples of common literary structures include the plot of a narrative, the acts and scenes of a drama, and such poetic forms as the Shakespearean sonnet and the Pindaric ode.

Sturm und Drang: A German term meaning "storm and stress." It refers to a German literary movement of the 1770s and 1780s that reacted against the order and rationalism of the enlightenment, focusing instead on the intense experience of extraordinary individuals. Highly romantic, works of this movement, such as Johann Wolfgang von Goethe's *Gotz von Berlichingen,* are typified by realism, rebelliousness, and intense emotionalism.

Style: A writer's distinctive manner of arranging words to suit his or her ideas and purpose in writing. The unique imprint of the author's personality upon his or her writing, style is the product of an author's way of arranging ideas and his or her use of diction, different sentence structures, rhythm, figures of speech, rhetorical principles, and other elements of composition. Styles may be classified according to period (Metaphysical, Augustan, Georgian), individual authors (Chaucerian, Miltonic, Jamesian), level (grand, middle, low, plain), or language (scientific, expository, poetic, journalistic).

Subject: The person, event, or theme at the center of a work of literature. A work may have one or more subjects of each type, with shorter works tending to have fewer and longer works tending to have more. The subjects of James Baldwin's novel *Go Tell It on the Mountain* include the themes of father-son relationships, religious conversion, black life, and sexuality. The subjects of Anne Frank's *Diary of a Young Girl* include Anne and her family members as well as World War II, the Holocaust, and the themes of war, isolation, injustice, and racism.

Subjectivity: Writing that expresses the author's personal feelings about his subject, and which may or may not include factual information about the subject. Subjectivity is demonstrated in James Joyce's *Portrait of the Artist as a Young Man,* Samuel Butler's *The Way of All Flesh,* and Thomas Wolfe's *Look Homeward, Angel.*

Subplot: A secondary story in a narrative. A subplot may serve as a motivating or complicating force for the main plot of the work, or it may provide emphasis for, or relief from, the main plot. The conflict between the Capulets and the Montagues in William Shakespeare's *Romeo and Juliet* is an example of a subplot.

Surrealism: A term introduced to criticism by Guillaume Apollinaire and later adopted by Andre Breton. It refers to a French literary and artistic movement founded in the 1920s. The Surrealists sought to express unconscious thoughts and feelings in their works. The best-known technique used for achieving this aim was automatic writing— transcriptions of spontaneous outpourings from the unconscious. The Surrealists proposed to unify the contrary levels of conscious and unconscious, dream and reality, objectivity and subjectivity into a new level of "super-realism." Surrealism can be found in the poetry of Paul Eluard, Pierre Reverdy, and Louis Aragon, among others.

Suspense: A literary device in which the author maintains the audience's attention through the buildup of events, the outcome of which will soon be revealed. Suspense in William Shakespeare's *Hamlet* is sustained throughout by the question of whether or not the Prince will achieve what he has been instructed to do and of what he intends to do.

Syllogism: A method of presenting a logical argument. In its most basic form, the syllogism consists of a major premise, a minor premise, and a conclusion. An example of a syllogism is: Major premise: When it snows, the streets get wet. Minor premise: It is snowing. Conclusion: The streets are wet.

Symbol: Something that suggests or stands for something else without losing its original identity. In literature, symbols combine their literal meaning with the suggestion of an abstract concept. Literary symbols are of two types: those that carry complex associations of meaning no matter what their contexts, and those that derive their suggestive meaning from their functions in specific literary works. Examples of symbols are sunshine suggesting happiness, rain suggesting sorrow, and storm clouds suggesting despair.

Symbolism: This term has two widely accepted meanings. In historical criticism, it denotes an early modernist literary movement initiated in France during the nineteenth century that reacted against the prevailing standards of realism. Writers in this movement aimed to evoke, indirectly and symbolically, an order of being beyond the material world of the five senses. Poetic expression of personal emotion figured strongly in the movement, typically by means of a private set of symbols uniquely identifiable with the individual poet. The principal aim of the Symbolists was to express in words the highly complex feelings that grew out of everyday contact with the world. In a broader sense, the term "symbolism" refers to the use of one object to represent another. Early members of the Symbolist movement included the French authors Charles Baudelaire and Arthur Rimbaud; William Butler Yeats, James Joyce, and T. S. Eliot were influenced as the movement moved to Ireland, England, and the United States. Examples of the concept of symbolism include a flag that stands for a nation or movement, or an empty cupboard used to suggest hopelessness, poverty, and despair.

Symbolist: See *Symbolism*

Symbolist Movement: See *Symbolism*

Sympathetic Fallacy: See *Affective Fallacy*

T

Tale: A story told by a narrator with a simple plot and little character development. Tales are usually relatively short and often carry a simple message. Examples of tales can be found in the work of Rudyard Kipling, Somerset Maugham, Saki, Anton Chekhov, Guy de Maupassant, and Armistead Maupin.

Tall Tale: A humorous tale told in a straightforward, credible tone but relating absolutely impossible events or feats of the characters. Such tales were commonly told of frontier adventures during the settlement of the west in the United States. Tall tales have been spun around such legendary heroes as Mike Fink, Paul Bunyan, Davy Crockett, Johnny Appleseed, and Captain Stormalong as well as the real-life William F. Cody and Annie Oakley. Literary use of tall tales can be found in Washington Irving's *History of New York,* Mark Twain's *Life on the Mississippi,* and in the German R. F. Raspe's *Baron Munchausen's Narratives of His Marvellous Travels and Campaigns in Russia.*

Tanka: A form of Japanese poetry similar to *haiku.* A *tanka* is five lines long, with the lines containing five, seven, five, seven, and seven syllables respectively. Skilled *tanka* authors include Ishikawa Takuboku, Masaoka Shiki, Amy Lowell, and Adelaide Crapsey.

Teatro Grottesco: See *Theater of the Grotesque*

Terza Rima: A three-line stanza form in poetry in which the rhymes are made on the last word of each line in the following manner: the first and third lines of the first stanza, then the second line of the first stanza and the first and third lines of the second stanza, and so on with the middle line of any stanza rhyming with the first and third lines of the following stanza. An example of *terza rima* is Percy Bysshe Shelley's "The Triumph of Love": As in that trance of wondrous thought I lay This was the tenour of my waking dream. Methought I sate beside a public way Thick strewn with summer dust, and a great stream Of people there was hurrying to and fro Numerous as gnats upon the evening gleam,...

Tetrameter: See *Meter*

Textual Criticism: A branch of literary criticism that seeks to establish the authoritative text of a literary work. Textual critics typically compare all known manuscripts or printings of a single work in order to assess the meanings of differences and revisions. This procedure allows them to arrive at a definitive version that (supposedly) corresponds to the author's original intention. Textual criticism was applied during the Renaissance to salvage the classical texts of Greece and Rome, and modern works have been studied, for instance, to undo deliberate correction or censorship, as in the case of novels by Stephen Crane and Theodore Dreiser.

Theater of Cruelty: Term used to denote a group of theatrical techniques designed to eliminate the psychological and emotional distance between actors and audience. This concept, introduced in the 1930s in France, was intended to inspire a more intense theatrical experience than conventional theater allowed. The "cruelty" of this dramatic theory signified not sadism but heightened actor/audience involvement in the dramatic event. The theater of cruelty was theorized by Antonin Artaud in his *Le Theatre et son double* (*The Theatre and Its Double*), and also appears in the work of Jerzy Grotowski, Jean Genet, Jean Vilar, and Arthur Adamov, among others.

Theater of the Absurd: A post-World War II dramatic trend characterized by radical theatrical innovations. In works influenced by the Theater of the Absurd, nontraditional, sometimes grotesque characterizations, plots, and stage sets reveal a meaningless universe in which human values are irrelevant. Existentialist themes of estrangement, absurdity, and futility link many of the works of this movement. The principal writers of the Theater of the Absurd are Samuel Beckett, Eugene Ionesco, Jean Genet, and Harold Pinter.

Theater of the Grotesque: An Italian theatrical movement characterized by plays written around the ironic and macabre aspects of daily life in the World War I era. Theater of the Grotesque was named after the play *The Mask and the Face* by Luigi Chiarelli, which was described as "a grotesque in three acts." The movement influenced the work of Italian dramatist Luigi Pirandello, author of *Right You Are, If You Think You Are*. Also known as *Teatro Grottesco*.

Theme: The main point of a work of literature. The term is used interchangeably with thesis. The theme of William Shakespeare's *Othello*—jealousy—is a common one.

Thesis: A thesis is both an essay and the point argued in the essay. Thesis novels and thesis plays share the quality of containing a thesis which is supported through the action of the story. A master's thesis and a doctoral dissertation are two theses required of graduate students.

Thesis Play: See *Thesis*

Three Unities: See *Unities*

Tone: The author's attitude toward his or her audience may be deduced from the tone of the work. A formal tone may create distance or convey politeness, while an informal tone may encourage a friendly, intimate, or intrusive feeling in the reader. The author's attitude toward his or her subject matter may also be deduced from the tone of the words he or she uses in discussing it. The tone of John F. Kennedy's speech which included the appeal to "ask not what your country can do for you" was intended to instill feelings of camaraderie and national pride in listeners.

Tragedy: A drama in prose or poetry about a noble, courageous hero of excellent character who, because of some tragic character flaw or *hamartia*, brings ruin upon him- or herself. Tragedy treats its subjects in a dignified and serious manner, using poetic language to help evoke pity and fear and bring about catharsis, a purging of these emotions. The tragic form was practiced extensively by the ancient Greeks. In the Middle Ages, when classical works were virtually unknown, tragedy came to denote any works about the fall of persons from exalted to low conditions due to any reason: fate, vice, weakness, etc. According to the classical definition of tragedy, such works present the "pathetic"—that which evokes pity—rather than the tragic. The classical form of tragedy was revived in the sixteenth century; it flourished especially on the Elizabethan stage. In modern times, dramatists have attempted to adapt the form to the needs of modern society by drawing their heroes from the ranks of ordinary men and women and defining the nobility of these heroes in terms of spirit rather than exalted social standing. The greatest classical example of tragedy is Sophocles' *Oedipus Rex*. The "pathetic" derivation is exemplified in "The Monk's Tale" in Geoffrey Chaucer's *Canterbury Tales*. Notable works produced during the sixteenth century revival include William Shakespeare's *Hamlet*, *Othello*, and *King Lear*. Modern dramatists working in the tragic tradition include Henrik Ibsen, Arthur Miller, and Eugene O'Neill.

Tragedy of Blood: See *Revenge Tragedy*

Tragic Flaw: In a tragedy, the quality within the hero or heroine which leads to his or her downfall. Examples of the tragic flaw include Othello's jealousy and Hamlet's indecisiveness, although most great tragedies defy such simple interpretation.

Transcendentalism: An American philosophical and religious movement, based in New England from around 1835 until the Civil War. Transcendentalism was a form of American romanticism that had its roots abroad in the works of Thomas Carlyle, Samuel Coleridge, and Johann Wolfgang von Goethe. The Transcendentalists stressed the importance of intuition and subjective experience in communication with God. They rejected religious dogma and texts in favor of mysticism and scientific naturalism. They pursued truths that lie beyond the "colorless" realms perceived by reason and the senses and were active social reformers in public education, women's rights, and the abolition of slavery. Prominent members of the group include Ralph Waldo Emerson and Henry David Thoreau.

Trickster: A character or figure common in Native American and African literature who uses his ingenuity to defeat enemies and escape difficult situations. Tricksters are most often animals, such as the spider, hare, or coyote, although they may take the form of humans as well. Examples of trickster tales include Thomas King's *A Coyote Columbus Story,* Ashley F. Bryan's *The Dancing Granny* and Ishmael Reed's *The Last Days of Louisiana Red.*

Trimeter: See *Meter*

Triple Rhyme: See *Rhyme*

Trochee: See *Foot*

U

Understatement: See *Irony*

Unities: Strict rules of dramatic structure, formulated by Italian and French critics of the Renaissance and based loosely on the principles of drama discussed by Aristotle in his *Poetics.* Foremost among these rules were the three unities of action, time, and place that compelled a dramatist to: (1) construct a single plot with a beginning, middle, and end that details the causal relationships of action and character; (2) restrict the action to the events of a single day; and (3) limit the scene to a single place or city. The unities were observed faithfully by continental European writers until the Romantic Age, but they were never regularly observed in English drama. Modern dramatists are typically more concerned with a unity of impression or emotional effect than with any of the classical unities. The unities are observed in Pierre Corneille's tragedy *Polyeuctes* and Jean-Baptiste Racine's *Phedre.* Also known as Three Unities.

Urban Realism: A branch of realist writing that attempts to accurately reflect the often harsh facts of modern urban existence. Some works by Stephen Crane, Theodore Dreiser, Charles Dickens, Fyodor Dostoyevsky, Emile Zola, Abraham Cahan, and Henry Fuller feature urban realism. Modern examples include Claude Brown's *Manchild in the Promised Land* and Ron Milner's *What the Wine Sellers Buy.*

Utopia: A fictional perfect place, such as "paradise" or "heaven." Early literary utopias were included in Plato's *Republic* and Sir Thomas More's *Utopia,* while more modern utopias can be found in Samuel Butler's *Erewhon,* Theodor Herzka's *A Visit to Free-land,* and H. G. Wells' *A Modern Utopia.*

Utopian: See *Utopia*

Utopianism: See *Utopia*

V

Verisimilitude: Literally, the appearance of truth. In literary criticism, the term refers to aspects of a work of literature that seem true to the reader. Verisimilitude is achieved in the work of Honore de Balzac, Gustave Flaubert, and Henry James, among other late nineteenth-century realist writers.

Vers de societe: See *Occasional Verse*

Vers libre: See *Free Verse*

Verse: A line of metered language, a line of a poem, or any work written in verse. The following line of verse is from the epic poem *Don Juan* by Lord Byron: "My way is to begin with the beginning."

Versification: The writing of verse. Versification may also refer to the meter, rhyme, and other mechanical components of a poem. Composition of a "Roses are red, violets are blue" poem to suit an occasion is a common form of versification practiced by students.

Victorian: Refers broadly to the reign of Queen Victoria of England (1837-1901) and to anything with qualities typical of that era. For example, the qualities of smug narrowmind-edness, bourgeois materialism, faith in social progress, and priggish morality are often considered Victorian. This stereotype is contradicted by such dramatic intellectual developments as the theories of Charles Darwin, Karl Marx, and Sigmund Freud (which stirred strong debates in England) and the critical attitudes of serious Victorian writers like Charles Dickens and George Eliot. In literature, the Victorian Period was the great age of the English novel, and the latter part of the era saw the rise of movements such as decadence and symbolism. Works of Victorian literature include the poetry of Robert Browning and Alfred, Lord Tennyson, the criticism of Matthew

Arnold and John Ruskin, and the novels of Emily Bronte, William Makepeace Thackeray, and Thomas Hardy. Also known as Victorian Age and Victorian Period.

Victorian Age: See *Victorian*

Victorian Period: See *Victorian*

W

Weltanschauung: A German term referring to a person's worldview or philosophy. Examples of *weltanschauung* include Thomas Hardy's view of the human being as the victim of fate, destiny, or impersonal forces and circumstances, and the disillusioned and laconic cynicism expressed by such poets of the 1930s as W. H. Auden, Sir Stephen Spender, and Sir William Empson.

Weltschmerz: A German term meaning "world pain." It describes a sense of anguish about the nature of existence, usually associated with a melancholy, pessimistic attitude. *Weltschmerz* was expressed in England by

George Gordon, Lord Byron in his *Manfred* and *Childe Harold's Pilgrimage,* in France by Viscount de Chateaubriand, Alfred de Vigny, and Alfred de Musset, in Russia by Aleksandr Pushkin and Mikhail Lermontov, in Poland by Juliusz Slowacki, and in America by Nathaniel Hawthorne.

Z

Zarzuela: A type of Spanish operetta. Writers of *zarzuelas* include Lope de Vega and Pedro Calderon.

Zeitgeist: A German term meaning "spirit of the time." It refers to the moral and intellectual trends of a given era. Examples of *zeitgeist* include the preoccupation with the more morbid aspects of dying and death in some Jacobean literature, especially in the works of dramatists Cyril Tourneur and John Webster, and the decadence of the French Symbolists.

Cumulative Author/Title Index

Gorki, Maxim
  The Lower Depths: V9
The Governess (Simon): V27
The Government Inspector (Gogol):
  V12
The Great God Brown (O'Neill): V11
The Great White Hope (Sackler): V15
The Green Pastures (Connelly): V12
Greenberg, Richard
  Take Me Out: V24
Gregg, Stephen
  This Is a Test: V28
Guare, John
  The House of Blue Leaves: V8
  Six Degrees of Separation: V13
Guys and Dolls (Burrows, Loesser,
  Swerling): V29

H

Habitat (Thompson): V22
Hackett, Albert
  The Diary of Anne Frank: V15
The Hairy Ape (O'Neill): V4
Hammerstein, Oscar II
  The King and I: V1
Hanff, Helene
  84, Charing Cross Road: V17
Hansberry, Lorraine
  A Raisin in the Sun: V2
  A Raisin in the Sun (Motion
    picture): V29
Hare, David
  Blue Room: V7
  Plenty: V4
  The Secret Rapture: V16
Harris, Bill
  Robert Johnson: Trick the Devil:
    V27
Hart, Moss
  Once in a Lifetime: V10
  You Can't Take It with You: V1
Harvey (Chase): V11
Havel, Vaclav
  The Memorandum: V10
*Having Our Say: The Delany Sisters'
  First 100 Years* (Mann): V28
Hay Fever (Coward): V6
Hayes, Joseph
  The Desperate Hours: V20
Heather Raffo's 9 Parts of Desire
  (Raffo): V27
Hecht, Ben
  The Front Page: V9
Hedda Gabler (Ibsen): V6
Heggen, Thomas
  Mister Roberts: V20
The Heidi Chronicles (Wasserstein):
  V5
Hell-Bent fer Heaven (Hughes): V31
Hellman, Lillian
  The Children's Hour: V3

  The Little Foxes: V1
  Watch on the Rhine: V14
Henley, Beth
  Crimes of the Heart: V2
  Impossible Marriage: V26
  The Miss Firecracker Contest: V21
Henrietta (Jones Meadows): V27
Highway, Tomson
  The Rez Sisters: V2
Hippolytus (Euripides): V25
Hollmann, Mark
  Urinetown: V27
Holmes, Rupert
  The Mystery of Edwin Drood: V28
The Homecoming (Pinter): V3
The Hostage (Behan): V7
Hot L Baltimore (Wilson): V9
The House of Bernarda Alba
  (GarcíaLorca, Federico): V4
The House of Blue Leaves (Guare):
  V8
How I Learned to Drive (Vogel): V14
*How to Succeed in Business without
  Really Trying* (Loesser,
  Burrows, Weinstock, Gilbert):
  V31
Howard, Sidney
  They Knew What They Wanted:
    V29
Hughes, Hatcher
  Hell-Bent fer Heaven: V31
Hughes, Langston
  Mulatto: V18
  Mule Bone: V6
Hurston, Zora Neale
  Mule Bone: V6
  Poker!: V30
Hwang, David Henry
  M. Butterfly: V11
  The Sound of a Voice: V18
  Trying to Find Chinatown: V29

I

I Am My Own Wife (Wright): V23
I Hate Hamlet (Rudnick): V22
I Never Saw Another Butterfly
  (Raspanti): V27
I Remember Mama (Van Druten):
  V30
I, Too, Speak of the Rose
  (Carballido): V4
Ibsen, Henrik
  Brand: V16
  A Doll's House: V1
  An Enemy of the People: V25
  Ghosts: V11
  Hedda Gabler: V6
  The Master Builder: V15
  Peer Gynt: V8
  The Wild Duck: V10
The Iceman Cometh (O'Neill): V5

An Ideal Husband (Wilde): V21
Idiot's Delight (Sherwood): V15
Icebound (Davis): V31
Iizuka, Naomi
  36 Views: V21
Ile (O'Neill): V26
I'm Not Rappaport (Gardner): V18
Imaginary Friends (Ephron): V22
The Imaginary Invalid (Molière): V20
The Importance of Being Earnest
  (Wilde): V4
The Importance of Being Earnest
  (Motion picture): V31
Impossible Marriage (Henley): V26
Inadmissible Evidence (Osborne):
  V24
India Song (Duras): V21
Indian Ink (Stoppard): V11
Indians (Kopit): V24
Indiscretions (Cocteau): V24
Inge, William
  Bus Stop: V8
  Come Back, Little Sheba: V3
  Picnic: V5
Inherit the Wind (Lawrence and Lee):
  V2
The Insect Play (Capek): V11
Into the Woods (Sondheim and
  Lapine): V25
Ionesco, Eugène
  The Bald Soprano: V4
  The Chairs: V9
  Rhinoceros: V25
Iphigenia in Taurus (Euripides): V4
Ives, David
  Time Flies: V29

J

J. B. (MacLeish): V15
Jarry, Alfred
  Ubu Roi: V8
Jensen, Erik
  The Exonerated: V24
Jesus Christ Superstar (Webber and
  Rice): V7
The Jew of Malta (Marlowe): V13
Joe Turner's Come and Gone
  (Wilson): V17
Jones, LeRoi
  see Baraka, Amiri
Jones Meadows, Karen
  Henrietta: V27
Jonson, Ben(jamin)
  The Alchemist: V4
  Volpone: V10

K

Kaufman, George S.
  Once in a Lifetime: V10
  You Can't Take It with You: V1
Kaufman, Moisés

Cumulative Nationality/ Ethnicity Index

Cumulative Nationality/Ethnicity Index

Subject/Theme Index

*When I Was a Little Girl and My
    Mother Didn't Want Me:*
    204–206
Hubris. *See* Pride
Human nature
    Beauty: 31
Humor
    Beauty: 32–34
    The Importance of Being Earnest:
        92, 109
    Passion Play: 148
    Rabbit Hole: 167, 171, 173
Hypocrisy
    *How to Succeed in Business
        without Really Trying:* 69
    The Importance of Being Earnest:
        97, 99, 108
    Why Marry?: 239

I

Idealism
    *When I Was a Little Girl and My
        Mother Didn't Want Me:* 216
Identity
    Beauty: 29–31
    The Importance of Being Earnest:
        99
    *When I Was a Little Girl and My
        Mother Didn't Want Me:* 204
Illegitimacy
    The Importance of Being Earnest:
        99
Imagery (Literature)
    Passion Play: 149–154
Immigrant life
    *When I Was a Little Girl and My
        Mother Didn't Want Me:* 201,
        203, 208–210
Independence
    The Importance of Being Earnest:
        107
    Why Marry?: 232
Injustice
    Passion Play: 146–147
Innocence
    Andre's Mother: 7
    Hell-Bent fer Heaven: 42
    Rabbit Hole: 169
    Romeo and Juliet: 193
Iraq War, 2003-2011
    Nine-Ten: 123
Irony
    Nine-Ten: 114, 121
    Why Marry?: 233
Islam
    Nine-Ten: 121–123
Isolation
    Rabbit Hole: 169, 174
    *When I Was a Little Girl and My
        Mother Didn't Want Me:* 218

J

Jazz
    Nine-Ten: 128–129
Jealousy
    Beauty: 19, 23–24, 31
    Hell-Bent fer Heaven: 36, 43
    Icebound: 71, 78
Joy
    Romeo and Juliet: 190
Judaism
    Passion Play: 135, 144

L

Language and languages
    Hell-Bent fer Heaven: 45
Lesbianism
    Passion Play: 139
Loss (Psychology)
    Andre's Mother: 1, 3, 5, 7, 10, 13
    Rabbit Hole: 160–161, 169, 170,
        174, 175
    Romeo and Juliet: 193
Love
    Andre's Mother: 1, 6, 7, 10, 12, 13
    Hell-Bent fer Heaven: 36
    Icebound: 71, 75, 76, 84, 85
    The Importance of Being Earnest:
        97, 99–101
    Passion Play: 141
    Rabbit Hole: 162, 168–170, 172
    Romeo and Juliet: 177, 182, 192,
        194
    *When I Was a Little Girl and My
        Mother Didn't Want Me:* 203,
        206
    Why Marry?: 223, 225, 226
Loyalty
    Hell-Bent fer Heaven: 36

M

Magical realism
    Passion Play: 144, 148
Marriage
    Why Marry?: 222–231, 236,
        238–242, 244
Melodrama
    Icebound: 85–89
Memory
    *When I Was a Little Girl and My
        Mother Didn't Want Me:*
        211–213
Metaphors
    Passion Play: 148
    Romeo and Juliet: 197
    *When I Was a Little Girl and My
        Mother Didn't Want Me:* 220
Metaphysics
    Rabbit Hole: 175
Morality

The Importance of Being Earnest:
    99
Mother-child relationships
    Andre's Mother: 11, 12
    Icebound: 75, 84
    *When I Was a Little Girl and My
        Mother Didn't Want Me:* 211
Music
    *How to Succeed in Business
        without Really Trying:* 60–61,
        66–69
    Nine-Ten: 128–129

N

Naïveté. *See* Innocence
Naturalism
    Rabbit Hole: 173
Nepotism
    *How to Succeed in Business
        without Really Trying:* 56, 58
Nihilism
    *When I Was a Little Girl and My
        Mother Didn't Want Me:*
        218–219
Northeastern United States
    Icebound: 71, 79, 82, 84, 89

O

Optimism
    Icebound: 84
Otherness
    Andre's Mother: 16
    *When I Was a Little Girl and My
        Mother Didn't Want Me:* 218

P

Pain
    Rabbit Hole: 172
Parent-child relationships
    Andre's Mother: 15–16
Passion
    Romeo and Juliet: 182, 184, 186,
        192
Political correctness
    *How to Succeed in Business
        without Really Trying:* 69
Politics
    Passion Play: 148
Postmodernism
    Passion Play: 143–144
Poverty
    *When I Was a Little Girl and My
        Mother Didn't Want Me:* 201
Prejudice
    Andre's Mother: 10
Pride
    *When I Was a Little Girl and My
        Mother Didn't Want Me:* 217
Psychoanalysis

Subject/Theme Index